UNDERSTANDING
HUMAN RESOURCES MANAGEMENT
A CANADIAN PERSPECTIVE

MELANIE PEACOCK
Mount Royal University

EILEEN B. STEWART
British Columbia Institute of Technology

MONICA BELCOURT
York University

NELSON

NELSON

Understanding Human Resources Management: A Canadian Perspective

by Melanie Peacock, Eileen B. Stewart, and Monica Belcourt

VP, Product Solutions, K–20:
Claudine O'Donnell

Director, Qualitative Publishing:
Jackie Wood

Publisher:
Alexis Hood

Executive Marketing Manager:
Amanda Henry

Content Manager:
Jacquelyn Busby

Photo and Permissions Researcher:
Julie Pratt

Senior Production Project Manager:
Natalia Denesiuk Harris

Production Service:
SPi Global

Copy Editor:
Holly Dickinson

Proofreader:
SPi Global

Indexer:
SPi Global

Design Director:
Ken Phipps

Higher Education Design PM:
Pamela Johnston

Interior Design:
Ken Cadinouche

Cover Design:
Courtney Hellam

Cover Image:
Diana Ong/SuperStock/Getty Images

Compositor:
SPi Global

Library and Archives Canada Cataloguing in Publication Data

Peacock, Melanie, author
    Understanding human resources management : a Canadian perspective / Melanie Peacock, Mount Royal University, Eileen B. Stewart, British Columbia Institute of Technology, Monica Belcourt, York University.

Includes bibliographical references and index.
Issued in print and electronic formats.
ISBN 978-0-17-679806-2 (softcover).—
ISBN 978-0-17-686191-9 (PDF)

    1. Personnel management—Canada—Textbooks. 2. Personnel management—Textbooks.
3. Textbooks. I. Belcourt, Monica, 1946–, author II. Stewart, Eileen B., 1943–, author III. Title.

HF5549.2.C3P43 2019   658.3
C2018-905996-6
C2018-905997-4

ISBN-13: 978-0-17-679806-2
ISBN-10: 0-17-679806-4

To my darling husband, Cam. I love the chapters of our life that we are writing during our journey together. To Miranda, Joely, and Eric, thank you for your love and support. Our family is the foundation that allows me to embrace life's opportunities.—MP

To my son, Jason Robertson, his wife, Andrea McLean, and my wonderful grandsons, Caleb and Adam Robertson, who are my anchor in life, and to the memory of my husband, Richard Robertson, who will always be my inspiration.—EBS

Key Features

Learning Outcomes are listed at the beginning of each chapter and are individually highlighted in the margin throughout the text to illuminate where the material is presented to address each specific LO. The Learning Outcomes Summary at the end of each chapter recaps and reinforces the outcomes to ensure students have successfully acquired the knowledge and abilities outlined.

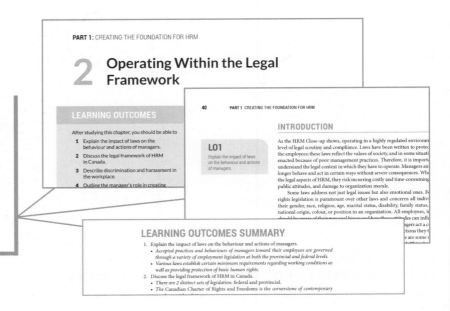

PART 1: CREATING THE FOUNDATION FOR HRM

2 Operating Within the Legal Framework

LEARNING OUTCOMES

After studying this chapter, you should be able to

1 Explain the impact of laws on the behaviour and actions of managers.
2 Discuss the legal framework of HRM in Canada.
3 Describe discrimination and harassment in the workplace.
4 Outline the manager's role in creating.

LO1 Explain the impact of laws on the behaviour and actions of managers.

INTRODUCTION

As the HRM Close-up shows, operating in a highly regulated environment... level of legal scrutiny and compliance. Laws have been written to protect... the employees; these laws reflect the values of society, and in some situations... enacted because of poor management practices. Therefore, it is important... understand the legal context in which they have to operate. Managers an... longer behave and act in certain ways without severe consequences. Whe... the legal aspects of HRM, they risk incurring costly and time-consuming... public attitudes, and damage to organization morale.

Some laws address not just legal issues but also emotional ones. Fo... rights legislation is paramount over other laws and concerns all indivi... their gender, race, religion, age, marital status, disability, family status,... national origin, colour, or position in an organization. All employees, in...

LEARNING OUTCOMES SUMMARY

1. Explain the impact of laws on the behaviour and actions of managers.
   • *Accepted practices and behaviours of managers toward their employees are governed through a variety of employment legislation at both the provincial and federal levels.*
   • *Various laws establish certain minimum requirements regarding working conditions as well as providing protection of basic human rights.*
2. Discuss the legal framework of HRM in Canada.
   • *There are 2 distinct sets of legislation: federal and provincial.*
   • *The Canadian Charter of Rights and Freedoms is the cornerstone of contemporary*

An HRM Close-up that relates a story about a manager's experience in human resources management opens each chapter. HRM Close-up Application questions are presented at the end of each chapter, highlighting how the material discussed could be used by the manager in the opening vignette.

HRM CLOSE-UP

"All I can say is, it's a good thing we have an outstanding HR department and integration function."

THE YEAR 2018 marked a major milestone in Canadian history with the legalization of marijuana. Previously availa... ical s... being... much...

4 facilities in Canada, we're building another one in Denmark, and we have a European distributor based in Berlin. We've also invested in Australia's largest licensed producer."

But such quick and dramatic growth isn't without its difficulties either.

"It's a good thing we have an outstanding HR department and integration function," Battley exclaims. "Our vice-president of HR, Debra Wilson, has assembled a top-notch human...

HRM CLOSE-UP APPLICATION

1. What are the 2 primary federal employment laws that apply to Aurora Cannabis?
2. What requirement did Health Canada initially require of Aurora?
3. What legal requirement did Aurora have to meet that was more stringent than for liquor producers?
4. What is an RPIC, and where was it required?

Chapters include a variety of visual elements, such as photos, charts, and figures, to reinforce key material and maintain visual interest.

Both employees and employers are responsible for promoting a safe work environment.

FIGURE 1.2 **Relationship of HR to Other Business Units**

FIGURE 2.2 **Provincial and Territorial Human Rights Agencies**

Organization	Website
Alberta Human Rights Commission	www.albertahumanrights.ab.ca
BC Human Rights Tribunal	www.bchrt.bc.ca
The Manitoba Human Rights Commission	www.manitobahumanrights.ca
New Brunswick Human Rights Commission	www2.gnb.ca
Newfoundland and Labrador Human Rights Commission	https://thinkhumanrights.ca
Northwest Territories Human Rights Commission	www.nwthumanrights.ca
Nova Scotia Human Rights Commission	https://humanrights.novascotia.ca
Nunavut Human Rights Tribunal	www.nhrt.ca
Human Rights Tribunal of Ontario	www.sjto.gov.on.ca/hrto
Prince Edward Island Human Rights Commission	www.gov.pe.ca/humanrights
(Québec) Commission des droits de la personne et des droits de la jeunesse	www.cdpdj.qc.ca/en

McClung, chief people officer at Capital One Canada, notes that HR professionals need

Toolkit boxes contain essential tips, resources, and strategies for effectively handling a multitude of HRM matters.

At Work with HRM boxes feature real-world applications relating to a specific topic, with critical thinking questions at the end.

HRM and the Law boxes help explain the legal implications of HRM and provide questions regarding legal considerations for HRM issues.

Ethics in HRM boxes highlight sensitive issues employees and managers might face and present questions to consider about these situations.

An **Emerging Trends** box provides information about trends in relation to each chapter's theme.

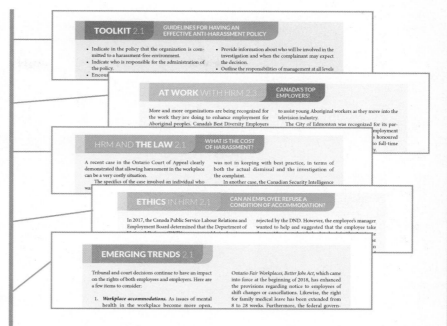

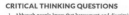

CRITICAL THINKING QUESTIONS

1. Although people know that harassment and discrimination are illegal, why would an employee or potential employee be reluctant to complain?
2. There is much concern about how people behave in the workplace and use words such as "respectful" to indicate how employees are to treat everyone. What does respectful look like to you?
3. You see a part-time job posted in your community for a tutor in a specific foreign language that also requires that the tutor be from the country of that language. Would being from a specific country be a justifiable BFOQ? Why or why not?
4. A friend of yours has heard you are taking a business course that focuses on human resources management and wants some help. Your friend, a parent of 2 small children, has learned that the daycare centre is changing its closing hours from 6:00 p.m. to

BUILDING YOUR SKILLS

1. Much attention is given to the issue of harassment and discrimination in the workplace. The cornerstone to addressing this is achieving organizational awareness. Training can help raise awareness. Working in groups of 3 or 4, develop the outline of a training session that would raise awareness for a small company with 75 employees. The outline should include (1) topics to be covered, (2) specific examples of harassment and/or discrimination, (3) how complaints are to be made and to whom, and (4) who would attend the training.
2. Companies are concerned about bullying at work and want to do what they can to prevent it. Watch the video *How I survived workplace bullying*, a TEDxWinnipeg talk by Sherry Benson-Podolchuk at **www.youtube.com/watch?v=YmRKlZEXVQM**. Working

End-of-chapter material includes the Learning Outcomes Summary as well as Critical Thinking Questions that promote basic recall and stimulate deeper thinking by providing questions for discussion. The Building Your Skills feature also appears at the end of each chapter and contains both text-based and Web-based experiential exercises.

Two case studies at the conclusion of each chapter present current HRM issues in real-life settings that allow for critical analysis. A running case throughout the text also highlights the complex and integrated application of human resources management topics and issues.

(Note: Cases are intended to serve as examples and discussion points. As such, the scenarios and details should not be used as benchmarks for business models or business plans.)

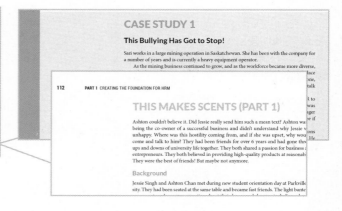

Students can stay organized with MindTap—a single destination with all the course material and study aids needed to succeed. Material is presented in an engaging way, and there is ample opportunity to review what is being learned to identify areas for further study to ensure success. The MindTap Mobile app allows students to learn on-the-go!

BRIEF CONTENTS

CONTENTS

Preface

How many times have you heard the expression "People are our greatest asset"? If this is true, then organizations need to pay attention to their employees and ensure that the right people join a company and are then provided with the correct resources and environment to be successful at work. Although this sounds like a simple concept, the complexities and intricacies of how to do this require a professional and well-thought-out approach to dealing with people. In doing so, businesses, the economy, and our country will continue to prosper and grow.

This book is written to help you understand HR "language"—the systems, processes, and policies necessary for the success of the people in an organization and therefore, ultimately, the success of an organization. It is written for those of you who will become (or are) employees, managers, business owners, and/or HR professionals. Since the text covers the major human resources management (HRM) topics, it provides a good overview if you are thinking about moving into the HR profession. For those working or going to work in other areas, this book will help you develop a deeper understanding of your role in implementing effective HRM practices as well as when to rely on and/or partner with HR professionals. The key point is that regardless of your role in a company, throughout your career you will be dealing with people; therefore, you need to understand how best to do this in order to create a meaningful and productive work environment for yourself and others.

The book has been authored by experienced, award-winning educators recognized by students and colleagues for their excellence in teaching and facilitating learning. The authors are also active HR practitioners who share business stories throughout to make the material interesting and relevant for you. Current Canadian scenarios are featured throughout the book, thereby presenting practical examples of how HRM is a critical function within an organization. Furthermore, different types of industries and different sizes of companies are discussed, including profit, non-profit/voluntary, public sector, unionized, and non-unionized organizations.

In summary, *Understanding Human Resources Management* is designed to cover the material you will need for an overall, general knowledge of the HRM systems, processes, and policies in a company, as well as your role in developing and implementing these—whether you are an employee, manager, owner, or HR professional. This book shows how theory applies to actual HRM practices in Canada in the 21st century and explains how these topics enable an organization to succeed through its people.

HIGHLIGHTS OF THE BOOK

- Canadian content with applicable questions posed, all of which illustrate the strategic nature of human resources management
- A running case* throughout the book that highlights the complex and integrated application of human resources management topics and issues
- Current Canadian references and cases* that focus on Canadian companies
- Figures and references that reflect up-to-date information
- Examples highlighting the importance of metrics in effective HRM practices
- Indigenous scenarios and references that honour this segment of the Canadian population
- Material that reflects current Canadian research from professional journals/periodicals and academic journals

*Note: The running case and the cases presented at the conclusion of each chapter are intended to serve as examples and discussion points. As such, the scenarios and details should not be used as benchmarks for business models or business plans.

SUPPLEMENTARY MATERIALS

INSTRUCTOR RESOURCES

The **Nelson Education Teaching Advantage (NETA)** program delivers research-based instructor resources that promote student engagement and higher-order thinking to enable the success of Canadian students and educators. Visit Nelson Education's **Inspired Instruction** website at nelson.com/inspired to find out more about NETA.

The following instructor resources have been created for *Understanding Human Resources Management*: *A Canadian Perspective*. Access these ultimate tools for customizing lectures and presentations at nelson.com/instructor.

NETA Test Bank

This resource was written by Lisa Bering, Humber College. It includes over 1000 multiple-choice questions written according to NETA guidelines for effective construction and development of higher-order questions. Also included are approximately 800 true/false questions and 80 essay questions.

The NETA Test Bank is available in a new, cloud-based platform. **Nelson Testing Powered by Cognero®** is a secure online testing system that allows instructors to author, edit, and manage test bank content from anywhere Internet access is available. No special installations or downloads are needed, and the desktop-inspired interface, with its drop-down menus and familiar, intuitive tools, allows instructors to create and manage tests with ease. Multiple test versions can be created in an instant, and content can be imported or exported into other systems. Tests can be delivered from a learning management system, the classroom, or wherever an instructor chooses. Nelson Testing Powered by Cognero for *Understanding Human Resources Management*: *A Canadian Perspective* can be accessed through nelson.com/instructor.

NETA PowerPoint

Microsoft® PowerPoint® lecture slides for every chapter have been created by one of the text's authors, Melanie Peacock, Mount Royal University. There is an average of 24 slides per chapter, featuring key points of information from *Understanding Human Resources Management*: *A Canadian Perspective*. NETA principles of clear design and engaging content have been incorporated throughout, making it simple for instructors to customize the deck for their courses.

Image Library

This resource consists of digital copies of figures, short tables, and photographs used in the book. Instructors may use these jpegs to customize the NETA PowerPoint or create their own PowerPoint presentations. An Image Library Key describes the images and lists the codes under which the jpegs are saved.

NETA Instructor Guide

This resource was also written by Melanie Peacock, Mount Royal University. It is organized according to the textbook chapters and addresses key educational concerns, such as student motivation, barriers to learning, and engagement strategies. Other features include lecture outlines, answers to end-of-chapter materials, notes for end-of-chapter case studies, and possible responses for the questions posed at the end of each part of the running case used throughout this text.

MindTap

Offering personalized paths of dynamic assignments and applications, **MindTap** is a digital learning solution that turns cookie-cutter into cutting-edge, apathy into engagement, and memorizers into higher-level thinkers. MindTap enables students to analyze and apply chapter concepts within relevant assignments and allows instructors to measure skills and promote better outcomes with ease. A fully online learning solution, MindTap combines all student learning tools—readings, multimedia, activities, and assessments—into a single Learning Path that guides the student through the curriculum. Instructors personalize the experience by customizing the presentation of these learning tools to their students, even seamlessly introducing their own content into the Learning Path.

MindTap contains interactive quizzes and exercises created by one of the text's authors, Eileen B. Stewart. Enda Soostar and Steve Robinson, both of Georgian College, also contributed valuable activities to this resource.

STUDENT ANCILLARIES

MindTap

Stay organized and efficient with **MindTap**—a single destination with all the course material and study aids you need to succeed. Built-in apps leverage social media and the latest learning technology. For example:

- ReadSpeaker will read the text to you.
- Flashcards are pre-populated to provide you with a jump start for review—or you can create your own.
- You can highlight text and make notes in your MindTap Reader. Your notes will flow into Evernote, the electronic notebook app that you can access anywhere when it's time to study for the exam.
- Self-quizzing allows you to assess your understanding.

Visit nelson.com/student to start using MindTap. Enter the Online Access Code from the card included with your text. If a code card is *not* provided, you can purchase instant access at NELSONbrain.com.

MINDTAP

ACKNOWLEDGMENTS

This book could not have happened without the hard work of many people. We are grateful to the managers and HR practitioners who shared their experiences and helped influence our writing and to all the individuals who told their stories to us.

Many thanks to Simon Vaughan and to the featured individuals for their work on the HRM Close-ups.

The efforts of the Nelson Education team were superb. Thanks to Jackie Wood, Alexis Hood, Jacquelyn Busby, and Natalia Denesiuk Harris for their guidance, wisdom, and patience.

The authors and publisher also wish to thank those who reviewed this project during its development and provided important insights and suggestions:

Lisa Bering, Humber College
Christine Coulter, Queen's University
Albert Elliott, Ambrose University
Edward Marinos, Sheridan College
Eddy Ng, Dalhousie University
John Predyk, Vancouver Island University
Chris P. Roubecas, Southern Alberta Institute of Technology
Vicky Roy, Southern Alberta Institute of Technology
Anne Zurowsky, Red River College

The greatest thanks go to the families of the current authors. Melanie Peacock is grateful to her husband, Cam, and children, Miranda, Joely, and Eric. They provided unwavering support throughout the creation of this book, and their encouragement was deeply appreciated. Eileen Stewart is indebted to her son, Jason Robertson, daughter-in-law, Andrea McLean, and grandsons, Caleb and Adam Robertson. They always provide help, support, research, and encouragement.

Melanie Peacock
Mount Royal University

Eileen B. Stewart
British Columbia Institute of Technology

Monica Belcourt
York University

ABOUT THE AUTHORS

Melanie Peacock

Melanie Peacock is an associate professor at the Bissett School of Business at Mount Royal University and president of the Mount Royal Faculty Association. Dr. Peacock has been extensively involved in professional HR initiatives as a senior manager, independent consultant, and educator. She obtained her BComm (with distinction) from the University of Alberta, her MBA from the Richard Ivey School of Business (Western University), and her PhD through the Faculty of Education at the University of Calgary.

As a senior manager and consultant, Dr. Peacock has led HR initiatives that create systems, processes, and policies that enable organizations to engage their employees and achieve strong results. With almost 30 years of experience, she has worked for industries including telecommunications, oil and gas, medical research, financial management, and not-for-profit entities and continues to work as an independent consultant. Due to her extensive knowledge and competencies, Dr. Peacock is a sought-after media contributor and commentator at the municipal, provincial, and national levels. In addition to this text, Dr. Peacock has authored books regarding training and development and change management.

Dr. Peacock enthusiastically promotes the value of an HR designation and has served on the board of directors for CPHR Alberta (formerly the Human Resources Institute of Alberta). As testimony to her exceptional work within the HR profession, Dr. Peacock was presented with the CPHR Alberta Distinguished Career Award in 2014 and was named to *HRD Canada* magazine's 2017 list of top 30 HR professionals across Canada. As well, in recognition of her passion for and dedication to teaching, Dr. Peacock was awarded the first Mount Royal Faculty Association Teaching Excellence Award in 2014. Furthermore, as testament to her accomplishments, Western University presented her with the Distinguished Alumni award in 2016.

Eileen B. Stewart

Eileen Stewart taught both full-time and part-time for many years at the British Columbia Institute of Technology (BCIT), where she was program head, Human Resource Management Programs. She is a senior human resources professional with extensive experience in all areas of human resources management (HRM), including labour relations in both the public and private sectors. As the HR executive, she has managed human resources units in several of British Columbia's large public sector organizations. With a diverse background that includes mining, banking, education, and municipal government, Ms. Stewart has a strong overall business orientation.

After receiving a BA in economics and commerce from Simon Fraser University, British Columbia, she joined Teck Mining as its first personnel manager. She then moved to BCIT, where she specialized in labour relations. She obtained her senior management experience at BCIT, as director of personnel and labour relations; the University of British Columbia, as director of human resources; and the City of Vancouver, as general manager of human resources.

While working full-time, Ms. Stewart completed her MBA at Simon Fraser University. She continues to provide consulting services to private, public, and not-for-profit organizations.

Ms. Stewart is active in the HR community through her continued involvement with the Chartered Professionals in Human Resources of British Columbia and Yukon (CPHR BC & Yukon). She was recognized by CPHR BC & Yukon in 2012 with the Award of Excellence for the HR Professional of the Year and became an Honorary Life Member in 2015. She has also served as president of the CPHR BC & Yukon's predecessor, the Human Resources

Management Association, as well as in other executive roles, for several years. In addition to her professional involvement, she is vice-chair, Board of Directors, B.C. Women's Hospital and Health Centre Foundation; sits on the Board of Directors, Community Living BC, where she chairs the Governance and Human Resources Committee; and is vice chair, Board of Directors, Douglas College. Previously, she was chair of the Board of Directors, YWCA of Vancouver, and sat on its board for many years.

Monica Belcourt

Monica Belcourt is the founding director of the School of Human Resource Management at York University. Additionally, she is a full professor, human resources management, and founding director of the Graduate Program in HRM at the Faculty of Liberal Arts and Professional Studies, York University. She has an extensive and varied background in HRM. After receiving a BA in psychology from the University of Manitoba, she joined the Public Service Commission as a recruitment and selection specialist. During her tenure with the federal government, she worked in training, HRM research, job analysis, and HR planning.

Dr. Belcourt alternated working in HRM with graduate school, obtaining an MA in psychology from York University, an MEd in adult education from the University of Ottawa, and a PhD in management from York University. Her research is grounded in the experience she gained as director of personnel for the 63,000 employees at CP Rail, as director of employee development at the National Film Board, and as a functional HR specialist for the federal government. She has taught HRM at Concordia University, Université du Québec à Montréal, McGill University, and York University, where she founded and managed the largest undergraduate program in HRM in Canada. She created Canada's first degrees in HRM: B.HRM, B.HRM (honours), and a master's in HRM. A full description of these degrees can be found at http://www.yorku.ca/laps/shrm.

Dr. Belcourt was director of the International Alliance for Human Resources Research (IAHRR), which was a catalyst for the discovery, dissemination, and application of new knowledge about HRM. This research centre has now been moved to the HRPA, where it is called the Human Resources Research Institute. Her research interests focus on strategic HRM, and she has published more than 100 articles, several of which received best paper awards.

Dr. Belcourt is series editor for the Nelson Series in Human Resources Management: *Managing Performance through Training and Development*; *Management of Occupational Health and Safety*; *Recruitment and Selection in Canada*; *Strategic Compensation in Canada*; *Strategic Human Resources Planning*; *Research, Measurement and Evaluation in HRM*; *International Human Resources Management: A Canadian Perspective*; and *Industrial Relations in Canada*. Additionally, she is lead author of the best-selling book *Managing Human Resources*, published by Nelson Education, from which this text is adapted.

Active in many professional associations and not-for-profit organizations, Dr. Belcourt was the president of the HRPA of Ontario, served on the national committee for HR certification, and was a board member of CIBC Insurance and the Toronto French School. She is a frequent commentator on HRM issues for Workopolis, CTV, *Canada AM*, CBC, *The Globe and Mail*, *Canadian HR Reporter*, and other media. She has been recognized as a champion of HR by *Canadian HR Reporter*. In 2009, the HRPA honoured Dr. Belcourt with the award of Right Management HR Academic of the Year, given for outstanding contributions to the HR profession and for thoughtful leadership. The following year, the association recognized her outstanding contribution to the HR profession by awarding her the Fellow Certified HR Leader designation (FCHRL). Dr. Belcourt was only the fourth person to receive the award since its inception in 1936. The award is given to CHRPs who have promoted best practices in the field, upheld the reputation, and made significant contributions in innovative ideas.

1 Exploring Why HRM Matters

LEARNING OUTCOMES

After studying this chapter, you should be able to

1 Define human resources management (HRM).

2 Identify HRM systems, practices, and policies.

3 Explain the importance of HRM to all employees.

4 Discuss the relationship between a manager and an HR professional.

5 Describe current business topics and their impact on HRM.

6 Outline demographic considerations.

7 Describe key employee expectations.

8 Illustrate the link between business strategy and HRM strategy.

OUTLINE

Introduction
What Is Human Resources Management?
What Are HRM Systems, Practices, and Policies?
Why Study Human Resources Management?
The Partnership of Managers and HR Professionals
Role of the Manager
Role of HR Professionals
The Ongoing Partnership
Current Business Topics Impacting HRM
Topic 1: Global Economy

Topic 2: Changes in Firms and Business Sectors
Topic 3: Technology and Quality
Topic 4: Sustainability
Topic 5: Human Capital and Talent Management
Topic 6: Demographics
Employee Expectations
Rights, Ethics, and Privacy
Fulfilling and Meaningful Work
Balancing Work and Family
Linking Business Strategy and HRM Strategy

"Human Resources is insurance. It can make you money, it can save you money."

IT'S NOT unusual to find awards proudly displayed throughout many workplaces. Trophies, acrylics, plaques; best employer, highest sales—you name it, many offices have at least one.

But few can boast a genuine Oscar!

Toronto-based 3D animation application software developer SideFX and its staff have received numerous Academy Awards and will shortly be adding another one to their collection. "We'll have to get a display case of some sort and put it somewhere," Kim Davidson, SideFX's cofounder, president, and CEO, exclaims with a broad smile.

Canada has long been known as Hollywood North for all of the movie and television productions made north of the 49th parallel. Although we may all know the Canadian actors and directors who have received recognition for their work, less familiar are the technology giants behind the scenes who make all that movie magic possible.

"Every visual effects award that's been given over the past dozen years has had Houdini in it," Davidson explains of the Houdini software program that SideFX is best known for. "If you see a movie with invisible effects, such as *The Shape of Water* or something like *Avatar, Doctor Strange, San Andreas, Captain America,* or *X-Men*—all the superhero stuff. Virtually every movie has some Houdini, especially if it's explosions, destructions, water, fluid, those sorts of things."

SideFX has come a long way since being founded by Davidson and business partner Greg Hermanovic in 1987 as Side Effects Software. Back then

Kim Davidson, President and CEO, SideFX

Courtesy of Kim Davidson

it was just the 2 programmers wearing all the hats, developing the software by night and searching for clients by day. "The first person we hired was basically just to put all our receipts in a box, simple admin, keeping track of things," Davidson reflects. "Our first real hire was a programmer, Mark Elendt, and he's still with us after 28 and a half years. And he's been recognized 4 times with an Academy Award!"

"In 1995 we hired a controller who also had a human resources background," explains Davidson. "Then we brought in a CFO about 12 years ago, and our controller moved full-time to HR, and then she hired someone to work with her."

Today, SideFX has more than 100 staff, interns, and co-op students scattered between Toronto and Santa Monica, California. "It's absolutely critical at the size we're at now to have an HR department," Davidson says. "There's just so much to do in a company of 100. I remember reading that you need 1 HR person for every 50 staff depending on the makeup of the company."

"We have support, education and training, marketing, sales, finance, and, obviously, the development group," he adds. "When you have all these diverse areas, it's very complex. And we have the US and Canada, so we have those regulations to worry about too. I think 3's the right number of HR professionals for our company at this stage. It's very helpful."

Although Davidson likes to keep an eye on every area of his business, he knows which ones to leave to the specialists. "Government policies and procedures are getting more onerous: accessibility training, sensitivity training—all that policy stuff is changing. It just makes it complex," he says. "Having a good HR department is a bit like your IT department," he explains. "How does that guy who's just fixing my computer make me money? If my computer never breaks down because he does regular maintenance, well, if it broke down once, then that kind of paid for that month of his time. I look at HR as not just preventative medicine for people who might otherwise move on but also maybe finding the right people for you, keeping you out of any downside if you get into any dismissal suit or anything of that nature. It's insurance. It can make you money, it can save you money."

A good human resources department isn't merely about the value to a company; it can also make the work environment better for employees and make sure they're a good fit for the organization.

"It's not just that it's a cool business to be in," Davidson points out. "People still quit really cool companies for any of a number of reasons."

"So it's very important to hire good people, and we spend a lot of time checking for fit," he says. That's one of the areas where Davidson depends on his HR team for assistance. "I think I have good people-sense, and so you

trust your Spidey-instinct, but you also make sure that other people are involved in that interview process, especially HR."

And if anyone knows anything about Spidey-senses, it's Davidson because SideFX's Houdini software also helps the legendary web-slinging superhero Spider-Man use his Spidey-senses to fight crime on the silver screen.

INTRODUCTION

This book will introduce you to the field of human resources management. Human resources management is a subject that affects people in all types of organizations (different sizes, profit or not for profit, and different industries) and will continue to impact you throughout your entire career. It is possible that you are taking this course along with other courses, such as general management, economics, organizational behaviour, or hospitality management. All the information you learn in those courses will be applicable to your fuller understanding of human resources management.

Some of the important things to know and understand about business today are that we live in a global world, that there is constant change, and that any of a number of factors can impact the success of any business. The economy in Canada, and in the rest of the world as well, continues to fluctuate. Competing forces affect the economy: a drop in the price of oil, changes in the value of the Canadian dollar, sluggish consumer sales, and increases in housing and food costs.[1] What happens in the economy has a direct impact on how many employees an organization hires. Without a healthy and prosperous economy, businesses won't thrive, and fewer jobs will be available.

The managing of people in any organization remains key to the business agenda—perhaps even more so now. New terms, such as "human capital," "intellectual assets," and "talent management," have crept into business jargon to emphasize the value that the people in the organization have.

As Kim Davidson says in the HRM Close-up, human resources management is a form of insurance and can protect an organization while helping it to grow and thrive. But what does this mean, and why is it important?

Just for a moment, imagine an organization without people—no employees, no managers, no executives, and no owners. It's a pretty tough assignment. Without people, organizations would not exist. Although this idea may not be much of a revelation, it brings home the point that organizations are made up of people. Successful organizations are good at bringing together different kinds of people to achieve a common purpose, which is to ensure that an organization achieves its goals. This is the essence of human resources management. As students, you are the future of any organization—whether you become employees, managers, or owners. Therefore, a deeper and thorough understanding of human resources management will help you be successful, regardless of your role(s) throughout your entire career.

WHAT IS HUMAN RESOURCES MANAGEMENT?

LO1

Define human resources management (HRM).

Human resources management is more than hiring, paying, and training people. **Human resources management (HRM)** is an *integrated* set of systems, practices, and policies in an organization that focuses on the effective deployment and development of its employees. In other words, HRM ensures that an organization will be successful by having the right people, in the right places, doing the right things at the right time. It is important to remember that a change in 1 HRM practice has an impact on the other systems, practices, and policies.

Throughout this book, the word "employee" is intended to cover anyone working for an organization. Today's workplace is far more fluid and flexible than the workforce 10 to 20 years ago, and all types of workers in an organization are important to its success. The term "manager" is intended to cover any person who has responsibility for, or authority over, other people. Depending on the organization, managers may be identified by different titles, including but not limited to team leaders, supervisors, or directors. It is important to remember that managers are employees too. Therefore, although managers have distinct and different roles (and therefore key responsibilities within an organization's HRM systems, practices, and policies), they are also impacted and influenced by HRM from the perspective of an employee.

Managers use a lot of words to describe the importance of people to their organizations. The term "human resources" implies that people are as important to the success of any business as other resources, such as money, materials, machinery, and information. However, unlike other assets, human beings have multi-faceted needs and motivations, thereby making the management of human resources a complex and dynamic subject to explore.

> **Human resources management (HRM)**
> An integrated set of systems, practices, and policies in an organization that focuses on the effective deployment and development of its employees

WHAT ARE HRM SYSTEMS, PRACTICES, AND POLICIES?

Before there can be a discussion about why to study HRM, let's look at the various systems, practices, and polices that fit together. You will notice that each of these topic is addressed in the various chapters of this book. Although these topics are examined individually, no system, practice, or policy stands alone as there is overlap among all the areas. At all times, legal requirements (as discussed in Chapter 2) must be considered and followed when developing and implementing systems, practices, and policies that address the following HRM topics:

> **LO2**
> Identify HRM systems, practices, and policies.

1. *Promoting employee health and safety through organizational culture.* Creating a work environment that promotes a sense of well-being and encouraging employee engagement. Ensuring that employees work in healthy and safe conditions (Chapter 3).
2. *Defining, analyzing, and designing the work.* Determining what tasks need to be done, in what order, with what skills, and how individual tasks fit together in work units. Creating high-performance work groups or teams as a form of defining and designing work (Chapter 4).
3. *Planning for, recruiting, and selecting employees.* Ensuring that the correct number of people with the correct skills are attracted to work for an organization. Choosing the right people to perform the required work (Chapter 5).
4. *Orienting, training, and developing employees.* Welcoming and socializing people to an organization. Providing the resources and opportunities to assist employees in developing the necessary knowledge, skills, and abilities to do their current and future job(s) (Chapter 6).
5. *Managing employee performance.* Ensuring that employees know what they are expected to accomplish and then providing appropriate mechanisms for regular feedback. Aligning employees' expected performance to the organization's goals (Chapter 7).
6. *Rewarding and recognizing employees.* Evaluating the worth of jobs and developing and administering a variety of rewards and recognition components, including pay and benefits, that will attract, retain, and engage employees (Chapter 8).
7. *Knowing your rights and responsibilities.* Ensuring that employees and management rights are protected and respected and that disciplinary issues are properly addressed. Effectively addressing conflict between employees and managers in order to maintain constructive relationships (Chapter 9).

FIGURE 1.1 HRM Topics

From STEWART/BELCOURT/PEACOCK/BOHLANDER/SNELL. *Essentials of Managing Human Resources*, 6E. © 2017 Nelson Education Ltd. Reproduced by permission. www.cengage.com/permissions.

8. *Understanding labour relations and collective bargaining.* Establishing effective negotiating practices and working relationships within unionized environments to create and sustain effective and efficient organizations (Chapter 10).

9. *Learning about international human resources management.* Customizing HRM systems, practices, and policies to address the various economic, political, legal, and cultural factors in different countries (Chapter 11).

As previously noted, and as shown in Figure 1.1, all of the above-noted HRM topics are interconnected and are not dealt with as isolated requirements within an organization. The running case (This Makes Scents) that you will see at the end of each part of this book also highlights this as the company featured is faced with many complex and overlapping HRM issues that cannot be dealt with in isolation.

Throughout this book, you will also be provided with information that links organizational performance to the various HRM topics, thereby reinforcing the requirement to have HRM systems, practices, and policies that fit the organization. The collective set of these activities, and how well they are linked to each other and the business, creates the setting for an organization to be successful through its employees.

WHY STUDY HUMAN RESOURCES MANAGEMENT?

LO3

Explain the importance of HRM to all employees.

To work with people in any organization, it is important to understand human behaviour and to be knowledgeable about the various systems, practices, and policies available to effectively use and build a skilled, knowledgeable, and motivated workforce. Managers must be aware of economic, technological, social, and legal issues that either help or hinder their ability to work with and guide others and thereby help an organization achieve its desired goals.

Employees need to understand what their work is, what development opportunities they can expect to receive, how their performance will be measured, how they will be rewarded, and what rights they have in the workplace. (Remember, managers are employees too, so they need to understand these topics from this perspective as well.)

You are the employees, managers, and business owners of tomorrow. Studying HRM will help you understand your work, responsibilities, and rights in an organization and how your contributions make the organization successful. In the process of managing human resources, increasing attention is being given to the individual needs of employees. For example, Simon Sinek (a well-known business consultant and speaker) stresses that knowing what to do is not sufficient; employees need to know *why* their work is valuable and needed.[2] People need to feel connected (to other people and to their work), need to be recognized, and need to understand that their work is important to the success of an organization.[3] This is not easy to accomplish, but effective HRM is required if this is to occur. Thus, this book will not only emphasize the importance of the contributions HRM makes to the organization but will also show how, through good people management in an organization, the individual and our overall society are improved. Consider how you feel and behave if your work isn't enjoyable and you don't feel that you understand your role in the organization or that your work doesn't appear to be valued. You might respond in a variety of ways, including being unconcerned about a customer complaint. By acting in this way, you are not contributing to the success of the organization, which includes your own success. If enough people do this, our overall productive capacity will decrease. So HRM isn't just about making employees feel good or keeping people happy. Effective HRM provides a work environment that allows people to be engaged, motivated, and successful in their work, ultimately resulting in profitable organizations and a prosperous society.

THE PARTNERSHIP OF MANAGERS AND HR PROFESSIONALS

Role of the Manager

The manager is the key link between the employee and the organization. Therefore, managers must have a thorough knowledge and understanding of contemporary HRM as well as the specific HRM systems, practices, and policies within their organizations. Although HR professionals may have responsibility for coordinating programs and policies pertaining to people-related issues, managers and employees themselves are ultimately responsible for making the organization successful. All managers—not HR professionals or HR—are people managers. Through the effective leadership of the manager, the talent or "intellectual capital" of the organization is enhanced. Remember that it is the manager who directly interacts with employees and is responsible for guiding and motivating their effective contribution to the organization. It is the manager's role to develop employees and make work a great place.[4] For example, when an organization wishes to place an increased emphasis on the growth and development of its people, it is the manager who is front and centre in identifying the gaps in any skill sets. It is also the manager who works with employees to ensure effective performance and, at times, improve performance. The key point is that managers are responsible for implementing various HRM systems, practices, and policies and must therefore work with, and rely upon, HR professionals to ensure that they have the right knowledge, tools, and resources to do so effectively.

Role of HR Professionals

It is important for managers to understand the role or function HR professionals play, whether these individuals are part of the organization or are external resources retained by the organization. Besides knowing how to recruit and pay people appropriately, HR professionals need sound business knowledge, good problem-solving and influence skills, and

LO4

Discuss the relationship between a manager and an HR professional.

personal credibility (trust and the ability to build personal relationships). The HR professional's primary role in today's organizations is to help equip the manager with the best people practices so that the organization can be successful. HR professionals can provide service activities, such as recruiting and training. Furthermore, they can be active in policy formulation and implementation in such areas as workplace harassment, healthy work environments, and change management. Lastly, an HR professional can be an employee advocate by listening to employee concerns and ensuring that the organization is aware of and responding to those concerns.

HR professionals are expected to fulfill their role by actively involving others in the organization, particularly managers, in the development and design of HRM systems, practices, and policies. For example, a company may want the HR professional to develop an overall recruitment approach to attract individuals with key skill sets. This approach would then generate a pool of applicants with the required skills. The HR professional would help develop appropriate interview questions and may be part of the interview process itself. However, it would be the manager who would select the best person for the job.

Dave Ulrich, a leading expert and author on human resources practices, states that an HR professional must be impactful and create value for the organization.[5] Above all else, HR professionals must be able to integrate business skills, HR skills, and skills in helping employees handle change so that their organization can build and maintain a competitive advantage through its people. One way to accomplish this is by providing key HR metrics. This data can be used to uncover useful insights in order to make well-informed business decisions. This includes information on the efficiency and effectiveness of recruitment and selection practices, data on absenteeism and turnover, and workplace injury statistics. HR professionals need to be able to show managers numerical information that can help identify what practices should be retained, as well as areas for improvement, and then provide HRM systems, practices, and policies for managers to use, thereby ultimately helping an organization to be successful.

The manager should make the hiring decision.

The Ongoing Partnership

As we next look at the competitive and social challenges facing any business, it is important to reinforce the idea that managing people is not something done in a back room or by HR professionals alone. It is important to remember that HR doesn't tell managers what to do, and proactive managers know when to involve an HR professional. Managing people is every manager's responsibility and obligation, and successful organizations are those that equip their managers with a thorough understanding of good HRM practices—either through having an HR unit or retaining expertise when needed. Even without an HR professional, the manager is still responsible for effective human resources management.

In organizations that have an HR unit, HR managers usually assume a greater role in top-management planning and decision making. There are, however, organizations that see HR as more an administrative matter than a key business section.[6] For HR to be seen as part of the business, it must have a solid understanding of the business and develop processes and practices that align with that business.[7] To this point, Christina

FIGURE 1.2 Relationship of HR to Other Business Units

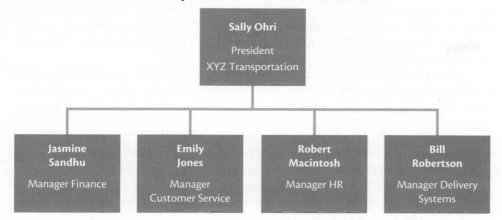

McClung, chief people officer at Capital One Canada, notes that HR professionals need to be vocal, need to actively share their combined business and HR expertise, and need to take an equally strategic role to that of other leaders within a business.[8] But many smaller organizations often wonder when they should hire an HR professional. Frequently, when an organization has 75 to 100 employees, the owners or senior management may think it best to get professional assistance. Figure 1.2 shows what the relationship between HR and other business units might be in a small organization. Even smaller organizations, those with fewer than 75 employees, will frequently retain an independent HR practitioner; this is typically done through the owner or president, and the manager may not have much interaction with the HR expert.

If Emily in Figure 1.2 needed to hire a customer service agent, she would work with Robert in confirming the job requirements, identifying possible recruitment sources, doing the final interviewing, and making the decision on which candidate to hire. Robert, on the other hand, would assist Emily as required, including the development of appropriate interview questions and conducting reference checks.

CURRENT BUSINESS TOPICS IMPACTING HRM

Organizations such as The Conference Board of Canada, CPHR Canada, and McKinsey & Company conduct ongoing studies of the most important competitive trends and issues facing Canadian organizations. As we move forward in an ever-evolving, connected world, the following business topics should be continuously monitored as they impact HRM systems, practices, and policies:

1. Global economy.
2. Changes in firms and business sectors.
3. Technology and quality.
4. Sustainability.
5. Developing human capital and talent management.
6. Demographics.

Topic 1: Global Economy

The Canadian economy is primarily built on exports, including those in natural resources, such as oil, gas, mining, and forestry. Because of this, for years many Canadian companies have been involved in global markets. As Canada has moved into other goods and services to

LO5

Describe current business topics and their impact on HRM.

export, many companies have created global operations or worked collaboratively with foreign companies to sell Canadian products. Canadian exports were valued at close to US$421 billion in 2017.[9] This figure represents just over 31% of Canada's gross domestic product (GDP).[10] At Work with HRM 1.1 provides insights into a number of Canadian companies that are successful in the global marketplace.

Although many companies, such as Starbucks, Walmart, and Lowe's, are coming to Canada to do business, some Canadian companies have acquired firms in other countries. An example is Brookfield, headquartered in Toronto and one of the largest owners/ managers of office properties and renewable energy–generating facilities.[11] The company recently acquired a large-scale gambling casino in Atlantic City and is investing heavily to induce people to come to that city for a full offering of entertainment as well as for gambling.[12] But **globalization** is not just something of interest to large firms. Although estimates vary widely, 70 to 80% of the Canadian economy is now affected by international competition. This means, for a small distributor in Kamloops, British Columbia, or a small manufacturer in Alliston, Ontario, that the competition today is no longer the distributor or manufacturer in the next town or province. Trade agreements that allow a freer flow of goods and services mean that competitors may be located anywhere around the world. Also, companies that had been doing business in Canada can move to other countries that may have lower production costs. For example, Ford Motor Co. decided to build a new engine plant in Mexico rather than in Windsor, Ontario, eliminating the creation of approximately 1000 jobs.[13]

Global growth continues to be vital for the Canadian economy, and according to the Business Development Bank of Canada, Europe will continue to be a driving force for

Globalization
Moving local or regional business into the global marketplace

---

AT WORK WITH HRM 1.1   OUR GLOBAL SUCCESS: GREAT EMPLOYEES!

Many Canadian companies acknowledge that their success in the global marketplace is attributable to the people they have hired. Employers actively strive now to have work environments that make them eligible for "best employer" status. For example, Cactus Restaurants, a western Canada restaurant chain, received such an award for the largest in-house apprenticeship pursuing Red Seal certification. Firms with an international presence, such as Atlantic Coated Papers, Fisherman's Market International, and The Woodbridge Group, were honoured in 2018 for being among the best managed companies in Canada.

As another example, Avison Young, a Canadian-owned commercial real-estate venture, is proud of its investment in people. It provides specialized training and workshops that allow its staff to provide exceptional service to clients. Furthermore, the company highlights the importance of collaboration to achieve the best expertise and intellectual capital. It also believes that its culture of team orientation helps it keep the most talented in the commercial real-estate business.

Global presence is also important to ECS Electrical Cable Supply, with operations as far away as Dubai. The company provides wire and cable products to specialty markets, such as shipping, mining, and critical life support with portable cables. It is successful because its professionals have deep knowledge of the various industries and superb customer service capabilities. To help with the deepening of its knowledge base, the company provides personal development and encourages everyone to take an active part in the company's success.

The above-noted companies serve as evidence that participating in the global economy is vital to many Canadian organizations.

CRITICAL THINKING QUESTIONS:
1. What other businesses in your geographic area have a global marketplace?
2. What types of skills would their employees need for them to continue being global players?

Sources: Adapted from "Canada's Best Managed Companies: Returning Winners," *Canadian Business*, March 8, 2018, accessed April 8, 2018, http://www .canadianbusiness.com/lists-and-rankings/best-managed-companies/requalified-winners; Avison Young, accessed April 8, 2018, http://www.avisonyoung.com/ enCA; and ECS Electrical Cable Supply, accessed April 8, 2018, https://www.ecswire.com.

enhancing our trade.[14] Furthermore, the other 2 most important global economies, the United States and China, have been expanding as well.[15]

Effect of Globalization on HRM

When an organization decides to operate in a different country, HRM practices need to address the different legal, political, and cultural requirements within this new location. As well, an organization needs to identify capable expatriate managers who can live and work overseas. Designing training programs and development opportunities to enhance managers' understanding of foreign cultures and work practices, adjusting compensation plans to ensure that pay schemes are fair and equitable across individuals in different geographic regions with different costs of living, and customizing performance management practices to align with workplace expectations must also be addressed.

So, although managing across borders provides new and broader opportunities for organizations, it also represents a quantum leap in the complexity of human resources management. Whether you are working for a large multinational company or a small parts distributor, HRM in other countries has an impact on you. Chapter 11 focuses on international human resources management.

Topic 2: Changes in Firms and Business Sectors

Although Canada exports its oil and minerals, much of Canada's economy over the past several years has relied upon housing and consumer spending. For real growth, Canada will need to increase its exports.[16] Currently, Canada is heavily dependent on the economic health of the United States since approximately 73% of Canada's GDP is exported there.[17] To put this in perspective, Canada exported 3.26 million barrels per day (bpd) of crude oil to the United States in November 2017 and 22,500 bpd to the United Kingdom in this same time period.[18] However, the price of crude oil continues to fluctuate, thereby causing further uncertainty within the Canadian economic landscape.[19]

Maintaining Canada's ability to export large quantities of oil and gas isn't easy given the environmental concerns about extracting and shipping. There is huge public resistance to pipelines, especially from environmentalists, farmers, and ranchers. The controversy surrounding the Keystone XL oil pipeline and TransCanada's ongoing expansion of its natural gas system in Alberta are examples of this.[20]

Changes to company ownership have produced some interesting outcomes. Several years ago, Sobeys, a grocery chain with headquarters in Nova Scotia, bought Safeway, thereby making Sobeys 1 of 2 national grocery retailers.[21] As other examples, Hudson's Bay Company bought Saks, LifeLabs Medical Laboratory bought CML, and TD Bank Group bought 50% of CIBC's Aeroplan credit card portfolio.[22] As companies change, so do the requirements for the capabilities of employees. Dealing with the consequences of changes impacts all HRM systems, practices, and policies.

Small and medium-sized businesses continue to be the lifeblood of a healthy economy. Gravitypope, a specialty shoe and clothing store headquartered in Edmonton, has grown from a small store in Edmonton to having stores in Calgary, Vancouver, and Toronto.[23] A brewery in Calgary that is noted for its specialty beers expanded its local operations while continuing to operate internationally as well.[24]

Productivity and Managing Costs

Companies continually look at ways to lower costs and improve productivity to maximize efficiency in order to be globally competitive. Labour costs are one of the largest expenditures of any organization, particularly in service and knowledge-intensive companies. Organizations have tried a number of approaches to lower costs, particularly labour costs. These include downsizing, outsourcing, and the use of contract employees, each of which has a direct impact on HRM systems, practices, and policies.

As companies grow and change, employees with new skills and experience will be required.

Downsizing
A strategic approach to decreasing the number of employees in a company

Downsizing is a strategic approach to decreasing the number of employees in a company. There is no company or business sector that hasn't experienced downsizing at some point. More downsizing will occur when the economy is poor, but sometimes downsizing might occur if the company decides to eliminate a product line or close a plant. For example, Saputo, a large dairy processor headquartered in Montréal, closed plants in both Alberta and the United States. It moved the production elsewhere so that efficiencies could be increased and costs reduced.[25] Although exact numbers were not given, in late 2017 and early 2018, Bell Media announced that employees, including prominent on-air personalities at radio and TV stations across Canada, would be let go.[26]

A number of lessons were learned in earlier downsizing situations, so organizations are being much more careful about changing operations. For a number of years, the general approach was to do an across-the-board reduction or to eliminate individuals on the basis of performance. However, research has found that why and how a company downsizes can create negative views of how responsible the company is.[27] Other lessons include communicating what is going to happen as soon as possible, being honest regarding why the downsizing occurs, treating everyone with respect, and being sure downsizing is the right solution.[28]

If jobs and employees have to be eliminated, the manner in which the action is taken also has to be carefully planned. This is known as *survivor syndrome* as much attention needs to be paid to those people who will still be employed as to departing employees. It is the people who are still employed who will make the company successful, so it is important that they feel the company has treated everyone well. It is also important that the remaining employees feel as if they matter; a good way to achieve this is to provide additional training and development opportunities.[29] Ethics in HRM 1.1 highlights the significance of this as Sears Canada faced severe criticism for how employees were treated when the company began shutting down operations across Canada. In contrast, in 2015, when Target announced it was leaving Canada, it created a fund that would guarantee severance payments to its 17,500 employees—a fund that would be safe from bankruptcy proceedings.[30]

Outsourcing and Contractors

Outsourcing
Hiring an external person (or a company) to do work that had previously been done by an internal employee

Outsourcing means hiring a person who does not work for the company (or hiring another company) to perform work that would normally have been performed by someone employed by the organization. Companies often hire the services of accounting firms, for example,

ETHICS IN HRM 1.1   THE END OF AN ERA

In early 2018, the final Sears Canada store in Canada was closed for good, thus marking the official end of the chain's historic retail reign of more than 65 years. As disappointing as it was to lose an iconic Canadian retailer, the treatment of employees during the months leading to the final closure is what gained the most attention.

In 2005, Sears Canada came under the control of a New York–based hedge fund run by former Goldman Sachs employee Edward Lampert. In that year and those that followed, billions were paid out to shareholders, while spending was slashed and little was invested in the ongoing operations of the company. According to some analysts, shareholders were getting rich while employees were getting cheated. Furthermore, the pension plan became underfunded, and the company failed to ensure that there was sufficient money to cover the health and medical allowances promised to retirees. Therefore, when it was announced that the store would be filing for creditors' court protection, 18,000 retirees learned that they were not only losing their benefits but also that their pension would be worth about 80 cents (or worse) on the dollar.

This has forced many of these former workers, some now into their seventies and beyond, to seek work in order to pay the bills. The plan they based their retirement on has collapsed.

As noted by reporter Gary Mason, "How can our governments sit back and allow corporations to treat their employees like total rubes? The business world could see what was happening to Sears, analysts could see the ruthless and deliberate winddown of the company, and yet no one thought to ask: what does this mean for retirees and their benefits?"

CRITICAL THINKING QUESTIONS:

1. What should the Canadian government do to ensure that business owners cannot protect their own (and shareholder) interests while ignoring the needs of employees?
2. What could be done to prevent this type of problem in the future in other iconic Canadian companies?

Sources: Adapted from Lisa Wright, "Final Sears Stores Close Sunday, Marking the End of an Era," *The Star*, January 12, 2018, accessed April 8, 2018, https://www.thestar.com/business/2018/01/12/final-sears-stores-close-sunday-marking-the-end-of-an-era.html; and Gary Mason, "The Inexcusable Treatment of Sears Employees: A Cautionary Tale," *The Globe and Mail*, January 19, 2018, accessed April 8, 2018, https://www.theglobeandmail.com/opinion/the-inexcusable-treatment-of-sears-employees-a-cautionary-tale/article37661479.

to take care of financial services. Increasingly, activities such as maintenance, security, catering, and payroll are being outsourced in order to increase the organization's flexibility and to lower administrative costs. For example, organizations such as Telus, Accenture, and IBM have business units that provide outsourced services such as technology support, management, and telephone operator services.[31]

Outsourcing can be a niche market for some entrepreneurs. Mindfield, a recruiting company in Burnaby, British Columbia, provides hourly workers for companies such as Canadian Tire, Sport Chek, Overwaitea Foods, and Mark's Work Wearhouse. Its focus is on retail and small to medium-sized companies, and it uses state-of-the-art technology to recruit and assess skills for hiring and placement.[32]

Although the use of outsourcing continues, there are examples of where outsourced work is returning to the home company. American Express Canada returned some activities to Canada from other countries.[33] Furthermore, in some cases, using

Organizations will often outsource their security requirements as this is a more effective and efficient way to fill this specialized requirement.

Africa Studio/Shutterstock.com

outsourced services can help with a business transformation, such as is occurring in Russia, where outsourcing has not traditionally been done.[34] However, since there is always a risk when outsourcing, here are some important things to examine:

1. What does the company want to outsource and why?
2. Who are the service providers, and what will the evaluation criteria be?
3. What are the risks of outsourcing, and how will the risks be mitigated?[35]

> **Independent contractor**
> A person who is hired by contract to perform a specific job and is not considered part of the employee base

In addition to downsizing and outsourcing, organizations will hire **independent contractors**. Generally speaking, independent contractors are hired to do a specific job for a specific period of time and have more flexibility in relation to hours of work, work location, and how the work is done. Independent contractors are not covered by mandatory employment deductions such as income tax and employment insurance premiums. However, independent contractors are still required to report all income and then to pay appropriate taxes. The Canadian government has strict rules regarding who may and may not be classified as an independent contractor and has been actively auditing companies to ensure that these regulations are being followed, with the burden of proof and compliance being required from employers.[36] The downside of using independent contractors is that they may not be as attached or committed to the work outcomes as an employee. Read HRM and the Law 1.1 for an overview of the legal requirements for a worker to be classified as an independent contractor.

HRM AND **THE LAW** 1.1   INDEPENDENT CONTRACTOR OR EMPLOYEE?

The Canadian government and several provinces (including British Columbia, Alberta, and Ontario) have amended legislation to ensure that workers are properly being classified as employees instead of being treated as independent contractors. Why does this matter? It is critical that the nature of the relationship between a worker and a company is properly defined as this has implications as to whether or not mandatory payroll deductions have to be taken from a person's pay, whether a worker is entitled to benefits, and requirements for notice of termination of the relationship, to name just a few of the considerations. However, if a business hires an independent contractor who is later deemed to be an employee, both parties lose big as unpaid taxes, penalties, interest, and CPP and EI premiums will all have to be paid. The big tax advantage for the independent contractor, of course, is the potential for certain tax deductions. Generally, a self-employed person can deduct all reasonable business expenses.

How is the nature of the relationship between a worker and an organization determined? The Canada Revenue Agency highlights the following factors that are typically considered: who controls the work (what, where, when, and how the work is performed), who owns the tools and physical resources used to complete the required work, who bears the risk of profit or loss for any work completed, and how integrated is the worker into the organization's ongoing business? (Does the independent contractor have other sources of revenue/other clients?)

The above-noted points are only consideration points, and companies are always encouraged to seek legal advice prior to hiring independent contractors. Incorrect classification and treatment of workers can be a costly mistake and can also damage an organization's employment brand.

CRITICAL THINKING QUESTIONS:

1. Would you want to work as an independent contractor? Why or why not?
2. If companies incorrectly classify workers as independent contractors, how could this damage their employment brand?

Sources: Adapted from Susan Ward, "Independent Contractor vs Employee: Which One Are You?," *The Balance*, September 7, 2017, accessed April 8, 2018, https://www.thebalance.com/are-you-a-contractor-or-an-employee-2948639; "Is It an Employee or Contractor? Learn CRA's Rules to Be Sure," *CFIB*, accessed April 8, 2018, https://www.cfib-fcei.ca/en/it-employee-or-contractor-learn-cras-rules-be-sure; and "RC4110 Employee or Self-employed?," Government of Canada, November 6, 2017, accessed April 8, 2018, https://www.canada.ca/en/revenue-agency/services/forms-publications/publications/rc4110-employee-self-employed.html.

Topic 3: Technology and Quality

Technology

Advancements in technology have enabled organizations to improve processes (both production and administrative), reduce costs, and improve quality. With computer networks, unlimited amounts of data can be stored, accessed, and used in a variety of ways, from simple record keeping to controlling complex equipment. The effect is so dramatic that, at a broader level, organizations are changing the way they do business. Use of the Internet for both large and small companies is now a way of doing business and is transforming the way traditional brick-and-mortar companies operate. For example, Amazon's rise was based on its having only an online presence, with no storefront. It is now considered one of the tech giants of the world as it not only sells books but also has developed electronic readers and Wi-Fi speakers.[37] Organizations are connected via computer-mediated relationships, which are giving rise to a new generation of "virtual" workers who work from home, hotels, cars, or wherever their work takes them.

The implications for HRM are at times mind-boggling. For example, in the early years, HRM was more administrative and involved a lot of time processing forms. Technology is now found in all the HRM practices, and many of you may have already experienced this, such as when applying online for a job. Support is also provided to all employees through technology, including intranets. Information is now also widely available to everyone regarding employment matters or anything to do with HRM. Toolkit 1.1 provides helpful website addresses regarding HRM.

In addition, cloud computing is a growing trend impacting the way organizations handle data and whether or not the company has in-house IT employees. There is even a suggestion that cloud computing can create organizations that are more agile and produce better business outcomes.[38]

Furthermore, it is important to remember the impact technology and the Internet have had on the way people work. Specifically, people can live in 1 location and "work" in another, including their own home. This kind of work is called **telecommuting**, in which people may have their job structured to allow them to work from home and to work at any time. Staples Canada conducted a survey regarding how employees feel about telecommuting. The survey revealed that 71% of employees consider telecommuting an important benefit as it enables them to have a better work–life balance.[39] Staples' use of telecommuting gives it an advantage in recruiting talent. However, not all companies are in favour of these types of working arrangements. Marissa Mayer, CEO of Yahoo, took away the ability for employees to telecommute as she believed that this detracted from team work, spontaneous creative exchange of ideas, and overall company performance.[40]

Figure 1.3 provides information about the skills important for contributing to innovation in the workplace.

> **Telecommuting**
> Conducting work activities away from the office (typically at home) through the use of technology

Quality

Meeting customer expectations and providing excellent customer service are essential for any organization. In addition to focusing on internal management issues, managers must also meet customer requirements of quality, innovation, variety, and responsiveness. These standards often separate the winners from the losers in today's competitive world. How well does a company understand its customers' needs? How fast can it develop and get a new product to market? How effectively has it responded to special concerns? "Better, faster, cheaper"—these standards require organizations to constantly align their processes with customer needs. Management approaches, such as quality management, Six Sigma, and Lean, outlined below, provide comprehensive approaches to responding to customers. These have direct implications for HRM: the requirement to hire staff that can work in teams, the necessity of having compensation systems that support quality objectives, and the need to

FIGURE 1.3   Innovation Skills Profile 2.0

The Conference Board of Canada, as a non-profit applied research organization, helps identify skills necessary to help organizations be more innovative and productive. Here are some of those skills:

Creativity, problem-solving, and continuous improvement skills—necessary to generate ideas

- Seeking different points of view and exploring options.
- Being adaptable.
- Asking questions.
- Putting forward own ideas.
- Looking for surprising connections.

Risk assessment and risk-taking skills—necessary for being entrepreneurial

- Being comfortable when pursuing new opportunities.
- Assessing and managing risk.
- Keeping goals in sight.
- Willing to experiment.
- Learning from experiences.

Relationship-building and communication skills—necessary to develop and maintain interpersonal relationships

- Engaging others.
- Building and maintaining relationships in and outside the organization.
- Sharing information.
- Respecting and supporting other ideas.

Implementation skills—necessary to turn ideas into capabilities, processes, products, and services

- Setting realistic goals.
- Accessing and applying knowledge.
- Using the right tools and technologies.
- Using measurements to show the value of a solution.
- Accepting feedback and learn from mistakes.
- Being accountable.

Source: Adapted from The Conference Board of Canada, *Innovation Skills Profile 2.0,* found at http://www.conferenceboard.ca/cbi/innovationskills.aspx. Reproduced with permission from The Conference Board of Canada.

have performance management systems that recognize the importance of customer satisfaction and service excellence.

The focus on quality began over 60 years ago with total quality management (TQM) and was based on a management philosophy that focused on understanding customer needs, involving employees, using fact-based decision making, communicating, doing things right the first time, and improving continuously. A number of studies, pioneered by management expert W. Edwards Deming, have demonstrated the strong positive link between a focus on quality and higher customer satisfaction.[41]

Companies such as Xerox, Hitachi, and Home Depot then adopted a more systematic approach to quality, called Six Sigma, which includes major changes in management philosophy and HRM systems, practices, and policies. **Six Sigma** is a statistical method of translating a customer's needs into separate tasks and defining the best way to perform each task in concert with the others. Six Sigma makes the improvements through measurement and data analysis.[42] The approach can also be used for internal organizational processes that deal with internal "customers." What makes Six Sigma different from other quality efforts is that it catches mistakes before they happen.

Six Sigma
A process used to translate customer needs into a set of optimal tasks performed in concert with one another

TOOLKIT 1.1   A GUIDE TO INTERNET SITES

The Internet offers employees and HR professionals a vast amount of resources for research, news, recruitment, and networking with people and organizations. Listed below are some Internet sites related to the HR field. Their addresses (URLs) are printed here for reference, but once you get started, it's easier to access the rest by following the links to related sites.

General HR Sites

www.workforce.com

This site posts articles regarding the latest trends and topics in human resources. It also provides links to HR specialist consultants.

www.hrreporter.com

Canadian HR Reporter is an excellent resource for current news, information on the latest trends and practices, expert advice, experiences, and insights from HR practitioners, research, and resources.

www.hrvillage.com

hrVillage is an excellent source of up-to-date human resources information, featuring online articles, discussion forums, book reviews, and links to related sites.

Specialized Sites

www.canoshweb.org

This site offers a variety of information regarding safety and health in the workplace, reports and statistics, and industry trends. It also provides online access to the workers' compensation legislation in Canadian jurisdictions.

www.canada.ca/en/services/jobs/workplace.html

This site provides online access to federal statutes and regulations, with links to provincial employment legislation.

www.statcan.gc.ca

The Statistics Canada site offers daily news updates, census information, and free tabular data on various aspects of the Canadian economy.

In addition to the above sites, this book's website, https://myhome.nelsonbrain.com/cb, provides useful and up-to-date links to accompany this text.

Monkey Business Images Ltd/Thinkstock

HRM systems, practices, and policies must support and reinforce teamwork.

Lean
Organizational system of improvements that maximize customer value and minimize waste

Benchmarking
Finding the best practices in other organizations that can be brought into a company to enhance performance

Lean is similar to Six Sigma but is a more inclusive organizational system of improvements that maximize customer value and minimize waste.[43] It was pioneered by Toyota as a way to look at not just individual machines but also the overall flow of the production through the total process.[44] Since then, Lean has been used by many organizations, from manufacturing to services. For example, the Saskatchewan healthcare system is using it to improve efficiency, quality, and customer service.[45] Another expert believes Lean builds trust and fosters employee engagement.[46]

Benchmarking looks at the "best practices" in other companies, whether competitors or not. By looking at other companies, managers and employees can assess if something might be used in their organization to improve overall performance. For example, the University of Calgary has benchmarked how the practice of law is changing and how adults learn so that its law school can create "excellence in lawyering."[47]

Key to all of these techniques are good and appropriate HRM systems, practices, and policies. One reason good HRM is so essential to programs such as Six Sigma is that it helps to balance 2 opposing forces: the needs of employees and the requirements of the company. Six Sigma's focus on continuous improvement drives the system toward disequilibrium, whereas Six Sigma's focus on customers, management systems, and the like provides the restraining forces that keep the system together. HRM helps managers balance these forces. Hence, the manager plays a key role in motivating employees to care about quality and helping the company foster a work environment that will allow employees to succeed in quality initiatives. Read At Work with HRM 1.2 to learn more about what organizations can do to become excellent at what they do.

AT WORK WITH HRM 1.2   BECOMING EXCELLENT AS A COMPANY!

As mentioned in this chapter, making use of initiatives that promote quality and efficiency is very dependent on the environment and culture of the company. So what can be done besides using Six Sigma and Lean?

Companies such as Apple and Amazon didn't become outstanding only by making sure their systems and processes were efficient—as 1 management author says, "Lean may eliminate waste but it doesn't help create value." Although there is no precise recipe, here are some things that can help:

- Ensure that the company's strategy and its actions work together and are measured to demonstrate success.
- Attract and retain the right people.
- Ensure that the environment supports and encourages collaboration and innovation at all levels.
- Get and keep customers that the company wants.

Symcor is a Canadian company founded in 1996 with a mission to "deliver value-added solutions for [its] clients that enable operational excellence and enhance their customers' experience." With locations across Canada, the company strives to add value to every client relationship through best-in-class service and the latest technology solutions. Arrow Electronics, a global company headquartered in British Columbia that provides services and solutions to commercial and industrial users of electronic components, has received awards for its focus on delivering solutions that fits its customer needs. Likewise, Ingram Micro Canada received a Microsoft award for its superior operational excellence.

And operational excellence isn't just in the for-profit sector. The University of Toronto makes sure its operations are aligned with the academic missions of the university. Furthermore, the university makes sure its budgeting process is driven by academic outcomes—not just a focus on financial constraints.

CRITICAL THINKING QUESTION:

Is use of any quality improvement initiatives just another management fad to get more work out of people? Explain the reasons for your answer.

Sources: Adapted from Symcor, accessed April 18, 2018, https://www.symcor.com/en; Andrew Miller, *Redefining Operational Excellence*, Amacon, 2014; Harvey Schachter, "Four Principles of Operational Excellence, *The Globe and Mail*, August 6, 2014, B11; Arrow Electronics, "About Arrow," accessed April 18, 2018, www .arrow.com/about_arrow; Michael Cusanelli, "Distribution Watch: Ingram Micro, Synnex, Arrow Electronics," *Distribution Watch*, accessed April 18, 2018, http:// thevarguy.com/distribution-watch/111414/distribution-watch-ingram-micro-synnex-arrow-electronics; and James Flynn, "The Man Who Keeps the University Running," *The Varsity*, November 10, 2014, accessed April 18, 2018, http://thevarsity.ca/2014/11/10/meet-the-man-who-keeps-the-university-running.

Another approach to overall quality in an organization is the Baldrige award for performance excellence, sponsored by the National Institute of Standards and Technology in the United States. This award looks at excellence from a systems perspective, with detailed criteria in the areas of leadership, strategic planning, customer focus, measurement and knowledge management, workforce focus, process management, and results. In Canada, the Baldrige awards are managed through Excellence Canada. Medium-sized organizations such as Archmill House Inc. in Ancaster, Ontario, to large organizations such as Bell Canada have been recipients.[48]

Topic 4: Sustainability

As the world progresses further into the 21st century, more and more attention is being paid to the health of our planet and the sustainability of economic growth. The world population is increasing, natural resources are declining, and the climate is changing. People are realizing that there might be limits to how life on our planet can be sustained. With this, businesses are examining the threats and opportunities presented by these concerns.

Canada's economy has benefited greatly from our ability to export oil and gas on global markets. Changing that would dislocate both employees and government revenues. A study done by *Corporate Knights*, a magazine dedicated to clean capitalism, indicates that Canada has a major opportunity to export clean energy generated by both wind and hydro power.[49]

With more focus on sustainability, there are new industries and companies on a global level looking at "clean" technology. Canada seems well positioned to move forward on the innovation front. For example, Westport Innovations, a Canadian company that specializes in natural gas engines and vehicles, has partnerships throughout the world to provide engine and vehicle technology that is better for the environment. It recently developed an enhanced spark-ignited natural gas system that is cost-competitive and provides the same levels of power and fuel economy as much larger engines.[50] Currently, the clean technology sector is the fastest-growing industry, with about 41,000 people in Canada, and it is projected to be worth $28 billion by 2022.[51]

Besides the environment, climate change is also on businesses' agendas. TD Bank Group achieved one of its environmental goals by creating TD Forests, which has increased the amount of forested lands by 10,500 hectares; more forests help reduce carbon dioxide.[52] Likewise, Mountain Equipment Co-op commits 1% of sales to conservation and outdoor recreation projects.[53] Moreover, as new business opportunities are created, new jobs and careers will also be created, such as environmental engineers and technologists, conservation biologists, and environmental communications officers.

To recognize the achievements of organizations that promote and take action for the "greening" of their businesses, *Corporate Knights* has been tracking, measuring, and ranking Canadian companies for several years. In this fashion, it has honoured a number of companies for being good corporate citizens in relation to the environment and the ability to be sustainable. In 2018, the Saskatchewan Research Council, the Canadian Broadcasting Corporation, and London Hydro were named the top 3 responsible companies in this regard.[54]

Topic 5: Human Capital and Talent Management

It is likely that you have heard many companies say, "People are our greatest asset." But what does this mean, and how do companies survive and then thrive because of people? The term **human capital** is used to describe the value that employees provide to an organization through their knowledge, skills, and abilities. Although this may not show up as a financial figure on a company's balance sheet, the people performing the work have the greatest impact on how successful an organization will be.[55]

Once again, it is important to emphasize that the manager is the link between the organization and its employees. Therefore, managers are key in helping the organization maintain and develop its human capital.

Human capital
The value that employees provide to an organization through their knowledge, skills, and abilities

To build and retain human capital, managers must find ways to help employees enhance their knowledge, skills, and abilities. Therefore, managers have to do a good job of providing developmental assignments to employees and ensuring that job duties and requirements are flexible enough to allow for growth and learning. Furthermore, more and more organizations are recognizing that sets of knowledge capabilities—**core competencies**—are part of their human capital. These competencies are necessary in order to be different from their competition and provide ongoing value to their customers. For example, a core competency might be as follows: *Focus on customer*—the ability to make an effort to identify internal and external customers and understand what adds value for them; to create an environment that appreciates delivery of good customer service.

Core competencies
A combination of knowledge, skills, and characteristics needed to effectively perform a role in an organization

An organization differentiates itself from competitors through the competencies of its employees.

iStock.com/wwing

Although many core competencies, such as a focus on customer or active listening skills, are similar from one organization to another, each organization will develop its own set and define the competency to fit that organization. Thus, the combination of competencies of all employees in that organization makes it stand out from its competition.

Once competencies are identified, organizations, through senior leadership, have to find ways of using and improving those competencies. Some organizations, such as Manulife Financial, encourage employees to volunteer in their local communities to gain additional skills.[56] Too often employees have skills that go unused; thus, they become outdated. Some of this can be eliminated by leveraging what people have by sharing and helping others learn.[57] Efforts to empower employees and encourage their participation and involvement use the human capital available more fully. David Cronin, cofounder of DevFacto Technologies, a small firm specializing in creative technology solutions, says, "If you give them a purpose that's larger than themselves, you can lead them to results."[58]

Companies such as Hitachi have included a no-layoff policy as part of their talent management approach. Hitachi's manufacturing manager, Nick Montecchia, states, "There's a cost associated with trying to retrain and spending all that to get someone to become proficient."[59] Hitachi made the decision to ensure that there were no declines in productivity and quality.

Studies have consistently demonstrated that firms with a focus on building and enhancing human capital demonstrate higher profitability and stronger overall organizational performance.[60] Developmental assignments, particularly those involving teamwork, can also be a valuable way of facilitating knowledge exchange and mutual learning. Effective communications (whether face to face or through information technology) are instrumental in sharing knowledge and making it widely available throughout the organization. Dave Ulrich, considered one of the foremost management gurus of our time, noted:

> When employees find meaning at work, they care enough about it to develop their competence; they work harder and are more productive; they stay longer and are more positive about their work experience. But there is more: when employees are more positive, customers generally respond in kind. Employee attitude is a key lead indicator of customer attitude, and satisfied customers help the businesses they patronize to survive and thrive.[61]

As companies continue to focus on their human capital, the concept of **talent management** has evolved. Talent management is concerned with leveraging the competencies in the organization by first ensuring that the competencies are in the right places in the organization and then measuring their impact against goals. Given the breadth of the concept, companies will look at various management and HRM systems, practices, and policies that have to be more clearly integrated than what might be found in many organizations. The practices that need to be considered in order to attract, keep, and engage employees include such things as:

Talent management
Leveraging competencies to achieve high organizational performance

- providing strong leadership
- providing opportunities for professional and personal development
- helping employees work better
- communicating all the time and at all levels
- allowing employees to perform powerfully
- ensuring that the rewards and recognition are appropriate[62]

Employee engagement is explored in greater detail in Chapter 3, and talent management, through providing opportunities for training and development, is explored in Chapter 6.

Topic 6: Demographics

In addition to the competitive challenges facing organizations, they need to be concerned about changes in the makeup of the overall population in Canada as these impact what types of employees are available to be hired. Some of these issues are discussed here; others are discussed in detail throughout other chapters in this book.

LO6
Outline demographic considerations.

Among the most significant challenges in organizations, more particularly affecting managers, are the demographic changes occurring in Canada. Key demographic considerations include employee background, multiple generations in the workforce, skills and labour shortage, gender distribution, and increasing levels of education.

Diversity of Backgrounds

Canadian workers will continue to be a diverse group. According to a recent report by Statistics Canada, it is predicted that by 2031, 33% of the labour force will be foreign-born and 15% will belong to a minority group.[63] Most of the immigration is from Asia—a sharp contrast to immigration that occurred 50 years ago, which was primarily from European countries. Immigrants tend to settle in large urban areas, such as Toronto, Montréal, and Vancouver. It has also been predicted that by 2031, 1 person in 3 in the labour force will be born outside Canada.[64] The majority of immigrants coming to Canada are from Asia and the Middle East.[65]

To ensure that skilled immigrants have access to employment opportunities, a number of partnerships have developed, such as the Toronto Region Immigrant Employment Council (TRIEC) and the Assisting Local Leaders with Immigrant Employment Strategies (ALLIES, modelled after TRIEC). The purpose of these agencies is to help immigrants make use of their skills and talents in the workforce so that Canada can become more prosperous as a nation.[66]

Aboriginal peoples make up 4.3% of the population and are predicted to be 5.3% by 2031.[67] Of note is the number of Aboriginal youths and the efforts of organizations to find ways to better involve Aboriginal peoples in the workforce. To assist with this, the Aboriginal Human Resource Council has a mandate to advance the full labour-market participation of Aboriginal peoples. Employers such as RBC, Syncrude, and IBM Canada are actively involved in the council's programs and as advocates to other employers. The recruitment and selection of immigrants and Aboriginal peoples are discussed in Chapter 5.

The diversity of the Canadian population also impacts how employees need to interact with one another and customers in a respectful manner. At Work with HRM 1.3 provides an example of how failing to prepare employees to appropriately deal with diversity can be detrimental to a company.

AT WORK WITH HRM 1.3 — STARBUCKS IS CLOSED!

What would cause a major business such as Starbucks to shut down 8000 stores across the United States in 1 afternoon? A huge backlash on social media to a corporate culture described as "racially insensitive" was the catalyst for this action.

A video went viral, and social media was filled with posts criticizing Starbucks after police in Philadelphia were called to remove 2 black customers who were not ordering anything but instead were waiting in a Starbucks for a friend to meet them there. The manager had apparently asked the men to leave, but they didn't. Therefore, law enforcement was called, and the men were removed in handcuffs, although this was done peacefully.

Posts, comments, and critiques were rampant after this event, with customers calling out Starbucks, stating that employees were racially insensitive and that type of behaviour should never be allowed. To protect its reputation in the marketplace (with both consumers and current and future employees), Starbucks decided to shut down all US stores in late May 2018 and provide mandated diversity sensitivity training to employees.

CRITICAL THINKING QUESTIONS:

1. Do you agree with Starbucks' response to this incident? Why or why not?
2. What else could Starbucks do to enhance diversity awareness and racial sensitivity in its various locations?
3. Could an incident like this occur in Canada? Why or why not?

Sources: "Starbucks to Close 8,000 US Stores for Racial Sensitivity Training," *RT*, April 18, 2018, accessed April 18, 2018, https://www.rt.com/business/424456-starbucks-stores-racial-training; and Sarah Whitten, "Starbucks to Close All Company-Owned Stores on the Afternoon of May 29 for Racial-Bias Education Day," *CNBC*, April 17, 2018, accessed April 18, 2018, https://www.cnbc.com/2018/04/17/starbucks-to-close-all-stores-on-may-29-for-racial-bias-education-day.html.

Generations at Work

The working-age population in Canada is getting older—there are more individuals than ever in the older age brackets (ages 45 to 64) and fewer than ever in the younger brackets. According to a 2018 report, there are more Canadians aged 55 to 64 than there are aged 15 to 24, meaning that there are more older people still in the workforce, making less room for the new entrants.[68] Furthermore, Canadians are working past age 65 according to the latest census data from Statistics Canada.[69]

The age distribution throughout the Canadian workforce means that there can be several generations working together—all with different values and expectations. It also means that organizations might not have the capacity to develop younger talent to prepare them to take on more significant roles when the older workers leave or that more attention has been given to the youngest cohort of workers at the expense of development of other generations.[70] As a result, organizational leaders will need to manage a wide spectrum of workforce diversity. However, some argue that there is too much focus on generational difference and that, ultimately, all workers (regardless of age) want and are motivated by the same things.[71]

The generations at work are typically baby boomers (born 1946–1964), Generation X (born 1965–1980), Generation Y/millennials (born 1981–1997), and Generation Z (born after 1997). Figure 1.4 provides a summary of the generational differences in relation to a number of factors.

FIGURE 1.4 **Generations at Work**

	Baby Boomers (Born 1946–1964)	Gen X (Born 1965–1980)	Gen Y/Millennials (Born 1981–1997)	Gen Z (Born after 1997)
Work ethic values	Question authority Question work ethic of younger people Accept promotion before questioning impact on life	View boss as expert	Tech-savvy Want work to have a greater purpose Flexibility Achievement oriented	Risk adverse and practical Stability
Interactive style	Team player Optimistic	Individualistic	Group or team oriented Self-assured	Highly reliant on online communication and social media
Idea of work	Adventure	"Live to work" Structured	Good at multi-tasking Not concerned about job security Want challenging work	Want work that is engaging and beneficial Incorporate technology into work for efficiency
View of work rewards	Loyal Expect advancement	Independent Want trappings of success	Continuous feedback Input into decision making	Purposeful and aligned with personal values
Work and family life	Work is first	Conservative	Expect work–life balance	Seek meaning and balance

Sources: Adapted from "Here Comes Gen Z: How to Attract and Retain the Workforce's Newest Generation," *Forbes Coaches Council*, February 27, 2018, accessed April 18, 2018, https://www.forbes.com/sites/forbescoachescouncil/2018/02/27/here-comes-gen-z-how-to-attract-and-retain-the-workforces-newest-generation/#349aa2911b2e; Jeremy Finch, "What Is Generation Z, and What Does It Want?," April 5, 2015, accessed April 18, 2018, https://www.fastcompany.com/3045317/what-is-generation-z-and-what-does-it-want; Robert Tanner, "Can Baby Boomers and Millennials Just Get Along?," November 6, 2015, accessed April 18, 2018, https://managementisajourney.com/new-millennium-trends-can-baby-boomers-and-generation-y-just-get-along; Jennifer Kilber, Allen Barclay, and Douglas Ohmer, "Seven Tips for Managing Generation Y," *Journal of Management Policy and Practice* 15, no. 4 (2014): 80–91; Rob Asghar, "Gen X Is from Mars, Gen Y Is from Venus: A Primer on How to Motivate a Millennial," *Forbes*, January 14, 2014, accessed April 18, 2018, www.forbes.com/sites/robasghar/2014/01/14/gen-x-is-from-mars-gen-y-is-from-venus-a-primer-on-how-to-motivate-a-millennial; and Paul Taylor and George Gao, "Generation X: America's Neglected 'Middle Child,'" *Fact Tank*, Pew Research Center, June 5, 2014, accessed April 18, 2018, www.pewresearch.org/fact-tank/2014/06/05/generation-x-americas-neglected-middle-child.

Companies are responding in a number of ways to this demographic shift. More attention is being paid to the corporate culture and ensuring that staff fit well with the **culture** and values of the organization. Culture has many definitions, but an easy one to remember is that it is the pattern of behaviours we see in an organization. (There will more about organizational culture in Chapter 3.) Culture is important as it drives the company's performance and results. For example, Whole Foods Market, which focuses on organic food, provides a culture where employees can align their personal values with those of the store.[72]

Skills and Labour Shortage

With the aging of the workforce and fewer new entrants, there is concern about shortages—primarily for skilled workers. Although Canada has a relatively high unemployment rate, employers say they can't find workers. Some economists also suggest that what is really occurring is a mismatch between what skills people have and what employers really want. A report by The Conference Board of Canada indicates that certain industries call for skill sets that will see shortages: health-related occupations, skilled labour such as crane and tower operators, plumbers, and work that requires scientific and mathematical skills.[73]

Some industries are more affected by shortages than others. The mining industry is expanding and will need more than 100,000 skilled workers over the next few years as many of the existing employees will be leaving. In response to this situation, a report by the Organisation for Economic Co-operation and Development (OECD) titled *Employment and Skills Strategies in Canada* stresses the importance of making students better informed regarding the skills necessary to find work.[74] This has been accomplished by New Gold, which entered into a partnership with the BC Aboriginal Mine Training Association, ensured that students knew what jobs would be available and what skills would be necessary, and provided apprenticeship opportunities.[75] Unfortunately, some organizations believe the problem can be addressed by more advertising or by dedicating more people to recruitment activities. However, as noted above, there are fewer new entrants due to fewer people being born.

To deal with these shortages, an employer can do a number of things—for example, provide more mentoring for millennials, ensure that the management style in the organization is suitable for both tech-savvy and other workers, and make better use of the skills that immigrants bring.[76] As mentioned earlier, TRIEC in Toronto showcases and recognizes employers for their leadership in recruiting and keeping skilled immigrants as a way to better address the skills shortage.[77]

Gender Distribution of the Workforce

According to Statistics Canada, more than 80% of women in Canada aged 25 to 54 participated in the labour market in 2015, compared to just over 20% in 1950. Women were also more likely than men to work on a part-time basis (18.9% versus 5.5%) and to do so for voluntary reasons (67.2% versus 53.0%). This meant that women spent an average of 5.6 fewer hours per week on paid work than men (35.5 hours versus 41.1 hours).[78] Employers are under constant pressure to ensure equality for women with respect to employment, advancement opportunities, and compensation. And since the rate is so high during women's childbearing years, employers also need to accommodate working mothers and fathers through parental leaves, part-time employment, flexible work schedules, job-sharing, telecommuting, and childcare assistance. Employers are also finding that many working people are now faced with being caregivers to aging parents. Thus, the whole area of "dependent care" is creating issues in organizations that will require creative solutions. In addition, because more women are working, employers are more sensitive to the growing need for policies and procedures to eliminate harassment in the workplace.

Rising Levels of Education

The educational attainment of the Canadian labour force has steadily risen over the years. Not coincidentally, the most secure and fastest-growing sectors of employment over the past decade have been in those areas requiring higher levels of education. In 2016, more than half (54.0%) of Canadians aged 25 to 64 had either college or university qualifications, up from 48.3% in 2006. As such, Canada continues to rank first among the OECD countries regarding the proportion of college and university graduates.[79] Furthermore, First Nations peoples, Métis, and Inuit all made gains in postsecondary education at every level. In 2016, 10.9% of Aboriginal peoples overall aged 25 to 64 had a bachelor's degree or higher, up from 7.7% in 2006. The proportion of Aboriginal peoples with a college diploma rose from 18.7% in 2006 to 23.0% in 2016.[80] As organizations become more sophisticated and use more technology, less and less employment is available for unskilled workers. The more education a person has, the greater the chances are of having work. For example, over 80% of people aged 25 to 64 with a university degree are employed.[81]

It is important to observe that although the educational level of the workforce has continued to rise, there is a widening gap between the educated and the non-educated, leading to different types of work experiences. At the lower end of the educational spectrum, many employers are coping with individuals who are functionally illiterate—unable to read, write, calculate, or solve problems at a level that enables them to perform even the simplest technical tasks, such as reading an operating manual or following safety procedures.[82] The topic of literacy is discussed in more detail in Chapter 6.

EMPLOYEE EXPECTATIONS

As Canadian workplaces continue to evolve and change, so have the expectations of employees.[83] Therefore, it is important to review key topics that need to be addressed, through effective HRM systems, practices, and policies, in order for organizations to be successful.

LO7
Describe key employee expectations.

Bruce Rogovin/Photolibrary/Getty Images

Organizations are aware that different families need different types of work flexibility to balance the demands of family and work.

Rights, Ethics, and Privacy

Over the past few decades, legislation has radically changed the rules for managing employees by granting them many specific rights. Among these are laws granting the rights to equal employment opportunity, union representation if desired, a safe and healthy work environment, minimum working conditions (hours of work, wages, vacations, etc.), and privacy in the workplace. More information on employee rights is presented in both Chapters 2 and 9.

With the various business scandals that continue to plague North America, increased attention is being paid to business ethics.[84] This important topic is explored throughout each chapter in this book, and examples are provided and questions posed to help you reflect upon important considerations that are applicable to the topics within HRM. Ethics in HRM 1.2 describes how some organizations respond to ethics violations.

HR professionals and managers need to understand their responsibilities when dealing with information about employees. The *Personal Information Protection and Electronic Documents Act* (PIPEDA) is a federal law that deals with the collection, use, and disclosure of personal information (note that Québec is the only province with similar laws, although Ontario and others have draft legislation in place). This law requires federally regulated organizations holding personal information on customers or employees to obtain their consent before they use, collect, or disclose this information. Chapter 2 explores more on privacy.

ETHICS IN HRM 1.2   ETHICS IN ACTION!

More and more focus is being put on ethical behaviour in organizations. Employees who do not adhere to a company's expected standards of behaviour are being disciplined, up to and including termination. For example, a Canadian Tire employee who was caught on tape racially profiling and harassing an Indigenous shopper was eventually fired. This story also raises the question about the ethics of being filmed while at work. Due to easy access to iPhones, people are questioning if it is ethical for customers to tape employees without their permission and then for a company to later use this material to discipline an employee. However, many experts feel that any inappropriate behaviour is wrong and that people should do the right thing whether being filmed or not.

Another aspect of ethics is ensuring that the organization has a whistleblower policy and that people are encouraged to bring concerns to senior managers. Furthermore, it is important that all employees receive ethics training in their particular organization so that

it can be clear what is expected regarding good ethical behaviour.

Ethics and Compliance Initiative, a non-profit organization dedicated to improving ethical practices, recently identified how leaders can enhance ethical practices. The organization found that millennials are the most at-risk generation when it comes to ethics in the workplace and that extra effort needs to occur when socializing them to the workplace. One of the reasons for this is that members of that generation can be daredevils and might think nothing of, for example, installing pirated software on company computers. Therefore, it is important that training occurs to help them understand the various business risks and how to behave.

CRITICAL THINKING QUESTION:

Can employees be taught to behave ethically, or is ethics a value system that either is, or is not, already engrained in people long before they begin working for a company?

Sources: Adapted from "Worker Who Confronted Indigenous Shopper Is No Longer with Canadian Tire," *CTV News*, July 29, 2017, accessed April 8, 2018, https://www.ctvnews.ca/canada/worker-who-confronted-indigenous-shopper-is-no-longer-with-canadian-tire-1.3524959; Julie Ireton, "Report Calls for Revamping of Whistleblower Law," *CBC News*, June 19, 2017, accessed April 8, 2018, http://www.cbc.ca/news/canada/ottawa/whistleblower-report-law-canada-1.4167847; and Ethics and Compliance Initiative, accessed April 8, 2018, www.ethics.org.

Fulfilling and Meaningful Work

As shown in Figure 1.4, people have different expectations, which means that they also have different attitudes toward work and different motivations. Organizations that create supportive and inclusive cultures are seen as great workplaces where people want to do their best.[85] For example, 360incentives, an information technology and software company in Ontario, was honoured as the #2 medium-sized employer in Canada's Best Workplaces.[86] The company treats new employees like rock stars by using a megaphone to announce their arrival as they are led through the offices. Likewise, Google Canada got the #1 ranking in large companies for the programs it offers to help employees cook and eat well at home.[87]

Another well-established trend is for employees to define success in terms of personal self-expression and fulfillment of potential on the job. They are frequently less obsessed with the acquisition of wealth and now view life satisfaction as more likely to result from balancing the challenges and rewards of work with those of their personal lives. Although most people still enjoy work and want to excel at it, they tend to be focused on finding interesting work and may pursue multiple careers rather than being satisfied with just "having a job." People also appear to be seeking ways of living that are less complicated but more meaningful.

These new lifestyles cannot help but have an impact on the way employees are motivated and managed. Employers are encouraged to provide mentoring (discussed further in Chapter 6) opportunities for younger employees so that they can acquire positive and constructive attitudes toward their employers.[88] Research has demonstrated that employees who are actively mentored report higher job and personal satisfaction and organizational commitment.[89] Furthermore, with the continued slow economic growth around the world, it is important to look at the morale of employees. Mentoring is a way to help build morale.[90]

Balancing Work and Family

Work and the family are connected in many subtle and not-so-subtle social, economic, and psychological ways. Because of the new forms that the family has taken—for example, the 2-wage-earner and the single-parent family—organizations find it necessary to provide employees with more family-friendly options. "Family-friendly" is a broad term that may include flexible work schedules, daycare, job-sharing, parental leave, executive transfers, spousal involvement in career planning, assistance with family problems, and teleworking. Another emerging issue is that of eldercare. Many employees not only balance work and childcare but also are responsible for aging parents. A recent study indicated that most employers want to help their employees with any caregiving responsibilities they might have.[91]

The Sunnybrook Health Sciences Centre and World Vision Canada were named Top Family-Friendly Employers for their initiatives supporting parents with young families. Some of the initiatives include alternative work arrangements, maternity and parental leave top-ups, and a strong focus on employee wellness.[92] Furthermore, other studies have demonstrated that flexible work schedules create higher levels of job satisfaction.[93] For small business owners, a variety of flexible work options not only helps with balancing work–family responsibilities but also benefits the business: it can save money, reduce turnover, and increase productivity; it is an attractive benefit; and it increases the talent pool.[94] However, it is important not to make assumptions about individual employee needs and to ensure that any type of mobile strategy works for them.[95]

The focus on balancing work and family life can also be seen as nearly half of all jobs created during the past 2 decades were non-traditional—that is, part-time, temporary, or contract work. With the change in the traditional notion of "job for life," job hopping is on the rise, and employees are being forced to be more flexible. This has led to employees having 2 or more part-time jobs, which is known as the **gig economy**. This, in turn, means that organizations will also need to be more flexible in how work is designed. Also, employers will need to rethink how to attract and retain these different types of employees.

Gig economy
Environment in which employees have many part-time jobs instead of 1 permanent full-time role

Although flexible work options can help organizations, 1 survey also suggested that there were other reasons employees wanted such arrangements. Although an improved work–life balance was the #1 reason (74% of respondents), the #2 reason was for health and exercise. Interestingly enough, 61% of those surveyed indicated that they would be more productive working from home because office politics would be reduced.[96]

LINKING BUSINESS STRATEGY AND HRM STRATEGY

LO8

Illustrate the link between business strategy and HRM strategy.

As you can see, there are many issues facing managers, as well as HR professionals, in today's business environment. To effectively address these issues, an organization develops a business strategy to enable it to achieve a high level of performance. The strategy helps the organization determine what business or businesses it will be in, why it exists, what its key goals are, and what actions it needs to take to realize those goals.

It is important to recognize the distinction between *corporate strategy* and *business strategy*.

Corporate strategy deals with questions such as these: Should we be in business? What business should we be in? Corporate strategies are company-wide and focus on overall objectives, such as long-term survival and growth. There are 2 main types of corporate strategies. The first is a restructuring strategy, to ensure long-term survival. Under this option, we can find turnaround situations (Harmac Pacific), divestitures (the Gillette empire getting rid of the Montreal Canadiens), liquidation (Circuit City), and bankruptcy (Magna Entertainment).

The second corporate strategy is growth. Organizations can grow incrementally (by adding new products or new distribution networks). For example, Procter & Gamble added skin care lotion and hair conditioners for babies and began to distribute to drugstores and grocery stores. Organizations can gain new customers by expanding internationally, as Finning International Inc. did when it started selling and renting Caterpillar equipment to the United Kingdom and Chile. Growth can also be achieved through mergers and acquisitions, such as when Rogers Communications acquired Fido and Best Buy Canada acquired Future Shop.

Unlike corporate strategy, business strategy focuses on 1 line of business and is concerned with the question "How should we compete?" Michael Porter developed a classification system that helps us understand 5 ways a business unit can compete.[97] Let us illustrate his model by analyzing how hamburgers are sold. Restaurants can compete by being a low-cost provider (McDonald's); by trying to differentiate products in a way that will attract a large number of buyers (Burger King introducing the Whopper); by being a best-cost provider through giving more value for the money (East Side Mario's sells hamburgers, but on a plate in an attractive environment); by focusing on a niche market on the basis of lower cost to a select group of customers (offering fish burgers or vegetarian burgers); or by offering a niche product or service, that is, one customized to the tastes of a narrow market segment (FleurBurger is sold in Las Vegas for $5000 and consists of a wagyu beef patty topped with foie gras and truffle).

Part of any business strategy is to be competitive. However, to be competitive, an organization needs to think of its people as part of its competitive advantage. Thus, the people in the organization need to be managed in a manner that enables achievement of the strategy.

Although people have always been central to organizations, today's employees are critical in helping to build a firm's competitive advantage. Competitive advantage is the capacity or quality that gives an organization an edge over its competition. The advantage might be productivity, price, quality, delivery, or service. Therefore, the focus of current HRM thinking and research is on identifying and implementing systems, practices, and policies that can make a particular firm stand out above the rest. HRM practices are expected to develop the employees' abilities and motivate them such that the organization is successful. For HRM to lead to organizational success, the HRM systems, practices, and policies must be supported, used, and highly regarded.

An HRM strategy aligned with the business strategy is particularly critical in organizations whose products or services rely upon the knowledge, skills, abilities, and competencies embedded in the employees—the knowledge workers. Furthermore, if an organization thinks of employees as assets, there is a higher likelihood that they will be invested in, supported, and nutured.[98] For example, companies such as CIBC are intentionally designed to increase the value employees add to the bottom line and to customer satisfaction. CIBC actively involves employees in day-to-day decisions, such as determining what specific steps can be taken to reduce customer complaints. Moreover, companies such as Four Seasons Hotels invest a great deal to hire and train the best and the brightest in order to gain advantage over their competitors.

What, then, is the link between business strategy and a human resources strategy? As stated earlier, a **human resources management strategy** involves the development and implementation of HRM systems, practices, and policies that enable the human capital (employees) to achieve the business objectives.[99] When 1 company buys another, often the success of the new business revolves around how well the people side of the merger was handled. Some of the people issues in the merger of 2 airlines in northern Canada, Canadian North and First Air, have delayed the actual merger. Both companies say that a tremendous amount of work remains to be done, including upping Inuit representation in senior staff, pilots, and flight engineers and increasing job stability as the merger occurs.[100]

Organizations of all sizes, public or private, should undertake a set of HRM systems, practices, and policies that enhance employees' contribution to organizational success—as defined by the business strategy. All managers play a tremendous role in developing and maintaining effective HRM and assisting the organization in creating a competitive advantage. If a manager believes employees have to be carefully monitored, when the business strategy suggests that employees need to be empowered, it is highly unlikely that the business will succeed. When a company (or a manager) doesn't link HRM to the business objectives, the company will be unable to leverage its knowledge capabilities and will not be innovative enough to achieve the necessary competitive advantage.[101] For example, if a company wished to focus on providing superb customer service, the employee selection process would tend to hire people with those skills. It might also have a training and development program that reinforced the expectations regarding customer service and a total rewards and performance management system that rated how well the employees did in that regard.

Linking HRM systems, practices, and policies to the business strategy isn't just about customer service. For example, ATB Investor Services realized that it needed to build its leadership capacity in order to achieve its business results.[102] Although this might be a natural outcome of slower business growth and fewer new employees, ATB identified it as a strategic gap. A survey by Mercer found that 64% of the respondents identified looking after the critical talent pool as key to their success. These same respondents also said they weren't doing as good a job as they might.[103] Likewise, Deloitte found that the relationship between employees and employers has shifted so that employees are more like business partners.[104] As previously discussed in this chapter, loyalty for employees is now about more than money—they want to feel valued.[105]

Although "competing through people" may be a key theme for HRM, the idea remains only a framework for action. On a day-to-day basis, managers frequently focus on specific business challenges and issues and may not always focus as critically on the people issues. You can see from Figure 1.1 that HRM helps blend many aspects of management–business pressures with the changing nature of the workforce. By balancing what are sometimes competing demands, HRM plays an important role in getting the most from employees for organizational success and providing a work environment that meets employees' short- and long-term needs.

For additional insights on important HRM topics and how these link to business strategy, read Emerging Trends 1.1.

Human resources management strategy
Identifying key HRM systems, practices, and policies and linking them to the overall business strategy

EMERGING TRENDS 1.1

1. ***Focusing on the employee experience.*** This involves everything employees experience throughout their connection to the organization, from the first contact as a potential recruit to the last interaction after the end of employment. Organizations are providing greater care and consideration to how they treat employees as this has an impact on how customers are treated and an organization's success and profitability.

2. ***The social contract between an employer and employees.*** The stability and consistency that once characterized the best employee–employer relationships are being disrupted by employees' tendency to change jobs more frequently. Therefore, employers must provide ongoing training and development, allow people to try different jobs for the same employer, and give employees more tools to manage their own careers.

3. ***Creating environmentally friendly office environments.*** Along with the ongoing development of clean technologies, more offices are looking at acquiring LEED certification, which means that the physical space has been designed and built to be as environmentally healthy and energy efficient as possible. For example, Earth Rangers in Ontario built a new building that uses close to 90% less energy than other similar-sized buildings.

4. ***Enhancing work flexibility.*** In response to the values and expectations of younger workers and the pace of economic growth, different forms of work flexibility are occurring. Some of this shows up in the growth of part-time work in a global and competitive economy.

5. ***Acceleration of social media technology.*** Social media has created both opportunities and threats within the business context. Companies use social media to inform their employees about business and to attract the type of employees they are looking for. However, social media has also created a way for employees to vent frustration with their work. Likewise, employers can use social media to get additional information about potential applicants. For example, Facebook is developing a platform that can be used in the workplace that better connects everyone, and Plasticity Labs in Toronto has made use of social technologies to track and measure employee engagement.

6. ***Increased use of analytics.*** Using data to draw inferences, make connections, and proactively identify trends and issues impacting employees will be critical to an organization's ongoing success and growth. HRM metrics are designed to help evaluate how effectively investment in people is being utilized. The better the return, the more value is being generated by employees and the more organizational goals are being supported across the board.

Sources: Adapted from Denise Lee Yohn, "2018 Will Be the Year of Employee Experience," *Forbes*, January 2, 2018, accessed April 23, 2018, https://www.forbes.com/sites/deniselyohn/2018/01/02/2018-will-be-the-year-of-employee-experience/#76a289841c8f; "2018 Global Human Capital Trends," Deloitte, accessed April 23, 2018, https://www2.deloitte.com/insights/us/en/focus/human-capital-trends.html; "Crunch These 6 HR Metrics to Measure Productivity (and Improve Your Bottom Line!)," *CPHR Canada*, July 14, 2017, accessed April 23, 2018, https://cphr.ca/blog/2017/07/14/profit-ability; Shane Douthitt, "4 HR Analytics Trends to Follow in 2018," *Talent Economy*, January 30, 2018, accessed April 23, 2018, http://www.talenteconomy.io/2018/01/30/4-hr-analytics-trends-follow-2018; Tavia Grant, "Hiring for the Future," *The Globe and Mail*, November 17, 2014, B1; Earth Rangers Centre, accessed April 23, 2018, www.ercshowcase.com; Jessica Barrett, "The Death of Lifelong Jobs," *Vancouver Sun*, November 1, 2014, B6–7; Daniel Tencer, "Canada Is A Job-Creating Powerhouse ... If You Like Part-Time Work," *Huffington Post Canada*, February 10, 2017, accessed April 23, 2018, https://www.huffingtonpost.ca/2017/02/10/unemployment-canada-january-2017_n_14676018.html; and William Watson and Susan MacMillan, "Avoiding the Pitfalls of Social Media," *Canadian Labour and Employment Law*, August 22, 2017, accessed April 23, 2018, https://www.labourandemploymentlaw.com/2017/08/avoiding-the-risks-an-outline-of-steps-to-employers-can-take-to-avoid-the-pitfalls-of-social-media.

LEARNING OUTCOMES SUMMARY

1. Define human resources management (HRM).
   - *Integrated set of systems, practices, and policies that focus on effective deployment and development of employees*
2. Identify HRM systems, practices, and policies.
   - *Operating within the legal framework*
   - *Promoting employee health and safety through organizational culture*

- *Defining, analyzing, and designing the work*
- *Planning for, recruiting, and selecting employees*
- *Orienting, training, and developing employees*
- *Managing employee performance*
- *Rewarding and recognizing employees*
- *Knowing your rights and responsibilities*
- *Understanding labour relations and collective bargaining*
- *Learning about international human resources management*

3. Explain the importance of HRM to all employees.
   - *All employees are affected by HRM systems, practices, and policies. Most employees have a manager who is the key link between the employee and the organization*
   - *Managers are employees too and are therefore concerned about employee rights and responsibilities, for themselves and for the people whom they are responsible for*
   - *HRM helps everyone understand their roles and responsibilities in the organization*
   - *People have always been central to organizations, but their strategic importance is growing in today's knowledge-based industries*

4. Discuss the relationship between a manager and an HR professional.
   - *Every manager's job is managing people*
   - *Successful organizations equip their managers with a thorough understanding of HRM*
   - *HR professionals help managers be good people managers by providing advice as well as direct services*
   - *Combining the expertise of HR professionals with the experience of managers can develop and utilize the talents of employees to their greatest potential*

5. Describe current business topics and their impact on HRM.
   - *Globalization is creating the requirement for managers to effectively lead people in locations throughout the world*
   - *Change in firms and business sectors will focus on maximizing utilization of employees*
   - *Technology has enabled organizations to focus on quality and enhanced customer service*
   - *Organizations use productivity improvements to help with sustainability*
   - *The environment and climate change are creating both threats and opportunities*
   - *Businesses are concerned about their human capital and talent management*

6. Outline demographic considerations.
   - *Diversity of backgrounds*
   - *Generations within the workforce*
   - *Skills and labour shortages*
   - *Gender distribution*
   - *Rising levels of education*

7. Describe key employee expectations.
   - *Rights, ethics, and privacy*
   - *Fulfilling and meaningful work*
   - *Balancing work and family*

8. Illustrate the link between business strategy and HRM strategy.
   - *Business strategy involves the formulation of a company's mission, goals, and action plans*
   - *Part of any business strategy is to be competitive; to be competitive, an organization needs to think about its people as part of its "competitive advantage"*
   - *HRM strategy focuses on linking and aligning the HRM systems, practices, and policies to the business strategy*
   - *HRM systems, practices, and policies will reflect a particular organizational strategy, such as growth*

KEY TERMS

benchmarking 18
core competencies 20
culture 24
downsizing 12
gig economy 27
globalization 10
human capital 19
human resources management (HRM) 4

human resources management strategy 29
independent contractor 14
Lean 18
outsourcing 12
Six Sigma 16
talent management 21
telecommuting 15

HRM CLOSE-UP APPLICATION

1. Kim Davidson states that hiring HR professionals is similar to hiring IT professionals. What does he mean?
2. Davidson notes that a good human resources department can make the work environment better for employees. What are 3 key HRM systems, policies, or practices that SideFX could implement?
3. Davidson also acknowledges that people leave "cool companies for a number of reasons." What are the key reasons employees leave a company?
4. SideFX wants to hire people who "fit" within the company. What does this mean, and what kind of person would be the best fit for this organization?

CRITICAL THINKING QUESTIONS

1. What are the reasons that all employees need to know about and understand HRM?
2. You are a manager in a major chain of coffee bars. What might your HR concerns be in attracting and retaining employees who have an understanding of the importance of the customer?
3. There have been a number of news reports about Canada's Temporary Foreign Worker Program and the suggestion that foreign workers are taking jobs from Canadian residents. If Canada eliminated this program, what would the HR implications be?
4. List at least 3 pros and 3 cons of having a more diverse workforce. Can Canada compete better globally with our diverse population? Why?

BUILDING YOUR SKILLS

1. Working in groups of 3 to 4, discuss the statement: "Employers need to be more concerned about how employees feel about their work and how they are treated." Do you agree with the statement? Why or why not?
2. As discussed in this chapter, employers make use of social media to gather additional information about potential job applicants. Is this ethical? Why or why not?
3. Using any search engine, search the phrase "Gen Z." Access each of the top 3 entries and create a list of 5 ways Gen Zs are described. Does the description sound like people you know in this generation? Why or why not?
4. A number of jobs and careers are being created in the "clean technology" sector. Using any search engine, research "jobs in clean technology." Prepare a short summary of what you found.

CASE STUDY 1

Does HR Provide Any Value?

Who do human resource professionals work for: the company or employees? Is it possible to properly represent the interests of divergent groups, and do the interests of employers and employees have to be in conflict with one other?

The recent outpouring of complaints from women about mistreatment in the workplace has included numerous accounts of being ignored by human resources departments, thereby characterizing these professionals as part of the problem, not the solution. Experts point to several contributing factors. Human resources departments, although officially responsible for fielding employee complaints, also work for a company that faces potential liability, which is an inherent conflict of interest. And for some human resource professionals, conducting an investigation into harassment allegations against a top executive or star performer can be hazardous to their own careers. The result can often be that human resources personnel are more inclined to suppress allegations than to get to the bottom of them.

"It can be very lonely being a human resources professional in an organization," said Carol Gordon, who spent three decades as a human relations officer in the banking industry and now runs a consulting firm. "It can be very isolating and very dangerous when you get into politics and harassment situations in the workplace. You need to have a strong sense of self to have the wherewithal to do this kind of work."

Yet others will argue that the human resources department is vital to an organization. It is only through effective HRM that an organization can truly bring employers and employees together in a united front that enables an organization to succeed. The areas that human resources departments are responsible for creating and helping others implement can enhance employees' experience at work while strengthening business operations. There's a good reason why management experts study firms such as 3M Canada and PepsiCo Canada, which have high worker satisfaction. These businesses are profitable in large part because of their employee engagement and the work HR professionals have done to ensure that this engagement occurs. Without strategic HRM systems, practices, and policies, a company's goals would merely be wishful thinking that is never brought to life. Ultimately, HRM is what keeps an organization productive, efficient, and thriving.

Sources: Adapted from "Canada's Top 100 Employers, 2018," *The Globe and Mail*, accessed April 23, 2018, http://www .canadastop100.com/national; Melanie Peacock, "#TimesUp for HR," *Inspired Teaching in Intro to HR Blog/Nelson Education*, February 1, 2018, accessed April 23, 2018, http://www.nelson.com/introhrblog/?p=823; Noam Scheiber and Julie Creswell, "Sexual Harassment Cases Show the Ineffectiveness of Going to H.R.," December 12, 2017, accessed April 23, 2018, https:// www.nytimes.com/2017/12/12/business/sexual-harassment-human-resources.html; Melanie Peacock, "The HR Professional's Guide to Change Management," *Business Expert Press*, 2017; and "HR's Increasing Importance in Successful Organizations," Georgetown University, June 2, 2016, accessed April 23, 2018, https://scs.georgetown.edu/news-and-events/ article/5634/hr-increasing-importance-successful-organizations.

Questions:

1. How do effective HRM systems, practices, and polices enable employees and employers to work toward the same goals?
2. What can an organization do to ensure that its HR department plays a vital and effective role in its operations?
3. What type of person should go into HR? Are there certain personality types best suited to this work?

CASE STUDY 2

Tim Hortons and Burgers—What Has This Meant for a Canadian Icon?

In 2014, news feeds went wild with the announcement that Tim Hortons and Burger King were merging. But what has this meant for such a visible icon of Canada?

When the merger was first announced, one of the more immediate concerns was what would happen to staff at both companies. Burger King, a subsidiary of a private Brazilian equity firm that has cut jobs at other companies when mergers have occurred, caused employees to question their future with Tim Hortons. Furthermore, shareholders were also concerned that there would be pressure on individual franchisees to cut corners and that executive pay would be excessive. From previous mergers done by the same company, including Heinz and Labatt, cost reductions did occur to make the companies more profitable. Furthermore, the company's stated commitment to maintain staff levels at Tim Hortons only applied to the 16 corporate-owned restaurants.

Other critics say that food items at both stores will become interchangeable, thereby reducing the need for separate distribution systems or separate physical locations. Revenues at Canadian Burger King restaurants were low, whereas Tim Hortons outlets were highly profitable. As such, there was some concern that any sharing of products would reduce the attraction consumers have for Tim Hortons, making it less profitable.

So what did happen? In early 2015, about 350 employees lost their jobs at Tim Hortons. Terminated employees were mainly from its headquarters and regional offices. Later that same year, 1 analyst noted that Tim Hortons had been able to cut costs and increase expansion to the US marketplace, neither of which would have occurred without the merger. In 2017, Tim Hortons' Canadian franchisees formed an association and filed class action lawsuits against the master franchisor, accusing the head office of misusing advertising funds and hiking the prices of products they buy through the company, such as sugar and bacon. Then in early 2018, it was determined that there had been slower than anticipated store growth for the coffee and doughnut chain across North America over the past few years. As well, the Tim Hortons brand was engulfed by negative publicity in 2018 after some of its Ontario franchisees cut employee benefits and paid breaks in response to the province's minimum wage hikes. At the time, its owner, Restaurant Brands International Inc., said the actions did not reflect the brand and blamed a "rogue group" of franchisees.

Clearly, the merger of 2 big brands has not been a smooth or simple process. It will be interesting to track the ongoing progress and profitability of Tim Hortons, to monitor which other major restaurant chains merge in the future, and to evaluate the success of these transactions.

Sources: Adapted from Hollie Shaw, "Restaurant Brands Jumps as Company Downplays Impact of Tims' Franchisee Fight," *Financial Post*, February 12, 2018, accessed April 23, 2018, http://business.financialpost.com/news/retail-marketing/tim-hortons-posts-weak-same-store-sales-for-the-fifth-quarter-in-a-row; James Cowan, "Why Foreign Ownership Has Been Great for Tim Hortons," *Canadian Business*, May 6, 2016, accessed April 23, 2018, http://www.canadianbusiness.com/blogs-and-comment/why-foreign-ownership-has-been-great-for-tim-hortons; "Tim Hortons Confirms It Cut 350 People in Layoffs This Week," *The Canadian Press*, January 29, 2015, accessed April 23, 2018, https://globalnews.ca/news/1801314/tim-hortons-cut-350-people-in-layoffs-this-week; "Tim Hortons Takeover by Burger King May Be Bad for Canada: Study," *CBC News*, October 30, 2014, accessed April 23, 2018, www.cbc.ca/news/business/tim-hortons-takeover-by-burger-king-may-be-bad-for-canada-study-1.2818036; and Jamie Sturgeon, "Tim Hortons Coffee Coming to a Burger King Near You?," *Global News*, November 10, 2014, accessed April 23, 2018, http://globalnews.ca/news/1663426/tim-hortons-coffee-coming-to-a-burger-king-near-you.

Questions:

1. What are the pros and cons when 2 major restaurant chains merge?
2. What are the HRM implications of this type of merger?
3. What, if any, significant changes to operations at Tim Hortons have you noticed since the merger?

NOTES AND REFERENCES

1. Government of Canada, "Canadian Business Network," accessed April 3, 2018, https://canadabusiness.ca/business-planning/market-research-and-statistics/canadian-economy.

2. Andy Partridge, "Executive Summary: The Golden Circle with Simon Sinek," Enviable Workplace website, August 27, 2014, accessed April 3, 2018, https://enviableworkplace.com/executive-summary-golden-circle-simon-sinek.

3. "Feeling Valued: The Dimensions Organisations Must Deliver On," Investors in People website, January 10, 2018, accessed April 3, 2018, https://www.investorsinpeople.com/resources/ideas-and-inspiration/feeling-valued-at-work-employees-recognition.

4. Suzanne Haywood, "Tom Peters on Leading the 21st-Century Organization," *McKinsey Quarterly*, September 2014, accessed April 3, 2018, http://www.mckinsey.com/insights/organization/tom_peters_on_leading_the_21st_century_organization.

5. Dave Ulrich, "5 of the Best Traits HR Professionals Have in Common," *HRM*, January 29, 2018, accessed April 3, 2018, http://www.hrmonline.com.au/section/featured/5-best-traits-hr-professionals-common.

6. Sarah Dobson, "Delving into HR's DNA," *Canadian HR Reporter*, October 20, 2014, 1.

7. Ibid.

8. Emily Douglas, "C-Suite Talks HR: Christina McClung, CPO at Capital One Canada," *HRD Canada*, March 20, 2018, accessed April 3, 2018, https://www.hrmonline.ca/hr-news/hr-technology/csuite-talks-hr-christina-mcclung-cpo-at-capital-one-canada-239350.

9. Daniel Workman, "Canada's Top 10 Exports," February 13, 2018, accessed April 8, 2018, http://www.worldstopexports.com/canadas-top-exports.

10. Ibid.

11. Barry Critchley, "Brookfield Gets Busy with $7.5 Billion of Acquisitions over Three Months," *Financial Post*, October 10, 2014, accessed April 8, 2018, http://business.financialpost.com/2014/10/10/brookfield-gets-busy-with-7-5-billion-of-acquisitions-over-three-months.

12. Tara Perkins, "Atlantic City Bust," *The Globe and Mail*, November 1, 2014, B8–9.

13. Greg Keenan and Adrian Morrow, "Ford Picks Mexico Over Windsor to Build New Engine," *The Globe and Mail*, October 25, 2014, B1.

14. Business Development Bank of Canada, "2018 Economic Outlook: Global Growth Brings Good News for Canadian Entrepreneurs," accessed April 8, 2018, https://www.bdc.ca/en/blog/pages/2018-economic-outlook-global-growth-brings-good-news-canadian-entrepreneurs.aspx.

15. Ibid.

16. Royal Bank of Canada, "Canada's Economy Ready to Keep Rolling in 2018, While On Track to Post the Strongest G-7 Performance in 2017," December 12, 2017, accessed April 8, 2018, http://www.rbc.com/newsroom/news/2017/20171212-econ-fcst.html.

17. Statistics Canada, "Imports, Exports and Trade Balance of Goods on a Balance-of-Payments Basis, by Country or Country Grouping," accessed April 8, 2018, https://www.statcan.gc.ca/tables-tableaux/sum-som/l01/cst01/gblec02a-eng.htm.

18. "Canadian Oil Exports to U.S. Dip in November: StatsCan Data," January 5, 2018, accessed April 8, 2018, https://www.reuters.com/article/us-canada-energy-trade/canadian-oil-exports-to-u-s-dip-in-november-statscan-data-idUSKBN1EU1NB.

19. "5 Year Crude Oil Prices," *InvestmentMine*, accessed April 8, 2018, http://www.infomine.com/investment/metal-prices/crude-oil/5-year.

20. Kevin Orland, "With Keystone XL Still in Limbo, TransCanada Moves Ahead with $2.4-Billion Natural Gas Expansion," *Financial Post*, February 15, 2018, accessed April 8, 2018, http://business.financialpost.com/commodities/energy/keystone-xl-on-hold-transcanada-turns-to-natural-gas-system.

21. "Helping Canadians Eat Better, Feel Better, and Do Better," Sobeys corporate website, accessed April 8, 2018, https://www.sobeyscorporate.com/en/Our-Company/At-A-glance.aspx.

22. Ahmad Hathout, "Big Deals," *Report on Business*, June 2014, 30–39.

23. Geoffrey Morgan, "Edmonton Abuzz Over Aspiring Entrepreneurs," *Vancouver Sun*, October 21, 2014, E3.

24. James Wood, "Minhas Brewery to Build New Distillery in Calgary," *Calgary Herald*, January 18, 2018, accessed April 8, 2018, http://calgaryherald.com/news/politics/minhas-brewery-to-build-new-distillery-in-calgary.

25. Ross Marowits, "Cheesemaker Saputo Closing Four Plants," *Global News*, March 26, 2014, accessed November 10, 2014, http://globalnews.ca/news/1232655/cheesemaker-saputo-closing-four-plants.

26. The Canadian Press, "Bell Media Confirms Layoffs of Local News and Sports Desk Employees," *Calgary Herald*, November 20, 2017, accessed April 8, 2018, http://calgaryherald.com/telecom/media/bell-media-confirms-it-is-laying-off-local-news-and-sports-desk-employees/wcm/1f67b727-2cd8-4312-b200-28d7d69e7877.

27. C. Lakshman, Aarti Ramaswami, Ruth Alas, Jean F. Kabongo, and J. Rajendran Pandian, "Ethics Trumps Culture? A Cross-National Study of Business Leader Responsibility for Downsizing and CSP Perceptions," *Journal of Business Ethics* 125, no. 1 (November 2014): 101–119.

28. Patricia M. Buhler, "Ten Tips for More Effective Downsizing," *Supervision*, August 2, 2014: 17–19.

29. Ibid.

30. Jeff Gray and Tim Shufelt, "Rare Move Protects Employees," *The Globe and Mail*, January 16, 2015, B7.

31. Telus International Outsourcing website, accessed April 8, 2018, https://www.telusinternational.com/; Accenture Outsourcing Services website, accessed April 8, 2018, https://www.accenture.com/ca/outsourcing/Pages/index.aspx; and IBM Global Technology Services website, accessed April 8, 2018, https://www-935.ibm.com/services/us/en/it-services/outsourcing.html.

32. Gail Johnson, "A Recruiting Niche Made This Company Recession-Proof," *The Globe and Mail*, October 15, 2014, H8.

33. American Express Canada website, accessed April 8, 2018, https://www.americanexpress.com/canada.

34. Eugeny Sokolove, "Transformation Through Outsourcing," *The Moscow Times*, April 17, 2012, accessed April 8, 2018, https://www.themoscowtimes.com/business/business_for_business/article/transformation-through-outsourcing/456840.html.

35. "Top Outsourcing Trends to Know in 2018," *Disrupter Daily*, December 18, 2017, accessed April 8, 2018, https://www.disrupterdaily.com/top-outsourcing-trends-know-2018.

36. Brenda Bouw, "How Contract Workers Navigate the Challenges of the CRA," *The Globe and Mail*, June 16, 2017, accessed April 8, 2018, https://www.theglobeandmail.com/report-on-business/small-business/sb-money/how-contract-workers-navigate-the-challenges-of-the-cra/article35152358.

37. Hayley Tsukayama, "How Closely Is Amazon's Echo Listening?," *The Washington Post*, November 11, 2014, accessed November 11, 2014, https://www.washingtonpost.com/blogs/the-switch/wp/2014/11/11/how-closely-is-amazons-echo-listening.

38. "The Impact of Cloud," *The Economist Intelligence Unit*, accessed April 8, 2018, http://www.economistinsights.com/technology-innovation/analysis/impact-cloud.

39. "Telecommuting Offers Edge to Companies Looking to Recruit Talent: Survey," *Canadian HR Reporter*, June 2, 2014, accessed November 11, 2014, https://www.hrreporter.com/articleview/21331-telecommuting-offers-edge-to-companies-looking-to-recruit-talent-survey.

40. Nicole Spector, "Why Are Big Companies Calling Their Remote Workers Back to the Office?," July 27, 2018, accessed April 8, 2018, https://www.nbcnews.com/business/business-news/why-are-big-companies-calling-their-remote-workers-back-office-n787101.

41. "Total Quality Management," ASQ website, accessed April 8, 2018, http://asq.org/learn-about-quality/total-quality-management/overview/overview.html.

42. Edwin Torres, "Deconstructing Service Quality and Customer Satisfaction: Challenges and Directions for Future Research," *Journal of Hospitality Marketing and Management* 23, no. 6 (August/September 2014): 652–677; and Po-Hsuan Wu, Ching-Yuan Huang, and Chen-Kai Chou, "Service Expectation, Perceived Service Quality, and Customer Satisfaction in Food and Beverage Industry," *International Journal of Organization Innovation* 7, no. 1 (July 2014): 171–180.

43. Matthew Daneman, "Xerox Cutting Back on Lean Six Sigma Program, Jobs," *Democrat & Chronicle*, October 13, 2014, accessed April 8, 2018, https://www.democratandchronicle.com/story/money/business/2014/10/13/xerox-cuts-popular-lean-six-sigma-program-jobs/17203841.

44. Lean Enterprise Institute, "What Is Lean?" accessed April 8, 2018, https://www.lean.org/WhatsLean.

45. Lean Enterprise Institute, "A Brief History of Lean," accessed April 8, 2018, https://www.lean.org/WhatsLean/History.cfm.

46. "Understanding Employee Engagement," Clarity Visual Management website, accessed April 8, 2018, http://www.clarityvisualmanagement.com/2018/03/13/understanding-employee-engagement.

47. Mallory Henry, "'Culture Change' Needed in Way Law Schools Assess, Revise Curriculum: Holloway," *Canadian Lawyer*, October 31, 2014, accessed April 8, 2018, http://canadianlawyermag.com/5339/Culture-change-needed-in-way-law-schools-assess-revise-curriculum-Holloway.html.

48. "Excellence Canada announces the 2017 Canada Awards for Excellence Recipients," November 6, 2017, accessed April 8, 2018, https://www.newswire.ca/news-releases/excellence-canada-announces-the-2017-canada-awards-for-excellence-recipients-655568773.html.

49. Tyler Hamilton, "Powering Up Canada's Exports," *Corporate Knights* 13, no. 4 (Fall 2014): 20–21.

50. "Westport Unveils Its Proprietary Enhanced Spark-Ignited Natural Gas System Targeting Medium-Duty Truck Applications," September 23, 2014, accessed April 18, 2018, https://www.westport.com/news/2014/enhanced-spark-ignited-natural-gas-system-targeting-medium-duty-truck-applications.

51. David Suzuki, "Clean Technology Fastest Growing Sector of Canadian Economy," *Net News Ledger*, October 26, 2014, accessed April 18, 2018, http://www.netnewsledger.com/2014/10/26/clean-technology-fastest-growing-sector-of-canadian-economy.

52. "Corporate Social Responsibility," *The Globe and Mail*, October 17, 2014, NCC1.

53. Ibid.

54. "2018 Future 40 Results," *Corporate Knights*, accessed April 18, 2018, http://www.corporateknights.com/reports/2018-future-40/2018-future-40-results-15241104.

55. "Human Capital Definition and Importance," Economics.help website, September 22, 2017, accessed April 18, 2018, https://www.economicshelp.org/blog/26076/economics/human-capital-definition-and-importance.

56. Paula Speevak Sladowski and Joanna Kaleniecka, "Employer-Supported Volunteering Builds Communities, Core Competencies," April 21, 2014, *Canadian HR Reporter*, accessed November 12, 2014, https://www.hrreporter.com/articleview/20880-employer-supported-volunteering-builds-communities-core-competencies.

57. Ibid.

58. Victor Lipman, "6 Good Reasons to Spend More Time Developing Your Employees," *Forbes*, March 8, 2018, accessed April 18, 2018, https://www.forbes.com/sites/victorlipman/2018/03/08/6-good-reasons-to-spend-more-time-developing-your-employees/#291e7646351b.

59. Greg Keenan, "For Hitachi, Keeping Skilled Workers Is Key," *The Globe and Mail*, September 8, 2014, B7.

60. Ravi Bapna, Nishtha Langer, Amit Mehra, Ram Gopal, and Alok Gupta, "Human Capital Investments and Employee Performance: An Analysis of IT Services Industry," *Management Science* 59, no. 3 (March 2013): 641–658.

61. Dave Ulrich and Wendy Ulrich, *The Why of Work* (New York: McGraw Hill, 2010), 5.

62. Karen Mishra, Lois Boynton, and Aneil Mishra, "Driving Employee Engagement: The Expanded Role of International Communications," *International Journal of Business Communication* 51, no. 2 (2014): 183–202; Harvey Schachter, "The Right HR Ingredients Can Boost Results," *The Globe and Mail*, August 18, 2014, B5; and Ruth Holmes, "Talent Management 4.0: Engaging and Leading in HR's Brave New World," *Relocate Global*, October 6, 2014, accessed April 18, 2018, https://www.relocatemagazine.com/articles/rh102014talent-management-4-0-engaging-and-leading-in-hrs-brave-new-world.

63. Statistics Canada, "Study: Projected Trends to 2031 for the Canadian Labour Force," *The Daily*, August 7, 2011, accessed April 18, 2018, http://www.statcan.gc.ca/pub/11-630-x/11-630-x2016006-eng.htm.

64. Ibid.

65. Statistics Canada, "Immigration and Ethnocultural Diversity in Canada, 2011," accessed April 18, 2018, http://www.statcan.gc.ca/pub/11-630-x/11-630-x2016006-eng.htm.

66. ALLIES Canada website, accessed April 18, 2018, http://alliescanada.ca.

67. Statistics Canada, "Population Projections by Aboriginal Identity in Canada 2006 to 2031," accessed April 18, 2018, http://www.statcan.gc.ca/pub/91-552-x/2011001/hl-fs-eng.htm.

68. Statistics Canada, "Population by Sex and Age Group," accessed April 18, 2018, http://www.statcan.gc.ca/tables-tableaux/sum-som/l01/cst01/demo10a-eng.htm.

69. "More Canadians Working Past Age 65: Statistics Canada," *Benefits Canada*, November 29, 2017, accessed April 18, 2018, http://www.benefitscanada.com/news/more-canadians-working-past-age-65-statistics-canada-107247.

70. Brian Kreissl, "Demographics and the Canadian Workforce," *Canadian HR Reporter*, October 15, 2014, accessed November 12, 2014, https://www.hrreporter.com/blog/HR-Policies-Practices/archive/2014/10/15/demographics-and-the-canadian-workforce.

71. Susan M. Heathfield, "Why Generational Differences Are a Workplace Myth," The Balance Careers website, April 8, 2018, accessed April 18, 2018, https://www.thebalancecareers.com/do-not-focus-on-workplace-generational-differences-4153271.

72. Jessica Barrett, "Work in Progress: Good Job versus Bad Job," *The Calgary Herald*, November 2, 2014, B2.

73. The Conference Board of Canada, "Growing Labour Shortages on the Horizon in Mature Economies," *The Chronicle Herald*, November 7, 2014, accessed April 18, 2018, http://thechronicleherald.ca/cream/home/1248944-growing-labour-shortages-on-the-horizon-in-mature-economies.

74. OECD, *Employment and Skills Strategies in Canada*, 2014, accessed April 23, 2018, https://www.keepeek.com/Digital-Asset-Management/oecd/employment/employment-and-skills-strategies-in-canada_9789264209374-en#page4; and "Canada Must Overcome Sector-Specific Skills Shortages," *Canadian HR Reporter*, June 12, 2014, accessed April 23, 2018, https://www.hrreporter.com/articleview/21469-canada-must-overcome-sector-specific-skills-shortages-oecd.

75. James Keller, "Labour Shortage Predicted for Mining Industry," *Global News*, accessed April 23, 2018, http://globalnews.ca/news/1031306/labour-shortage-predicted-for-mining-industry.

76. "Faced with Skills Shortage, Canadian Employers Are Recognizing the Value of Immigrants," Canada Bound website, accessed April 23, 2018, http://canadaboundimmigrant.com/breakingnews/article.php?id=654.

77. Ibid.

78. Statistics Canada, "Women in Canada: Women and Paid Work," March 8, 2017, accessed April 23, 2018, http://www.statcan.gc.ca/daily-quotidien/170308/dq170308b-eng.htm.

79. "Education in Canada: Key Results from the 2016 Census," November 29, 2017, accessed April 23, 2018, http://www.statcan.gc.ca/daily-quotidien/171129/dq171129a-eng.pdf.

80. Ibid.

81. Ibid.

82. Angie Seth, "Rising Concerns Over Literacy Rates in Canada," *Global News*, September 15, 2017, accessed April 23, 2018, https://globalnews.ca/news/3748748/rising-concerns-over-literacy-rates-in-canada.

83. Daniel Roth, "LinkedIn Top Companies 2018: Where Canada Wants to Work Now," LinkedIn website, March 21, 2018, accessed April 23, 2018, https://www.linkedin.com/pulse/linkedin-top-companies-2018-where-canada-wants-work-now-daniel-roth.

84. Joe Azam, "Why Ethical Conduct Is Good Business," *The Infor Blog*, February 8, 2018, accessed April 23, 2018, http://blogs.infor.com/insights/2018/02/why-ethical-conduct-is-good-business.html.

85. Dan K. Williams, "How to Help Employees Find Meaning in Work," *Forbes*, June 25, 2017, accessed April 23, 2018, https://www.forbes.com/sites/davidkwilliams/2017/06/25/defining-and-finding-meaning-in-work/#3b31c3543aa5.

86. "Canada's Best Workplaces," *The Globe and Mail*, April 27, 2017, accessed April 23, 2018, https://www.greatplacetowork.ca/images/article/2017_globemail_feature.pdf.

87. Ibid.

88. Peter Cheese, "Get 'Em While They're Young," *People Management*, 5.

89. Ann Rolfe, "Taking Mentoring to the Next Level in Organisations," *Training and Development* 41, no. 2 (April 2014): 26–27.

90. Dan Carrison, "The Challenge of 2014: Sustaining Morale," *Industrial Management*, July 1, 2014, 6.

91. Gloria Galloway, "Employers Want to Help Caregivers," *The Globe and Mail*, January 20, 2015, A4.

92. "Canada's Top Family-Friendly Employers, 2014," accessed November 14, 2014, http://www.canadastop100.com/family.

93. Clare Koning, "Does Self-Scheduling Increase Nurses' Job Satisfaction?," *Nursing Management* 21, no. 6 (October 2014): 24–28.

94. Brittney Helmrich, "5 Ways Flexible Work Options Benefit Small Businesses," *Business News Daily*, October 23, 2014, accessed April 23, 2018, https://www.businessnewsdaily.com/7339-job-flexibility-benefits.html.

95. Leah Eichler, "Mobile Workspace Boon for Some, Not All," *The Globe and Mail*, February 28, 2015, B18.

96. Sarah Sutton Fell, "Your Workers Want More Flexibility But Companies Benefit Most," *Entrepreneur*, accessed April 23, 2018, https://www.entrepreneur.com/article/239111.

97. Michael E. Porter, *On Competition* (Boston: Harvard Business Press, 2008).

98. Brian Kreissl, "Human Capital Management Is Starting to Grow on Me," *Canadian HR Reporter*, August 11, 2014, accessed April 23, 2018, https://www.hrreporter.com/21938-human-capital-management-is-starting-to-grow-on-me.

99. Jeffrey A. Mello, *Strategic Human Resource Management*, 4th ed. (Independence, KY: Cengage Learning), 2015.

100. Jane George, "Canadian North: Merger with First Air Might Take Another Two Years," *Nunatsiaq News*, September 24, 2014, accessed April 23, 2018, http://nunatsiaq.com/stories/article/65674canadian_north_merger_with_first_air_might_take_another_two_years.

101. Mizuki Kobayashi, "Relational View: Four Prerequisites of Competitive Advantage," *Annals of Business Administrative Science*, 13 (2014): 77–90.

102. Sarah Dobson, "Few Successors Lined Up for Top Roles: Report," *Canadian HR Reporter*, August 11, 2014, accessed April 23, 2018, https://www.hrreporter.com/articleview/21951-few-successors-lined-up-for-top-roles-report.

103. "Want to Be a Better Manager?" *Mercer*, August 21, 2017, accessed April 23, 2018, https://www.mercer.com/our-thinking/career/voice-on-talent/stop-trying-to-motivate-your-employees.html.

104. Leah Eichler, "The Brave New World of 'On Demand' Work," *The Globe and Mail*, April 25, 2015, B16.

105. Romina Maurino, "Employee Loyalty about More Than Money," *Vancouver Sun*, August 13, 2014, D4.

2 Operating Within the Legal Framework

LEARNING OUTCOMES

After studying this chapter, you should be able to

1 Explain the impact of laws on the behaviour and actions of managers.

2 Discuss the legal framework of HRM in Canada.

3 Describe discrimination and harassment in the workplace.

4 Outline the manager's role in creating a work environment that is free from harassment and discrimination.

5 Identify the general types of employment laws in Canada.

6 Explain the relationship between employment equity, diversity, and inclusion.

7 Discuss the concept of ethics in the management of human resources.

OUTLINE

"All I can say is, it's a good thing we have an outstanding HR department and integration function."

THE YEAR 2018 marked a major milestone in Canadian history with the legalization of marijuana. Previously available only by prescription as a medical substance, cannabis was suddenly being distributed across the country in much the same way as alcohol.

That legalization opened up the need for an entirely new industry.

"The only thing I can think of that compares with the birth and growth of the cannabis industry in Canada was the advent of the personal computer," explains Cam Battley, chief corporate officer of Aurora Cannabis Inc. "When Microsoft and Apple were born, it was the birth of a global industry, and the pace at which the legalization of cannabis happened is like nothing else I've ever seen."

Cremona, Alberta–based Aurora Cannabis is one of the world's leading licensed medical and consumer marijuana producers. Founded in 2006, Aurora now has a staff of more than 480 in Canada and around the world and operations that range from a 40,000 square foot production facility in Québec to the enormous 800,000 square foot Aurora Sky facility in Edmonton.

In late 2017, Aurora acquired Saskatoon's CanniMed Therapeutics Inc. for $1.1 billion—a record amount for the country's fledgling cannabis industry. That acquisition—only one of a number in quick succession for the firm—came as a challenge for a company that was a fraction of the size when Battley had arrived not long before.

"When I joined the company in March of 2016, we had about 35 employees and 1 facility," Battley recalls. "We now have 4 facilities in Canada, we're building another one in Denmark, and we have a European distributor based in Berlin. We've also invested in Australia's largest licensed producer."

But such quick and dramatic growth isn't without its difficulties either.

"It's a good thing we have an outstanding HR department and integration function," Battley exclaims. "Our vice-president of HR, Debra Wilson, has assembled a top-notch human resources group, and they've done an amazing job of on-boarding hundreds of people in a very short period of time. I'm astonished by how seamless and smooth that process has been. It's a testament to her and her team."

Integrating staff from new acquisitions is only 1 aspect of the employment challenges that the rapidly expanding Aurora faces, however. The other are the legal restrictions and security regulations present in the highly regulated cannabis industry.

"All of our production facilities had to be surrounded by security fencing," Battley says. "We had to have cameras covering every square inch of our existing production facilities as one of the regulations that Health Canada has since dialled back. Now, based on those changes, we only have to cover ingress and egress, but previously we had cameras every square inch within that facility 24 hours a day and had to keep all the video data for 2 years."

Those regulations were far more stringent than anything required of pharmaceutical companies or even liquor producers and also extended to Aurora's hiring practices.

"In addition to the security, the requirements for what are known as RPICs—responsible persons in charge—were that they have to be background-checked by the RCMP, and it's a deep, deep background check," explains Battley. "We had to have an RPIC present anywhere cannabis was, and you can imagine in a cannabis

Cam Battley, Chief Corporate Officer, Aurora Cannabis Inc.

production facility there are a lot of places that cannabis is present."

Fortunately for Aurora, operating within that stringent legal framework was not an impediment to staffing the quickly growing company.

"We've had no difficulty finding people; in fact, we've brought people into Aurora who came from the dispensary system in Vancouver, for example," Battley says. "It is actually one of the strengths and one of the interesting things about Aurora—one of our differentiators from our peers—that we have a unique, hybrid culture of suits like me, people who come from mature industries, and people who came from the cannabis community. It's been very gratifying to me to see the harmonious hybrid company culture that we've managed to establish at Aurora."

For all of Aurora's growing pains in a growing industry and the hard work that that has necessitated, Battley is enjoying the challenge immensely.

"You don't get a lot of opportunities in life to be part of inventing a new industry," he says. "And that's what we're doing right here. We're inventing a brand new industry in real time, not just for Canada but for the world, because hands down, Canada's the leader in this space."

INTRODUCTION

LO1

Explain the impact of laws on the behaviour and actions of managers.

As the HRM Close-up shows, operating in a highly regulated environment creates another level of legal scrutiny and compliance. Laws have been written to protect the employer and the employees; these laws reflect the values of society, and in some situations, laws have been enacted because of poor management practices. Therefore, it is important for managers to understand the legal context in which they have to operate. Managers and employees can no longer behave and act in certain ways without severe consequences. When managers ignore the legal aspects of HRM, they risk incurring costly and time-consuming litigation, negative public attitudes, and damage to organization morale.

Some laws address not just legal issues but also emotional ones. For example, human rights legislation is paramount over other laws and concerns all individuals regardless of their gender, race, religion, age, marital status, disability, family status, sexual orientation, national origin, colour, or position in an organization. All employees, including managers, should be aware of their personal biases and how these attitudes can influence their dealings with one another. It should be emphasized that whether managers act a certain way unintentionally or intentionally, they are responsible for any illegal actions they take. Being ignorant of the law is not a valid excuse. As Cam Battley describes, there are some unique employment law challenges when an industry that was illegal is legalized. This chapter focuses on the various employment laws at both the federal and provincial levels that affect how a manager practises human resources management.

Beyond legislation, there is also an expectation in today's society that treating employees in certain ways is just "good business." Thus, the concept of diversity management and inclusion in a multicultural society has become part of business simply because it makes good business sense. It is important to remember that we have gone beyond what is required by law in our human resources management practices.

THE LEGAL BACKGROUND OF HRM

LO2

Discuss the legal framework of HRM in Canada.

Canada has 2 distinct sets of laws that govern: federal and provincial. Federal laws apply to everyone who resides in Canada. For example, everyone who earns income must pay taxes. Other laws are handled at the provincial level. For example, the provinces are responsible for determining who can get a driver's licence. Although this chapter discusses specific employment laws, other kinds of laws, such as common law (our body of law that has developed from judicial decisions), contract law (the laws that relate to legal and binding agreements, such as the purchase of a car), and government regulations (called statutory law), can also have an impact on HR. For example, common law establishes the basic employee–employer relationship of trust. Contract law governs a person engaged in a fee-for-service activity for a company. Statutory law creates employment conditions, such as providing minimum wages or holidays with pay (e.g., Canada Day on July 1).

There are a total of 14 different jurisdictions (government authorities), which means 14 different sets of laws.

Federal legislation applies to only about 10% of Canadian workers who work in federal government departments and agencies, Crown corporations, and other businesses and industries under federal control, such as banks, airlines, railway companies, and insurance and communications companies. Examples of companies governed by federal legislation are CIBC, Scotiabank, Air Canada, WestJet, Bell, and CBC.

In addition, each province and territory has its own legislation that covers employment standards, human rights, labour relations, and worker health and safety. Companies covered under provincial legislation include the corner 7-Eleven, the local McDonald's, and others, such as Canadian Tire, RONA, and Walmart. Despite a great deal of similarity across provinces and territories, there are some notable variations in minimum wage and vacation entitlement. For example, Ontario's minimum wage increased to $14 (per hour) in 2018 and is scheduled to increase to $15 in 2019, whereas Nova Scotia has the lowest at $10.85.[1] Also, some aspects of human rights legislation differ from one jurisdiction to another. Some provinces and territories have employment equity legislation, whereas others do not. For example, Ontario and Québec have stringent pay equity legislation. In Alberta and British Columbia, however, there is no such legislation. Therefore, any pay equity adjustments are the decision of the organization.

Although federal law regulates both Employment Insurance (EI) and the Canada Pension Plan (CPP), all employers and employees are covered, not just federal employees. EI provides for wage payment should you lose your job, and CPP provides for a small pension when you retire. Québec has its own pension plan similar to the CPP. Changes to EI over the past several years have had an impact on human resources practices in organizations. For example, compassionate care benefits are available to employees who need time off to care for or support a family member who is gravely ill or at risk of dying within 6 months.[2] In late 2017, parental leave was extended to a total of 78 weeks (18 months), which can be used by either parent or shared between them.[3] In both cases, the job is held open for the person until the leave is over.

Federal Employment Laws

For companies that are federally regulated, there are 2 basic employment laws: the *Canada Labour Code* and the *Canadian Human Rights Act*. The *Canada Labour Code* covers basic employment conditions, labour relations, and health and safety in the federal sector. The Canada Industrial Relations Board administers this law.

The *Canadian Human Rights Act*, like the *Canada Labour Code*, applies to all federal government departments and agencies, Crown corporations, and businesses and industries under federal jurisdiction, such as banks, airlines, railway companies, and insurance and communications companies. It is administered by the Canadian Human Rights Commission, which makes decisions on complaints involving discrimination and harassment. The concept of a certain level of basic human rights is part of the very fabric of Canadian society. It is also an area that is constantly expanding. For example, in May 2017, the federal government passed the *Genetic Non-Discrimination Act*, which protects individuals who suffer from a predisposition to certain diseases from being discriminated against, whether being denied employment or being denied health benefits.[4]

Of increasing concern for managers and HR professionals is privacy legislation. There are 2 primary laws: one that applies to only federally regulated companies (e.g., banks, airlines) and one that extends the federal legislation to provinces and businesses within the provinces. These laws are the *Personal Information Protection and Electronic Documents Act* (*PIPEDA*) and provincial legislation commonly called the "Personal Information Privacy Act." These acts have a direct influence on how companies and managers handle employee information and the rights of employees regarding this information. Both acts enhance the protection granted to employees on their personal information that a company retains. Organizations can use the information (such as a social insurance number) only for its intended purpose (to remit premiums to the Canada Pension Plan). Organizations can no longer collect personal information without disclosing the full use to employees. Furthermore, organizations must seek written permission from employees to disclose personal information. For example, if you want to get a car loan, your employer is obliged to seek your written authorization to disclose your pay to the lending agency.

These acts have been most noted in the monitoring of emails, use of social media, and website visits of employees while at the worksite. More information on this is covered in Chapter 9.

Provincial Employment Legislation

Each province and territory has relatively similar legislation that provides certain rights and guarantees regarding employment. For example, each province has maximum limits regarding hours per day or hours per week that a person can work before the organization is obliged to pay overtime wages. Similarly, the health and safety of workers are also covered by provincial legislation. In addition, provinces and territories have legislation dealing with human rights and legislation that covers unions and their relationships with employers. The following sections provide information about these major types of employment laws, whether provincial or federal. Figure 2.1 provides a summary of the various federal and provincial employment laws referred to in the previous 2 sections. In addition, websites for accessing the legislation can be found in the appendix at the end of this chapter.

FIGURE 2.1 Major Employment Laws in Canada

Jurisdiction	Basic Employment Conditions	Labour Legislation	Occupational Health and Safety and Workers' Compensation	Human Rights
Federal	Canada Labour Code	Canada Labour Code	Canada Labour Code	Canadian Human Rights Act
Alberta	Employment Standards Code	Labour Relations Code	Occupational Health and Safety Act	Alberta Human Rights Act
British Columbia	Employment Standards Act	Labour Relations Code	Workers Compensation Act	Human Rights Code
Manitoba	The Employment Standards Code	The Labour Relations Act	The Workplace Safety and Health Act/The Workers Compensation Act	The Human Rights Code
New Brunswick	Employment Standards Act	Industrial Relations Act	Occupational Health and Safety Act/Workers' Compensation Act	Human Rights Act
Newfoundland and Labrador	Labour Standards Act	Labour Relations Act	Occupational Health and Safety Act	Human Rights Act
Nova Scotia	Labour Standards Code	Trade Union Act	Occupational Health and Safety Act/Workers' Compensation Act	Human Rights Act
Nunavut	Labour Standards Act	Labour Standards Act	Safety Act/Workers' Compensation Act	Human Rights Act
Ontario	Employment Standards Act	Labour Relations Act, 1995	Occupational Health and Safety Act/Workplace Safety and Insurance Act	Human Rights Code
Prince Edward Island	Employment Standards Act	Labour Act	Occupational Health and Safety Act/Workers Compensation Act	Human Rights Act
Québec	Act Respecting Labour Standards	Labour Code	Act Respecting Occupational Health and Safety/Workers' Compensation Act	Charter of Human Rights and Freedoms
Saskatchewan	The Saskatchewan Employment Act	The Saskatchewan Employment Act	The Saskatchewan Employment Act	The Saskatchewan Human Rights Code

Note: Websites for legislation and agencies can be found in the appendix at the end of this chapter.

HUMAN RIGHTS LEGISLATION

The legislation that has had the most far-reaching impact on employment conditions has been the *Canadian Charter of Rights and Freedoms*, particularly the area of human rights. The *Charter*, passed in 1982, guarantees certain rights and freedoms in our society. What it has done for employment legislation is to ensure that such legislation is consistent with its principles.[5] Rights under the Charter were reinforced when the first human rights legislation was passed. Although the original human rights legislation was at the federal level, all provinces have enacted similar laws.

The basic foundation of human rights legislation is that "all individuals should have an opportunity equal with other individuals to make for themselves the lives that they are able and wish to have and to have their needs accommodated, consistent with their duties and obligations as members of society, without being hindered in or prevented from doing so by discriminatory practices based on race, national or ethnic origin, colour, religion, age, sex, sexual orientation, gender identity or expression, marital status, family status, genetic characteristics, disability or conviction for an offence for which a pardon has been granted or in respect of which a record suspension has been ordered."[6] Although the legislation is designed to protect individuals, it does not cover every situation. For example, "age" had been defined to be the ages between 19 and 65 in most jurisdictions. However, most jurisdictions have now eliminated the "65," which means that, in most cases, the notion of "mandatory retirement" would now be illegal. Employers now need to be vigilant regarding how older workers are treated so that organizations do not have complaints based on age discrimination. For example, the tech industry was recently in the news with complaints of "ageism" as companies target millennials for hiring and bypass older, more experienced tech workers.[7]

Human rights legislation is enforced through human rights commissions (or tribunals) and is achieved via a complaint process (explained in detail later). Since human rights legislation is paramount over other employment laws, the decisions of these commissions and tribunals have a huge influence over all types of employment issues. It is important to note that commission decisions have changed expectations regarding the proper treatment of employees. As a result, organizations now have higher standards to meet. For example, a recent Ontario Human Rights Commission policy decision reminded employers that requiring female employees to dress in a gender-specific way at work may violate the *Ontario Human Rights Code*.[8]

Discrimination

The essence of human rights legislation, both federally and provincially, is to prohibit discrimination on a number of grounds, such as race, religion, gender, age, national or ethnic origin, disability, or family status. Prohibited grounds continue to evolve as changes occur in Canadian society. For example, Alberta, British Columbia, Newfoundland and Labrador, Nova Scotia, Ontario, and Prince Edward Island include "gender identity and gender expression" as prohibited grounds; Manitoba and Saskatchewan only include gender identity.[9] Note that some jurisdictions include pardoned convictions (e.g., federal, British Columbia, Ontario, and Québec) and records of criminal convictions (British Columbia, Québec, Prince Edward Island, and Yukon) as prohibited grounds. A person's political beliefs are protected in some jurisdictions, such as British Columbia, Manitoba, Now Scotia, New Brunswick, Newfoundland and Labrador, Northwest Territories, Québec, and Prince Edward Island. Often a company may have operations in more than 1 province and may need to be aware of the different prohibited grounds. By looking at the complete list of prohibited grounds for each jurisdiction at the human rights agencies listed in Figure 2.2, a comparison can be made.

Many employment barriers are hidden, unintentionally, in the rules and procedures that organizations use in their various human resources management practices. These barriers, referred to as **systemic discrimination**, have prevented the progress of these designated

LO3
Describe discrimination and harassment in the workplace.

Systemic discrimination
The exclusion of members of certain groups through the application of employment policies or practices based on criteria that are not job related

FIGURE 2.2 Provincial and Territorial Human Rights Agencies

Organization	Website
Alberta Human Rights Commission	www.albertahumanrights.ab.ca
BC Human Rights Tribunal	www.bchrt.bc.ca
The Manitoba Human Rights Commission	www.manitobahumanrights.ca
New Brunswick Human Rights Commission	www2.gnb.ca
Newfoundland and Labrador Human Rights Commission	https://thinkhumanrights.ca
Northwest Territories Human Rights Commission	www.nwthumanrights.ca
Nova Scotia Human Rights Commission	https://humanrights.novascotia.ca
Nunavut Human Rights Tribunal	www.nhrt.ca
Human Rights Tribunal of Ontario	www.sjto.gov.on.ca/hrto
Prince Edward Island Human Rights Commission	www.gov.pe.ca/humanrights
(Québec) Commission des droits de la personne et des droits de la jeunesse	www.cdpdj.qc.ca/en
Saskatchewan Human Rights Commission	http://saskatchewan humanrights.ca
Yukon Human Rights Commission	http://yukonhumanrights.ca

Source: "Provincial & Territorial Human Rights Agencies," Canadian Human Rights Commission, accessed January 12, 2018, www.chrc-ccdp.gc.ca/eng/content/provincial-territorial-human-rights-agencies.

groups. Inequity can result if these barriers discourage individuals on the basis of their membership in certain groups rather than their ability to do a job the employer needs done. An example of systemic discrimination would occur when an employer's workforce represents 1 group in our society and the company recruits new employees by posting job vacancies within the company or by word of mouth among the employees. This recruitment strategy is likely to generate a candidate similar to those in the current workforce, thereby unintentionally discriminating against other groups of workers in the labour market. A better approach might be to vary recruitment methods by contacting outside agencies and organizations.

Bona Fide Occupational Requirement

Although it is necessary to ensure that discrimination does not occur, there is a provision in all human rights codes for employers to have certain employment qualifications that are discriminatory. This is called a **bona fide occupational qualification (BFOQ)** or *bona fide occupational job requirement*. For example, Alberta requires that liquor store employees must be at least 18 years of age to sell alcohol.[10] A BFOQ is justified if the employer can establish its necessity for business operations. Business necessity is a practice that includes the safe and efficient operation of an organization. In other words, differential treatment is not discrimination if there is a justifiable reason. This can apply to any and all prohibited grounds under human rights legislation. For example, a recent complaint before the BC Human Rights Tribunal alleged that the employer was being discriminatory under the provisions of disability by not allowing an employee to use medical marijuana. The employee insisted that they needed to regularly smoke marijuana at work. Employers are required to protect employees' rights when medication is required; however, employers also have a responsibility

Bona fide occupational qualification (BFOQ)
Job qualifications that may be discriminatory due to business or safety reasons

to protect employees at work and ensure a safe work environment. The tribunal, although sympathetic to the employee's illness, determined that the employer did not need to take accommodation to the point that others at work might be put at a safety risk.[11] Therefore, an employer needs not only to examine job requirements and demonstrate that a certain characteristic is absolutely essential but also to consider the work environment. The federal government, for example, has been allowed to hire only women as guards in prisons for women; however, a retail store specializing in women's fashions would not be allowed to hire only women. Frequently, the HR professional and the manager would work together to review job requirements to determine if the qualifications met the BFOQ requirement. For recruitment and hiring purposes, it is important that job requirements not create a discriminatory situation. Likewise, even the process of hiring can be considered discriminatory if inappropriate questions are asked. These topics are discussed more fully in Chapter 5.

Most of the decisions made by the Supreme Court of Canada, human rights tribunals, and arbitrations have looked at whether the discrimination was "intentional" or "unintentional." Intentional discrimination is very clear and direct, such as a requirement that only males 5 foot 9 and taller could apply or that airline pilots could not be older than 60. An age limit as a BFOQ was initially upheld for airlines almost 20 years ago. However, the Canadian Human Rights Tribunal in late 2017 decided that it will reconsider whether Air Canada was wrong to force pilots to retire at age 60.[12] Conversely, some discriminatory employment situations are unintentional. Another example is the requirement that a firefighter be able to run a certain distance within a fixed amount of time.

A Supreme Court of Canada decision several years ago changed this approach from previous court decisions, and the result remains the standard when determining BFOQ.[13] The case (*Meiorin*) involved a female forest firefighter in British Columbia who was terminated after performing successfully on the job for 3 years. As a consequence of a coroner's report, new fitness standards had been instituted requiring that all firefighters be able to run 2.5 km in 11 minutes. Meiorin failed the standard on 4 attempts and was terminated, even though she had been doing the work successfully. The court decided that the test was discriminatory because females have a lower aerobic capacity than males and would therefore be unable to meet the standard. The decision went on to establish a new approach to BFOQ. From now on, an employer is required to demonstrate that it is impossible to accommodate individuals discriminated against without undue hardship. This means that whatever the standard is, the employer must provide for individual accommodation if possible.[14]

Duty to Accommodate

Another concept that has arisen from human rights decisions is that of the duty to accommodate, also known as reasonable accommodation. **Duty to accommodate** is a requirement that employers adjust employment practices so that no employee is discriminated against on the prohibited grounds. This is a legal obligation, so as new prohibited grounds are added to any human rights legislation, they, too, become eligible for accommodation. When an accommodation request is made, an employer needs to thoroughly investigate and consider methods by which the employee's particular needs (e.g., family status, gender expression, disability) can be accommodated in the workplace, including whether the specific tasks can be organized in a way to deal with the need.

It is important to remember that accommodation works both ways: both the employee and the employer must live up to the agreement. In an interesting case dealing with accommodation due to a disability and a requested return-to-work, the Human Rights Tribunal of Ontario determined that the employer had a duty to accommodate and could require the employee to attend a medical examination by a doctor of the employer's choosing. The employee alleged that to do so was discriminatory by not being allowed to return to work based on a recommendation by the employee's doctor. The tribunal's decision was recently upheld by the Court of Appeal for Ontario.[15] The court reaffirmed the tribunal's decision that it was reasonable to seek a medical assessment by another doctor. Although reasonable,

Duty to accommodate
Requirement that employers adjust employment practices to avoid discrimination

accommodation is expected unless "undue hardship" is created for the employer. Undue hardship is typically based upon financial grounds or health and safety issues. However, most midsized-to-large organizations would have difficulty saying that an accommodation request would create undue hardship. For example, if someone does not have the necessary eye–hand coordination to do detailed electronics work, the employer may be obliged to reconfigure the tasks so that the person can do the work. Whether an employer can accommodate the work to fit the individual needs is ultimately a decision made by human rights tribunals. Ethics in HRM 2.1 describes what happened when the federal government denied an accommodation request on family status.

Undue hardship, however, may be something different for a small organization compared to a larger organization. For example, it may be a hardship for a small firm to modify a washroom to accommodate a person in a wheelchair, but it may be reasonable to expect a large organization, with its own building, to renovate or install a washroom that can accommodate a wheelchair.

In exploring a duty to accommodate, the employer may redesign the job duties; adjust the work schedules; provide technical, financial, and human support services; and upgrade physical facilities. Furthermore, with the aging workforce, people are working longer, and there will be a need to accommodate older workers with health issues.[16]

Businesses are becoming more aware of the value that individuals with disabilities can bring to the workplace. To help make this happen, many not-for-profit organizations in Canada support and encourage employment opportunities for people with disabilities, among them the Canadian Association for Community Living, Canadian Abilities Foundation, and Canadian Council on Rehabilitation and Work. Although many employers tend to think of accommodation in terms of physical disabilities, it is important to remember that the duty to accommodate includes all the prohibited grounds of discrimination, including mental illness. The focus on mental illness is more prominent as its impact in the workplace is better understood. As a result, organizations are being reminded that mental illness qualifies for accommodation.[17] Other organizations, such as Mental Health Works, can also

ETHICS IN HRM 2.1   CAN AN EMPLOYEE REFUSE A CONDITION OF ACCOMMODATION?

In 2017, the Canada Public Service Labour Relations and Employment Board determined that the Department of National Defence (DND) was reasonable in denying a request by an employee to leave work 30 minutes early to help their spouse care for special-needs children. Specifically, the spouse had health problems, and 2 of the couple's 4 children had developmental difficulties. The employee wanted to take the 2 paid 15-minute breaks at the end of the day and stated that the accommodation was necessary to relieve the spouse of some tasks. The DND refused the request because it would be a violation of the collective agreement and that rest periods throughout the day were for health and safety reasons. The employee filed a grievance, which was rejected by the DND. However, the employee's manager wanted to help and suggested that the employee take the two 15-minute breaks back to back (with a 1-minute interval) and take a 30-minute unpaid lunch break at the end of the day. The employee rejected this suggestion and pursued the grievance, which the union advanced to the board. The board determined that the request was for the spouse's health, not necessarily child care, and that the refusal didn't prevent the employee from fulfilling their legal obligations toward the children.

CRITICAL THINKING QUESTION:

What is your opinion of the decisions by the DND and the employee? Why?

Sources: *Pascal Guilbault and Treasury Board (Department of National Defence)*, 2017 PSLREB1, January 10, 2017, accessed January 14, 2018, http://pslreb-crtefp .gc.ca/decisions/fulltext/2017-1_e.asp; and Jeffrey Smith, "Government Employee Faces Limits of Family Status Accommodation," *Canadian HR Reporter*, July 10, 2017, accessed January 14, 2018, www.hrreporter.com/workplace-law/33898-government-employee-faces-limits-of-family-status-accommodation.

provide advice and guidance regarding workplace issues. A further discussion on healthy workplaces is provided in Chapter 3.

Reasonable accommodation benefits all employees. The provision of allowances for childcare expenses when employees take company-sponsored courses not only removes a barrier that blocks many women but also may assist any employee with sole parenting responsibilities. The flexible work schedules adopted by some companies in northern Canada benefit First Nations employees, who are prepared to work unusual hours in exchange for significant breaks away from the worksite in order to take part in traditional hunting and fishing activities. Many other employees also benefit from these flexible work schedules. Furthermore, with the cultural and religious diversity of the Canadian population, more and more employers are being asked for accommodation for religious or creed purposes, including time off to attend religious/creed services.[18]

At Work with HRM 2.1 provides another example of what happens when an employer doesn't consider all the prohibited grounds when making a decision.

Reverse Discrimination

In pursuing initiatives to avoid discrimination, employers may be accused of **reverse discrimination**, or giving preference to members of certain groups such that others feel they are being discriminated against. For example, if a company feels that it has too few women employees, it may take active steps to hire more women. By hiring more women, however, the company may hire fewer men, opening it up to criticism that it is discriminating against men. When these charges occur, organizations are caught between attempting to correct past discriminatory practices and handling present complaints that they are being

Reverse discrimination
Giving preference to members of certain groups such that others feel they are the subjects of discrimination

AT WORK WITH HRM 2.1 — WHAT IF THE PERSON IS RETIRING?

A recent decision by the Public Sector Labour Relations and Employment Board reinforces the need to consider all the prohibited grounds in human rights legislation when making decisions.

An employee at the Canadian Border Services Agency (CBSA) indicated that she was willing to take a cash payment to leave as part of the CBSA decision to downsize certain jobs. The manager refused the request even though the cash incentive plan was written into the various collective agreements. The decision was based on the manager's perspective that the position could be eliminated as part of the cost cutting because the person was going to retire. Under the downsizing plan, employees could post their position on the internal website if they were willing to give up their job to employees who were going to be laid off. The employee did this, on the advice of the union, and the manager was obliged to consider the various applicants. In reviewing the applications, the manager found that none qualified for the position. Furthermore, the manager informed the employee that the

position was going to be eliminated, so there was no need to try to find someone to take the job. The union grieved the decision on the basis that the employee was being discriminated against due to age.

The grievance advanced to the board, which determined that age played a major role in the decision. According to the board, the employee was identified as someone who was retiring soon (although the employee never indicated this) and that the position could be eliminated. In its view, this was a stereotype of age, and since the CBSA continued to support the manager, it was a discriminatory practice. The board ordered the CBSA to pay $15,000 for the discrimination and another $10,000 as special compensation for the pain and suffering caused to the employee.

CRITICAL THINKING QUESTIONS:
1. Do you think this was an appropriate decision? Why or why not?
2. Do you think the monetary award was appropriate? Why or why not?

Source: Jeffrey R. Smith, "Manager's Assumption of Pending Retirement Leads to Age Discrimination," *Canadian HR Reporter*, December 11, 2017, 5.

Businesses can benefit from having individuals with diverse skills and capabilities.

Belushi/Shutterstock.com

unfair. If an organization is required to comply with any type of employment equity legislation (discussed later), it can be quite legal to discriminate and hire certain individuals.

In some cases, organizations may identify the need to hire a certain proportion of people from specific groups, such as visible minorities. Although these organizations may state that they wish to find a larger pool of qualified applicants from a particular group, the organizations may, in fact, create a type of quota system for hiring. If it is perceived that there are hard numbers attached to hiring, then it is easy for individuals not in a targeted group to feel they are being discriminated against. Charges of reverse discrimination have occurred in fire and police services as those organizations try to achieve a workforce more reflective of the residents in their communities.

Harassment

LO4

Outline the manager's role in creating a work environment that is free from harassment and discrimination.

Harassment
Any conduct or comment that a reasonable person would consider objectionable or unwelcome

Besides prohibiting discrimination, human rights legislation prohibits harassment as harassment is a form of discrimination. However, some provinces have enacted legislation (usually through an occupational health and safety act) that broadens harassment beyond just prohibited grounds. For example, bullying is considered a type of harassment and is also specifically identified in occupational health and safety legislation. **Harassment** is usually considered to be any conduct or comment that a reasonable person would consider objectionable or unwelcome, including any unnecessary physical contact.[19] Harassment can take many forms and can be 1 incident or several incidents. It is not acceptable, for instance, for one coworker to strike another, and it is not acceptable to make personal comments that are offensive to the other person. When dealing with harassment in the workplace, a manager needs to ask whether a "reasonable person" would consider a certain behaviour or action as harassment. If the answer is yes, then the manager is expected to act accordingly. It is interesting to note that what is considered harassment in today's workplace was sometimes considered acceptable behaviour not long ago. For example, it used to be acceptable to call someone a name that reflected the person's ethnic background.

Although for some time, discussions of harassment have focused on general harassment and bullying, the concern that sexual harassment is still very prevalent became news headlines recently. Many individuals, particularly women, publicly described their experiences of sexual harassment in many different industries, including Parliament.[20] One of the more prominent arts industries identified was film and TV when leaders came together to acknowledge how prevalent it was and that they were committed to changing the culture to prevent it.[21] In addition, Facebook's COO, Sheryl Sandberg, cautioned employers to ensure that there isn't a backlash to a woman's career if she speaks about sexual harassment.[22] A recent study also linked sexual harassment to mental health in the workplace.[23] HRM and the Law 2.1 describes the financial cost of harassment complaints.

With the heightened attention to sexual harassment, it is important to remember general harassment in the workplace. Organizations have developed policy statements and guidelines for dealing with this. To reinforce the importance of dealing with harassment in the workplace, the Supreme Court of Canada recently ruled that employees harassed by workers of other companies can file a human rights complaint.[24]

The Canadian Human Rights Commission defines harassment as follows:

Harassment is any unwanted physical or verbal behaviour that offends or humiliates you. Generally, harassment is a behaviour that persists over time. Serious one-time incidents can also sometimes be considered harassment.

Harassment occurs when someone:

- makes unwelcome remarks or jokes about your race, religion, sex, age, disability or other of the grounds of discrimination
- threatens or intimidates you because of your race, religion, sex, age, disability or any other of the grounds of discrimination
- makes unwelcome physical contact with you, such as touching, patting, or pinching[25]*

HRM AND **THE LAW** 2.1 — WHAT IS THE COST OF HARASSMENT?

A recent case in the Ontario Court of Appeal clearly demonstrated that allowing harassment in the workplace can be a very costly situation.

The specifics of the case involved an individual who was awarded $60,000 in moral damages by the Ontario provincial court. The court not only determined that the employee was entitled to $35,000 for having been wrongfully dismissed but also that the employee had been sexually harassed; therefore, an additional $25,000 was awarded. During the hearing, the employee described the harassment over a 9-year period. At the same time as the employee filed the sexual harassment complaint, the employer was considering terminating the employee as a result of a reorganization of the company. As a result, the employer undertook a very superficial investigation of the complaint without allowing the employee to provide their story.

The employer appealed the court's award, and the appeal court determined that the employer's conduct was not in keeping with best practice, in terms of both the actual dismissal and the investigation of the complaint.

In another case, the Canadian Security Intelligence Service (CSIS) voluntarily agreed to pay $35,000,000 to staff for workplace harassment. The employees who launched the discrimination lawsuit indicated that managers had created a culture of discrimination, harassment, and bullying by their actions and behaviours at all levels of management. Several employees met with the director of CSIS to describe the types of behaviours against Muslims, people of colour, and employees who are gay. The director stated that he would work to ensure that the behaviour of everyone reflected respect for people.

CRITICAL THINKING QUESTION:
What do you think of the decisions? Why?

Sources: Shreya Patel, "Whopper Damages for Harassment, then Dismissal," *Human Resources Director Canada*, October 13, 2017, accessed January 19, 2018, www.hrmonline.ca/hr-business-review/employment-litigation-and-advice/whopper-damages-for-harassment-then-dismissal-232310.aspx; and Emily Douglas, "CSIS Settles 435m Suit with Staff Alleging Workplace Harassment," *Human Resources Director Canada*, December 15, 2017, accessed January 19, 2018, www.hrmonline.ca/hr-news/csis-settles-35m-suit-with-staff-alleging-workplace-harassment-235532.aspx.

*Canadian Human Rights Commission, www.chrc-ccdp.ca/eng/content/what-harassment-1.

When considering whether the behaviour is harassing, the test used is this: "Would a reasonable person know that the conduct was not welcomed by the other?" What this means for managers is that they are expected to work with employees to ensure that they are behaving and acting acceptably.

It is important for organizations to have policies dealing with harassment. For example, the Newfoundland and Labrador government has an extensive policy dealing with harassment and a discrimination-free workplace,[26] including definitions, responsibilities, and information about how complaints are filed and handled.

Furthermore, harassment is defined by the *Ontario Human Rights Code, 1962*, as engaging in a course of vexatious comment or conduct that is known or ought reasonably to be known to be unwelcome (Section 10(1)(f)). Some examples of harassment are:

- unwelcome remarks, jokes, slurs, innuendoes, or taunting
- hazing, stalking, or shunning
- the repeated mistreatment of 1 employee, targeted by 1 or more employees with a malicious mix of humiliation, intimidation, and sabotage of performance (bullying)
- displaying derogatory or offensive pictures, graffiti, or materials either through printed copy or personal computer
- verbal abuse
- insulting gestures or practical jokes that cause embarrassment or awkwardness
- unauthorized and/or unnecessary physical contact
- an impassioned, collective campaign by coworkers to exclude, punish, and humiliate a targeted worker

For harassment policies to succeed, confidentiality is necessary, as is the need to do a thorough investigation. For example, a Manitoba First Nation was fined $10,000 for not doing a thorough investigation when a workplace incident occurred.[27] Without organizational commitment to zero tolerance of harassment, such policies are meaningless. It is also important to remember that harassment is against the law. As the Province of Saskatchewan reminds employers: "[I]t's against the law" and "If you violate the *Code* you could be liable for the harm caused. . . ."[28]

Toolkit 2.1 presents some suggestions for developing an effective harassment policy.

TOOLKIT 2.1   GUIDELINES FOR HAVING AN EFFECTIVE ANTI-HARASSMENT POLICY

- Indicate in the policy that the organization is committed to a harassment-free environment.
- Indicate who is responsible for the administration of the policy.
- Encourage employees to come forward with complaints.
- Provide a clear definition of harassment.
- Provide guidelines for individuals about making a complaint, including to whom it goes.
- Outline employee obligations and responsibilities.
- Provide a step-by-step procedure for making a complaint, including timelines.

- Provide information about who will be involved in the investigation and when the complainant may expect the decision.
- Outline the responsibilities of management at all levels of the organization.
- Train managers and employees.
- Maintain confidentiality.
- Guarantee fair and prompt action.
- Communicate and consistently enforce the policy.
- Review the policy annually.

Additional resources from the various human rights commissions are available at the websites listed in Figure 2.2.

Sources: Adapted from "Developing an Anti-Harassment Policy," Canadian Human Rights Commission, accessed January 20, 2018, www.chrc-ccdp.gc.ca/eng/content/template-developing-anti-harassment-policy; "Workplace Harassment Policy," Government of New Brunswick, accessed January 20, 2018, www.chrc-ccdp.gc.ca/eng/content/template-developing-anti-harassment-policy; and "Bullying and Harassment Prevention Training," Harris & Company, October 10, 2017.

The concepts of harassment in the workplace are being broadened to include **psychological harassment**, such as bullying, yelling at subordinates, excluding employees from certain activities, making derogatory comments, and other similar actions. As mentioned earlier in this chapter, **bullying** has become very prominent as a particular type of harassment. Chapter 3 provides information on bullying as a health and safety matter and discusses the implications for an organization's culture. It is important to note that psychological harassment can create a poisoned work environment and a toxic culture that can result in a significant response by the employer. For example, an external investigation of an Edmonton maximum-security prison identified the work environment as toxic and recommended a number of changes, including more training. To reinforce the seriousness of the situation, several staff were fired in early 2018.[29] Although the concept of psychological harassment is based on prohibited grounds in human rights legislation, several jurisdictions have also included psychological harassment in health and safety legislation, for example, Ontario and British Columbia. Sometimes there is a fine line between bullying and strong management, but the difference appears to be whether feedback is constructive to help employees with their work.[30] It is important to know that expressing differences of opinion or taking reasonable disciplinary action does not constitute bullying.[31] However, spreading gossip or rumours and vandalizing another employee's belongings can be. For additional information on psychological harassment in the workplace, resources can be found at the Psychological Harassment Information Association's website.

> **Psychological harassment**
> Repeated and aggravating behaviour that affects an employee's dignity or psychological or physical integrity that makes the work environment harmful
>
> **Bullying**
> Actions and verbal comments that can hurt or isolate a person in the workplace

Enforcement of Human Rights Legislation

The federal government and each province and territory have a commission or similar agency to deal with complaints concerning discriminatory practices covered by legislation. For example, the Canadian Human Rights Commission (CHRC) deals with complaints from those employees and businesses (e.g., airlines, banks, telecommunications, etc.) covered by the *Canadian Human Rights Act*. These commissions can act on their own if they feel there are sufficient grounds for a finding of discrimination. The agencies also have the ability to interpret the act. Figure 2.3 presents a flow chart of a process used to resolve complaints.

The steps are as follows:

1. *Complaint received.* An individual contacts the human rights commission/tribunal to file a complaint.
2. *Screening and investigation.* A commission/tribunal representative works with the complainant to determine what occurred.
3. *Employer notified.* The representative contacts the employer to determine its perspective.
4. *Mediation/conciliation/settlement.* Specialists are assigned by the commission/tribunal to assist the parties in finding a mediated solution. This is a voluntary and confidential step.
5. *Tribunal hearing.* When a case is referred to a tribunal, there is no guarantee that the complaint will be upheld. Furthermore, if the tribunal decides the complaint is valid, it can order corrective measures, such as human rights training, a change in the employer's human rights policies, or payment for lost wages, pain, and/or suffering.[32]

Human rights laws are enforced in both federal and provincial jurisdictions in a manner similar to that described in Figure 2.3. The majority of cases are resolved at the investigation stage. If no agreement can be reached, the case is presented to the human rights tribunal. The tribunal studies the evidence and then makes a decision. Failure to comply with the remedies prescribed by the tribunal are enforceable through the judicial system and may result in prosecution in provincial court. Individuals may be fined between $500 and $1000 and organizations or groups between $1000 and $10,000. These levies may vary across provinces.

FIGURE 2.3 Human Rights Commission Dispute Resolution Process

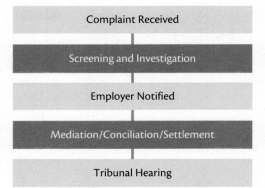

Complaint Received

Screening and Investigation

Employer Notified

Mediation/Conciliation/Settlement

Tribunal Hearing

AT WORK WITH HRM 2.2 — HOW MUCH MORE?

Small and large organizations throughout Canada are expected to do more than they have to create and maintain work environments that are free from discrimination and harassment. Recently, a well-known lawyer indicated that although employers are expected to bear the responsibility of protecting their employees, this is complicated due to concerns of relationships and reputations. Specifically, if someone within the organization is the investigator of the complaint, can the person be totally unbiased about the employer's conduct?

This also means that employers are expected to do more regarding accommodation. One of the areas where employers frequently misstep is dealing with sick leaves—whether short- or long-term. Often there is a reluctance to have a conversation with the employee, especially regarding what can be done to get the person back to work, and an assumption that accommodation refers to physical disabilities.

Other experts remind employers that it is crucial that all managers are trained and updated on what constitutes prohibited grounds. Many employers may not be aware that older employees could feel discriminated against and that age discrimination can occur. As more grounds are included, such as genetics in the *Ontario Human Rights Code*, governments are expecting a higher standard for employers in the future.

CRITICAL THINKING QUESTIONS:

1. Do you think employers will do more to eliminate discrimination and harassment? Why or why not?
2. How do you think employers feel about doing more? How do you think employees feel about whether employers should do more?

Sources: Adapted from Adelle Chua, "Workplace Is Wrong Venue to Address Harassment," *Human Resources Director*, November 21, 2017, accessed January 20, 2018, www.hrmonline.ca/hr-law/discrimination/workplace-is-wrong-venue-to-address-harassment-234221.aspx; Adelle Chua, "Age Discrimination Case a Warning for Employers," *Human Resources Director*, November 8, 2017, accessed January 20, 2018, www.hrmonline.ca/hr-law/discrimination/age-discrimination-case-a-warning-for-employers-233571.aspx; Laura McQuillan, "Ask a Lawyer: Am I Accommodating Disabilities Correctly?," *Human Resources Director*, September 27, 2017, accessed January 20, 2018, www.hrmonline.ca/hr-law/accommodation/ask-a-lawyer-am-i-accommodating-disabilities-correctly-231526.aspx; "Legal Experts Reveal What Employers Must Learn," *Human Resources Director*, September 26, 2017, accessed January 20, 2018, www.hrmonline.ca/hr-law/accommodation/legal-experts-reveal-what-employers-must-learn-231478.aspx; and Adelle Chua, "What Ontario's New Discrimination Bill Means for HR," *Human Rights Director*, October 13, 2017, accessed January 20, 2018, www.hrmonline.ca/hr-law/discrimination/what-ontarios-new-discrimination-bill-means-for-hr-232317.aspx.

The impact of fines can be particularly difficult on small businesses. For example, the Human Rights Tribunal of Ontario recently awarded almost $60,000 in damages to an employee who was forced to resign after repeated harassment and discrimination.[33]

As issues of discrimination and harassment continue to occur in workplaces, more and more emphasis will be put on employers to do something more than they are. Read At Work with HRM 2.2 to gain a better understanding of what is expected.

EMPLOYMENT STANDARDS LEGISLATION

LO5

Identify the general types of employment laws in Canada.

All federal, provincial, and territorial jurisdictions have passed employment standards laws specifying the minimum obligations of employers. The names of the laws usually include the term "employment standards" or something similar. However, the minimum obligations for federal companies are covered under the *Canada Labour Code*.

Usually included in this type of legislation are items such as hours of work, minimum wages, overtime pay, vacation pay, public holidays, and who is covered by the legislation. Standards vary between provinces. In Alberta, for instance, certain provisions, such as keeping overtime records, do not apply to architects or engineers.[34]

The legislation also typically reflects the views of the specific government with regard to its social policy. For example, British Columbia's legislation provides the right for a person to take a limited number of days off to tend to childcare needs, and Ontario recently enacted a provision whereby personal emergency leave was expanded to 10 days per calendar year, with at least 2 paid days per year.[35] Both British Columbia and Ontario have legislation that provides 9 statutory or public holidays. Usually, a separate branch or agency administers and interprets the legislation for both employers and employees. All the websites are listed in the appendix at the end of this chapter.

This legislation is important as it applies to all employers, unionized or not. And because it specifies minimum obligations of employers, every employer—large or small—needs to be aware of the legislation. This is particularly true if the organization also uses contractors (see Chapter 1). There might be circumstances in which the contractor is considered an employee. Even though the use of contractors has been popular with organizations and individuals, Alberta and Ontario recently passed legislation that will have more protection for contractors. For example, in Alberta, the law has changed so that contractors can unionize, and in Ontario, employers are prohibited from misclassifying employees as independent contractors.[36]

An agency or commission that both interprets and enforces the law administers the legislation. For example, if employees feel that they are not receiving the right amount of vacation pay, they can contact the agency and find out what the right amount should be. If they are getting the wrong amount, then the agency can contact the employer and start an investigation. Furthermore, other legislation may influence what standards must be met. A case involving a collective agreement that allowed the employer to adjust automatic wage adjustments during parental leave was deemed to be violating human rights legislation, and it was ruled that the employment standards requirement must be met.[37]

Sometimes organizations think a certain provision in these standards does not apply. For example, there have been many instances in which an employer thinks a manager paid by salary is not entitled to overtime. This applies only if the person is truly doing managerial work and isn't just titled "manager" while doing non-managerial work.[38]

LABOUR RELATIONS LEGISLATION

Labour relations legislation governs both the process by which a trade union acquires bargaining rights and the procedures by which trade unions and employers engage in collective bargaining.

In some jurisdictions, such as Ontario, the legislation (*Labour Relations Act, 1995*) applies primarily to workplaces in the private sector but also covers certain parts of the public sector (e.g., municipal workers, hospital employees, school boards). Ontario has separate legislation for certain types of employers in the public sector, such as hospitals and Crown corporations.[39] However, in other jurisdictions, such as British Columbia, the legislation can apply to any workplace, whether in the public or the private sector.

Labour relations legislation applies only to unionized employees and to employers with unionized employees. Currently, approximately 4.8 million employees (or 32% of the Canadian workforce) belong to a union primarily in the public sector (71%).[40] Unionization continues to decline in Canada, with the lowest rate of unionization being among young workers.[41]

Labour relations legislation is usually administered through an agency called a labour relations board, which is responsible for administering and enforcing the legislation. This board makes decisions on a variety of complaints from either a union or an employer. An employer might complain about the location of a trade union's picket, or union members might complain that the union has not fairly represented them. The board hires the people making these decisions, who are usually lawyers or have some type of legal training.

More information on labour relations legislation is provided in Chapter 10.

HEALTH AND SAFETY LEGISLATION AND WORKERS' COMPENSATION

As you will read in Chapter 3, the work environment and well-being of employees are the responsibility of employers. This responsibility is partially governed by legislation that describes the expected standards for health and safety in the workplace, as well as outlining the role and involvement of employees in health and safety.

The federal, provincial, and territorial governments regulate occupational health and safety. Although statutes and standards differ slightly from jurisdiction to jurisdiction, attempts have been made to harmonize the various acts and regulations. Health and safety legislation has had an impact on workplace injuries and illnesses. The number of workplace accidents in Canada has declined even though there has been an increase in the number of workers.

All managers and HR professionals should become familiar with the occupational health and safety legislation governing the jurisdiction under which their organization operates. The fundamental duty of every employer is to take every reasonable precaution to ensure employee safety.

In addition to providing a hazard-free workplace and complying with the applicable statutes and regulations, employers must inform their employees about health and safety requirements. Employers are also required to keep certain records, to compile an annual summary of work-related injuries and illnesses, and to ensure that managers are familiar with the work and its associated hazards (the manager, in turn, must ensure that workers are aware of those hazards). In most jurisdictions, employers are required to ensure that employees are knowledgeable about workplace health and safety.

Violations of health and safety statutes are administered through a government agency, frequently called the Workers' Compensation Board. As part of the legislation, workers can receive a monetary payment if they are injured or get a disease that can be attributed to their work. Thus, the employer is responsible not only for the health and safety of the workplace but also for financial compensation if the worker is injured or gets a disease from the job. In all jurisdictions, employers are required to report any accidents that cause injuries and diseases to the Workers' Compensation Board. An accident resulting in death or critical injury must be reported immediately; the accident must then be investigated and a written report submitted. Finally, employers must provide safety training and be prepared to discipline employees for failing to comply with safety rules. Web addresses for the various provincial agencies can be found in this chapter's appendix.

The legislation also identifies the duties of workers, which include complying with all applicable acts and regulations; reporting hazardous conditions or defective equipment; and following all employer safety and health rules and regulations, including those prescribing the use of protective equipment, such as wearing hard hats or steel-toed boots at a construction site or protective eyewear in a laboratory. Workers have many rights that pertain to requesting and receiving information about safety and health conditions. They also have the right to refuse unsafe work without fear of reprisal.

Occupational health and safety laws also require managers to advise employees of potential workplace hazards; ensure that workers use or wear safety equipment, devices, or clothing; provide written instructions where applicable; and take every reasonable precaution to guarantee the safety of workers. As you will read in Chapter 3, the manager is key in creating a healthy and safe work environment. The manager is the point of contact for almost every question regarding health and safety. Furthermore, the manager will reinforce safety and health training and will be the person held accountable for employees' understanding and behaviour regarding health and safety in the workplace.

Lastly, most jurisdictions require the formation of health and safety committees operated jointly by employee and management representatives. This arrangement is intended to create a non-adversarial climate in which labour and management work together to create a safe and healthy workplace.

Both employees and employers are responsible for promoting a safe work environment.

Cineberg/Shutterstock.com

EMPLOYMENT AND PAY EQUITY

Central to Canada's economic growth and prosperity in a highly competitive global marketplace will be a barrier-free environment in which all Canadians can fully explore and develop their career potential. Labour force statistics, described in Chapter 1, indicate changing patterns of immigration, the rising labour force participation rates of women, and an aging population with a proportionately higher incidence of disabilities. Women, members of visible minorities, Aboriginal peoples, and people with disabilities are the designated groups under the federal employment equity legislation. These designated-group members entering Canada's labour pool constitute a vital resource, and their full participation in the workplace will be fundamental to an organization's ability to understand and respond to the needs of a rapidly changing marketplace.

Employment Equity

Equity, by definition, means fairness or impartiality. In a legal sense, it means justice based on the concepts of ethics and fairness and a system of jurisprudence administered by courts and designed primarily to decrease the rigidity of common law. The implementation of **employment equity** has involved the establishment of policies and practices designed to ensure equitable representation in the workforce and to redress past discriminations as they relate to employment and employment practices.

> **Employment equity**
> A distinct Canadian process for achieving equality in all aspects of employment

The Law on Employment Equity

The *Employment Equity Act* requires that the federal government, federal agencies, and Crown corporations with 100 employees or more that are regulated under the *Canada Labour Code* must implement employment equity and report on their results. Some of the companies covered by the *Employment Equity Act* are Royal Bank, Rogers Foods Ltd., GE Canada, Brink's Canada Limited, and Vancouver Fraser Port Authority. Under the act, the employer is required to develop plans to better represent the **designated groups** mentioned above. In creating the plan, the employer must identify and remove any employment barriers, such as a keyboarding test for jobs in which no keyboarding is required. Furthermore, the plan must have a timetable for achieving these changes. Although this law does not extend to the provinces, the federal government, through its Federal Contractors Program, expects organizations that do more than $1 million in business with the federal government to implement employment equity principles.[42]

Although there are no specific provincial acts pertaining to employment equity, the concept of employment equity is rooted in federal and provincial employment standards legislation, human rights codes, and the *Canadian Charter of Rights and Freedoms*. Employment equity involves the identification and removal of systemic barriers to employment opportunities that adversely affect designated groups. It also involves the implementation of special measures and reasonable accommodation (discussed earlier under "Discrimination"). The employment equity legislation identified 4 designated groups in Canada that had not received equitable treatment in employment—women, members of visible minorities, Aboriginal peoples, and people with disabilities—recognizing that they faced significant but different disadvantages in employment. Some of the disadvantages included high unemployment, occupational segregation, pay inequities, and limited opportunities for career progress. Although there has been progress since the introduction of the legislation in the mid-1980s, some of the original concerns have not been advanced very far.

Although in Canada, women represent 50% of people employed,[43] the employment tends to be concentrated in education (68%), accommodation and food services (57%), and healthcare (82%).[44] On the other hand, women tend to be underrepresented in mining, oil and gas (18%), and manufacturing (28%). But they are close to being equally represented (48%) with men (52%) in wholesale and retail trade jobs.[45]

The number of Aboriginal peoples is about 5%[46] of the population, with an increase of 43% between 2006 and 2016.[47] The numbers of young Aboriginal workers will increase, and in western Canada, they will account for a substantial portion of labour market growth. However, many Aboriginal peoples face major employment barriers, which may be compounded by low educational achievement and a lack of job experience, as well as language and cultural barriers. In urban centres, many Aboriginal workers are concentrated in low-paying, unstable employment. Economic self-sufficiency and participation in the economy are seen as essential to the development of Aboriginal peoples. At Work with HRM 2.3 describes the success of several organizations in assisting Aboriginal peoples to become an integral part of their workforces.

Visible-minority groups vary in their labour force profiles and in their regional distributions. Toronto and Vancouver have large visible-minority populations. Studies have shown that Latin Americans and Southeast Asians experience lower-than-average incomes, higher rates of unemployment, and reduced access to job interviews, even for those persons with the same qualifications as other candidates. Systemic barriers that have a negative employment impact on visible minorities can include culturally biased aptitude tests, lack of recognition of foreign credentials, and excessive levels of language requirements. Recent statistics indicate that 22% of the Canadian population are identified as visible minorities, of which 50% lived in Toronto, Montréal, and Vancouver.[48]

People with disabilities represent approximately 14% of the Canadian population, and only about one-half of them are employed, as against 74% of Canadians without a disability.[49] This number is growing as people age and live longer.[50] People with disabilities face attitudinal barriers, physical demands unrelated to job requirements, and inadequate access to the technical and human support systems that would make productive employment possible. It is encouraging to note that more and more businesses are hiring people with a disability, which helps create a more inclusive and diverse workforce that leads to better business performance.[51]

AT WORK WITH HRM 2.3 — CANADA'S TOP EMPLOYERS!

More and more organizations are being recognized for the work they are doing to enhance employment for Aboriginal peoples. Canada's Best Diversity Employers 2017 honoured a number of companies for this work. Among the award recipients was Cameco Corporation for employing Aboriginal Elders at their northern sites so that there are dedicated resources familiar with the culture for maintaining a dedicated team focused on workforce development for communities in northern Saskatchewan.

Aboriginal Peoples Television Network Inc. (APTN) also was recognized for helping its staff achieve a better work–life balance through a number of alternative work schedules and painting the interior walls in an Aboriginal colour scheme. It has also excelled in creating mentorships to assist young Aboriginal workers as they move into the television industry.

The City of Edmonton was recognized for its participation in a partnership to increase the employment of Aboriginal peoples, and Jazz Airlines was honoured for creating scholarships that are awarded to full-time Aboriginal students in their final year of study.

CRITICAL THINKING QUESTIONS:

1. What has the company you are working for (or have recently worked for) done to assist visible minorities, people with disabilities, and Aboriginal peoples in getting hired?
2. Is there more they could do? If so, please explain.

Sources: Adapted from "Canada's Top 100 Employers 2018," November 6, 2017, accessed January 23, 2018, www.canadastop100.com/national; "RBC, Shaw Among Winners for Employment Equity Awards," *Canadian HR Reporter*, October 5, 2017, accessed January 28, 2018, www.hrreporter.com/hr-trends/34754 -rbc-shaw-among-winners-for-employment-equity-awards; and "Canada's Best Diversity Employers 2017," March 28, 2017, accessed January 23, 2018, www.canadastop100.com/diversity.

The employment experiences of people with disabilities are also dependent on their level of education. In most cases, people with minor limitations who are university graduates do not experience as many barriers as those with little education or more extreme limitations.[52]

As mentioned earlier in the chapter, these employment practices can unintentionally exclude certain segments of our population from employment opportunities. Toolkit 2.2 gives examples of suggested solutions to systemic barriers.

TOOLKIT 2.2 — EXAMPLES OF EMPLOYMENT PRACTICES

1. *Word-of-mouth recruiting.* Although this is a common form of making job opportunities known to family and friends, it is better to have a formal job posting that can also be targeted to particular underrepresented groups.
2. *Job requirements.* Employers that require Canadian experience may be excluding visible minorities, particularly recent immigrants. It is important to assess all previous experiences and have culturally neutral qualifications.
3. *Training and development.* It is important to review the organization's approach to training of its employees and ensure that appropriate training is available to all.
4. *Promotion and advancement.* Opportunities for changes should be widely communicated in the organization. Also, when reviewing performance, all employees need to be measured using the same criteria.
5. *Organizational environment.* It is a good idea to have flexible work arrangements to handle work and family obligations.

Sources: Adapted from Ontario Human Rights Commission, "Appendix—Workplace Policies, Practices and Decision-Making Processes and Systemic Discrimination," accessed January 25, 2018, www.ohrc.on.ca/en/policy-and-guidelines-racism-and-racial-discrimination/appendix-%E2%80%93-workplace-policies -practices-and-decision-making-processes-and-systemic-discrimination; and Manitoba Civil Service Commission, "Principles & Policies for Managing Human Resources: 1.5.2 Removing Employment Barriers," accessed January 25, 2018, www.gov.mb.ca/csc/policyman/removbar.html#one.

First Nations University is a unique Canadian university that creates an environment for learning about First Nations culture and values.

Frazer Harrison/Getty Images

Benefits of Employment Equity

Many employers are finding that employment equity is beneficial for the overall success of the business as there is a larger pool of qualified people for employment, training, and promotions. Most provinces now take an active approach to ensuring that there is appropriate representation in their workforces. For example, the Manitoba Civil Service Commission believes a diverse employee base can better serve the citizens of Manitoba.[53] Likewise, organizations such as Loblaw Companies Limited in Ontario have created a dedicated network for female staff that helps with their development in the company.[54]

Employment and Social Development Canada administers the federal *Employment Equity Act*, and through annual reports, it provides statistical information about the successes of organizational initiatives in achieving a more representative workforce. In the most recent report, the participation rate of members of visible minorities has been achieved, and Aboriginal peoples' participation rate increased significantly, whereas women and people with disabilities are still underrepresented.[55]

Pay Equity

Pay equity
The practice of equal pay for work of equal value

As a result of a 1978 amendment to the *Canadian Human Rights Act*, **pay equity**—equal pay for work of equal value—became law. Federal pay equity law makes it illegal for federally regulated employers to discriminate against individuals on the basis of job content. The focus of pay equity legislation is to narrow the wage gap between men and women, on the basis that women's work historically has been undervalued and therefore underpaid relative to work primarily done by men. For example, the average hourly wage of men who worked full time in 2017 was $28.69 but only $24.65 for women.[56] One of the principles behind pay equity is gender neutrality, designed to reduce systematic discriminatory pay practices.[57] Iceland was the first country to enact a law to force employers to pay women and men equally.[58]

Pay equity is based on 2 principles. The first is equal pay for equal work. Equal pay for equal work means that if a woman and a man are doing substantially the same work for the same organization or company, they must receive the same wage unless the difference is due to a formal seniority system, a temporary training assignment, or merit pay.[59] Equal pay for equal work is regulated through basic employment conditions legislation, usually titled *Employment Standards Act*.

The second principle of pay equity is equal pay for work that may be comparable in value to the organization. Pay equity compares the value and pay of different jobs. This means that male and female workers must be paid the same wage rate for jobs of comparable value, such as nurse (historically female-dominated work) and electrician (historically male-dominated work).

Implementation of pay equity is based on comparing jobs performed mostly by women with jobs performed mostly by males. Comparisons require the use of a gender-neutral job comparison system to evaluate the jobs in the organization.[60] The value of the work is based on the skills and effort required, the responsibilities of the job, and the conditions under which the work is performed. It is important to remember that the comparisons are made on job content, not on the performance of the employee. The comparison must be done in such a way that the characteristics of "male" jobs, such as stockroom attendants who lift and organize groceries, are valued fairly in comparison with the characteristics of "female" jobs, cashiers who lift and bag groceries.[61] For example, under pay equity, Canadian National Railway would need to compare the work of an accounts payable clerk to that of a person who repairs the train cars.

Federal pay equity legislation applies to the workforce under its jurisdiction and covers all organizations regardless of the number of employees. The system is complaint based, meaning that an employee, a group of employees, or a union can raise complaints. However, it can take years for complaints to be resolved.

For example, it took 28 years to resolve a pay equity case involving Canada Post! The case was originally filed with the Canadian Human Rights Tribunal in 1983 and involved pay comparisons with clerical workers (primarily female) to operations jobs, such as letter carriers (primarily male). The tribunal initially upheld the complaint, and then the issue went through years of various appeals. Finally, in 2005, a decision that upheld the complaint was made, and it was appealed to the Supreme Court of Canada. In November 2011, the court reinstated the original award, which will now cost Canada Post approximately $250 million.[62] However, as of 2018, Canada Post was still not implementing pay equity throughout the entire organization, with its union claiming that there is inequity between the wages of rural and urban carriers.[63]

Pay equity legislation is in 6 provinces: Manitoba, New Brunswick, Nova Scotia, Ontario, Prince Edward Island, and Québec.[64] Although British Columbia, Newfoundland, and Saskatchewan have no legislation, they've developed frameworks for negotiations with some public sector unions. Alberta has no legislation.[65]

DIVERSITY AND INCLUSION

Managing diversity goes beyond any legislation in addressing the need to create a fair work environment. The terms "diversity" and "employment equity" are often used interchangeably, but there are differences. **Diversity** is about voluntarily having a more representative workforce; employment equity is not. Managing diversity is a broader concept encompassing such factors as religion, personality, lifestyle, and education. Frequently, you will hear organizations talk about **inclusion** as part of diversity. Whereas diversity refers to our differences, inclusion is putting into action all those differences to create a very successful organization.[66] An inclusive environment leads to better organizational performance.[67] In 2017, Deloitte, a professional services firm, released a report concluding that Canada could become the best place in the world to live and work if everyone truly embraced inclusion.[68] The report noted

Diversity
The combination of organizational policies and practices that supports and encourages employee differences in order to reach business objectives

Inclusion
Putting the concept of diversity into action

LO6
Explain the relationship between employment equity, diversity, and inclusion.

that in being more deliberate in what a company did regarding inclusion, the company could drive its own and general society's economic growth.

According to Statistics Canada, much of the increase in our total population over the next 25 years will be due to immigration.[69] In this context, utilizing all of the individuals with the necessary skills and abilities is not about doing something because the law requires it but rather is a requirement for company success. It is also not just about racial and cultural background but also about accepting and understanding differences. One of the more progressive firms is SAP Canada, a company that provides a variety of information technology solutions for companies to do business better and uses its diversity to drive innovation, engage employees, and enable business success. It believes having a culture of inclusion allows more different insights, leading to new ideas.[70] Many organizations understand the societal and business imperative as research continues to demonstrate that diverse and inclusive teams outperform competitors.[71] See At Work with HRM 2.4 for a fuller description of more thinking about diversity and inclusion.

Many different types of organizations in Canada recognize the importance of diversity and inclusion in their overall business strategy. For example, a job fair was recently held in Toronto that focused on making the transgender community aware of career opportunities in a number of organizations, including Parks Canada, the Canadian Forces, and Indigo.[72] Another example is the emphasis that Bill McFarland, CEO of PricewaterhouseCoopers (PwC) Canada, places on diversity. He feels strongly that it is important for PwC to create an environment where people can be their real selves and use their different experiences to

AT WORK WITH HRM 2.4 — ISN'T IT ABOUT NUMBERS?

It is still too often that some employers think diversity and inclusion are about numbers. Well, they can be, depending on what numbers someone is looking at. Diversity and inclusion aren't about how many women, members of visible minorities, Aboriginal peoples, or people with disabilities a company employs. They are, however, about the success of the company and its performance—which is about numbers.

A good example of ensuring that diversity and inclusion are in the DNA of the organization is HP Canada. Mary Yule, president and CEO, is encouraging all Canadian business leaders to entrench practices throughout the organization that allow diversity and inclusion to enable companies to grow, innovate, attract top talent, and connect with customers.

She reminds everyone that we all have unconscious biases and that we must acknowledge them in order to create a less biased work culture. This also means being specific about the bias. Is it women? People of colour? People in the LGBTQ community? Immigrants? Anyone who doesn't look or think like me? Whatever the bias is, it can't be the "elephant in the room" that everyone walks around. Also, as stressed by the executive director of Pride at Work Canada, an organization that works with others to promote LGBTQ workplace acceptance, there are many different practices that can support diversity and inclusion, and each employer needs to determine the gaps and identify the priorities.

Another example of getting stereotypes into the open is through the educational system. Part of the curriculum in the School of Engineering at the University of Waterloo are discussions about women being in STEM (science, technology, engineering, and mathematics), including what people think or feel if a female student gets a job before a male student. One of the directors in its Velocity start-up initiative noted that using different language is more welcoming and has substituted words such as "start-up" with phrases such as "has social impact."

CRITICAL THINKING QUESTION:

Can you think of other initiatives that organizations can adopt to help create a positive work environment that supports diversity and inclusion?

Sources: Adapted from Cassandra Szklarski, "Canadian Tech Sector Not Immune to Sexism, Discrimination of Silicon Valley," *The Globe and Mail*, August 9, 2017, accessed January 26, 2018, www.theglobeandmail.com/technology/canadian-tech-sector-not-immune-to-sexism-and-discrimination-of-silicon-valley/article35919577; Mary Anne Yule, "Diversity and Inclusion Is About More than Meeting Numbers," *The Globe and Mail*, October 27, 2017, B15; and Susan Goldberg, "Pride Guide," *Corporate Knights*, Summer 2017, 40–42.

reach their full potential. As he states, "diversity is also good for business."[73] Several not-for-profit organizations, such as the YWCA Calgary and the Museum of Vancouver, also note that it is important to involve employees as initiatives are being developed to create a more diverse and inclusive work environment.[74] The importance of leadership in any organization cannot be understated. The CEO of Chestermere Utilities in Alberta, Leigh-Anne Palter, indicates that "leadership is everything because people will model the behaviours that are expected of them."[75]

Although CEOs may recognize the importance of diversity and inclusion, there are still ample examples of immigrants struggling to gain employment opportunities in their chosen field of study or experience and to feel accepted when they do find work. There is, therefore, a continuing need to create programs and other ways to tap into a vital and talented component of our population and maximize the country's human capital. Canada's economic growth will be dependent on employers making use of the talent immigrants bring. That is why organizations such as Toronto Region Immigrant Employment Council (TRIEC) created the Inclusive Workplace Competencies, which helps employers make their workplaces more inclusive.[76] The initiative has a set of competencies that demonstrate what inclusive behaviour in a work environment looks like. TRIEC also stresses that these competencies can be used in a variety of ways, including during hiring and when helping employees determine their training and development needs.[77]

It is important to remember that in Canada, diversity also includes Aboriginal peoples. In 2017, the federal government created a training program in skilled trades that will support apprenticeships with a focus on Aboriginal peoples. It is designed to be focused on what is needed for the future in construction and is undertaken in cooperation with trade unions.[78] Another example of diversity success is described in At Work with HRM 2.5, which showcases the business successes of an Aboriginal group in the interior of British Columbia.

AT WORK WITH HRM 2.5 — BECOMING SELF-SUFFICIENT!

Chief Clarence Louie is very proud of the successes his community has achieved. As chief of the Osoyoos Indian Band and CEO of Osoyoos Indian Band Development Corporation in British Columbia, he has provided leadership and vision for the band to excel in a number of enterprises. The band has achieved the distinction of being Canada's most successful and diverse First Nation in its economic endeavours. Chief Louie has been recognized with numerous awards, including chairman of the Aboriginal Business Canada Board.

During the past 30 years, the band, in the southern Okanagan region in British Columbia, has created a large and successful business enterprise on the band's 13,000 ha of land, of which about a third is vineyards. The band businesses include Nk'Mip vineyards, Nk'Mip Gas & Convenience Store, Nk'Mip construction, Oliver Readi-Mix, Nk'Mip Canyon Desert Golf Course, Nk'Mip Campground & RV Park, the first Aboriginal winery in North America—Nk'Mip Cellars and Nk'Mip Desert Cultural Centre—an ecocultural centre that promotes Okanagan Native heritage and culture, and Spirit Ridge Vineyard Resort and Spa. All of the band's business interests are handled through the Osoyoos Indian Band Development Corporation, of which Spirit Ridge Vineyard Resort and Spa is its premium accommodation.

The variety of businesses provide the band with numerous jobs, countless career opportunities for its members, and $26 million in annual revenue. The Osoyoos Indian Band prides itself on having low unemployment rates, a healthy economic outlook, and the potential for more business development. The band states that one of its goals is to "decrease the dependency on government funding through increased level of self generated income, joint ventures, leasing, land and resource development so that economically we can one day be self sufficient." Chief Louie is a strong believer in education that he sees as making Aboriginal peoples employable. He also is a strong believer in individuals being independent and self-sufficient. He does speak out about the need to teach Aboriginal peoples how to work, how to have a work

continued

ethic, and how to focus on the economy—not just handing out money.

Louie is also quick to say that the band hasn't done everything on its own but has partnered wisely with outside business leaders. He brought in experts to help the band develop financial controls and created the Nk'Mip Cellars as a joint venture with Vincor.

What is the band's most profitable revenue stream? Its biggest source of revenue is from land leases, including a new BC provincial prison and race-track. Through the relationship, Louie is hoping that there will be employment opportunities for band members. This new initiative has had its share of criticism given

Chief Clarence Louie

the history many First Nations have with justice systems throughout Canada. His response: "We need our band members working in that prison as role models."

Sources: Adapted from Osoyoos Indian Band Development Corporation, accessed January 27, 2018, www.oibdc.com; Keith Lacey, "Chief Louie to Tell His Story in Autobiography," *The Oliver Chronicle*, October 13, 2017, accessed January 28, 2018, www.oliverchronicle.com/chief-louie-to-tell-his-story-in-autobiography; Osoyoos Indian Band, accessed January 27, 2018, oib.ca/about-oib; and Shelby Thom, "Osoyoos Indian Band Generates More Revenue Than It Receives from Federal Government," *Global News*, November 24, 2017, accessed January 28, 2018, globalnews.ca/news/3880509/osoyoos-indian-band-generates-more-revenue-than-it-receives-from-federal-government.

Creating an Environment for Success

Transforming an organizational culture into one that embraces diversity and inclusion can be a complex and lengthy process. Diversity and inclusion initiatives should be taken slowly so that everyone can understand that this change is an evolutionary process and that expectations should be realistic.

Leadership is one of the most important variables in an organization's ability to successfully incorporate the value of diversity into its business strategy. And it is important not to make any assumptions. For example, Hubba, a Toronto business, decided to conduct its own diversity study to determine how diverse it truly was. The survey found that 67% of the employees were male, 25% of all staff were not born in Canada, and 80% of its people and operations staff are women.[79] Even though the company trained its hiring teams about bias, the survey identified other things that it could work on.

For any organization to become more diverse and inclusive, the process is one of changing culture. This is not done overnight and needs considerable and consistent attention and support from all leaders in the organization.[80] Given that becoming more diverse and inclusive is a culture shift, all efforts need to be integrated—everything from recruitment to training to performance management.[81] As part of its commitment to its staff and clients, KPMG, a global consulting firm, understands the importance of diversity and inclusion and was named one of Canada's best diversity employers in 2017 for initiatives such as its Aboriginal Education Accounting Mentorship Program (now the Martin Aboriginal Education Initiative Accounting Mentorship Program), which is designed to encourage Aboriginal students to pursue accounting, as well as a development program that focuses on leadership coaching for women.[82] Likewise, Jazz Aviation LP was honoured for its corporate strategy to support mental health and pilots with disabilities.[83] TD Bank Group is distinctive among employers for maintaining LGBT employee resource groups and an organization-wide Employee Pride Network.[84]

Training is essential to the success of diversity implementation. One area of training that we sometimes don't think about is the training and experiences that military veterans can bring to an organization. You might ask: what does this have to do with diversity and inclusion? Think about the number of Canadian military veterans who have disabilities. This is the very group that Sage, a software company, has focused on with providing support to veterans' entrepreneurial desires. The company feels strongly that these individuals are owed a duty of thanks and need assistance in transitioning into their lives outside the military.[85]

Breaking down barriers is also an important part of diversity initiatives. Enbridge in Alberta (one of the Top 100 Employers in Canada) has undertaken a number of initiatives. Two of the more notable ones are Females in Engineering, an outreach program that encourages young, female Aboriginal students to consider science, technology, engineering, and math (STEM), and the Indigenous Partnership Strategy, which spotlights Indigenous employment and awareness training.[86]

As noted earlier in this section, diversity and inclusion are now a business imperative in our global environment. Canada, as described in the Deloitte report, has a unique opportunity to leverage its multicultural society and become more prosperous and stronger.[87] The same report reinforced the financial success of those organizations that make diversity and inclusion part of all that they do.[88] Again, the success of creating a more diverse and inclusive work environment comes from the leaders of those organizations—who must drive the culture to be one of belonging.[89]

When determining that the organization needs to be more inclusive, it is necessary to set expectations regarding behaviours for leaders—they must "walk the talk" and be held accountable for those behaviours.[90] And as noted earlier, it will be important to define and describe exactly what those behaviours look like. Within its own organization, Deloitte has launched a national workplace strategy (Orbis) with the goal of having a high level of interaction and collaboration with far fewer physical locations.[91] To achieve a lot less office space, the organization must create an environment where people can be their very best all the time.

Another element of successful diversity and inclusion approaches is evaluating the performance of behaviours on an ongoing basis.[92] Measuring everyone's performance with regard to diversity and inclusion will instill those values in the minds of all employees and demonstrate that valuing diversity is part of day-to-day business. In doing this, it will be important to provide regular and ongoing feedback and to encourage dialogue and discussion on how well people are doing. Deloitte reinforces its commitment to behaviours by encouraging its employees to promote diversity and inclusion to its clients and suppliers.[93] Additional insights regarding the issues of diversity and inclusion can be found in Ethics in HRM 2.2.

ETHICS IN HRM 2.2 — BUT DOESN'T THIS DISADVANTAGE SOMEONE ELSE?

There is much emphasis put on diversity in organizations. Part of the emphasis revolves around increasing the workforce and increasing the capabilities of everyone. If one looks at the definition of *diversity*, it means having different elements or variety. Businesses feel that by having a variety of different perspectives, the business will be more successful.

On the other hand, employers in Canada also know that there is a shortage of skilled labour. As people retire from the workforce, there are fewer people to replace

continued

those retirees. Therefore, employers are looking for individuals in various demographic sectors that may have been overlooked before. For example, only about 50% of individuals with disabilities are employed compared to 79% for the general population. To facilitate more inclusion, Electricity Human Resources Canada created a Web-enabled portal that provides resources and information for employers so that they can establish successful means to achieve accessible and accommodating workplaces.

Although corporate Canada may be moving forward on individuals with disabilities, what about other differences? What about individuals from the LGBTQ community? Organizations that have taken great steps to ensure inclusivity for these individuals indicate that inclusion needs to be a systemic change and not just done by one-at-a-time initiatives. For example, if the company uses gender-neutral language and doesn't train its managers on using an inclusive hiring approach, which includes paying attention to their own biases, the desired outcome may not be achieved.

Then there is the recent case of Walmart Canada when it announced it would no longer be involved with a Québec program of job training for individuals with intellectual disabilities. In doing so, Walmart also indicated that the individuals in the program who worked with Walmart would no longer be employed with it. Walmart stated that it wanted to find other ways to help participants. Yet this program was referenced in its "Diversity and Inclusion Report" as an example of its commitment to an inclusive environment.

Hiring people from a number of different communities in and of itself will not make an inclusive workplace. It has to be created.

CRITICAL THINKING QUESTIONS:

1. If a person from a diverse employment pool is hired, it means that someone else wasn't hired from another diverse pool of applicants. Is this acceptable? Why or why not?
2. Comment on the statement "Diversity initiatives are reverse discrimination."

Sources: Adapted from *Merriam-Webster Dictionary*, accessed April 3, 2018, www.merriam-webster.com/dictionary/diversity; Michelle Branigan and Julia Aitken, "Enabling Change: From Disability to Inclusion," *Canadian HR Reporter*, October 2, 2017, 16; "2015 Diversity & Inclusion," Walmart, accessed April 3, 2018, https://cdn.corporate.walmart.com/01/8b/4e0af18a45f3a043fc85196c2cbe/2015-diversity-and-inclusion-report.pdf; Kamil Krzaczynski, "Walmart sorry for 'confusion' over end of program for people with disabilities," *Canadian HR Reporter*, April 2, 2018, accessed April 3, 2018, www.hrreporter.com/hr-trends/36459-walmart-sorry-for-confusion-over-end-of-program-for-people-with-disabilities; and Susan Goldberg, "Pride Guide," *Corporate Knights*, Summer 2017, 40–42.

ORGANIZATIONAL ETHICS

LO7

Discuss the concept of ethics in the management of human resources.

Ethics
Things that matter to us that motivate our behaviour

Throughout this chapter, the legal requirements of HRM are emphasized. Laws and court decisions affect all aspects of the employment process—recruitment, selection, performance appraisal, safety and health, labour relations, and testing. Managers must comply with government regulations to promote an environment free from litigation.

However, beyond what is required by the law is the question of organizational ethics and the ethical—or unethical—behaviour engaged in by all employees. **Ethics** are usually defined as a system of moral values—the things that matter to us that motivate our behaviour.[94] Therefore, ethics, like the legal aspects of HR, permeate all aspects of the employment relationship. For example, managers may adhere to the organization's objective of hiring more members of designated groups, but how those employees are supervised and treated once employed gets to the issue of managerial ethics. Compliance with laws and the behavioural treatment of employees are completely different aspects of the manager's job.

Although ethical dilemmas will always occur in the supervision of employees, how employees are treated is what largely distinguishes the ethical organization from the unethical one. An ethical organization recognizes and values the contributions of employees and respects their personal rights. Certainly, some of the cases mentioned earlier in this chapter reinforce this belief.

Many organizations have their own codes of ethics that govern relations with employees and the public at large. These codes are formal written statements of the organization's primary values and provide a basis for the organization's and individual managers' behaviours and actions. For example, the Canadian Centre for Ethics and Corporate Policy is designed to promote and practise ethical decision making and in doing so ensures that its members have codes that are widely publicized. Among its members are Investors Group, Loblaw Companies Limited, BMO Financial Group, Hydro One, Deloitte LLP, and Siemens Canada Limited.[95] Organizations now have ethics committees and ethics ombudspersons to provide training in ethics to employees.

In addition, the Government of Canada has an ethics commissioner, reporting directly to the prime minister. The role of the commissioner is to help appointed and elected officials prevent and avoid conflicts between their public and private interests.[96] Provincial governments such as Alberta, Ontario, and New Brunswick also have ethics commissioners. The ultimate goal of ethics training and ethics commissioners is to avoid unethical behaviour and adverse publicity; to gain a strategic advantage; and, most of all, to treat employees in a fair and equitable manner, recognizing them as productive members of the organization.

Whistleblowing

Even with codes of ethics and ethics committees, people do not always behave ethically. Organizations such as Canada Post encourage high standards of business conduct by providing examples of actions and behaviours that might be unethical.[97] When something unethical happens, employees will sometimes report an organization's unethical practices outside the organization. This is referred to as **whistleblowing**. People will sometimes not report unethical actions or behaviours as they are concerned about revenge from those involved, but sometimes the unethical actions are so high profile that they cannot be ignored. For example, recently, a former manager of a Carl's Jr. restaurant in Alberta contacted the Alberta Health Service with videos that showed one of the co-owner's using his hands to mix a sauce, dipping raw chicken into a batter with bare hands, and picking up cooked chicken from the floor and putting it into a warming tray. The former manager had earlier approached the other co-owner, who ignored the health concerns. The agency investigated the situation and determined that the person was to be prevented from handling any more food until he had successfully completed a food safety course.[98]

Although some organizations install special hotlines or create other confidential ways that employees can whistleblow, that may not be enough. If employees can't trust that their story will be truly heard and acted upon, they may not come forward. Also, if they don't know who is answering the hotline, they may refrain from complaining.[99] If the organization does have a hotline, it is important to have it open to anyone—customers, public, suppliers—and let people know it is there to serve them.[100]

To ensure that employees understand the importance of dealing with unethical behaviour, leaders play a crucial role in reinforcing ethical behaviour by their own actions, as well as playing a role in encouraging and supporting whistleblowing.[101] Whether an organization is small or large, there are basic guidelines to follow: (1) be trustworthy, (2) maintain confidences, (3) be impartial and objective, (4) be fair, and (5) avoid any real or potential conflict of interest.[102]

Even though there have been recent changes in employment legislation described at these sites, changes will continue as Canadian social values change. Emerging Trends 2.1 provides examples of ongoing issues that continue to be addressed.

Whistleblowing
Reporting unethical behaviour outside the organization

EMERGING TRENDS 2.1

Tribunal and court decisions continue to have an impact on the rights of both employees and employers. Here are a few items to consider:

1. ***Workplace accommodations.*** As issues of mental health in the workplace become more open, employers are having to learn about how to discuss mental health issues with the person and what information they may need to accommodate the person. With many young parents in the workforce, as well as individuals who are looking after aging parents and a workforce that is getting older, employers will need to pay careful attention to requests for accommodation—particularly those involving "family status" and "disability." Requests due to mental illness and addictions are also increasing. Furthermore, more and more employers are recognizing that people with varying degrees of disability are ignoring the "dis-" and looking at abilities. In doing so, employers are making all aspects of the work environment and culture barrier-free.

2. ***Harassment.*** With such high-profile media commentary on harassment in the workplace, increased attention is being paid to what employers do regarding allegations of harassment and the health of the workplace. Some experts are even suggesting that employees need to receive training on what may or may not be appropriate when greeting people at work. With the increased focus on all types of harassment, employers are increasingly under pressure to conduct independent investigations and not rely upon internal staff to conduct an unbiased review.

3. ***Employment legislation.*** With the continued focus on creating healthy and safe work environments, governments are passing additional employment legislation to accelerate what employers do. The Ontario *Fair Workplaces, Better Jobs Act*, which came into force at the beginning of 2018, has enhanced the provisions regarding notice to employees of shift changes or cancellations. Likewise, the right for family medical leave has been extended from 8 to 28 weeks. Furthermore, the federal government has undertaken an online consultation process to modernize labour legislation to align with evolving workplaces.

4. ***Diversity and inclusion.*** It is sometimes difficulty and discouraging to realize that workplaces are not as inclusive and welcoming as they could be. And it isn't just 1 or 2 of the prohibited grounds. A recent report by Deloitte challenged employers to become more courageous: "they must choose to fundamentally change the culture—their way of acting and being"—in promoting diversity and inclusion and acknowledge that to do so will allow Canada to remain competitive. The study also noted that one-half of millennials consider diversity and inclusion as important criteria when searching for work. Another study by KornFerry confirmed that a direct correlation exists between diversity and financial performance. Finally, another study by Deloitte Global noted that diversity and inclusion impact corporate purpose, brand, and performance.

5. ***Substance abuse.*** With the projected legalization of marijuana, attention is once again focusing on workplace impacts of substance abuse. Several major court cases upheld employers' actions when dealing with employees who use substances, whether legal or not. For example, a nurse was terminated for stealing narcotics from their employer even though the person had an addiction. The arbitrator upheld the termination and did not determine that an accommodation had to be done.

Sources: Adapted from Brad Fedorchuk, "Getting Employees Back to Work," *Canadian HR Reporter*, November 27, 2017, accessed January 14, 2018, www.hrreporter.com/workplace-health-and-wellness/35259-getting-employees-back-to-work; Emily Douglas, "What Are the Biggest Employment Issues of 2018?," *HRD Canada*, January 15, 2018, accessed January 16, 2018, https://www.hrmonline.ca/hr-news/employee-engagement/what-are-biggest-employment-law-issues-of-2018-236248.aspx; Shreya Patel, "2017 in Review: Top Legal Cases that Impacted Your Workplace," *HRD Canada*, January 8, 2018, accessed January 16, 2018, https://www.hrmonline.ca/hr-general-news/2017-in-review-the-top-legal-cases-that-impacted-your-workplace-235913.aspx; Fasken, "Major Labour and Employment Changes Become Law: What You Need to Know About Bill 148," *Labour, Employment, and Human Rights Bulletin*, December 15, 2017, https://www.fasken.com/en/knowledgehub/2017/12/major-labour-and-employment-changes-become-law; Laura McQuillan, "Mental Health Accommodations: What You Need to Know," *HRD Canada*, August 16, 2017, accessed January 26, 2018, www.hrmonline.ca/hr-law/accommodation/mental-health-accommodations-what-You-need-to-know-229496.aspx; Laura McQuillan, "Should Your Workplace Ban Hugs?," *HRD Canada*, December 10, 2017, accessed January 26, 2018, www.hrmonline.ca/opinion-and-best-practice/should-your-workplace-ban-hugs-234841.aspx; "Ottawa Looks for Feedback on Modernizing Federal Labour Standards," *Canadian HR Reporter*, January 17, 2018, www.hrreporter.com/workplace-law/35668-ottawa-looks-for-feedback-on-modernizing-federal-labour-standards; "Be More 'Courageous' About Diversity, Deloitte Report Urges Canadian Companies," November 22, 2017, accessed January 26, 2018, www.cbc.ca/news/business/deloitte-diversity-report-1.4413914; "Outcomes Over Optics: Building Inclusive Organizations," Deloitte, 2017; "Rewriting the Rules for the Digital Age," *Deloitte University Press*, 2017, 107; and "Compensation Trends and Strategies for 2018," KornFerry webcast, September 20, 2017.

LEARNING OUTCOMES SUMMARY

1. Explain the impact of laws on the behaviour and actions of managers.
   - *Accepted practices and behaviours of managers toward their employees are governed through a variety of employment legislation at both the provincial and federal levels*
   - *Various laws establish certain minimum requirements regarding working conditions as well as providing protection of basic human rights*
2. Discuss the legal framework of HRM in Canada.
   - *There are 2 distinct sets of legislation: federal and provincial*
   - *The* Canadian Charter of Rights and Freedoms *is the cornerstone of contemporary employment legislation*
3. Describe discrimination and harassment in the workplace.
   - *Discrimination is denying someone something because of race, ethnic background, gender, marital status, or other prohibited grounds under human rights legislation*
   - *Harassment is any behaviour that demeans, humiliates, or embarrasses a person*
   - *Harassment includes bullying*
   - *Discrimination and harassment are illegal under human rights legislation*
4. Outline the manager's role in creating a work environment that is free from harassment and discrimination.
   - *Managers need to ensure that unacceptable behaviours are dealt with*
   - *Managers are expected to work with employees to ensure that they are behaving and acting in an acceptable fashion*
   - *The manager is the key link in creating an appropriate work environment*
5. Identify the general types of employment laws in Canada.
   - *Employment standards legislation describes the basic obligations of employers*
   - *Labour legislation governs both the process by which a trade union acquires bargaining rights and the procedures by which trade unions and employers engage in collective bargaining*
   - *Health, safety, and workers' compensation legislation describes the expected standards for health and safety in the workplace and the impact if an employee is injured*
   - *Human rights legislation prohibits discrimination on the basis of such areas as race, ethnic origin, marital status, and gender*
   - *Human rights legislation is paramount over other employment laws*
   - *Human rights legislation also protects individuals from all types of harassment*
6. Explain the relationship between employment equity, diversity, and inclusion.
   - *Managing diversity not only incorporates but also goes beyond employment equity*
   - *The goal of diversity is to make optimal use of an organization's multicultural workforce in order to realize strategic business advantages*
   - *Inclusion is putting diversity into action*
7. Discuss the concept of ethics in the management of human resources.
   - *Ethics in HRM extends beyond the legal requirements of managing employees*
   - *Managers engage in ethical behaviour when employees are treated in a fair and objective way and when an employee's personal and work-related rights are respected and valued*

KEY TERMS

bona fide occupational qualification (BFOQ) 44

bullying 51

designated groups 56

diversity 59

duty to accommodate 45

employment equity 55

ethics 64

harassment 48

inclusion 59

pay equity 58	systemic discrimination 43
psychological harassment 51	whistleblowing 65
reverse discrimination 47	

HRM CLOSE-UP APPLICATION

1. What are the 2 primary federal employment laws that apply to Aurora Cannabis?
2. What requirement did Health Canada initially require of Aurora?
3. What legal requirement did Aurora have to meet that was more stringent than for liquor producers?
4. What is an RPIC, and where was it required?

CRITICAL THINKING QUESTIONS

1. Although people know that harassment and discrimination are illegal, why would an employee or potential employee be reluctant to complain?
2. There is much concern about how people behave in the workplace and use words such as "respectful" to indicate how employees are to treat everyone. What does respectful look like to you?
3. You see a part-time job posted in your community for a tutor in a specific foreign language that also requires that the tutor be from the country of that language. Would being from a specific country be a justifiable BFOQ? Why or why not?
4. A friend of yours has heard you are taking a business course that focuses on human resources management and wants some help. Your friend, a parent of 2 small children, has learned that the daycare centre is changing its closing hours from 6:00 p.m. to 5:30 p.m. Your friend's work ends at 5:00 p.m., and it takes approximately 45 minutes to get to the centre. The organization at which your friend works has a large office complex with more than 1000 employees. Is this a case for reasonable accommodation? Why or why not?

BUILDING YOUR SKILLS

1. Much attention is given to the issue of harassment and discrimination in the workplace. The cornerstone to addressing this is achieving organizational awareness. Training can help raise awareness. Working in groups of 3 or 4, develop the outline of a training session that would raise awareness for a small company with 75 employees. The outline should include (1) topics to be covered, (2) specific examples of harassment and/or discrimination, (3) how complaints are to be made and to whom, and (4) who would attend the training.
2. Companies are concerned about bullying at work and want to do what they can to prevent it. Watch the video *How I survived workplace bullying*, a TEDxWinnipeg talk by Sherry Benson-Podolchuk at **www.youtube.com/watch?v=YmRKIZEXVQM**. Working in groups of 2 or 3, determine whether you have encountered bullying at work. If so, what did you do and why? Did your actions improve the workplace environment?
3. Working in pairs, list as many jobs as you can in which an employer could justify "female-only" applicants based on a BFOQ.
4. Using any search engine, conduct a search on the term "workplace inclusion." Review the first 10 matches and determine if they would be helpful resources. Prepare a 1- to 2-page summary of the results of your search indicating whether the sites were useful and how an employer might make use of the information.
5. Access the Fair Measures, Inc. site at **www.fairmeasures.com**, go to the "Workplace Issues" drop-down menu, and click on "Business Ethics." Read the various FAQs and

pick 1 to explore further. Access the FAQ you selected and read the explanations. Prepare a 1-page analysis about why you picked the question and what you learned.

6. Working in a group of 4 to 5 students, identify some of the ethical dilemmas that might arise in the areas of selection, performance reviews, health and safety, privacy rights, and compensation.

APPENDIX

Websites for Employment Legislation

1. Federal Government
   - *Canada Labour Code:* **http://laws-lois.justice.gc.ca/eng/acts/L-2/index.html**
   - *Canadian Human Rights Act:* **http://laws-lois.justice.gc.ca/eng/acts/h-6**
   - Workers' compensation agency: **www.canoshweb.org**
2. Province of Alberta
   - *Employment Standards Code:* **www.qp.alberta.ca/1266.cfm?page=e09 .cfm&leg_type=Acts&isbncln=9780779783366&display=html**
   - *Labour Relations Code:* **www.qp.alberta.ca/1266.cfm?page=l01.cfm&leg _type=Acts&isbncln=9780779782628&display=html**
   - *Occupational Health and Safety Act:* **www.qp.alberta.ca/1266.cfm?page=O02P1 .cfm&leg_type=Acts&isbncln=9780779800865&display=html**
   - Workers' Compensation Board of Alberta: **www.wcb.ab.ca**
   - *Alberta Human Rights Act:* **www.qp.alberta.ca/documents/Acts/A25P5.pdf**
3. Province of British Columbia
   - *Employment Standards Act:* **www.bclaws.ca/EPLibraries/bclaws_new/document/ ID/freeside/00_96113_01**
   - *Labour Relations Code:* **www.bclaws.ca/civix/document/id/complete/ statreg/96244_01**
   - *Workers Compensation Act:* **www.bclaws.ca/Recon/document/ID/freeside/96492_00**
   - WorkSafeBC: **www.worksafebc.com/en**
   - *Human Rights Code:* **www.bclaws.ca/Recon/document/ID/freeside/00_96210_01**
4. Province of Manitoba
   - *The Employment Standards Code:* **web2.gov.mb.ca/laws/statutes/ccsm/e110e.php**
   - *The Labour Relations Act:* **web2.gov.mb.ca/laws/statutes/ccsm/l010e.php**
   - *The Workplace Safety and Health Act:* **web2.gov.mb.ca/laws/statutes/ccsm/w210e.php**
   - *The Workers Compensation Act:* **web2.gov.mb.ca/laws/statutes/ccsm/w200e.php**
   - Workers Compensation Board of Manitoba: **www.wcb.mb.ca**
   - *The Human Rights Code:* **web2.gov.mb.ca/laws/statutes/ccsm/h175e.php**
5. Province of New Brunswick
   - *Employment Standards Act:* **http://laws.gnb.ca/en/ShowPdf/cs/E-7.2.pdf**
   - *Industrial Relations Act:* **http://laws.gnb.ca/en/showdoc/cs/I-4**
   - *Occupational Health and Safety Act:* **http://laws.gnb.ca/en/showdoc/cs/O-0.2**
   - *Workers' Compensation Act:* **http://laws.gnb.ca/en/showdoc/cs/W-13**
   - *Human Rights Act:* **http://laws.gnb.ca/en/ShowPdf/cs/2011-c.171.pdf**
6. Province of Newfoundland and Labrador
   - All statutes accessible with links to each law: **www.assembly.nl.ca**
   - WorkplaceNL: **www.workplacenl.ca/default.whscc**
7. Province of Nova Scotia
   - All statutes accessible with links to each law: **http://nslegislature.ca/legislative -business/bills-statutes/consolidated-public-statutes**
   - Workers' Compensation Board of Nova Scotia: **www.wcb.ns.ca**
8. Province of Ontario
   - All statutes accessible with links to each law: **www.ontario.ca/laws**
   - Workplace Safety and Insurance Board: **www.wsib.on.ca**

9. Province of Prince Edward Island
   - Electronic versions of legislation accessible by downloading PDF files: **www.gov.pe.ca/law/statutes**
   - Workers Compensation Board of PEI: **www.wcb.pe.ca**
10. Province of Québec
    - All statutes accessible with links to each law: **www.publicationsduquebec.gouv.qc.ca**
    - Commission des norms, de l'équité, de la santé et de la sécurité du travail au Québec: **www.csst.qc.ca**
11. Province of Saskatchewan
    - *The Saskatchewan Employment Act:* **www.qp.gov.sk.ca/documents/English/Statutes/Statutes/s15-1.pdf**
    - Saskatchewan Workers' Compensation Board: **www.wcbsask.com**
    - *The Saskatchewan Human Rights Code:* **www.qp.gov.sk.ca/documents/English/Statutes/Statutes/S24-1.pdf**
12. Government of Nunavut
    - All statutes accessible with links to each law: **www.nunavutlegislation.ca**
    - Workers' Safety and Compensation Commission: **www.wscc.nt.ca**

CASE STUDY 1

This Bullying Has Got to Stop!

Sari works in a large mining operation in Saskatchewan. She has been with the company for a number of years and is currently a heavy equipment operator.

As the mining business continued to grow, and as the workforce became more diverse, senior leaders in the company also determined it was important to ensure that the workplace did not engage in discrimination or harassment. Training was initially done with everyone, and then the company also created ongoing discussion groups with the managers to talk about discrimination and harassment and reinforce the role they play.

Shortly after the initial training for all employees, Sari approached someone in HR to report that her boss (a man) had bullied her on several occasions. An investigation was undertaken to determine what had occurred, what had been said, and what the manager had to say. Part of the investigation included conversations with Sari's coworkers to see if they had experienced any bullying.

The investigation determined that the manager had met with Sari on several occasions to talk about her work performance and the way in which she operated the equipment. He _____ essed concern that she was driving the equipment in an unsafe manner and that _____ nued, he would have to discipline her. Sari did not agree with him and indicated _____ was only doing what all the other heavy equipment operators did. He told her _____ d not supervise the others, that he supervised her, and that she was working in _____ manner. He also reminded her that bragging about doing "wheelies" with the _____ t was not appropriate behaviour under his supervision. He stated clearly that he _____ ant to see this kind of behaviour again and concluded the meeting. The investi- _____ ermined that coworkers drove equipment unsafely and that Sari's manager only _____ n her about her driving, whereas the other managers ignored what was going on. _____ re, the investigation determined that Sari's manager was very firm in his views _____ ty.

Questions:

1. Was Sari bullied? Why or why not?
2. Is there anything else that should be part of the investigation?
3. If you were Sari, what would you do now?
4. If you were the manager, what would do now?

CASE STUDY 2

Whistleblowing and the Environment: The Case of Avco Environmental

Chantale Leroux works as a clerk for Avco Environmental Services, a small toxic-waste disposal company.

The company has a contract to dispose of medical waste from a local hospital. During the course of her work, Chantale comes across documents that suggest that Avco has actually been disposing of some of this waste in a local municipal landfill. Chantale is shocked. She knows this practice is illegal. And even though only a small portion of the medical waste that Avco handles is being disposed of this way, any amount at all seems a worrisome threat to public health.

Chantale gathers together the appropriate documents and takes them to her immediate superior, Dave Lamb. Dave says, "Look, I don't think that sort of thing is your concern or mine. We're in charge of record-keeping, not making decisions about where this stuff gets dumped. I suggest you drop it."

The next day, Chantale decides to go one step further, and talk to Angela van Wilgen-burg, the company's operations manager. Angela, clearly irritated, says, "This isn't your concern. Look, these are the sorts of cost-cutting moves that let a little company like ours compete with our giant competitors. Besides, everyone knows that the regulations in this area are overly cautious. There's no real danger to anyone from the tiny amount of medical waste that 'slips' into the municipal dump. I consider this matter closed."

Chantale considers her situation. The message from her superiors was loud and clear. She strongly suspects that making any more noise about this issue could jeopardize her job. Further, she generally has faith in the company's management. They've always seemed like honest, trustworthy people. But she is troubled by this apparent disregard for public safety. On the other hand, she asks herself whether maybe Angela was right in arguing the danger was minimal. She looks up the phone number of an old friend who works for the local newspaper.

Source: Reprinted by permission of Chris MacDonald, Businessethics.ca.

Questions:

1. What should Chantale do?
2. What are the reasonable limits on loyalty to one's employer?
3. Would it make a difference if Chantale had a position of greater authority?
4. Would it make a difference if Chantale had scientific expertise?

NOTES AND REFERENCES

1. Retail Council of Canada, "Minimum Wage by Province," accessed January 6, 2018, https://www.retailcouncil.org/quickfacts/minimum-wage-by-province; and "Major Labour and Employment Changes Become Law: What You Need to Know About Bill 148," *Fasken newsletter*, December 4, 2017.

2. Government of Canada, "EI Compassionate Care Benefit—Overview," accessed January 6, 2018, https://www.canada.ca/en/services/benefits/ei/ei-compassionate.html.

3. Government of Canada, "Employment Insurance Maternity and Parental Benefits," accessed January 6, 2018, https://www.canada.ca/en/employment-social-development/programs/ei/ei-list/reports/maternity-parental.html#h2.0.

4. Michael Adams, "Hands-Off my Chromosomes!," *Fasken newsletter*, August 29, 2017.

5. Government of Canada, The Canadian Charter of Rights and Freedoms, accessed January 7, 2018, http://www.justice.gc.ca/eng/csj-sjc/charter-charte/index.html.

6. "*Canadian Human Rights Act*, Section 3, Prohibited Discrimination," accessed January 7, 2018, http://laws-lois.justice.gc.ca/eng/acts/h-6/page-1.html#h-4.

7. Sarah Dobson, "Older Tech Workers Face Ageism in Hiring," *Canadian HR Reporter*, October 30, 2017, accessed January 7, 2018, https://www.hrreporter.com/recruitment-and-retention/34985-older-tech-workers-face-ageism-in-hiring.

8. Ontario Human Rights Commission, "OHRC Policy Position on Sexualized and Gender-Specific Dress Codes," accessed January 7, 2018, http://www.ohrc.on.ca/en/ohrc-policy-position-sexualized-and-gender-specific-dress-codes.

9. Trans Equality Society of Alberta, "Fact Page: Human Rights Across Canada," accessed January 12, 2018, http://www.tesaonline.org/human-rights-across-canada.html.

10. Alberta Human Rights Commission, "Bona Fide Occupational Requirement," accessed January 13, 2018, https://www.albertahumanrights.ab.ca/employment/employee_info/employment_contract/Pages/bfor.aspx.

11. Norm Keith, "Put to the Test," *OHS Canada*, December 23, 2015, accessed January 14, 2018, https://www.ohscanada.com/features/put-to-the-test.

12. Michelle McQuigge, "Human Rights Tribunal to Revisit Air Canada Retirement Age Issue," *Canadian HR Reporter*, September 17, 2017, 4; Laura McQuillan, "Was Air Canada Wrong to Force Pilots to Retire?," *HRD Canada*, September 20, 2017, accessed January 19, 2018, https://www.hrmonline.ca/hr-general-news/was-air-canada-wrong-to-force-pilots-to-retire-231183.aspx.

13. Canadian Human Rights Commission, "Bona Fide Occupational Requirements and Bona Fide Justifications Under the *Canadian Human Rights Act*: The Implications of *Meiorin* and *Grismer*," accessed January 14, 2018, https://www.chrc-ccdp.gc.ca/eng/content/bona-fide-occupational-requirements-and-bona-fide-justifications-under-canadian-human-rights.

14. For students who wish to understand the *Meiorin* case in more detail, access http://scc-csc.lexum.com/scc-csc/scc-csc/en/item/1724/index.do.

15. Sean Bawden, "Ontario's Top Court Confirms That Employees May Sometimes Be Required to Attend Medical Examination by Doctor of Employer's Choosing," *CanLIIConnects*, September 2, 2017, accessed January 14, 2018, http://canliiconnects.org/en/summaries/46620; and *Marcello Bottiglia and Ottawa Catholic School Board*, accessed January 14, 2018, https://www.canlii.org/en/on/onhrt/doc/2015/2015hrto1178/2015hrto1178.html?autocompleteStr=Bottiglia%20v.%20Ottawa%20Catholic%20School%20Board%20&autocompletePos=2.

16. Adrian Ishak, "The Aging Workforce," *HR Professional*, September 2017, accessed January 14, 2018, http://hrprofessionalnow.ca/index.php/legal-words/478-the-aging-workforce.

17. Shana French and Brian Wasyliw, "Mental Health Accommodation: Taking a New Approach," *Canadian HR Reporter*, April 17, 2017, accessed January 14, 2018, https://www.hrreporter.com/workplace-health-and-wellness/33163-mental-health-accommodation-taking-a-new-approach; and Workplace Strategies for Mental Health, "The Duty to Accommodate," accessed January 14, 2018, https://www.workplacestrategiesformentalhealth.com/managing-workplace-issues/the-duty-to-accommodate.

18. Tim Mitchell, "Accommodating Creed Requests," *Canadian HR Reporter*, April 18, 2016, accessed January 14, 2018, https://www.hrreporter.com/article/27377-accommodating-creed-requests-toughest-hr-question.

19. BC Human Rights Clinic, "What Is Harassment?," accessed January 14, 2018, http://www.bchrc.net/harassment; and Canadian Human Rights Commission, "Harassment: A Discriminatory Practice," accessed January 14, 2018, http://www.chrc-ccdp.gc.ca/eng/content/your-guide-understanding-canadian-human-rights-act-page1.

20. Joanna Smith, "MPs Speak Out on Harassment on the Job," *Vancouver Sun*, January 3, 2018, NP3.

21. Victoria Ahearn, "Canadian Film, TV Leaders to Meet About Industry's 'Prevalent' Sexual Harassment," *Canadian HR Reporter*, October 31, 2017, accessed November 2, 2017, https://www.hrreporter.com/culture-and-engagement/35004-canadian-film-tv-leaders-to-meet-about-industrys-prevalent-sexual-harassment; and Adelle Chua, "Artists Condemn Harassment Culture," *HRD Canada*, November 1, 2017, accessed January 19, 2018, https://www.hrmonline.ca/hr-general-news/artists-condemn-harassment-culture-233237.aspx.

22. Adelle Chua, "Facebook's Sheryl Sandberg: 6 Ways to End Sexual Harassment, *HRD Canada*, December 12, 2017, accessed January 19, 2018, https://www.hrmonline.ca/hr-general-news/facebooks-sheryl-sandberg-6-ways-to-end-sexual-harassment-235304.aspx.

23. Adelle Chua, "Is Sexual Harassment Affecting Your Organisation?," *HRD Canada*, September 28, 2017, accessed January 19, 2018, https://www.hrmonline.ca/international-news/is-sexual-harassment-affecting-your-organization-231620.aspx.

24. Adelle Chua, "Supreme Court Broadens Scope of Workplace Harassment in B.C. Ruling," *HRD Canada*, December 18, 2017, accessed January 19, 2018, https://www.hrmonline.ca/hr-news/mental-health/supreme-court-broadens-scope-of-workplace-harassment-in-b-c--ruling-235574.aspx.

25. Canadian Human Rights Commission, "What Is Harassment? About Human Rights," accessed January 20, 2018, http://www.chrc-ccdp.ca/eng/content/what-harassment.

26. Newfoundland and Labrador Human Resource Secretariat, "Harassment and Discrimination-Free Workplace Policy," accessed January 20, 2018, https://www.exec.gov.nl.ca/exec/hrs/working_with_us/harassment.html.

27. Jeffrey R. Smith, "Investigations: The Proper Path to Discipline and Dismissal," *Canadian HR Reporter*, October 30, 2017, accessed January 20, 2018, http://www.hrreporter.com/columnist/employment-law/archive/2017/10/30/investigations-the-proper-path-to-discipline-and-dismissal.

28. Saskatchewan Human Rights Commission, "A Guide to Human Rights for Employers," accessed January 20, 2018, http://saskatchewanhumanrights.ca/learn/fact-sheets/a-guide-to-human-rights-for-employers.

29. The Canadian Press, "4 Workers Fired at Edmonton Maximum Security Prison Over Alleged Bullying," *Canadian HR Reporter*,

January 10, 2018, accessed January 20, 2018, https://www.hrreporter.com/workplace-law/35618-4-workers-fired-at-edmonton-maximum-security-prison-over-alleged-bullying; and Canadian Centre for Occupational Health and Safety, "Bullying in the Workplace," accessed January 20, 2018, https://www.ccohs.ca/oshanswers/psychosocial/bullying.html.

30. "Bullying and Harassment Prevention Training," Harris & Company webinar, October 10, 2017.

31. Ibid.

32. Alberta Human Rights Commission, "The Human Rights Complaint Process," accessed January 20, 2018, https://www.albertahumanrights.ab.ca/publications/bulletins_sheets_booklets/sheets/complaints/Pages/process.aspx; BC Human Rights Tribunal, "Steps in the Human Rights Complaint Process," accessed January 20, 2018, http://www.bchrt.bc.ca/complaint-process/steps.htm; Human Rights Tribunal of Ontario, "Application and Hearing Process," accessed January 20, 2018, http://www.sjto.gov.on.ca/hrto/application-and-hearing-process; and Saskatchewan Human Rights Commission, "How to File a Complaint," accessed January 20, 2018, http://saskatchewanhumanrights.ca/learn/fact-sheets/how-to-file-a-complaint.

33. Stuart Rudner and Nadia Zaman, "Whose Onus Is It Anyways?," *Canadian HR Reporter*, October 23, 2017, accessed January 20, 2018, https://www.hrreporter.com/columnist/canadian-hr-law/archive/2017/10/23/whose-onus-is-it-anyways.

34. Province of Alberta, Employment Standards Regulation, accessed January 20, 2018, http://www.qp.alberta.ca/1266.cfm?page=1997_014.cfm&leg_type=Regs&isbncln=9780779800216&display=html.

35. Ontario Ministry of Labour, "Ontario Passes Legislation to Create Fair Workplaces, Better Jobs," November 22, 2017, accessed January 21, 2018, http://news.ontario.ca/mol/en/2017/11/ontario-passes-legislation-to-create-fair-workplaces-better-jobs.html; and "Breaking: Landmark Workplace Legislation in Ontario," *HRD Canada*, November 22, 2017, accessed January 21, 2018, https://www.hrmonline.ca/hr-news/breaking-landmark-workplace-legislation-passed-in-ontario-234345.aspx.

36. Cailynn Klingbeil, "Alberta Small-Business Owners Chafe at New Labour Laws," *The Globe and Mail*, December 26, 2017, B9; and Sarah Dobson, "Contractors in Spotlight with Legislative Changes," *Canadian HR Reporter*, August 7, 2017, accessed January 21, 2018, https://www.hrreporter.com/workplace-law/34173-contractors-in-spotlight-with-legislative-changes.

37. Colin Gibson, "Employer Obligations for Maternity Leave," *Canadian HR Reporter*, October 20, 2014, accessed January 21, 2018, https://www.hrreporter.com/articleview/22557-employer-obligations-for-maternity-leave.

38. Ontario Ministry of Labour, "Overtime Pay," accessed January 21, 2018, https://www.labour.gov.on.ca/english/es/tools/esworkbook/overtime.php.

39. Ontario Ministry of Labour, "Laws—Labour Relations," accessed January 21, 2018, https://www.labour.gov.on.ca/english/lr/laws/index.php.

40. Government of Canada, "Labour Organizations in Canada 2015," accessed January 21, 2018, https://www.canada.ca/en/employment-social-development/services/collective-bargaining-data/reports/union-coverage.html; and Statistics Canada, "Unionization Rates Falling," March 7, 2017, accessed January 21, 2018, http://www.statcan.gc.ca/pub/11-630-x/11-630-x2015005-eng.htm#def2.

41. Statistics Canada, "Unionization Rates Falling."

42. Government of Canada, "Federal Contractors Program," accessed January 22, 2018, https://www.canada.ca/en/employment-social-development/programs/employment-equity/federal-contractor-program.html.

43. Statistics Canada, "Labour Force Survey Estimates, Average Usual Hours and Wages of Employee by Age Group, Sex, Union Coverage, Job Permanency, and National Occupational Classification (NOC)," January 5, 2018, accessed January 23, 2018, http://www5.statcan.gc.ca/cansim/a26?lang=eng&retrLang=eng&id=2820167&&pattern=&stByVal=1&p1=1&p2=31&tabMode=dataTable&csid=.

44. Statistics Canada, "Employment by Industry and Sex, 2017," accessed January 23, 2018, http://www.statcan.gc.ca/tables-tableaux/sum-som/l01/cst01/labor10a-eng.htm.

45. Ibid.

46. Statistics Canada, "Aboriginal Peoples in Canada: Key Results from the 2016 Census," *The Daily*, October 25, 2017, accessed January 23, 2018, http://www.statcan.gc.ca/daily-quotidien/171025/dq171025a-eng.htm.

47. Ibid.

48. Statistics Canada, "Immigration and Ethnocultural Diversity: Key Results from the 2016 Census," October 25, 2017, accessed January 23, 2018, http://www.statcan.gc.ca/daily-quotidien/171025/dq171025b-eng.htm.

49. Statistics Canada, "A Profile of Persons with Disabilities Among Canadians Aged 15 Years or Older, 2012," updated February 15, 2017, accessed January 25, 2018, http://www.statcan.gc.ca/pub/89-654-x/89-654-x2015001-eng.htm.

50. Ibid.

51. Ingrid Muschta and Joe Dale, "Win the War on Talent: Hire People with Disabilities," *HRD Canada*, October 10, 2017, accessed January 25, 2018, https://www.hrmonline.ca/opinion-and-best-practice/win-the-war-on-talent-hire-people-with-disabilities-232102.aspx.

52. Statistics Canada, "Study: Persons with Disabilities and Employment," December 3, 2014, https://www150.statcan.gc.ca/n1/daily-quotidien/141203/dq141203a-eng.htm.

53. Manitoba Civil Service Commission, "Diversity and Inclusion," accessed January 25, 2018, http://www.gov.mb.ca/csc/employment/emplequity.html.

54. "Canada's Top 100 Employers 2018," November 6, 2017, accessed January 25, 2018, https://content.eluta.ca/top-employer-loblaws.

55. Government of Canada, "Employment Equity Act: Annual Report 2016," accessed January 25, 2018, https://www.canada.ca/en/employment-social-development/services/labour-standards/reports/employment-equity-2016.html#h2.4.

56. Statistics Canada, "Average Hourly Wages of Employees by Selected Characteristics and Occupation," December 2017, accessed January 25, 2018, http://www.statcan.gc.ca/tables-tableaux/sum-som/l01/cst01/labr69a-eng.htm.

57. Adelle Chua, "Iceland Makes It Illegal to Pay Women Less Than Men," *HRD Canada*, January 4, 2018, accessed January 25, 2018, https://www.hrmonline.ca/hr-general-news/iceland-makes-it-illegal-to-pay-women-less-than-men-235768.aspx.

58. Ibid.

59. Ontario Pay Equity Commission, "An Overview of Pay Equity in Various Canadian Jurisdictions," accessed January 19, 2015, http://www.payequity.gov.on.ca/en/about/pubs/genderwage/pe_survey.php.

60. Government of Canada, "Introduction to Pay Equity," accessed January 25, 2018, https://www.canada.ca/en/employment-social-development/programs/pay-equity/intro.html.

61. Government of New Brunswick, "What Is Pay Equity?," accessed January 28, 2018, http://www2.gnb.ca/content/gnb/en/corporate/promo/pay_equity_bureau/Pay_Equity.html.

62. "Human Resources Year in Review," *Canadian HR Reporter*, January 13, 2014, accessed January 28, 2018, https://www.hrreporter.com/articleview/19898-human-resources-year-in-review.

63. Vanessa Lu, "Pay Equity Fight at Canada Post Heads to Review Process," *Toronto Star*, September 9, 2016, accessed January 25, 2018, https://www.thestar.com/business/2016/09/09/pay-equity-fight-at-canada-post-heads-to-review-process.html.

64. Miriam Yosowich, "Pay Equity for Men and Women," FindLaw-Canada website, accessed January 25, 2018, http://employment.findlaw.ca/article/pay-equity-for-men-and-women.

65. Ibid.

66. Laura Sherbin and Ripa Rashid, "Diversity Doesn't Stick Without Inclusion," *Harvard Business Review*, February 1, 2017, accessed January 28, 2018, https://hbr.org/2017/02/diversity-doesnt-stick-without-inclusion.

67. Emily Douglas, "The Business Case for Investing in Equality," *HRD Canada*, November 17, 2017, accessed January 15, 2018, https://www.hrmonline.ca/hr-news/diversity-and-inclusion/the-business-case-for-investing-in-equality-234649.aspx.

68. Deloitte, "Outcomes Over Optics: Building Inclusive Organizations," 2017, 10, https://www.canada175.ca/sites/default/files/download/files/inclusion_aoda_en.pdf.

69. Statistics Canada, "Immigration and Diversity: Population Projections for Canada (2011 to 2036)," January 25, 2017, accessed January 26, 2018, http://www.statcan.gc.ca/pub/91-551-x/91-551-x2017001-eng.htm.

70. Adelle Chua, "Why These Companies Are Winning at Diversity," *HRD Canada*, October 10, 2017, accessed January 26, 2018, https://www.hrmonline.ca/hr-news/diversity-and-inclusion/why-these-companies-are-winning-at-diversity-232099.aspx; "Canada's Top 100 Employers 2018," *The Globe and Mail*, November 6, 2017, accessed January 23, 2018, http://www.canadastop100.com/national; and Lauren Acurantes, "How Diversity Affects a Company's Bottom Line," *HRD Canada*, September 28, 2016, accessed January 26, 2018, https://www.hrmonline.ca/hr-news/how-diversity-affects-a-companys-bottom-line-214455.aspx.

71. "Rewriting the Rules for the Digital Age," Deloitte University Press, 2017, 109, https://www2.deloitte.com/content/dam/Deloitte/us/Documents/human-capital/hc-2017-global-human-capital-trends-us.pdf.

72. Sarah Dobson, "Job Fair Focuses on Transgender Community," *Canadian HR Reporter*, December 11, 2017, accessed January 27, 2018, https://www.hrreporter.com/recruitment-and-retention/35394-job-fair-focuses-on-transgender-community.

73. Sarah Dobson, "Dedicated to Diversity," *Canadian HR Reporter*, October 30, 2017, accessed January 27, 2018, https://www.hrreporter.com/culture-and-engagement/34988-dedicated-to-diversity.

74. Ibid.

75. Ibid.

76. Adelle Chua, "Is Your Workplace Inclusive Enough," *HRD Canada*, October 30, 2017, accessed January 27, 2018, https://www.hrmonline.ca/hr-law/discrimination/is-your-workplace-inclusive-enough-233393.aspx.

77. Ibid.

78. Marcel Vander Wier, "Federal Government Turns Focus to Trades," *Canadian HR Reporter*, July 10, 2017, accessed January 28, 2018, https://www.hrreporter.com/hr-trends/33897-federal-government-turns-focus-to-trades.

79. Laura McQuillan, "What This Company's Diversity Survey Found," *HRD Canada*, September 7, 2017, accessed January 28, 2018, https://www.hrmonline.ca/hr-news/diversity-and-inclusion/what-this-companys-diversity-survey-revealed-230432.aspx.

80. Laura McQuillan, "Why Diversity Programs Don't Stick," *HRD Canada*, August 16, 2017, accessed January 28, 2018, https://www.hrmonline.ca/hr-news/diversity-and-inclusion/why-diversity-programs-dont-stick-229495.aspx.

81. Ibid.

82. "Canada's Top 100 Employers 2018."

83. Ibid.

84. Ibid.

85. Marcel Vander Wier, "Transition to Employment Difficult for Vets," *Canadian HR Reporter*, October 16, 2017, accessed January 28, 2018, https://www.hrreporter.com/recruitment-and-retention/34852-transition-to-employment-difficult-for-vets.

86. "Canada's Top 100 Employers 2018."

87. Outcomes Over Optics: Building Inclusive Organizations," 8.

88. Ibid., 13.

89. Ibid., 18.

90. Ibid., 32.

91. Ibid., 36.

92. Ibid., 37.

93. Ibid., 38.

94. Critical Thinker Academy, "What Are Moral Values?" accessed January 28, 2018, https://criticalthinkeracademy.com/courses/moral-arguments/lectures/659294.

95. Canadian Centre for Ethics and Corporate Policy, "Current Membership," accessed January 28, 2018, http://www.ethicscentre.ca/EN/membership/current_membership.cfm.

96. Office of the Conflict of Interest and Ethics Commissioner, "Welcome to the Office," accessed January 28, 2018, http://ciec-ccie.parl.gc.ca/EN/Pages/default.aspx.

97. Canada Post, "Canada Post Code of Conduct: Our Values and Business Ethics," accessed January 28, 2018, https://www.canadapost.ca/assets/pdf/aboutus/cocobc_en.pdf.

98. Laura McQuillan, "Burger Giant Blasts Food Safety Whistleblower," *HRD Canada*, August 25, 2017, accessed January 28, 2018, https://www.hrmonline.ca/hr-general-news/burger-giant-blasts-food-safety-whistleblower-229927.aspx.

99. "1-800 You Have a Problem," *Canadian HR Reporter*, August 25, 2017, accessed January 28, 2018, https://www.hrreporter.com/columnist/editor/archive/2017/04/25/1-800-you-have-a-problem.

100. Ibid.

101. Sheng-min Liu, Jian-qiao Liao, and Hongguo Wei, "Authentic Leadership and Whistleblowing: Mediating Roles of Psychological Safety and Personal Identification," *Journal of Business Ethics*, January 2015, accessed January 28, 2018, http://link.springer.com/article/10.1007/s10551-014-2271-z.

102. Larry Colero, "A Framework for Universal Principles of Ethics," W. Maurice Young Centre for Applied Ethics, University of British Columbia, accessed January 28, 2018, http://ethics.ubc.ca/papers/invited/colero-html.

3 Promoting Employee Health and Safety Through Organizational Culture

After studying this chapter, you should be able to

1   Define organizational culture.

2   Explain the impact of organizational culture on employees.

3   Discuss the relationship between an organization's culture and employee engagement.

4   Describe the link between an organization's culture and health and safety in the workplace.

5   List the key components within occupational health and safety.

6   Explain the various ways to protect employees.

7   Describe the programs and services that promote overall health of employees.

OUTLINE

HRM CLOSE-UP

"Changing people's lives is the very core of our company culture."

AS MAYOR of G Adventures, Kristopher Martinez knows success begins with a strong sense of purpose. As such, G Adventures is very clear about its vision of *changing the world through travel*. As Martinez says, "We place as much focus on the life-changing employee experience as we do the life-changing traveller experience. We need a highly engaged workforce to fulfill our vision."

G Adventures is the largest small-group adventure travel company in the world. From humble beginnings 28 years ago, the Toronto-based company now has 2200 employees in 28 offices across the world. With more than 200,000 travellers a year and revenues of over $500 million, the company is driven by the following core values: *We Love Changing People's Lives, Lead with Service, Embrace the Bizarre, Create Happiness and Community*, and *Do the Right Thing*. Martinez and his team, known as G Force, are responsible for enhancing employee engagement and the culture at G Adventures. G Force needs to ensure that all employees feel aligned and connected to the core values, and Martinez notes that this is accomplished by "listening to our people."

G Adventures recognizes that happy employees are more satisfied with their work. This results in satisfied customers (travellers) and benefits the communities where customers visit, which, in turn, encourages more people to travel to these locations. Martinez says, "This is known as the loop tail effect, and it all begins with our employees."

As further acknowledgment of the importance of satisfied employees, in 2009, the company introduced a happiness business model. Based upon 4 pillars (freedom, ability to grow, being connected, and being part of something greater than yourself), a community of employees is created with a higher shared purpose to use travel as a force for good.

The company also understands that people are continuously looking for opportunities to grow and develop. Martinez appreciates that "employees want to be the best version of themselves—personally and professionally." To support this, G Adventures offers leadership development camps throughout the year. As well, the company provides opportunities for CEOs (chief experience officers) from different regions to meet in order to exchange ideas and share best practices. This program, known as CEO Exchange, allows these employees to learn from one another and form meaningful connections to each other and to the work that they do.

"We have great people, and we want to retain them. We want them to grow in the company and be ready to be leaders," Martinez explains.

Familiarization trips are also important. G Adventures sponsors 1 trip a year for each employee, thereby allowing people to experience a travel adventure themselves. The company also holds an annual G Stock conference. During this 5-day event, employees, who are chosen to attend based upon their contributions and being visible champions of company culture, participate in team-building activities. The conference ends with a State of G Nation keynote speech from founder Bruce Poon Tip, which celebrates what has been accomplished during the past year and outlines the company's future goals.

Connection Camps are another way that G Adventures supports employee engagement. Employees from different offices or departments form teams of 3 to 6 people and work on completing challenges designed to create stronger connections between group members. This can be as basic as making a meal

Kristopher Martinez, Mayor, G Adventures

from a recipe provided by one of the group members. The team then posts about the experience on G Nation, an internal social media platform that is similar to Facebook.

Teams are awarded points based upon what they post, and each year the top-scoring 120 employees are invited to attend a connection camp, which is a week of team building at one of the company's destinations.

G Adventures also recognizes that a safe work environment is important to employees. Martinez is proud that the company "has monthly joint health and safety committee meetings and offers CPR and first-aid training to all employees. As well, during the recent renovation of the Toronto office, ergonomic principles were considered to ensure that appropriate work spaces are provided to all employees."

Martinez shares great advice he was given from Leah Shelly, the director of global engagement at G Adventures, which is to "always put people first. When you prioritize people and people issues, you build effective teams and support individuals to do their best work. It's the core of everything."

INTRODUCTION

Although this chapter provides a fuller discussion of healthy and safe work environments, it does so from the perspective of the culture of the organization and how that impacts the well-being of employees. Chapter 2 discussed the legal requirements pertaining to health and safety, but an organization needs to think about more than just adhering to legal standards. To have a workplace that truly attends to and promotes the well-being of employees, the collective values, actions, and behaviours need to reflect that. As such, employee well-being involves much more than simply following the law.

As you continue in this chapter, you will note that job stress and concern about the mental health of employees are increasing and that how these issues are dealt with will depend greatly on everyone in the organization. In Chapter 2, you also learned about the increasing attention to harassment, including psychological harassment and bullying. Again, how these concerns are handled reflects an organization's work environment and its culture. You will note from the HRM Close-up that G Adventures is very serious about its culture and the work it takes to ensure that all employees remain engaged and committed to changing the world through travel.

Although there are sometimes hidden costs if the work environment allows unhealthy or unsafe behaviour (turnover, loss of productive time), the costs associated with an unhealthy and/or unsafe work environment are direct and very tangible. For example, approximately 233,000 incidents of lost-time claims occurred throughout Canadian workplaces in 2015.[1]

Although the laws safeguarding employees' physical and emotional well-being are an incentive to provide desirable working conditions, many employers are motivated to create a culture of well-being as it makes good business sense. The more cost-oriented employer recognizes the importance of avoiding accidents and illnesses wherever possible. Costs associated with sick leave, disability payments, replacement of employees who are injured or killed, and workers' compensation far exceed the costs of creating a culture of well-being and having a healthy and safe work environment. Accidents and illnesses attributable to the workplace may also have pronounced effects on employee engagement and morale and on the goodwill that the organization enjoys in the community and in the business world.

Although leaders at all levels throughout a company are expected to know and enforce health and safety standards throughout the organization, the immediate manager plays the biggest role. The manager must ensure a work environment that protects employees from physical hazards, unhealthy conditions, and unsafe acts of others. Through effective safety and health practices, the physical and emotional well-being of employees may be preserved and even enhanced. As such, in this chapter, you'll be presented with information about how to attend to the well-being of employees through the creation of an organizational culture that promotes a healthy and safe work environment.

LO1
Define organizational culture.

Organizational culture
Collective understanding of beliefs and values that guide how employees act and behave

ORGANIZATIONAL CULTURE AND ITS IMPORTANCE

Organizational Culture

For those of you who have had an organizational behaviour course, you'll probably easily be able to answer the question, What is **organizational culture**? For those of you who have not, the simplest way to describe culture is the "personality" of the organization—the collective understanding of beliefs and values that guide how employees act and behave. As such, the culture of an organization sets the standards of behaviour and helps people understand how they are expected to conduct themselves and interact with others.

Origin of Organizational Culture

Organizational culture doesn't just happen or appear overnight. It usually starts with the original business owner and then builds over time as new people come into the organization and interpret the beliefs and values of the original owner. Depending on how aligned newer actions are with established expectations, culture can change over time, and based upon the original founder's beliefs and values, it can take great effort to ensure that those beliefs and values remain over time. A good example of ensuring that the culture remains over time is SC Johnson, the worldwide company that produces a variety of household products, such as Drano, Pledge, Raid, etc. It is a family-owned business that has built its reputation on trust for quality and excellence in its products. The fifth generation of family members continues that culture, even if it means discontinuing a highly profitable product due to safety concerns.[2] SC Johnson did this when it ceased making its top-selling Saran product when consumer advocates expressed grave concern about the product containing polyvinyl chloride (PVC). It didn't, but it did contain a product that could be confused with PVC, so its owners decided to "act in the best interests of our customers, whose trust in our company is a primary reason they buy our products."[3]

Impact of Organizational Culture on Work Environment and Employees

Since culture influences actions and behaviours, it provides the compass for guiding what employees do and say. Culture addresses such questions as "What is the appropriate amount of personal disclosure?" or "Can I informally speak to my boss, or should I book an appointment?"[4] There are several dimensions of culture, all which contribute to the personality of the organization. For example, does management take into consideration the impact of decisions on employees, or does it focus on getting the work done at all costs? Another dimension is whether rules and regulations are used to control employee behaviour or the organization supports empowerment. A further dimension is how much the organization focuses on team versus individual effort. A final dimension that will be mentioned is the willingness of the organization to encourage employees to be innovative and to take risks.[5]

LO2

Explain the impact of organizational culture on employees.

Monkey Business Images/Shutterstock.com

Encouraging employees to work in teams is 1 indicator of an organization's culture.

As mentioned earlier in this chapter, culture derives from the original founders' visions. And whether it changes over time is a function of how new leaders behave and act. A good example of this is when Steve Jobs, founder of Apple Inc., died and Tim Cook became CEO. Apple's culture was very much aligned with Jobs's vision, yet Cook has created a more inclusive and open company. His particular style is more like a coach who trusts his staff, and he isn't manipulative the way Jobs was.[6] Cook indicates that the culture is measured by excellence, helpfulness, ambition, innovativeness, ability to admit mistakes, and integrity and is more important than just making money.[7]

Culture has a profound impact on the success of any organization. Specifically, when employees are empowered to innovate and failures are expected and tolerated as part of learning, research has demonstrated that organizations are more successful.[8] Risks become a way that ideas become actions. But as you will see later in this chapter, there are some areas of the running of the business in which certain types of risks, which impact the health and safety of employees, are not acceptable.

You will remember from Chapter 1 that the values and expectations of the different generations affect how employees relate to their companies. Likewise, the various components of culture also affect the attraction and retention of employees. For example, the cofounder of Klick Health, a digital marketing firm in Toronto, wanted a culture that was open and employee centred, where people could be involved and engaged in the business.[9] This focus is kept at the forefront when new people are hired—it is necessary to have people who will fit into the culture and enable others to grow and succeed.

Read At Work with HRM 3.1 to learn more about how culture is exhibited and what it does for the organization.

AT WORK WITH HRM 3.1 — IS CULTURE REALLY THAT IMPORTANT?

Think about any work that you've done and what the work environment was like. Were you encouraged to learn from your mistakes? Were you encouraged to innovate? Were you asked to be and function as part of a team? Were you allowed to dress casually, or were you expected to wear proper business attire at all times? Were you allowed to make decisions that helped the customer, or did you always have to ask a manager even when you knew the answer?

These are all examples of what culture "looks like" every day in all organizations. Some of the most successful companies ensure that their cultures support innovation, learning, risk taking, and being part of a team. They know that the culture has been a factor in their success.

Fibernetics clearly understands the link between employee satisfaction, business outcomes, and customer satisfaction. The data telecommunications provider, located in Cambridge, Ontario, ensures that each employee feels valued and recognized and believes that work can and should be fun. In addition to a work-hard, play-hard value system, employees are offered unique benefits, such as having their birthdays off and being sponsored to engage in volunteer activities. The company also provides activities for employees to get together, socialize, and get to know one another in non-work settings.

Likewise, Vancity, a credit union in British Columbia, has a culture that encourages employees to take care of their personal lives. Employee well-being is a focus—no matter what stage of life someone is at. The organization also feels very strongly that employee well-being drives both business results and employee engagement.

Both organizations also understand the importance of considering the organizational culture when managing different generations in the workforce. Since many employees want respect, understanding, and flexibility, how people are treated and how people act and behave demonstrate whether the culture can support those wants.

CRITICAL THINKING QUESTIONS:

1. If you're currently working or have worked, how would you describe the company's culture?
2. How would you describe the type of organizational culture you'd like to work in?

Sources: Adapted from Laura McQuillan, "Why Outstanding Culture Makes a Difference," *Human Resources Director Canada*, October 12, 2017; Tracy White, "Authenticity and Fairness Key Elements of Organizational Culture," *Canadian HR Reporter*, August 8, 2017; Isabelle St-Jean, "Flexible Thinking Drives Workplace Futures," *People Talk*, Winter 2014, 20–21; Robert Hackett, "KPMG's Viral Morale Meme," *Fortune*, March 1, 2015, 26; and Brian Kreissl, "Managing a Multi-generational Workforce," *Canadian HR Reporter*, April 6, 2015, 19.

EMPLOYEE ENGAGEMENT

Attending to the well-being of employees requires being aware of, and enhancing, the way they feel about their work and the organization they work for. As such, more and more organizations are paying attention to the concept of **employee engagement**—employees' commitment and dedication to their roles and to achieving overall organizational outcomes. Engagement is used to refer to the interplay of attitudes, behaviours, and dispositions that relate to organizational outcomes such as turnover and productivity. As discussed in Chapter 1, it is important to use metrics to enhance human resource practices. As such, HRM consulting firms, such as Aon Hewitt and Willis Towers Watson, conduct engagement surveys and publish studies identifying factors that drive employee engagement. These studies, which are an example of using metrics to evaluate an organization, present a wide array of drivers and definitions that make the term "engagement" complicated. Some of the drivers include the organization's reputation for social responsibility, leadership, trust and integrity, nature of the job, and total rewards—all factors that are part of the organization's culture. Certain studies focus on particular drivers and their impact on specific organizational outcomes, such as employee turnover, absenteeism, tenure and retention, customer satisfaction, loyalty, sales, company productivity, and financial performance. Although an organization can conduct its own survey, many choose to be involved in top-employer surveys administered by a third party in order to have an independent external assessment of their employees' engagement compared to other organizations.

Cisco Systems Canada has been recognized as one of Canada's top employers from 2009 to 2017 because of its focus on collaboration, strong leadership, and a commitment to providing challenging and interesting opportunites.[10] Aon Hewitt, a global HR consulting and outsourcing solutions business of Aon Corporation, conducts an annual national Canadian workplace study that measures employee engagement. Aon claimed that employers need to focus on specific behaviours and actions ("culture") in order to drive business success and create an engaged workforce.[11] Figure 3.1 illustrates what helps drive better employee engagement and the cultural factors that improve engagement.

To achieve a high level of employee engagement, it is critical that leadership practices focus on key engagement drivers such as empowerment and not control.[12] But why do

LO3

Discuss the relationship between an organization's culture and employee engagement.

Employee engagement
Amount of commitment and dedication an employee has toward the job and the organization

Asking employees to complete a survey is 1 way to measure engagement.

FIGURE 3.1 Employee Engagement

Employee Engagement and Organizational Culture

Psychometrics Canada Inc. conducted a study on the perspectives of human resources professionals on employee engagement in the Canadian workplace. The study showed that when employees are engaged, they demonstrate higher levels of performance, commitment, and improved work relationships. Some themes for increasing engagement are identified below.

What Makes Employees Engaged?

- Positive work relationships with coworkers and management.
- Good fit between skills, job requirements, and the organization's culture.
- Regular feedback on employee performance.
- Opportunities to learn new skills.
- Employees having control over their work.
- Celebrations of progress.
- Communication of the direction and strategy of the organization.
- Trust and mutual respect among employees.

What Can Managers Do to Improve Employee Engagement?

- Design jobs to include employees' skills and strengths.
- Listen to and incorporate employee opinions.
- Communicate clear expectations.
- Give recognition and praise.
- Provide learning and career development opportunities.
- Provide resources and support in finding solutions to problems.
- Clarify roles and decision-making authority.
- Provide flexible work schedules and workloads.

Sources: Adapted from "Engagement Study: Control Opportunity & Leadership, 2011," with permission of Psychometrics Canada Ltd.; Melanie Peacock, *The Human Resource Professional's Guide to Change Management*, Business Expert Press, 2017; Karen Mishra, Lois Boynton, and Aneil Mishra, "Driving Employee Engagement," *International Journal of Business Communication* 51, no. 2 (2014): 183–202.

employees want to be engaged? A further study by Psychometrics Canada, a Canadian firm specializing in employee assessments, provided information about what makes employees engaged and what leaders can do to improve engagement. Figure 3.1 identifies a number of areas for consideration. Furthermore, engagement leads to less frustration at work, thereby creating greater impact at the work level, which becomes increasingly important as employers strive to create a healthier work environment.

As you can see from Figure 3.1, the drivers for employee engagement and cultural components are the same ones necessary to foster a healthy and safe work environment. Therefore, the link between an organization's culture and its practices to ensure the health and safety of employees is critical.

OCCUPATIONAL HEALTH AND SAFETY

Legal Framework

Although the focus on creating a healthy and safe work environment needs to be addressed from the perspectives of organizational culture, it cannot be ignored that there is a legal requirement to have a healthy and safe work environment. As mentioned in the introduction to this chapter, close to 233,000 workplace injuries occurred in Canada throughout 2015. Also, in that year, 852 employees died in work-related accidents.[13] The burden on Canada's

LO4

Describe the link between an organization's culture and health and safety in the workplace.

LO5

List the key components within occupational health and safety.

economy as a result of lost productivity and wages, medical expenses, and disability compensation is staggering. And there is no way to calculate the human suffering involved.

As described in Chapter 2, the federal, provincial, and territorial governments regulate occupational health and safety. Although statutes and standards differ slightly from jurisdiction to jurisdiction, attempts have been made to harmonize the various acts and regulations. Health and safety legislation has had an impact on workplace injuries and illnesses as the number of workplace accidents in Canada has declined even though there has been an increase in the number of workers.

Definitions

In order to understand occupational health and safety, it is important to recognize key terms used to describe what can happen to employees. An **occupational injury** is any cut, fracture, sprain, or amputation resulting from a workplace accident or from an exposure involving an accident in the work environment. An **occupational illness** is any abnormal condition or disorder, other than one resulting from an occupational injury, caused by exposure to environmental factors associated with employment. It includes acute and chronic illnesses or diseases that may be caused by inhalation, absorption, ingestion, or direct contact. With regard to parts of the body affected by accidents, injuries to the back occur most frequently, followed by leg, arm, and finger injuries. An **industrial disease** results from exposure to a substance relating to a particular process, trade, or occupation in industry. Correct use of these terms helps ensure that people discussing occupational health and safety understand each other and are aware of issues being addressed.

> **Occupational injury**
> Any cut, fracture, sprain, or amputation resulting from a workplace accident
>
> **Occupational illness**
> Abnormal condition or disorder resulting from exposure to environmental factors in the workplace
>
> **Industrial disease**
> A disease resulting from exposure relating to a particular process, trade, or occupation in industry

Responsibility for Workplace Health and Safety

All managers and HR professionals should become familiar with the occupational health and safety legislation governing the jurisdiction under which their organization operates. The fundamental duty of every employer is to take every reasonable precaution to ensure employee safety, also known as due diligence. The motivating forces behind workplace legislation were effectively articulated in the landmark case *Regina v. Wholesale Travel Group*, which dealt with the legal liability and obligation of employers to behave in accordance with legislation:

> Regulatory legislation is essential to the operation of our complex industrial society; it plays a legitimate and vital role in protecting those who are most vulnerable and least able to protect themselves. The extent and importance of that role have increased continuously since the onset of the Industrial Revolution. Before effective workplace legislation was enacted, labourers—including children—worked unconscionably long hours in dangerous and unhealthy surroundings that evoke visions of Dante's inferno. It was regulatory legislation with its enforcement provisions that brought to an end the shameful situations that existed in mines, factories and workshops in the nineteenth century.[14]

As discussed earlier in this chapter, there is a very strong link between the values and culture of the organization to employee behaviours. Culture sets the context for what employees do and don't do. When the culture supports cost cutting and getting the product out at all costs, employees will probably not take safety concerns seriously. At Work with HRM 3.2 describes how UPS focuses on employee involvement and a safety culture as the foundation of its health and safety program and not just a legalistic perspective of its responsibilities.

Although employers must display due diligence when it comes to occupational health and safety, it is important to note that all employees have responsibility for this important part of the workplace. Figure 3.2 summarizes the legally required duties and responsibilities regarding health and safety issues, as well as of those directly involved in health and safety issues.

There is a strong link between employees' behaviour regarding health and safety and the culture of an organization.

AT WORK WITH HRM 3.2 — LOOK WHAT EMPLOYEE INVOLVEMENT CAN DO!

UPS Canada, an express carrier and package delivery company, has more than 1100 stores, 11,000 employees, and 2624 vehicles. The company was confronted with high injury rates, particularly sprains and strains from loading and unloading packages and getting into and out of trucks. How did they reduce their injury rates?

UPS implemented the Comprehensive Health and Safety Process (CHSP) to improve health and safety by involving employees first. The results are impressive: lost-time injuries have been reduced by 35% since 2006. In addition, UPS has created a "Circle of Honor" to encourage road safety for its drivers. There are now over 7200 employees in the circle; each has driven 25 years or more, and collectively they have travelled more than 5.3 billion miles of road, with a total of 198,000 years of safe driving. The circle also has 394 members with 35 years or more of driving with no roadside incidents.

How does CHSP work? For one thing, it provides a vast amount of training each year. For example, UPS tractor-trailer drivers received 80 hours of both computer-based and on-the-road training before ever going out on the road as equipment operators. For another, UPS also bases the CHSP on a culture of commitment to safety—creating values in which safety is first no matter

what. This is especially true when drivers are faced with bad weather or package handlers with high production demands.

Employee involvement is the foundation of the health and safety process established by UPS. The company's approach can be illustrated as a pyramid, of which the base consists of employees' personal values toward safety practices. The next level is built on management commitment and employee involvement. The remaining 3 tiers are worksite analysis, hazard prevention and control, and education and training. Worksite analysis is based on past data, prevention reports, audits, employee concerns, observation, and feedback. Hazard assessment and control utilize an employee concern logbook as well as observation and feedback processes. And it is important to remember that CHSP is considered a process, not a program.

With both management and front-line employees involved and focusing jointly on safety, the practices and values of placing safety above operational concerns are reinforced. If an incident occurs, UPS conducts a formal investigation to look at possible root causes to prevent a recurrence.

When a person walks through any of the distribution centres, it is obvious that safety is in the company's DNA.

continued

Lester Lefkowitz/Stone/Getty Images

Weekly communication meetings always end with a senior manager reminding drivers to be safe as they travel the various roadways and routes. With support like that, no wonder employees are involved and help reinforce the safety culture!

CRITICAL THINKING QUESTIONS:
1. If you're working or have worked, would this approach work at your company?
2. What characteristics of organizational culture are necessary for this approach?

Sources: Adapted from UPS Canada, "Fact Sheet," accessed October 10, 2017, www.ups.com/content/ca/en/about/facts/canada.html; Jayanth Jayaram, Jeff Smith, Sunny Park, and Dan McMackin, "A Framework for Safety Excellence: Lessons from UPS," **SupplyChain** 247 (October 20, 2013), accessed October 10, 2017, www.supplychain247.com/article/framework_for_safety_excellence_lessons_from_ups.

Focus on Younger Workers

Much concern has been expressed about the high incidence of youth injuries. The statistics are alarming: teenagers are twice as likely as older workers to be injured on the job; young workers get hurt more than anybody else. This is usually attributable to a lack of work experience and insufficient training. So it is even more important for organizations that employ young people to ensure that they are oriented to any dangers at work and to ensure that young people receive

FIGURE 3.2 Health and Safety Duties and Responsibilities

Employers
- Provide a hazard-free workplace.
- Comply with laws and regulations.
- Inform employees about safety and health requirements.
- Keep records.
- Compile an annual summary of work-related injuries and illnesses.
- Ensure that managers are familiar with work and associated hazards.
- Report accidents to the Workers' Compensation Board.
- Provide safety training.

Employees
- Comply with all laws and regulations.
- Report hazardous conditions or defective equipment.
- Follow employer safety and health rules.
- Refuse reasonably unsafe work.

Managers
- Advise employees of potential workplace hazards.
- Ensure that employees follow health and safety protocols.
- Ensure that employees use or wear safety equipment.
- Provide written instructions.
- Take every reasonable precaution to guarantee the safety of workers.

Joint Health and Safety Committees
- Advise employer on health and safety matters.
- Create a non-adversarial climate to foster a safe and healthy work environment.
- Investigate accidents.
- Train others in safety obligations.

appropriate safety training. And it is important that young workers know that it is okay to say no if they are asked to do any work that is unsafe. But the biggest solution to helping young workers to stay safe is ensuring that safety is part of the company's culture.[15]

To help build awareness of safety at work in young people, the Alberta government created a series of videos entitled *Bloody Lucky*. Its objective is to create awareness and to encourage younger workers to protect themselves and others in the workplace. The poster in Toolkit 3.1 in an example of another resource as it is targeted toward young people, making them aware of workplace risks.

Consequences for Occupational Health and Safety Violations

Even though this chapter stresses the critical role of organizational culture in creating a healthy and safe work environment, it is important to remember that there are financial penalties for violations of occupational health and safety regulations. These penalties vary across provinces and territories. For example, the Ontario *Occupational Health and Safety Act* provides for fines of up to $500,000, and offenders can be sent to jail. Manitoba has a similar provision.

Saskatchewan and Manitoba continue to have the 2 highest workplace injury rates in the country. Both provinces have proposed increased penalties to reflect the serious nature of violating laws that protect worker health and safety. The maximum fines under Manitoba's *Workplace Safety and Health Act* are $250,000 for the first offence and $500,000 for a second or subsequent offence and the possibility of jail time.[16] The Province of Saskatchewan recently combined various employment laws, including occupational health and safety, into 1 law called

the *Saskatchewan Employment Act*. The province also increased penalties for causing a serious injury or fatality to $500,000 for individuals and $1,500,000 for corporations.[17] Financial penalties for federally regulated companies range from $100,000 to $1,000,0000.[18] Furthermore, early in 2015, British Columbia introduced new workplace legislation that also expands a court's authority to bar the worst offenders from operating in a particular industry.[19] HRM and the Law 3.1 describes what happened to an organization in relation to safety violations.

The federal government was so concerned about employers' responsibilities for workplace health and safety that the *Criminal Code* (Bill C-45) was changed to make it easier to bring criminal charges against coworkers, managers, executives, and employers when a worker is killed or injured on the job. The legislation was a direct result of a public inquiry into the Westray Mine disaster in 1992 that killed 26 workers. Numerous safety infractions occurred at Westray, and it was determined that senior managers and executives knew of the infractions but did nothing to fix them. There is no doubt that violations of health and safety laws can have significant consequences.

Workers' Compensation

In addition to penalties for safety violations, workers' compensation provides financial benefits to injured workers or workers who become ill as a result of their work environment. These benefits can be in the form of a cash payout (if the disability is permanent) or wage-loss payments (if the worker can no longer earn the same amount of money). Unlimited medical aid is also provided, along with vocational rehabilitation, which includes physical, social, and psychological services. The goal is to return the employee to the original job (or some type of modification) as soon as possible. For example, the Nova Scotia Liquor Corporation received a safety award for its return-to-work program. The program has resulted in a reduction of lost days by 73% and reduced the premiums the corporation paid by 87%.[20]

Equally problematic is compensation for stress, which is discussed in more detail later in the chapter. Stress-related disabilities are usually divided into 3 groups: physical injuries

HRM AND **THE LAW** 3.1 — HOW MUCH IS THE PENALTY?

The amounts of penalties vary when an employer is found to have violated safety protocols. But how much is appropriate when a person is burned?

Bridgestone Canada Inc., which manufactures textile products, was found to be in violation of following health and safety requirements when a technician was working with sulfuric acid to be used in the lab for conducting tests. The sulfuric acid was contained in a 45-gallon drum equipped with an electric pump, hose, and nozzle to transfer the acid into the desired container. The worker was filling a plastic bottle in this way when the hose nozzle attached to the bottle detached under pressure. The worker, who was not wearing the apparel required to be protected from injury, suffered minor chemical burns and was exposed to the hazard of injury from contact of skin with acid, a noxious liquid.

The court found that Bridgestone failed to ensure that the measures and procedures required by law were carried out at the workplace. The company was fined $70,000 and a 25% victim fine surcharge as required by the *Provincial Offences Act* in Ontario. The surcharge is credited to a special provincial government fund to assist victims of crime.

CRITICAL THINKING QUESTIONS:

1. Do you think companies should be fined for safety violations? Are financial penalties truly a deterrent? Why or why not?
2. Do you think owners or key managers in companies should be charged under the *Criminal Code* when the death of a worker occurs and safety violations have been confirmed? Why or why not?

Sources: Adapted from "Worker Suffers Burns, Company Fined $70,000," *Court Bulletin*, *Ontario Newsroom*, September 29, 2017, accessed October 12, 2017, https://news.ontario.ca/mol/en/2017/09/worker-suffers-burns-company-fined-70000.html?_ga=2.16184688.711051350.1507819605-803080844.1507819605.

FIGURE 3.3 Ways to Reduce Workers' Compensation Costs

1. Perform an audit to assess high-risk areas within a workplace.
2. Prevent injuries by proper ergonomic design of the job (such as position of keyboard) and effective assessment of job candidates.
3. Provide high-quality medical care to injured employees by physicians with experience and preferably with training in occupational health.
4. Manage the care of an injured worker from the injury until return to work. Keep a partially recovered employee at the worksite.
5. Provide extensive worker training in all related health and safety areas.

leading to mental disabilities (e.g., clinical depression after a serious accident); mental stress resulting in a physical disability (ulcers or migraines); and mental stress resulting in a mental condition (anxiety over workload or downsizing leading to depression). Most claims, it should be pointed out, result from accidents or injuries.

Compensation has become a complex issue. Since workers can receive payment if they have contracted an industrial disease, cause and effect can be difficult to determine. Consider, for example, the case of a mine worker who has contracted a lung disease but who also smokes heavily. Although the number of Canadians injured at work every year is decreasing, there are still many people injured, and the cost of these injuries is in the billions of dollars of compensation claims. This has left workers' compensation boards with a huge deficit to pay existing claims. To encourage employers to introduce better prevention and claims management practices, the emphasis of workers' compensation has been shifting from assessments and payments to the creation of a safety-conscious environment intended to reduce the number of work-related accidents, disabilities, and diseases. Figure 3.3 lists some ways employers can reduce their workers' compensation costs.

PROTECTING EMPLOYEES

LO6

Explain the various ways to protect employees.

Occupational health and safety legislation was clearly designed to protect the health, as well as the safety, of employees. Because of the dramatic impact of workplace accidents, however, managers and employees alike may pay more attention to these kinds of immediate safety concerns than to job conditions or work environments that may be dangerous to their health. It is essential, therefore, that health hazards be identified and controlled.

Largely because of the growing public awareness of the efforts of environmentalists, factors in the work environment that affect health are receiving greater attention. Unprecedented air and water pollution throughout the world has made everyone more conscious of the immediate environment in which they live and work. Articles about workers who have been exposed to potential dangers at work can frequently be found in the newspapers. Pressure from the federal government and unions, and increased public concern, has given employers a definite incentive to provide the safest and healthiest work environment possible.

As part of Building Your Skills at the end of this chapter, you will be asked to explore the website for the Canadian Centre for Occupational Health and Safety.

Safety Programs

As we've already learned, most employers have a formal safety program. The success of a safety program depends largely on managers of operating departments, even though an HR department may have responsibility for coordinating the safety communication and training programs and maintaining the safety records required by occupational health and safety regulations. Above all else, the CEOs and other senior leaders in unique positions of influence set the tone for safe and healthy work practices. Bill Borger, president and CEO of the Borger

Increased public awareness and accountability about air and water pollution have expanded pressure to provide safe and healthy work environments.

Group of Companies, is very pleased and proud to have been awarded a Canadian Occupational Safety Gold Medal in the building and construction category. He states, "To me, safety is a leading indicator of the entire organization's health. That's how I measure it, so I put a lot of effort into it."[21] Borger feels that the weekly company-wide phone broadcast, with contests, jokes, safety tips, and company news, goes a long way to achieving the company's safety goals.

Organizations with formal safety programs generally have a joint health and safety committee that includes members from management, each department or manufacturing or service unit, and the pool of employees. Committees are typically involved in investigating accidents and helping to publicize the importance of safety rules and their enforcement.

Both the Canada Safety Council and *Canadian Occupational Safety* magazine provide resources to assist in the development of a safe work environment, as does the Canadian Centre for Occupational Health and Safety mentioned above.

Creating Awareness

Probably the most important role of a safety program is motivating managers and subordinates to be aware of safety considerations. Although there is a requirement by law to do this, success comes when a manager willingly promotes a safe work environment. If managers fail to demonstrate awareness, their subordinates can hardly be expected to do so. Unfortunately, most managers wear their "safety hats" far less often than their "production, quality control, and methods improvement hats."

Although discipline may force employees to work safely, the most effective enforcement of safety expectations occurs when employees willingly obey and champion safety rules and procedures. This goal can be achieved when management actively encourages employees to participate in all aspects of the organization's safety program and the organization provides incentives to do so.

As an example, Hydro One in Ontario has identified employee health and safety as one of its core values. It acknowledges that some of the work is done in hazardous situations and wants its employees to go home safely every day. Hydro One promotes a strong safety culture by training staff and equipping them appropriately for any work hazards.[22]

Ontario Power Generation, the other electrical company in Ontario, also promotes a strong safety culture. It does so by ensuring that its leaders are committed to safety, are doing

Protective clothing is required in some work settings.

extensive employee training, and are using safety investigations for continuous learning and improvement.[23] Once again highlighting the importance of metrics (as discussed in Chapter 1), Ontario Power Generation widely publishes the fact that it has had a zero-injuries record for some years.

Toolkit 3.2 provides some steps in setting up a health and safety incentive program.

No matter what types of incentive programs are developed, the key to success is the employees' manager. One of a manager's major responsibilities is to communicate to every employee the need to work safely. Beginning at new-employee orientation (as discussed in Chapter 6), safety should be continually emphasized. Proper work procedures, the use of protective clothing and devices, and potential hazards should be explained thoroughly. Furthermore, employees' understanding of all these considerations needs to be verified during training sessions, and employees should be encouraged to take some initiative in

TOOLKIT 3.2   CREATING A SUCCESSFUL HEALTH AND SAFETY INCENTIVE PROGRAM

- Obtain the full support and involvement of management by providing cost benefits.
- Review current injury and health statistics to determine where change is needed.
- Decide on a program of action and set an appropriate budget.
- Select a realistic safety goal, such as reducing accidents by a set percentage, improving safety suggestions, or achieving a period of time without a lost-time injury. Communicate your objectives to everyone involved.
- Select incentive rewards on the basis of their attractiveness to employees and their fit with your budget.
- Communicate continually the success of your program. Provide specific examples of positive changes in behaviour.
- Reward safety gains immediately. Providing rewards shortly after improvements reinforces changed behaviour and encourages additional support for the safety program.
- Include safety goals and discussions in the organization's ongoing coaching conversations and in the formal performance management system.

AT WORK WITH HRM 3.3 — IT MAKES GOOD BUSINESS SENSE!

Does a healthy work environment help a company succeed? Manulife Financial (Manulife), a global financial services company, thinks so, and it recently won an award for its accomplishments. As described in Chapter 1, Excellence Canada recognizes and honours a variety of organizations for quality initiatives. It also has a special Healthy Workplace Award granted from time to time to companies that have attained a high standard in creating a healthy work environment. The criteria for the award include a broad-based approach to health and wellness in the workplace with specific factors of physical, environmental, mental, safety, and social issues. The overall goal of the award is to promote healthy employees, and there is evidence of a positive link between health and business growth, productivity, and business excellence. Manulife expresses its core values through the acronym PRIDE (Professionalism, Real Value to Customers, Integrity, Demonstrated Financial

Strength, Employer of Choice) and recognizes the strong relationship between personal financial wellness, physical and emotional health and productivity. Furthermore, Manulife is committed to providing a work environment in which each employee feels appreciated, supported, healthy, and comfortable. The company wants each member of the organization to have an exceptional employee experience.

As well, Manulife displays a high level of corporate social responsibility. In doing so, the company is involved in a variety of programs and initiatives that make a difference in the places where their employees live and work. The company believes that it makes good business sense to have healthy people who work in an environment that allows them to thrive.

CRITICAL THINKING QUESTION:
Do you think employers only create healthy workplaces to receive awards? Why or why not?

Sources: Adapted from "Award Categories," *Excellence Canada*, accessed October 11, 2017, http://excellence.ca/en/awards/about-the-canada-awards-for-excellence/Award%20Categories-en; "Canadian Health Workplace Criteria—Overview," *Excellence Canada*, accessed October 11, 2017, http://excellence.ca/awards/about-the-canada-awards-for-excellence/Award%20Categories-en#HW; and "2016 CAE Recipient Profile - Manulife Canada," *Excellence Canada*, accessed October 11, 2017, http://excellence.ca/en/awards/2016-cae-recipients/2016-cae-profiles/2016-caeprofile-manulife.

maintaining a concern for safety. Since training by itself does not ensure continual adherence to safe work practices, managers must observe employees at work and reinforce safe practices. Where unsafe acts are detected, managers should take immediate action to find the cause. Managers need to foster a team spirit of safety among the work group. Again, it is important to state that although this is a legal requirement, the success of any safety awareness depends on the willingness of the manager to actively support the employees in creating a safe work environment.

Many organizations advocate employee involvement when designing and implementing safety programs as well as ensuring that the top leaders support and promote a healthy and safe work environment.[24] Employees can offer valuable ideas regarding specific safety and health topics to cover, instructional methods, and proper teaching techniques. Furthermore, acceptance of safety training is heightened when employees feel a sense of ownership in the instructional program.

At Work with HRM 3.3 describes how Manulife Financial won an award for its approach and commitment to employee health and safety.

Monitoring and Investigating

Safety programs, and awareness of them, are a good starting point. However, how employees are, or are not, following health and safety requirements needs to be continuously monitored and investigated. Ongoing communication is critical to monitoring and specific expectations, and standards concerning occupational health and safety must be communicated through managers, bulletin-board notices, employee handbooks, and signs attached to equipment. Safety expectations are also emphasized in regular health and safety meetings, at new-employee orientations, and in paper and online manuals of standard operating procedures. Such expectations typically refer to the following types of employee behaviours:

- using proper safety devices
- using proper work procedures
- complying with accident- and injury-reporting procedures
- wearing required safety clothing and equipment
- avoiding carelessness or horseplay

Penalties for violation of health and safety rules are usually stated in the employee handbook. In a large percentage of organizations, the penalties imposed on violators are the same as those imposed for violations of other standards and expectations. They include an oral or written warning for the first violation, suspension or disciplinary layoff for repeated violations, and, as a last resort, dismissal. However, for serious violations—such as smoking around volatile substances—even the first offence may be cause for termination.

When an incident happens, the manager and a member of the safety committee should investigate even if the incident is considered minor. Such an investigation may determine the contributing factors and reveal what preventive measures are needed, such as rearranging workstations, installing safety guards or controls, or, more often, giving employees additional training and ensuring that they understand the importance of healthy and safe work practices.

Employers are also required to keep certain records and to compile and post an annual summary of work-related injuries and illnesses. From these records, organizations can compute their *incidence rate*, the number of injuries and illnesses per 100 full-time employees during a given year. Incidence rates are useful for making comparisons between work groups, between departments, and between comparable units within an organization. They also provide a basis for making comparisons with other organizations doing similar work. Occupational health and safety departments in each province and Employment and Social Development Canada compile data organizations can use as a basis for comparing their safety record to those of other organizations. Progressive organizations can also use this information to benchmark "best practices," once again showing the importance of metrics.

Best practices help with safety preparedness.

Identifying Health and Safety Hazards

At one time, health and safety hazards were associated primarily with jobs found in industrial processing operations, such as coal mining. In recent years, however, hazards in jobs outside the plant, such as in offices, healthcare facilities, and airports, have been recognized and preventive methods adopted. Substituting materials, altering processes, enclosing or isolating a process, issuing protective equipment, and improving ventilation are some common methods to prevent problems. General conditions of health with respect to sanitation, housekeeping, cleanliness, ventilation, water supply, pest control, and food handling are also important to monitor.

Believing that workers have the right to know about potential workplace hazards, industry, labour, and government joined forces several years ago to develop a common information system for labelling hazardous substances. The Workplace Hazardous Materials Information System (WHMIS) is based on 3 elements:

1. *Labels.* Labels are designed to alert the worker that the container holds a potentially hazardous substance. WHMIS class symbols and subclass designations are shown in Figure 3.4.
2. **Safety Data Sheets (SDS).** The SDS identifies the product and its potentially hazardous ingredients and suggests procedures for the safe handling of the product.
3. *Training.* Employees must be trained to check for labels and to follow specific procedures for handling spills. As detailed in Chapter 6, training employees is part of the due diligence required of employers; it also becomes an important factor in the event of a lawsuit.

Safety Data Sheets (SDS)
Documents supplied by the supplier containing detailed information regarding hazardous material

Canada has aligned WHMIS with the Globally Harmonized System of Classification and Labelling of Chemicals (GHS). Specific requirements to ensure compliance can be found through the Canadian Centre for Occupational Health and Safety.[25]

Exposure to secondhand smoke is also considered to be a workplace hazard. Although smoking in the workplace has been eliminated, there are still some concerns about people walking through smokers in front of buildings. Many provinces and municipal bylaws now restrict people from smoking too close to building entrances.

FIGURE 3.4 WHMIS Pictogram

Exploding bomb (for explosion or reactivity hazards)	**Flame** (for fire hazards)	**Flame over circle** (for oxidizing hazards)
Gas cylinder (for gases under pressure)	**Corrosion** (for corrosive damage to metals, as well as skin, eyes)	**Skull and Crossbones** (can cause death or toxicity with short exposure to small amounts)
Health hazard (may cause or suspected of causing serious health effects)	**Exclamation mark** (may cause less serious health effects or damage the ozone layer*)	**Environment*** (may cause damage to the aquatic environment)
Biohazardous Infectious Materials (for organisms or toxins that can cause diseases in people or animals)		

* The GHS system also defines an Environmental hazards group. This group (and its classes) was not adopted in WHMIS 2015. However, you may see the environmental classes listed on labels and Safety Data Sheets (SDSs). Including information about environmental hazards is allowed by WHMIS 2015.

Pictogram names reproduced by permission of the Canadian Centre for Occupational Health and Safety. http://images.ccohs.ca/oshanswers/pictogram_names.gif.

ETHICS IN HRM 3.1   WHY DO I NEED TO DRESS LIKE THIS?

Although employers want to present a polished and professional image to customers, it is important to think about the consequences for employees. Enforcement of dress codes is an example of how workplace requirements may harm workers. Women have been arguing that the requirement to wear high heels is dangerous due to tripping and slipping hazards and also causes them to experience various types of pain and blisters on their feet.

This issue was addressed by the British Columbia government in 2017 when it amended footwear rules under the province's 1996 *Workers Compensation Act*. Ontario passed similar legislation, by amending Bill 148,

in 2017 as well. Discussions examining if women are held to higher standards when it comes to dress, therefore resulting in greater health and safety issues, will continue to be addressed throughout Canadian workplaces.

CRITICAL THINKING QUESTIONS:

1. Do you think that the dress expectations for men and women are different? If so, why does this occur? Is this appropriate?
2. What types of dress code requirements could cause health and safety problems for employees?
3. What do strict dress codes indicate about a company's organizational culture?

Sources: Adapted from Tim Lawson and Matthew Demeo, "Bill 148 Passes (But Not Before a Few Last-Minute Changes Were Made)," *Lexology, Ontario Employment Advisor*, November 24, 2017, accessed March 22, 2018, https://www.lexology.com/library/detail.aspx?g=661cffba-7d83-4397-8142-6a46234738de; Jill Slattery, "Women Working in Restaurants Should Not Be Required to Wear High Heels: BC Green Party," *Global News*, March 10, 2017, accessed October 18, 2017, https://globalnews.ca/news/3302769/women-working-in-restaurants-should-not-be-required-to-wear-high-heels-bc-green-party; and Pádraig Collins, "Canadian Province Makes It Illegal to Require Women to Wear High Heels," *The Guardian*, April 8, 2017, accessed October 18, 2017, https://www.theguardian.com/fashion/2017/apr/08/canadian-province-makes-it-illegal-to-require-women-to-wear-high-heels.

As well, more attention is now given to keeping fragrances such as perfumes, colognes, oils, and other personal care products with scents clear of the workplace. Many people can suffer painful reactions even if the scent is at a very low concentration. If an employee expresses concern about fragrances, it is important for the organization to treat the concern seriously, openly, and honestly.

Ethics in HRM 3.1 addresses how company-enforced dress codes may create health and safety problems for employees. Therefore, it is important for employers to think about what the policies are asking of their employees and how this can impact their experiences at work.

Ergonomics

Ergonomics examines the design of equipment and systems to ensure that they can be easily and efficiently used by people, while focusing on the physical safety and comfort of employees.[26] For example, some organizations are purchasing adjustable desks for employees who sit for long periods of time.[27] And recent research has confirmed that prolonged sitting correlates with bad health even when people exercise frequently.[28] Mini-breaks involving exercise and changing one's working position have been found helpful. Importantly, these kinds of injuries often go away if caught early. If they are not, they may require months or years of treatment or even surgical correction.

The increasing use of technology has been associated with increased health risks ranging from musculoskeletal injuries caused by repetitive movements involved in using computer and technical devices, often leading to carpal tunnel syndrome. Therefore, organizations will often do an audit of employees' workstations to ensure that this is not occurring. This review also ensures that appropriate lighting is available to avoid eye strain and other related issues.

Simply put, ergonomics displays an organization's commitment to providing employees with a work environment and working conditions that support their physical well-being while conducting the tasks associated with their jobs in an effective and productive way.

It is important to provide working conditions that support an employee's physical well-being.

OTHER SAFETY CONSIDERATIONS

Employees need to feel secure and safe at work. Without this, people are not able to effectively work, and the behaviour and standards of what employees should or should not do (i.e., the culture of the organization) may become toxic. Therefore, organizations need to focus on workplace security and create a work environment that is free from violence and bullying.

Workplace Security

Significant events have affected workplace security, including the events that occurred on September 11, 2001, and the mass shooting in Las Vegas on October 1, 2017. These tragic events have caused organizations throughout Canada to put renewed emphasis on personal safety and security at work. Heightened workplace security often involves screening people before they are allowed access into certain buildings and security clearance, which is required before being able to work in certain industries and roles. Enhanced security is also reflected in documented procedures to follow in the case of an emergency, increased presence of security on site, and key areas being locked down and accessible only to certain workers.

Terrorism, once largely confined to foreign countries, is now a major concern to many Canadian employers, such as airlines, sporting facilities, energy plants, high-tech companies, and financial institutions. Heightened security procedures include increased video surveillance, blast-resistant glass, tightened garage security, and off-site emergency backup offices.

And the concerns of employees are not restricted to terrorism or bomb threats. In fact, changes to the *Canada Labour Code* have provided an expanded definition of the reasons employees can refuse work they perceive as dangerous. Employees can now refuse "any hazard, condition or activity that could reasonably be expected to be an imminent or serious threat to the life or health of a person exposed to it before the hazard or condition can be corrected or the activity altered."[29]

Workplace Violence

In Canada, some tragic incidents—such as that at L'École polytechnique, in which 14 women were shot and killed, and the death of Maryam Rashidi, who was killed after chasing a car that drove away from the Calgary gas station without paying—have brought our attention to workplace violence.

Furthermore, a recent study found that only about 10% of employers are aware that domestic abuse impacts the safety of those at work and that domestic violence can occur at work.[30] Since it costs Canadian employers almost $78 million every year due to direct and indirect domestic violence, employers are having to learn more about domestic violence and what can happen at work.[31]

The challenge of understanding workplace violence is that it has so many forms, not all of which are legislated against—for example, bullying, aggression, intimidation, ganging, and emotional abuse. Many people think of workplace violence as a physical assault, but there are many forms, including these:

- threatening behaviour, such as shaking fists or throwing objects
- verbal or written threats
- harassment—any behaviour that demeans, embarrasses, or humiliates
- verbal abuse, including swearing, insults, or condescending language
- physical attacks, including hitting, shoving, pushing, or kicking[32]

Recent legislative changes have broadened the responsibility of employers to ensure that their work environment is free of violence. Several provinces, including Alberta, British Columbia, Saskatchewan, Manitoba, Nova Scotia, Prince Edward Island, Québec, and Newfoundland and Labrador, as well as federally regulated workplaces, have implemented regulations dealing with workplace violence as part of their occupational health and safety regulations. As well, Bill 168 details legislated requirements in Ontario, thereby highlighting the legal requirements to have a workplace that is free from violence. Among the requirements of these regulations are a risk assessment, development of policies and procedures to handle the risks identified, instruction and training of workers in handling violence, an emergency response plan, and a requirement that incidents be reported.[33] As well, many provinces have implemented legislation requiring an organization to give an employee who is the victim of domestic violence unpaid leave to address and recover from this type of incident. Furthermore, most provinces have begun to expand legislation requiring procedures to be in place to eliminate or reduce the risks associated with working alone and at night. Here are some of the risk factors in organizations that increase the risk of violence:

- working with the public
- handling valuables such as money or prescription drugs
- carrying out enforcement duties, such as parking meter enforcement
- working alone
- working in a mobile environment, such as a taxicab
- working during times of organizational uncertainty, such as strikes[34]

Exposure to workplace violence results in employees fearing more incidents of violence, leading to personal strains (such as stress) and organizational strains (such as reduced commitment). To implement some preventive measures, the Canadian Centre for Occupational Health and Safety suggests the following:

- workplace designs, such as locks or physical barriers, lighting, and electronic surveillance
- administrative practices, such as keeping cash register funds to a minimum, varying the time of day at which cash is emptied, and using a security firm to deliver cash
- work practices (particularly for those working alone or away from an office) that include having a designated contact, checking the credentials of a client, and having an emergency telephone source[35]

TOOLKIT 3.3 "NO" TO VIOLENCE AT WORK!

There are some very specific things employers can do to minimize and prevent violence in the workplace:

1. Establish violence, including domestic violence, prevention policy and standards.
2. Conduct a risk assessment.
3. Control violence hazards through workplace design and work practices.
4. Regularly inspect the workplace and review the violence education program to ensure that standards are maintained.
5. Educate employees on these policies and programs and appropriate actions to take, including signs of domestic violence, how to prevent violence, and resources for victims of any form of violence.
6. Develop a workplace safety plan to help keep the workplace and all employees safe from threats of any form of violence.
7. Develop a personal safety plan, if an employee reports domestic violence, to ensure that the victim is protected while at the workplace.
8. Ensure that all employees are aware that the employee assistance provider is available.
9. Encourage the victim to contact a professional.
10. In cases of domestic violence, screen for the abuser (with the victim's permission) by providing a photo or description to reception and security.
11. Inform all workplace parties that they must report any abuse or violent behaviour.
12. Act upon any reports immediately.

Sources: Adapted from Government of Canada, "Guide to Violence Prevention in the Workplace," accessed October 12, 2017, https://www.canada.ca/en/employment-social-development/services/health-safety/reports/violence-prevention.html; Public Services Health and Safety Association, "Addressing Domestic Violence in the Workplace: A Handbook," 2010, accessed October 12, 2017, www.pshsa.ca/products/addressing-domestic-violence-in-the-workplace; and WorkSafeBC, "Addressing Domestic Violence in the Workplace: A Handbook for Employers," 2014.

It is also important for all employees to be vigilant regarding potential workplace violence. For example, if an employee is agitated and shouting, others can respond by defusing the situation, establishing clear boundaries around appropriate behaviour, and accessing help from a manager. If an employee is shouting and swearing, others should remove themselves from the situation and alert security. Awareness of such threatening behaviours can provide an opportunity to intervene and prevent disruptive, abusive, or violent acts.

Finally, organizations can establish formalized workplace violence prevention policies, informing employees that aggressive employee behaviour will not be tolerated. Toolkit 3.3 lists violence prevention measures that organizations can take.

Organizations are also using a number of different ways to inform employees about security issues. For example, Seneca College in Ontario uses its intranet as a communication tool to inform employees of internal and external security issues in the surrounding geographic area of the college. Another innovative approach to learning more about preventing workplace violence is the Canadian Initiative on Workplace Violence. The initiative is a research firm with partners from universities, unions, and employers. It researches the impact of workplace violence and provides educational resources to help organizations eliminate such violence. Furthermore, the Canadian Labour Congress and Western University undertook a comprehensive survey to gather data about the prevalence and impact of domestic violence at work that can better inform employers about the impact, once again showing the strategic use of metrics.

Workplace Bullying

Although bullying in the workplace was discussed in Chapter 2 as an example of psychological harassment, it also needs to be examined in the context of workplace safety and security. Bullying is prevalent in the workplace, and some estimates suggest that bullying at work impacts 25% of employees.[36] It is unclear whether bullying is more prevalent or that it is no longer acceptable anyplace in a civil society.

There is also the probability that ongoing bullying might create stress in the workplace and that the employee (or employees) might launch compensation claims. Although most provincial agencies are rejecting claims for psychological stress, there have been a few cases in which claims have been accepted. For example, although WorkSafeBC has traditionally rejected mental health claims, it has recently accepted some for mental disorder that arose from "cumulative series of significant work-related stressors,"[37] and, certainly, regular and persistent bullying could qualify. Similarly, a tribunal in Ontario recently ruled that workplace-related stress might be a valid workers' compensation claim.[38] In this situation, it is also important to recognize that the word being used is "workplace" and not "work." What is being signalled is that it isn't necessarily the work the person is doing but the environment in which it is undertaken. Hence, the emphasis in this chapter is on the culture of the organization and the acceptable behaviours and actions.

Of growing concern is the emergence of cyberbullying in the workplace, which is also a cause of stress in the workplace (to be discussed later). We don't often think of adults as vulnerable to it, but bullying is an extreme form of harassment and can happen anywhere. What is **cyberbullying**? It is a certain way of using information and technology. On sites such as Twitter, Instagram, and Facebook, most postings are benign. But what happens when the message is anonymous and a particular person is targeted with taunts, untruths, etc.? This form of harassment, depending on the severity, can cause stress, anxiety, depression, insomnia, and low self-esteem.[39] As Ethics in HRM 3.2 indicates, organizations that allow bullying in the workplace do face consequences.

Some organizations have formal crisis management teams that conduct initial risk assessment surveys, develop action plans to respond to violent situations, and perform crisis intervention during violent or potentially violent encounters. As well, organizations have created emergency telephone lines for their employees and families in the event of a crisis, such as a blackout or severe weather conditions.

Cyberbullying
Bullying by using communication technology and information

ETHICS IN HRM 3.2 — BULLIES GET OUT!

What is it like to be bullied at work? Ask Meredith Boucher, who went public with her story. She worked at Walmart in Ontario and saw great progress for herself after winning a number of awards for her work. But all that changed when she became a target of harassment and abuse by her manager. She stated that the behaviour and actions started when she refused to falsify certain records as the manager was concerned about a poor audit of the store. Then, she reports, the bullying behaviour started—and continued every day for 6 months. Ms. Boucher also noted that it took an emotional, mental, and physical toll over that time.

She documented the occurrences and provided the information to a senior manager, including confirmations from other employees. Eventually, Walmart did an investigation and concluded that the complaint was unfounded, which led to discipline for Boucher. She

then quit and filed a lawsuit against both the manager and Walmart.

As the case went through the various stages, an appeals judge did conclude that the behaviour was abusive and that Boucher suffered a "visible and provable illness as a result." The judge awarded $1.4 million in compensation, which was later downgraded to $400,000. After the decision, Walmart reported that the manager had been moved to another store, and there have been no further issues regarding the workplace behaviour.

Depending on the extent, harassment, and bullying in particular, can lead to a criminal charge under Canada's **Criminal Code**. There is a continuum of behaviours that range from harassment to assault. The actions can be overt, such as somebody saying something to someone, or less visible, such as someone texting something very hurtful about someone to someone

continued

else—for example, sending a picture altered with the intent to ridicule.

More attention is now being paid to bullying at work, particularly as various tribunals and courts continue to award money when complaints are upheld. There is also now the possibility that under workers' compensation, further claims could be made for psychological injuries.

Clearly, more than ever, there is no place for bullies at work.

CRITICAL THINKING QUESTIONS:
1. Have you ever felt bullied at work or school? What did you do?
2. What would you now do if you faced the same situation?

Sources: Adapted from "Workplace Bullying a Major Concern in Canada, Says Woman Who Sued Wal-Mart," *CBC News*, June 14, 2014, accessed October 12, 2017, www.cbc.ca/news/business/workplace-bullying-a-major-concern-in-canada-says-woman-who-sued-wal-mart-1.2673109; Jennifer Newman, "Why Bullying Persists in the Workplace," *CBC News British Columbia*, February 28, 2016, accessed October 12, 2017, http://www.cbc.ca/news/canada/british-columbia/jennifer -newman-why-bullying-persists-in-the-workplace-1.3468466; Liz Bernier, "From the Schoolyard to the Office," *Canadian HR Reporter*, March 23, 2015, accessed October 12, 2017, www.hrreporter.com/articleview/23856-from-the-schoolyard-to-the-office; and Stuart Rudner, "Workers' Compensation for Harassment, Mental Distress?," *Canadian HR Reporter*, January 12, 2015, accessed October 12, 2017, www.hrreporter.com/blog/Canadian-HR-Law/archive/2015/01/12/ workers-compensation-for-harassment-mental-distress.

When violent incidents, such as the death of a coworker, happen at work, employees can experience anxiety, shock, guilt, grief, apathy, resentment, cynicism, isolation, and a host of other emotions. Such incidents may require the violence response team to perform crisis intervention through positive counselling techniques. It is also important that employees are provided with the opportunity and time to grieve.[40]

STRESS IN THE WORKPLACE

According to a report on the main sources of workplace stress, Sun Life's Health Index found that 77% of those surveyed experienced excessive or uncomfortable stress at work.[41] People frequently talk about being stressed at work yet are unable to explain what they mean. **Stress** can be defined as physiological, mental, and/or emotional tension caused in response to a demanding environment. For example, while running 5 km, an individual may become short-winded after 3 km. Thus, the body is "stressed" as the individual deals with being short of breath. Likewise, a student may have just received a special award at school and be excited about the recognition. Again, the student has to cope with this. Stress can be either positive or negative, and each person handles stress differently.

In the Sun Life survey, respondents indicated that the top driver of excessive stress was personal finances and that the level of stress was impacting their work performance.[42] A large-scale international study of 22,000 professionals in more than 100 countries confirmed that employees globally feel more stressed at work than they did 5 years ago.[43] So, then, what work processes (the way work is designed and performed) and organizational practices are stressing the stressed at work? The international study found that technological advances are keeping employees connected 24/7.[44] The constant use of email can be a psychological strain on workers. Employers are beginning to reduce after-work use of company-issued smartphones through mandated blackout periods, expressing concerns ranging from unpaid overtime to encroachment on family time. Furthermore, people understand the need to escape their cellphones for thinking and relaxing—and getting away from data overload.[45]

Angst and the feeling that things might be better someplace else are also fuelled by job postings on LinkedIn and other online job postings, further increasing stress levels.

Stress
Physiological, mental, and/ or emotional tension caused in response to a demanding environment

Technology can be a source of stress for employees.

Consequences of Stress

Stress can lead to mental health issues, which are increasing in the workplace. A survey conducted by the Centre for Addiction and Mental Health (CAMH) revealed that 40% of employees would not tell their manager if they had a mental health problem or similar problems that were impacting their performance.[46] Recognizing and dealing with **workplace stressors** is the first step toward managing workplace stress. A corporate culture and work environment that promote a healthy, safe, and environmentally protected work environment can have a positive impact on worker stress.

Workplace stressors
A workplace event, process, or practice that has the potential to cause worker stress

Coping with Stress

To reinforce the concern that stress has on the health of the workplace, a research study was presented in 2014 to the federal, provincial, and territorial ministers of labour indicating that the economic cost of workplace stress in Canada is over $51 billion every year.[47] This study noted that laws aren't enough to improve the psychological well-being of the work environment and that it was the culture of the work environment that would improve the psychological environment of work. Toolkit 3.4 provides some suggestions about what employers can do to improve the psychological health of the workplace.

Several years ago, a new National Standard of Canada for Psychological Health and Safety in the workplace was launched, giving organizations the tools to achieve measurable improvement in the psychological health and safety of Canadian employees. It will help employers prevent the loss and liability associated with mental injuries—estimated at $11 billion a year in workplace losses alone—by nurturing psychologically safe working environments.[48]

Stress management programs involve employees and employers working together to take initiatives to reduce aspects of their work environments that result in negative impacts on employee health. Organizational techniques, such as flexible work hours and reduced overtime, should not be overlooked in the process of dealing with stress in the workplace.[49] Formal training programs for time management, dealing with conflict, and effectively communicating are other resources that may be provided to employees.

TOOLKIT 3.4 — WE NEED A PSYCHOLOGICALLY HEALTHY WORKPLACE!

Employers can develop a number of strategies to reduce stress in the work environment. Since stress is part of everyday life, it cannot be eliminated, but it can be reduced. Here are "best practices" from various research studies to have a healthier workplace:

- Managers learning to be more responsive and supportive to employees.
- Recognizing employee issues that need referral to an employee assistance program.
- Managers communicating more openly about organizational changes.
- Keeping workloads reasonable, controlling for overtime
- Allowing for more work flexibility.

- Training managers and employees on mental health so that employees can discuss stress and mental health issues.
- Assessing workplace stressors so that actions can be taken to mitigate them.
- Ensuring that senior leaders affirm the need for a healthier work environment.
- Ensuring that all efforts for an improved work environment are seamless—from occupational health and safety committees to wellness services, employee assistance programs, etc.
- Ensuring that expectations regarding a healthier work environment are part of the culture.

Sources: Adapted from "Psychological Health and Safety in the Workplace – a LEADS Perspective," *CHA Learning*, posted on June 6, 2017, accessed October 17, 2017, https://www.chalearning.ca/news/psychological-health-safety-workplace-leads-perspective; Dr. Ted Harvey and Neil Gavigan, "Minimizing Workplace Stress, Injuries and Violence in Canada: Towards a New Standard for Occupational Health and Safety," submission to the Mental Health Commission of Canada and Federal-Provincial-Territorial Ministers of Labour, September 2014; Sarah Dobson, "Health Cultures, Reduced Costs," *Canadian HR Reporter*, November 17, 2014, accessed October 13, 2017, www.hrreporter.com/articleview/22808-healthy-cultures-reduced-costs; and Sarah Dobson, "Manager Relationships Key to Mentally Healthy Workplace," *Canadian HR Reporter*, February 23, 2015, 2.

Before concluding this discussion, we should observe that stress that is harmful to some employees might be healthy for others. Most managers learn to handle stress effectively and find that it can stimulate better performance. However, there will always be those unable to handle stress, who need help learning to cope with it. The increased interest of young and old alike in developing habits that will enable them to lead happier and more productive lives will undoubtedly be beneficial to them as individuals, to the organizations where they work, and to a society where people are becoming more and more interdependent. Progressive companies are also discovering that other interventions, such as creating a culture of celebration and reinforcing values, help with the overall workplace environment.[50] Furthermore, as discussed earlier in this chapter, employee well-being and health are more likely in organizations with highly engaged staff. Therefore, there is additional rationale to ensure that work stressors are kept to a minimum. Figure 3.5 provides some suggestions on how individuals can reduce stress.

FIGURE 3.5 Tips for Reducing Job-Related Stress

- Encourage open communication between and among employees and between employees and managers.
- Ensure that all employees have the right tools and resources to properly do their jobs.
- Provide ongoing feedback to employees and ensure that they know what is expected of them.
- Make sure that employees take breaks, including using their allocated vacation time.
- Respond to feedback and employee concerns in a timely manner.
- Be transparent and regularly communicate with employees. Ensure that they know and understand what the organization is doing to keep them safe and healthy.
- Encourage employees to have interests and activities that are not related to their work.

SUPPORTING OVERALL HEALTH OF EMPLOYEES

LO7

Describe the programs and services that promote overall health of employees.

Along with improving working conditions that are hazardous to employee health and safety, many employers provide a variety of services and support that encourage employees to improve their overall health. It is recognized that better health benefits not only the individual but also the organization through reduced absenteeism, increased efficiency, and better morale. An understanding of the close relationship between physical and emotional health and job performance has made broad health-building programs attractive to employers as well as to employees. And with recent research from the Mental Health Commission of Canada indicating that every week in Canada, 500,000 people miss work due to a mental health problem or illness, unions are also getting involved in providing programs that encourage their members to be involved in making the work environment healthy and safe.[51] As public expectations for ethical business practices are increasing, organizations are beginning to follow through on their social and environmental commitment responsibilities, creating new opportunities to improve the quality of work life and organizational performance. These organizations are using individual health promotion programs as the first step toward a more comprehensive approach to employee well-being. Health services, alternative health care, wellness, disability management, and employee and family assistance programs can begin to address the underlying causes of presenteeism, absenteeism, stress, and work–life imbalance. Also critical is the understanding of the work environment and how work processes and practices can be improved to enhance employee health and organizational performance. Graham Lowe, a leading researcher on healthy organizations, states that a supportive culture that values employees, employee involvement, commitment from senior leadership, communication, and an understanding of the strategic link between organizational goals and health outcomes are the building blocks of a healthy organization.[52]

Studies have demonstrated a strong link between high-performance work systems with employee well-being and a reduction in burnout.[53] In such a system, employees who are treated respectfully and experience quality interpersonal relationships tend to be more committed and to participate more fully.[54]

As described in At Work with HRM 3.4, 2 organizations have won awards for creating a healthy work environment.

Health Services

One of the supports that an employer can provide is health services. The type of health services that an employer provides is primarily related to the size of the organization and the importance of such services. Small organizations have only limited facilities, such as those needed to handle first-aid cases, whereas many larger firms offer complete diagnostic, treatment, and emergency medical services. Since employers are required to provide medical services after an injury, the larger firms may have nurses and physicians on full-time duty or certainly have arrangements with local physicians for preferred attention. Small and medium-sized organizations have 1 or more physicians on call.

Wellness Programs

Another support is wellness programs. Typical elements in a wellness program are access to flexible work hours, healthy food, fitness facilities, health professionals, health groups, activities, relaxation techniques, chiropractic, therapeutic massage, acupuncture, and homeopathy. Some suggest that wellness programs may not achieve the desired results, but recent research indicates that if the employer is clear about the goals and that the culture supports wellness, a well-designed and well-executed program can achieve both health and financial results.[55] Since Canada has a publicly funded healthcare system, these same critics argue that employers ought not to do this. However, wellness programs can take a preventive approach

AT WORK WITH HRM 3.4 — WHAT DOES A HEALTHY ORGANIZATION LOOK LIKE?

Throughout this chapter, you've been provided with a number of reasons why it is important to have healthy organizations. But is this just a theory, or do businesses really believe it makes a difference?

Ask John Mannarino, who founded Mannarino Systems & Software Inc. in Montréal. As a company that sells safety-critical systems and software engineering services to a number of sectors, including power generation, aerospace, and space, the organization believes it is important to have a culture that reflects the importance of safety in their products. Not only must the work be of the highest quality, but the work environment must also provide an atmosphere that enables employees to do and be their best. The senior managers focus on a team atmosphere, including allowing flex-time to have a healthy work–life balance. The company believes strongly that a healthy work environment has enabled it to become a leader in its field.

Healthy work environments are not just for the private sector. Take NB Power, for example, which won the 2016 Gold Award for Canada's Safest Employers in the category of psychological safety. From formal training to daily breathing exercises, the company believes it is important for employees to be mindful of each other and of their work surroundings. Minimizing anxiety and distractions is viewed as critical to creating a workplace that is healthy and safe. What do these examples mean for other employers? Build the business case with hard data to demonstrate that a healthy and safe work environment does mean better business results.

CRITICAL THINKING QUESTION:

If a healthy work environment is good for business, why don't more organizations have one? Explain your answer.

Sources: Adapted from "Mannarino Flourishes Amid the Aerospace Giants," Canada's 2015 Top Small & Medium Employers, **The Globe and Mail**, March 15, 2015, 43; "Making Mental Health a Priority at Work," **Canadian HR Reporter**, December 1, 2014, www.hrreporter.com/articleview/22959-making-mental-health-a-priority-at-work; and Psychological Safety 2016 = NB Power, **Canadian Occupational Safety**, October 25, 2016, accessed October 12, 2017, http://www.cos-mag.com/personal-process-safety/31584-psychological-safety-2016-nb-power.

that the Canadian healthcare system mostly cannot. Also, it may now be the more socially responsible thing to increase the organization's stature as a good employer that attracts and retains staff and has high employee engagement.[56]

Some organizations provide on-site medical services for employees.

iStock/Getty Images Plus

Although early wellness programs attempted to develop a return-on-investment (ROI) metric to justify the expense, many organizations and benefits professionals suggest that an ROI isn't as important as seeing improved employee health and productivity.[57]

Disability Management

Disability management
Integrated approach to managing disability-related benefits

More and more organizations are taking an integrated approach to dealing with short- and long-term absences. Initially, **disability management** programs were linked to workplace injuries as a way to get employees back to work as soon as possible. These programs have now evolved to an approach that combines a strong organizational commitment centred on managers, overseen by expert internal resources, and supported by clinical case management.[58] This means that the focus is also on creating a work environment where employees want to return to work as soon as they are medically able. Professionals have long known that being off work is unhealthy.[59] Part of an effective disability management program includes a graduated return to work in which the employee works fewer hours and, in some situations, is accommodated by being assigned to a different shift.[60] Even in difficult economic times, a carefully designed and well-managed program can be effective in getting capable staff back to work while communicating that the employer is interested in their well-being.[61]

Facilitating a return-to-work plan would include maintaining contact with employees while they are on leave, providing organizational support to the manager and team by discussing implementation and anticipated challenges and solutions, understanding the tasks and responsibilities that need to be modified, and having a clear diagnosis and plan. This approach would reduce any anxiety, alienation, fears of reinjury and job loss, and stigma that the employee involved might feel.

Employee Assistance Programs

A broad view of health includes the emotional as well as the physical aspects of one's life. Although emotional problems, personal crises, financial problems, and substance abuse are considered personal matters, they become organizational problems when they affect behaviour at work and interfere with performance. It is estimated that psychological problems, including depression, anxiety, mental illness, and stress in the workplace, cost the Canadian economy about $50 billion every year, about 30% of which is attributed to productivity losses.[62]

Employee assistance programs (EAP)
Program to provide short-term counselling and referrals to appropriate professionals

Employee assistance programs (EAPs) or more inclusive ones called "employee and family assistance programs" (EFAPs) can provide a useful way to deal with problems, such as stress and depression, that might lead to more serious mental health problems. Managers are often given training and policy guidance in the type of help they can offer. Figure 3.6 outlines the types of EAP services offered to employees in Canada. Although many companies do not offer programs due to concerns over the costs/benefits of such initiatives, research has shown that 80% of mental health problems can be successfully treated with early detection and treatment.[63]

The most prevalent problems among employees are personal crises involving marital, family, financial, or legal matters. Such problems often come to a manager's attention. In some instances, the manager can provide help simply by being understanding and supportive and by helping the individual find the type of assistance needed. In many cases, the person is referred to the EAP or EFAP. Many organizations that have an EAP also have operations and offices that are in many different locations yet want to use the same EAP provider. Therefore, in recent years, many EAP providers have begun to offer 24/7 telephone access to bilingual expert counsellors, telephonic counselling sessions, and online assistance to support managers.[64] Managers would want to ensure that they leverage the online support services offered by EAP providers; these include training, guides, checklists, videos, assessment tools, and articles.

As mentioned earlier in this chapter, emotional and/or mental health issues are on the rise and creating direct and indirect costs to the Canadian economy. A persistent focus on awareness, communication, and education would begin to reduce the fear, stigma, and discrimination around mental illness.

FIGURE 3.6 **Employee Assistance Programs**

Listed below are some of the usual services in EAPs:
- Personal issues.
- Job stress.
- Relationship issues.
- Eldercare, childcare, and parenting issues.
- Harassment.
- Substance abuse.
- Separation and loss.
- Balancing work and family.
- Financial or legal.
- Family violence.

In addition, and depending on the wishes of the company, there may be services for retirement and layoff assistance, wellness and health promotion, fitness, and disability issues. Also, depending on the service provider, training is provided for managers.

Sources: "Employee Assistance Programs," Canadian Centre for Occupational Health and Safety, accessed October 16, 2017, www.ccohs.ca/oshanswers/hsprograms/eap.html; and ComPsych, accessed October 16, 2017, www.compsych.com/canada.

It is also important to pay attention to the mental well-being of managers. Too often the focus is on the employees and not the leaders.[65] Whether leaders will be able to perform their jobs must be determined on an individual basis and by qualified professionals. Once again, the culture of an organization is important as this will provide managers with indicators of how much they are valued and what behaviours are expected from them. Business and industry lose billions of dollars every year because of substance abuse. According to the most recent study by the Canadian Centre on Substance Abuse and Addiction, the total cost is close to $40 billion yearly, or $1267 for every Canadian. In addition, legal substances such as tobacco and alcohol account for 80% of the abuse. Specifically, the following losses occur:

- $14.6 billion from alcohol abuse
- $8.2 billion from illicit drugs
- $17 billion from tobacco[66]

In confronting the problem, employers must recognize that substance addiction follows a rather predictable course, and they can take specific actions to deal with employees showing its symptoms at particular stages of its progression. Substance abuse typically begins with social drinking or drug taking that gets out of control. As the abuse progresses, the person loses control over how much to use and when. The person uses denial to avoid facing the problems created by the substance abuse and often blames others for them. The first step in helping the abuser is to awaken the person to the reality of the situation.

To identify substance abuse as early as possible, it is essential that managers monitor the performance, attendance, and behaviour of all employees regularly and systematically. A manager should carefully document evidence of declining performance, behaviour, and/or attendance and then bring the matter to the attention of the employee with evidence that the work is suffering. The employee should be assured that help will be made available without penalty. In fact, through court decisions concerning substance addiction, the courts have confirmed that substance addiction is a disability, and employers are legally obliged to deal with the problem. This means the employer can no longer terminate someone because of an abuse problem. Specifically, a manager needs to set clear expectations, be consistent, act, and follow any other health and safety regulations. Since the assessments are made solely with regard to poor job performance, attendance, or behaviour, a manager can avoid any mention of the abuse and allow such employees to seek aid as they would for any other problem. A manager cannot discipline an employee for suspicion of abusing a substance; discipline is dependent on the degree of the problem with job performance, attendance, or behaviour. Therefore, it is important for managers to recognize that any discipline, whether a verbal warning or a termination, has to be related to the job. Furthermore, as mentioned in previous chapters, there are many constraints on employers to legally ensure that the workplace is safe, secure, and free of discrimination.

In conclusion, it is important to remember the role leaders play in creating a culture that supports well-being. Building organizational processes and systems is a difficult task at the best of times. They must be able to respond well to immediate needs and help propel the organization toward a desirable future. In addition, these processes and systems must be simple to manage and maintain. When this doesn't happen, the result is too much time, resources, and attention spent on ineffective activities. In a culture that enables good health and safety in the workplace, employees will work together to maintain it, and there will be less focus on the legislated requirements.

Consider Emerging Trends 3.1 for information about what is on the horizon for workplace health and safety.

EMERGING TRENDS 3.1

1. ***Increasing attention to the culture of the organization.*** More organizations are finding that the culture of the organization can have a large impact on employee engagement and the well-being of the organization. It is no longer enough to pay attention to the legal requirements of health and safety legislation; it is also necessary to focus on how people interact. Through appropriate and acceptable workplace actions and behaviour, culture can change to support a healthy and safe work environment. Research has demonstrated that employees who are empowered and engaged take more responsibility for their own health and safety at work.

2. ***Expanding employee and family assistance programs (EAP, EFAP).*** With the increasing demands on employees and their families, EAP services have expanded to include services and resources for the entire family—particularly financial and stress counselling. Other types of addiction beyond substance abuse (i.e., gambling) are also being recognized and treated.

3. ***Increasing attention to mental health in the workplace.*** Many organizations have worked with and supported the Mental Health Commission of Canada to have open dialogue about mental health and the impact on the work environment—everything from harassment to bullying and violence. It is also recognized that treatment alone won't solve the issues and that supportive work environments need to be involved.

4. ***Ensuring that employees take time off from work.*** For the workplace to be healthy and safe, individuals need to have breaks. As such, some organizations are implementing email blackout periods when no communication to or from employees can be done. Also, some organizations are offering employees to choose when and how much vacation they take.

5. ***Ensuring that assessments are done to prevent violence in the workplace.*** As more attention is paid to preventing violence in the workplace, the Canadian government has created a special committee that has identified key areas for employers to pay attention to: organizational risk assessments, individual and customer (client) risk assessments, security assessment, and having a personal safety response team.

Sources: Carolyn All, "Women in Business: Tackling Mental Health in the Workplace," **Business Vancouver**, September 20, 2017, accessed October 17, 2017, https://www.biv.com/article/2017/9/women-business-tackling-mental-health-workplace; J. Anitha, "Determinants of Employee Engagement and Their Impact on Employee Performance," **Journal of Productivity and Performance Management** 63, no. 3 (2014): 308–323; Mental Health Commission of Canada, "Changing Directions, Changing Lives: The Mental Health Strategy for Canada," accessed October 15, 2017; Association of Workers' Compensation Boards of Canada, "Emerging Trends," accessed October 15, 2017, http://awcbc.org/?page_id=91&lcp_page0=2#lcp_instance_0; Institute for Work & Health; "IWH Research on Vulnerable Workers Leads to Tool for Measuring Risk Factors," **At Work**, 80 (Spring 2015): 3; Nadine Wentzell, "Dealing with Prescription Drug Abuse in the Workplace," **Canadian HR Reporter**, September 8, 2014, 13; and Chloe Taylor, "Workplace Violence—Breaking the Silence," **HRM Online**, May 13, 2015, accessed October 15, 2017, www.hrmonline.ca/hr-news/workplace-violence--breaking-the-silence-191279.aspx.

LEARNING OUTCOMES SUMMARY

1. Define organizational culture.
   - *Organizational culture is the collective understanding of beliefs and values that guide how employees act and behave—the personality of the organization*
2. Explain the impact of organizational culture on employees.
   - *Culture provides the compass or guide for actions and behaviours*
   - *Supportive cultures enable a positive approach to a healthy and safe work environment*
3. Discuss the relationship between an organization's culture and employee engagement.
   - *Cultures that focus on social responsibility, leadership, and trust tend to have more engaged employees*
   - *Employees that are more engaged tend to enjoy their work, have higher productivity, stay with the organization longer, and support the organization*
4. Describe the link between an organization's culture and health and safety in the workplace.
   - *Culture guides actions and behaviours*
   - *Cultures that openly demonstrate a commitment to a healthy and safe work environment will have employees who act and behave in a healthy and safe way*
5. List the key components within occupational health and safety.
   - *Adhering to legal requirements*
   - *Shared responsibility among employees, including the use of health and safety committees*
   - *Consequences for violations*
   - *Workers' compensation*
6. Explain the various ways to protect employees.
   - *Development and awareness of safety programs*
   - *Monitoring and investigating health and safety violations*
   - *Identifying health and safety hazards*
   - *Providing an ergonomically approved work environment*
   - *Attending to workplace security and preventing bullying and violence at work*
7. Describe the programs and services that promote overall health of employees.
   - *Health services*
   - *Wellness programs*
   - *Disability management*
   - *Employee assistance programs*

KEY TERMS

cyberbullying 98
disability management 104
employee assistance program (EAP) 104
employee engagement 81
industrial disease 83
occupational illness 83

occupational injury 83
organizational culture 78
Safety Data Sheet (SDS) 93
stress 99
workplace stressor 100

HRM CLOSE-UP APPLICATION

1. Kristopher Martinez notes that it is important to listen to employees. How can an organization effectively do this?
2. G Adventures believes that employees want to develop themselves personally and professionally. What types of personal development programs should the company offer to employees?

3. Are there any downsides to offering a familiarization trip to employees? If so, what could these be?

4. Given the nature of its business, what are some of the key health and safety concerns that G Adventures should address?

CRITICAL THINKING QUESTIONS

1. You've just been hired by Rim Auto Parts as the manager of its largest store in a major city. Part of your responsibility is to continue to foster an organizational culture that focuses on a healthy and safe work environment. How would you approach this, and what might you do?

2. You recently started working in a large retail store as a management trainee. You are asked to develop a series of actions to improve employee engagement. What might you consider and why?

3. You work in the medical equipment and pharmaceutical department at a local hospital. Your department is responsible for dispensing medical supplies and prescriptions to patients. There have been recent incidents in which patients have been quite vocal and threatening in their behaviour toward staff. As a consequence, you and 4 other staff have been appointed to a task group to undertake a workplace violence audit and then develop appropriate procedures. What steps might you take to do the audit, and what procedures might you use to minimize the possibility of workplace violence?

4. You recently joined a community recreational centre that hires many young workers. You are told of a growing concern about the health and safety of these employees. What would you do and why?

BUILDING YOUR SKILLS

1. On an individual basis, review Hofstede's organizational cultural model as described at **https://www.quickbase.com/blog/6-dimensions-of-organizational-culture-which -one-is-right-for-you**. The model consists of 6 dimensions or variables of culture. Which one most represents your preferred way of working and why? Share the results with your classmates.

2. Using any search engine, search on the phrase "employee engagement." Look at each of the top 10 sites. Write a 1-page summary of your results, including which site provided the best information or most interesting information on employee engagement.

3. On an individual basis, access **http://excellence.ca/en/awards/2016-cae -recipients/2016-cae-profiles/2016-caeprofile-manulife** and review the information about Manulife Financial. What 1 thing about the company impressed you? Why?

4. Access the Province of Alberta's interactive health and safety quiz at **http://work .alberta.ca/ohs-quiz/index.html**. Pick 2 to 3 categories and take the quiz. Identify which quiz was the most useful and why. Share your results with the rest of your classmates.

5. Access the following websites or your provincial workers' compensation site and list 3 items/3 points of information that surprised you from each website:
   - **https://canadasafetycouncil.org (Canada Safety Council)**
   - **www.ccohs.ca (Canadian Centre for Occupational Health and Safety)**
   - **http://awcbc.org (Association of Workers' Compensation Boards of Canada)**

6. Identify 3 companies that have violated health and safety regulations in your province. Prepare a 1-page summary describing the losses to the organizations in work (hours), the dollar penalties, and any other considerations, such as family impact.

CASE STUDY 1

Why Is Everyone So Stressed?

Lisa Harcourt sat at her desk and could not believe the feedback received from the recent employee survey. As HR director for Top Notch Storage, she has always thought that the company had highly engaged and happy workers. However, the data were presenting a very different picture.

Top Notch Storage had been in business for 10 years and had been rapidly growing. The company employed over 2000 people, ranging from office workers who did bookings, to people who were in charge of placing and retrieving items from storage, to a group of 30 managers who supervised the various employees. Lisa noted that only 400 people (or about 20%) of the workforce responded to the employee survey, but she couldn't understand why this was the case. The low response rate also caused her to wonder if the information presented was accurate and a true indication of problems at Top Notch Storage.

From the responses received, employees indicated that they received constant calls from the office (even on weekends) indicating that clients needed access to their storage units; therefore, someone had to go to the office and provide this service. Employees also indicated that they felt unsafe going to the units at the back of the facility to meet a client alone on a weekend. Also, feedback indicated that the work environment contained many safety hazards, such as improper equipment (forklifts and poor lighting), and that the software used for booking and tracking storage units was outdated and very difficult to operate. Furthermore, some employees indicated that they hadn't had a vacation in a long time and that their boss encouraged them not to take time away from work.

Lisa was concerned and wondered what the next steps should be. The response rate was so low that she wondered if any action was required.

Questions:

1. What should Lisa do next? How would you prioritize the issues that need to be addressed?
2. What are the possible consequences if Lisa chooses to ignore the results from the employee survey given the low response rate?
3. Why was the response rate so low, and how could this be improved for future surveys?
4. How would you describe the culture at Top Notch Storage? What key actions are required in order to change the culture, particularly regarding health and safety?

CASE STUDY 2

Culture and Healthy Organizations

It is easy to say that supportive and people-centred cultures typically have more engaged and productive employees. But does that mean that the organization has an environment of well-being? As with most answers, "it all depends."

Senior leaders in particular need to act and behave in a way that creates and maintains a great work environment—one that values and puts trust in its people and ensures that there is open communication at all levels. But where are such leaders found?

Sun Life Financial, a financial services company with headquarters in Toronto, takes great pride in making employee health the core of its positive work culture—one that it says makes the company so successful. Its health focus includes physical and psychological well-being for its employees and their families. In order to maintain this focus, managers are trained to recognize and be able to respond to unusual situations, to communicate effectively, and to engage employees in work activities that sustain the culture. The managers are also critical in helping employees understand the company's values and what is important to everyone. Managers are also trained to acknowledge and thank employees on a regular basis; it isn't enough to just do this occasionally.

Another well-known company with a positive culture that has become a competitive advantage is IKEA. The company is known for creating and sustaining a culture that blends employees' individual qualities with its values. The company wants its employees to be down to earth and always prepared to contribute to its positive culture, proud to work there, and be part of a team. IKEA's values of respect for both employees and customers, leading by example, being willing to change, being cost-conscious, learning from mistakes, and working together with enthusiasm were instilled by its founder, Ingvar Kamprad.

Sources: Adapted from Jim Riley, "Ikea's Distinctive and Positive Organizational Culture," May 6, 2015, accessed October 15, 2017, http://beta.tutor2u.net/business/blog/would-you-fit-into-the-organisational-culture-at-ikea; Sarah Dobson, "Health Cultures, Reduced Costs," *Canadian HR Reporter*, November 17, 2014, 6; "Employee Health Is Core to Organizational Success," *Canadian HR Reporter*, November 17, 2014, 9; and "Our Values," Ikea.com, accessed October 15, 2017, www.ikea.com/ms/en_US/the_ikea_story/working_at_ikea/our_values.html#.

Questions:

1. If you are working or recently worked, how would you describe the culture of the organization?
2. Do you think you'd fit into Ikea's culture? To assess, go to **www.ikea.com/ms/en_US/the_ikea_story/working_at_ikea/our_values.html#** and answer the 10 questions. What did you learn about yourself?

NOTES AND REFERENCES

1. Association of Workers' Compensation Boards of Canada (AWCBC), National Work Injury/Disease Statistics Program (NWISP), "2015 Number of Accepted Lost Time Claims, by Jurisdiction," accessed October 3, 2017, http://awcbc.org/?page_id=14.
2. Fisk Johnson, "SC Johnson's CEO on Doing the Right Thing, Even When It Hurts Business," *Harvard Business Review*, April 2015, 60–72.
3. Ibid.
4. Melanie Peacock, *The Human Resource Professionals Guide to Change Management* (New York: Business Expert Press, 2017).
5. For those interested, a full description of the various dimensions of culture identified by Geert Hofstede can be found at The Hofstede Centre, https://geert-hofstede.com.
6. Adam Lashinsky, "Becoming Tim Cook," *Fortune*, April 1, 2015, 60–72.
7. Ibid.
8. Clark Quinn, "Learning's Role in Innovation," Chief Learning Officer website, May 11, 2017, accessed October 5, 2017, http://www.clomedia.com/2017/05/11/learnings-role-innovation.
9. Clark Quinn, "Learning's Role in Innovation"; Diane Jermyn, "Company Culture a Magnet for Talent, Not a Frill," *The Globe and Mail*, October 15, 2014, E3; and "Canada's Best Workplaces," *The Globe and Mail*, April 10, 2015.
10. "Top 100 Canadian Employers Unveiled for 2017," *Canadian HR Reporter*, November 7, 2016, accessed October 5, 2017, https://www.hrreporter.com/article/28929-top-100-canadian-employers-unveiled-for-2017.
11. "2014 Trends in Global Employee Engagement," Aon Hewitt website, 2014, accessed September 12, 2015, http://www.aon.com/human-capital-consulting/thought-leadership/talent_mgmt/2014-trends-in-global-employee-engagement.jsp.
12. Amelia Chan, "Remove the Roadblocks to Engagement," *PeopleTalk*, Winter 2014, 14–15.
13. Association of Workers' Compensation Boards of Canada (AWCBC), National Work Injury/Disease Statistics Program (NWISP), "2015 Number of Fatalities, by Jurisdiction," accessed October 5, 2017, http://awcbc.org/?page_id=14.
14. *R. v. Wholesale Travel Group Inc.* [1991] 3 S.C.R. 154 (Supreme Court of Canada, October 24, 2991).
15. Liz Bernier, "Engaging Young Workers in a Safety Culture," *Canadian HR Reporter*, April 6, 2015, 13.
16. Government of Manitoba, "The Workplace Safety and Health Act," Manitoba.ca, accessed October 15, 2017, http://web2.gov.mb.ca/laws/statutes/ccsm/w210e.php.
17. Government of Saskatchewan, "Understanding Occupational Health and Safety in Saskatchewan," 2015.
18. Government of Canada, "Overview, *Canada Labour Code*, Part II," accessed October 15, 2017, https://www.canada.ca/en/employment-social-development/services/health-safety/reports/summary.html.
19. Gordon Hoekstra, "Liberals Introduce New Workplace Safety Laws," *Vancouver Sun*, February 12, 2015, D1.
20. Workers' Compensation Board of Nova Scotia, "Employer Return-to-Work Award Nova Scotia Liquor Corporation," May 2014, accessed October 15, 2017, http://worksafeforlife.ca/Home/Programs-Awards/Mainstay/Winners.
21. "Building and Construction 2014: Borger Group of Companies," *Canadian Occupational Safety*, October 20, 2014, accessed October 15, 2017, https://www.cos-mag.com/safety/safety-stories/4160-building-and-construction-2014-borger-group-of-companies.html.

22. Hydro One, "Putting Safety First," accessed October 5, 2017, https://www.hydroone.com/power-outages-and-safety/corporate-health-and-safety.

23. Ontario Power Generation, "Corporate Safety," accessed October 15, 2017, http://www.opg.com/about/safety/corporate-safety/Pages/corporate-safety.aspx.

24. Canadian Centre for Occupational Health and Safety, "Workplace Health and Wellness Program—Getting Started," accessed October 15, 2017, https://www.ccohs.ca/oshanswers/psychosocial/wellness_program.html.

25. Canadian Centre for Occupational Health and Safety, "WHMIS 2015 - General," accessed October 15, 2017, https://www.ccohs.ca/oshanswers/chemicals/whmis_ghs/general.html.

26. Chartered Institute of Ergonomics and Human Factors, "What Is Ergonomics?," http://www.ergonomics.org.uk/what-is-ergonomics.

27. Doni Bloomfield, "Employees Take a Stand Against Being Desk Jockeys," *Van couver Sun*, January 24, 2015, H5.

28. Ibid.

29. Government of Canada, "Definition of 'Danger'," *Canada Labour Code*, October 2014, accessed October 15, 2017, http://www.labour.gc.ca/eng/resources/ipg/062.shtml.

30. Liz Bernier, "Domestic Violence Spills into Workplace," *Canadian HR Reporter*, January 26, 2015, accessed October 15, 2017, https://www.hrreporter.com/articleview/23333-domestic-violence-spills-into-workplace.

31. Canadian Labour Congress, "Domestic Violence at Work," accessed October 15, 2017, http://canadianlabour.ca/issues-research/domestic-violence-work; and Social Sciences and Humanities Research Council of Canada, "Can Work Be Safe When Home Isn't?" 2014.

32. Canadian Centre for Occupational Health and Safety, "Violence in the Workplace," accessed October 15, 2017, https://www.ccohs.ca/oshanswers/psychosocial/violence.html.

33. Government of Canada, "Canada Occupational Health and Safety Regulations," *Justice Laws website*, accessed October 15, 2017, http://laws.justice.gc.ca/eng/regulations/sor-86-304/page-114.html.

34. Canadian Centre for Occupational Health and Safety, "OSH Answers Fact Sheets: Violence in the Workplace," accessed October 15, 2017, https://www.ccohs.ca/oshanswers/psychosocial/violence.html.

35. Ibid.

36. Liz Bernier, "From the Schoolyard to the Office," *Canadian HR Reporter*, March 23, 2015, accessed April 26, 2015, https://www.hrreporter.com/articleview/23856-from-the-schoolyard-to-the-office.

37. Erin Ellis, "Working in a Stressful Job Can Be Hard on an Employee's Head," *Vancouver Sun*, June 21, 2014, D1.

38. Yamri Taddese, "Are You Ready for a Flood of Stress-Related Compensation Claims?," *Canadian HR Reporter*, July 14, 2014, 5.

39. Sarah Shearman, "Cyberbullying in the Workplace," *The Guardian*, accessed October 16, 2017, https://www.theguardian.com/careers/2017/mar/30/cyberbullying-in-the-workplace-i-became-paranoid.

40. Brenda Bouw, "Dealing with Death at Work," *The Globe and Mail*, October 8, 2014, B15.

41. Susan Stefura, "Money Issues Top Source of Stress: Survey," *Canadian HR Reporter*, September 8, 2014, 25.

42. Ibid.

43. Liz Bernier, "High Stress, High Stakes," *Canadian HR Reporter*, April 6, 2015, 3.

44. Ibid.

45. Arianna Huffington, "How to Keep E-Mail from Ruining Your Vacation," *Harvard Business Review*, August 23, 2017, accessed October 15, 2017, https://hbr.org/2017/08/how-to-keep-email-from-ruining-your-vacation.

46. Sarah Dobson, "Manager Relationships Key to Mentally Healthy Workplace," *Canadian HR Reporter*, February 23, 2015, 2.

47. Dr. Ted Harvey and Neil Gavigan, "Minimizing Workplace Stress, Injuries and Violence in Canada: Towards a New Standard for Occupational Health and Safety," submission to the Mental Health Commission of Canada and Federal-Provincial-Territorial Ministers of Labour, September 2014.

48. Mental Health Commission of Canada, "National Standard of Canada for Psychological Health and Safety in the Workplace," accessed October 15, 2017, https://www.mentalhealthcommission.ca/English/issues/workplace/national-standard.

49. Brielle Buis, "Here's How a Flexible Work Schedule Can Reduce Stress," *The Cheat Sheet*, January 26, 2016, accessed October 15, 2017, https://www.cheatsheet.com/health-fitness/heres-how-a-flexible-work-schedule-can-reduce-stress.html/?a=viewall.

50. Melanie Peacock, *The Human Resource Professional's Guide to Change Management*.

51. Carmen Chai, "500,000 Canadians Miss Work Each Week Due to Mental Health Concerns," *Global News*, May 5, 2017, accessed October 16, 2017, https://globalnews.ca/news/3424053/500000-canadians-miss-work-each-week-due-to-mental-health-concerns.

52. The Lowe Group, "Ten Guiding Principles for Healthy Organizations," accessed April 22, 2015, http://grahamlowe.ca/documents/298/GLG%20Healthy%20Org%20Guiding%20 Principles %20rev_Mar15.pdfGraham.

53. Di Fan, Lin Cui, Mike Mingqiong Zhang, et al., "Influence of High Performance Work Systems on Employee Subjective Well-Being and Job Burnout," *The International Journal of Human Resource Management* 25, no. 7 (2014): 931–950.

54. Ibid.

55. Ron Z. Goetzel, Rachel Mosher Henke, Maryam Tabrizi, et al., "Do Workplace Health Promotion (Wellness) Programs Work?," *Journal of Occupational & Environmental Medicine* 56, no. 9 (September 2014): 927–934.

56. Brian Kreissl, "Are Employee Wellness Initiatives Effective?," *Canadian HR Reporter*, December 16, 2014, accessed October 16, 2017, https://www.hrreporter.com/blog/HR-Policies-Practices/archive/2014/12/16/are-employee-wellness-initiatives-effective.

57. Bruce Jacobs, "RIP Wellness ROI?," *BenefitsPro*, February 10, 2014, accessed October 15, 2017, https://www.benefitspro.com/2014/02/10/rip-wellness-roi/?slreturn=20180724200533.

58. Laurie Down, "The Disability Case Manager's Tool Box," *Canadian HR Reporter*, April 20, 2015, 14.

59. Nancy Gowan, "Defining 'Light Duties' in Return-to-Work Programs," *Canadian HR Reporter,* October 20, 2014, 12.

60. Ibid.

61. Ibid.

62. Carmen Chai, "500,000 Canadians Miss Work Each Week Due to Mental Health Concerns."

63. Mental Health Association in Greensboro, "Mental Health Facts," accessed October 16, 2017, http://www.mhag.org/mental-health-facts.

64. "GuidanceResources ® Services in Canada," ComPsych, accessed October 15, 2017, https://www.compsych.com/canada.

65. Nicola Middlemiss, "Too Little Attention Paid to Managers' Mental Health," *HRM Online*, April 27, 2015, accessed October 13, 2017, https://www.hrmonline.ca/hr-news/too-little-attention-paid-to-managers-mental-health-190639.aspx.

66. Canadian Centre on Substance Abuse and Addiction, "Costs of Substance Abuse in Canad," accessed October 15, 2017, http://www.ccsa.ca/Eng/topics/Costs-of-Substance-Abuse-in-Canada/Pages/default.aspx.

THIS MAKES SCENTS (PART 1)

Ashton couldn't believe it. Did Jessie really send him such a mean text? Ashton was thrilled being the co-owner of a successful business and didn't understand why Jessie would be unhappy. Where was this hostility coming from, and if she was upset, why wouldn't she come and talk to him? They had been friends for over 6 years and had gone through the ups and downs of university life together. They both shared a passion for business and were entrepreneurs. They both believed in providing high-quality products at reasonable prices. They were the best of friends! But maybe not anymore.

Background

Jessie Singh and Ashton Chan met during new student orientation day at Parkville University. They had been seated at the same table and became fast friends. The light banter quickly gave way to a deeper conversation about their hopes and dreams, including why they had each decided to attend Parkville University. As it turned out, both Jessie and Ashton were enrolled in the bachelor of business undergraduate degree program. Neither of them had decided on a major, but both expressed a keen interest in learning more about accounting and finance.

Throughout the next 5 years, Jessie and Ashton were in many of the same classes and therefore had numerous opportunities to work on group projects together. As they did, they discovered that they had a lot of personal interests in common. They liked the same grunge bands, they liked the same type of food, and they both listed Las Vegas as their favourite vacation spot. On top of this, they both had a strong work ethic and always strived to do well on group projects. "Anything but an A is not okay" was their motto, and through their hard work and dedication, both finished each year of the program on the dean's list.

Graduation was just around the corner, and neither Jessie nor Ashton had selected a major throughout their program. Nothing had really appealed to them, so they had both decided to finish with a general business degree. Therefore, when Jessie approached Ashton with the idea of starting their own business, they both thought it was a terrific chance to use all the knowledge they had acquired over the past years while being their own bosses. They agreed that "Friends to the end!" would be their new motto as they began the process of starting their new company.

The Company

Many of Jessie's friends had commented that the price of high-quality perfumes was ridiculous. Body sprays were a cheaper option but certainly didn't provide the same quality or aroma as perfume. Therefore, when Jessie read an article about a company in Mexico that specialized in making knock-off perfume, she was intrigued. Market research showed that the products were of high quality and that consumers really couldn't tell the difference between a brand name and the mock fragrance. Jessie and Ashton quickly took this product idea and put together a very financially solid and viable business plan, being careful not to infringe on trademarks and to clearly market their products as "mock" perfume and not counterfeits. A small store space in a busy strip mall was leased, profit margins on products were calculated, expenses (including a reasonable annual salary for both Jessie and Ashton, who would split the shifts) were accounted for, and a bank loan was easily secured to get the company off the ground.

The company, *This Makes Scents*, opened for business on March 1, and in just 8 months, business had increased beyond initial projections. Sales were growing, and it was often difficult to keep enough inventory on hand. Both Jessie and Ashton agreed that this was a terrific problem to have as they rarely had items sitting on the shelf for long periods of time. The growth in business had also meant that 4 new employees were hired to help with the various shifts. As such, the store was now open 7 days a week, from 9:00 a.m. to 4:00 p.m. on each day.

The Current Situation

Jessie was furious! When she started the company with Ashton, she assumed that they would be partners and share in the responsibilities. However, she was responsible for all the product ordering and inventory tracking, and to make matters worse, all the complaints from their 4 employees and all the problems seemed to be directed at her. This wasn't the type of environment she wanted to work in, and the stress was taking a toll on her physical and mental health.

The strip mall where the store was located just sent out notification that the stores had to be open from 9:00 a.m. to 6:00 p.m. each day or leases would not be renewed. One employee told Jessie that he could not work past 4:00 p.m. on any day as he had to pick up his children from daycare. He muttered something about requiring accommodation and expected the company to follow the law. He also suggested that an employee handbook be developed so that clear policies were available to everyone. Another employee sent Jessie an email stating that she wanted clarification on overtime payments and statutory holidays. Specifically, this employee wanted to know why the store wasn't closed on the last Canada Day and demanded explanations regarding scheduling and payments. "I used to like working here, but now the hours are a grind, and I don't have any input into when I work." A third employee was upset because he wasn't getting enough overtime and felt the distribution of extra shifts was unfair. He wanted to be able to bank his extra time and then take time off at a later date. He also wanted to book 2 weeks of vacation, had asked Ashton about this, and had been told "no." As such, he was threatening to sue the company and told Jessie, "You better get your partner in line as employees are entitled to 2 weeks of vacation according to the law. I don't care that I didn't receive a written offer letter when I started this job, but I know my rights! I thought this would be a neat place to work, but the customers are mean and the owners are worse." The fourth employee had sent Jessie an email noting that a customer dropped a bottle of perfume, and while cleaning up the broken glass, this employee got a bad cut and later had to receive 5 stitches at the local emergency room. Jessie wondered what she was supposed to do with this information. Also, Ashton had just sent her an email indicating that they should think about hiring more people. "What, now I have to do this as well?" thought Jessie.

Jessie was exhausted. "When the company first opened, I had fun working with Ashton, and it was rewarding to watch the sales expand. Now I dread coming to work and am anxious every time I open my emails. I can't take this anymore!" Jessie grabbed her phone and sent the following text to Ashton: "It is time that you took responsibility for this company and its problems. You are a horrible partner, and I'm sorry that we went into business together. In fact, it **doesn't make 'scents'** to me anymore. So there!"

Questions:

1. What issues, in order of priority, should Jessie and Ashton address?
2. In addition to the problems identified by employees, what other actions should Jessie and Ashton take? Why?
3. What can be done to change the culture within the company?
4. Why are all the employees going to Jessie with their problems? How can a more equitable partnership and sharing of responsibilities be established?
5. What can Jessie and Ashton do to enhance the communication between the two of them?
6. What can Jessie and Ashton do to enhance communication to employees?

*Note: This case, including all subsequent parts throughout the text, does not represent a real-life situation or real people. Any resemblance to actual circumstances is purely coincidental. As such, the scenario and details should not be used as an example for a business model or business plan.

4 Defining, Analyzing, and Designing the Work

LEARNING OUTCOMES

After studying this chapter, you should be able to

1 Explain the manager's and the employee's role in defining and designing work.

2 Discuss the relationship between job analysis and HRM processes.

3 Explain the relationship between job analysis and a job description.

4 Define and describe the sections in a job description.

5 Describe the uses of information gained from job analysis.

6 Explain the relationship of job design to employee contributions.

7 Discuss the different types of work designs to increase employee contribution.

OUTLINE

HRM CLOSE-UP

"Narrowing the gap between the executives and the front line provided the employees with a sense that management does really care, and that's very important to them and also to us."

IN 2006, the government of Ontario decided there needed to be a better way to provide the people of the province with access to government services and information. The result was ServiceOntario, a division of the Ministry of Government and Consumer Services that streamlines not just its own services but also those of most other ministries in an efficient one-stop-shopping experience.

Today, ServiceOntario is one of the largest government customer service operations in North America, with more than 80 in-person service centres, over 200 privately operated service provider centres, a robust website, and telephone call centres located in Toronto, Oshawa, Thunder Bay, and Kingston. In one recent year, ServiceOntario handled more than 35 million transactions, and it now represents more than a dozen ministries assisting people with everything from health cards and driver's licences to acquiring government publications.

Mary Ben Hamoud is director, Central Region Contact Centre Services, for ServiceOntario. Out of a total ServiceOntario staff of more than 2000 people, the call centres within her responsibility account for approximately 220 employees, all of whom must undergo intensive training before handling inquiries.

"With so much falling under the ServiceOntario umbrella, our contact centres must not only be knowledgeable on the products and services that we provide to the broader public, but we're also mandated to be consistently fair and respectful," Ben Hamoud says. "We also must remain current with new legislation and government policies, and this makes our environment very dynamic, both at the senior management level, where requirements are constantly reviewed and assessed, and at the front line, where the information is disseminated."

Prior to joining the government, Mary Ben Hamoud had more than 15 years of experience managing various state-of-the-art call centres, including those of one of the country's largest automotive manufacturers and a leading telecommunications company. ServiceOntario was her first venture into the public sector, however.

"As a public-sector service, I quickly learned that our service principles commit us to providing everyone with equitable and superior services and a clear explanation of our decisions, all while maintaining the utmost security of the public's private information," Ben Hamoud explains. "All of this must be done in the most efficient, cost-effective, and time-sensitive manner as we know that when people contact us, they need accurate answers or assistance quickly."

Meeting the needs of Ontarians and the requirements of the various ministries with their unique and multiple service offerings was a significant challenge for those who established ServiceOntario and its overall brand awareness. But that wasn't the only difficulty encountered.

"Aside from defining the work, we had to consider how to create our own culture while respecting and maintaining the culture that was coming to us from our partner ministries," Ben Hamoud says. "I think that was one of the biggest challenges."

Used by permission of Mary Ben Hamoud

Mary Ben Hamoud, Director, Central Region Contact Centre Services, ServiceOntario

As ServiceOntario continues to evolve, there have been other changes, including a recent effort to promote more direct contact between upper management, the front-line staff, and, ultimately, the customers.

"Our deputy minister was very much interested in what was happening on the front line," Ben Hamoud explains. "In an organization as large as ServiceOntario, the challenge was how best to do that while not overloading anyone."

The chosen outcome was to restructure a layer of management. That redistribution of the work not only succeeded in immediately giving senior management and executives a better grasp of how things were at the front line, but it also achieved other valuable benefits.

"The redistribution exercise provided an opportunity to really get connected to the front line, and that experience allowed us to be more engaged with staff," Ben Hamoud says. "I think it was one of the most brilliant things that happened in the organization. I unfortunately didn't know too many of my front-line staff before because of that layer of management, but now I know almost all of my agents by first name."

"I'm intimately aware and involved with their success and their performance. That feels really good, and it also provides the employees with a sense that management does really care, and that's very important to them and also to us."

INTRODUCTION

As Mary Ben Hamoud from ServiceOntario noted, work needs to be designed in a manner that enhances customer service, promotes communication, and supports the appropriate distribution of tasks. This being so, organizations are transforming themselves in an attempt to become more effective. Companies such as Wild Rose Brewery, a Calgary-based company specializing in craft beer, are paying attention to the structure and culture of their organizations. Wild Rose Brewery practises what it preaches by promoting team work and encouraging employees to recognize coworkers' accomplishments. The company focuses on the way employees work and the culture that this creates and was recognized as one of Canada's top small and medium employers in 2017.[1]

As organizations reshape themselves, managers want employees to operate more independently and have flexibility to meet customer demands. To do this, managers require that decisions be made by the people who are closest to the information and are directly involved in the product or service delivered. The objective is to develop jobs and basic work units adaptable enough to thrive in a world of high-speed change.

This chapter discusses how jobs can be analyzed and also designed to best contribute to the objectives of the organization while satisfying the needs of the employees who perform them. You will learn about the role of the manager and the employee in defining and designing work and the terminology used to describe how jobs are defined. Several innovative job design and employee contribution techniques that increase job satisfaction and employee empowerment while improving organizational performance are discussed. Teamwork and the characteristics of successful teams are highlighted. The chapter concludes with a brief discussion on the future design of organizational work.

DEFINING WORK

Job
A group of related activities and duties

Position
Specific duties and responsibilities performed by only 1 employee

Work
Tasks or activities that need to be completed

Organizations are complex systems composed of numerous and varied tasks. A **job** consists of a group of related activities and duties. Ideally, the duties of a job should consist of natural units of work that are similar and related. They should be clear and distinct from those of other jobs to minimize misunderstanding and conflict among employees and to enable employees to recognize what is expected of them. For some jobs, several employees may be required, each of whom will occupy a separate position. A **position** consists of the specific duties and responsibilities performed by only 1 employee. In a city library, for example, 4 employees (4 positions) may be involved in reference work, but all of them have only 1 job (reference librarian).

In many ways, the words "job" and "position" are relics of the industrial age. As organizations need to be more flexible and adaptable and utilize their people resources well for a competitive advantage, managers also need to think in terms of "work." By thinking of **work**, employers have more flexibility to define what needs to be done and when and to change employee assignments on a short-term basis.

In Chapter 1, you were introduced to the concept of "competencies"—characteristics or behaviours necessary for successful work performance in an organization. Competencies become very important when focusing on "work" compared to a job. For example, individuals seeking one of the levels within the certified human resource professional (CHRP) designation in Ontario or seeking a chartered professional in human resources (CPHR) designation within all other Canadian provinces must display professional competencies that are organized into functional areas of knowledge and enabling competencies. Proficiency levels for each knowledge area and competency are outlined as well. Instead of organizations focusing on job descriptions, companies will use "work profiles" or "work agreements" to describe the work to be done. Furthermore, the concept of "roles" is also linked to competencies. Your **role** is the part you play in the organization, and it will have certain expected behaviours. For example, your role as a customer service representative includes active listening as an expected behaviour. You will continue to see more references to work and work processes, project management, tasks, and task analysis than to "job."

Whether thinking in terms of "job" or "work," a manager needs to describe what tasks need to be done and in what order, the skills a person needs to successfully perform the work requirements, and the role a person plays in the company. This is the essence of organizational success. For all HRM processes, you will need to have this type of information.

Role
The part played by an employee within an organization and the associated expected behaviours

THE MANAGER'S AND THE EMPLOYEE'S ROLE IN DEFINING WORK

The manager is the primary individual who determines what tasks and activities need to be performed, and in what order, to reach the company's goals or objectives. Therefore, it is critical that the manager understand what steps need to be implemented to design jobs in order to maximize organizational performance. Although the manager will take an active role in determining what skills and abilities are needed to successfully perform the work, often an employee (the **job incumbent**, the person doing the work) will be asked for information regarding the job and its requirements. The person performing the job is often able to contribute information regarding the work that only they would know. Furthermore, through job analysis, the manager will play an integral role in developing and/or writing a job description and will rely upon input from the job incumbent to ensure that information regarding the job is accurately collected and documented.

LO1
Explain the manager's and the employee's role in defining and designing work.

Job incumbent
The employee hired to do a job

JOB ANALYSIS

Job analysis is referred to as the cornerstone of HRM because the information it collects informs and supports so many HRM processes. **Job analysis** is the process of obtaining information about jobs (or work) by determining what the duties, tasks, or activities of those jobs are and the necessary skills, knowledge, training, and abilities to perform the work successfully. The procedure involves undertaking a systematic approach to gathering specific job information, including the work activities, worker attributes, and work context.[2] This being the case, when job information is accurate, it will be easier to recruit, select, manage performance, plan for training and development and health and safety issues, and compensate an individual doing this work. The ultimate purpose of job analysis is to improve organizational performance and productivity. Figure 4.1 illustrates how job analysis is done and what the information is used for.

Job analysis is concerned with objective and verifiable information about the requirements of a job (compared to "job design," which reflects subjective opinions about the ideal requirements of the job). Job analysis is not done in a vacuum: it is important that the organization's goals and strategies be known and understood. Without the organizational context or an understanding of the organization as a whole, the requirements identified may not reflect foreseeable future requirements. A proactive strategic approach would link the jobs to the organization's performance.[3]

Job analysis is typically undertaken by trained HR people; however, a manager with good analytical abilities and writing skills can also do it. The HR professional can provide assistance to the manager in gathering the relevant information by ensuring that appropriate questions are asked and that the job is not "inflated" (made to sound more difficult

LO2
Discuss the relationship between job analysis and HRM processes.

Job analysis
Process of obtaining information about jobs by determining the duties, tasks, or activities and the skills, knowledge, and abilities associated with the jobs

FIGURE 4.1 The Process of Job Analysis

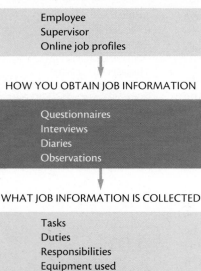

WHERE YOU GET JOB INFORMATION

Employee
Supervisor
Online job profiles

HOW YOU OBTAIN JOB INFORMATION

Questionnaires
Interviews
Diaries
Observations

WHAT JOB INFORMATION IS COLLECTED

Tasks
Duties
Responsibilities
Equipment used
Skills required
Knowledge required
Experience required
Working conditions
Effort
Job context
Performance standards

WHERE THE INFORMATION GOES

Written Job Description, Including:
Job title
Summary of job
Job duties and responsibilities
Job specification (skills, knowledge, abilities)
Standards of performance

HOW INFORMATION IS USED

Recruitment
Selection
Performance management
Training and development
Health and safety
Compensation

LO3

Explain the relationship between job analysis and a job description.

or important than it really is). Therefore, as previously noted, the employee performing the work also has a critical part to play to ensure that accurate information about the job is collected. It is also valuable to have the person doing the work (and the manager or team leader) review the data gathered to ensure that it is accurate and complete. Online resources providing job profiles are another source of information. For example, the Government of Canada provides a resource of National Occupational Classification (NOC) codes that lists detailed information regarding various jobs. Regardless of the source of information, prior to any job analysis being conducted, it is critical that the manager and employees have received transparent communication to inform them of how the analysis will be conducted and what the information will be used for.

Performing Job Analysis

Job data can be collected in a range of ways. Individual interviews may be conducted (asking questions such as "What duties do you perform every day?" or "What tools do you use to complete these duties?") with employees performing the jobs, or groups of employees who perform the same job may be interviewed to collect information. Alternatively, the incumbent may fill out a questionnaire or be observed in order to better understand the work required. Or the incumbent may be asked to keep a diary or log of work performed. In larger organizations, a uniform approach is frequently used, such as asking people to fill out an electronic or hard-copy questionnaire that requests a list of work activities. Review Toolkit 4.1 for examples of questions that might be posed either in an interview or on a questionnaire.

When deciding which method of job analysis should be used, the time and money spent versus the quality of information collected should be taken into consideration. Efficiency and effectiveness should be balanced. It is also important that the manager review the information collected in order to ensure accuracy. Ethics in HRM 4.1 describes what can happen if a job is inflated.

JOB DESCRIPTIONS

Once all the information on a particular job has been collected, it is organized into a **job description**—a written document. This description includes the types of duties or responsibilities and the skills, knowledge, and abilities or competencies (job specifications; see below) needed to successfully perform the work. Since no standard format applies to job descriptions, they tend to vary in appearance and content from one organization to another. However, typical headings are the following:

I. *Job Title.* Provides an indication of the general nature of the job, for example, "night manager," "salesperson," "lab assistant," or "team leader."

II. *Reports To.* Listing of the position that this job is accountable to.

III. *Date.* Date that the description was written. Indicates currency of information.

IV. *Written By and Approved By.* Names and titles of individuals involved in writing the document. Provides points of contact for future questions or clarification.

V. *Summary.* Two or three sentences describing the overall purpose of the job. Answers the question, "Why does this job exist?"

VI. *Duties and Responsibilities.* Individual statements, usually listed in order of importance, of the key duties and responsibilities. You would expect to see between 10 and 15 statements.

VII. *Job Specification.* The required knowledge, skills, and abilities.

VIII. *Performance Standards.* A prioritized list outlining several expected results of the job.

TOOLKIT 4.1 JOB ANALYSIS QUESTIONS

Here are some questions a person might ask when conducting a job analysis:

1. In 3 to 4 brief sentences, describe the basic purpose of your position. Do it in a way that answers the question, "Why does my position exist?"
2. What are the most important responsibilities of your position, and how much time do you spend on each of these? Please list each main responsibility in order of importance. Start each statement with an action verb, such as "provides," "determines," "verifies."
3. What are the key tasks for each of the responsibilities? What percentage of your time each month do you spend on each task?
4. What are the physical surroundings and/or hazards of your position? (This can include travel, exposure, danger, and environmental risks.)
5. Describe the mental and physical efforts you expend in performing your work. For example, do you have long periods of intense concentration? Is there a lot of routine? Is the position physically demanding? Please include the frequency of the effort.
6. What are the knowledge and basic skills required to successfully fulfill the responsibilities?
7. Describe 2 or 3 of the more difficult problems you must solve to get your job done. Include situations that are a constant challenge and situations that require judgment and time to consider alternative solutions before problems can be resolved.

The specific skills, knowledge, and abilities required to successfully perform the job become the **job specifications**. Skills relevant to a job can include education and experience, specialized training, and specific abilities, such as manual dexterity. If there are any physical demands, such as walking long distances or reaching high shelves, these would also be mentioned. Many organizations now view job specifications as including "employability" skills and knowledge, such as problem-solving abilities.

Toolkit 4.2 provides an example of a job description for the manager of retail operations at a sports arena. Note that this example includes specific HR responsibilities, as noted in the first section under "People Management." It includes both duties and specifications and should satisfy most of the job information needs of managers while providing information for other critical HRM processes, as discussed later in this chapter.

LO4

Define and describe the sections in a job description.

Job description
A document that lists the tasks, duties, and responsibilities of a job to be performed along with the skills, knowledge, and abilities or competencies needed to successfully perform the work

ETHICS IN HRM 4.1 INFLATING THE JOB

At some point in your working life, you will be asked to describe your job, perhaps when being interviewed by a job analyst or by answering questions on a form. Most employees have a reasonable expectation that their answers will affect their lives in significant ways. The information obtained may be used to reclassify the job to either a higher or a lower pay level. Most employees believe that standards of performance may change, and the employer will expect them to work faster or to do more, although that is not the goal of job analysis. As a result of these beliefs and expectations, employees have a vested interest in "inflating" their job descriptions by making the job sound very important and very

difficult. Thus, night clerks in hotels become "auditors," and receptionists become "administrators." Job inflation might reflect an employee's sincere belief in the significance of their contribution, or it may be an attempt to lobby for higher pay.

CRITICAL THINKING QUESTIONS:
1. Do you believe employees intentionally inflate their jobs, or do they genuinely believe their jobs to be significant, as per their descriptions?
2. As a manager, how can you ensure that job information is correct if the employee and you view the job differently?

TOOLKIT 4.2   **SAMPLE JOB DESCRIPTION**

Plumage Games
Job: Manager, Retail Operations
Reports To: Director, Retail Operations
Date: February 1, 2019
Written By: Hank Rovers, HR Analyst
Approved By: Helen Richards, HR Director & Lola Mercer, Director Retail Operations

SUMMARY

The manager, retail operations, is responsible for all aspects of retail operations for game nights and events. The manager ensures that the store, booths, and kiosks are staffed with well-trained sales and service professionals and are visually attractive, with appropriate merchandise for the customer environment. Although staff development, sales, and service are primary focus areas, administrative activities, such as payroll and scheduling, are also part of this role.

ESSENTIAL DUTIES AND RESPONSIBILITIES

People Management

1. Recruit, train, motivate, and develop a professional and knowledgeable part-time and on-call service and sales workforce.
2. Coach and communicate with employees in a fair and consistent manner (e.g., mentoring sessions, performance evaluations).
3. Work closely with senior retail management and human resources regarding disciplinary and other sensitive employee issues.
4. Identify and implement employee recognition and incentive programs.
5. Ensure that staff are trained in all key areas of the business.

Business Management

1. Ensure that selling areas are open for business on time and are clean and visually attractive.
2. Identify opportunities for increasing revenue.
3. Create sales and promotional programs.
4. Work with marketing staff regarding event details, such as expected attendance levels, merchandise deals, internal and external event contacts.
5. Produce sales reports.

Administration

1. Schedule staff in a transparent, fair, and consistent manner
2. Input payroll information into a payroll time-management system
3. Monitor payroll against budget and sales
4. Develop and maintain an employee manual

REQUIRED EXPERIENCE AND QUALIFICATIONS (JOB SPECIFICATIONS)

1. Four to 6 years' retail experience, with at least 2 years' management experience.
2. Degree or diploma in business administration or related field.
3. Excellent leadership skills with the ability to coach, mentor, and motivate a sales service team.
4. Excellent communication, interpersonal, and problem-solving skills.
5. A solid understanding of the business and customer environment.
6. Must be able to identify and implement new business opportunities and promotions.
7. Flexible and adaptable.
8. Computer-literate, with a working knowledge of MS Word, MS Excel, point-of-sale software, and electronic mail systems.
9. Must be able to work evenings and weekends.

STANDARDS OF PERFORMANCE

1. Meets on a weekly basis with all staff to review sales results.
2. Orients new staff during the first shift on customer-service requirements.
3. Meets or exceeds monthly sales targets.
4. Submits sales data within 24 hours of each event.
5. Trains staff on any new procedures within 1 week of hiring.
6. Keeps customer satisfaction levels at 80% or above.

Problems with Job Descriptions

Although many managers consider job descriptions a valuable tool for performing HRM activities, several problems are frequently associated with these documents, including the following:

1. They can become out of date as work requirements quickly evolve and change.
2. They do not contain standards of performance, which are essential for selecting, training, evaluating, and rewarding jobholders.
3. They do not adequately capture the complete requirements and complexity within a job. Vague terms may be used, thereby not providing adequate information.
4. They may not address expected behaviours and can be the basis for conflict, including union grievances.

Writing Clear and Specific Job Descriptions

In writing a job description, it is essential to use statements that are concise, direct, and simply worded. Unnecessary words or phrases should be eliminated. Typically, the sentences that describe job duties begin with a present-tense and action-oriented verb, with the implied subject of the sentence being the employee performing the job. An example for an accounting clerk for a small company might read, "Deposits cheques on a daily basis" or "Prepares month-end financial statements by the 10th of the following month." (Note that these 2 statements include performance standards.) The term "occasionally" is used to describe those duties that are performed once in a while. The term "may" is used in connection with those duties performed by only some workers on the job. Other examples of action-oriented, present-tense verbs are "coordinates," "handles," "researches," "conducts," "generates," and "evaluates."

Legal Considerations for Job Descriptions

Even when put in writing, job descriptions and specifications can still be vague. To the alarm of many employers, however, today's legal environment has created what might be called an "age of specifics." Human rights legislation requires that the specific performance requirements of a job be based on valid job-related criteria. Decisions that involve either job applicants or employees and that are based on criteria that are either vague or not job related are increasingly being successfully challenged. Managers of small businesses, in which employees may perform many different job tasks, have to be particularly concerned about writing specific job descriptions. In a very small business, such as Aquinox Pharmaceuticals in British Columbia, the focus is not so much on writing a job description but on identifying the core activities and then describing the attributes needed to be successful.[4]

When preparing job descriptions, managers must be aware of human rights legislation. In addition to adhering to legal requirements, consideration of appropriate and acceptable ways to describe jobs is often given. Ethics in HRM 4.2 highlights how the Toronto School Board addressed this issue.

Written job descriptions must match the requirements of the job. Also, position descriptions may need to be altered to meet the standard of "reasonable accommodation." Reasonable accommodation is used most frequently to match religious or disability needs, although any prohibited ground for discrimination under human rights legislation would have to be considered for reasonable accommodation.

The 2010 case *Fiona Johnstone v. Canada Border Services* made it clear that reasonable accommodation for family-status reasons is valid.[5] In a judicial review in 2014, the Federal Court upheld this decision, reinforcing the requirement to fully consider the requirements for, and what constitutes grounds for, reasonable accommodation.[6]

Job specifications
Statement of the needed knowledge, skills, and abilities of the person who is to perform the position

Based upon legal requirements, specific job requirements must be based on valid job-related criteria, such as airplane pilots having a certain level of eyesight.

Job descriptions written to match the needs for reasonable accommodation reduce the risk of discrimination. The goal is to match and accommodate human capabilities to job requirements. For example, if the job requires the jobholder to read extremely fine print, to climb ladders, or to memorize stock codes, these physical and mental requirements should be stated within the job description. Read HRM and the Law 4.1 to understand more about the legal implications of inappropriate job requirements.

ETHICS IN HRM 4.2   DO JOB TITLES REALLY MATTER?

Canada's largest school board is phasing out the word "chief" from senior staff job titles, saying the move is being made out of respect for Indigenous peoples.

The Toronto District School Board's decision raised eyebrows in some quarters, but a spokesperson said the action was taken due to recommendations made by the Truth and Reconciliation Commission. Although the word "chief" may not have originated as an Indigenous word, it may be used as a slur or demeaning way to describe Indigenous people; therefore, this title is being removed as a proactive measure. New titles, such as "manager" and "executive officer," will be used in job descriptions going forward.

CRITICAL THINKING QUESTIONS:

1. Do you agree with the Toronto School Board's decision to remove the word "chief" from job titles? Why or why not?
2. Do the Toronto School Board's actions have implications for other organizations? What are the consequences, if any, for sports teams that continue to use this word?

Source: Nicole Thompson, "TDSB to Remove 'Chief' from Job Titles Out of Respect for Indigenous People," *The Globe and Mail*, October 11, 2017, accessed October 23, 2017, https://beta.theglobeandmail.com/news/toronto/tdsb-to-remove-chief-from-job-titles-out-of-respect-for-indigenous-people/article36540732/?ref=http://www.theglobeandmail.com&.

HRM AND **THE LAW** 4.1   JOB DESCRIPTION TENSIONS

As the following examples show, tensions may arise in the workplace due to disability or family-related issues that place limitations on an employee's ability to perform or availability for work.

Dr. Kelly was a resident in family medicine at the University of British Columbia (UBC) in 2016. He suffered from attention-deficit/hyperactivity disorder (ADHD) and a non-verbal learning disorder (NVLD). Despite the school's attempts to alter the program to meet his needs, it was decided that he lacked the skills to complete the program and could not be further accommodated without undue hardship to the school. This led to Dr. Kelly's removal from the program. Dr. Kelly initiated proceedings against UBC, alleging discrimination in employment in breach of the province's *Human Rights Code*. The tribunal found that Dr. Kelly's disabilities were a factor in the decision to terminate his participation in the program and that UBC breached its duty to accommodate those disabilities to the point of undue hardship. In addition to reinstatement in the program and payment of lost wages, the tribunal awarded Dr. Kelly $75,000 for the injury to his "dignity, feelings, and self-respect," the highest-ever award for injury to dignity in British Columbia.

As another example, in 2014, a case was decided in favour of an employee (Denise Seeley) seeking accommodation (due to family status and childcare responsibilities) from her employer, Canadian National Railway (CNR). CNR requested that Seeley temporarily relocate from Alberta to Vancouver to cover a staff shortage. CNR's request posed a problem for Ms. Seeley as she was not able to arrange for adequate childcare during her absence. Initially, Ms. Seeley requested an extension of time to relocate to Vancouver and then eventually requested that she be exempted from having to relocate to Vancouver due to her childcare obligations. Although CNR granted Ms. Seeley an extension, she was eventually dismissed for failing to relocate to Vancouver. Ms. Seeley alleged that the CNR had discriminated against her on the basis of her family status because her requests for accommodation were not granted even though other employees with medical conditions had been accommodated in the past.

CRITICAL THINKING QUESTIONS:

1. Do you think these decisions were appropriate? Provide and explain reasons for your answer.
2. Is it fair to other employees (i.e., single or childless people) if their coworkers are given accommodations due to family status, potentially resulting in more work and responsibilities for those not asking for accommodations?

Sources: Carman J. Overholt and Victoria Petrenko, "The Growing Cost to Employers for Failing to Accommodate Disabled Employees," *Overholt Law*, April 7, 2017, accessed October 28, 2017, http://www.mondaq.com/canada/x/584046/employment+litigation+tribunals/The+Growing+Cost+to+Employers+for+Failing+to+Accommodate+Disabled+Employees; *Kelly v. University of British Columbia* (No. 4), 2013 BCHRT 302 (CanLII), accessed October 28, 2017, https://www.canlii.org/en/bc/bchrt/doc/2013/2013bchrt302/2013bchrt302.html; and *Canadian National Railway Company v. Seeley*, 2014 FCA 111 (CanLII), accessed November 23, 2014, http://canlii.ca/t/g6sdq.

USES OF INFORMATION FROM JOB ANALYSIS

As stated earlier in the chapter, a variety of HRM processes make use of the output of job analysis. Therefore, job analysis provides critical information that is required for all other HRM processes as follows: recruitment, selection, performance management, training and development, health and safety, and compensation. These are discussed below.

LO5

Describe the uses of information gained from job analysis.

Recruitment

Recruitment is the process of locating and encouraging potential applicants to apply for job openings. Because job specifications establish the qualifications required of applicants for a job opening, they serve an essential role in the recruiting function as they define "who" will be successful doing the job and provide a basis for attracting qualified applicants. From a legal perspective, it is critical that the requirements listed for the job reflect necessary components. For example, requirements that labourers have a high-school diploma, that firefighters be at least 6 feet tall, and that truck drivers be male discriminate against members of certain designated groups, many of whom have been excluded from these jobs in the past. Further details are discussed in Chapter 5.

Selection

After you have located individuals interested in working for you, you must now hire someone. Selection is the process of choosing the individual who has the relevant qualifications and who can best perform the job. Therefore, a manager will use the information collected through job analysis as a basis to compare the skills and abilities of each applicant. Given changes to our society and the various employment laws, employers must be able to show that the specifications used in selecting employees for a particular job relate specifically to the duties of that job. Because managers usually help define the specifications, they must ensure that the job requirements recruit the best candidate and do not discriminate. Managers must be careful to ensure that they do not hire employees on the basis of "individualized" job requirements that satisfy personal whims but bear little relation to successful job performance. Further details about how to properly select new employees are discussed in Chapter 5.

Performance Management

The job requirements obtained from the job analysis provide the criteria for evaluating the performance of the job incumbent. These individual performance standards are linked to the business performance goals and strategies incorporated in the performance management systems, as discussed in Chapter 7. Evaluating an employee's ongoing performance is a major responsibility of the manager. From the employer's standpoint, written job descriptions can serve as a basis for minimizing the misunderstandings that occur between managers and their subordinates concerning job requirements. They also establish management's right to

michaeljung/Shutterstock.com

Linking the organization's goals to information gathered from the people who do the work is important when analyzing jobs.

take corrective action when the duties covered by the job description are not fulfilled as required by performance standards. The results of the performance evaluation may reveal whether certain requirements, or **standards of performance** listed on a job description, for a job continue to be valid. For example, a job may require an employee to word-process at the rate of 30 words per minute (wpm), but the performance review may determine that 60 wpm is necessary. If the criteria used to evaluate employee performance are vague and not job related, employers may find themselves being charged with unfair discrimination.

> **Standards of performance**
> Set out the expected results of the job

Training and Development

Any discrepancies between the knowledge, skills, and abilities (referred to as KSAs) demonstrated by a jobholder and the requirements obtained through job analysis provide clues to training needs. Also, if the job specification section contains competencies (such as "focuses on customer" or "demonstrates excellent customer service skills"), these competencies could provide the basis for training. As managers are often responsible for training the new employee, accurate job specifications and descriptions are essential. Also, as career development is often a concern for both the manager and the employee, the formal qualification requirements set forth in higher-level jobs serve to indicate how much more training and development are needed for employees to advance to those jobs. This topic is discussed further in Chapter 6.

Health and Safety

The job analysis identifies the health and safety related physical and mental capabilities required to perform the job and the work environment conditions in which the job is performed. The job analysis describes the existing and potential safety and health hazards associated with workplace injuries or illnesses, which are particularly important in redesigning jobs to improve employee wellness and eliminate or reduce exposure to hazards.

An example of how job analysis addresses health and safety requirements occurred in 2011 when the Air Canada pilots' case of discrimination due to the mandatory retirement age of 60 was dismissed. The Canadian Human Rights Tribunal determined that extra staffing, scheduling, and health and safety requirements would constitute an undue hardship for the airline and that mandatory retirement of pilots at age 60 is a "bona fide occupational requirement" (BFOR). However, this continues to be contentious issue. In 2017, the Canadian Human Rights Tribunal revisited the issue of whether Air Canada was wrong to force some pilots to retire at age 60. Due to lengthy court proceedings and deliberations, legal decisions and conversations regarding this issue are expected to continue well into the future.[7]

Compensation

Job analysis and the resulting job descriptions are often used for compensation purposes. In determining the rate at which a job is paid, the relative worth of the job is one of the most important factors. This worth (*pay rate*) is based on what the job demands of an employee in skill, effort, and responsibility and on the conditions and hazards under which the work is performed. Systems that measure the worth of jobs are called *job evaluation systems* (see Chapter 8). Job descriptions and job specifications are used as sources of information in evaluating jobs. Often the HR department designs these job evaluation systems. Ultimately, however, it is the manager who makes pay decisions based on performance relative to the standards of performance that have been established.

Job Analysis in a Changing Environment

The traditional approach to job analysis assumes a static job environment within a large organization in which jobs remain relatively stable even though incumbents who might hold these jobs perform them differently. Here jobs can be meaningfully defined in terms of tasks, duties, processes, and behaviours necessary for job success. Unfortunately, this assumption discounts technological advances, which are often so accelerated that jobs as defined today may be obsolete tomorrow. Furthermore, downsizing, the adoption of teams, the demands of small organizations, or the need to respond to global change can alter the nature of jobs and their requirements. For organizations using "virtual" jobs or "virtual" teams, there is a shift away from independently performed jobs with narrow job specifications and descriptions to a focus on the relationships among workers and their work environments.[8] In a dynamic environment where job demands rapidly change, job analysis data can quickly become inaccurate, and outdated information can hinder an organization's ability to adapt to change. Job information must be regularly reviewed and adjusted as needs change.

For organizations that operate in a fast-moving environment, several novel approaches to job analysis may accommodate needed change.

First, managers might adopt a future-oriented or strategically oriented approach to job analysis in which managers have a clear view of how jobs should be restructured to meet future organizational requirements.[9]

Second, organizations might adopt a competency-based approach in which emphasis is put on characteristics or behaviours of successful performers rather than on standard job duties and tasks and so on. As described in Chapter 1, these competencies would be customized to the organization's culture and strategy and include the tailoring of broad competencies such as communication skills, decision-making ability, project management, conflict resolution skills, adaptability, and self-motivation. Competencies are developed using a top-down rather than a bottom-up approach, with the goal of integrating organizational and human resources management objectives, strategies, and systems.[10]

Neither of the above 2 approaches is without concerns, including the ability of managers to predict future job needs accurately and the need for job analysis to comply with human rights legislation.

A third and perhaps more practical method might be to have a "living job description" or a "role description" that is updated as the nature of the work changes. The manager and the employee would then ensure that substantial changes in duties, responsibilities, skills,

Dmitry Kalinovsky/Shutterstock.com

Job analysis needs to keep up with the changing requirements within a job.

and other work characteristics are documented on an ongoing basis. One type of living job or role description is a behavioural one that describes how the work is to be done and what results are expected. Often these descriptions also address typical issues and problems that may occur and the results that can be expected in dealing with the issues. By doing this, the manager and the employee can also establish standards of performance. These descriptive and evaluative job descriptions can be linked to the organization's online performance management system, allowing for continuous updating by all users.

As previously discussed, determining the work to be done involves an approach that links the organization's future goals to information gathered from the people who do and supervise the work.

In order to have "the right people with the right skills at the right time," contemporary managers must take the time to think about the work and the skills required to do the work. Organizational success depends on capable people. Managers want to be sure that they have the correct number of employees and the correct skills mix. Clearly identifying the work duties and the skills needed to perform the work can help managers achieve that objective. It is important to remember that the purpose of identifying who does what is to bring all the talent together in order to capitalize on synergy among employees and achieve the company's goals.[11] This leads to considerations of how work should be designed in order to most effectively achieve results while keeping employees motivated.

DESIGNING THE JOB

An outgrowth of job analysis, **job design** is the process of defining and arranging tasks, roles, and other processes to achieve employee goals and organizational effectiveness. For example, organizations engaged in self-managed teams, continuous improvement, or process reengineering may revamp their jobs in order to eliminate unnecessary job tasks or find better ways of performing work. Job design should facilitate the achievement of organizational objectives and at the same time recognize the capabilities and needs of those who are to perform the job. Job design is concerned with appropriately altering and modifying the job so that there is a good person–job fit and a good person–organization fit. Improving the quality of work life facilitates positive worker attitudes and behaviours, leading to organizational effectiveness. Historically, the focus has been on analyzing and defining specific jobs within physical "brick-and-mortar" structures. Today, with rapid advances in communication technology, the meaning of the word "job" is in flux, with workers working in more distributed, unconstrained work environments.[12] These fundamental changes in the relationships between workers, the type of work they do, how they perform their work, when the work is scheduled, and the organizational environment are increasing the use of non-standard employment forms and non-traditional strategies for job design. Job design strategies can include the following:

- job rotation (in which people move from one job to another to learn new tasks)
- job enlargement (in which a person's job expands in the types of tasks he or she is expected to perform)
- job enrichment (in which a person's job takes on higher-order responsibilities)
- job crafting (in which a person chooses how to complete work in a way that is most engaging and stimulating)
- leadership teams (in which a leader takes on multiple responsibilities and activities rather than 1 well-defined functional leadership role)

As Figure 4.2 illustrates, job design is a combination of 3 basic considerations: (1) the overall purpose of the job and how it contributes to an organization's success; (2) ergonomic requirements, including workers' mental and physical requirements or restrictions; and (3) employees' attitudes and behaviours that can impact their success in the job.

LO6

Explain the relationship of job design to employee contributions.

Job design
Process of defining and organizing tasks, roles, and other processes to achieve employee goals and organizational effectiveness

FIGURE 4.2 Considerations in Job Design

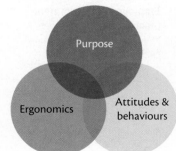

Job Characteristics

Job design was further advanced when behavioural scientists focused on various job dimensions that would simultaneously improve the efficiency of organizations and the job satisfaction of employees. The **job characteristics model** is an approach to job design that recognizes the link between motivational factors and components of the job to achieve improved work performance and job satisfaction.

There are 5 job characteristics in this model that should be considered when designing a job:

1. *Skill variety:* the variety of different activities, which require a number of different skills and talents.
2. *Task identity:* completion of a whole and identifiable piece of work, that is, doing a job from beginning to end with a concrete outcome.
3. *Task significance:* the impact on the lives or work of other people, whether in the immediate organization or in the external environment.
4. *Autonomy:* the amount of independence, freedom, and discretion.
5. *Feedback:* comments and clear information provided based upon output and accomplishments.[13]

The job characteristics model seems to work best when certain conditions are met. One of these is that employees must have the psychological desire for the autonomy, variety, responsibility, and challenge of enriched jobs. When this personal characteristic is absent, employees may resist the job redesign effort. Job redesign efforts almost always fail when employees lack the physical or mental skills, abilities, or education needed to perform the job. Forcing enriched jobs on individuals who lack these traits can lead to their frustration. The advances in information technology resulting in increased flexible work arrangements have expanded the scope of these characteristics to employees doing front-line work, thereby showing the ongoing importance of the job characteristics model in today's workplaces.[14]

DESIGNING WORK FOR ENHANCED CONTRIBUTIONS

Although a variety of techniques have been developed to involve employees more fully in their organizations, all these techniques have 2 characteristics in common: enhancing collaboration and increasing synergy. By increasing the degree of collaboration in the work environment, these techniques can improve work processes and organizational decision making. Also, by increasing synergy, they underline the adage that the contributions of 2 or more employees are greater than the sum of their individual efforts. Greater involvement in their jobs and/or working in a group setting strengthen employee commitment to an organization's goals, increase employee acceptance of decisions, and encourage a cooperative approach to workplace tasks. Two collaborative techniques are discussed below: employee empowerment and employee teams.

Employee Empowerment

Employee empowerment is a technique for involving employees in their work through a process of inclusion. Empowerment has been defined as pushing down decision-making responsibility to those close to internal and external customers and is therefore a very intentional form of job design. *Job crafting* is 1 example of empowerment, by which workers do not wait for management initiatives but customize their work to meet both their own needs and the organization's goals.[15] Empowerment and job crafting strategies are more fluid in nature, a departure from other job design methods that are generally top-down and fixed in nature. Interviews with employees in both a small service organization and a large manufacturing organization found that senior employees felt more constrained than front-line employees in their ability to craft their jobs even though they had greater autonomy and power.[16]

Job characteristics model
An approach to job design that recognizes the link between motivational factors and components of the job to achieve improved work performance and job satisfaction

LO7
Discuss the different types of work designs to increase employee contribution.

Employee empowerment
Granting employees power to initiate change, thereby encouraging them to take charge of what they do

Although defining empowerment can become the first step to achieving it, in order for empowerment to grow and thrive, organizations must encourage these conditions:

1. *Ownership*. Employees must be encouraged to be responsible for their work tasks.
2. *Risk taking*. The organization should be receptive to new ideas and encourage people to take reasonable risks at reasonable costs. Creativity and innovation are encouraged.
3. *Information sharing*. Employees must be able to determine what information they need to do their jobs and be given this when it is requested.
4. *Responsibility*. Employees should be held accountable for their achievements and their behaviour toward others.

Additionally, employee empowerment succeeds when the culture of the organization is open and receptive to change. As discussed in Chapter 3, an organization's culture is created largely through the philosophies of senior managers and their leadership traits and behaviours. In an empowered organization, effective leadership is exemplified by managers who are honest, caring, and receptive to new ideas and who treat employees with dignity and respect and as partners in organizational success. Furthermore, for empowerment to work, it must be aligned directly with the strategy of the organization and individual accountability throughout the enterprise.

However, some organizations will have difficulty promoting empowerment as managers are sometimes unwilling to give up power or give employees the authority to make decisions. Toolkit 4.3 provides some additional examples of employee empowerment.

TOOLKIT 4.3 EXAMPLES OF EMPLOYEE EMPOWERMENT

Many types of organizations have successfully empowered their employees. Empowered employees have improved product and service quality, reduced costs, increased productivity, and modified or, in some cases, designed products. The following companies (under the category of the "Top 39 Large Companies") were recognized as Canada's Best Employers in 2017:

PURDYS CHOCOLATIER: MAKE INNOVATION A CONTEST

Like many firms, Vancouver-based Purdys Chocolatier puts a high value on its employees' suggestions to make it better, but the confectioner ups the ante by making innovation a competition. Through a program called "Make us better ideas," Purdys awards points to warehouse and production employees—redeemable for everything from coffee cards to paid days off—based on the impact of their suggestions. Once an idea is acted on, the firm measures the significance of the result. The more beneficial it is to the company, the more points the employee receives. The perks make people more inclined to think of the big picture and to speak up when they get a great idea. Best of all, the whole process gives employees a clear indicator of the importance of their work to the company as a whole.

COSSETTE COMMUNICATION INC.: GOING BEYOND

Headquartered in Québec City, Cossette Communication is a fully integrated marketing communications agency with a leading role in Canada. The company provides a full and integrated range of innovative communications services to some of the most prestigious brands in the world, including McDonald's, General Motors, Aeroplan, and Via Rail. With a desire to "go beyond," the company encourages employees to be innovative and thrives due to a culture of creativity.

BIRCHWOOD AUTOMOTIVE GROUP: NO PLACE FOR MEDIOCRITY

Over the past 50 years, Birchwood Automotive Group has grown to become Winnipeg's largest network of automotive retailers, with 17 franchised operations. The company is committed to enhancing the community in which it operates and believes in continuous improvement. Employees are expected to show personal responsibility and accountability while demonstrating respect for the uniqueness of every person they encounter.

Sources: "Canada's Best Employers 2017: The Top 39 Large Companies," accessed October 23, 2017, http://www.canadianbusiness.com/lists-and-rankings/best-jobs/best-employers-2017-top-large-companies/; Purdys Chocolatier, accessed October 23, 2017, https://www.purdys.com/?affiliate_id=3897&click_id=2112115741; Cossette Communication, "Working at Cossette Communication Overview," accessed October 23, 2017, https://www.glassdoor.ca/Overview/Working-at-Cossette-Communication-EI_IE18509.11,33.htm; and Birchwood Automotive Group, accessed October 23, 2017, https://www.birchwood.ca/dealership/about.htm.

EMPLOYEE TEAMS

Employee teams
An employee-contributions technique in which work functions are structured for groups rather than for individuals and team members are given discretion in matters traditionally considered management prerogatives, such as process improvements, product or service development, and individual work assignments

During the past decade, perhaps one of the more radical changes to how work is done has been the introduction of **employee teams**. These are a logical outgrowth of employee involvement and the philosophy of empowerment. Although many definitions of teams exist, an employee team may be defined as a group of employees working toward a common purpose, whose members have complementary skills, whose work is mutually dependent, and who have discretion over tasks performed. Furthermore, a team seeks to make members of the work group share responsibility for the group's performance. Inherent in the concept of employee teams is that employees, not managers, are in the best position to contribute to workplace improvements.

Two issues important in the design of work for teams are (1) the appropriate use of teams and (2) the types of teams.[17] Job tasks that require specialized individual expertise may be inappropriate for teams. Teams should be used when the work is amenable to teamwork and is adequately structured and supported by both managers and employees.[18] Transitioning to distributed workplaces requires more effort on the part of managers to ensure that practices and processes capitalize on team communication, collaboration, and collective knowledge. Teams can operate in a variety of structures, each with different strategic purposes or functional activities. Figure 4.3 describes 6 different team forms.

Virtual team
A team with widely dispersed members linked through computer and telecommunications technology

One form, the **virtual team**, also called a *distributed team*, consists of dispersed team members who need to meet regularly but do not require high levels of interdependency among members. Communication technology is integrated so that workers are able to constantly consult each other. Managers must establish common communication processes and practices that work effectively as well as create a sense of collaborative communication.

FIGURE 4.3 Work Design and Types of Teams

Surgical teams require coordinated interaction among all members in real time with the responsibility and accountability for outcomes lying primarily with 1 person. Appropriate for work that requires a high level of individual insight, expertise, and/or creativity but is too large or complex to be handled by any 1 member working alone.

Coaching groups are individual members who do not depend upon what the others do; the output of a group is simply the aggregation of members' individual contributions. Appropriate only when there is little need for interdependent work by group members.

Face-to-face teams have members with complementary expertise, experience, and perspectives who work together interdependently in real time to generate a product for which they are collectively accountable. Appropriate for a wide variety of tasks for which creating a high-quality product requires coordinated contributions in real time.

Virtual, or distributed, teams use communication technologies to exchange observations, ideas, and reactions at times of their own choosing. Teams are collectively responsible and accountable for work products and are useful when it is difficult for team members to meet regularly and the work does not require high levels of interdependence.

Leadership teams include all significant leaders who share responsibility for leading an entire organization or a large organizational unit. This kind of team addresses the expanding pace and scope of leadership.

Sand dune teams are dynamic and fluid social systems that change in number and kind of members as business requirements and opportunities change. Well suited for fast-changing environments.

Source: Adapted with permission of John Wiley & Sons Ltd., from Greg R. Oldham and J. Richard Hackman, "Not What It Was and Not What It Will Be: The Future of Job Design Research," *Journal of Organizational Behavior* 31 (2010): 463–479; permission conveyed through Copyright Clearance Center, Inc.

Virtual teams provide these organizations with access to previously unavailable diverse and collective expertise and knowledge and may be especially useful in bringing geographically dispersed employee talent together.[19] More organizations are forming leadership teams to address the challenges faced by those in leadership roles. A cross-national study of senior leadership teams suggests that particular attention needs to be given to the design, dynamics, and performance of these senior-level teams.[20]

Characteristics of Effective Teams

Regardless of the type of team, the following should occur in order for the group to operate effectively:

- clear goals, which the team understands and is committed to, have been set
- team members support and trust one another
- communication is open, honest, and respectful
- team has a strong sense of cohesion while respecting individual opinions and differences
- effective decision making and conflict resolution occur
- ongoing evaluation of team performance occurs, and unproductive or dysfunctional behaviour is corrected[21]

Therefore, in adopting the work team concept, organizations must address several issues that could present obstacles to effective team function. For example, new team members must be retrained to work outside their primary functional areas, and compensation systems must be constructed to reward individuals for team accomplishments. Another consideration is that work teams alter the traditional manager–employee relationship. Managers often find it hard to adapt to the role of leader and sometimes feel threatened by the growing power of the team and the need to hand over authority. Furthermore, some employees may have difficulty adapting to a role that includes traditional managerial responsibilities. As team members become capable of carrying out processes, such as strategic planning, that were previously restricted to higher levels of management, managers must be prepared to design work that utilizes their new-found expertise. In designing work teams, special attention needs to be given to the more fluid relationships and communication among workers and their work activities.[22]

Role of Management

Leadership issues arise at several levels when employees are involved in decision making. At both the executive and management levels, there needs to be clear support for employee involvement and teams as changes may be required in processes and actions to support this new way of doing business. For many years, managers have played the role of decision maker. Thus, organizations will need to redefine the role of managers when employees are participating more in the operations of the company. For example, Mike Moore Construction works closely with its owners, subtrades, and partners to ensure that everyone from management to labourer is involved in workplace decisions and practices.[23] Decisions within the company are based on a process of inclusion.

Therefore, in order to capitalize on employee empowerment and employee teams, it is critical that the organization be clear on what is expected of managers and the skills necessary to be successful. Furthermore, it needs to carefully consider its overall design and structure. Research has demonstrated that the organizational structure and context (size, centralization, and hierarchical levels) are key determinants of behaviours in the organization.[24] If the organization wants a more committed and engaged workforce, then the way it is structured—who reports to whom and who makes decisions—will greatly influence the effectiveness of the leaders.

AT WORK WITH HRM 4.1 — BEST EMPLOYERS

Would you like to work for one of Canada's #1 companies? Most of us would answer yes.

Earls Restaurants Ltd. was included in the listing of Canada's Best Employers in 2017. What led to this honour? Some of the reasons were as follows:

- Restaurant employees receive at least 24 hours of training every year; the company's Red Seal apprenticeship program pays the full cost of knives, books, and technical culinary training.
- All workers can participate in leadership or personal development courses.

- Company awards include food-and-wine tours to destinations such as Japan, Bordeaux in France, and California's Napa Valley.

CRITICAL THINKING QUESTIONS:

1. What would your current or past company need to do to go out of its way to meet the needs of the employees and be considered a top employer?
2. Given what you know or have heard about the restaurant business, would you want to work for Earls?

Sources: "50 Best Employers in Canada, 2017," *The Globe and Mail*, March 26, 2017, accessed October 23, 2017, https://beta.theglobeandmail.com/report-on-business/rob-magazine/50-best-employers-in-canada/article4297262/?ref=http://www.theglobeandmail.com&#table; and "Canada's Best Employers 2015: The Top 50 Large Companies," accessed November 22, 2014, www.canadianbusiness.com/lists-and-rankings/best-jobs/2015-best-employers-top-50.

Organizations have found that the success of employee involvement depends on first changing the roles of managers and team leaders. With fewer layers of management and a focus on team-based organizations, the role of managers is substantially different. Managers are expected to be open to suggestions, actively support 2-way communication, and encourage risk taking. Rather than autocratically imposing their demands on employees and closely watching to make sure that the workers comply, managers share responsibility for decision making with employees. Typically, "team leader" has replaced the term "manager."

In a growing number of cases, leadership is shared among team members. Some organizations rotate team leaders at various stages in team development. Alternatively, different individuals can assume functional leadership roles when their particular expertise is needed most.

A clear example of the role senior managers play in creating an involved organization is described in At Work with HRM 4.1.

FUTURE DESIGN OF WORK

There have been changes in jobs and work contexts over the past few decades. Globalization, technology, and demographics have given rise to new questions about how, where, when, and what work is done. Organizations have been responding by replacing traditional (permanent full-time, full-year) jobs with a range of non-traditional employment forms and flexible arrangements such as these:

- contract or freelance work
- e-work
- temporary work
- job or work sharing
- telework
- compressed workweek
- mobile work
- home-based work

- flex-time or flex-year
- time-limited projects
- partnership arrangements

The increasing use and convergence of social, mobile, and cloud computing technologies are creating unique ways to work—ways so new that their definitions have yet to be agreed upon. These contingent employment options are associated with improved work–life balance and increased job insecurity. Organizations are therefore being challenged to provide meaningful work to engage and motivate a diverse group of employees who structure their work in differing ways.[25] Future job design will shift its focus away from traditional jobs, in which individuals worked independently within bounded organizational structures, toward the more dynamic fluid relationships among workers and their work activities that utilize networked communication technology. Consequently, future job design practices will require more attention to job crafting, thereby allowing employees to utilize their strongest competencies and skills. This, in turn, will enhance employees' motivation while still achieving the organization's desired goals. In addition, the broader organizational context and culture (e.g., technology, work flow, decentralization, and control systems); distributed teams; the social and relational aspects and attributes of work; diversity; and the linking of competencies, work, and organizational strategy must continue to be considered when designing work.[26] For information about what might be in the future for job or work design, read Emerging Trends 4.1.

EMERGING TRENDS 4.1

1. ***Diversity and generational differences.*** Managers will be continually challenged by the changing nature and mix of their workers. Millennials are entering the workplace in significant numbers, and research suggests that they hold different work values and motivations from the Gen X and baby boom generations. For example, social values (building interpersonal relationships) and intrinsic values (having an interesting, results-oriented job) were rated lower by millennials than by boomers. Differing value systems have implications for how jobs are designed, what will motivate different groups of employees, and how they can best work together. Most of the Canadian baby boom generation is continuing to work part-time or is returning to work during their retirement years. Baby boomers are working in a wide range of employment forms and for diverse reasons; therefore, job design must be considered to entice them to continue participating in the workforce. In designing work, caution needs to be taken to ensure that generations are not viewed too narrowly as homogeneous groups and that recognition is given to the broader aspects of human diversity.

2. ***Increasing use of competencies.*** As work becomes more fluid, organizations will incorporate the core competencies needed for success in each job. These competencies will be the skills, knowledge, abilities, and other behaviours (KSAOs) that lead to the organization's desired results. Competencies are developed top-down by senior managers to ensure that they are strategic, future oriented, and linked to the organization's strategy. An attempt is made to distinguish the KSAOs of top performers while keeping employees motivated within their jobs.

3. ***Artificial intelligence.*** Organizations will need to find ways to incorporate automation and robotics in meaningful, strategic ways. The ability to embrace new technologies while successfully mitigating their harmful side effects will create added prosperity and opportunities for meaningful work.

4. ***The gig economy, employee classification, and job crafting.*** With decreased full-time work available to some people, employees are taking on a number of temporary or part-time jobs. As such, attention must be given to ensure that people are given opportunities to craft meaningful work and provided with

continued

ample access to different jobs. Furthermore, organizations must continue to examine how they classify workers to ensure that independent contractors are not really employees under legislative requirements.

As well, when designing work, attention will need to be given to social and collaborative aspects within changing workplace contexts (i.e., where and when employees work).

Sources: Adapted from Linda Nazareth, "The Gig Economy Is Here – and We Aren't Ready," *The Globe and Mail*, October 20, 2017, accessed October 23, 2017, https://beta.theglobeandmail.com/report-on-business/rob-commentary/the-gig-economy-is-here-and-we-arent-ready/article36678505/?ref=http://www.theglobeandmail.com&; Jason Spencer, "How to Telecommute without Isolating Office Employees," *Brampton Guardian*, September 12, 2017, accessed October 26, 2017, https://www.bramptonguardian.com/news-story/7549597-how-to-telecommute-without-isolating-office-employees; Susan Ward, "Independent Contractor vs Employee: Which One Are You?," *The Balance*, September 7, 2017, accessed October 23, 2017, https://www.thebalance.com/are-you-a-contractor-or-an-employee-2948639; Drew Hasselback, "Automation Will Have Significant Impact On Jobs, But Don't Fear the Robots Says Bank of Canada's Wilkins," *Financial Post*, April 16, 2017, accessed October 25, 2017, http://business.financialpost.com/news/economy/automation-will-have-significant-impact-on-almost-half-of-all-jobs-within-20-years-bank-of-canada-warns; Armina Ligaya, "Most Older Workers Who Leave Career Jobs Return to Work within a Decade: Statistics Canada," *Financial Post*, January 28, 2014, accessed October 23, 2017, http://business.financialpost.com/personal-finance/retirement/rrsp/most-older-workers-who-leave-career-jobs-return-to-work-within-a-decade-statistics-canada; Dan Schawbel, "10 Workplace Trends You'll See In 2017," *Forbes*, November 1, 2016, accessed October 23, 2017, https://www.forbes.com/sites/danschawbel/2016/11/01/workplace-trends-2017/#47f190cd56bd; Jean Twenge, Stacy Campbell, Brian Hoffman, and Charles Lance, "Generational Differences in Work Values: Leisure and Extrinsic Values," *Journal of Management* 36 (2010): 1117–1142; Peter Bamberger and Samuel Bacharach, "Predicting Retirement upon Eligibility: An Embeddedness Perspective," *Human Resource Management* 53, no. 1 (2014): 1–22; David Harrison and Stephen Humphrey, "Designing for Diversity or Diversity for Design? Tasks, Interdependence, and Within-Unit Differences at Work," *Journal of Organizational Behavior* 31 (2010): 328–337; Paul Sparrow and Lilian Otaye-Ebede, "Lean Management and HR Function Capability: The Role of HR Architecture and the Location of Intellectual Capital," *International Journal of Human Resource Management* 25, no. 21 (2014): 2892–2910; Brian Becker and Mark Huselid, "SHRM and Job Design: Narrowing the Divide," *Journal of Organizational Behavior* 31 (2010): 379–388; Adam Grant et al., "Putting Job Design in Context: Introduction to the Special Issue," *Journal of Organizational Behavior* 31 (2010): 145–157; and Elizabeth Redmont, "Competency Models at Work: The Value of Perceived Relevance and Fair Rewards for Employee Outcomes," *Human Resource Management* 52, no. 5 (2013): 771–792.

LEARNING OUTCOMES SUMMARY

1. Explain the manager's and the employee's role in defining and designing work.
   - *The manager is the primary individual who determines what work needs to be done*
   - *The manager takes an active role in determining what skills and abilities are needed to successfully perform the work*
   - *As the person performing the work, an employee contributes knowledge and information regarding the elements within a specific job*
2. Discuss the relationship between job analysis and HRM processes.
   - *The requirements of a job are central to, and inform, all HRM processes*
3. Explain the relationship between job analysis and a job description.
   - *Job analysis is the process of obtaining information about jobs (or work) by determining what the duties, tasks, or activities are*
   - *The outcome is a job description—a written document listing the types of duties, responsibilities, and the skills (job specifications) needed to successfully perform the work*
4. Define and describe the sections in a job description.
   - *Company name*
   - *Position title—indication of what the duties might be or the nature of the work*
   - *Date document is completed*
   - *Summary of job—2 or 3 sentences describing the overall purpose of the job*
   - *List of duties and responsibilities—statements of the key duties and responsibilities*
   - *Job specifications—statement of the needed knowledge, skills, and abilities or competencies of the person who is to perform the work*
   - *Standards of performance*
5. Describe the uses of information gained from job analysis.
   - *Job specifications establish the qualifications required of applicants for a job opening and play an essential role in the recruiting function*
   - *Information on the job description is used as a basis for comparing the skills and abilities of each applicant in the selection process*

- *Managers must be careful to ensure that they do not hire employees on the basis of "individualized" job requirements that satisfy personal whims but bear little relation to successful job performance. Performance management should align with the job requirements*
- *Requirements contained in the job description and specifications provide clues to training needs*
- *Job requirements highlight health and safety issues and necessities*
- *The pay of a job is based on what the job demands in skill, effort, and responsibility and on the conditions and hazards under which the work is performed*

6. Explain the relationship of job design to employee contributions.
   - *Job design is the process of defining and arranging tasks, roles, and other processes to achieve both organizational and employee goals*
   - *Job design strives to incorporate the motivational and behavioural needs of employees, which leads to improved performance*
   - *Job design can enhance or take away from the employee's ability to participate in decision making*

7. Discuss the different types of work designs to increase employee contribution.
   - *Employee empowerment is a method of involving employees in their work and encouraging them to take charge of what they do*
   - *Employee teams are groups of employees who assume a greater role in the production or service process*
   - *Non-traditional employment forms and arrangements are addressing employee and employer needs for work flexibility*

KEY TERMS

employee empowerment 128	job incumbent 117
employee teams 130	job specifications 119
job 116	position 116
job analysis 117	role 117
job characteristics model 128	standards of performance 125
job description 118	virtual team 130
job design 127	work 116

HRM CLOSE-UP APPLICATION

1. What job information would you collect when conducting a job analysis for call centre employees at ServiceOntario?
2. What could be some potential problems when developing written job descriptions for call centre employees?
3. How could ServiceOntario ensure that call centre employees' jobs are designed according to the job characteristics model?
4. Would working in teams be effective for call centre employees at ServiceOntario? Why or why not?
5. Could call centre employees work from home? What potential problems could this cause to the design of their work?

CRITICAL THINKING QUESTIONS

1. Assume that you are a new manager in a hotel and you have been asked to prepare a job description for room attendants. What would you include as 5 key duties, and what would you list as 3 key skills? Would you involve the current room attendant in the preparation of the job description? Why?

2. If a job incumbent inflates their work when submitting information for job analysis, why should this person be included in the process? Why shouldn't the information for job analysis only be collected from the job incumbent's manager?
3. What are some of the pitfalls of employee teams? How can these be managed or lessened?
4. How is the increasingly mobile workforce changing how, when, where, and what work is done? What opportunities and challenges face managers and mobile workers?

BUILDING YOUR SKILLS

1. In groups of 4 or 5, identify the job specifications (knowledge, skills, and abilities) for the position of college or university instructor. (You will have approximately 20 minutes to complete the exercise.) Each group will then present its findings to the rest of the class. Discuss and compare the requirements and develop a single list of job specifications.
2. Use the job analysis questions in Toolkit 4.1 to interview someone, perhaps another student who is working, about their job. What did you discover about the job analysis interview process and the information required?
3. For a job you currently have (or for a past job), list 3 new or different things that your employer might do to redesign your job to make you feel more empowered. How would you convince your employer to implement your ideas?
4. Access and use current research about a non-standard work option (e.g., telework, mobile work, flexible schedules) that you would like your current or future employer to consider. Write a 1-page proposal to your employer that illustrates the benefits of your chosen employment form (e.g., teleworkers are more satisfied than office workers).

CASE STUDY 1

If Only I Had Known

A few months ago, Maria Turks, manager of client care at Willowpark Retirement Centre, was asked to review a job description for *caregiver* as 25 people in this job report directly to her. Maria was busy, so she quickly skimmed the document, which had been written by the HR director, and thought it was fine. However, Maria quickly learned that when the duties and responsibilities listed in the job description do not reflect current job content, disagreements and other problems can arise.

Jane Freemont joined Willowpark 3 months ago, and during her recent probationary performance review, Maria had to convey to Jane that her work as a caregiver was not meeting expectations. Jane was not properly cleaning the rooms she was assigned, was not ensuring that the residents were arriving for meals in a timely manner, and was not checking on her assigned residents at least 4 times per day as required.

Jane's response to Maria's feedback was not what she had anticipated. Instead of welcoming the comments and wanting to improve, Jane lashed out and said none of these functions were noted in the job description she had been given on her first day of work. Furthermore, Jane indicated that she had been "told a very different story" regarding what her work would entail and that she felt micro-managed and constantly watched. Jane found this to be demeaning and far beneath her capabilities. Jane also stated that she had left a good job to work at Willowpark and never should have done this as she was "sold a bill of goods." "If only I had known, I would never have accepted this job."

Maria could relate. "If only I had known, I would have been more careful when reviewing and approving the job descriptions."

Questions:

1. Why are the job descriptions for caregivers inaccurate? Going forward, what should be done differently to ensure that these documents are correct?
2. What could be done to enhance the job of caregiver so that it isn't as "demeaning" based upon Jane's feedback?
3. Does Jane have any recourse if she was provided with an inaccurate job description? If so, what actions could she take?

CASE STUDY 2

What Should a New Manager Do?

Jack Deppster arrived for his first day of work as store manager at Buzz, one of the largest and most popular retail stores at a local mall. Buzz, operating various locations throughout Canada, sold clothing and accessories targeted to people between 18 and 24 years old. Jack, who had a business administration degree, was seen as a motivated and self-directed person who got results. On the basis of his strong GPA, volunteer experience, and previous retail experience working as a salesperson for a grocery store, the management group at Buzz expected a strong performance from him. Jack impressed the HR hiring manager and district manager during the interview process, and they believed he would have no problem in achieving the target of increasing store sales by 5% over the next 6 months. Jack also believed he could achieve this goal and was excited about the opportunity to take on his first management role.

However, the honeymoon did not even last a few hours. During the morning, Jack noticed quite a bit of chaos in the store. Some of the cashiers did not know how to operate the registers; others seemed to be circumventing established processes and cashing out customers out in unique ways. When Jack questioned them about this, they said they had discovered different, easier methods to utilize the technology that allowed them to spend more time talking to customers as they paid and that this was their favourite part of the job.

However, the sales staff did not seem interested in helping customers and seemed very bored. Jack noticed that many of the salespeople would spend time talking to each other, even when it was apparent that customers were in need of assistance. The situation in the inventory room was no better. The shelves were a mess, and items were pulled out of boxes by various employees in a random fashion whenever store displays began to look empty. The employees told Jack it was his job as store manager to order and track inventory, so the storage room was his responsibility. However, Jack felt all employees should be involved in inventory management.

To further complicate matters, Jack knew that Buzz would soon be implementing new technology, which would impact the cash registers and the inventory tracking and ordering system. Jack was confused and disappointed. This was not what he had anticipated!

Questions:

1. How could Jack use the job characteristics model to redesign the job of salespeople in the store?
2. Explain how Jack might utilize employee teams to increase employee empowerment.
3. Should Jack allow some cashiers to determine how they cash out customers? Is this a good idea given that new technology will soon be implemented? What are the consequences of allowing, or not allowing, this to continue?

NOTES AND REFERENCES

1. Richard Yerema and Kristina Leung, "Recognized as One of Canada's Top Small & Medium Employers (2017)," Mediacorp Canada Inc., April 24, 2017, accessed October 28, 2017, http://content.eluta.ca/top-employer-wild-rose-brewery.

2. Juan I. Sanchez and Edward L. Levine, "The Rise and Fall of Job Analysis and the Future of Work Analysis," *Annual Review of Psychology* 63 (November 30, 2011).

3. Greg R. Oldham and Richard R. Hackman, "Not What It Was and Not What It Will Be: The Future of Job Design Research," *Journal of Organizational Behavior* 31 (2010): 463–479.

4. Jason Robertson (Director, Business Development, Aquinox), interview with the author, October 2017.

5. Customs and Immigration Union, "Duty to Accommodate – Johnstone Decision," accessed October 28, 2017, https://www.ciu-sdi.ca/representation/duty-accommodate-johnstone-decision.

6. *Canada (Attorney General) v. Johnstone*, 2014 FCA 110 (Federal Court of Appeal, May 2, 2014).

7. "Canadian Human Rights Tribunal to Revisit Air Canada Retirement Age Issue," *National Post*, September 15, 2017, accessed March 22, 2018, http://nationalpost.com/pmn/news-pmn/canada-news-pmn/canadian-human-rights-tribunal-to-revisit-air-canada-retirement-age-issue.

8. Oldham and Hackman, "Not What It Was and Not What It Will Be."

9. Ibid.

10. Michael A. Campion et al., "Doing Competencies Well: Best Practices in Competency Modeling," *Personnel Psychology* 64, no. 1 (Spring 2011): 225–262.

11. M. Armstrong, *Armstrong's Handbook of Human Resource Management Practice* (Philadelphia: Kogan Page, 2014).

12. Oldham and Hackman, "Not What It Was and Not What It Will Be."

13. Martin, "Understanding the Job Characteristics Model (Including Job Enrichment)," *Cleverism*, March 13, 2017, accessed October 23, 2017, https://www.cleverism.com/job-characteristics-model.

14. Oldham and Hackman, "Not What It Was and Not What It Will Be."

15. Madeleine L. van Hooff and Edwin van Hooft, "Boredom at Work: Proximal and Distal Consequences of Affective Work-Related Boredom," *Journal of Occupational Health Psychology* 19, no. 3 (2014): 348–359.

16. Justin M. Berg, Amy Wrzesniewski, and Jane E. Dutton, "Perceiving and Responding to Challenges in Job Crafting at Different Ranks," *Journal of Organizational Behavior* 31, nos. 2–3 (February 2010): 158–186.

17. Oldham and Hackman, "Not What It Was and Not What It Will Be."

18. Maria Paasivaara and Casper Lassenius, "Communities of Practice in a Large Distributed Agile Software Development Organization," *Information & Software Technology* 56, no. 12 (2014): 1556–1577.

19. Rikkel Duus and Mudithal Cooray, "Together We Innovate: Cross-Cultural Teamwork Through Virtual Platforms," *Journal of Marketing Education* 36, no. 3 (2014): 244–257.

20. Oldham and Hackman, "Not What It Was and Not What It Will Be."

21. Susan M. Heathfield, "10 Tips for Better Teamwork," *The Balance*, August 1, 2017, accessed October 23, 2017, https://www.thebalance.com/tips-for-better-teamwork-1919225.

22. Oldham and Hackman, "Not What It Was and Not What It Will Be."

23. "Moore Wins 2011 OGCA Doug Chalmers Award," *Daily Commercial News*, September 26, 2011.

24. Frederick P. Morgeson, Erich C. Dierdorff, and Jillian L. Hmurovic, "Work Design In Situ: Understanding the Role of Occupational and Organizational Context," *Journal of Organizational Behavior 31*, nos. 2–3 (February 2010): 351–360.

25. "Effective Engagement Strategies for an Increasingly Dispersed Workforce," *Public Manager* 43, no. 3 (2014): 62–65.

26. Oldham and Hackman, "Not What It Was and Not What It Will Be."

5 Planning For, Recruiting, and Selecting Employees

LEARNING OUTCOMES

After studying this chapter, you should be able to

1 Describe the relationship between HR planning, recruitment, and selection.

2 Discuss the steps in human resource planning.

3 Compare the advantages and disadvantages of recruiting from within the organization.

4 Compare the advantages and disadvantages of external recruitment.

5 Describe the typical steps in the selection process.

6 Identify the various sources of information used for selection decisions.

7 Discuss the different methods and types of questions for conducting an employment interview.

8 Illustrate the value of different types of employment tests.

9 Outline key considerations when making a hiring decision.

OUTLINE

HRM CLOSE-UP

"When I find someone with the right personality..., I'm very emotional and say, 'Oh, I love this person; let's just hire them!' While my second-in-command...is very good with her HR hat on making sure they have the right skills for us to have in the company...."

WHAT HAPPENS when you can't expand your business until you've added a key new member to your workforce, but you can't add that key new member until you've expanded your business? It's a bit of a catch-22, one that Susan Webb faces quite often.

Webb is the president and cofounder of VoX International, a marketing company based in Toronto that represents travel and tourism companies across Canada.

"If we have a request for proposal from a potential client who's interested in having us represent them, we look at the scope of work they need, and usually they want a dedicated account manager," Webb explains.

Although Webb will have to immediately start considering who can best do that job, she generally can't hire anyone new until she has a signed contract with the client.

"We usually can't just have someone inside in the company assigned to the new contract because they already have another position," Webb says. "Sometimes we can move them, but that's not always the case."

"Most times, the potential client really wants to know who the person is going to be on the account, but we can't tell them," she adds. "So what we often do is put forward the name of one of our senior account directors and explain that that person will hire an account manager. The client gets to see that someone on the team here that has the experience will oversee the account, and that seems to work fine." Only once the contract is signed can Webb usually pursue her newest member of the team.

Founded in 2002, VoX now has nearly 30 employees across the country and has clients that include the tourism boards of Australia, Hawaii, Germany, Portugal, Kenya, and Texas, among others. The reason that those large government agencies choose VoX instead of a rival or doing it themselves is because of VoX's experienced and knowledgeable team. "We have the experience, we know the market," Webb says. "We have all the relationships in Canada with the travel agents, tour operators, airlines, the media, so we know Canada. We've got languages covered, we've got people in Québec. You can't just move into Canada and all of a sudden just open an office and think that you can manage the country from coast to coast."

"And if a client wants to invest more money into a market or less money, we're able to help them because we can scale up or down as needed." Hiring staff to fill those positions and make the clients happy can be demanding, however. "I think with any company the challenge is always your staff," Webb says. "Making sure they're motivated, they're looking after our clients because the client is king in this type of a business. So our people really have to be service orientated, and they have to be dedicated and positive and confident and be good at what they do."

Susan Webb, President and Cofounder, VoX International

For the account managers, Webb often looks within the travel and tourism sector for staff, but for other positions, her search tends to move further afield. "There are some aspects of the positions that really need to have the travel background," she says. "They need an in-depth understanding of how we work, and they have the networking because travel really is a small industry. But for a lot of our people, it doesn't really matter. Our accounting people just have to know how to manage accounting, so they don't need travel experience at all for that. We have a social media team member who doesn't have any travel background but has picked it up very quickly. Even one of our PR people came from technology start-ups and the fashion industry so didn't have any travel media background but has all the skills of being able to manage media relations and PR, which is transferable into the travel scope."

Regardless of whether her new employees are travel and tourism veterans or not, there's always one thing that Webb looks for in every new hire. "I'm very much about the relationship," Webb says. "When I find someone with the right personality who's going to get along with everyone and the client's going to love them and the industry will work well with them, I'm very emotional and say, 'Oh, I love this person; let's just hire them!' While my second-in-command, who has been with me for over 20 years, is very good with her HR hat on at making sure that they have the right skills for us to have in the company and to provide our clients with what they need."

Together they make a great team, and that helps VoX to be one of the best travel and tourism marketing teams in the country.

INTRODUCTION

In earlier chapters, we stressed that the structure of an organization and the design of the work within it affect the organization's ability to reach its objectives. These objectives, however, can be achieved only through the efforts of people. VoX International is a clear example as the company must continuously seek and hire people qualified to do the work and meet changing customer needs and demands. To achieve this, defining the core competencies for any work is critical to the recruitment and selection processes, and this starts with the manager, who is also encouraged to think about current and future people requirements. As such, planning for human resources requirements is a critical first step.

Recruitment and selection continue to be some of the top concerns of all levels of management within an organization. Despite the economic challenges of the past several years, about two-thirds of Canadian companies are finding it difficult to secure qualified and appropriate applicants to fill job openings in their organizations, and this is having a significant impact on their ability to operate effectively and efficiently.[1] Given legal requirements, ethical considerations, and the complex economic environment, managers must carefully plan how to fill job openings and make careful hiring decisions. This chapter discusses the process of planning for staffing requirements and then finding, attracting, and selecting applicants.

HUMAN RESOURCE PLANNING

You will recall from Chapter 1 that a company becomes competitive by means of its people. Therefore, it is essential that an organization look strategically at its people and the skills they require to accomplish the strategic and operational goals of the organization.

But what is meant by "strategic"? Strategic plans tend to be broader in scope and longer in time frames (2 to 3 years), provide overall direction, and apply to the entire organization. Basically, a company's strategy lies in determining its key goals and the actions it needs to take to achieve those goals. The importance of strategic planning is highlighted by Target's failure in the Canadian marketplace; the company's inability to properly implement strategic planning had devastating consequences.[2] The demise of Sears Canada was also due to a lack of strategic planning and inability to focus on the demands of the current marketplace.[3] These 2 examples clearly show that when a company fails to plan, disastrous outcomes will result. Strategic HRM, as noted in Chapter 1, includes all the HR policies, processes, and practices that help the company achieve those goals through its employees. Therefore, it is important that the manager link the goals of the company to the competencies of the people employed.

In linking goals to competencies, the manager will need to anticipate the current and future needs of the company and develop the road map to get there. What the manager is really doing is ensuring that the company has people with the right competencies for the present and for future organizational growth.[4] This is called **human resource planning**—a process to ensure that the organization is employing the people required to run the company and that employees are being used as effectively as possible, where and when they are needed, in order to accomplish the organization's goals. In other words, the goal is to have the right

Human resource planning
Process to ensure that an organization has people available (employed) who have the right competencies and that these people are being effectively utilized in the right capacities in order for the company to achieve its desired objectives

people with the right skills in the right jobs at the right time. In times of economic uncertainty, organizations might sometimes want to ignore this. However, it is even more important in difficult financial circumstances to ensure that they have the appropriate staff to achieve success both in the short term and into the future.[5]

Linking HR Planning to Strategic Planning

Organizations will undertake strategic planning where major objectives are identified and comprehensive plans are developed to achieve these goals. Because strategic planning involves the allocation of resources, including the people resources of the organization, HR planning is aligned to ensure that the objectives are met. From the overall organizational objectives, divisions and/or departments will also set subordinate objectives that support the attainment of organizational ones. Thus, the manager will need to make plans not only for business objectives but also for the necessary staffing resources. For example, if the organization has strategically decided to enter a new market, it needs to ensure that it has the people with the right skill sets to gain a foothold in that market. Consequently, the HR plan must have an activity that assesses the skill of current employees and possibly a recruitment activity that attracts new employees with the necessary skills.

Likewise, through HR planning, all HR processes, systems, and practices can be aligned to the overall business strategy. In doing this, the organization ensures that it has the people capabilities to adjust to changes in the environment. An area of strategic HR planning receiving much attention is succession planning. Organizations are concerned about developing leaders for the future and are focusing efforts on leadership development so that the leaders have the competencies necessary to keep pace with the direction and overall strategy of the organization.[6] In the best companies, such as Fairmont Hotels, BMO, and IBM, virtually no distinction exists between strategic planning and HR planning; the planning cycles are the same, and HR issues are seen as inherent in the management of the business.

Importance of HR Planning

Why is it important for the manager to be involved in human resource planning? Consider these facts about the Canadian labour force, which highlight the requirement to understand the diversity (gender, age, geographic location) within this landscape:

1. Canada has a population of about 35 million, with an unemployment rate of 6.2% in September 2017.
2. In September 2017, employment rose by 25,000 jobs for people aged 55 and older, mostly in full-time work.
3. For men aged 25 to 54, employment declined by 29,000 in September 2017, all in part-time work. The unemployment rate for men in this age group rose by 0.4 percentage points to 5.9%.
4. In September 2017, employment rose in Ontario but fell in Manitoba, Prince Edward Island, and Alberta. Québec was overall unchanged.
5. The workforce is aging—by 2031, it is projected that 25% of the workforce will be 55 or older.
6. Of Canadians who left their long-term jobs, defined as lasting 12 years or more, within the traditional retirement period between age 60 and 64, 44% were re-employed within a decade.
7. Approximately 35% of workers are part-time employees or self-employed, with Intuit Canada estimating that 45% of Canadians will be self-employed by 2020.[7]

These dramatic shifts in the composition of the labour force require that managers become more involved in planning their need for employees because such changes affect not only employee recruitment but also methods of employee selection, training, compensation, and motivation.

LO1

Describe the relationship between HR planning, recruitment, and selection.

AT WORK WITH HRM 5.1   THE IMPORTANCE OF PLANNING

Changes in the Canadian workforce and the availability of people to fill jobs in the company meant that PTI Group in Alberta had to think outside the box and be innovative about HR planning. PTI supplies remote-site services such as food services and worker accommodations, particularly within the resource industry. Since much of its work in Canada occurs on or near Indigenous land, the company decided that it was in its long-term best interest to create employment opportunities for the local communities. As such, PTI determined that the hiring of Indigenous peoples should be a strategic imperative.

Indigenous and Northern Affairs Canada (INAC) is a resource to connect employers with the Indigenous workforce. INAC's mandate is to improve the quality of life of Indigenous peoples and their communities and assists employers to access qualified Indigenous candidates and support their HR planning requirements. This, in turn, increases Indigenous employment opportunities, helps employers, and helps the Canadian economy in general.

PTI also partnered with the Northern Alberta Institute of Technology to create training programs where it can employ the graduates. Without doing its own workforce planning, PTI would not have known there was a problem in acquiring enough workers with the correct skill sets and would not have implemented strategic responses.

Sources: Shannon Klie, "Aboriginals a 'Strategic Imperative,'" *Canadian HR Reporter*, April 25, 2011, accessed October 31, 2017, www.hrreporter.com/articleview/10088-aboriginals-a-strategic-imperative; and "Aboriginal Employment," *Indigenous and Northern Affairs Canada – Government of Canada*, accessed November 2, 2017, https://www.aadnc-aandc.gc.ca/eng/1100100033790/1348508851503.

Read At Work with HRM 5.1 to learn more about how HR planning helped an organization respond to the changes in the Canadian workforce in order to meet its ongoing strategic goals.

An organization may incur several intangible costs as a result of inadequate or no people planning. For example, inadequate planning can cause vacancies to remain unfilled. The resulting loss in efficiency can be costly, particularly when lead time is required to train replacements or when customers become frustrated with a lack of service, thereby causing them to seek out other providers and/or an organization to lose goodwill in the marketplace. Situations also may occur in which employees are laid off in one department while applicants are hired for similar jobs in another department.

Realistically, planning occurs more systematically in medium-sized and larger organizations. Small, entrepreneurial organizations tend to approach HR staffing needs on a more short-term basis. These businesses tend to spend the most time in creating the business and give little time to creating staffing plans.[8]

An example of a small organization that does pay attention to its staffing needs is Brainworks Software. The company received a small business excellence award within the Avaya and International Avaya User Group Customer Innovation Awards. Brainworks is a geographically distributed company, with more than half of its employees working remotely. Its ability to select staff on the basis of skills and expertise rather than location allows it to achieve the highest levels of customer satisfaction.[9]

Approaches to HR Planning

Since the overall outcome of HR planning is to have the right people with the right competencies at the right time in the right jobs, there is a need to forecast the demand for employees. Forecasting can be done through quantitative approaches, such as a **trend analysis**, or qualitative approaches, such as **management forecasts**.

A trend analysis will forecast employment requirements on some type of organizational index, such as sales or units of production. Previous years' experiences will be analyzed, and projections will be made for the future. This type of numerical analysis is often accomplished

LO2

Discuss the steps in human resource planning.

Trend analysis
Using past numerical data to look for patterns in order to predict future demand for employees

Management forecasts
Asking managers for their predictions regarding the future demand for employees

Gorodenkoff/Shutterstock.com

Managers often use trends to predict future needs.

through the use of software. In management forecasts, the opinions and judgments of people knowledgeable about the organization's future needs will develop scenarios that can be used for planning purposes. The Delphi and the nominal group technique are 2 forecasting methods in which managers' opinions regarding employment demands are obtained.

Besides forecasting the demand for employees, an organization will also need to look at the supply of employees. This activity includes looking both internally, in the organization, and externally, to the larger labour market. Two techniques to assess the internal supply are the **staffing table** and **Markov analysis**. Staffing tables use graphs to display the jobs in an organization and show the number of people currently in these jobs. Anticipated demand for the number of people to fill each job in the organization may be shown as well. Markov analysis describes how employees typically move into, within, and out of the organization. This information highlights numerical data regarding employees who remain in a job from year to year as well as the number of employees who are promoted, demoted, moved to another job in the company, or have left the organization.

Whereas staffing tables and Markov analysis focus on numbers of employees, another technique focuses on the skill mix or **skills inventory**. When assessing supply, organizations will identify the key skills or core competencies necessary for organizational success. Without knowing the core competencies required for business success, the other HR processes may not be successful. All other HR needs are based on the identified competencies of employees to ensure good organizational performance. Organizations such as Hewlett-Packard and DuPont Canada use HR information and enterprise systems to assist in this task. Information taken from skills inventories assists an organization with succession planning, which is discussed later in this chapter.

Figure 5.1 describes the steps in the planning process.

Results of HR Planning

The outcome of HR planning is to achieve a usable balance between the demand for and supply of employees. It is here that organizations can see the results of good HR planning.

The demand for and supply of labour are very much a function of the economic environment. The dynamics within the Canadian economy are complex, and it is often difficult to forecast impending changes. Global economies, the world's political climate, and the increasing Canadian household debt load are just 3 factors that need to be considered when examining national economic conditions (e.g., think of Brexit and tensions caused by North Korea).[10]

Staffing table
Graphs displaying the jobs in an organization and showing the number of people currently in these jobs. Anticipated demand for the number of people to fill each job in the organization may be shown as well

Markov analysis
Description of how employees typically move into, within, and out of the organization

Skills inventory
Information about the education, experiences, skills, etc., of employees

FIGURE 5.1   The HR Planning Steps

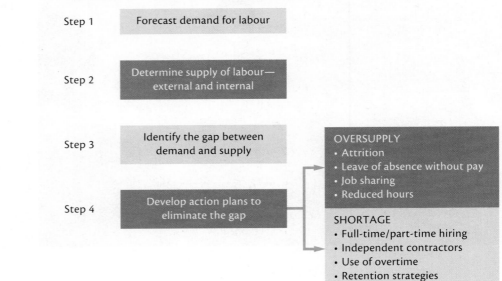

Step 1 — Forecast demand for labour

Step 2 — Determine supply of labour— external and internal

Step 3 — Identify the gap between demand and supply

Step 4 — Develop action plans to eliminate the gap

OVERSUPPLY
- Attrition
- Leave of absence without pay
- Job sharing
- Reduced hours

SHORTAGE
- Full-time/part-time hiring
- Independent contractors
- Use of overtime
- Retention strategies

These scientists have knowledge and expertise that will enable the company to achieve its goals.

Purestock/Thinkstock

But HR planning is no guarantee that the organization will never have too many employees for its immediate or long-term needs. This situation can be the result of severe economic conditions (i.e., the decreased price of oil, which caused an oversupply of employees in Alberta), as mentioned in Chapter 1, or major company collapses, such as Sears Canada's 2017 bankruptcy or the 2014 merger between Burger King and Tim Hortons. In such cases, a company must choose how to deal with having more employees than needed.

Dealing With Oversupply of Labour

When an organization has more employees than required, this is known as an **oversupply of labour**. In this scenario, a company must take steps to deal with the excess people. Some organizations have decided that since employees are key to their success,

Oversupply of labour
Occurs when an organization's demand for employees is less than the number of employees currently employed

any need to reduce employee numbers would be done by attrition. Attrition is the natural departure of employees through people quitting, retiring, or dying. Usually, organizations can estimate how many people leave and for what reasons. Therefore, an organization may be able to avoid downsizing because it knows that people will leave. This was easier to do when people left the organization at the age of retirement, usually 65. However, with many people postponing retirement, it is more difficult to predict what the natural attrition rate will be.

Not all attrition is good. If too many people leave—if there is *high turnover*—it can cost the company more money than intended. Replacing an employee is a costly and time-consuming activity. It is estimated that the costs of turnover can be as high as 2 times the annual compensation, particularly in high-demand skill areas or professionals.[11] And the costs are not just financial: they can include the loss of key knowledge. One of the more serious business issues of the 21st century has been the concern with retaining key employees.[12]

If the organization can predict that the excess supply of employees is more short-term, it may suggest that some employees take a leave of absence (without pay), job-share, or reduce working hours (and pay), or it can redeploy people to units that have a need.

Dealing With Shortage of Labour

Even though human resource planning frequently focuses on the surplus of employees, attention must also be given to projected labour shortages, particularly in certain occupations and industries. When an organization has fewer employees than required, this is known as a **shortage of labour**. For example, British Columbia is projecting that there will be almost 62,000 more jobs than people to fill them by 2020, with a shortage of skilled trades much sooner.[13] Therefore, an organization may need to recruit from outside the company. However, if the need might be short-term or temporary, the organization will not want to hire for the longer term and may request that current employees work extra hours, such as during peak periods.

As mentioned in Chapter 1, the number of part-time employees has increased a great deal. Therefore, it is not unusual for companies to hire part-time staff to cover labour shortages. Likewise, organizations will utilize the services of a temporary employment agency to acquire short-term staff, particularly in areas where a certain type of expertise is required, such as software programming. In addition, an organization might enhance retention strategies, or as mentioned in Chapter 1, people might be hired as independent contractors for a set period of time. When doing so, careful attention must be given to the criteria for independent contractors to ensure that these people should not, in fact, be classified as employees of the company.

Ultimately, when dealing with a shortage of labour (notwithstanding the temporary measures noted above to deal with short-term gaps), an organization must respond to the lack of human resources through recruitment and selection, which we will now address.

RECRUITMENT

Once an organization has determined its needs, it must then recruit potential employees. The manager, together with HR professionals, will identify where a company might look for these candidates. **Recruitment** is the process of locating and encouraging people to apply for existing or anticipated job openings. The purpose of recruitment is to have a sufficient pool of qualified applicants. Figure 5.2 provides an overview of the process.

The process informs the applicants about the qualifications required to perform the job and the career opportunities the organization can offer. **Employment branding** is another key consideration.[14] An organization's reputation in the employment landscape and what applicants believe their employment experience will be like (i.e., work–life balance, fairness

Shortage of labour
Occurs when an organization's demand for employees is greater than the number of employees employed

Recruitment
The process of locating and encouraging people to apply for jobs

Employment branding
An organization's reputation as an employer

FIGURE 5.2
The Recruitment Process

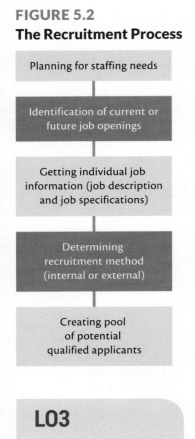

Planning for staffing needs

Identification of current or future job openings

Getting individual job information (job description and job specifications)

Determining recruitment method (internal or external)

Creating pool of potential qualified applicants

LO3

Compare the advantages and disadvantages of recruiting from within the organization.

and equity, communication norms) influence their decision to apply to job opportunities. This being so, organizations should be aware of how they are perceived by those seeking employment.

Whether a vacancy will be filled by someone within the organization or from outside will, of course, depend on the availability of people, the organization's HR practices, and the requirements of the job.

Recruiting Within the Organization

Most public-sector organizations, and many private-sector ones, try to follow a policy of filling job vacancies above the entry-level position through promotions and transfers from within. For example, promotion-from-within policies at CIBC and Canada Mortgage and Housing Corporation have contributed to the companies' overall growth and success.

Advantages of Recruiting from Within

Promotion serves to reward employees for past performance and is intended to encourage them to continue their efforts. Promoting from within makes use of the people who already know the organization and the contribution they have made. It also gives other employees a reason to anticipate that similar efforts by them will lead to promotion, thus improving morale within the organization and decreasing voluntary resignations. This is particularly true for members of designated groups who have had difficulty finding employment and often faced even greater difficulty in advancing. Many organizations have integrated promotion policies as an essential part of their employment equity programs.

Transfers can also serve to protect employees from layoff or to broaden their job experiences. This strategy becomes more noticeable as organizations become flatter, with fewer layers between front-line employees and executives. Furthermore, the transferred employee's familiarity with the organization and its operations can eliminate the orientation and training costs that recruitment from the outside would entail. Most importantly, the transferee's performance record is likely to be a more accurate predictor of the candidate's success than the data gained about outside applicants.

Job vacancies filled from within the organization capitalize on employees' knowledge and provide recognition to employees for their past accomplishments.

Methods of Locating Qualified Internal Job Candidates

The effective use of internal sources requires a system for locating qualified job candidates and for enabling those who consider themselves qualified to apply for the opening. Qualified job candidates within the organization can be located by using computerized record systems, using information from succession planning processes, and using internal job postings.

Human Resources Management Systems Information technology has made it possible for organizations to create databases that contain the complete records and qualifications of each employee. Using increasingly user-friendly search engines, managers can access this information and identify candidates for available jobs. Organizations have developed resumé-tracking systems that allow managers to query an online database of resumés. Companies such as Oracle and SAP Canada are leaders in developing technology for staffing and skills management. Similar to the skills inventories mentioned earlier, these systems allow an organization to rapidly screen its entire workforce to locate suitable candidates for an internal opening. This data can also be used to predict the career paths of employees and to anticipate when and where promotion opportunities may arise. Since the value of the data depends on its being up to date, the systems typically include provision for recording changes in employee qualifications and job placements as they occur.[15]

Succession Planning As mentioned earlier, many organizations conduct succession planning—the process of identifying, developing, and tracking key employees for future promotions or transfers. Therefore, when a job opening occurs in a particular part of the organization, it might make use of the succession plan and put the internal employee into the vacancy. Succession plans rely upon the organization identifying its long-term goals, outlining the competencies required to achieve those goals, and making sure that employees are developed in order to assume other roles and take on other responsibilities in the future.

Internal Job Posting Organizations may advertise about job openings through a process referred to as internal job posting. In the past, this process has consisted largely of posting vacancy notices on company employment boards in an HR department or common area, such as a lunchroom. In addition, internal advertising can also be done through a company's intranet, emails or other types of internal memos, and company newsletters.

Posting a job internally can provide many benefits to an organization. However, these benefits may not be realized unless employees believe the process is being administered fairly. Furthermore, it is more effective when internal job posting is part of a career development program in which employees are made aware of opportunities available to them within the organization. For example, the organization may provide new employees with literature on potential job progression that describes the lines of job advancement, training requirements for each job, and skills and abilities needed as they move up the job-progression ladder.

Limitations of Recruiting from Within the Organization

Sometimes certain jobs that require specialized training and experience cannot be filled from within the organization and must be filled from outside. This situation is especially common in small organizations. Also, for certain openings, it may be necessary to hire individuals from another organization who have gained the knowledge and expertise required for these jobs.

Even though the company may encourage job openings to be filled from within, outside candidates should be considered in order to prevent the inbreeding of ideas and attitudes. Applicants hired from the outside, particularly for certain technical and managerial positions, can be a source of new ideas and may bring with them the latest knowledge. Indeed, excessive reliance on internal sources can create the risk of "employee cloning." Furthermore, it is not uncommon for firms in competitive fields, such as high technology or retailing, to attempt to gain secrets and managerial talent from competitors by hiring away their employees.

Recruiting Outside the Organization

LO4
Compare the advantages and disadvantages of external recruitment.

Frequently, organizations will decide to fill positions by bringing people in from outside the organization. For example, RONA decided to hire someone new to the organization as its chief commercial officer in order to bring in new ideas, a different leadership style, and new energy.[16] External recruitment may also be necessary when a current employee leaves, causing a chain reaction of promotions to occur and thereby creating other openings throughout the organization.

Usually, external recruitment is organized and coordinated by an HR department, with the manager frequently giving suggestions about where to recruit, such as an ad in a newspaper or professional journal. However, if there is no HR department, these managers need to be aware of such things as labour-market conditions and external sources of recruitment.

Advantages and Disadvantages of Recruiting Outside the Organization

Like recruiting from within, recruiting outside the organization (external recruitment) has advantages and disadvantages.

One advantage is that the individual brings certain unique skills the company needs now. Likewise, it is possible to bring in people with a variety of different experiences and perspectives.

A disadvantage is the lack of solid information about the person's performance on the job. That information is likely to be available only through secondhand sources, such as what the applicant volunteers and what references might say. Also, the person may not know the industry or organization, necessitating more extensive orientation and training. Furthermore, there may be constraints in the organization, such as salary levels, that prevent the organization from accessing a large pool of applicants. Significant costs are usually associated with external recruitment. These include time, the cost of advertising (sometimes as much as $9000 per newspaper), and the cost of familiarizing the person with the organization. Lastly, there may also be legislative requirements, such as employment equity, which lead to certain applicant pools.

The Labour Market

Labour market
Area from which applicants are recruited

The **labour market**, or the area from which applicants are recruited, will vary with the type of position to be filled, the amount of compensation to be paid, and, as mentioned earlier, the economic environment. Recruitment for executives and technical personnel who require a high degree of knowledge and skill may be national or even international in scope. Recruitment for jobs that require relatively little skill, however, may encompass only a small geographic area, such as within a city or a province. The reluctance of people to relocate may cause them to turn down offers of employment, eliminating them from consideration beyond the local labour market.

The condition of the labour market may also help determine which recruiting sources an organization will use. During periods of high unemployment, organizations may be able to maintain an adequate supply of qualified applicants from unsolicited resumés alone. A tight labour market, one with low unemployment, may force the employer to advertise heavily and/or seek assistance from local employment agencies. How successful an organization has been in reaching its employment equity goals may be still another factor in determining the sources from which to recruit. For a number of years, Canada has relied on immigration to assist in meeting the demand for labour. In addition, the department responsible for immigration, Immigration, Refugees, and Citizenship Canada, has worked with businesses to create processes that are more responsive to labour-market shortfalls. In 2014, Canada's Temporary Foreign Worker Program was reorganized into 2 distinct programs that provided a temporary measure by which foreign workers could enter Canada at the request of employers given approval through a new Labour Market Impact Assessment (LMIA). A new International Mobility Program was also introduced, which included streams in which foreign nationals were not subject to an LMIA, with the goal of advancing Canada's broad economic and cultural national interests rather than filling particular jobs.[17] As mentioned in Chapter 1, Canada has an aging population with insufficient younger workers to fill the work requirements in the future. Furthermore, as more and more individuals become part of a global talent pool, companies will seek a number of ways to recruit beyond their home country.

The dynamics of the labour market mirror the general economy. When there is a poor economic climate with many people unemployed, there may be a larger pool of applicants; if the economy is strong, with few unemployed, the pool of applicants may be much smaller. There are also training and education programs that aim to provide an appropriate number of skilled applicants so that most of those graduates can be hired, such as nurses and other medical specialists. This does not mean that everyone is always hired, however, as the person may not have the skills needed by a particular employer. However, employers who make good use of their HR planning activities will continue to look for qualified applicants whether the economy is good or poor.

Outside Sources of Recruitment

The outside sources from which employers recruit will vary with the type of position to be filled. A software developer, for example, is not likely to be recruited from the same source as a retail service person. Trade schools can provide applicants for entry-level positions, although these recruitment sources are not as useful when highly skilled employees are needed. Networking, referrals from previous and existing staff, information from customers or clients, and involvement in the community are a few ways organizations seek outside people. As well, social network sites such as Facebook, Twitter, and LinkedIn continue to evolve as recruitment tools. Some of the major outside sources of recruitment are discussed below.

Advertisements One of the frequent methods of attracting applicants is through advertisements. Advertisements may be posted on websites, in newspapers, or in trade journals or transmitted by radio, television, billboards, posters, and email. And it is no longer unusual to see an ad on the side of a bus. Advertising has the advantage of reaching a large audience of possible applicants. Some degree of selectivity can be achieved by using newspapers and journals directed to a specific readership. Professional journals, trade journals, and publications of unions and non-profit organizations fall into this category.

Well-written advertisements can highlight the major assets of the position while showing the responsiveness of the organization to the job and career needs of applicants. Advertisements in all types of media should follow the AIDA principle: provoke Attention, Interest, Desire, and Action in those seeing the ad.[18] Part of the information typically included is a statement that the organization is an equal-opportunity employer and that only those candidates selected to move forward in the process will be contacted.

Employment and Social Development Canada (ESDC) is responsible for administering the Employment Insurance program through its Service Canada agency, found in most communities. Individuals who become unemployed must register at one of these offices and be available for "suitable employment" in order to receive their weekly employment insurance cheques. Service Canada has created a national job bank that lists information about employment opportunities across the country province by province, thereby providing another source of job advertisements.

Internet There is no doubt that the Internet has had an impact on external recruitment practices. Not too many years ago, a person would see 5 to 10 pages of career ads in all the major newspapers. Now you might find no more than 1 or 2 pages a week. Companies such as WestJet, Mountain Equipment Co-op, Finning Canada, and the federal government use the Internet to attract people. Employers indicate that the reason is to increase the opportunity to attract the people with the right skill sets for their organizations. Furthermore, large Canadian recruiting sites include Monster.ca, Workopolis, Jobs.ca, and Working.com.

Employers say that the Internet is faster (some job applicants respond within 30 minutes of the job posting), that it generates higher-quality candidates, and that it is cheaper (by as much as 80%) than traditional advertising media. An Internet posting can be as low as $50 per month, as against a newspaper ad at $6000 per day, with Monster and Workopolis being about $750 per job posting. There is also an interesting side benefit for the job seeker given the difficult employment landscape: according to 1 study, a person is unemployed 25% less time by making use of Internet job postings.[19]

Social Media Given the prevalence of technology, it is important for organizations to explore using social media to post external advertisements. According to a recent study, Canadians actively use LinkedIn, Facebook, and Twitter as sources for employment opportunities.[20] Facebook and LinkedIn have created apps where employers can post jobs inside the 800-million-member social network.[21] Such a situation has created an incredibly large labour pool with relatively low cost to organizations. It is therefore important that employers develop a strategic approach to use social media to promote employment opportunities and encourage people to apply for job vacancies.

Employment Agencies Employment agencies, including executive search firms and temporary employment agencies, attempt to match applicants with the specific needs of a company. A fee is charged to the employer for services that are tailored to the employer. By law, job seekers cannot be charged for help in finding work. It is common for such agencies to specialize in serving a specific occupational area, such as office staff or technical computer people. Private agencies usually focus on clerical, technical, and junior–middle management, whereas executive search firms tend to focus on senior and executive management. These agencies may charge an employer 25% to 30% of the annual salary if they find a candidate who gets hired. Since these agencies differ in the services they offer, job seekers would be wise to take the time to find a recruiter who is knowledgeable, experienced, and professional. When talking with potential recruiters, individuals should openly discuss their philosophies and practices with regard to recruiting strategies, including advertising, in-house recruiting, screening procedures, and costs for these efforts.

Executive search firms (also called "headhunters") are employment agencies that typically focus on senior-level and executive-level managerial positions. The search tends to be very focused to that employer. The fees charged the employer by the agencies may range from 30% to 40% of the annual salary for the position to be filled. The employer pays this fee.

Agencies that provide temporary employees are one of the fastest-growing recruitment sources. Companies such as Imperial Oil Ltd., Home Depot, and SaskTel use temporary employees extensively. These temporary workers ("temps") are used for short-term roles such as filling in for employees who are on leave or completing work during times when there are additional projects or extra customer demands that need to be addressed. Temporary workers can be laid off quickly, and with less cost, when work lessens. The use of temps thus becomes a viable way to maintain proper staffing levels. Also, the employment costs of temps are often lower than those of permanent employees because temps are usually not provided with benefits and can be dismissed without the need to file Employment Insurance claims.

The drawbacks of temporary employees are that their commitment to the company may be lower than that of full-time employees, and they may take confidential information to their next employer, possibly a competitor. Further difficulties may be encountered in getting full-time and contract employees to effectively work together.

Educational Institutions Educational institutions, at both the high school and postsecondary level, can provide a rich source of job applicants. An organization may choose to recruit at one or both of these levels based upon the typical competencies required to fulfill job requirements and the types of programs offered at the institutions. For example, Humber College in Etobicoke, Ontario, and the British Columbia Institute of Technology offer a human resource management training program and are therefore ideal resources for recruiting people with specialized knowledge and skills in human resources management.

It is important for employers to be aware of what attracts students to employers. Universum, a global survey company, conducts research on students' perceptions of employers. Part of the survey asks about the ideal company. Some of the top "ideal companies" in Canada for 2017, as rated by Canadian students, were Google, Microsoft, and Apple.[22]

Open Houses and Job Fairs Organizations may also use open houses and job fairs to recruit new employees—particularly if the organization is expanding or is looking for particular types of skills. For example, with the shortage of skilled trades, an organization might participate in a job fair at an educational institution that graduates tradespeople. Or the organization might have an open house where potential applicants are encouraged to visit the company and see what might be available. Seasonal resort operations such as Whistler Blackcomb in British Columbia use open houses at the start of each ski season as a way to attract people with a variety of skills, and Home Depot typically holds recruitment open houses at key points throughout the year.

As an innovative example combining the concept of an open house with the use of technology, a job fair was created in which 20 employers from a wide array of industries (e.g., financial services, insurance, and retail) attracted over 18,000 job applicants throughout Canada.[23] Although the event had virtual employer booths describing the opportunities, job seekers could access the information at any time during the event, no matter where they lived or worked. This ability represents an example of the evolving use of technology in recruitment.

David Paul Morris/Bloomberg via Getty Images

Job fairs are 1 method to source external applicants.

Employee Referrals The recruitment efforts of an organization can be aided by employee referrals or recommendations made by current employees. Managers have found that the quality of employee-referred applicants is normally quite high because employees are generally hesitant to recommend individuals who might not perform well. According to a management professor, 88% of employers rate employee referrals as their #1 source of quality candidates.[24] The effectiveness of this recruitment effort can be increased by paying commissions or bonuses to employees when they make a successful "recruitment sale." In utilizing employee referrals, however, an organization needs to ensure that it is not creating a situation of systemic discrimination.

Unsolicited Applications and Resumés Many employers receive unsolicited applications and resumés from individuals who may or may not be good prospects. Even though the percentage of acceptable applicants from this source may not be high, the source cannot be ignored. Many job-search strategies suggest that individuals use this method to introduce themselves to organizations that are of interest to them.[25]

Good public relations dictate that any person who contacts an organization for a job be treated with courtesy and respect. If there is no possibility of employment in the organization at present or in the future, the applicant should be tactfully and frankly informed of this fact.

Professional Organizations Many professional organizations and societies offer a placement service to members as one of their benefits. For example, CPHR Alberta (the provincial HR association) provides members with weekly emails of job opportunities. The system enables employers to connect with HR professionals and inform them of job prospects.

Unions If a company is unionized and has employees that belong to labour unions, those unions can be a principal source of applicants for blue-collar jobs (such as welders, electricians, and plumbers) and for some professional jobs. Unions may hold hiring events, similar to career fairs, to support employment opportunities for their members. Employers wishing to use this recruitment source should contact their local union for employer eligibility requirements and applicant availability.

Recruitment Considerations

When recruiting applicants, organizations must ensure that all legal requirements, as addressed in Chapter 2, are met. For example, an advertisement should not specify height or weight requirements unless this is a bona fide occupational requirement within the role. As previously noted, systemic discrimination might occur if employee referrals are the only recruitment source used. Also, as organizations continue to develop diverse workforces, employers will often focus on attracting staff in communities of different ethnic and cultural backgrounds. Those employers that fall under the federal employment equity legislation (see Chapter 2) are expected to have a recruitment program that focuses on the designated groups of women, visible minorities, people with disabilities, and Aboriginal peoples. Although Canada (unlike the United States) does not have a quota system, under employment equity legislation, there is an expectation that over time those organizations that fall under the legislation will have a workforce reflective of the general population of Canada. Therefore, recruitment initiatives should take this into consideration, and it is important for managers to be knowledgeable about and supportive of their organization's objective to have employees with diverse ethnic and cultural backgrounds. Managers need to be held accountable for the success (or failure) of creating a more diverse workforce.[26] Managers may also be actively involved in recruitment "outreach" programs, where they speak at ethnic community centres to let people know about employment opportunities with their company. Other avenues are ethnic-community newspapers and TV stations. Maple Leaf Sports & Entertainment extended itself into the South Asian community by ensuring that hockey games were broadcast in Punjabi.[27]

A particularly effective organization in bridging the immigrant gap is the Toronto Region Immigrant Employment Council (TRIEC). The council represents an innovative partnership between employers, unions, postsecondary institutions, other community organizations, and government. The organization came into existence in 2003 when the city realized that to have well-settled and satisfied immigrants, it was necessary for immigrants to have successful employment opportunities. The mission of the organization is to create and facilitate solutions to better the integration of immigrants into the regional workforce.[28] It is unique in that it doesn't work directly with immigrants but provides a collaborative approach to engaging the various parties that can help immigrants get settled, find work, and succeed in Canada.

SELECTION

Once the recruitment process has yielded applicants whose qualifications appear to fit the organization's requirements, organizations have to assess those qualifications and decide whom to hire. This is usually the manager's responsibility. If there is an HR department, it will usually play a supporting role by arranging for and sitting in during interviews, doing reference checking, administering employment tests, and so on. However, if no HR professional is there to help, the manager needs to know these steps and their importance.

Matching People and Jobs

Making hiring decisions is not a scientific process, so it cannot be structured to achieve perfect results. However, a systematic hiring process increases the possibility of acquiring staff committed to the vision and business plans.[29] **Selection** is the process of choosing from the pool of applicants and hiring individuals who are best able to fulfill the requirements of the job. Those responsible for making selection decisions should have adequate information about the jobs to be filled, and as much relevant information as possible about the applicants themselves, in order to be able to predict the candidate's job performance.

Prior to the selection process, it is important to reconfirm the necessary knowledge, skills, and abilities for the job. As mentioned in Chapter 4, these requirements are identified through job analysis. Various tools and processes ranging from pre-employment tests to interviews to references help assess an applicant's competencies and match these against the requirements of the job and the needs of the organization.[30]

The Selection Process

In most organizations, selection is a continuous process. Turnover inevitably occurs, leaving vacancies to be filled by applicants from inside or outside the organization or by individuals whose qualifications have been assessed previously. In some situations, organizations will have a waiting list of applicants who can be called when permanent or temporary positions become available.

Based upon the type and level of the job to be filled, how selection is done may vary. The typical steps in the selection process are outlined in Figure 5.3. For each selection process, it needs to be determined if a specific step will be used and why this process is being used (i.e., what is the expected outcome that will support the selection decision). In other words, not all applicants will go through all steps in the selection process. For example, applicants may be rejected after a review of their resumé or after a pre-employment test.

As Figure 5.3 shows, the selection process provides different tools to evaluate candidates. These include application forms and resumés, interviews, tests, and reference checks. Regardless of the method used, it is essential that it conform to accepted ethical standards, including privacy and confidentiality, as well as legal requirements. Above all, it is essential that the information obtained be sufficiently reliable and valid.

Selection
Selection is the process of choosing from the pool of applicants and hiring individuals who are best able to fulfill the requirements of the job

LO5
Describe the typical steps in the selection process.

FIGURE 5.3   Steps in the Selection Process

Completion of application form or submission of resumé

Pre-screening

Employment tests

Interview: one-on-one, panel, telephone, or Internet

Reference checks

Hiring decision

Note: Steps may vary. An applicant may be rejected after any step in the process.

Obtaining Reliable and Valid Information

It is important that selection tools used provide comparable data over time, which is known as **reliability**. For example, unless an interviewer would assess the suitability of a candidate to be the same today as was the outcome yesterday, this judgment is unreliable—that is, not consistent. Likewise, a test that results in vastly different outcomes when administered to the same job candidate a few days apart is unreliable.

In addition, information pertaining to a person's suitability must be as valid as possible. **Validity** refers to how well a selection procedure measures what it is intended to measure. In the context of employee selection, validity is essentially an indicator of the extent to which data from a procedure (e.g., interview or test) predict job performance. However, whether something is valid depends upon the selection tool's overall reliability. The bull's-eye scenario is a helpful way to remember these important concepts. Someone may hit the same area of a target every time a dart is thrown (very reliable), but if the dart continues to land outside the targeted area, the desired results are not achieved (not valid). Therefore, whatever selection procedures or tools are used—whether an interview or an employment test—they must be both reliable and valid in order to provide useful information about predicting the applicant's performance in the organization.

Although it is important that all information used during the selection process be both reliable and valid, organizations are especially concerned about the reliability and validity of any employment tests they might conduct. This topic is discussed later in the chapter.

SOURCES OF INFORMATION ABOUT APPLICANTS

Many sources of information are used to provide as reliable and valid a picture as possible of an applicant's potential for success on the job. This section looks at the usefulness of application forms and resumés, interviews, employment tests, and reference checks.

Application Forms

Many organizations require application forms to be completed because they provide a fairly quick and systematic means of obtaining a variety of information about the applicant. Application forms serve several purposes:

- they provide information for deciding whether an applicant meets the minimum requirements for experience, education, and other competencies

Reliability
The degree to which selection procedures provide consistent and comparable outcomes over time

Validity
How well a selection procedure measures what it is intended to measure

LO6
Identify the various sources of information used for selection decisions.

- they provide a basis for questions the interviewer will ask about the applicant's background
- they also offer sources for reference checks. For certain jobs, a short application form is appropriate

Many managers remain unclear about the questions they can ask on an application form. Although most know that they should steer clear of issues such as age, race, marital status, and sexual orientation, other issues are less clear. The following are some suggestions for putting together an application form:

1. *Date.* The form should require the applicant to fill in the date as this provides information regarding when the form was completed and how current the information is.
2. *Education.* The applicant should be asked to provide information regarding schools attended and specific credentials received. Certifications and other designations could be included in this section.
3. *Experience.* The applicant should be asked to provide an employment history, including dates worked and responsibilities within each job listed.
4. *Arrests and criminal convictions.* Questions about arrests, convictions, and criminal records are to be avoided. If bonding is a requirement, ask if the individual can be bonded.
5. *Country of citizenship.* Such questions are not permitted. It is allowable to ask if the person is legally entitled to work in Canada.
6. *References.* It is both permissible and advisable that the names, addresses, and phone numbers of references be provided. (References are covered in more detail later in the chapter.)
7. *Disabilities.* Employers should avoid asking applicants if they have physical disabilities or health problems, if they have ever received psychiatric care or have been hospitalized, or if they have ever received workers' compensation.

Just as many organizations are using the Internet for recruitment, as noted earlier in this chapter, they are also having job seekers apply for work directly online. In some cases, there is an electronic application, and in other cases, job seekers send their resumé to an email address.

Resumés

A resumé is a document that summarizes and highlights relevant information about an individual who is seeking employment. Contact information, education, previous work experiences, volunteer experiences, and personal interests are typical components. However, individuals frequently exaggerate or overstate their qualifications on a resumé; in a tight labour market, candidates sometimes even delete advanced qualifications. One survey indicated that 45% of individuals in the 18 to 34 age range "stretch" the truth on their resumés,[31] in spite of legal consequences (including termination) and ethical considerations.[32] Ethics in HRM 5.1 discusses some of these issues.

Although resumés should be accurate, applicants can still ethically display creativity in how they present themselves. In addition, most employers ask applicants to submit a cover letter with the resumé.[33] This document introduces the job candidate to a potential employer, provides an example of writing and communication skills, and highlights how the applicant has the required knowledge, skills, and abilities to do the job.

Although resumés, along with cover letters, are an important tool, modern selection processes are looking at different ways to use technology to gather information about job candidates without asking for these formal documents. Look at Emerging Trends 5.1 for the latest techniques used in developing resumés and evolving selection practices.

ETHICS IN HRM 5.1   WHEN DOES "STRETCHING" BECOME LYING?

Most candidates for white-collar jobs prepare a resumé and submit it to prospective employers. They also complete the application form, answering questions required by employers for comparison purposes. Some recruitment agencies noticed during the last recession that resumé padding increased. Applicants were "stretching" the dates of their employment, misleading employers about the nature of their duties, and misrepresenting their salaries. When you are writing a resumé, adding 3 months to your previous employment, saying you were a night auditor instead of a clerk, and adding $950 to your last salary might seem relatively harmless.

But what are the facts? Studies of "creative" resumé writing indicate that about 30% of resumés report incorrect dates, 11% misrepresent reasons for leaving, and others exaggerate education attainments or omit criminal records. The probability is that about two-thirds of employers check references. Some former employers give only dates of employment and previous salary ranges.

Most organizations require you to sign a statement saying that the information you supply is true and that if it is not, you will be dismissed. Some cases of resumé padding have been heavily publicized. A Toronto Stock Exchange manager was dismissed for lying about having a master's degree. A member of Parliament listed an ILB on his resumé, which normally stands for International Baccalaureate of Law, but which he claimed stood for Incomplete Baccalaureate of Law. In a heart-wrenching case, a person who was ready to retire was found to have lied about his age decades earlier to get a job. On discovery, he was dismissed and lost his pension. In another case, a Canadian businessman was sentenced to 8 months in jail in New Zealand for lying on his resumé: he had listed false qualifications, such as an MBA.

In a labour market where too many people are chasing too few jobs, candidates will also lie on their resumes, but do so by dropping experience and educational qualifications. This practice, called "stripping," is used because job seekers are ready to take any job in order to survive or to hold them over until the jobs they really want are available.

Here are some tips for employers when reviewing resumés:
1. Watch for ambiguity—probe on the use of general or vague terms.
2. Look for unexplained gaps in the work and/or educational history.
3. Ask questions more than once—rephrase similar questions and compare answers.
4. Be factual—ask references to confirm basic information, such as employment history.

CRITICAL THINKING QUESTION:

Have you ever overstated information on your resumé? Explain your reason.

Source: Adapted from "Almost One-Half of Workers Know Someone Who Lied on Resume," *Canadian HR Reporter*, September 27, 2011, accessed November 2, 2017, www.hrreporter.com/articleview/11315-almost-one-half-of-workers-know-someone-who-lied-on-resume.

EMERGING TRENDS 5.1

1. *The candidate experience.* Organizations are paying attention to how job applicants are treated throughout the selection process. Even if a candidate is not offered a job, companies are aware that how they treat people will impact their employment brand and reputation in the marketplace. A recent study shows that 91% of employers believe the candidate experience can impact consumer-purchasing decisions.

2. *Mobile platforms.* Both job seekers and employers are making use of apps. Job seekers can apply wherever they happen to be and manage their job search process from anywhere, and employers can manage postings and applications through mobile apps.

3. *Video resumés.* With the evolution of so many different technologies, job seekers, especially those in creative fields, are using video technology to present their resumés. Although there can be a number of

legal issues associated with this for the potential employer, it has had some appeal for certain organizations. Employers also have tools that allow them to assess the candidates by using pop-up video comments while reviewing the resumé.

4. ***Video interviewing.*** Given the potential for geographic diversity among applicants, video interviewing will allow employers to "meet" candidates in an efficient (both from a time and a cost perspective) manner.

5. ***Increased use of social networks.*** More and more job seekers are using their contacts on social networks both to get recommendations and to post their resumés. For example, a LinkedIn profile might be used in lieu of a resumé when applying. Likewise, many organizations will search the various social network sites to gather information about applicants.

Sources: Dan Schawbel, "10 Workplace Trends You'll See In 2018," *Forbes*, November 1, 2017, accessed November 3, 2017, https://www.forbes.com/sites/danschawbel/2017/11/01/10-workplace-trends-youll-see-in-2018/#73ed106d4bf2; Che Caparas, "The Top Recruiting Trends to Look Out for in 2017," *Hire Rabbit*, accessed November 2, 2017, http://blog.hirerabbit.com/the-top-recruiting-trends-to-look-out-for-in-2017; "Emerging Trends in Recruitment," March 3, 2015, accessed November 2, 2017, www.allaboutpeople.net/emerging-trends-in-recruitment; and J. Freeborn, "How to Master Social Media Recruitment in 2015," February 5, 2015, accessed November 2, 2017, www.social-hire.com/social-recruiting-advice/5103/how-to-master-social-media-recruitment-in-2015.

Interviews

Interviews are an important part of the selection process. Depending on the type of job, applicants may be interviewed by 1 person, by members of a work team, or by other individuals in the organization.

Nevertheless, interviews are plagued by problems of subjectivity and personal bias. Some interviewers' judgment is more valid than others'. Remember, the purpose of the interview is to gather relevant information to determine whether the candidate has the skills, abilities, and knowledge to be successful on the job in the organization. However, it is also critical that the interview questions be based on the work requirements (as determined through the job analysis) and specific knowledge required. As well, interviewers have their own biases and therefore need to have been appropriately educated to ensure that they are not influenced by such issues as a candidate's appearance or how well-spoken the candidate is.[34] Toolkit 5.1 shows some of the typical errors that interviewers make and should be trained to avoid.

TOOLKIT 5.1   INTERVIEWER ERRORS

Although not intentional, untrained interviewers may display subjectivity or bias against certain job candidates. The following are examples of the types of errors that may occur during an interview. It is important that interviewers be trained about these potential issues to ensure that selection processes are valid:

1. Similar to me: Interviewers tend to favour candidates who remind them of themselves.
2. Halo effect: Interviewers like 1 specific thing about a candidate and, in turn, minimize or negate all other aspects that should be considered.

3. Telegraphing: Interviewers convey, through body language or through responses to the candidate's answers, what they want the job candidate to say.
4. Leading questions: Interviewers phrase questions in such a way that it is obvious what they want the job candidate to say.
5. Central tendency: Interviewers rate every person as average and find it difficult to differentiate amongst job candidates.
6. Contrast effect: Interviewers compare job applicants to one another instead of evaluating each candidate based upon the requirements of the job.

Source: Adapted from Dartmouth Human Resources, "Common Rater Errors," accessed November 2, 2017, http://www.dartmouth.edu/~hrs/profldev/performance_management/rater_errors.html.

INTERVIEWING METHODS

Employment or selection interviews differ according to the methods used to obtain information and to find out an applicant's attitudes, feelings, and behaviours. Organizations have a variety of methods to choose from. Furthermore, depending on the number of interviews, more than 1 method may be used.

One-on-One

Most often, the first face-to-face interview occurs between the applicant and an interviewer. The interviewer could be an HR professional or a manager. Questions are asked and observations are made of both the interviewer and the applicant. The structure of the questions could be a behavioural description interview (BDI), situational, or non-directive. (The different types of questions are explained below.)

Panel

Panel interview
An interview in which a board of interviewers questions and observes a single candidate

This type of interview involves a panel of interviewers who question and observe a single candidate. In a typical **panel interview**, the candidate meets with several interviewers, who take turns asking questions. After the interview, the interviewers pool their observations to reach a consensus about the suitability of the candidate.[35] During the interview, the panel may use structured questions, situational questions, BDI questions, or a combination of all 3.

Telephone

Many companies use a telephone interview as the first step in the selection process. This interview provides the opportunity to ask job applicants further details about their qualifications for the job and to conduct an initial assessment about their verbal communication skills.

Lucky Business/Shutterstock.com

Panel interviews allow several people to meet with a job applicant at the same time.

Technology Based

Increased use of technology has not only helped in creating a way to recruit job applicants but has also enabled organizations to engage with job candidates online. Asking applicants to submit a video responding to preset questions and using Skype or Google Hangouts to conduct interviews are just 2 examples of how technology can be used to interview job candidates. As an example, Monster makes use of online interviewing; given that its business is Web-based services, this practice is consistent with its use of technology.[36] In addition to the benefits of objectivity, some research evidence suggests that applicants may be less likely to engage in "impression management" in computerized interviews than in face-to-face interviews.[37]

INTERVIEW QUESTIONS

Regardless of the type of interview method used, questions must be asked of the applicant. In addition, for an interview to be reliable, the questions must be stated in such a way that the same questions are asked of each applicant. The questions can be very specific to get specific answers (structured), or they can be less structured where broad and open-ended questions are asked. Listed below are the types of interview questions typically used.

Structured Questions

Since the objective of an interview is to gather data for making a decision, companies will look at the interview process as an investment and therefore create structured questions to determine if the person has the competencies to do the work.[38] Because structured questions are based on job requirements and an established set of answers against which applicant responses can be rated, they provide a more consistent basis for evaluating job candidates. Structured questions are more likely to provide the type of information needed for making sound decisions. They also help reduce the possibility of legal charges of discrimination. Employers must be aware that any interview is highly vulnerable to legal attack and that more challenges (human rights and grievances) in this area can be expected in the future. The 2 main types of structured questions are discussed below.

The leading type of structured interview question being used is a **behavioural description interview (BDI) question**. A BDI question focuses on real work incidents, not hypothetical situations, as a situational interview question does. The BDI format asks job applicants what they did in a given situation. For example, to assess a potential manager's ability to handle a problem employee, an interviewer might ask, "Tell me about the last time you disciplined an employee." Or the format might be this sequence:

> **Behavioural description interview (BDI) question**
> Question about what a person actually did in a given situation

1. Describe a situation when you disciplined an employee.
2. What was the action taken?
3. What were the results?

Toolkit 5.2 provides an example of a BDI question and approach for interviewing someone for a front-desk position in a hotel.

Such an approach to interviewing is based on solid research that past performance is the best predictor of future performance. You will notice that with this type of interview, the questions can produce a variety of responses. The interviewer will usually clarify or ask further questions to get the necessary information. Many more organizations are using BDI questions to better assess the applicant's ability to perform successfully in the organization's environment. If you have recently looked for work, you may have encountered BDI questions.

TOOLKIT 5.2   SAMPLE BDI INTERVIEW QUESTION

You are being considered for work in our hotel. As we encounter difficult situations with our customers, please describe a time you had to tell a customer that there was no reservation for a room. What action did you take? What were the results?

Some additional clarification might be gained from the following questions:

1. Was there any aspect of your decision that you were uncertain about?
2. Did the customer have information that you didn't have?
3. Could anyone overhear the customer?
4. What decision did you finally make?

This type of question is criticized by some individuals who argue that people can change and therefore should not be evaluated based upon past behaviour. However, this type of interview question is still being used for a number of reasons:

1. Answers can provide a rich source of information. Questions are based on the job requirements directly related to the skills and competencies needed to successfully perform the work.
2. Responses provide a clear view of the candidate's past behaviour and results.
3. Responses provide consistency to the selection process due to the format of questions.
4. Answers are noted and rated on the basis of previously established guidelines.
5. Such questions provide a high degree of validity when done properly.[39]

Situational question
Question in which an applicant is given a hypothetical incident and asked how he or she would respond to it

Another variation is the **situational question**, in which an applicant is given a hypothetical incident and asked to respond. The response is evaluated relative to preestablished benchmarks. Interestingly, many organizations are using situational questions to select new college graduates. Toolkit 5.3 shows sample situational questions used to select systems analysts at a chemical plant.

Unstructured Questions

These types of questions are broad and open-ended and allow the candidate to talk freely, with little interruption from the interviewer. For example, an interviewer might ask, "Tell me more about your experiences on your last job." The applicant is allowed a great deal of latitude in guiding the discussions. Generally, the interviewer listens carefully and does not argue, interrupt, or change the subject abruptly. The interviewer also uses follow-up questions to allow the applicant to elaborate, makes only brief responses, and permits pauses in the conversation. This last technique is the most difficult for the beginning interviewer.

A study conducted by Western University indicated that unstructured questions might result in inconsistent and subjective responses that can disadvantage minority candidates, particularly for those organizations with employment equity programs.[40,41]

TOOLKIT 5.3   SAMPLE SITUATIONAL INTERVIEW QUESTIONS

1. You work in an environment where deadlines are part of everyone's work. The project you are working on has a deadline that you feel is not realistic. What would you do in this situation?

2. A team member is constantly arriving at work late and is not actively contributing to a project that you are both working on. How would you react to these circumstances?

Which Type of Questions to Use?

The greater freedom afforded to the applicant in the non-directive interview is particularly valuable in bringing to the interviewer's attention any information, attitudes, or feelings that may often be concealed by more structured questioning. However, because the applicant determines the course of the interview and no set procedure is followed, little information that comes from these interviews enables interviewers to cross-check agreement with other interviewers.

Thus, the reliability and validity of the non-directive interview may be expected to be minimal. Based on experiences in hiring, it is probably a better approach to use both types of questions—structured to get good information about skills and competencies to do the work and unstructured to help in determining the candidate's fit in the organization.[42]

INTERVIEW GUIDELINES

Studies on the employment interview tend to look at questions such as "What traits can be assessed in the interview?" and "How do interviewers reach their decisions?" The purpose of the studies is to assess how an interview can be structured to improve the overall process. Toolkit 5.4 presents some of the major findings of these studies. It shows that information is available that can be used to increase the reliability and validity of interviews.

Employers have found it advisable to provide interviewers with instructions on how to avoid potentially discriminatory questions in their interviews. The examples of appropriate and inappropriate questions shown in Figure 5.4 may serve as guidelines for application forms as well as pre-employment interviews. Complete guidelines may be developed from current information available from the office of the Canadian Human Rights Commission. Once the individual is hired, the information needed but not asked in the interview may be obtained if there is a valid need for it and if it does not lead to discrimination.

As a final helpful hint for interviews, applicants need to be provided with information on all aspects of the job, both desirable and undesirable (this is called a *realistic job preview*),

---

TOOLKIT 5.4   **WHAT ARE SOME OF THE FINDINGS FROM RESEARCH STUDIES ON THE INTERVIEW?**

1. Understand that there is difficulty in gathering the right information and in making an informed decision.
2. Use appropriate and good questions to get the necessary information. Structured interviews are more reliable than unstructured interviews.
3. Review candidate information (such as the resumé) after the interview. To do so before the interview can lead to certain impressions and therefore certain conclusions, such as where the person went to school.
4. Impressions and judgments need to come from the interview and applications or resumés.
5. Take time to come to a conclusion. Don't make early judgments.

6. Observe the behaviour and actions of the candidate during the interview. Sometimes candidates will behave in a way intended to strengthen their credentials, for example, name-dropping or projecting an image of the ideal candidate.
7. Practise asking questions before the interview.
8. Ask questions to determine fit with the organization, particularly about interpersonal skills and motivation.
9. Allow the applicant time to talk, which provides a larger behaviour sample.
10. Be aware that non-verbal as well as verbal interactions influence decisions.

Sources: Adapted from Nicole Fallen, "Hiring? 4 Tips for a Successful Candidate Interview," *Business Daily News*, September 28, 2017, accessed November 3, 2017, http://www.businessnewsdaily.com/5212-job-interviews-techniques.html; Allen Hullcutt, "From Science to Practice," *Canadian HR Reporter*, June 6, 2011, accessed November 3, 2017, www.hrreporter.com/articleview/10442-from-science-to-practice; and Scott Erker, "Do's and Don'ts of Recruitment," *Canadian HR Reporter*, November 15, 2010, accessed November 3, 2017, www.hrreporter.com/articleview/8457-dos-and-donts-of-recruitment.

FIGURE 5.4 Appropriate and Inappropriate Interview Questions

Type of System	Appropriate Questions	Inappropriate Questions
National or ethnic origin	Are you legally entitled to work in Canada?	Where were you born?
Age	Have you reached the minimum or maximum age for work, as defined by the law?	How old are you?
Sex	How would you like to be referred to during the interview?	What are your childcare arrangements?
Marital status	As travel is part of the requirement of our position, would you foresee any problems meeting this obligation?	What does your spouse do for a living? Is there travel involved? Who takes care of the children when you are away?
Disabilities	Do you have any conditions that could affect your ability to do the job?	Do you use drugs or alcohol?
Height and weight	(Ask nothing)	How tall are you? How much do you weigh?
Address	What is your address?	What were your addresses outside Canada?
Religion	Would you be able to work the following schedules?	What are your religious beliefs?
Criminal record	Our job requires that our employees be bonded.	Are you bondable? Have you ever been arrested?
Affiliations	As an engineer, are you a member of the engineering society?	What religious associations do you belong to?

so that they may opt out of the selection process if they feel they would not be satisfied with the job. This reality check helps avoid production losses and costs associated with low job satisfaction that can result in the person leaving the organization.

EMPLOYMENT ASSESSMENTS

An employment assessment is an objective and standardized way to assess a person's KSAs (knowledge, skills, and abilities), competencies, and other characteristics in relation to other individuals.[43] When an organization decides to use a particular employment assessment or test, it is critical that the attribute or skill being tested is used in the work. For example, if someone's keyboarding skills are tested, yet the job doesn't have any tasks that require keyboarding, it would be inappropriate to use that test. Again, the purpose of tests is to gather additional information on the candidate so that job performance in the organization can be predicted.

As mentioned earlier in this chapter, there continue to be concerns about the reliability and validity of employment tests. The concern is focused on whether these tests are biased and appropriate for the job under consideration.[44] In a court decision in 2010, the court held that the written examination of applicants for a firefighter position adversely affected certain minority groups.[45] Although an organization is certainly able to design and use any test it chooses, without ensuring the validity and reliability of the test through on-the-job performance, over time employers are creating legal challenges for themselves.[46]

Organizations use assessments or tests to gather more in-depth information on applicants.[47] However, the information from the assessment will not be useful if there are challenges of bias and discrimination. To better understand the legal implications of pre-employment testing, read HRM and the Law 5.1.

HRM AND **THE LAW** 5.1   WAS THIS DISCRIMINATION?

When making a hiring decision, managers must ensure that the use of pre-employment assessments does not create a complaint of discrimination. In a case involving the Toronto District School Board and an applicant, it was determined by the Ontario Human Rights Tribunal that although the assessment was valid and reliable, pre-employment accommodation needed to be done with that particular applicant.

Specifically, the applicant, with a diagnosed learning disability and attention-deficit disorder, applied for a part-time caretaker role. As part of the screening process, the employer used literacy and numeracy assessments. The applicant informed the school board of the learning disability and asked that there be some accommodation to write the test: "specifically, to write in a separate room, to have someone break down the questions so that they could be understood, and to use a calculator." The applicant was informed that the board does not accommodate. The person administering the tests suggested that the applicant just write the tests, see what the results were, and then further consider any accommodation needs. The applicant felt that this was being "set up to fail."

At the time of the application, the job seeker was working with an agency that assists adults with learning disabilities. The executive director of the agency contacted the school board, confirmed the need for accommodation, and indicated that medical documentation could be provided. Even after the documentation was received and reviewed, the school board refused to provide accommodation.

In making its decision, the tribunal first determined that the applicant had been discriminated against in the application process. The tribunal indicated that the applicant had a documented learning disability that makes it difficult to perform on written tests without assistance and that to be forced to do so would mean that the applicant would perform poorly. The tribunal concluded that the applicant had fulfilled the responsibility by informing the school board that accommodation was required. Although the tribunal accepted that to do so for a pre-employment screening test would be difficult, such accommodation could have occurred. Finally, the tribunal confirmed that the employer did not seek information about the nature of the disability, as it was required to.

And the consequence of this decision to the Toronto District School Board? The tribunal awarded $7500 in compensation to the job applicant for injury to dignity.

CRITICAL THINKING QUESTIONS:

1. Given what you were informed about in Chapter 2 on accommodation, do you think the decision is reasonable? Why?
2. What are some of the potential issues with other candidates who do not or may not be aware of the ability to seek accommodation when being assessed for a job?

Source: *Human Rights Tribunal of Ontario, David Mazzei, Applicant, and Toronto District School Board, Melanie Stoughton and Silvana Filice, Respondents*, February 24, 2011, TR-0527-09, 2011 HRTO 400.

Types of Employment Assessments

Employment assessments, or tests, may be classified in different ways. Generally, **aptitude tests** (capacity to learn or acquire skills) or **achievement tests** (what a person knows or can do right now) are used to measure a person's abilities.

Cognitive Ability Tests

Cognitive ability tests evaluate brain-based skills such as memory, problem solving, and numerical ability. A variety of tests—both paper-and-pencil and computer-administered—measure cognitive abilities, including the General Aptitude Test Battery (GATB), the Graduate Management Admission Test (GMAT), the Bennett Mechanical Comprehension Test, and the Wonderlic Cognitive Ability Test.

One of the more interesting uses to which measuring general mental ability has been put is the National Football League's administering of the Wonderlic to measure the brain-power of its recruits to ensure that they can keep up with both the physical and the mental demands of the game.[48]

LO8
Illustrate the value of different types of employment tests.

Aptitude tests
Measures of a person's capacity to learn or acquire skills

Achievement tests
Measures of what a person knows or can do right now

Personality and Interest Inventories

Whereas cognitive ability tests measure a person's mental capacity, personality tests measure personal characteristics, such as extroversion, agreeableness, and openness to experience. Although the ability of such tests to predict job performance has been quite low, recent research indicates that people tend to blame themselves and react inappropriately when something goes wrong. This type of awareness can be useful when assessing candidates for managerial roles.[49] Personality tests can be problematic if they inadvertently discriminate against individuals who would otherwise perform effectively. Therefore, although it is generally not recommended that personality tests be used for background information when selecting employees, they can be very useful as part of a career development program and for enhancing teamwork.[50]

Emotional Intelligence/Emotional and Social Competence

One of the newer, and greatly debated, types of employment tests measures the *emotional intelligence* of the applicant, particularly for leadership roles. Emotional intelligence (EI) has many definitions, but the one most commonly used describes it as a set of personal qualities distinct from cognitive ability and important for success.[51] Researchers, including those who originally developed the concept, believe there is more to success at work than mere intellect. This being so, the concept of EI is evolving into *emotional and social competence* (ESC), which consists of a range of personality characteristics and is not just a single measurement.[52] Emerging from the research is the question as to whether any 1 type of employment assessment can measure ESC and the idea that what might be better is a set of different tests that measure the broad spectrum of personality and social competence. The research also suggests that emotional and social competence is more appropriately assessed for leadership roles.[53]

Physical Ability Tests

Employers may need to evaluate a person's physical abilities due to the requirements of the job. Specific jobs, such as warehouse worker and police officer, typically require job incumbents to have specific physical abilities, such as strength and endurance. These physical abilities are needed not only to do the job properly but also to minimize injury due to the demands of these positions.[54]

A physical ability test is not the same as a medical exam. Some organizations may still require a medical exam before starting employment to ensure that there is no medical condition that might preclude the employee from successfully performing the work or due to requirements from insurance providers if the employee is to qualify for benefits. However, many organizations are no longer doing medical exams due to privacy issues or potential challenges of discrimination. It is critical to note that a medical exam may only be requested after a conditional offer of employment has been given to a job applicant.

Job Sample Tests

Job sample tests, or work sample tests, require the applicant to perform tasks that are part of the work required on the job. Like job knowledge tests, job sample tests are constructed from a carefully developed outline that, experts agree, includes the major job functions; the tests are thus considered content valid. They are often used to measure skills for office and clerical jobs. Job sample tests have been devised for many diverse jobs: a map-reading test for traffic control officers, a lathe test for machine operators, a complex coordination test for pilots, an in-basket test for managers, a group discussion test for managers, and a judgment and decision-making test for administrators, to name a few.

Assessments, such as the applicants' keyboarding skills, can provide additional information in the selection process.

Substance Abuse (Drug and Alcohol) Testing

The Canadian Human Rights Commission and some of its provincial counterparts have issued policies on employment-related drug testing. Further complexities within Canadian workplaces are being experienced due to the legalization of recreational marijuana.[55] Even if the employer has established that substance testing is job related and there is a requirement for the employee to have no substances in his or her system (i.e., this is a bona fide occupational requirement as discussed in Chapter 2 and typically revolves around safety issues), when this is used as part of the selection process, the candidate must be informed that job offers are conditional on the successful passing of a drug test. To comply with legal issues in Canada, any policies in relation to substance abuse testing during the selection process must have a clear and legitimate purpose. As well, the testing must be administered in a reasonable manner, including not being invasive or done in a discriminatory fashion. Furthermore, addiction to drugs or alcohol is considered a disability, and during the selection process, if substance abuse is detected, the employer must adhere to legislation requiring workplace accommodation, to the point of undue hardship, for the applicant who was given a conditional offer of employment.

Employer obligations and employee rights pertaining to drug and alcohol testing are discussed in greater detail in Chapter 9.

REFERENCE CHECKING

Organizations use a variety of ways to check references, including electronic and telephone. At Intuit, the Edmonton, Alberta, software company that produces Quicken, managerial applicants are asked to provide between 5 and 9 references, who are then called and asked specific questions.

An employer has no legal obligation to provide a former employee with a reference. To avoid liability, many employers are providing a perfunctory letter of reference, which supplies only the name, employment dates, last position with the company, and final salary. It is important for employers to be understanding of the handling of reference information so that the employer does not create legal issues for itself. The best way to do this is to have a consent form that the applicant signs that provides the reference names and contact information.[56] By using sources in addition to former employers, organizations can obtain valuable information about an applicant's character and habits. Telephone interviews are most effective, and 1 key question that is particularly effective in screening is to ask, "Would you rehire this employee?" Some employers prefer to outsource reference checking to professional firms, such as Intelysis Employment Screening Services in Toronto, to obtain information that is as accurate as possible. A survey conducted by Robert Half International, an employment agency, identified that 20% of job seekers were eliminated from consideration after reference checks.[57] Toolkit 5.5 provides some sample questions to use when doing reference checks.

Those individuals supplying references must do so in a responsible manner without making statements that are damaging or cannot be substantiated. To aid employers in ensuring that appropriate reference checks are done, a number of companies provide screening services. Among these are Informed Hiring, BackCheck, and Hire Performance. With an increasing number of companies providing pre-employment screening, the National Association of Professional Background Screeners was formed to create and promote standards when screening job applicants.[58]

Inadequate reference checking can contribute to high turnover or difficulties with the employee. Furthermore, organizations might face legal liability issues if inadequate checks were done. It is important to remember, however, that such investigation needs to be in relation to the work. For example, Mark's Work Wearhouse in Alberta was banned from having credit checks done on candidates for sales positions.[59] The company indicated that credit checks were important to see whether the salesperson could handle financial responsibilities and identify risk for store theft. The Alberta commission disagreed and determined that this was an invasion of privacy.

TOOLKIT 5.5   SAMPLE REFERENCE CHECK QUESTIONS

1. How long has the person been employed in your organization?
2. Describe the person's attendance pattern.
3. Can you give me some examples of how the candidate demonstrated initiative?
4. What are the person's strengths?
5. How did the person get along with others in the work unit?
6. What are some areas the person needs to develop?
7. Was the person successful in their role?
8. Why did the person leave your employment?
9. Would you rehire?
10. Describe the person's ability to work with others or in a team.

Sources: "Checking References: Top 10 Questions to Ask," Hcareers.com, August 7, 2014, accessed November 3, 2017, www.hcareers.com/us/resourcecenter/tabid/306/articleid/298/default.aspx; adapted from Public Service Commission, "The Right Choice!," accessed November 3, 2017, www.psc-cfp.gc.ca/ppc-cpp/acscmptnc-evl-cmptnc/chck-ref-eng.htm; and "Sample Reference Check Questions," Best-Job-Interview, accessed November 3, 2017, www.best-job-interview.com/reference-check-questions.html.

ETHICS IN HRM 5.2   **IS THIS AN INVASION OF PRIVACY?**

Many employers report that reviewing a job applicant's social media postings is a common practice. These mechanisms provide insight into how candidates communicate, their belief systems, and how they conduct themselves outside of work.

Job applicants have argued that this is an invasion of privacy and that without permission, it is improper for a prospective employer to check out and assess a job candidate through these means. Although Canadian laws value and protect individual's privacy, experts warn that online privacy is essentially a misnomer and that information posted to a relatively secure profile could be accessed by any member of the public.

CRITICAL THINKING QUESTIONS:

1. Is it right for employers to use social media sites to assess job candidates?
2. If you were hiring someone, what problems could be avoided by looking through the candidate's social media posts during the selection process?
3. Would you want a prospective employer to look through your social media sites? Why or why not?
4. Knowing that this happens, what changes or safeguards will you make to your social media activities?

Sources: Adapted from the Canadian Press, "Facebook-Snooping Employers Limited in Canada," *CBC News*, March 25, 2012, accessed November 3, 2017, http://www.cbc.ca/news/technology/facebook-snooping-employers-limited-in-canada-1.1161720.

A final caution on reference checks: accessing social media sites to see what candidates have posted not only may be inaccurate but also might be considered an invasion of privacy.[60] With this in mind, as Ethics in HRM 5.2 addresses, using social media sites for background checking is still a common practice, and therefore job candidates cannot ignore this matter.

MAKING THE HIRING DECISION

Although all steps of the selection process are important, the most critical one is who will be hired to fill a job vacancy. Because of the cost of placing new employees on the payroll, the short probationary period in many organizations, and human rights considerations, the final decision must be as sound as possible. Thus, it requires systematic consideration of all the relevant information about applicants. Summary forms and checklists are commonly used to ensure that all the pertinent information has been included and that all applicants for a specific job are evaluated and compared in a fair and consistent manner.

It is also helpful to remember that summarizing the information about the candidates is not a mechanical process. The decision maker needs to be sure that any employment assessments are appropriate for the work and that any challenges to their use can be defended, that the weighting of any criterion is done consistently for all applicants, and that job performance indicators are appropriate for all stages of the job.[61]

Of primary importance is ensuring that the entire process is well structured. Recent research indicates that by improving the overall structure of the decision process, including structured interview questions, the validity and reliability of the process improve.[62]

It is much easier to measure what individuals can do than what they will do. The can-do factors are readily evident from test scores and verified information. What the individual will do can only be inferred. Motivation-based interview questions are another tool to help determine how a job applicant will ultimately perform in the job.[63] Given the uncertainty

LO9

Outline key considerations when making a hiring decision.

around a hiring decision, the selection process may be described as a risk-management process. The goal is to hire the best person for the job by using a variety of sources of valid and reliable information.

As such, the hiring decision is typically approached in 1 of 2 ways:

1. A "clinical approach," in which each person involved will give different weights to the applicants' background. This approach can lead to different decisions and frequently demonstrates biases and stereotypes as it is based on personal judgment.
2. A "statistical approach," in which criteria for successful job performance are listed and weighting factors are assigned. Information gathered from interviews and assessments are then combined, with the person receiving the highest score being offered the job. In this approach, it is important to identify any threshold or cut-off—the point at which a person is no longer considered.

Although different people, including HR professionals, may be involved in the selection process, ultimately, the manager decides who gets hired. Therefore, it is important that this person understand the importance of the steps necessary to make a good decision. In large organizations, notifying applicants of the decision and making job offers are often the responsibility of the HR department. This department will confirm the details of the job, working arrangements, wages, and so on and specify a deadline by which the applicant must reach a decision. In smaller organizations without an HR practitioner, the manager will notify the candidates. Therefore, if there is an HR department, it is valuable to forge a strong partnership with HR in order to gain its valuable technical and legal assistance.

EVALUATING SELECTION PROCESSES

As noted in Chapter 1, metrics (or measurements) are a critical part of effective HR management. Therefore, after a hiring decision is made, it is important to evaluate the effectiveness and efficiency of a company's selection process. Toolkit 5.6 provides some common measurements to do this.

Making a selection decision is no different than making any other type of management decision: identifying criteria and weighting them need to be done. It is of interest to note

---

TOOLKIT 5.6   MEASURING SELECTION EFFECTIVENESS AND EFFICIENCY

In order to evaluate the effectiveness and efficiency of selection processes, various measurements have been developed. The following are common ways to conduct this assessment:

Yield ratios: The percentage of applicants who proceed to the next stage of the selection process.

Selection ratios: The proportion of applicants for 1 or more positions who are hired or the number of hired employees to the number of applicants.

Source analysis: Number of applicants from each source and number of qualified applicants from each source.

Cost per hire: The expenses incurred per successful hiring decision.

Time to hire: Elapsed time from when the job is advertised to when the selected person begins working for the organization.

Sources: Sandra Hess, "8 Key Hiring Metrics to Quantify Your Talent Selection Process," *FurstPerson*, June 13, 2016, accessed November 3, 2017, https://www.furstperson.com/blog/key-hiring-metrics-to-quantify-your-hiring-process; and Paul Slezak, "7 Recruiting Metrics You Should Really Care About," *RecruitLoop*, October 8, 2013, accessed November 3, 2017, http://recruitloop.com/blog/7-recruiting-metrics-you-should-really-care-about.

that even when all legal, ethical, and procedural considerations are taken into account, bad hiring decisions may still occur. A study by CareerBuilder revealed that approximately "68% of employers fell victim to bad hires" at one point.[64] This being so, the processes of recruitment and selection will continue to evolve and advance.

LEARNING OUTCOMES SUMMARY

1. Describe the relationship between HR planning, recruitment, and selection.
   - *As organizations plan for their future, managers at all levels must play an active role in planning for future people requirements*
   - *It is critical that the organization have the right number and types of employees available to ensure that the organization meets its short- and long-term strategic goals*
   - *Managers play a key role in planning for the human resources necessary to achieve the business plan*

2. Discuss the steps in human resource planning.
   - *Forecast demand for labour in the organization*
   - *Determine the supply of labour—both external and internal to the organization*
   - *Identify the gap between demand and supply*
   - *Develop action plans to close or eliminate the gap*

3. Compare the advantages and disadvantages of recruiting from within the organization.
   - *By recruiting from within, an organization can capitalize on previous investments made in recruiting, selecting, training, and developing its current employees*
   - *Internal promotions can reward employees for past performance and send a signal to other employees that their future efforts will pay off*
   - *A disadvantage can be the inbreeding of ideas and attitudes*

4. Compare the advantages and disadvantages of external recruitment.
   - *External recruitment can bring in new ideas and acquire people with specialized skills*
   - *Constraints on the organization, such as a legislated employment equity plan, may lead to a different pool of applicants than what the manager may want*

5. Describe the typical steps in the selection process.
   - *Typical steps start with the receipt of an application (form and/or resumé), an initial interview, possible employment tests, an interview with the manager, reference checks, and then a hiring decision*

6. Identify the various sources of information used for selection decisions.
   - *Application forms or resumés*
   - *Employment tests*
   - *Interviews*
   - *References*

7. Discuss the different methods and types of questions for conducting an employment interview.
   - *One-on-one, in which there is only the candidate and 1 interviewer*
   - *Panel, in which more than 1 interviewer is present*
   - *Telephone, in which an initial screening is done*
   - *Internet, in which a variety of technologies, including video streaming, are used*
   - *Unstructured, in which the interviewer is free to pursue whatever approach and sequence of topics might seem appropriate*
   - *Structured, in which each applicant receives the same set of questions, which have pre-established answers*
   - *Situational, in which candidates are asked about hypothetical situations and how they would handle them*

- *Behavioural descriptions of previous work experiences*
- *Motivational, in which candidates' attitudes and desires to achieve certain outcomes are assessed*

8. Illustrate the value of different types of employment tests.
   - *More objective than the interview*
   - *Can provide a broader sampling of behaviour and skills*

9. Outline key considerations when making a hiring decision.
   - *Important to establish fair and consistent selection criteria for all job applicants*
   - *Ensure that the selection process is well structured*

KEY TERMS

achievement tests 165

aptitude tests 165

behavioural description interview (BDI) question 161

employment branding 147

human resource planning 142

labour market 150

management forecasts 144

Markov analysis 145

oversupply of labour 146

panel interview 160

recruitment 147

reliability 156

selection 155

shortage of labour 147

situational question 162

skills inventory 145

staffing table 145

trend analysis 144

validity 156

HRM CLOSE-UP APPLICATION

1. How could VoX International enhance its HR planning so that recruitment and selection are not always done in response to changing or new customer demands?
2. Should VoX International use employee referrals as a recruitment strategy? Why or why not?
3. What employment tests could VoX International use when selecting a new account manager?
4. Susan Webb indicates that she wants to hire people with the right personality. Is this a legally allowable and defensible requirement?

CRITICAL THINKING QUESTIONS

1. You recently applied for work at a medium-sized clothing retail store as a full-time salesperson. Part of the screening process will include a group interview with some of the people you would be working with. What questions do you think they will ask you? What questions would you ask them?
2. When a labour shortage is experienced, a company may ask current employees to work overtime. What are the legal and ethical considerations of this strategy? How long would this type of strategy be sustainable?
3. A candidate may be unwilling to relocate due to family obligations and considerations. This being so, is it viable for an organization to offer employment to both spouses in order to employ the chosen candidate? What are the strategic, ethical, and legal considerations?
4. You recently applied for a barista position in a local coffee shop and have been asked to supply the names of references. Who would you select to be your references? Why did you choose these people?

BUILDING YOUR SKILLS

1. Here is your opportunity to take personality tests. Access the Jung Typology Test at Human Metrics (**www.humanmetrics.com/cgi-win/JTypes2.asp**) and the Big Five Personality Test (**www.outofservice.com/bigfive**). Complete each online assessment. Review the results. Is this consistent with your understanding and awareness of yourself? Are there any surprises? If so, what are they?

2. Working in groups of 4 or 5, list 3 recent times you have been interviewed. Working with this list, identify the type of interview conducted. Determine whether the interview questions were appropriate for the work and whether the interview was effective in attracting you to work for the organization.

3. Working in pairs, 1 person will access **easyjob.net** and click on "Resume Templates," and the other person will access **resume-now.com** and click on "Create Resume." For EasyJob Resume Builder, pick 1 of the related links with sample resumés. Review the sample resumé and then prepare your own. For Resume-Now, follow the instructions and prepare a resumé. Bring your resumé to class. Working in your pair, critique each other's resumés and identify what is similar and what is different in their formatting. Share your findings with the rest of the class.

4. Access the corporate website for Bombardier, one of Canada's premier aerospace and transportation companies, at **bombardier.com**, and click on "Careers." Watch the short video and read the rest of the information about working at Bombardier. Prepare a 1 to 2-page summary explaining why you would or would not want to work there. Comment on how effective the video was in helping you make your decision.

CASE STUDY 1

What Went Wrong?

Joseph Bloom was confused and disappointed. As IT director for a medium-sized technology firm, he knew that he had to recruit and select 3 junior analysts as the people filling these roles had all quit within the past week. Joseph couldn't believe that each person doing this job had left the company at the same time. This caused a huge gap in the workforce, and employees on this team were complaining that they would not be able to meet customer demands. Joseph knew he had to fix the problem and fix it fast!

As such, Joseph had convinced senior management that attending the local career fair was a strategic approach to generating interest in the company and acquiring resumés from students who would be graduating in the near future. The costs (registration fee, booth materials, salaries of employees who attended) were substantial, yet the response from students was dismal. Only about 20 people stopped by the booth, and of those who did, only 4 handed over a resumé.

The city's 1 university and employers from all sectors had hosted the fair. Joseph did note that representation from employers was lower than in previous years but thought that this might be due to the poor economy and that there would be fewer employment opportunities for new graduates. However, Joseph had spread word through his contacts and network in the industry and thought that students would know that his company was actively seeking to hire junior analysts and would therefore be keen to stop by his company's booth.

Joseph noticed that some companies were giving away items (pens, cellphone holders) at their booths, and this seemed to attract more students. "Well, this is just silly promotion and a waste of money," thought Joseph, but at the same time, he did wonder why the booths with items to be given to students seemed more popular. "Technology is such an exciting and dynamic profession, so we shouldn't need to entice people to stop by and hand over a resumé. Who wouldn't want to work for such a great company as ours?" Joseph knew that senior management would not be pleased when he reported the outcome from the career fair and wondered what he should do next.

Questions:

1. Going forward, what method of HR planning should Joseph use to ensure that he is not surprised when people suddenly quit, thereby causing problems due to significant gaps in the workforce?
2. Should Joseph consider internal employees to fill the current junior analyst vacancies? Why or why not?
3. Why didn't many students stop by the booth at the career fair? List 3 key reasons that can be determined based upon information provided in the case.
4. Based upon the 3 reasons you have selected, what might Joseph do differently to address each issue if the company were to attend a career fair again?

CASE STUDY 2

It Isn't Rocket Science!

Pizza Barn provides upscale takeout pizzas and has locations in major cities all across Canada. Miranda Jones, an HR analyst working at the corporate offices in Vancouver, was concerned as she reviewed statistics pertaining to the workforce during the past 6 months.

    She noted that over the past half-year, pizza makers (known as "dough masters" within the company) had a high turnover rate. Miranda compared Pizza Barn's numbers to those of other companies in the industry and found that employees were leaving at 3 times the industry average. Furthermore, pizza makers were staying with the company for an average of only 3 weeks.

    To better understand what was happening, Miranda began talking to managers at various locations across the country. Eric Anders, the manager of the Regina location, could not understand why he had such difficulty keeping staff. "Being a pizza maker is such a simple and basic job. It isn't rocket science! However, people just don't seem to like working here. When they quit, the pizza makers keep telling me that this just 'isn't their scene,' whatever that means. It seems like dough experts think this is going to be some type of exciting job and dynamic place to work and are then disappointed once they actually start doing the job." When Miranda asked about Eric's recruitment and selection process, he told her that he places advertisements at the local high schools and universities, goes through the resumés that come in, and selects the best candidates to interview. To save time, he invites 4 or 5 people to meet with him at the same time and spends about 20 minutes asking each a few behavioural questions. Eric asks for 1 or 2 references, which he does check before hiring anyone. The interview also involves a test for manual skills as pizza makers need to be coordinated. Conversations with managers at different locations across Canada yielded the same results. All managers followed processes similar to those Eric had outlined and were experiencing high levels of turnover.

Miranda was perplexed. The recruitment and selection processes were thorough, yet something wasn't working.

Questions:

1. What changes would you suggest to the recruitment and selection processes for dough masters? Why?
2. Should all Pizza Barn locations across Canada use the same recruitment and selection processes? Do geographic diversity and differences in the labour market mean that these processes should differ on the basis of location? Why or why not?
3. Should Miranda be concerned about the turnover of pizza makers? Why or why not?

NOTES AND REFERENCES

1. Peter Harris, "Labour Shortage: The 10 Hardest Jobs for Canadian Employers to Fill in 2015," Workopolis website, May 19, 2015, accessed November 1, 2017, https://careers.workopolis.com/advice/help-wanted-the-10-hardest-jobs-for-canadian-employers-to-fill-in-2015.
2. Phil Wahba, "Why Target Failed in Canada," *Fortune*, January 15, 2015, accessed February 8, 2015, http://fortune.com/2015/01/15/target-canada-fail.
3. Hollie Shaw, "'Following the Eaton's Death Spiral' Sears to End 65 Years of Retail History," *Financial Post*, October 11, 2017, accessed November 2, 2017, http://business.financialpost.com/news/retail-marketing/brief-sears-canada-to-seek-court-approval-for-liquidation.
4. P.A. Bamberger, *Human Resource Strategy: Formulation, Implementation, and Impact*, 2nd ed. (New York: Routledge, 2014).
5. Harvey Deutschendorf, "5 Ways to Boost Employee Engagement and Satisfaction in Tough Times," Business 2 Community website, April 5, 2014, accessed November 2, 2017, https://www.business2community.com/human-resources/5-ways-boost-employee-engagement-satisfaction-tough-times-0781213#vksH8gChAsKybV1w.99.
6. Heather Stockton and Karen Pastakia, "Leadership Development: A Top Concern in Canada," *Deloitte Perspectives*, accessed November 2, 2017, https://www2.deloitte.com/ca/en/pages/human-capital/articles/leadership-development-in-canada.html.
7. Statistics Canada, "Canada at a Glance," accessed October 31, 2017, http://www.statcan.gc.ca/pub/12-581-x/2017000/pop-eng.htm; Statistics Canada, "Labour Force Survey, September 2017," accessed October 31, 2017, http://www.statcan.gc.ca/daily-quotidien/171006/dq171006a-eng.htm; Josh McConnell, "Intuit Says 45% of Canadians Will Be Self-Employed by 2020, Releases New App to Help with Finances," *Financial Post*, January 23, 2017, accessed October 31, 2017, http://business.financialpost.com/technology/personal-tech/intuit-says-45-of-canadians-will-be-self-employed-by-2020-releases-new-app-to-help-with-finances; and Armina Ligaya, "Most Older Workers Who Leave Career Jobs Return to Work Within a Decade: Statistics Canada," *Financial Post*, January 28, 2014, accessed October 31, 2017, http://business.financialpost.com/2014/01/28/most-older-workers-who-leave-career-jobs-return-to-work-within-a-decade-statistics-canada.
8. "Three-Quarters of Small Businesses Lack Succession Plans," *Canadian HR Reporter*, October 17, 2011, accessed October 31, 2017, https://www.hrreporter.com/articleview/11461-three-quarters-of-small-businesses-lack-succession-plan-survey.
9. Deb Kline, "Avaya and International Avaya User Group Announce Winners of the 2014 Customer Innovation Awards," April 30, 2014, accessed November 2, 2017, https://www.avaya.com/usa/about-avaya/newsroom/news-releases/2014/pr-140430.
10. Economic Development Canada, "The Top 10 Risks for Canadian Companies Abroad," August 8, 2017, accessed October 30, 2017, https://edc.trade/top-10-company-risks; and "Here are the Top 4 Risks Facing Canada's Economy, according to the Bank of Canada," *Financial Post*, July 17, 2013, https://business.financialpost.com/2013/07/17/bank-of-canada-economy-risks.
11. Stephen King, "Accounting for the Real Cost of Employee Turnover (It's More Than You Think)," *GrowthForce*, accessed October 30, 2017, https://www.growthforce.com/blog/the-real-cost-of-employee-turnover-its-more-than-you-think.
12. "The True Cost of Employee Turnover," *Psychometrics*, accessed October 30, 2017, https://www.psychometrics.com/true-cost-employee-turnover.
13. Tara Carman, "B.C. Faces Vast Labour Shortages Unless It Can Attract More Workers," *Vancouver Sun*, February 3, 2012.
14. J. Rokkaa, K. Karlssonb, and J. Tienarib, "Balancing Acts: Managing Employees and Reputation in Social Media," *Journal of Marketing Management* 30, nos. 7–8 (2014), 802–827.
15. Interested readers can check out the websites of these companies at https://www.oracle.com/index.html and https://www.sap.com/canada/index.epx.
16. The Canadian Press, "Rona Hires Alain Brisebois to Help Improve Efficiency," *Vancouver Sun*, May 3, 2013, accessed November 2, 2017, http://www.vancouversun.com/life/Rona+hires+Alain+Brisebois+help+improve+efficiency/8332866/story.html.
17. Government of Canada, "Temporary Workers," accessed November 2, 2017, http://www.cic.gc.ca/english/resources/tools/temp/work/index.asp.
18. Lois Geller, "The AIDA Principle: Roadmap for a Lot of Great Advertising," *Forbes*, June 2, 2014, accessed February 23, 2015, https://www.forbes.com/sites/loisgeller/2014/06/02/the-aida-principle-roadmap-for-a-lot-of-great-advertising.
19. Leigh Goessl, "Study Finds Internet Job Search Reduces Time Spent Unemployed," *Digital Journal*, October 5, 2011, accessed November 2, 2017, http://digitaljournal.com/article/312400.
20. "Why Using Social Media for Recruiting Is Important," Aspire Recruitment Solutions website, February 12, 2016, accessed November 2, 2017, https://www.aspirehiring.ca/social-media-for-recruiting.
21. Susan Grant, "Technology Streamlines Recruitment," *Canadian HR Reporter*, April 11, 2011, accessed November 2, 2017, https://www.hrreporter.com/articleview/9962-technology-streamlines-recruitment.
22. "2017 Canada Top 100 Ideal Employer Ranking," accessed November 2, 2017, https://universumglobal.com/rankings/canada.

23. Robin Waghorn, "Internet Puts Spin on Traditional Career Fair," *Canadian HR Reporter*, November 21, 2011, accessed November 2, 2017, https://www.hrreporter.com/articleview/11769-internet-puts-new-spin-on-traditional-career-fair.

24. Sioffra Pratt, "How to: Unleash the Power of 'The Talent Graph,'" *Social Talent*, November 11, 2014, accessed November 2, 2017, https://www.socialtalent.com/blog/recruitment/employee-referrals-and-the-talent-graph.

25. "How to Succeed with Unsolicited Applications," Graduateland website, May 11, 2015, accessed November 2, 2017, https://graduateland.com/article/success-with-unsolicited-applications.

26. Amanda Silliker, "Making Managers Accountable for Diversity," *Canadian HR Reporter*, August 15, 2011, accessed November 2, 2017, https://www.hrreporter.com/articleview/10997-making-managers-accountable-for-diversity.

27. Marina Jiménez, "Scoring Points with Newer Canadians," *The Globe and Mail*, March 13, 2009, L1.

28. "About Us," TRIEC website, accessed November 2, 2017, http://triec.ca/about-us.

29. John Ewing, "The First Steps to Growing Your Company," *Green Industry PRO* 10 (October 2011): 11–12.

30. Farah Naqvi, "Competency Mapping and Managing Talent," *Journal of Management Research* 8, no. 1 (2009): 85–94.

31. Anne Fisher, "Are Young Job Seekers Less Ethical or Just Desperate?," *Fortune*, July 12, 2011, accessed November 3, 2017, http://management.fortune.cnn.com/2011/07/12/are-young-job-seekers-less-ethical-or-just-desperate.

32. Kate Rogers, "Why Lying on Your Resume Is Never Worth It," *Fox Business*, September 13, 2013, accessed November 2, 2017, www.foxbusiness.com/personal-finance/2013/09/13/why-should-never-lie-on-your-resume.

33. Mark Swartz, "Are Cover Letters Still Relevant?," Monster.ca website, accessed November 2, 2017, https://www.monster.ca/career-advice/article/is-writing-a-cover-letter-necessary.

34. "Bias-Free Hiring and Assessment: Removing the 'Canadian Experience' Barrier," September 24, 2013, accessed November 2, 2017, http://www.hireimmigrants.ca/resources-tools/webinars/register-now-bias-free-hiring-and-assessment-removing-the-canadian-experience-barrier.

35. Don Georgevich, "Panel Interview Tips—Five Essential Steps to a Great Panel Interview," accessed November 2, 2017, https://www.jobinterviewtools.com/blog/panel-interview-tips-five-essential-steps-great-panel-interview.

36. Tim Halloran, Director of Recruiting, Monster.com, video accessed January 10, 2012, through YouTube and GreenJobInterview.com.

37. Nita Wilmott, "Interviewing Styles: Tips for Interview Approaches," About.com: Human Resources, accessed November 2, 2017, http://humanresources.about.com/cs/selectionstaffing/a/interviews.htm.

38. Murray R. Barrick, Brian W. Swider, and Greg L. Stewart, "Initial Evaluations in the Interview," *Journal of Applied Psychology* 95, no. 6 (2010): 1163–1172.

39. Hanna Dunn, "Behavioural Interviews Deserve Accolades," *Canadian HR Reporter*, July 12, 2010, accessed November 2, 2017, https://www.hrreporter.com/articleview/8031-behavioural-interviews-deserve-accolades.

40. "Interview Format Influences Perception of Hiring Fairness: Study," *Canadian HR Reporter*, May 21, 2010, accessed November 3, 2017, https://www.hrreporter.com/articleview/7872-interview-format-influences-perception-of-hiring-fairness-study.

41. "Bias-Free Hiring and Assessment: Removing the 'Canadian Experience' Barrier."

42. Wallace Immen, "Want Better Employees? Ask Better Questions," *The Globe and Mail*, January 6, 2012, B14.

43. For additional resources on employment testing, see Robert M. Guion, *Assessment, Measurement and Prediction for Personnel Decisions*, 2nd ed. (New York: Routledge, 2011).

44. Jana Szostek and Charles J. Hobson, "Employment Test Evaluation Made Easy," *Employee Relations Law Journal* 37, no. 2 (Autumn 2011): 67–74.

45. Arthur B. Smith, Jr. and Michael H. Cramer, "Supreme Court Rules on Pre-employment Tests and Disparate Impact," *Texas Employment Law*, July 2010, 6.

46. Yanseen Hemeda and Joan Sum, "Understanding Pre-employment Testing," *Canadian HR Reporter*, November 21, 2011, accessed November 3, 2017, https://www.hrreporter.com/articleview/11765-understanding-pre-employment-testing.

47. "Hiring Assessments: Setting Your Team Up For Success," Corvirtus website, April 14, 2017, accessed November 3, 2017, http://corvirtus.com/hiring-assessments-for-team-success.

48. David W. Freeman, "Wonderlic Test on Tap for NFL Hopefuls: What It Is and Who Has Highest Score?," *CBC News*, February 24, 2011, accessed November 3, 2017, https://www.cbsnews.com/8301-504763_162-20035953-10391704.html?tag=mncol;lst;7.

49. Ben Dattner and Robert Hogan, "Can You Handle Failure?," *Harvard Business Review*, April 2011, 117–121.

50. Rick Smith, "Building on Your Strengths," *HR Professional* 27, no. 1 (January 2010): 22–25.

51. Cary Cherniss, "Emotional Intelligence: New Insights and Further Clarifications," *Industrial and Organizational Psychology* 3 (2010): 183–191.

52. Ibid.

53. Frank Walter, Michael S. Cole, and Ronald H. Humphrey, "Emotional Intelligence: Sine Qua Non of Leadership or Folderol?," *Academy of Management* (February 2011): 45–59.

54. Norman D. Henderson, "Predicting Long-Term Firefighter Performance from Cognitive and Physical Ability Measures," *Personnel Psychology* 3 (2010): 999–1039.

55. Lisa Stam, "Pot in the Workplace," *Employment and Human Rights Law in Canada*, August 2, 2017, accessed November 3, 2017, https://www.canadaemploymenthumanrightslaw.com/2017/08/pot-in-the-workplace.

56. Ken Cahoon, "Pre-employment Screening—What Is Necessary?" *Canadian HR Reporter*, July 18, 2011, accessed November 3, 2017, https://www.hrreporter.com/articleview/10784-pre-employment-screening-what-is-necessary.

57. John Hollon, "How Important Are Reference Checks? They Knock Out 20% of Job Candidates," *Talent Management and HR*, June 23, 2010, accessed November 3, 2017, https://www.tlnt.com/how-important-are-reference-checks-they-knock-out-20-of-job-candidates.

58. The National Association of Professional Background Screeners website, accessed November 3, 2017, https://www.napbs.com.

59. Shannon Klie, "Tread Carefully with Credit Checks: Privacy Commissioner," *Canadian HR Reporter*, March 22, 2010, accessed November 3, 2017, https://www.hrreporter.com/articleview/7670-tread-carefully-with-credit-checks-privacy-commissioner.

60. Michael Overell, "Reference Checks and Social Media: On Shaky Ground?," RecruitLoop website, November 10, 2011, accessed November 2, 2017, http://recruitloop.com/blog/reference-checks-and-social-media-on-shaky-ground.

61. Paul R. Sackett and Filip Lievens, "Personnel Selection," *Annual Review of Psychology* 59 (2008): 16.1–16.32.

62. Robert M. Guion, *Assessment, Measurement and Prediction for Personnel Decisions*, 2nd ed. (New York: Routledge, 2011), 427.

63. "Be Prepared for Motivation-Based Interviews; They Are Tough and Get to the Core of the Applicant," January 8, 2013, accessed November 3, 2017, http://thingscareerrelated.com/2013/01/08/be-prepared-for-motivation-based-interviews-they-are-tough-and-get-to-the-core-of-the-applicant.

64. Ibid.

THIS MAKES SCENTS (PART 2)

After receiving Jessie's harsh email, Ashton asked her to come to the store so that they could talk in person. When Jessie opened up about all of her concerns and frustrations, they were able to talk things out and design a more equitable way to divide the work and responsibilities of owning and operating the store. A list of how to split responsibilities was developed for Jessie and Ashton, and this information was shared with employees. This allowed everyone to fully understand which owner was responsible for different workplace issues.

Furthermore, Jessie and Ashton worked together and successfully wrote an employee handbook, which included policies regarding safety, overtime, holidays, and respect in the workplace. Creating this document as a team helped remind Jessie and Ashton that they worked well together and really did have the same vision to provide high-quality mock perfume at reasonable prices. As well, they had taken all employees out for a night of pizza and bowling, and the event was a huge success. Everyone got along well, and the atmosphere in the store seemed better after this evening out.

More Employees Needed?

Ashton was still convinced that they needed to hire more employees, so he emailed Jessie about this. He wanted to hire 2 more sales clerks and an inventory specialist. Jessie wrote back indicating that these people would cut into profits and they shouldn't hire more people until they were sure that they were needed. "Besides, our current employees seem to be managing inventory, so we don't need someone specifically in charge of this task," wrote Jessie. Ashton wrote back indicating that on 3 separate occasions when he was in the store customers had asked for a specific product only to be told that it wasn't in stock. Ashton noted, "Business is being lost because of ineffective inventory management. I happen to know that my cousin Ashley could take on this role and would enhance and grow our profits." Jessie once again replied and suggested that they interview each employee individually to gain a better understanding of the work each performs. "Only then can we determine if we need more sales clerks and an inventory specialist. Also, other employees will find out if we hire your cousin, and this could be seen as unfair."

Ashton was becoming frustrated with the back-and-forth communication. Maybe things weren't going as well as he thought. One more email back to Jessie was worth a try, so he responded, "We will figure out what each employee does. If we need to hire an inventory specialist (and I'm betting we do), we can put together an effective and efficient recruitment plan to hire the best person for the job. I'm not sure why employees would care whom we hire, but I'm putting an action plan in place to address all of your ongoing concerns."

Questions:

1. Is meeting with each employee individually the best method of job analysis? What other method(s) could be used and why?
2. Should written job descriptions be developed for each employee's position? Why or why not?
3. If an inventory specialist is needed, should Jessie and Ashton hire Ashley for this role? Why or why not?
4. If external recruitment is used, where should Jessie and Ashton advertise this opportunity?
5. Who should be involved in interviewing people for any new positions? Why?
6. What other key recruitment and selection considerations should Jessie and Ashton address?

6 Orienting, Training, and Developing Employees

LEARNING OUTCOMES

After studying this chapter, you should be able to

1 Describe the benefits of employee orientation.

2 Outline the steps in the instructional systems design approach (ADDIE model) to training and development.

3 Describe the components of a needs assessment.

4 Explain the 3 key issues that should be focused on during program design.

5 Discuss various types of training methods.

6 List 4 methods to evaluate training.

7 Explain how a career development program integrates individual and organizational needs.

OUTLINE

Introduction
Orientation
Benefits of Orientation
Continuous Process
Cooperative Endeavour
Careful Planning
Training and Development: Instructional Systems Design
Phase 1: Conducting the Needs Assessment
Phase 2: Designing the Program
Phase 3: Developing the Program
Phase 4: Implementing the Program
Training Methods
Phase 5: Evaluating the Program
Internal versus External Resources

Training Focus
Basic Skills
Teamwork
The Training Landscape
Investment
Career Development—Individual and Organizational Needs
Creating Favourable Conditions
Management Support
Goal Setting
HRM Practices to Enhance Career Development
Mentorship to Enhance Career Development
Keeping a Career in Perspective

HRM CLOSE-UP

"It's really about continuous learning and trying to create the energy and the belief that people should strive to be lifelong learners in order to maximize their success."

IN 2006, BC Ferries' *Queen of the North* sank south of Prince Rupert. Although 99 passengers and crew were saved, 2 passengers disappeared and were presumed drowned. The accident precipitated an overhaul of every aspect of BC Ferries that has resulted in the company becoming an industry leader not just in Canada but around the world.

Prior to the accident, BC Ferries' onboarding process was the same as that in many other organizations. "If you were new to the company, were moving to another vessel, or being promoted, you would be hooked up with someone and follow that person around, observe, and listen and eventually try things out under that person's oversight," explains Jeff Joyce, director of terminal engineering. "When it was reasonably felt that you were capable of safely doing the job yourself, you were given a clearance for that position."

As customary as that was at the time, it was too reliant on the skills of the person being shadowed. If that staff member wasn't sufficiently experienced, was too busy, or just didn't enjoy being shadowed, the results could be inconsistent. Although it had worked well enough for 45 years, it became apparent that a more standardized training system might produce more consistent results.

The outcome was BC Ferries' Standardized Education and Assessment (SEA) program and its Simulator Training Centres (STC).

"What we do now in almost all of our entry-level positions is put them through a bit of training before we even decide to hire them, just to see how they perform," says Joyce. That pre-hiring training is the first phase of SEA and requires candidates to immerse themselves in an online self-study workbook. Only once they have passed a multiple-choice exam can they advance further in the hiring process.

"It really ups the ante for the candidate recognizing that we're serious about our training and that we want to make sure that we have effective people and safe people with the right qualities," says Joyce.

Once hired, new employees undergo a day-long orientation program. From there they advance to the second phase of SEA, on-board or on-site education.

"The third phase of the program is the clearance phase, which includes the exam as well as demonstrative activities that they have to do," Joyce explains. "It's sort of like a board approach, where they have to respond to scenarios that are given to them verbally. Employees have to be successful in every phase in order to be cleared and officially allowed to work."

SEA continues well beyond hiring, however. The fourth phase focuses on skill enhancement and career progression, providing BC Ferries' more than 4000 employees with the constant opportunity for professional advancement. "It's a process that ensures that for those that want it, there's always hope and a career path," Joyce says. "It's about continuous learning and trying to create the energy and the belief that people should strive to be lifelong learners in order to maximize their success."

As mentioned, along with SEA, BC Ferries also rolled out their state-of-the-art Simulator Training Centres.

Courtesy of Jeff Joyce

Jeff Joyce, Director, Terminal Engineering, BC Ferries

"The simulation training program started as an idea to improve bridge team effectiveness, and we went through a planning and procuring process to eventually start delivering curriculum in October 2011," Joyce says. Today, the company has 3 bridge simulators, and during the summer, when all hands are literally on deck carrying customers, the centres' instructors head out to the fleet to observe the bridge teams in action and to evaluate if the STC lessons are being incorporated into daily use.

Not only have SEA and STC improved the company's safety record, but since their introduction, there has been a drop in absenteeism, an improvement in staff retention levels, and an increase in the number of staff involved in delivering training, from 67 to 425. In addition, other marine service providers have expressed an interest in using BC Ferries' excess capacity in the simulators, providing the company with a possible extra revenue stream.

"We've also had 2 international awards presented to us as a result of both the SEA program and the STC," Joyce adds with quiet pride. "Due to our practice of involving front-line employees in the development of SEA material and STC curricula, both have proven to be powerful employee engagement tools as well. The sustainment of both is largely due to our employees' efforts in continuously improving the products."

INTRODUCTION

The ability of an organization to ensure that its people continue to learn, grow, and develop has become critical to business success. As noted in Chapter 1, organizations often compete on competencies—the core sets of knowledge and expertise that give them an edge over their competitors. Frequently, they refer to "intellectual capital," the combination of the "human capital" (the competencies) and the organizational support that enables human capital to flourish.[1] Furthermore, as individuals learn (e.g., the human capital increases), the organization has the potential to learn. Only through individuals does the organization gain knowledge.[2] Therefore, learning and development are a critical part of any organization, with **orientation**, **training**, and **development** playing a central role in enabling, nurturing, and strengthening the human capital in the organization. As shown in the HRM Close-up, BC Ferries understands the strategic importance of this and actively supports the learning, growth, and development of employees.

Furthermore, as will be discussed in this chapter, it is critical that organizations approach learning and development in a systematic way. Doing so will ensure a clear linkage to the organization's strategic direction. Rapidly changing technologies require that employees continuously hone their KSAs (knowledge, skills, and abilities), or "competencies," to cope with new processes and systems. Jobs that require little skill are rapidly being replaced by ones that require technical, interpersonal, and problem-solving skills. And, as described, the business world is constantly changing, requiring improved skills and abilities. As noted in Chapter 4, careful job analysis and job design provide information regarding the required competencies within a job; therefore, these processes identify potential areas where employees require enhanced learning and development.

A carefully designed learning and development program can also be a key lever in attracting and retaining people with the key competencies that will keep the organization's competitive advantage. Succession planning, as discussed in Chapter 5, is also linked to strategic learning and development as employees who have been identified to take on higher-level jobs within a company may require opportunities to enhance their abilities in order to take on increased roles and responsibilities.

The manager plays a key role in ensuring that learning and development efforts are appropriate and reinforced for the individuals for whom they are responsible. Without the manager's involvement, organizational growth, success, and sustainability might be at risk. Other trends toward empowerment, total quality management, teamwork, and globalization make it necessary for managers as well as employees to develop the skills that will enable them to handle new and more demanding work.

ORIENTATION

Orientation, or employee onboarding, is a very particular type of training. The first objective in the process is to get new employees off to a good start, and this is generally achieved through a formal orientation program. As discussed in Chapter 5, employers should approach recruitment and selection of new employees with a strategic and well-planned

Orientation
A structured process for new employees to become familiar with the organization and their work; critical to socialization, which is the embedding of organizational values, beliefs, and accepted behaviours

Training
The acquisition of skills, behaviours, and abilities to perform current work

Development
The acquisition of skills, behaviours, and abilities to perform future work or to solve an organizational problem

approach. After hiring people, through effective recruitment and selection, it is important to then make sure that these employees are properly welcomed into, and informed about, their new workplaces. As such, orientation is a structured process for new employees to become familiar with the organization and their work. Socialization, or the embedding of organizational values, beliefs, and accepted behaviours, is also a key outcome. The benefit for new employees is that it allows them to get "in sync" so that they become productive members of the organization. Orientation is a process—not a 1-day event. Furthermore, it is important to remember that how employees are treated when they first come on board makes a huge impact on their views of managers and the organization.

Benefits of Orientation

In some organizations, a formal new-hire orientation process is almost non-existent or, when it does exist, is performed in a casual manner. Some employees may show up for the first day on a new job, being told to work, but receiving no instructions, introductions, or support. This situation is unfortunate because a number of practical and cost-effective benefits can be derived from conducting a well-run orientation. Benefits frequently reported by employers include the following:[3]

LO1

Describe the benefits of employee orientation.

1. Lower turnover.
2. Increased productivity.
3. Improved employee morale and identification with the company.
4. Lower training costs.
5. Facilitation of learning.
6. Reduction of anxiety.

The more time and effort an organization devotes to making new employees feel welcome, the more likely they are to identify with the organization and the more quickly they are to become productive. Orientation is designed to help employees acquire a certain attitude about the work and their role in the organization. It defines the philosophy behind the rules and provides a framework for their work in that organization.

Continuous Process

Since an organization is faced with ever-changing conditions, its plans, policies, and procedures must change with these conditions. Unless current employees are kept up to date with these changes, they may find themselves embarrassingly unaware of activities to which new employees are being oriented. Although the discussion that follows focuses primarily on the needs of new employees, it is important that all employees be continually reoriented to changing conditions.

Cooperative Endeavour

For a well-integrated orientation process, cooperation between managers and HR professionals is essential. HR professionals usually design an overall orientation program and make sure that new employees receive complete information regarding their pay and benefits, which includes ensuring that all proper employment forms are signed. However, the manager has the most important role in the orientation process. New employees are interested primarily in what their manager says and does and what their new coworkers are like. Before the arrival of a new employee, the manager should inform the work group that a new worker is joining the unit. It is also common practice for managers to ask another employee to be guide or mentor to a new person. This approach conveys an emphasis on teamwork and provides a new employee with direct access to colleagues who can continue to assist them and respond to questions.

A coworker acting as a sponsor or buddy for a new employee can be an important part of orientation.

Careful Planning

An orientation process can make an immediate and lasting impression on an employee that can mean the difference between the employee's success and failure. Thus, careful planning—with an emphasis on goals, topics to be covered, and methods of organizing and presenting them—is essential. Successful orientation processes emphasize the individual's needs for information, understanding, and a feeling of belonging. Using checklists is a tool used by many organizations to ensure that all important information is given to a new employee and that key information is not overlooked. Orientation information can also be printed and given to the new employee. Companies are also beginning to use their intranets to make the information more readily available to their employees.

Toolkit 6.1 suggests items to include in an orientation checklist for managers. Orientation should focus on matters of immediate concern, such as important aspects of the job and organizational behaviour expectations (e.g., attendance and safety). Since orientation focuses on helping the new employee become familiar, comfortable, and productive, it is important not to overwhelm or provide too much information at one time. Those planning an orientation process should take into account the anxiety employees feel during their first few days. Anxiety is natural, but if employees are too anxious, training costs, turnover, absenteeism, and even production costs may increase. Anxiety reduction can be accomplished by establishing specific times at which the manager will be available for questions or coaching. Furthermore, reassuring newcomers that the performance levels they are observing among their coworkers will be attained within a predetermined time frame, based on experiences with other newcomers, can decrease anxiety. This reassurance is particularly important for employees with limited work experience who are learning new skills.

Also, as discussed in Chapter 3, organizations need to pay special attention to the health and safety of employees who must be made aware of their rights and responsibilities. The general legislation states that health and safety orientation and training must occur before employees begin working and that the manager must continue to coach and train the new workers after the initial orientation and training. HRM and the Law 6.1 highlights the importance of health and safety training and the disastrous outcomes when this is not done.

TOOLKIT 6.1   MANAGER'S ORIENTATION CHECKLIST

1. Formal greeting, including introduction to colleagues.
2. Explanation of job procedures, duties, and responsibilities.
3. Training to be received (when and why).
4. Manager's and organization's expectations regarding attendance and behaviour norms.
5. Job standards and production and service levels.
6. Performance appraisal criteria, including estimated time frame to achieve peak performance.
7. Conditions of employment, including hours of work, pay periods, and overtime requirements.
8. Organization and work unit rules, regulations, and policies.
9. Overview of health and safety expectations, as well as when specific training will occur.
10. Those to notify or turn to if problems or questions arise.
11. Chain of command for reporting purposes.
12. An overall explanation of the organization's operation and purpose.
13. A review of the organizational chart or structure indicating departments and work flow.
14. Offers of help and encouragement, including a specific time each week (in the early stages of employment) for questions or coaching.

HRM AND THE LAW 6.1   COMPANY DIRECTOR SENTENCED TO JAIL

In 2017, a precedent-setting occupational health and safety (OHS) case was decided, and for the first time in Alberta's history, a worker who was also a company director was sentenced to jail for a period of 4 months following his conviction under Alberta's *Occupational Health and Safety Act*.

In April 2015, Frederick Tomyn had been hired as a day labourer by Sukhwinder Singh Nagra to dig a trench behind a home development in Edmonton and install a new water and sewer connection. Mr. Tomyn was an Assured Income for the Severely Handicapped (AISH) recipient who had no experience with this type of work, did not have any safety training, and did not receive any relevant training from Mr. Nagra or the employer.

Despite having no previous training in construction or excavation, Mr. Nagra proceeded to dig a deep trench using a backhoe and directed that Mr. Tomyn enter the trench to connect pipes. The trench collapsed, burying Mr. Tomyn alive and resulting in his death.

The Crown prosecutor sought a $425,000 fine together with a victim fine surcharge of $63,750, which was eventually awarded. However, the Court concluded that the extreme facts of the case also warranted jail time and ordered Mr. Nagra to serve 4 months in incarceration. The court made it clear that this level of sentencing was required to ensure that others would be deterred from engaging in similar violations of this critical legislation and made note that Mr. Tomyn was a particularly vulnerable worker.

This case is a reminder to employers and employees that understanding and complying with OHS laws is vital, including the requirement to provide employees with proper training, and that infractions can result in extremely serious outcomes for everyone involved.

CRITICAL THINKING QUESTIONS:

1. Was the penalty of jail time too harsh in this case?
2. Will the financial penalty and jail time serve as motivators for other employers to provide appropriate health and safety training? Why or why not?

Source: Adapted from Jennifer Miller, Q.C., Simon Foxcroft, and Mathieu LaFleche, "Precedent Setting Alberta OHS Case: Excavation Company Director Sentenced to Jail," accessed November 12, 2017, https://www.bennettjones.com/en/Blogs-Section/Precedent-Setting-Alberta-OHS-Case-Excavation-Company-Director-Sentenced-to-Jail.

Learning
A relatively permanent change in knowledge or behaviour

TRAINING AND DEVELOPMENT: INSTRUCTIONAL SYSTEMS DESIGN

Training typically refers to skills, behaviours, and abilities employees can apply to their current work; *development* is typically focused on assisting employees in fulfilling future job requirements or solving an organization's problems. The wording "training and development" is often used to capture the various processes and activities used by organizations to increase the abilities and capabilities of their employees.

You often hear the word **learning** as well. Learning refers to an ongoing change in behaviour and thinking: ultimately the goal of training and development.

The primary reason organizations train new employees is to bring their KSAs and competencies up to the level required for satisfactory performance. As these employees continue on the job, development provides opportunities for them to acquire new knowledge and skills to perform jobs in other areas or at higher levels.

For help in understanding the importance of training in today's business environment, refer to Figure 6.1, which lists the skills many employers seek.

The primary goal of training and development is to contribute to the organization's overall goals; therefore, programs and opportunities should be structured with an eye to attaining desired organizational outcomes and strategies. Unfortunately, many organizations never make the connection between their strategic objectives and their training and development programs. Instead, fads, fashions, or "whatever the competition is doing" sometimes drives the agenda. As a result, much of an organization's investment can be wasted.

FIGURE 6.1 Workplace Skills and Capabilities

Employees want to know what employers are looking for today in skill sets. Although all employers do not look for all of these, employees are expected to have many of the following:

Core Skills

- Read and understand information presented in different forms (e.g., words, graphs).
- Write and speak so that others understand.
- Use computer software and hardware to produce useful information.
- Use relevant knowledge and skills (scientific, technological) to explain and clarify.
- Use numerical data to evaluate possibilities and make a decision.
- Manage time effectively and efficiently operate basic office equipment to implement effective work processes.

Interpersonal and/or Soft Skills

- Be flexible and adaptable.
- Be honest and ethical.
- Be open to working with a diverse group of people.
- Be respectful to the thoughts and opinions of others.
- Be able to effectively manage conflict.
- Be able to consistently demonstrate a positive attitude and willingness to embrace change.
- Be willing to keep learning.

Sources: Adapted from Lori Jazvac, "Marketable Skills for the Future," Career Professionals of Canada, accessed November 14, 2017, https://careerprocanada.ca/trends-future-marketable-skills; "What Do Canadian Employers Want?," Settlement.org, accessed November 14, 2017; and "Employability Skills," The Conference Board of Canada, accessed November 14, 2017, http://www.conferenceboard.ca/spse/employability-skills.aspx?AspxAutoDetectCookieSupport=1.

The amount of training employees require in order to do their jobs will vary from person to person. As well, employees will require different levels and types of development in order to fulfill future roles in the organization. It is important to note that *all* employees need some type of training and development on an ongoing basis to maintain effective performance, or to adjust to new ways of work, and to remain motivated and engaged in their work. Therefore, to ensure that investments in training and development have the maximum impact on individual and organizational performance, a systems approach should be used. The instructional systems design approach (often referred to as the ADDIE model) involves 5 phases: (1) needs assessment, (2) program design, (3) program development, (4) training delivery or implementation, and (5) evaluation of training.[4] Although the word "training" will be used in the discussion on the systems approach, all elements refer to orientation and development as well. Figure 6.2 illustrates the ADDIE model.

Each phase of the systems approach will now be reviewed.

Phase 1: Conducting the Needs Assessment

Managers and HR professionals should stay alert to the kinds of training needed, where the training is needed, who needs the training, and which methods will best deliver increased abilities to employees. Typically, a problem or customer complaint signals that training may be required. For example, if employees frequently miss sales target or if complaints regarding poor customer service are received, this might indicate that employees require training in order to do their jobs properly.

To make certain that training is timely and focused on priority issues and that training is the right solution for the concern, managers should approach a needs assessment systematically. You might think of this as trying to identify the training problem. The needs assessment can occur at the organizational level (examining the environment and strategy of the company to see where to put training emphasis), the task level (reviewing the activities of the work to determine the competencies needed), and the person level (reviewing which employees need training).

A needs assessment can be done by asking (and answering) the following 4 questions:

1. How important is this issue to the success of the organization? If it is important, proceed to questions 2, 3, and 4.
2. What competencies or knowledge, skills, and abilities do employees *need*?
3. What competencies or knowledge, skills, and abilities do the employees currently *have*?
4. What is the gap between the desired (need) and the actual (have)?

Once answers have been determined, then specific action plans can be developed to address the gap. For example, since the vehicular attacks in Toronto and Edmonton, training for police officers has increased in order to help these employees learn how to deal with unforeseen circumstances that threaten public safety and security.

Toolkit 6.2 provides some suggestions for an approach to identifying training needs.

Other training issues tend to revolve around the strategic initiatives of an organization. Mergers and acquisitions, for example, frequently require that employees take on new roles and responsibilities and adjust to new cultures and ways of conducting business. Nowhere is this more prevalent than in grooming new leaders within organizations. Other issues, such as technological change, globalization, re-engineering, and total quality management, all influence the way work is done and the types of skills needed to do it. Still other concerns may be more tactical but no less important in their impact on training. Organizational restructuring, downsizing, empowerment, and teamwork, for example, have immediate training requirements.

Finally, trends in the workforce itself have an impact. As mentioned in Chapter 1, employees increasingly value self-development and personal growth, and with this has come an enormous desire for learning. At the same time, as older workers may decide to postpone

FIGURE 6.2 ADDIE Model

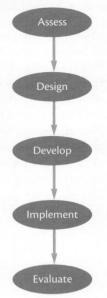

LO3

Describe the components of a needs assessment.

TOOLKIT 6.2 — IDENTIFYING TRAINING NEEDS

The following steps may be taken to discover an organization's requirements for training:

1. Invite key stakeholders (i.e., job incumbents and managers) to a brainstorming session. Be sure to advise attendees of the purpose of the meeting in advance and have a trained facilitator lead the discussion.
2. With the group, review the organization's strategic plans and desired outcomes.
3. Through discussion, conduct a gap analysis and identify training opportunities to assist employees in achieving these key goals. Determine the training priorities. This step may be done using the nominal group technique.
4. Training priorities and outcomes should be as detailed as possible. For example, do not list "communication skills" as a desired outcome. Instead, as examples, list oral presentation skills or report writing skills.
5. Encourage attendees to suggest ways to conduct the training and ensure that support and resources are available to ensure successful implementation.

retirement, training will need to be done for a variety of different generations. Because no company in the private sector can count on stable employment levels, organizations as diverse as Inco and Boeing are facing situations in which they need to prepare the next generations of employees as the current groups approach retirement.

It is important that the manager be knowledgeable about the organization's needs, the requirements of the work, and the capabilities of an employee in order to assess that training is the right solution. Training efforts (and dollars) can be wasted if the manager has not adequately determined whether training is appropriate. The question to ask here is something like: "If Joe receives more training on how to handle customer complaints, will his performance improve?" If performance issues are due to ability problems, training may likely be a good intervention. However, if an employee's poor performance is caused by other issues, such as a lack of resources to properly do the job or a lack of desire to do

diego_cervo/Thinkstock

A thorough needs assessment should be done before any training occurs.

the job properly, training may not solve the problem. Managers need to communicate with employees and have frank conversations regarding performance concerns in order to ensure that any training provided will actually improve the situation.[5]

Phase 2: Designing the Program

Once the training needs have been determined, the next step is to design appropriate training programs. The success of training programs depends on more than the organization's ability to identify training needs. Success hinges on taking the information gained from the needs analysis and utilizing it to design first-rate training programs. Starting a training program without considering design is like building a house without a blueprint. It makes much more sense to start with a clear plan of how everything in the training program will be laid out and how all of the content will fit together. As well, learner engagement, length and sequence of material, and time provided for each component of training are other examples of issues that should also be addressed. Experts believe that training design should focus on at least 3 related issues: (1) instructional goals, (2) trainee characteristics, and (3) learning principles.

Instructional Goals

As a result of conducting needs analysis at 3 levels (organization, task, and person), managers will better understand an organization's training needs. Based upon this information, desired training outcomes, through written **instructional goals**, can be developed. Generally, instructional goals describe the skills and knowledge the company wants people to have and the behaviours employees should acquire or change. For example, a stated goal for 1 training program might be "Employees trained in team methods will be able to demonstrate the following skills within 6 months: problem-solving, conflict resolution, and effective team meetings."

Frequently, managers will seek external resources to design the training program and write the instructional goals. However, they will contribute help and guidance. It is therefore important for managers to be able to specifically describe what they want the person to do or how they want the person to act after completing a training program.

Trainee Characteristics

When designing training, the characteristics of the trainees must be considered, with specific attention to readiness and motivation. Trainee readiness refers to both maturity and experience factors in the trainee's background. Prospective trainees should be screened to determine that they have the right skills and experiences that will allow them to learn what is being delivered. **Trainee readiness** will also be impacted by previous success, or lack of success, encountered in previous training situations. Motivation is also an important consideration if optimum learning is to take place as trainees must recognize the need for new knowledge or skills and must maintain a desire to learn as training progresses. By focusing on the trainees rather than on the trainer or training topic, the opportunity for learning will be enhanced. Six strategies can be essential:

1. Use positive reinforcement.
2. Eliminate threats and punishment.
3. Be flexible.
4. Have participants set personal goals.
5. Design interesting instruction.
6. Break down physical and psychological obstacles to learning.

Although most employees are motivated by certain common needs, they differ from one another in the relative importance of these needs at any given time. Training objectives that are clearly related to trainees' individual needs will increase the motivation of employees to succeed in training programs. Again, the manager plays a vital role in ensuring that the training is suitable for the person and that the person is ready to take on the training initiative.

LO4
Explain the 3 key issues that should be focused on during program design.

Instructional goals
Desired outcomes of a training program

Trainee readiness
The consideration of trainees' skills and experiences when assessing their ability to benefit from training

Learning Principles

The success or failure of a training program is frequently related to certain learning principles. Therefore, managers as well as employees should understand that different training methods or techniques vary in the extent to which they utilize these concepts. When investing in effective and efficient training programs, it is important that they incorporate the following principles of learning:

1. *Clear outcomes.* It is important that the goals for the training are clear.
2. *Relevance.* People need to know why outcomes have been set. Application and usefulness of learning are critical.
3. *Activity.* Engaging with other people and exchanging ideas and active exploration are important. Listening to someone else explain concepts is not enough.
4. *Focus on solving problems.* Although content is important, the application of what is being learned to resolve difficulties is important. A practical, results-based approach to learning is required.
5. *Feedback.* People need to know how they are doing. Feedback (e.g., verbally from the instructor, through tests, from peers) helps keep learners focused and motivated.

> **Behaviour modification**
> Belief that the consequences of behaviour determine if it will be repeated or discontinued

When designing training, organizations may consider the concept of **behaviour modification**. This practice is based on the premise that the consequences of behaviour determine if it will be repeated or not. For example, if a behaviour is rewarded, it is more likely to continue, whereas if a behaviour results in punishment, then it is likely to stop. For example, in customer service training, it is possible to identify specific actions that are examples of going the extra mile to serve guests. After training occurs, or during the actual training, trainers and managers can use rewards to ensure that the desired behaviour continues.

Phase 3: Developing the Program

Once training needs have been identified and the program has been designed, the next step is to create the content. This involves various processes, such as writing the lesson plans or creating the online subject matter and supporting technological platforms. During this stage, the proposed training should be tested on a group of employees, reviewed by a subject matter expert, or benchmarked against other programs that have achieved desired outcomes. The goal is to ensure that the planned training will deliver the required results.

Phase 4: Implementing the Program

The choice of how to deliver, or implement, a training program is critical to its success. A major consideration in choosing among various training methods is to examine what is to be learned. For example, if the goal is to have trainees remember a large amount of factual data, a lecture may be an appropriate method. However, if the training requires significant behavioural change, a more active method, such as on-the-job training, would be more suitable.

Furthermore, the success of any training activity will depend in large part on the skills and personal characteristics of those responsible for conducting the training. Good trainers, whether staff persons, managers, or external facilitators, need to be knowledgeable about the subject, be well prepared, have good communication skills, and be enthusiastic about the subject matter. Therefore, careful consideration as to who will deliver the training must be given during the implementation phase.

Various methods to implement or deliver training (and/or development) will now be reviewed.

Training Methods

A wide variety of methods can be implemented for training employees at all levels. Some of the methods have a long history of use. Newer methods have emerged as the result of a greater understanding of human behaviour, particularly in the areas of learning, motivation, and interpersonal relationships. More recently, technological advances, especially in Web 2.0 technologies and social media, from blogs to virtual collaboration environments, have resulted in emerging learning approaches that, in many instances, are more effective and economical than the traditional training methods. It is now becoming increasingly common for organizations to use several different delivery methods, and it is expected that the way people learn and receive training will continue to evolve as learning becomes increasingly learner driven and collaborative.[6] The awareness and prevalence of informal learning (e.g., seeking information from coworkers or the Internet) continue to grow, prompted by the increased need of organizations to transfer and retain knowledge as leaders from the baby boom cohort approach retirement.[7] Informal e-learning through communities of practice, sharing of experiences, and self-learning is growing rapidly.[8]

The following are various types of training methods that can more or less blend formal, informal, and social learning.

On-the-Job Training

On-the-job training (OJT) is a common method for providing active experience to trainees while they learn new skills. Trainees are given the opportunity to perform work under the guidance of a more experienced employee. Three common drawbacks of OJT are (1) the lack of a well-structured training environment, (2) poor training skills of managers, and (3) the absence of well-defined job performance criteria.

Toolkit 6.3 describes some basic steps that can be taken to effectively provide OJT.

Apprenticeship Training

Apprenticeship training is typically used when an employee needs to learn a specific skill or trade. Many former fishers left the declining East Coast fishery to join in a seafarers' training program funded by several companies, the federal government, and the Nova Scotia government to learn new skills working in the engine rooms of larger vessels. Magna International, the auto parts giant, pays students to train as millwrights and tool-and-die makers. Learning is offered in shops, laboratories, and classrooms. Employers in the oil industry in Alberta

> **LO5**
> Discuss various types of training methods.

> **On-the-job training (OJT)**
> Method by which employees are given hands-on experience with instructions from their manager or another trainer

> **Apprenticeship training**
> System of training in which a worker entering the skilled trades is given thorough instruction and experience, both on and off the job, in the practical and theoretical aspects of the work

---

TOOLKIT 6.3   **ON-THE-JOB TRAINING**

T   *Talk.* Spend time explaining the job to a new employee. Provide documentation or manuals that provide written instructions. Explain how these resources can be used. It is important to spend time conversing and not jump right into showing how the job should be done.

R   *Review.* Go over the key elements of the job. Provide an overview of what is required.

A   *Answer.* Let the employee ask a lot of questions and patiently respond to these inquiries.

I   *Initiate.* When the employee is comfortable and ready to do so, he or she should try to do the job.

N   *Nurture.* Continue to assist the employee and provide ongoing feedback and reassurance. Training should continue until the employee feels confident in doing the job without someone continuously observing.

goodluz/Shutterstock.com

Apprenticeship training provides the opportunity for a younger employee to learn by working beside a more experienced person.

have established an apprenticeship approach to ensure that oil-patch workers have the appropriate training. The Banff World Media Festival and Shaw Media have developed a Corus Writer's Apprentice Program that provides emerging Canadian writers with the opportunity to gain experience by apprenticing in the story department of a prime-time series.[9]

Co-operative and Internship Programs

Co-operative programs
Training programs that combine practical, on-the-job experience with formal education

Internship programs
Programs jointly sponsored by colleges, universities, and other organizations that offer students the opportunity to gain real-life experience while allowing them to find out how they will perform in work organizations

Co-operative programs and **internship programs** provide trainees with a combination of on-the-job experience and formal education. Typically, co-op programs are offered at colleges and universities; as part of their education, students work at selected organizations. Although they don't get course credit, they do earn a salary for their work and graduate with an indication that they have been involved in a co-op program. They can thereby demonstrate to prospective employers that they have work experience. The pioneer in co-op education is the University of Waterloo, but there are now co-op programs throughout Canada. Syncrude Canada, Harley-Davidson, and Canadian Microelectronics Corporation are among the many companies that have formed partnerships with education. Furthermore, organizations benefit by getting student-employees with new ideas, energy, and eagerness to accomplish their assignments. Humber College in Toronto, Red River College in Manitoba, and many other colleges and universities allow students to earn credits on the basis of successful job performance and fulfillment of established program requirements.

Internship programs have recently received considerable attention due to the legal and ethical considerations of having interns work for no pay with the promise of providing valuable work experience.[10] Guidelines for interns are governed by employment standards legislation, and employers must pay careful attention to these requirements in order to determine if a person qualifies to be classified and treated as an intern.[11] Ethics in HRM 6.1 highlights these considerations.

Classroom Instruction

This method lends itself particularly to training in areas where information can be presented in lectures, demonstrations, films, and videotapes or through computer instruction. A special type of classroom facility is used in "vestibule training." Trainees are given instruction in the

ETHICS IN HRM 6.1   **ARE UNPAID INTERNSHIPS LEGAL?**

According to legislation in Ontario, if an employer provides a person with training in skills that are used by the workers in the company, the intern will generally also be considered to be an employee (and therefore should be paid) unless **all** of the conditions below are met:

1. The training is similar to that which is given in a vocational school.
2. The training is for the benefit of the intern.
3. The employer derives little, if any, benefit from the activity of the intern while he or she is being trained.
4. The training doesn't take someone else's job.
5. The employer isn't promising the intern a job at the end of the training.
6. The intern has been told that no compensation will be given.

   Another exception applies to college and university programs, and interns who work under a program approved by a college of applied arts and technology or a university do not have to be paid. This exception exists to encourage employers to provide students enrolled in a college or university program with practical training to complement their classroom learning.

CRITICAL THINKING QUESTIONS:

1. Do the above-noted guidelines provide enough detail and clarity to determine when an intern should, or should not be, compensated?
2. Is it ethical for an employer to have an unpaid intern under any circumstances? Are there certain groups or people who could be disadvantaged because of this?
3. Would you take an unpaid internship? Why or why not?

Source: Adapted from "Are Unpaid Internships Legal in Ontario?," Ontario Ministry of Labour, June 2011, accessed November 12, 2017, https://www.labour.gov.on.ca/english/es/pubs/internships.php.

operation of equipment like that found in operating departments. The emphasis is on instruction. For example, a checkout clerk in a supermarket first learns how to use the cash register.

Self-Directed Learning

Self-directed learning occurs when individuals work at their own pace at programmed instruction. Such learning typically involves the use of books, manuals, or computers to break down subject-matter content into highly organized, logical sequences that demand a continuous response on the part of the trainee.

Audiovisual

Audiovisual methods are used to teach the skills and procedures required for a number of jobs. An example would be golf and tennis coaches using video recorders or camcorders so that their students can see their mistakes. Telehealth, a shared British Columbia Ministry of Health video-conferencing system, connects patients through live video conferencing to clinical, administrative, and educational consultations in more than 100 communities across the province. Video conferencing can deliver faster service, allow for desktop conversations and meetings across distances, and enhance the management, sharing, and archiving of digital content.[12,13]

Simulation

Simulation is used when it is not practical or safe to train people on the actual equipment or within the actual work environment. Examples include training pilots and new surgeons. In these examples, trainees may practise how to fly an aircraft or how to perform an operation in an artificial situation using fake equipment that mirrors what an actual work situation would require.

Simulation training provides exposure to realistic equipment and operations.

E-Learning

> **E-learning**
> Training that uses computers and/or online resources

E-learning typically involves using online resources and encompasses a wide variety of training methods, such as computer-based training (CBT) and virtual classrooms. This includes delivering training via the Internet, videotape, satellite and broadcast interactive TV, DVD, and CD-ROM. E-learning makes it possible to provide drill and practice, problem solving, simulation, gaming forms of instruction, and certain sophisticated forms of individualized instruction in a way that is more engaging for learners than traditional classroom instruction. It is also cheaper for employers to administer because, in many instances, it can be delivered directly via the employees' computers.

E-learning has become firmly established as a delivery method within organizations: 78% are self-paced, 48% are instructor led, 34% are blended, and 27% are collaborative, becoming an alternative to, not a replacement for, classroom delivery methods.[14] Furthermore, with the use of mobile devices, e-learning provides the opportunity for training in multiple locations and at times suited to learners' schedules and preferences.[15] There are also systems that can track the progress of learners and then adjust or alter the training provided to suit the needs of the trainee.

Through this type of training, employees are able to search through a virtual sea of information in order to customize their own learning in their own time and space. More companies are demanding access to individual training components for employees to use at their own discretion and as their schedules permit. This type of availability allows trainees to learn material in shorter increments and to access material when they are able to focus on the information. It is also important to ensure that the strategies and culture of the organization support and encourage e-learning.

E-learning can also be revised rapidly, thereby providing continuously updated training material. This capability not only makes it easier and cheaper to revise training curricula but also saves travel and classroom costs. When combined with other communications technology, such as e-mail, teleconferencing, video conferencing, and groupware, this type of training can be even more effective.

Special Projects or Tasks

Specific experiences at work present employees with opportunities to perform under pressure and to learn from their mistakes. Such experiences are some of the most powerful and commonly used techniques. However, just as on-the-job training can be problematic if not well planned, these experiences should be well organized, supervised, and challenging to the participants. Examples of special projects or tasks include the following:

1. *Understudy assignments* groom an individual to take over a manager's job by helping the individual gain experience in handling important functions of the job.
2. *Job rotation* provides, through a variety of work experiences, the broadened knowledge and understanding required to manage more effectively.
3. *Lateral transfer* involves horizontal movement through different departments, along with upward movement in the organization.
4. *Special assignments* and *junior boards* provide an opportunity for individuals to become involved in the study of current organizational problems and in planning and decision-making activities.
5. *Action learning* gives managers release time to work full time on projects with others in the organization. In some cases, action learning is combined with classroom instruction, discussions, and conferences.
6. *Planned career progressions* utilize all of these different methods to provide employees with the training and development necessary to progress through a series of jobs requiring higher and higher levels of knowledge and/or skills.

Seminars and Conferences

Seminars and conferences typically bring large groups of people together to exchange and share ideas and information. Speakers are usually selected based upon their expertise in a specific subject; therefore, these types of opportunities help employees learn new, innovative, and leading-edge practices, which then can be incorporated into their own work processes.

Case Studies

Case studies use documented examples, which may have been developed from the experiences of participants in their own organizations. Cases help trainees examine a situation, evaluate key factors and considerations, weigh alternatives, and then recommend a solution or best course of action.

This book uses case studies as a way for you, with the help of your instructor, to better understand and integrate the information covered in each chapter.

Management Games

Management games are valuable for bringing a hypothetical situation to life and provide experiential learning. Many games have been designed for general use. For example, TD Bank uses a simulation called Desert Kings to encourage more open communication, to increase levels of team performance, and to increase commitment to both internal and external customer service.

Role-Playing

Role-playing involves assuming the attitudes and behaviour of a person in a particular situation or trying to solve a specific problem. By acting out another's position, participants in the role-playing can improve their ability to understand and cope with others. Role-playing can also help participants learn how to counsel others by helping them see situations from a different point of view. Role-playing is used widely in training healthcare professionals to be empathetic and sensitive to the concerns of patients. It is also used widely in training managers to handle employee issues relating to absenteeism, performance appraisal, and conflict situations.

Coaching

As the need for continuous and timely feedback increases, coaching may be used as a form of training. **Coaching** involves a more experienced person closely observing a less experienced employee, typically during a shorter or set period of time, and providing ongoing, customized feedback to enhance job performance. Research shows that coaching provides greater opportunities for employees to reach their goals and increases their desire for ongoing learning.[16] Furthermore, coaching has been shown to help employees develop enhanced self-awareness while increasing specific skills and competencies.[17] As is discussed in Chapter 7, coaching is also an important component of managing an employee's performance.

Phase 5: Evaluating the Program

LO6

List 4 methods to evaluate training.

Training, like any other HRM process, should be evaluated to determine its effectiveness. Unfortunately, few organizations adequately evaluate their training programs. In many ways, this lack of evaluation goes beyond poor management; it is poor business practice. Given the substantial monetary stake that organizations have in training, it would seem prudent that managers would want to maximize the return on that investment. At Work with HRM 6.1 provides an example of how various Canadian organizations are strategically evaluating their return on investments in training.

Four Levels of Evaluation

Donald Kirkpatrick developed 4 basic methods to evaluate training: (1) reactions, (2) learning, (3) behaviour, and (4) results.[18] Recently, he presented a fifth level, return on investment, although others believe this is considered within the "results" evaluation or fourth level.[19] When these various levels of evaluation are used together, an organization can determine

---

AT WORK WITH HRM 6.1   **DEMONSTRATING THE VALUE OF INVESTING IN PEOPLE**

In response to the increasing demand to show the financial impact of training programs, or investments in people, the ROI Methodology is an evaluation solution that has been implemented in more than 60 countries. The ROI Methodology was developed by Dr. Jack J. Phillips in the 1970s, refined through application and use in the 1980s, and implemented around the world during the 1990s. The ROI Institute, founded in 1992, is a service-driven organization that strives to assist organizations in improving their programs and processes through the use of the ROI Methodology.

The ROI Methodology is a balanced approach to measurement that captures 6 types of data:

1. Reaction and Planned Action—Level 1
2. Learning—Level 2
3. Application and Implementation—Level 3
4. Business Impact—Level 4

5. Return on Investment—Level 5
6. Intangibles

The process always includes a technique to isolate the effects of a training program in a tangible, measurable way. Clients of the ROI Institute of Canada include Canada Post, Canada Border Services Agency, and Employment and Social Development Canada. These Canadian organizations find value in having hard data to measure the outcomes of their training initiatives.

CRITICAL THINKING QUESTIONS:

1. Which of the above-noted types of data would be most difficult to measure? Why?
2. What do you think is meant by "intangibles," as noted in step 6 of the process? Provide an example of an intangible benefit that results from a training program.

if business results are improving, what parts of training should be continued, what needs to change about a training program, and whether or not the training should even be continued.[20] Organizations' learning evaluation efforts are becoming more challenging with the growth in different learning techniques and the diversity of participants.[21] Even though contending with complex environments is not simple, an overview of Kirkpatrick's evaluation model is warranted.

Level 1: Reactions Assessing participants' reactions is a relatively straightforward way to evaluate training. Happy trainees are more likely to focus on training principles and to utilize the information on the job. However, participants can do more than say whether they liked a program or not. Comments regarding which parts of the training were most useful can be given, and trainees can also critique the instructors or make suggestions about the training facilities or length of the training and indicate if they would recommend the training to others.

Although evaluation methods based on reactions are improving, too many conclusions about training effectiveness are based on broad satisfaction measures that lack specific feedback. Furthermore, it should be noted that positive reactions are no guarantee that the training has been successful. Collecting glowing comments from trainees may be easy, but as gratifying as this information is to management, the training received needs to result in improved behaviour and job performance.

Level 2: Learning Beyond what participants *think* about the training, it might be a good idea to see whether they actually learned anything. Testing knowledge and skills before a training program provides a baseline standard on trainees that can be measured again after training to determine improvement. This approach also means that whatever the person is learning must be used at work. For example, if an employee was learning new software and the employee's computer did not have the software, the employee's inability to perform was a result of inadequate resources, not of an absence of learning.

Level 3: Behaviour Much of what is learned in a training program never gets used on the job. It's not that the training was necessarily ineffective. In fact, on measures of employee reactions and learning, the program might score quite high. But for any of several reasons, trainees may not demonstrate **transfer of training** (also called *transfer of learning*)—effective application of principles learned. Although measuring the extent of the behaviour change may not be necessary, it is important for the manager to expect the behaviour change and to reinforce it.

> **Transfer of training**
> Applying what is learned to enhance performance on the job

Ultimately, the success or failure of any training is whether there has been a transfer of that training. To ensure transfer of training, the following considerations need to be addressed:

1. Training needs to reflect what an employee experiences on the job.
2. Managers need to encourage employees to use new skills and knowledge, provide the correct resources for this to occur, and provide positive feedback when this happens.[22]

Level 4: Results (Return on Investment) Both the people responsible for training and the managers are under continual pressure to show that their programs produce "bottom line" results. Most organizations measure their training in terms of its return on investment (ROI). This measure becomes even more important during economic downturns. As noted in At Work with HRM 6.1, organizations want to know that the training has increased business results, whether they be profit, customer satisfaction, or decreased costs.

In order to effectively use metrics, Figure 6.3 illustrates an example of the costs and benefits of a training program and how to calculate the ROI. The Business Development Bank of Canada takes ROI very seriously, spending 5% of its payroll on training, with the goal to improve business outcomes. A meta-study conducted by Investors in People found that the Business Development Bank achieved a 74% ROI on training efforts to improve branch managers' coaching skills.[23]

Calculating return on investment of training is important.

FIGURE 6.3 Measuring Return on Investment

In assessing the value of training (or development), organizations will look at the costs and benefits and assign a dollar value.

Typical Costs Included

- Trainer's salary.
- Trainees' salaries.
- Materials for training (e.g., handouts, flip charts, pens and flip charts).
- Expenses for trainers/trainees (e.g., travel, meals, and accommodation).
- Cost of facilities and equipment (e.g., room rental and LCD projector).
- Lost productivity (opportunity cost).

Typical Benefits Included

- Increase in quality.
- Increase in quantity.
- Decrease in turnover.
- Enhanced employee motivation.
- Improved safety record.

For example, a revised safety training program might have the following costs: trainer time ($10,000), trainees' time ($20,000), materials ($5000), and facilities ($1000), for a total of $36,000. If the training covered 2 years and during that time the company saved $50,000 in workers' compensation insurance and the costs of other, related safety infractions, the benefits outweigh the costs.

Return on training investment is calculated through the following formula:

ROI: ((Benefits − Cost)/Cost) × 100. For the above-noted example, the ROI would be (($50,000 − $36,000)/$36,000) × 100 = 38.8%.

Increasingly, organizations with sophisticated training systems look to training to support long-term strategy and change more than they look for short-term financial returns from their investments. For example, WestJet believes that investment in good training helps create an atmosphere in which people can do their best work.[24]

As training and development are viewed more and more from a strategic standpoint, there is heightened interest in benchmarking these services and practices against those of recognized leaders in industry. Although no single process for exact benchmarking exists, the simplest models are based on the late W. Edwards Deming's classic 4-step process. The 4-step process advocates that managers do the following:

1. *Plan.* Conduct a self-audit to define internal processes and measurements, decide on areas to be benchmarked, and choose the comparison organization.
2. *Do.* Collect data through surveys, interviews, site visits, and/or historical records.
3. *Check.* Analyze data to discover performance gaps and communicate findings and suggested improvements to management.
4. *Act.* Establish goals, implement specific changes, monitor progress, and redefine benchmarks as a continuous-improvement process.

To use **benchmarking** successfully, managers must clearly define the measures of competency and performance and must objectively assess the current situation and identify areas for improvement.

> **Benchmarking**
> Evaluating and comparing processes and practices against those that represent high standards or those that deliver strong performance outcomes

Internal versus External Resources

During all phases of training, an evaluation of when to use internal and/or external resources should be made. At times, it is beneficial for an organization to hire people from outside the company to perform a needs assessment, design and develop training, deliver the training, or conduct an evaluation of the results. External experts often have the knowledge, tools, and experience to effectively and efficiently perform these functions. When engaging the services of external people, it is important for an organization to evaluate the costs versus the benefits of doing so. Developing a request for proposal helps ensure that enough options are considered and a choice of who will provide services is made in a fair and thorough manner.

Using internal people to perform any or all phases of training requires that current employees have the correct skills and expertise to do so. Internal people often understand the organization's culture and norms (as addressed in Chapter 3), can better relate to employees, and are able to provide ongoing follow-up to the processes. Therefore, a careful evaluation of the positive aspects versus the potential downfalls of using internal resources must be done.

TRAINING FOCUS

Although this chapter has focused almost exclusively on the processes underlying a systems model of training, it is also useful to discuss some of the more popular topics covered in these training programs. As noted in Figure 6.1, a wide variety of skills and capabilities are required in today's workplace. In addition to the training that addresses the competencies associated with a particular job, many employers develop training programs to meet the needs of a broader base of employees. This section summarizes some of these programs, including basic skills training and team training. Emerging Trends 6.1 provides information regarding evolving training issues.

EMERGING TRENDS 6.1

As investment in training evolves, so will the type of training that organizations focus on. Not only "what" will be offered is changing, but also "how" training is delivered continues to be altered. This being so, the following key trends are emerging:

1. *Leadership development.* The unexpected retirement of several high-profile CEOs continues to raise concern about the loss of organizational leadership experience and knowledge as the baby boom generation prepares to withdraw from the workplace. Hence, it is critical that organizations take time to develop leaders and allow them to grow and adapt to future needs and demands. Leadership development will continue to be a top priority in order to ensure that people who are digitally competent, adaptable, and able to guide and motivate others are readily available.[25]

2. *Change management.* Increasingly, employees are expected to be able to adapt to and thrive in changing work conditions and requirements. Training opportunities of how to plan and enact successful transition, as well as how to address the potential barriers or points of resistance to change, enable organizations to grow and thrive in a dynamic environment.[26]

3. *Learning 2.0.* Learning 2.0 is a term used to describe the reinvention of learning and development in the 21st century. It represents the paradigm shift from face-to-face and/or online instructor–controlled, structured, 1-way adaptive training to the learner-driven, collaborative, and problem-focused learning made possible by Web 2.0 technologies that provide a massive forum for sharing information and working collaboratively.[27]

4. *Online and mobile learning.* Social, mobile, and cloud-computing technological advances, convergence, and the increase in collaborative work have led to changes in how organizations approach learning. They have also expanded the breadth and diversity of delivery methods: blogs, communities of practice, podcasts, instant messaging, wikis, and team learning. Tablets and emerging mobile technology tools will allow employees to manage their professional development digitally. *MOOCs* (massive open online courses) are an example of how thousands of people may enroll in 1 online course offering. As well, combining in person and online learning, known as blended delivery, will be utilized to a greater extent.[28]

5. *Gamification and virtual reality.* Using technology to create "mock" experiences that incorporate concepts from games holds the promise to provide increased access to, and more engaging, learning platforms.[29]

Basic Skills

Experts define an illiterate individual as having a sixth-grade education or less. Working adults who improve their literacy gain better pay and more promotions and are employed for longer periods of time. Furthermore, people of low literacy tend to have lower rates of employment and tend to work in occupations with lower skill requirements.[30] Ontario WorkInfoNET (OnWIN) is an example of a resource that is available to address this issue and provides links to resources for basic skills and literacy training.[31]

These figures on literacy have important implications for society at large and for organizations that must work around these skill deficiencies. This is especially true given labour-market considerations on the one hand and increasing skill requirements (related to advances in technology) on the other. Basic skills have become essential occupational qualifications, having profound implications for product quality, customer service, internal efficiency, and workplace and environmental safety.

In the past several years, the number of businesses that require a high level of knowledge has grown due to globalization and a knowledge-based economy.[32] A recent study by the Canadian Chamber of Commerce found that Canada's slipping global competitiveness is due to the shortage of skilled and educated workers.[33] As such, attention to basic skills training will continue to be of strategic importance.

Teamwork

As discussed in Chapter 4, employees must work together in order for an organization to achieve its goals. As such, the success of an organization is a function not only of the skills and capabilities (competencies) of each individual but also of the interaction of the team members. To give an example of how important this can be to an organization, Dofasco had 6700 employees participate in 4-day workshops on interpersonal and group skills over a 3-year period. The company wanted all its employees to learn to work with one another in new and different ways.

Teamwork skills fall under 2 broad categories: task related and relationship related. Teamwork skills that characterize effective teams include a balance between the use of technical skills, such as time management and problem solving, and interpersonal skills, such as conflict resolution and collaboration. Teams need to evaluate themselves periodically to ensure that the goal(s) is being achieved and that there are no concerns about interpersonal relationships.

Managers who want to design team training for their organization should keep the following points in mind:

1. Team building is a difficult and comprehensive process. Since many new teams are under pressure to produce, there is little time for training. Everything cannot be covered in a 24-hour blitz. Team training works best when it is provided over time and parallels team development.
2. Team development is not always a linear sequence of "forming, storming, norming, and performing." Training initiatives can help a team work through each of these stages, but managers must be aware that lapses can occur.
3. Additional training is required to assimilate new members. Large membership changes may result in teams reverting to a previous developmental stage.
4. Skills need to be acquired through practice and reviewing and rewarding the performance of the teams.[34]

Learning to work in teams is important in today's dynamic workplaces.

THE TRAINING LANDSCAPE

The context in which training (and development) occurs in Canada is ever-evolving. Therefore, it is important to review the amount of time, energy, and resources (both financial and non-financial) that companies commit to training employees.

Investment

Canadian employers recognize the need to prioritize workplace learning and development to ensure their competitiveness in the rapidly changing global economy. Furthermore, employers recognize that these opportunities provide employees with greater job satisfaction, enhanced security, and better pay.[35] Even with this in mind, a recent Conference Board of Canada study suggested that, on average, Canadian employers spend roughly two-thirds as much as their US counterparts on employee training and education. Employers that took part in the Conference Board study said they invested an average of 1.4% of their annual payroll in structured, formal training and education.[36]

With the relative lack of priority Canadian organizations are giving to learning and development, combined with Canada's fluctuating economy and lagging global competitiveness and innovation, the issue of whether training should be legally enforced arises. Ethics in HRM 6.2 describes the debate surrounding decisions to force organizations to provide training and employees to take training.

It is worth noting that organizations that make "Best Employers in Canada" lists tend to put a much higher value on the continued learning and development of their employees. A study conducted by The Conference Board of Canada showed that organizations with

---

ETHICS IN HRM 6.2   **LEGISLATING LEARNING?**

In recent years, widespread public concern has led to the development and passing of more laws that require workplace training in areas such as health and safety, the environment, and human rights. Although legislation enacted to date deals with strict minimal standards, enforcement, and penalties to employers that do not comply with the training requirements, the larger purpose of the legislation is to widely educate owners, managers, and workers about acceptable safe and non-discriminatory workplace behaviours.

In June 2010, Bill 168, which amended the Ontario *Occupational Health and Safety Act* to deal with the prevalence of, impact of, and risks associated with workplace violence and harassment, came into effect. It requires organizations to provide training in employer and employee obligations and related workplace policies and

programs. Most recently, other provinces are requiring training that addresses violence in the workplace, including assessment of the risks of a domestic violence situation spilling over into the workplace. As an example of a response to this type of mandated training, Western University provides a variety of online courses that faculty, staff, and volunteers have to take in order to learn how to create a safe, healthy, diverse, and respectful workplace.

CRITICAL THINKING QUESTIONS:

1. Do you think mandatory training is right? Why or why not?
2. How would you react if your employer wanted you to participate in a training program that you thought was a waste of time? Why?

Sources: Adapted from "OH&S Legislation in Canada—Introduction," accessed November 12, 2017, www.ccohs.ca/oshanswers/legisl/intro.html; "Workplace Violence and Workplace Harassment," Ontario Ministry of Labour, accessed November 12, 2017, www.labour.gov.on.ca/english/hs/sawo/pubs/fs_workplaceviolence .php; "Domestic Violence in the Workplace," WorkSafe BC, accessed November 12, 2017, www2.worksafebc.com/Topics/Violence/Resources-DomesticViolence .asp#Readmore; and "Human Resources—Required Training," Western University, accessed November 12, 2017, www.uwo.ca/hr/learning/required/index.html.

strong learning cultures invest more in their learning and development and are realizing greater returns for their investment.[37] Overall, these organizations have superior employee performance, have higher levels of customer satisfaction, and provide higher-quality products and services to their customers.[38]

Part of a strong learning culture in an organization also includes attention to career development, which is the focus of the remainder of this chapter.

CAREER DEVELOPMENT—INDIVIDUAL AND ORGANIZATIONAL NEEDS

Career development programs, with their greater emphasis on the individual, introduce a personalized aspect to the term "development." Most training and development programs have a career development component. Most career development programs should be viewed as a dynamic process that attempts to meet the needs of managers, their employees, and the organization. As such, the needs of an organization should be linked to the individual career needs in a way that joins the personal effectiveness and satisfaction of employees with the achievement of the organization's strategic goals.

Career planning, on the other hand, is a systematic approach in which you would assess your values, interests, abilities, and goals and identify the path(s) you would need to take to realize your career goals. John Holland posited 6 personality types, or career anchors, into which people could be categorized: realistic, investigative, artistic, social, enterprising, and conventional.[39] Along these lines, Schein believed there are 8 career anchors or considerations: autonomy/independence, security/stability, technical–functional competence, general managerial competence, entrepreneurial creativity, service or dedication to a cause, pure challenge, and lifestyle.[40] Through a deeper understanding of your type, or favourite activities that aligned with these anchors, you could then determine which careers would provide the best matching to your values and preferences. Through career development programs, you would then journey along the career path.

Ultimately, in today's organizations, individuals are responsible for initiating their own career planning. It is up to individuals to identify their knowledge, skills, abilities, interests, and values and seek out information about career options in order to set goals and develop career plans. Managers should encourage employees to take responsibility for their own careers by offering continuing assistance in the form of feedback on individual performance and making available information about the organization, the job, and career opportunities that might be of interest.

The organization should be responsible for supplying information about its mission, policies, and plans and for providing support for employee self-assessment, training, and development. Significant career growth can occur when individual initiative combines with organizational opportunity. Career development programs benefit managers by giving them increased skill in managing their own careers, greater retention of valued employees, increased understanding of the organization, and enhanced reputations as people developers.

Some organizations make use of leadership career development programs. Enbridge, an Alberta-based company in the energy transportation and distribution business, changed how it provided leadership development. For several years, it sent a few executives every year to Queen's University for a 3-week residential program. However, in assessing ways to maximize the training budget, the organization decided it could provide leadership training to a larger number of employees by custom-developing a program that could be delivered in-house. By changing the approach to delivery, Enbridge is now able to offer a leadership development program to employees every year instead of every 5 years. In recognition of their strategic approach, Enbridge got the 2014 WOW! Award for their program.[41]

LO7

Explain how a career development program integrates individual and organizational needs.

Creating Favourable Conditions

Although a career development program requires many special processes and techniques, some basic elements must be present if it is to be successful, ones that create favourable conditions for the program.

Management Support

If career development is to succeed, it must receive the complete support of top management. The system should reflect the goals and culture of the organization, and a "people philosophy" should be woven throughout. A people philosophy can provide employees with a clear set of expectations and directions for their own career development. For a program to be effective, managerial staff at all levels must be trained in the fundamentals of job design, performance appraisal, career planning, and coaching.

Goal Setting

Before individuals can engage in meaningful career planning, they must have not only an awareness of the organization's philosophy but also a clear understanding of the organization's more immediate goals. Otherwise, they may plan for personal change and growth without knowing if or how their own goals match those of the organization.

For example, if the technology of a business is changing and new skills are needed, will the organization retrain to meet this need or hire new talent? Is there growth, stability, or decline in the number of employees needed? How will turnover affect this need? Answers to these kinds of questions are essential to the support of individual career planning.

HRM Practices to Enhance Career Development

To ensure that its career development program will be effective, an organization can implement various HRM practices. For example, a practice of job rotation can counteract obsolescence and maintain employee flexibility. Another practice that can aid development involves job transfers and promotions. A **transfer** involves moving an employee into a different job that is similar to the previous role in terms of responsibility and complexity. As such, although an employee may have to work in a new team or a new area of the company, thereby developing new skills and experiences, a transfer does not usually involve an increase in pay.

A **promotion** involves moving an employee into a more complex job that has increased responsibilities, and this role is typically higher in the organizational hierarchy; therefore, this move usually involves an increase in compensation and status. Promotions enable an organization to utilize the skills and abilities of its staff more effectively, and the opportunity to gain a promotion serves as an incentive for good performance. The 2 principal criteria for determining promotions are merit and seniority. Often the problem is to determine how much consideration to give to each factor.

As organizations continue to change, including their structure and number of employees, it is becoming more difficult to promote people as part of career development. The issues of balancing work and family, mentioned in Chapter 1, can become paramount when considering a promotion. Even though there has been growth in the number of women working, the proportion of women in senior management positions has not changed over the past 2 decades. A report by The Conference Board of Canada outlined practices organizations are using to encourage the advancement of women: succession planning, mentoring, coaching, job rotation, and training.[42] Canadian Pacific Railway, Manitoba Liquor & Lotteries Corporation, and TD Financial Group use a range of these practices to recruit and retain diverse talent, supporting their organizational goals of equity and performance.[43]

Transfer
Moving an employee to a different role in the organization. The new job is typically similar to the previous role in terms of responsibility and complexity

Promotion
Moving an employee into a job that is more complex, has increased responsibilities, and therefore typically provides increased compensation and status

Mentorship to Enhance Career Development

As mentioned earlier in this chapter, "development" is a long-term approach for acquiring and utilizing new skills. Since the purpose of a development program is to give employees enhanced capabilities, there are a number of ways this can occur. The responsibility to develop the talent lies with all managers in the organization—not just the person's immediate manager or team leader.

When one talks with men and women about their employment experiences, it is common to hear them mention individuals at work who influenced them. They frequently refer to immediate managers who were especially helpful as career developers. But they also mention others at higher levels who provided guidance and support. These managers (and executives) who advise and encourage less experienced employees are called **mentors**.

Although a mentoring relationship can develop informally between a more and less experienced employee, many organizations emphasize formal mentoring plans that assign a mentor to those employees considered for upward movement in the organization. Mentoring differs from coaching in that coaching typically focuses on specific work-related tasks and short-term performance outcomes, whereas mentoring provides general advice and guidance to a less experienced employee over a long period of time. A good mentorship is a reciprocal relationship, with both the *mentee* and the mentor learning from each other. In recent years, there has been a growth in the different types of mentoring relationships, from reverse mentoring (in which the roles are switched) to peer and team mentoring. Done well, the process is beneficial for both parties.

It is important to remember that a mentor relationship is very personal. Toolkit 6.4 provides guidelines for establishing and maintaining successful mentor and mentee relationships.

Organizations with formal mentoring programs include Shell International, Johnson & Johnson, and the Bank of Montreal. Alternatively, given the importance of the issue, a number of mentoring organizations have begun to spring up. A new form of mentoring, sponsored by the Ms. Foundation for Women, provides an opportunity for both girls and boys, 8 to 18 years old, to spend a day with parents or friends on the job. The program is designed to give young people more attention and provide them with career role models. American Express, Chevron, and Estée Lauder participate in this program.

Not surprisingly, mentoring is also being done electronically. *E-mentoring* brings experienced business professionals together with individuals needing advice and guidance. Participants in e-mentoring typically never meet, but many form long-lasting email connections that can be very beneficial. Still, most participants see these connections as supplements to—rather than substitutes for—in-person connections.

Mentors
Experienced employees who provide advice and guidance to encourage and support less experienced workers

TOOLKIT 6.4   MENTORING GUIDELINES

Successful mentoring is built on a common understanding of interests and "ground rules." Here are some to consider before establishing a mentor–mentee relationship:

1. Formalize the expectations with a written agreement that outlines the behaviours of each person.
2. Monitor progress. Understand that either party can withdraw from the relationship at any time, and it is not necessary to provide an explanation.
3. All documents exchanged, such as company plans or resumés, will be treated as confidential.
4. The mentor cannot be solicited for a job. Doing so is grounds for breaking the relationship. There must be dedication to the process.
5. Respect each other's time. Arrive on time and prepare with a list of questions or topics to be discussed.
6. Provide feedback honestly. For example, the mentee might state, "This is not the kind of information I need at this stage," or the mentor might advise, "You should not skip meetings just because they are tedious. It is an important part of this company's culture to be visible at these meetings."

Mentoring is important to help develop people at all levels in an organization.

There are a number of resources for mentoring. A few examples include the following:

1. *Society for Canadian Women in Science and Technology (SCWIST)* is an association that has assembled thousands of women in technology fields who act as online mentors.
2. *National Mentoring Partnership* is an online site for a variety of different resources for mentors and mentees, including information about how to find a mentor.
3. *Women's Enterprise Centre* is an organization that encourages, helps, and supports women in British Columbia who want to own, operate, and grow their own business.

Keeping a Career in Perspective

It is important in any training and development program to keep everything in perspective. Although work is a very important part of someone's life, it is only a part. Organizations want people who maintain an appropriate balance between their work life and their personal life and therefore can continue to grow and develop for personal satisfaction and success for the organization.

Some of the other areas of life that must be considered are the following:

1. Off-the-job interests can provide a break from the demands of a career while allowing employees to gain satisfaction from non-work-related activities.
2. Family life can be negatively affected if the organization does not provide recognition of a person's life outside of work. Conflict between work and family may arise over such issues as number of hours worked per week, the need to relocate for career advancement, and the amount of overtime that may be required.
3. Planning for retirement is an important consideration given the aging workforce. Many companies are now providing pre-retirement programs to allow an employee to be productive in the organization while minimizing problems that can arise in the retirement years.
4. Dual-career families are a factor in the contemporary business world. Therefore, career development and progress may need to take the goals of the partner into consideration.

As mentioned in Chapter 1, the workforce of today is very different from that of yesterday. The organization might have as many as 4 generational cohorts, each with its own view and expectations about career development. Therefore, it will be important to maintain a balanced perspective on career development and to structure opportunities to fit the needs of both the diverse employee base and the organization.

LEARNING OUTCOMES SUMMARY

1. Describe the benefits of employee orientation.
   - *Lower turnover*
   - *Increased productivity*
   - *Improved employee morale and identification with the company*
   - *Lower training costs*
   - *Facilitation of learning*
   - *Reduction of anxiety*

2. Outline the steps in the instructional systems design approach (ADDIE) to training and development.
   - *Assess*
   - *Design*
   - *Develop*
   - *Implement*
   - *Evaluate*

3. Describe the components of a needs assessment.
   - *Organizational level*
   - *Task or job level*
   - *Person level*

4. Explain the 3 key issues that should be focused on during program design.
   - *Instructional goals*
   - *Trainee characteristics*
   - *Learning principles*

5. Discuss various types of training methods.
   - *On-the-job*
   - *Apprenticeship*
   - *Co-operative and internship programs*
   - *Classroom instruction*
   - *Self-directed*
   - *Audiovisual*
   - *Simulation*
   - *E-learning*
   - *Special projects or tasks*
   - *Seminars and conferences*
   - *Case studies*
   - *Management games*
   - *Role-playing*
   - *Coaching*

6. List 4 methods to evaluate training.
   - *Reaction*
   - *Learning*
   - *Behaviour*
   - *Results (return on investment)*

7. Explain how a career development program integrates individual and organizational needs.
   - *It blends employee effectiveness and satisfaction with the achievement of the organization's strategic objectives*
   - *HRM practices must fit so that both individual and organizational needs can be achieved.*
   - *Mentorship can enhance career development for employees*

KEY TERMS

apprenticeship training 189

behaviour modification 188

benchmarking 197

coaching 194

co-operative programs 190

development 180

e-learning 192

instructional goals 187

internship programs 190

learning 184

mentors 203

on-the-job training (OJT) 189

orientation 180

promotion 202

trainee readiness 187

training 180

transfer 202

transfer of training 195

HRM CLOSE-UP APPLICATION

1. What changes would you make to the orientation program at BC Ferries? Why are you making these specific recommendations?
2. How could BC Ferries evaluate the return on investment for their simulation training?
3. BC Ferries involves front-line employees in the development of SEA material and STC curricula. What could be a potential downfall with this approach?
4. What specific types of future training should BC Ferries focus on to ensure ongoing success?

CRITICAL THINKING QUESTIONS

1. What have been the biggest changes that you have noticed in how you learn as a post-secondary student? What do you think has been the key driver of these changes?
2. Would you be willing to take a blended delivery (partially in person and partially online) postsecondary course? Why or why not? What would be some of the potential benefits and problems that you foresee?
3. Your employer has approached you to assume a managerial role. Although flattered, you are also concerned about your ability to carry out the role successfully. What type of training or development might you want to help you succeed? What would be the "core skills" and "soft skills"?
4. What are some creative, and low cost/no cost, ways that an organization could make a new employee feel welcome?

BUILDING YOUR SKILLS

1. In groups of 3 or 4, develop a list of behaviours or skills that would improve your performance as a team member. For each behaviour or skill, identify 1 or 2 training methods that would be appropriate for learning that behaviour or skill.
2. Providing training to employees is a significant retention tool in a tight labour market. In groups of 4 to 5, discuss the benefits of training for individuals and organizations. Prepare a response, including the ethical considerations, to the following statement: "Employees should be required to repay the cost of any training if they leave the organization before 1 year."

3. In groups of 3 or 4, prepare a new student orientation program for your campus. How long would the orientation program be, and who would be involved? What would be included before, during, and after the formal orientation?

4. You work in an organization that focuses on wine sales and marketing. Recently, there have been a number of complaints about a particular customer service representative in terms of the accuracy of wine knowledge shared with customers and the timeliness of work orders. Complete the 5 steps in the systems approach to training and development. Specifically, consider the following: (1) How will you determine whether training is the answer? (2) What is a possible learning or training objective you could identify? (3) What materials need to be developed? (4) What methods would you use to implement training? (5) How would you evaluate if the training was effective?

CASE STUDY 1

E-Learning at Elevated Software

After 15 years of managing one of the leading sales departments, Priya Bandali was excited about her promotion to the position of learning and development manager for Elevated Software. Elevated had over 300 salespeople and an overall workforce of 2000 employees working in 3 locations across Canada: Victoria, Regina, and Charlottetown. Although located in the head office in Regina, Priya had always been able to deploy new sales practices across the country to keep Elevated ahead of its competitors and felt her knowledge and experience would be valuable to her new position.

Elevated continued to experience more competition as there were more companies that were also selling accounting software to small and medium-sized businesses. This increase in competition resulted in lower profits, and Priya was now tasked with finding a way to streamline learning and development programs and lower expenditures by 10%.

In strategic planning meetings with the leadership team, it was clear to Priya that Elevated was not decreasing its commitment to learning but needed a new, more cost-effective learning strategy able to meet the "on-demand" learning needs of all employees and managers at varying and distant locations. All employees' roles, not just salespeople's, were increasingly complex, thereby requiring excellent communication skills, superior problem-solving abilities, and the willingness to collaborate effectively with other employees. The president of Elevated clearly stated that one of Priya's first tasks was to conduct a thorough review of the learning and development function within the organization. The president wanted hard evidence, a "return on investment," to back up learning and development initiatives.

Through her research and conversations with colleagues, Priya knew that a few competitors had introduced a learning approach that provided online training modules for employees. Priya felt this approach could realize the president's productivity goals and would also allow all employees in the 3 locations across the country to receive the same training, but at their convenience and on their own time. Perhaps this was too good to be true. Priya wondered if the investment in online training would really provide effective learning and development opportunities to employees and what next steps she should take.

Questions:

1. What is the first thing that Priya should do before proceeding with implementing online learning across the company? Why is this important?

2. Given the increased complexity of employees' work and the demand for certain competencies, will online modules be an effective way to train employees at Elevated? What other cost-effective methods of training could be used?
3. If implemented, how can employees be motivated to utilize the online training?
4. If implemented, how should Priya measure the return on investment of online training?

CASE STUDY 2

Welcome to the Jungle

Jason was excited about his first day of work at Jimmy's Jungle Gym. As a second-year kinesiology student, this job would provide Jason with the opportunity to work with young children and teach them about active and healthy play.

Jimmy's Jungle Gym was a play centre targeting 3- to 6-year-olds and provided numerous types of "play pits" and equipment for these youngsters to use. A café was also located on site, where parents could visit with each other, grab a snack, and wait for their children to burn off some energy. Located in a local strip mall, the Jungle Gym had opened 3 months ago and employed 1 manager and 12 general employees. During each shift, there would be 5 or 6 employees on site, with each person expected to welcome guests, collect cash, manage the café, and interact with the children in the play pits.

Jason arrived for his first day and introduced himself to Bob, another employee who had been working at the Jungle Gym since it opened. The manager, Todd, eventually arrived and appeared surprised to see Jason. Todd then told Jason to go into the staff room and spend an hour or so reading through manuals that described safety protocol and explanations about how the equipment in the play pits worked. Jason was concerned about this as he was more of an active learner and found it difficult to learn new material merely by reading. However, as a new employee, he did not want to rock the boat. After about 90 minutes, Bob told Jason that he "was on" and to join the other 5 employees working.

Things were chaotic, to say the least. The children (over 50 of them) were loud and boisterous. As well, there was a long lineup in the café, and parents were becoming agitated as they had to wait for some service. Jason asked Bob about how to use some of the ropes on the climbing wall and was told, "Figure it out. We are all expected to be competent, and you were hired for your knowledge." Todd was also yelling at Jason to get to the café and help serve coffee to the adults. Jason had no idea how to use the special coffee maker and when serving a latte burnt his hand on the steam. For the rest of his 6-hour shift, he ran back and forth between the play pits and the café trying to keep children and parents happy. Ten minutes before his shift ended, a child was "lost," and all employees ran around in a panic trying to locate the youngster, who was eventually found hiding under a table in the café.

As he was leaving, Jason wanted to talk to Todd, but Todd was in his office, and there was a "Do not disturb" sign posted on the door.

Jason walked home. His hand and head hurt! This was not what he had envisioned, and he wondered whether he should even bother showing up for his next shift tomorrow.

Questions:

1. Who should be in charge of orienting new employees at the Jungle Gym? Why?
2. What tools and resources might be used in lieu of manuals to orient new employees?
3. Outline an effective orientation process that Jimmy's Jungle Gym should use. Consider what should be done prior to, on, and after the first day of employment.
4. What possible legal liabilities is the company facing? Why?

NOTES AND REFERENCES

1. E. Fragouli, "Intellectual Capital & Organizational Advantage: An Economic Approach to Its Valuation and Measurement," *International Journal of Information, Business and Management* 7, no. 1 (2015): 36–57.
2. Ibid.
3. A. Ferdous and M. Polonsky, "The Impact of Frontline Employees' Perceptions of Internal Marketing on Employee Outcomes," *Journal of Strategic Marketing* 22, no. 4 (2014): 300–315, doi:10.1080/0965 254X.2013.876077.
4. Jack Shaw, "Formal Training Processes—Instructional Systems Design (ISD) and ADDIE," accessed November 13, 2017, https://managementhelp.org/training/methods/formal-isd-and-addie.htm.
5. Susan M. Heathfield, "Performance Development Planning," About .com website, accessed November 12, 2017, http://humanresources .about.com/cs/perfmeasurement/a/pdp.htm.
6. Tony Bates, "2020 Vision: Outlook for Online Learning in 2014 and Way Beyond," January 12, 2014, accessed November 12, 2017, https://www.tonybates.ca/2014/01/12/2020-vision-outlook-for -online-learning-in-2014-and-way-beyond.
7. The Conference Board of Canada, "Learning and Development Outlook 2011: Are Organizations Ready for Learning 2.0?," October 2011.
8. Tony Bates, "2020 Vision."
9. "The Banff World Media Festival and Shaw Media Announce Recipients for Mentorship Programs," *Shaw Media*, June 5, 2015, accessed November 12, 2017, http://www.newswire.ca/news-releases/the -banff-world-media-festival-and-shaw-media-announce -recipients-for-mentorship-programs-517867621.html.
10. Ezra Stoller and Lily Sugrue, "Unpaid Internships: A Priceless Experience?," *The Harvard Crimson*, April 3, 2014, accessed November 12, 2017, https://www.thecrimson.com/article/2014/4/3/ unpaid-internships-experience.
11. Canadian Intern Association, "What Is the Law?," accessed November 12, 2017, http://internassociation.ca/what-is-the-law.
12. "Embracing Opportunities for Better Patient Care," *News Canada's Healthcare Newspaper*, April 3, 2012, accessed November 1,7, 2017, http://www.hospitalnews.com/embracing-opportunities -for-better-patient-care.
13. "6 Best Web Conferencing in 2017," ezTalks website, accessed November 12, 2017, https://www.eztalks.com/video-conference/ best-web-conferencing-in-2017.html.
14. The Conference Board of Canada, "Learning and Development Outlook 2011."
15. James Ramussen, "Why e-Learning on Tablets?," *Upside Learning*, March 19, 2015, accessed November 12, 2017, https://www.upside learning.com/blog/index.php/2014/03/19/why-elearning-on-tablets.
16. "Benefits of Coaching," accessed November 12, 2017, http://www .abetterperspective.com/Benefits_of_Coaching.htm.
17. Ibid.
18. Jim Kirkpatrick and Wendy Kirkpatrick, "The Kirkpatrick Philosophy," Kirkpatrick Partners website, accessed November 12, 2017, https://www.kirkpatrickpartners.com.
19. "More on Re-evaluating Evaluation—Jack Phillips and ROI," August 19, 2011, accessed November 12, 2017, https://www.dashe.com/blog/ evaluation-2/more-on-re-evaluating-evaluation-jack-phillips-and-roi.
20. Jim Kirkpatrick and Wendy Kirkpatrick, "The Kirkpatrick Philosophy."
21. A. Vasconcelos, "Older Workers: Some Critical Societal and Organizational Challenges," *The Journal of Management Development* 34, no. 3 (2015): 352, http://search.proquest.com/ docview/1664767789?accountid=1343.
22. Monica Belcourt, George Bohlander, and Scott Snell, *Managing Human Resources*, 6th Canadian ed. (Toronto: Nelson Thomson, 2011), 298.
23. Lynette Gillis and Allan Bailey, "Business Development Bank of Canada: Measuring the ROI of a Coaching Program for Banking Branch Managers," Canadian Society for Training and Development website, accessed November 12, 2017, http://www.cstd.ca/resource/ resmgr/iip/bdc_report_final_english.pdf.
24. "WestJet Once Again Canada's Most Attractive Employer," May 3, 2013, accessed November 13, 2017, http://westjet2.mediaroom .com/index.php?s=43&item=769.
25. William C. Byham, "The Business Case for Leadership Development," Chief Learning Officer website, August 17, 2017, accessed November 12, 2017, http://www.clomedia.com/2017/08/17/ business-case-leadership-development.
26. "Change Management," Queen's University website, accessed November 12, 2017, http://irc.queensu.ca/training/change -management-training-courses-management-of-change -process-organizational-change-management-plan.
27. The Conference Board of Canada, "Learning and Development Outlook 2011."
28. Tony Bates, "2020 Vision."
29. Tess Taylor, "4 learning and development trends for HR leaders to watch in 2017," *HR Drive*, November 15, 2016, accessed November 12, 2017, https://www.hrdive.com/news/4-learning-and -development-trends-for-hr-leaders-to-watch-in-2017/430471.
30. "Adult Literacy Facts," Life Literacy Canada website, accessed November 12, 2017, https://abclifeliteracy.ca/workplace-literacy.
31. "WELCOME to the Ontario WorkInfoNET (OnWIN)!," accessed November 12, 2017, http://onwin.ca/en.
32. Kate McFarlin, "The Effects of Globalization in the Workplace," accessed August 7, 2018, https://smallbusiness.chron.com/ effects-globalization-workplace-10738.html.
33. Canadian Chamber of Commerce, "Top 10 Barriers to Competitiveness," Skills Development Discussion Paper, March 2012.
34. Susan M. Heathfield, "How to Build a Teamwork Culture," accessed November 12, 2017, http://humanresources.about.com/od/ involvementteams/a/team_culture.htm.
35. Business Council of Canada, "Canadian Employers Launch National Initiative on Workplace Learning and Development," accessed November 12, 2017, http://thebusinesscouncil.ca/news/ canadian-employers-launch-national-initiative-on-workplace -learning-and-development.
36. Ibid.
37. The Conference Board of Canada, "Learning and Development Outlook, 13th Edition," December 10, 2015, accessed November 12, 2017, http://www.conferenceboard.ca/e-library/abstract .aspx?did=7542.
38. Ibid.
39. Dawn Rosenberg McKay, "The Holland Code," accessed November 12, 2017, http://careerplanning.about.com/od/selfassessment/a/ holland-code.htm.
40. Edgar H. Schein, *Career Anchors (Discovering Your Real Values)* (San Francisco: Jossey-Bass Pfeiffer, 1990).
41. Enbridge, "Employee Development," accessed November 12, 2017, http://www.enbridge.com/WorkwithEnbridge/CareersatEnbridge/ Why-Enbridge/EmployeeDevelopment.aspx.
42. The Conference Board of Canada, "Women in Senior Management: Where Are They?" Conference Board of Canada, August 2011.
43. Ibid.

7 Managing Employee Performance

HRM CLOSE-UP

"As a small business, it's less about a written performance review of a type you might see in a large corporation and more about really in-the-moment coaching."

IT'S HARD to say what first grabs your attention when you step into a Prairie Girl Bakery. It could be the tantalizing scent of fresh baking that drifts through the air, the bright colours and splendid perfection of the yummy wares, or the genuine warmth of the welcome.

Baked with all-natural ingredients, including salted butter, eggs, and Belgian chocolate, a visit to one of these blissful baking boutiques is like stopping by your grandmother's house as a child. If your grandmother was a master baker, that is.

Prairie Girl Bakery was founded by Jean Blacklock in 2011. Born in Saskatoon and having earned degrees in commerce and law from the University of Saskatchewan, Blacklock took the plunge into entrepreneurship after a successful career with a top Calgary law firm and as a wealth manager with BMO.

"I was very passionate about the food business," Blacklock explains. "And I found a niche for cupcakes. I thought I could make a go of it if I had a really great website and if I had a really great product."

Now, with 3 stores, a successful online business that accounts for more than a quarter of the company's sales, a best-selling cookbook, and plans to distribute her products across the country, Blacklock likes to "live life one cupcake at a time," as her company's motto exclaims. Baking the perfect cake is only part of Prairie Girl's recipe for success, however.

"It's always been 50% the product and 50% the service," Blacklock explains. "We are really a luxury product. I mean people are paying a lot for our product, so I want them to be a little bit happier when they leave the store than when they go in. Customer service is just really important to me." But finding the right people to fulfill Blacklock's aim was easier said than done.

"There's no sort of magic to finding really good people," Blacklock says. "We hire very carefully. We look for people who really can't keep the smile off their face in the interview. Initially, in the first year or two, I thought that attribute of friendliness could be taught because in my corporate career technical things could be taught. But I've learned over the years that you actually can't teach people who are reserved by nature to be friendly."

Once welcomed into the Prairie Girl world and properly trained, it's very important that staff are constantly evaluated to make sure that they really are a good fit and can grow and be rewarded within the organization.

"As a small business, it's less about a written performance review of a type you might see in a large corporation and more about really in-the-moment coaching," Blacklock explains of Prairie Girl's approach to evaluating staff performance.

"Any feedback we may have is always done in a respectful, friendly manner and never in front of the public. Just ongoing positive or constructive feedback. I strongly believe in the 'praise in public, coach in private' model," she says.

And if Blacklock sees something that troubles her when visiting one of her stores, she sticks to the company's structure when it comes to rectifying it.

"I am clearly the owner, but the staff's interactions with me are as a friendly, respectful, nice person. If I see something that I don't like, I don't tell them; I will tell their manager. I don't go behind their managers' backs."

Courtesy of Jean Blacklock

Jean Blacklock, Founder, Prairie Girl Bakery

To reward those top performers, Blacklock takes a few different avenues.

"We have annual salary reviews, and at that time, a person's performance or goals in the company—like whether they'd like to become a manager or whatever—are discussed. Plus we try to pay above the average. And we provide financial bonuses."

Providing recognition of a staff member's contribution is always very important to Blacklock. "We always reward good staff through acknowledgment," she says. "Acknowledgment in our all-employee newsletter by email, acknowledgment of everyone's hard work or a particular person's hard work."

It's that effort to attract high-quality staff and to properly recognize their performance that has given Prairie Girl Bakery a family atmosphere.

"Working here is not the destination career for most of our employees," Blacklock admits. "They'll work here while they're studying for their degree or whatever. But often, when they're leaving, they'll say they'll always remember their time at Prairie Girl, that it felt like a family, and that they made friends."

And perhaps also developed a bit of a sweet tooth as well.

INTRODUCTION

In the preceding chapters, we discussed how an organization hires and develops a productive workforce. In this chapter, we turn to performance management, which is a critical process that managers use to maintain and enhance productivity and facilitate progress toward strategic goals. Although we will focus mainly on a formal system, as noted by Jean Blacklock of Prairie Girl Bakery, the processes of managing and reviewing performance can be informal as well. All managers monitor the way employees work and assess how this matches organizational needs. Managers form impressions about the relative value of employees to the organization and seek to maximize the contribution of every individual. Yet although these ongoing informal processes are vitally important, most organizations also have a system that includes a formal review of the person's performance once or twice a year or on an ongoing basis.

The success or failure of a performance management system depends on the philosophy underlying it, its connection to business goals, the attitudes and skills of those responsible for using it, and the individual components of the system. A performance management system is more than the actual review—it is an overall approach to getting the maximum contribution from each employee.

A PERFORMANCE MANAGEMENT SYSTEM

LO1

Define a performance management system.

Performance management system
A set of integrated management practices designed to help employees maximize performance, thereby allowing the organization to reach its goals

A **performance management system** is a set of integrated management practices designed to help employees maximize performance, thereby allowing the organization to reach its goals. Although reviewing employees' performance is a key component, this is only 1 part of a good performance management system. A systems approach to performance management (1) allows the organization to integrate the management functions in order to maximize employee potential and (2) helps increase employees' satisfaction with their work and with the organization.

Formal programs for managing performance are by no means new to organizations. Performance management programs are used in large and small organizations in both the public and private sectors. Advocates see these programs as among the most logical means to coach, review, develop, and thus effectively utilize the knowledge and abilities of employees as well as monitor the healthiness of the work culture. A senior manager at Softchoice, a technology company in Toronto, feels that performance management issues can be related to a toxic work environment.[1] Robert Bacal, a long-time observer of performance management systems, reminds us that the primary purpose for managing employees' performance is to improve their future performance.[2]

It is important that the organization be clear about the purpose, but this is not always the case. Sometimes companies want systems to communicate what work is valued; at other times, performance management systems are used to make decisions about employees' pay. For example, an organization that employs a team-based structure might have a performance management system that focuses on reviewing individual performance. This focus gives mixed messages about who owns the responsibility for the results and what is being valued in the performance review. Performance management needs to align everyone's work toward organizational goals and objectives and to ensure that employees are not working at cross-purposes.[3]

There is no doubt that managing performance is not always easy. Managers frequently avoid this process, yet when done properly, the organization improves and the employee's engagement and development are enhanced.[4,5] Managing performance is not an added activity in the busy manager's life—it is central to the everyday work of managers. A number of different research studies in a variety of industries, including engineering, healthcare, and education, demonstrate the strong link between performance management systems and organizational success.[6] These studies consistently demonstrate, however, that an employee's performance needs to be connected to achieving the larger goals of the organization and that it is critical to have measurable performance criteria that are applied to everyone in the work unit.[7] Furthermore, there is evidence that an effective system includes leadership behaviours where managers are more concerned with employees' job performance than their own.[8] With such clear evidence of the value of performance management systems, it will be useful for managers and HR practitioners to use these research findings when building a business case for the implementation of such a system.

PURPOSES OF MANAGING PERFORMANCE

Performance management has several purposes, all intended to benefit both the organization and the employee and to ensure that any decisions resulting from the system are based on objective, reliable, and valid information. As such, performance management provides key information that should be strategically used with other HRM processes. The purposes of managing performance will now be reviewed.

LO2
Explain the purposes of managing performance.

Compensating

The most frequent use of performance management systems is to make compensation decisions. If the organization indicates that it is paying for performance, then it is necessary that pay and performance are linked. Furthermore, it will also be necessary to ensure that differences in performance levels can be measured, communicated, and then converted into pay decisions.[9]

Planning

A performance management system can be used as part of HR planning—particularly when the organization has a succession plan. Performance management provides information on which employees have specific competencies and therefore helps identify how current employees can best use their knowledge, skills, and abilities. Performance management also identifies competency gaps and unfilled needs within an organization.

Documenting

A performance system provides a "paper trail" for documenting HRM processes and decisions, for information purposes, and in case of any resulting legal action. It is important that managers keep a record of performance discussions with employees (both informal and formal conversations regarding performance) as this provides evidence that these conversations took place. (Note: There are times when a very informal or quick coaching conversation with an employee could occur, and this may or may not be documented by the manager. But it is recommended that managers always document performance discussions.) Employees should also be asked to sign a document to verify that the discussion occurred and that they understood what they were told. For example, if a person were being disciplined regarding very poor customer service, the performance management system would be able to identify what the goals were, how well the person met the goals, and what discussions and coaching sessions took place to improve performance in relation to customer service. Legal responsibilities and rights, for both employees and employers, when dealing with ineffective performance are discussed in Chapter 9. Although documentation regarding an

A performance management system provides a paper trail.

employee's performance is always important, it is even more critical in a unionized environment. If an employee grieves a performance rating, managers must be able to prove that goals were written down and communicated to the employee and that the employee's performance was assessed in a fair manner.

Coaching and Developing

From the standpoint of individual development, a performance system provides the feedback essential for discussing strengths and areas where performance needs improving. In this way, ongoing coaching from a manager to an employee can occur. As well, more formal training and development needs can be highlighted through needs assessment, as was discussed in Chapter 6. For example, if, through setting objectives, many managers determine that people have to improve their computer literacy skills, then the organization can provide a solution that meets those needs. From this information, the organization may set up a formal training program for all employees. This approach can be better than having each manager deal with each person on an individual basis. Without such a step in the system, the manner in which developmental needs are identified can be hit-and-miss.

Regardless of the employee's level of performance, the system provides an opportunity to identify issues for discussion, eliminate any possible problems, and work on ways of achieving high performance. Newer approaches to performance management emphasize training and development and growth plans for employees. A developmental approach recognizes that the purpose of a manager is to support and help the person (or team) achieve results for good organizational performance. Having a sound basis for identifying performance goals, coaching, reviewing, and recognizing performance leads to successful organizations. Effective use of performance management to support development also assists with opportunities for transfers or promotions. These types of moves within a company are strategically implemented when performance management is used to inform decisions about placing employees in new positions.

Figure 7.1 provides a summary of the purposes of managing performance.

FIGURE 7.1 **Purposes of Managing Performance**

Compensating
- Determining salary increases.
- Structuring bonuses and pay-for-performance awards.

Planning
- Implementing succession plans.
- Identifying knowledge, skills, and abilities of current employees.
- Identifying competency gaps in the organization.

Documenting
- Creating a paper trail for documenting HRM decisions and actions.
- Providing evidence to support layoff decisions.

Coaching and Developing
- Proving ongoing coaching to employees, discussing strengths, and identifying areas needing improvement.
- Setting formal training programs.
- Creating plans for growth and development.
- Informing transfer and promotion decisions.

STEPS IN AN EFFECTIVE PERFORMANCE MANAGEMENT SYSTEM

The HR department ordinarily has primary responsibility for overseeing and coordinating the performance management system. HR may also design or select a performance management system to use. It is important to note that although HR has a critical role to play, managers implement the performance management system and are therefore ultimately responsible for the process and outcomes. As such, managers from the operating departments must also be actively involved in helping to establish the objectives for the system. Furthermore, employees are more likely to accept and be satisfied with the performance management system when they have the chance to participate in its development.

The following sections describe the key steps in an effective performance management system.

LO3

Describe the steps in an effective performance management system.

Clarifying the Work to Be Done

Before any goals can be established or performance standards identified, it is important to clarify the work to be accomplished. Information from job analysis and job descriptions (as discussed in Chapter 4) or information obtained from conversations between managers and employees will help identify the expected outcomes or results and determine how those results will be measured. For example, an expected result for a cook at a fast-food restaurant might be "no food wastage." The manager and cook would then decide how this would be measured. It might be measured by determining the number of kilograms of food in the garbage pail or the number of voided customer orders.

Setting Goals and Establishing a Performance Plan

Once the manager and the employee(s) are clear on expected results and how those results will be measured, goals must be set. For the system to really work, these goals must be linked to overall business objectives. For example, an overall business objective for the

A key step in performance management is setting goals and establishing a performance plan.

fast-food restaurant is to reduce costs. Since food costs are a large proportion of overall costs, the restaurant may decide to focus on reducing food costs. Therefore, for the individual employee, cutting down on wasted food will contribute to this, so the goal may be "to reduce food waste by 10% within the next 3 months." You will note that this is a very specific goal that includes a time frame.

To ensure a strong link to business goals, the manager may also need to establish performance measures that are qualitative, such as customer relations, rather than quantitative (e.g., revenue).[10] With the use of both financial results (e.g., cost of food) and soft measures (e.g., customer satisfaction), the results are more strongly linked to the overall restaurant outcomes. This step also involves discussion between both the manager and the employee, which leads to greater involvement and commitment to the specific goals.

With the ongoing concern about business ethics, more and more organizations are including standards of performance related to ethics and reviewing ethical behaviour as part of the performance management system. Ethics in HRM 7.1 discusses what can happen if ethical behaviour or action isn't included, or supported, in the performance management system.

There are other types of methods, such as trait and behavioural, in addition to results, that can be used in establishing the performance plan. These are discussed later in the chapter.

Providing Frequent Coaching

Coaching sessions are designed to help employees achieve their results. Coaching should not involve fault-finding or blaming. Most people want to do a good job; therefore, it is important that a manager approach coaching in a helpful and supportive way. If the employee is having

ETHICS IN HRM 7.1 — WHAT ABOUT THE ETHICS OF OUR SYSTEM?

Most organizations use some type of performance management system to assess the performance of employees. And most of us assume that any system supports ethical behaviours and decisions. But what if it doesn't?

As part of any performance management system, employees have established goals geared to help the company succeed in its business performance. Many of the goals are quantitative measures, such as the number of items sold in a retail store or the number of transactions in a financial institution. Goals such as these often are linked to bonuses, in which employees earn more when they sell more products or the value of the sales is higher than the goal. Does this always mean that the employee is doing the right thing for the customer? Unfortunately, it does not.

For example, current and former TD Bank Group employees exposed performance goals and described their work environment as "poisoned," "stress inducing," and "insane," with "zero focus on ethics." "Some employees admitted they broke the law, claiming they were desperate to earn points towards sales goals they have to reach every three months or risk being fired." Examples of unethical behaviour included creating overdrafts on customer accounts without their knowledge or permission.

Although it is necessary that employees be assessed on what they accomplish, it is also critical that they be assessed on how the work is accomplished. To make this happen, the performance management system needs to be grounded in the company's values and ethics.

CRITICAL THINKING QUESTIONS:

1. What type of performance management systems have you experienced?
2. Do you feel the system incorporated the organization's values and ethics?
3. What should employees do if they believe performance goals are requiring them to act in an unethical manner?

Source: Adapted from Erica Johnson, "We Do It Because Our Jobs Are at Stake: TD Bank Employees Admit to Breaking the Law for Fear of Being Fired," *CBC News*, March 10, 2017, accessed November 22, 2017, http://www.cbc.ca/news/business/td-bank-employees-admit-to-breaking-law-1.4016569.

difficulty reaching a goal, the manager and the employee can explore together the reasons why and what can be done to fix the difficulty.

Coaching is also a good way to avoid the costs of firing employees and hiring new employees. It is difficult for employees to improve their performance if the manager does not take the time to help them understand what they need to do. For coaching to be effective, the manager needs to listen carefully and ask probing, open-ended questions so that conversation and dialogue can occur.[11] Encouraging and supporting an environment where coaching is a partnership mean that the employee is more likely to develop and gain from the coaching relationship. Read Toolkit 7.1 for some coaching tips.

Conducting a Formal Review of Performance

Most performance management systems include an annual formal review of an employee's overall performance. This occasion allows both the manager and the employee to consider the employee's accomplishments and to discuss development areas and goals for the next year. As such, a formal performance review is an opportunity to evaluate, discuss, and document what an employee has accomplished in relation to the goals that were set. It is also usually at this point that the organization uses the results of the annual performance review for salary adjustments. Since the employee was involved in the original goal setting, and since there has been regular and frequent feedback and coaching, this step is more of a review. There shouldn't be any surprises.

How to conduct an effective performance review is discussed later in this chapter.

TOOLKIT 7.1   EFFECTIVE COACHING

1. Coaching is between 2 people.
2. Coaching is based on a relationship of trust and respect between the 2 people, not on control.
3. Coaching is about personal development for the person being coached.
4. Coaching is designed to fit the individual needs of each person.
5. Both people must want to be involved in the coaching relationship.
6. The coach asks open-ended questions and doesn't "tell."
7. Coaching draws out the person's potential.
8. Coaching is about helping people come to their own conclusions: the coach does not impose a solution.
9. Coaching requires active listening and full participation for both people.
10. Coaching is helping the other person learn and become self-sufficient.
11. Coaching is enabling—not training.
12. Coaching is about reflection and conversation.
13. Coaching builds accountability and creates stronger bonds between managers and employees.
14. Coaching focuses on real-world situations so that the person can learn and act or behave differently.
15. Coaching provides specific and timely feedback and includes both positive and constructive comments.
16. Coaching aligns desired outcomes with business objectives.

Sources: Adapted from Victor Lipman, "The Most Fundamental Quality A Good Coach Needs," *Forbes*, February 19, 2017, accessed November 22, 2017, https://www.forbes.com/sites/victorlipman/2017/02/19/the-most-fundamental-quality-a-good-coach-needs/#6e697d54399e; Susan M. Heathfield, "Tips for Effective Coaching," *About.com*, accessed November 22, 2017, http://humanresources.about.com/od/coachingmentoring/a/coaching.htm; Monique Valcour, "A Great Manager Must Be a Great Coach: Here's 5 Tips to Get You Started," *Financial Review*, July 25, 2014, accessed November 22, 2017, www.brw.com.au/p/leadership/great_manager_must_you_great_coach_vmJ9hRBE5Qie0IaWwi3D0L; "Introduction to Coaching," Society for Industrial and Organizational Psychology, accessed November 22, 2017, www.siop.org/Workplace/coaching/introduction.aspx; and Jennifer Osborn, "Developing Workplace Coaching Skills," LIScareer.com, accessed November 22, 2017, www.liscareer.com/osborn_coaching.htm.

Recognizing and Rewarding Performance

No system will be effective without recognition of accomplishments. Although we usually think of recognition in monetary terms, some non-financial rewards for the employee include the following:

- being considered for a promotion
- being given the opportunity to work on a special project
- being praised by the manager
- being profiled in a business journal or a company newsletter about a particular achievement

These types of rewards cost little or no money. People like to know that their good work and achievements are noticed. For example, in a recent study, employees indicated that they had not received any verbal or written appreciation from their manager, and this was very discouraging.[12] By careful use of praise and positive feedback, the manager can energize the individual, and employees can feel they are making a difference.[13]

Creating an Action Plan

Action plans regarding future training and development and discussions regarding career development should be an outcome from a review of performance. As well, clarifying work and setting goals for the upcoming year or performance cycle (i.e., starting again at the first steps of the performance management system) should also be done. A well-integrated performance management system concludes with a plan for the next performance cycle.

In situations where an employee is not meeting performance expectations, an action plan would need to be developed to ensure that there is a clear understanding between the manager and the employee regarding what is necessary to improve performance. Unless these deficiencies are brought to the employee's attention, they are likely to continue until they become quite serious. Sometimes underperformers do not understand exactly what is expected of them. However, once their responsibilities are clarified, they are in a position to take the corrective action needed to improve their performance. For an improvement plan to be useful, any behaviours or results requiring change need to be clearly identified, expectations about what change looks like need to be clear, and clear timelines need to be set. It is also important that both the manager and the employee are clear on what types of supports will be available.[14]

Identifying Reasons for Ineffective Performance

There are many reasons why an employee's performance might not meet the standards. First, everyone has a unique pattern of strengths and weaknesses. In addition, other factors—such as the work environment, the external environment (including home and community), and personal problems—have an impact. See Figure 7.2 for a list of possible reasons for ineffective performance.

LO4

Identify possible reasons for ineffective performance.

FIGURE 7.2 Reasons for Ineffective Performance

Organizational Policies and Practices
- Ineffective placement.
- Insufficient job training.
- Ineffectual employment practices.
- Permissiveness with enforcing policies or job standards.
- Heavy-handed management.
- Lack of attention to employee needs or concerns.
- Inadequate communication within organization.
- Unclear reporting relationships.

Job Concerns
- Unclear or constantly changing work requirements.
- Boredom with job.
- Lack of job growth or advancement opportunities.
- Management–employee conflict.
- Management–union conflict.
- Problems with fellow employees.
- Unsafe working conditions.
- Unavailable or inadequate equipment or materials.
- Inability to perform the job.
- Excessive workload.
- Lack of job skills.

Personal Problems
- Marital problems.
- Financial worries.
- Emotional disorders (including depression, guilt, anxiety, fear).
- Conflict between work demands and family demands.
- Physical limitations, including disabilities.
- Low work ethic.
- Other family problems.
- Illness.

Once the cause(s) of performance problems are known, a plan of action to address this can be developed. This may include training, providing new or better resources or tools, offering counselling through an employee assistance program, or providing clearer goals and performance standards. Any plan of action to improve employee performance should also include planned meetings during which the manager and the employee track progress, discuss ongoing concerns, and ensure that support mechanisms are being provided and are useful to support the employee in meeting performance expectations.

If ineffective performance persists, it may be necessary to transfer the employee, take disciplinary action, or terminate the person's employment. Whatever action is taken, it should be done with objectivity, fairness, and consideration of the employee's feelings. More information on dealing with ineffective performance is covered in Chapter 9.

WHY PERFORMANCE MANAGEMENT SYSTEMS CAN FAIL

LO5

Explain possible reasons why performance management systems can fail.

In actual practice, formal performance management systems sometimes yield disappointing results. Figure 7.3 shows that some of the reasons include the manager believing that it is only for the HR department, that it is used to punish employees, or that it isn't clear what is expected. Furthermore, if the performance review is used to provide a written assessment for salary action and at the same time to motivate employees to improve their work, the compensation and developmental purposes may be in conflict. As a result, the review interview may become a discussion about salary in which the manager seeks to justify the action taken. In such cases, the discussion might have little influence on the employee's future job performance.

One of the main concerns of employees is the fairness of the performance management system because the process is central to so many HRM decisions. Employees who believe the system is unfair may consider a performance review to be a waste of time and leave the interview feeling anxious and frustrated. They may also view compliance with the system as mechanical and thus play only a passive role during the entire process. By addressing these employee concerns during the planning stage of the system, the organization will help the performance management system succeed in reaching desired goals.

As with all HR processes and systems, if the support of top management is lacking, the system will not be successful. Even the best-conceived process will not work in an environment where managers are not encouraged and expected by their superiors to take their responsibilities seriously in managing performance. To underscore the importance of this responsibility, top management should ensure that managers are also part of the overall performance management system and that their performance will be reviewed for how well they are managing their employees' performance.

In many organizations, performance management is a once-a-year activity in which the review interview becomes a source of friction for both managers and employees. As noted earlier in this chapter, an important principle of performance management is that continuous feedback and employee coaching must be a positive regular activity—be it daily or hourly. The annual or semi-annual performance review should be a logical extension of the day-to-day supervision process. For example, Mead Johnson Canada, a subsidiary of Bristol-Myers Squibb, a large pharmaceutical firm, changed its performance management system so that employees receive ongoing feedback. This system now has a future growth and expectations focus with immediate and specific feedback. At Work with HRM 7.1 describes how some companies are making use of more frequent feedback.

Whether performance feedback is given formally (i.e., once per year) or is given more informally and continuously, the process of meeting with employees to provide this information is a critical part of the performance management system. As such, conducting performance reviews will now be discussed.

FIGURE 7.3   Reasons Performance Management Systems Can Fail

1. Performance management is not well defined and may not encourage outcomes.

2. Objectives are not prioritized.

3. The process is complex and not connected to the company strategy.

4. The system is not aligned with business performance.

5. Employees are not involved in developing the system and setting performance goals and therefore think the system is unfair or a waste of time.

6. The system isn't designed to adapt as needs change.

7. The system focuses on blame rather than helping employees.

8. Not enough time is spent on planning and communicating.

9. Not enough time is spent on coaching employees.

10. Performance management has competing and different purposes.

11. The focus is on annual review and not on the entire integrated system.

12. The performance process does not help employees develop skills and abilities.

13. Managers feel little or no benefit will be derived from the time and energy spent on the process.

14. Managers dislike the face-to-face discussion and performance feedback.

15. Managers are not sufficiently adept in setting goals and performance measures, coaching and supporting, or providing performance feedback.

16. Managers are not properly trained, and rating errors can occur.

17. The judgmental role of a review can conflict with the helping role of developing employees.

Sources: Adapted from Bill Schiemann, "Why Do Performance Management Systems Fail?," *Association for Talent Development*, January 27, 2016, accessed November 23, 2017, https://www.td.org/Publications/Blogs/Human-Capital -Blog/2016/01/Why-Do-Performance-Management-Systems-Fail; Scott Engler, "5 Reasons Your Performance Management Is a Failure," *Executive Board*, February 4, 2014, accessed November 23, 2017, www.executiveboard.com/blogs/5 -reasons-your-performance-management-is-a-failure; and "Why Does Most Performance Management, or Appraisal, Fail?," Performance Management Help Centre, *Bacal & Associates*, accessed November 23, 2017, http://performance-appraisals .org/faq/failure.htm.

Pressmaster/Shutterstock.com

Continuous feedback and coaching are an important part of performance management.

AT WORK WITH HRM 7.1   **TELL ME HOW I'M DOING**

Employees and managers frequently indicate their frustration with only doing annual performance reviews. So what is the answer?

Much of the frustration could be reduced if managers spent more time meeting with their staff so that the manager knows what is going on and providing assistance to keep employees focused on what needs to be accomplished. This can be as simple as asking, "How are things going?" and "What do you need from me?" It is also important to ask probing questions.

Some experts suggest that a manager set aside an hour a day for meeting one-on-one with 3 or 4 employees. It is also suggested that the manager prepare for the meeting and expect employees to do the same. Keep the discussions focused on what is within the employees' control. The manager also needs to use a coaching-type feedback approach.

Although it is important for the manager to provide feedback, it is also necessary to ensure that there is more positive than negative feedback. The feedback needs to be ongoing and include praise and thanks for a job well done.

Managers need to be trained to provide more ongoing coaching and feedback. They do not just automatically know. When managers take the time to check in with employees, it also provides the employee with an opportunity to discuss any issues in relation to work, the organization, or even other employees. When managers are appropriately trained on providing effective feedback, both the manager and the employee learn that performance feedback is not a yearly, form-driven process but a management process that keeps everyone's eyes on the ball.

It is also important to be aware of the demographics of the employee population. For example, Pricewaterhouse-Coopers understands that its young professionals want frequent feedback—annually isn't good enough and won't keep them at the firm.

CRITICAL THINKING QUESTIONS:

1. If you've had work experience, how frequently did your manager provide you feedback? Did you feel it was often enough? Why?

2. What other ideas do you have for encouraging managers to provide more frequent feedback to employees?

Sources: Adapted from Marcus Buckingham and Ashley Goodall, "Reinventing Performance Management," *Harvard Business Review*, April 2015, accessed November 23, 2017, https://hbr.org/2015/04/reinventing-performance-management; Harvey Schachter, "The Solution to All Management Problems? Talk with Your Staff," *The Globe and Mail*, January 6, 2015, accessed February 14, 2015, www.theglobeandmail.com/report-on-business/careers/management/the-solution-to-all-management-problems/article22168929; Michelle Ray, "The Five Biggest Mistakes Leaders Make with Their Staff," *The Globe and Mail*, November 16, 2014, accessed February 14, 2015, www.theglobeandmail.com/report-on-business/careers/leadership-lab/the-five-biggest-mistakes-leaders-make-with-their-staff/article21606639; Brian Kreissl, "Ongoing Performance Management," *Canadian HR Reporter*, September 22, 2014, accessed February 14, 2015, www.hrreporter.com/articleview/22323-ongoing-performance-management; and David Ciccarelli, "Why the Annual Performance Review Doesn't Work," *The Globe and Mail*, October 8, 2014, accessed February 14, 2015, www.theglobeandmail.com/report-on-business/careers/leadership-lab/why-the-annual-performance-review-doesnt-work/article20980895.

CONDUCTING PERFORMANCE REVIEWS

Providing employees with feedback regarding their performance (i.e., conducting a performance review) is a critical step in the performance management system. As noted earlier in the chapter, feedback can be continuously given to employees in a more informal manner (i.e., coaching) or during a more formal performance interview. Therefore, when performance feedback is provided, consideration must be given to employees, managers, and legal requirements.

Employees

Employees can help ensure that the performance review is fair by being well prepared. This can include keeping track of positive (and negative) feedback and keeping records of courses, workshops, and any other training activities. As well, employees should be encouraged to be active participants during the performance review and be asked to share their ideas and comments. One way to ensure that this is done is to ask employees to complete a self-assessment of their performance prior to the actual performance review meeting.

Managers

As noted earlier in the chapter, managers need to understand that performance management is an integrated system and that they are expected to take an active role in helping employees achieve results. That said, managers can have biases even in a well-run system.[15] For example, managers may inflate reviews because they desire higher salaries for their employees or because higher ratings make them look good as managers. Alternatively, managers may want to get rid of troublesome employees, passing them off to another department by inflating their ratings. Managers have to be watchful for the same types of errors in performance reviews as in selection interviews. The manager may make decisions about a person's performance based on recent events (the recency error) or judge performance favourably or unfavourably overall by putting emphasis on only 1 area that is important in the manager's mind (the halo error). Likewise, the manager may be unwilling to give either extremely low or extremely high assessments and decide to rate everyone as "above average" (the central tendency). A manager can also be biased by comparing one employee's performance to another's (the contrast error) instead of assessing the employee against a set of standards.

Not just biases can create problems with performance management. Organizational politics and how the manager wants to be perceived can also creep into performance reviews. For example, managers may base the assessment on how they feel about the employee—whether they like the person or not.[16] Or they may want to maintain as much discretion as possible and therefore not use the performance management system as intended. Likewise, they may want to avoid any conflict and therefore delay the annual review for months.[17]

Given the numerous errors or problems that can occur, it is important that managers receive training on how to deliver effective performance feedback. The training needs to help remove the barriers of time constraints, lack of knowledge, and interpersonal conflicts. Overcoming these barriers makes the review process more effective. As noted earlier (see Why Performance Management Systems Can Fail), managers may not be aware of some of the rater errors that can occur. Part of the training needs to include such information as well as the ability to practise giving feedback. Training can also serve to remind managers to deliver performance feedback in a private setting, to focus on behaviours, not the person, and to encourage an employee to actively participate in the discussion.

Legal Requirements

Since performance assessments are used as a basis for HRM actions and decisions, they must meet certain legal requirements. The legality of any performance feedback is measured against the criteria of reliability, fairness, and validity. *Reliability* refers to whether performance is measured consistently among the employee participants. *Fairness* refers to the extent to which the system avoids bias caused by any factors unrelated to performance. *Validity* refers to the extent to which the system is job related and accurate. Under the *Canadian Charter of Rights and Freedoms* and other federal and provincial human rights requirements, performance assessment must be, above all, valid. Worker performance must be assessed on the basis of job requirements to ensure legal compliance.

Although currently there are few lawsuits pertaining to performance management in Canada, the spillover effect of lawsuits in the United States has prompted organizations to try to eliminate vagueness in descriptions of traits, such as attitude, cooperation, dependability, initiative, and leadership. For example, "dependability" can be made much less vague if it is spelled out as absence of employee tardiness or unexcused absences. In general, reducing room for subjective judgments will improve the entire process.

Employers might face legal challenges when reviews indicate acceptable or above-average performance but employees are later passed over for promotion, disciplined for poor performance, or terminated from the company. In these cases, the reviews can undermine the legitimacy of the subsequent decision. And legal challenges can be very costly. For example, if an organization terminated someone due to downsizing, but then subsequently said it was for poor performance, the company would not be successful in defending its action if the personnel file did not contain a performance review backing that up. More information regarding performance reviews and discipline is discussed in Chapter 9.

Formal performance reviews should therefore meet the following guidelines:

1. Employees should be given a copy of performance expectations.
2. Employees should be encouraged to actively contribute to performance review discussions.
3. Employees should have the opportunity to appeal or disagree with assessments about their performance.
4. Performance ratings must be job related (as determined through job analysis) and be based on observable behaviour and measurable results.
5. Managers should be trained on how to effectively evaluate, and provide feedback about, performance.

Employees should have the opportunity to appeal or disagree with assessments about their performance. As noted earlier in the chapter, organizations must ensure that managers document reviews and reasons for subsequent HRM actions and decisions. This information may prove decisive should an employee take legal action. An employer's credibility is strengthened when it can support performance results by documenting instances of poor performance. Read HRM and the Law 7.1 to gain an understanding of some other dimensions of poor performance.

HRM AND **THE LAW** 7.1 — DOES POOR PERFORMANCE INCLUDE ACTIONS AND BEHAVIOURS?

Most people think that poor performance is only about work output. However, poor performance can include any aspect of one's performance, including behaviours and actions.

This was demonstrated very clearly when a truck driver employed by a liquor distribution centre was terminated for harassment and bullying of coworkers. Initially, when the matter was first brought to the attention of the employer, an investigation was conducted. The truck driver had been employed for over 24 years and had had a good work record. When the company hired a female truck driver, the employee began to make derogatory remarks about her in her role as a union committee chair, which escalated to attempted shoving and threats. When both the union and the employer investigated, the employee confirmed that he had been trying to intimidate her and that he had made vulgar comments.

Although he did apologize for his behaviour, he continued with these comments and actions, not only to the same worker but also to other female workers. He was warned that his performance was unacceptable and that further incidents could lead to termination. Things did not improve, and he was eventually terminated.

The union filed a grievance about the employer's action, and the arbitrator concluded that the employee's actions constituted the most serious form of inappropriate workplace behaviour and upheld the dismissal.

On the other hand, in a case involving a railroad, the employer terminated an employee for harassing and verbally abusing other workers through phone calls. An investigation by the employer concluded that although the complaints had no merit, the conduct of the employee was confrontational and adversarial. Again, the union filed a grievance, and the arbitrator concluded that although the insults were inappropriate, they were not threats and therefore didn't warrant termination. The employee was reinstated with back pay and ordered to undertake anger management.

CRITICAL THINKING QUESTION:

Why was one employee termination upheld, whereas the other was not? Do you agree with the outcome in both scenarios? Why or why not?

Sources: Adapted from Jeffrey Smith, "B.C. Employer Puts an End to Worker's Ongoing Harassment," *Canadian HR Reporter*, February 15, 2015, accessed November 23, 2017, www.hrreporter.com/articleview/23592-bc-employer-puts-an-end-to-workers-ongoing-harassment-legal-view; and Jeffrey Smith, "Worker's Angry Phone Calls Not Just Cause," *Canadian HR Reporter*, February 9, 2015, accessed November 23, 2017, www.hrreporter.com/articleview/23470-workers-angry-phone-calls-not-just-cause-legal-view.

SOURCES OF INFORMATION REGARDING AN EMPLOYEE'S PERFORMANCE

For many years, the traditional approach to reviewing an employee's performance was to base it solely on information the manager had gathered first-hand. However, given the complexity of today's jobs, it is often more realistic to gather information directly from those best acquainted with the person's performance, such as managers, the employee being reviewed, peers, team members, subordinates, and customers. The Canadian Institute of Chartered Accountants and the Ontario Ministry of Energy, Northern Development and Mines have begun using this approach.

Since managers spend a lot of their time gathering information for evaluating performance, we will now focus on various way that managers can do this.

Manager Review

Employees typically receive performance feedback from their direct manager. As such, a **manager review** is common in many organizations. However, managers often do not observe the day-to-day performance of employees or do not have the time to do this. In these cases, managers may use information acquired from other resources. For example, American Express Canada uses telephone monitors to assess the quality of the communication between a service centre representative and a customer. Employees are aware that they are being monitored for developmental purposes. If such reliable and valid measures are not available, the review may be less than accurate.

Self-Review

Sometimes employees are asked to assess themselves on some or all aspects of their performance. **Self-review** is beneficial when managers seek to increase an employee's involvement in the review process. Such an approach may require an employee to complete a review form prior to the performance interview. At a minimum, this gets the employee thinking about strengths and areas for improvement and may lead to discussions about barriers to effective performance. During the performance interview, the manager and the employee discuss job performance and agree on a final assessment. This approach also works well when the manager and the employee jointly establish future performance goals or employee development plans.

Critics of self-review argue that employees are more lenient than managers in their assessments and tend to present themselves in a highly favourable light. However, some research has found that people tend to underrate their own overall performance, thereby lessening the value of this type of assessment.[18]

Subordinate Review

Some organizations use **subordinate review** to give managers feedback on how their employees view them. Subordinates are often able to provide performance feedback about their managers regarding leadership and communication skills. However, aspects of performance related to managers' specific job tasks, such as planning and organizing, budgeting, creativity, and analytical ability, are not usually appropriate for subordinate feedback. To ensure that subordinate feedback is as objective as possible, it is important that everyone understand how feedback is written and collected.[19] It is important that subordinates know that information collected from them will remain anonymous and that their own jobs will not be threatened based upon the comments they provide.

LO6
Describe the various sources of information regarding an employee's performance.

Manager review
Performance review done by the employee's manager

Self-review
Performance review done by the employee being assessed, generally on a form completed by the employee prior to the performance interview

Subordinate review
Performance review of a superior by an employee, which is more appropriate for developmental than for administrative purposes

Peer Review

Peer review
Performance feedback collected from an employee's colleague

Colleagues, or people who work together, may be asked to assess each other. A **peer review** provides information that is somewhat different from that provided by a superior because employees working together often see different dimensions of performance. For example, a manager asked to provide input about a server in a restaurant on a dimension such as "dealing with the public" may not have had much opportunity to observe it. Fellow servers, on the other hand, have the opportunity to observe this behaviour regularly.

Many believe 1 advantage of peer input is that it furnishes more accurate and valid information than assessments by superiors. The manager often sees employees putting their best foot forward, whereas those who work with their fellow employees on a regular basis may see a more realistic picture. With peer input, coworkers are asked to provide input on specific areas, usually in a structured, written format.

Despite evidence that peer reviews are possibly the most accurate method of judging employee behaviour, often they are not used. Some of the reasons commonly cited are as follows:

1. Peer reviews can be biased toward or against the employee.
2. Too much pressure is put on reviewers to meet time deadlines.
3. Too many people are involved.
4. Anonymous ratings can be less objective.[20]

When peers are in competition with one another (e.g., sales associates), peer reviews may not be advisable for administrative decisions, such as those relating to salary or bonuses. Also, employers who use peer reviews must make sure to safeguard confidentiality in handling the review forms. A breach of confidentiality can foster interpersonal rivalries, hurt feelings, or hostility among fellow employees.

Customer Review

Customer review
Performance review that seeks information from both external and internal customers

Also driven by quality and customer satisfaction concerns, an increasing number of organizations use internal and external **customer reviews** as a source of performance review information. Although external customers' information has been used for some time to review restaurant, hotel, and car rental company personnel, companies such as FedEx have begun utilizing external customers as well. Customer information can also tell an organization if employees are following procedures. As an example, secret shoppers at the Radisson Hotel Saskatoon provided feedback to hotel management that employees were failing to provide accurate accounting on some customers' bills.

Managers establish customer service measures (CSMs) and set goals for employees that are linked to company goals. Often the CSM goals are linked to employee pay through incentive programs. Customer survey data are then incorporated into the performance evaluation. By including CSMs in their performance reviews, managers focus on what is important, and business results improve. For example, AMF Canada, a manufacturer of automated bakery equipment, uses customer feedback to drive the technology behind its success.[21]

In addition to seeking performance feedback from external customers, internal customers can also provide important information. Internal customers are employees inside an organization who depend on an employee's work output. For example, managers who rely on the HR department to develop and deliver training programs could be asked to provide performance feedback. Ethics in HRM 7.2 discusses some of the problems that can occur when asking for customer feedback about employees' performance.

360-Degree Review

360-degree review
Provides employees with performance feedback from a variety of people or sources

Many companies are combining various sources of performance appraisal information to create multi-person, 360-degree appraisal and feedback systems. A **360-degree review** is intended to provide employees with feedback about their performance from various sources,

Customer reviews can be a valuable source of information about an employee's performance.

ETHICS IN HRM 7.2   CUSTOMERS ALWAYS COMPLAIN

Providing excellent customer service would seem like a reasonable performance expectation; therefore, many organizations are encouraging customers to provide reviews, either by filling out forms available at the business or through online surveys. However, research has found that people are most likely to give feedback only when they have something negative to share. Also, providing anonymous feedback seems to bring out the worst in people and provide them with the opportunity to be overly critical.

This leads to questions about the reliability and validity of customer feedback. Critics of this type of review claim that it is not appropriate to assess employees' performance based upon customers' comments due to the likelihood of negative feedback being received. This type of review only serves to demotivate and discourage employees, who only hear about what they have done wrong and only get input from unhappy people. Given the importance of performance feedback, some argue that it is inappropriate to allow this type of criticism to influence how an employee's performance is evaluated.

CRITICAL THINKING QUESTIONS:
1. Do you agree that people are only likely to comment and provide feedback when they receive poor customer service? What have been your experiences?
2. How can organizations encourage customers to provide feedback regarding positive or exceptional customer service?

Source: Adapted from "Bad Customer Service Interactions More Likely to Be Shared Than Good Ones," April 15, 2013, accessed November 26, 2017, https://www.marketingcharts.com/digital-28628.

such as managers, peers, team members, and customers. Although in the beginning, 360-degree systems were purely developmental and restricted mainly to management and career development, they have migrated to performance appraisal and other HR purposes. For example, Starwood Hotels and Resorts uses a 360-degree performance review system and uses the information to deliver training programs that address areas where employees most need development.[22]

Because the system combines more information than a typical performance appraisal, it can become administratively complex. To handle the amount of information, software has been developed. For example, Cornerstone has developed a system that allows managers and employees to develop performance plans, goals, and objectives and then track their progress over time. Managers can see all of an employee's goals and action steps on a single screen, and self-appraisals and multiple-rater reviews can be combined into a 360-degree format. After rating an employee's performance on each goal, raters can provide summary comments in 3 categories: victories and accomplishments, setbacks and frustrations, and general comments. To ensure security, a user ID and password are required, and all the data are captured and saved in the employee's history file. And with the introduction of social media, organizations are making use of the technology to seek input from a variety of sources.[23]

Figure 7.4 is a graphical depiction of 360-degree input sources.

Although 360-degree feedback can be useful for both developmental and administrative purposes, most companies start with an exclusive focus on development. Employees may be understandably nervous about the possibility of everyone "ganging up" on them in their evaluations. If an organization starts with only developmental feedback—not tied to compensation, promotions, and the like—employees will become accustomed to the process and will likely value the input they get from various parties.

Grand Challenges Canada, an organization that focuses on global health projects, makes use of social media to assist in its 360-degree performance review system. The advantage of this, according to one of its program managers, is that input can be collected throughout the year, not just at performance review time. The company also found that it could "tag" people and projects that allowed it to compare the person's self-assessment to the manager's assessment.[24]

Based on the experiences of companies such as Celestica, Allstate Insurance, and Canadian Tire, it appears that 360-degree feedback can provide a valuable approach to performance review. Its success, as with any performance review method, depends on how managers use the information and how fairly employees are treated. Furthermore, it is important to remember that there may be inconsistencies in the feedback depending on the rater. For example, the rater may not have worked with the employee long and so may rate differently than raters who have known the person longer. Research has also indicated that if the rating isn't kept confidential from the employee, the rating might be inflated. In addition, raters may have more or less confidence in the accuracy of their rating if the rating is lower. Finally, research has indicated that the most "accurate" of raters is the boss, whereas any direct reports tend not to see much difference between high and low

FIGURE 7.4 360-Degree Review Information

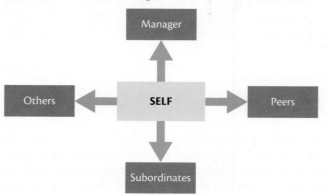

TOOLKIT 7.2   SAMPLE 360-DEGREE STATEMENTS WITH DESCRIPTORS

Based on interactions that you have had with the individual, select the level that best describes the individual's performance in each competency area.

Level 4. Consistently demonstrates the behaviour.

Level 3. Usually demonstrates the behaviour.

Level 2. Sometimes demonstrates the behaviour.

Level 1. Rarely demonstrates the behaviour.

Competency 1—Teamwork. Works effectively with others within own department and across departments for benefit of company. Specifically, displays an openness to ideas, works collaboratively with team members, participates in development of the team, celebrates team successes, and treats team members with respect.

Competency 2—Customer service. Shows a commitment to understanding customer needs and strives to exceed their expectations. Specifically, displays knowledge of customer needs, provides exceptional service to customers, exhibits knowledge of products, and shows steady gains in response time without sacrificing positive interaction.

performers.[25] Also, if performance feedback is to be obtained from various sources, then these people should have access to the performance expectations that were set and also receive training regarding performance management, how to provide effective feedback, and how the feedback will be used. In other words, anyone who provides performance feedback should have a complete understanding of the entire performance management system. As noted earlier in the chapter, managers also need to be trained about how to provide feedback as this will allow them to properly share information, received from other sources, with employees.

Toolkit 7.2 provides sample competency descriptors and how they might be assessed on a 360-degree performance review.

PERFORMANCE REVIEW METHODS

Since the early years of their use by the federal government, methods of reviewing staff have evolved considerably. Old systems have been replaced by new methods that reflect technical improvements and legal requirements and are more consistent with the purposes of a performance management system. In the discussion that follows, you will be introduced to methods to review performance that can be classified as measuring traits, behaviours, results, or a combination of methods.

LO7
Describe various methods to review performance.

Trait Methods

Reviewing performance based upon traits assesses the extent to which an employee displays certain characteristics, such as enthusiasm, dependability, and creativity. The traits should be required for the employee to do the job, and although simple to develop, trait methods can be very subjective or biased.

Frequently in the trait method, the manager is asked to numerically rate the person on the specific characteristics. For example, on the characteristic of "dependable," the manager might be asked to rate the person on a scale of 1 to 5, with 1 being unsatisfactory and 5 being exceptional. This is called a **graphic rating scale**, a sample of which is shown in Toolkit 7.3. The manager may also be asked to provide a few written comments regarding each trait that is being evaluated.

Graphic rating scale
A trait approach to performance review where an employee is rated, typically on a numerical scale, regarding key elements within the job

A customer service representative may be reviewed on being helpful when using the trait method of performance review.

TOOLKIT 7.3 SAMPLE GRAPHIC RATING SCALE

Trait	Exceptional (5)	Above Average (5)	Average (3)	Below Average (2)	Requires Improvement (1)
Dependability					
Problem Solving					
Written Communication					
Verbal Communication					
Initiative					
Ability to Work with Others					

Behavioural Methods

Behavioural methods describe which specific actions should (or should not) be displayed by an employee. Since behavioural methods are common, this section describes 2 approaches that use them: the behavioural checklist method and behaviourally anchored rating scale (BARS).

Behavioural Checklist

This method consists of having the manager review statements on a list and place a check mark beside those behaviours that the employee displays. A checklist developed for a server at a restaurant might include a number of statements like these:

_____ Is able to explain menu choices clearly

_____ Keeps up to date with changes to the menu

_____ Arrives at work on time

_____ Responds quickly and accurately to customer questions

_____ Places orders correctly

Behaviourally Anchored Rating Scale (BARS)

The **behaviourally anchored rating scale (BARS)** method consists of a series of scales, 1 for each performance dimension or component within a job. These components are then given a numerical scale based on critical incidents of on-the-job performance. Toolkit 7.4 displays an example of using BARS to evaluate performance, regarding communication, for an employee in a service-based industry.

> **Behaviourally anchored rating scale (BARS)**
> A performance review method that consists of a series of scales for each performance dimension or component within a job

Results Methods

Many organizations review an employee's performance based upon accomplishments or the results achieved through work. Examples of results include sales figures and items produced. Using results to assess performance is based upon objective measurements; therefore, this method may be less open to bias. Furthermore, this approach often gives employees responsibility for their outcomes while giving them discretion (within limits) over the methods they use to accomplish them.

TOOLKIT 7.4   EXAMPLE OF BARS FOR SERVICE-BASED INDUSTRY

High	6	Consistently demonstrates exceptional verbal and written communication skills. Demonstrates exceptional sensitivity and empathy. Improves lines of communication throughout hotel.
	5	Frequently demonstrates exceptional verbal and written communication skills. Correctly assesses and responds to sensitive situations.
Average	4	Facilitates the clear, concise communication of information in appropriate forms in a timely fashion. Adapts communication style to meet the needs of others.
	3	Inconsistent ability to communicate effectively or in a timely manner. Does not always adapt communication style to meet the needs of others.
Low	2	Frequently receives and imparts information inaccurately.
	1	Consistently unable to receive, record, and share information in an accurate and timely manner.

Sales figures are 1 way to use results to evaluate performance.

Results methods may inadvertently encourage employees to look good on a short-term basis while ignoring the long-term results. For example, workers may let their equipment deteriorate in order to reduce maintenance costs. Furthermore, in any job requiring working with others, how an employee interacts with others should also be considered. In other words, although results matter, *how* the results are achieved should also be considered.

Management by Objectives

Management by objectives (MBO)

Employees and managers agree on an individual's goals, which support the organization's objectives, and employee performance is assessed upon results achieved in relation to these goals

A method that was very popular for a number of years attempted to overcome some of the limitations of results-oriented reviews. **Management by objectives (MBO)**, pioneered by management guru Peter Drucker, focused on employees establishing objectives (e.g., production costs, sales per product, quality standards, profits) through discussion and communication with their superiors and related to the business objectives of the company.[26]

Over time, as organizations became more mature and management styles actively involved employees in making decisions, the concept of MBO evolved into that of the Balanced Scorecard (see below). However, depending on the maturity and management style of the organization, the principles of MBO can be helpful in involving employees in setting objectives. MBO also helps ensure that an employee's goals are linked to departmental and/or organizational goals. As well, the goals should be SMART: Specific, Measurable, Attainable, Relevant, and Time-Bound.[27] These types of goals give employees clear targets to aim for and provide explicit guidelines against which performance results will be evaluated.

The Balanced Scorecard

Balanced Scorecard (BSC)

A measurement framework that helps managers translate strategic goals into operational objectives

One of the most enthusiastically adopted performance management innovations over the past decade has been the **Balanced Scorecard (BSC)**, developed by Harvard professors Robert Kaplan and David Norton. The BSC is a measurement framework that helps managers translate strategic goals into operational objectives. The generic model, shown in Figure 7.5, has 4 related categories: (1) financial, (2) customer, (3) processes, and (4) learning.[28] The logic of the BSC is that learning and people management help organizations improve their internal processes. These internal processes—product development, service, and the like—are critical for creating customer satisfaction and loyalty. Customer value creation, in turn, is what drives financial performance and profitability.

FIGURE 7.5 The Balanced Scorecard

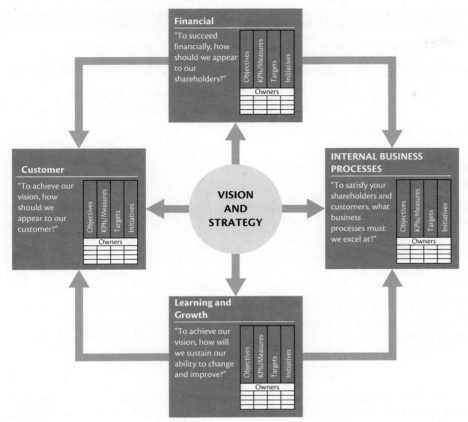

Source: Reprinted by permission of *Harvard Business Review*. Balanced Scorecard. From "Using the Balanced Scorecard as Strategic Management System" by R.S. Kaplan and D.P. Norton, Jan–Feb 1996. Copyright © 1996 by the Harvard Business Publishing; all rights reserved.

The BSC—which, as mentioned above, evolved from the MBO—enables managers to translate broad corporate goals into divisional, departmental, and team goals in a cascading fashion. The value of this is that individuals can see more clearly how their performance ties into the overall performance of the firm.

The effectiveness of a BSC framework is also highly dependent on the culture of the organization. Organizations that have a high degree of integration among work units, good communication, linkage with employee's performance, and continual review and revision of BSC metrics improve the effectiveness of the BSC.[29]

Which Performance Review Method to Use?

The approach used should be based largely on the purpose of the system. Figure 7.6 provides a helpful summary of the advantages and disadvantages of the specific performance review methods discussed in this section. Note that the simplest and least expensive techniques often yield the least accurate information and focus only on the actual review. Although there has been a lot of discussion about which approach to use, whatever method is chosen needs to fit the organization's culture and values.[30] For example, designing and producing a form for managers to use in reviewing an employee's performance are relatively simple and inexpensive. On the other hand, implementing a 360-degree performance management system may require a change in management thinking and philosophy. This could take a long time, with many meetings and the involvement of expensive consultants.

FIGURE 7.6 Summary of Various Review Methods

	Advantages	Disadvantages
Trait Methods	1. Simple and inexpensive to develop.	1. Strong possibility of rater error.
	2. Easy to use and understand.	2. Difficult to use for compensation decisions.
		3. Difficult to use for transfer and promotion decisions.
Behavioural Methods	1. Specific, observable performance dimensions.	1. Can be time-consuming to develop and implement.
	2. Useful for providing detailed, job-specific feedback.	2. Possibility of rater error.
	3. Useful for decisions relating to compensation, transfers, and promotions.	
Results Method	1. Objective measurements.	1. Can be time-consuming to develop and implement.
	2. Usually accepted and understood by employees and managers.	2. May encourage short-term thinking and behaviour.
	3. Useful for decisions relating to compensation, transfers, or promotions.	3. Measurement of results may not include all relevant criteria or may use incorrect information.

Although you are being presented with all the positive reasons to have a formal performance review, as noted earlier in this chapter, some organizations believe such processes are ineffective and are therefore eliminating what has become a once-a-year activity. Read At Work with HRM 7.2 to learn more.

AT WORK WITH HRM 7.2   OUT WITH PERFORMANCE REVIEWS!

As was mentioned earlier, there has been much criticism about performance reviews. Because of this, some organizations, such as Microsoft, PricewaterhouseCoopers, and Juniper Networks, have started doing something different.

In a recent study, over 58% of organizations said that performance management processes were not effective use of time. Furthermore, in the same study, leading organizations indicated that they were eliminating the annual cycle and ensuring that managers provide ongoing feedback and coaching for continuous development of employees.

Some of the criticism has been both that meaningful feedback only occurs once a year and that managers were having to force-rank their staff. Critics believe that making sure there is a bell curve on performance rankings undervalued top performers and pushed average performers to the bottom, creating some amount of

demotivation. Furthermore, neuroscience research suggests that numerical ranking generates an automatic "fight-or-flight" response, and any constructive discussions or actions do not register with the employee.

Another reason for the changed view of performance appraisal is that today's workforce, especially certain generations within it, expects regular feedback, coaching, and development. Deloitte has addressed the issue of ongoing feedback by eliminating annual performance reviews and instead uses an online rating system with managers providing feedback to employees at the conclusion of a project. By asking 4 specific questions, the focus is on asking leaders what they'd do with their team members, not what they think of them, and employees receive feedback continuously instead of once a year at preset times.

Moving toward a model of continuous coaching and development also means a different role for managers and leaders as well as ensuring that they have the skills to execute this new role. It also means that senior leaders need to have a different mindset regarding employee development. They need to be clear how the model fits into the strategy and the importance of the manager's role in employees' achievement.

CRITICAL THINKING QUESTIONS:

1. Should organizations eliminate the annual performance review? Why or why not?
2. How would you feel about continuous feedback and development? Explain your answer.

Sources: Adapted from Peter Cappelli, "Why We Love to Hate HR … and What HR Can Do About It," *Harvard Business Review*, July/August 2015, 59; Marcus Buckingham and Ashley Goodall, "Reinventing Performance Management," *Harvard Business Review*, April 2015, accessed November 23, 2017, https://hbr.org/2015/04/reinventing-performance-management; Alex Nabaum, Lisa Barry, Stacia Garr, and Andy Liakopoulos, "Performance Management Is Broken," *Deloitte University Press*, March 4, 2014, accessed November 23, 2017, http://dupress.com/articles/hc-trends-2014-performance-management; Julie Bort, "Why Some Microsoft Employees Still Fear the Controversial 'Stack Ranking' Employee Review System," *Business Insider*, August 27, 2014, accessed November 23, 2017, www.businessinsider.com/microsofts-old-employee-review-system-2014-8; Lucie Mitchell, "Are Annual Appraisals Losing Impact?," *HR Magazine*, November 25, 2014, accessed November 23, 2017, www.hrmagazine.co.uk/hr/features/1148344/annual-appraisals-losing-impact; and David Rock, Josh Davis, and Beth Jones, "Kill Your Performance Ratings," *Strategy + Business* 76 (August 2014), accessed July 3, 2015, www.strategy-business.com/article/00275?gko=c442b.

For additional information on current trends in performance management, read Emerging Trends 7.1.

EMERGING TRENDS 7.1

1. ***Annual performance reviews will continue to fall out of favour.*** As noted throughout this chapter, many organizations are moving away from a formalized, annual performance review and instead encouraging ongoing communication (i.e., coaching conversations) between managers and employees.

2. ***Changes in mindsets regarding managing performance.*** As organizations evolve in their structure and culture, people are reexamining how performance is measured. A revised way of thinking is looking at performance management as part of a talent management strategy. As organizations have a multitude of employees and other types of workers (e.g., contractors, business process providers, consultants), more attention is being given to how these individuals have their performance reviewed. This includes ensuring that there are key performance indicators (appropriate ways to measure or rate performance) and appropriate oversight.

3. ***Reexamining components of feedback.*** Companies have for some time looked at all components of 360-degree feedback as the same. However, organizations are questioning whether everyone involved in the feedback is necessary or whether certain key people,

such as team leaders, are more critical. Furthermore, organizations are asking different questions to better assess performance-related behaviours.

4. ***Better aligning performance management system with organizational objectives.*** Many companies are reviewing their systems to ensure that the overall organizational objectives are being helped versus hindered by the existing system. The review is looking not just at what is achieved but also "how" to make sure that the company's values are reflected.

5. ***Confirming the strategic importance of managing performance.*** Companies are reaffirming the strategic performance of managing performance as part of their talent strategy, coupled with a better alignment of any performance management system with their organization's objectives. Companies are recognizing the need for capable employees in order to achieve growth and evolution. One way of identifying and enhancing employees' capabilities is through a well-designed and executed performance management system. Use of technology (i.e., online performance management platforms) will continue to evolve as organizations seek efficient and effective ways to provide, and document, performance feedback.

6. ***Using analytical tools.*** Just as metrics are used to measure organizational performance, more and more organizations are understanding the importance of using data analysis to measure the link of individual employee performance to organizational performance.

Sources: Adapted from Stuart Hearn, "5 Performance Management Trends for 2017," *Clear Review*, December 30, 2016, accessed November 23, 2017, https://clearreview.com/latest-performance-management-trends-2017; Jennifer Gerves-Keen, "Reimagining Performance Management," *PeopleTalk*, Spring 2015, 16–17; Dorien Van De Mieroop and Eveline Vrolix, "A Discourse Analytical Perspective on the Professionalization of the Performance Appraisal Interview," *Journal of Business Communication* 51, no. 2 (April 2014): 159–182; Ruth Steinholtz, "Is Your Performance Management System Supporting or Undermining an Ethical Culture?," *HR Bullets*, November 26, 2014, accessed November 23, 2017, www.hrbullets.co.uk/blog/is-your-performance-management-system-supporting-or-undermining-an-ethical-culture.html; "Fresh Thinking Needed to Fix Performance Management," *Canadian HR Reporter*, April 15, 2014, accessed November 23, 2017, www.hrreporter.com/blog/Compensation-Rewards/archive/2014/04/15/fresh-thinking-needed-to-fix-performance-management; Brian Kreissl, "Ongoing Performance Management," *Canadian HR Reporter*, September 22, 2014, accessed November 23, 2017, www.hrreporter.com/articleview/22323-ongoing-performance-management; Todd Hunter, "Fixing the Broken Performance Review," *Canadian HR Reporter*, March 23, 2015, 6; Nicola Middlemiss, "Legal Advice—Implementing Performance Objectives," *HR Online*, January 5, 2015; Marcus Buckingham and Ashley Goodall, "Reinventing Performance Management," *Harvard Business Review*, April 2015, 40–50; and "Building Capabilities for Performance," *McKinsey Insights*, January 2015, accessed November 23, 2017, www.mckinsey.com//insights/organization/building_capabilities_for_performance.

LEARNING OUTCOMES SUMMARY

1. Define a performance management system.
   - *Set of integrated management practices designed to help employees maximize performance, thereby allowing the organization to reach its goals*
2. Explain the purposes of managing performance.
   - *Allows employees to maximize their performance and allows the organization to get the right things done*
   - *Helps increase employees' satisfaction with their work and the organization*
3. Describe the steps in an effective performance management system.
   - *Clarifying the work to be done*
   - *Setting goals and establishing a performance plan*
   - *Providing frequent coaching*
   - *Conducting a formal review of performance*
   - *Recognizing and rewarding performance*
   - *Creating an action plan*
4. Identify possible reasons for ineffective performance.
   - *Organizational policies and procedures*
   - *Job concerns*
   - *Personal problems*
5. Explain possible reasons why performance management systems can fail.
   - *Performance management is not well defined and may not encourage outcomes*
   - *Objectives are not prioritized*
   - *The process is complex and not connected to the company strategy*
   - *The system is not aligned with business performance*
   - *Employees are not involved in developing the system and setting performance goals and therefore think the system is unfair or a waste of time*
   - *The system isn't designed to adapt as needs change*
   - *The system focuses on blame rather than helping employees*
   - *Not enough time is spent on planning and communicating*
   - *Not enough time is spent on coaching employees*
   - *Performance management has competing and different purposes*

- *The focus is on annual review and not on the entire integrated system*
- *The performance process does not help employees develop skills and abilities*
- *Managers feel little or no benefit will be derived from the time and energy spent on the process*
- *Managers dislike the face-to-face discussion and performance feedback*
- *Managers are not sufficiently adept in setting goals and performance measures, in coaching and supporting, or in providing performance feedback*
- *Managers are not properly trained, and rating errors can occur*
- *The judgmental role of a review can conflict with the helping role of developing employees*
- *Managers feel there is a lack of support from top management*

6. Describe the various sources of information regarding an employee's performance.
   - *Manager review*
   - *Self-review*
   - *Subordinate review*
   - *Peer review*
   - *Customer review*
   - *360-degree review*

7. Describe various methods to review performance.
   - *Trait approaches are designed to measure the extent to which an employee possesses certain characteristics*
     - i. Graphic rating scale
   - *Behavioural methods specifically describe which actions should (or should not) be exhibited on the job*
     - i. Behavioural checklist
     - ii. Behaviourally anchored rating scales (BARS)
   - *Results methods review an employee's performance based upon accomplishments or the results achieved through their work*
     - i. Management by objectives
     - ii. Balanced Scorecard

KEY TERMS

Balanced Scorecard (BSC) 232
behaviourally anchored rating scale
  (BARS) 231
customer review 226
graphic rating scale 229
management by objectives 232

manager review 225
peer review 226
performance management system 212
self-review 225
subordinate review 225
360-degree review 226

HRM CLOSE-UP APPLICATION

1. Why does informal, in-the-moment coaching work as an effective method of managing performance at Prairie Girl Bakery?
2. What does Jean Blacklock mean by "praise in public, coach in private"? Are there any drawbacks to this approach?
3. If Prairie Girl Bakery implements a more formal performance appraisal system, which method should be used? Why?
4. Other than an employee's direct manager, who else could be involved in assessing an employee's performance at Prairie Girl Bakery?

CRITICAL THINKING QUESTIONS

1. What should happen when a manager and an employee cannot agree on performance goals?
2. Could a 360-degree review be used to assess the performance of a bartender? Why or why not? If implemented, who should be providing feedback?
3. Will formal performance reviews become obsolete? Why or why not?
4. Why are managers uncomfortable with providing performance feedback? What can be done to address this?

BUILDING YOUR SKILLS

1. You have just been hired as a customer service representative at a major retail chain store. The branch manager has asked that you work with a small task force to develop an appropriate set of performance standards and an appropriate review method. What would you recommend and why?
2. You've just started working at a high-end grocery store in a large city. The store manager wishes to develop a graphic rating scale for cashiering staff. Identify 3 critical areas of the job (e.g., "interactions with customers") that should be evaluated using this performance management method. Is this the best method to evaluate performance of cashiers? Why or why not?
3. Your friend works as a manager in a small credit union and has asked your advice on how to give feedback to a staff member who did not handle a customer request particularly well. What suggestions would you give?
4. Working in groups of 4, review the following descriptions of 3 different employees. Describe the possible causes of poor performance in each case. Then pair off and create a role-playing scenario to practise giving performance feedback. (For assistance, review the role-playing information in Chapter 6.) Whereas one pair conducts the performance feedback session, the other pair is asked to observe and then provide feedback to the role-playing pair.

   A. *Carl Spackler* is the assistant greens keeper at Bushwood Country Club. Over the past few months, members have been complaining that gophers are destroying the course and digging holes in the greens. Although Carl has been working evenings and weekends to address the situation, the problem persists. Unfortunately, his boss is interested only in results. Because the gophers are still there, he contends that Carl is not doing his job. He has accused Carl of slacking off and threatened his job.

   B. *Sandeep Dhillon* works in research and development for a chemical company that makes non-nutritive food additives. His most recent assignment was the development of a non-stick aerosol cooking spray, but the project is way behind schedule and seems to be going nowhere. CEO Frank Shirley is decidedly upset and has threatened that if things don't improve, he will suspend bonuses this year just like he did last year. Sandeep is dejected because without the bonus, he won't be able to take his family on vacation.

   C. *Soon Tan* is the host of a local television talk show called *Morning Winnipeg*. Although she is a talented performer and comedian, Soon has an unacceptable record of tardiness. The show's producer, David Bellows, is frustrated because the problem has affected the quality of the show. On several occasions, Soon was unprepared when the show went on the air. Bellows has concluded that Soon is not a morning person and has thought about replacing her.

CASE STUDY 1

I Can't Believe It

Charlie Lu sat at his desk staring at his resumé. He wondered if he should immediately quit his job and start looking for a new position. "That doesn't make sense," thought Charlie, as he had bills to pay and needed the income. That wasn't the only thing that didn't make sense to Charlie, who had just finished his annual performance review with his manager, John Carlton.

As a salesperson for Onway Stationery, Charlie had met all of his sales quotas for the year. He had shown up for work on time, had been respectful to customers, and had only missed 2 weeks of work when his wife was really sick and he needed to care for her. Charlie had expected to receive positive feedback during the meeting, but instead John rated him as "average" on most categories. Then to make things even worse, John rated Charlie as "needs improvement" on 2 categories: customer service and dependability.

When Charlie asked John to explain the poor ratings, John indicated that he had received several customer complaints about Charlie. Charlie wanted to know who complained and what the issues were, but John stated that this information was confidential and that he couldn't share any details. When asked about the poor rating regarding dependability, John explained that Charlie suddenly took 2 weeks off work during the past year and left his coworkers with extra work.

"Wow, John has no clue. This whole thing is a joke," thought Charlie. Having 2 "needs improvement" ratings meant that Charlie would not be eligible for a pay increase or any type of bonus payment. Feeling both angry and depressed, Charlie began writing a cover letter. "I have to get out of here," thought Charlie as he began pounding on his keyboard.

Questions:

1. Instead of looking for a new job, what other action could Charlie take?
2. What could have been done to prevent Charlie from being surprised during the performance review?
3. What type of performance method should Onway Stationery use for salespeople? Why?
4. Does Charlie have any responsibility for the poor performance review he received? Why or why not?

CASE STUDY 2

Results Count!

What if all organizations focused their performance approaches on results? Would that work in all cases?

It does work at Mabel's Labels, an Ontario company that designs, manufactures, and sells waterproof labels for identifying personal belongings. In its brief 13 years in business, it has expanded into Walmart in both Canada and the United States. Recognizing that people have many priorities in their lives—personal and work—the company has ensured that its business success is measured by results. This means that individual performance is also measured by results. In this way, Mabel's people can work at almost any location. To quote one of them, "Work is what you do, not where you go."

Every week, staff determine where they will work. In making the decision, consideration is given to whether the team's needs are being met and whether the person's own goals and deliverables can be met. One individual indicated that their best design work is done when alone; however, this same person expressed the value of office collaboration in coming up with design ideas.

Does such a focus create a culture of results only? Not according to the employees. People get together outside of work for socializing as well as volunteering for such things as food drives and helping at a local charity for seniors.

The company's approach to performance and employee engagement earned it an award as one of Canada's Top 100 Small & Medium Employers.

Sources: Adapted from "2015 Canada's Top Small & Medium Employers," *The Globe and Mail*, March 2015, accessed November 23, 2017; and Mabel's Labels, accessed November 23, 2017, www.mabelslabels.com.

Questions:

1. Would a results focus work in a financial services institution? Why or why not?
2. If Mabel's Labels decided to use a different approach to performance, what approach would you suggest? Why?

NOTES AND REFERENCES

1. Sarah Dobson, "Healthy Cultures, Reduced Costs," *Canadian HR Reporter*, November 17, 2014, accessed November 21, 2017, https://www.hrreporter.com/articleview/22808-healthy-cultures-reduced-costs.
2. Robert Bacal, "What Is the Point of Performance Appraisal," accessed November 21, 20175, http://work911.com/articles/pointperformance.htm.
3. Brian Kreissl, "Ongoing Performance Management," *Canadian HR Reporter*, September 22, 2014, accessed November 21, 2017, https://www.hrreporter.com/articleview/22323-ongoing-performance-management.
4. Ron Ashkenas, "Stop Pretending That You Can't Give Candid Feedback," *Harvard Business Review*, February 28, 2014.
5. Courtney Bigony, "Driving Employee Engagement Through Effective Performance Management," *Human Resources Today*, accessed November 21, 2017, http://www.humanresourcestoday.com/employee-engagement/performance-management/?open-article-id=7537793&article-title=driving-employee-engagement-through-effective-performance-management&blog-domain=15five.com&blog-title=15five.
6. Ibid.
7. Zanina Kirovska and Nedzmije Qoku, "System of Employee Performance Assessment, Factor for Sustainable Efficiency of Organization," *Journal of Sustainable Development* 5, no. 11 (December 2014): 25–51.
8. Shane Thornton, "The Importance of Reliability in Performance Appraisals," *bizfluent*, September 26, 2017, accessed November 21, 2017, https://bizfluent.com/about-5445066-importance-reliability-performance-appraisals.html; and Robert C. Liden, Sandy J. Wayne, Chenwei Liao, and Jeremy D. Meuser, "Servant Leadership and Serving Culture: Influence on Individual and Unit Performance," *Academy of Management Journal* 57, no. 5 (2014): 1434–1452.
9. John Crowley, "The Odd Relationship Between Compensation and Performance," *People*, April 25, 2017, accessed November 21, 2017, https://www.peoplehr.com/blog/index.php/2017/04/25/the-odd-relationship-between-compensation-and-performance.
10. Brian Kreissl, "Ongoing Performance Management," *Canadian HR Reporter*, September 22, 2014, accessed November 24, 2017, https://www.hrreporter.com/articleview/22323-ongoing-performance-management; and Monique Valcour, "A Great Manager Must Be a Great Coach: Here's 5 Tips to Get You Started," *Financial Review*, July 25, 2014, accessed November 24, 2017, https://www.afr.com/leadership/a-great-manager-must-be-a-great-coach-heres-5-tips-to-get-you-started-20140725-jycf8.
11. Sara Stibitz, "How to Really Listen to Your Employees," *Harvard Business Review*, January 20, 2015, accessed November 24, 2017, https://hbr.org/2015/01/how-to-really-listen-to-your-employees.
12. Amy Adkins and Brandon Rigoni, "Managers: Millennials Want Feedback, but Won't Ask for It," *Business Journal*, June 2, 2016, accessed November 24, 2017, http://news.gallup.com/businessjournal/192038/managers-millennials-feedback-won-ask.aspx.
13. Nicole Fallon, "Employee Performance Reviews: Tips for Bosses," *Business News Daily*, January 1, 2015, accessed November 23, 2017, https://www.businessnewsdaily.com/5366-performance-review-tips-for-bosses.html.
14. Teresa Ewington, "Poor Performance," *Training Journal*, October 2014, 27–30.
15. Dane Jensen, "How Do You Manage Someone You Don't Like?," *Canadian HR Reporter*, February 9, 2015, accessed November 22, 2017, https://www.hrreporter.com/articleview/23468-how-do-you-manage-someone-you-dont-like.

16. Ibid.

17. Susan M. Heathfield, "Performance Appraisals Don't Work," *About.Com*, accessed November 24, 2017, http://humanresources.about.com/od/performanceevals/a/perf_appraisal.htm.

18. Kate Fehlhaber, "Studies Find High Achievers Underestimate Their Talents, While Underachievers Overestimate Theirs," June 9, 2017, accessed November 24, 2017, https://qz.com/992127/studies-find-high-achievers-underestimate-their-talents-while-underachievers-overestimate-theirs.

19. Neil Kokemuller, "The Advantage of Subordinate Evaluations," accessed November 24, 2017, https://yourbusiness.azcentral.com/advantage-subordinate-evaluations-11609.html.

20. Alex Csiszar, "Peer Review: Troubled from the Start," April 19, 2016, accessed November 24, 2017, https://www.nature.com/news/peer-review-troubled-from-the-start-1.19763.

21. Edie L. Goldberg, "Performance Management Gets Social," *HR Magazine*, August 2014, 35–38.

22. Karen N. Caruso, "Case Study: Starwood Hotels Takes 360 Degree Feedback to a New Level," August 29, 2011, accessed November 23, 2017, http://web.viapeople.com/viaPeople-blog/bid/65018/Case-Study-Starwood-Hotels-Takes-360-Degree-Feedback-to-a-New-Level.

23. Liz Bernier, "5 Areas Where Social Media Shines," *Canadian HR Reporter*, January 27, 2014, accessed November 24, 2017, https://www.hrreporter.com/articleview/20016-5-areas-where-social-media-shines.

24. "Who We Are," Grand Challenges Canada website, accessed November 24, 2017, http://www.grandchallenges.ca/who-we-are; and Susan Heathfield, "What Is a 360 Review in the Workplace?," *The Balance Careers*, October 27, 2016, accessed November 24, 2017, https://www.thebalance.com/what-is-a-360-review-1917541.

25. Nikhat Afshan, Diganata Chakrabarti, and J.S. Balaji, "Exploring the Relevance of Employee Productivity-Linked Firm Performance Measures," *Journal of Transnational Management* 19, no. 1 (2014): 24–37.

26. Anastasia, "Introduction to Management by Objectives," *Cleverism*, January 5, 2017, accessed November 24, 2017, https://www.cleverism.com/introduction-management-objectives.

27. "SMART Goals," accessed November 24, 2017, http://www.yourcoach.be/en/coaching-tools/smart-goal-setting.php.

28. Yuanhong Chen, Zengbiao Yu, and Thomas W. Lin, "How Zysco Uses the Balanced Scorecard," *Strategic Finance* 97, no. 1 (January 2015): 27–36.

29. "Balanced Scorecard Basics," Balanced Scorecard Institute, Strategy Management Group website, accessed November 24, 2017, http://www.balancedscorecard.org/BSC-Basics/About-the-Balanced-Scorecard.

30. "Building Capabilities for Performance," *McKinsey Insights*, January 2015, accessed November 27, 2017, https://www.mckinsey.com//insights/organization/building_capabilities_for_performance.

8 Rewarding and Recognizing Employees

LEARNING OUTCOMES

After studying this chapter, you should be able to

1 Explain an organization's strategic considerations in developing a strategic rewards program.

2 Identify the various factors that influence the setting of pay levels.

3 Describe the major job evaluation systems.

4 Illustrate the compensation structure.

5 List the types of incentive plans.

6 Explain the employee benefits that are required by law.

7 Describe voluntary benefits.

OUTLINE

Introduction
Rewards as Part of Company Strategy
Linking Rewards to Organizational Objectives
The Motivating Value of Compensation
Equity Theory
Pay for Performance
Bases for Compensation
Determining Compensation
Internal Factors
External Factors
Job Evaluation Systems
Job Ranking System
Job Classification System
Point System
Factor Comparison System
Determining Wage Rates
Salary Surveys
Collecting Survey Data
The Wage Curve
Pay Grades
Pay Ranges
Broadbanding

Other Ways to Determine Wages
Incentive Plans
Employee Benefits
Linking Benefits to the Overall Rewards
    Program
Cost Concerns
Benefits Required by Law
Canada and Québec Pension Plans (CPP/QPP)
Employment Insurance (EI)
Provincial Hospital and Medical Services
Leaves without Pay
Other Required Benefits
Voluntary Employee Benefits
Health and Welfare Benefits
Retirement and Pension Plans
Pay for Time Not Worked
Wellness Programs
Employee Assistance Programs
Educational Assistance Plans
Childcare and Eldercare
Employee Recognition Programs
Other Services

"...APTN really makes a work environment that's pleasant, that's comfortable."

SINCE ITS creation in 1999, APTN has been named among Manitoba's Top Employers each year since 2009, has been noted as one of Canada's Top 100 Employers since 2013, and has most recently featured in Canada's Top Employers for Young People. That headline-grabbing success hasn't happened by accident, however.

"For a lot of people, APTN is like a second family because it's where you spend most of your time during the day," explains Monika Ille, APTN's executive director of programming and scheduling. "You see less of your husband or wife and your kids than you do your work colleagues, so APTN really makes a work environment that's pleasant, that's comfortable."

Although some companies may reward their employees with financial bonuses, APTN takes a more holistic position, which includes creating a healthy work environment, encouraging personal advancement, and ensuring that all staff feel a part of the organization and can take pride in its accomplishments.

Upon receiving its national broadcast licence in 1999, APTN became the world's first national Indigenous broadcaster. With its head office in Winnipeg and satellite offices across the country, APTN today has more than 11 million Canadian TV subscribers and directly employs more than 120 full-time staff.

Ille began with APTN in 2003.

"I've been here 15 years," she says. "I've never stayed at a place as long as here, but I'm staying because, professionally, I'm very satisfied, it's fulfilling, and I'm giving back to my community.

I feel like I'm bringing my community to a better way of life as well."

Part of APTN's approach is to not merely encourage their staff to make a difference in the community but to make it easy for them to do so. "If you want to be a volunteer for an Indigenous organization or for an event that has to do with Indigenous peoples, APTN will automatically say, 'Yeah, do it!'" Ille says. "You don't have to take a vacation day; you get paid to do it. That's important too. You want people to be involved and give back to their community, so we highly support that."

Although First Nations status is not a requirement to work at APTN, 65% of the company's staff are Indigenous. "As an Indigenous person, you can work somewhere else and you feel a bit out of it," Ille admits. "Sometimes you can't really relate, but even the non-Indigenous people that work here do relate to the Indigenous culture and way of doing things, and I just feel people are happy. A lot of people stay for a long time."

APTN is big on recognizing people's potential, and staff are encouraged to grow by participating in mentoring opportunities and ongoing training. That investment in personnel can be a financial gamble, but it's one that has worked for APTN and is reflected in their high employee retention rate.

"We do train a lot of people, and sometimes they leave, but that's fine," Ille says. "We don't take it personally. Hey, if you've got an opportunity elsewhere, go for it. If we were able to give you the skills needed to do it, fine. We'll go and train somebody else, and for us it's very important. We will cut other budget-line items before we cut our training plan."

A couple of years ago, APTN introduced peer-to-peer recognition within the company. "You notice that someone you work with went beyond their job description, so you send a little note that goes in their file that just says, 'Hey, I really appreciated what you did,'" Ille

Monika Ille, Executive Director of Programming and Scheduling, APTN

Courtesy of Monika Ille

explains. "Then they get a little gift. It's cute; it could be a pencil, it could be a cup, it could be a chocolate. . . . It's just a little recognition, and when people get it, they're just so happy."

APTN productions have won countless awards for journalism and have also been recognized at numerous festivals, including the Hot Docs Canadian International Documentary Festival, the Sundance Film Festival, and the Boulder International Film Festival. Those successes are felt throughout the company, not just in Winnipeg, but at other offices in Vancouver, Ottawa, and Montréal, and they contribute to the employees' sense of belonging.

"People really feel they belong. Even though you work in a satellite office, you know you belong to something bigger," Ille says. "You're a part of the company, you work for the company, you're part of it." "When we win awards, we all feel we won it."

INTRODUCTION

You will note from the HRM Close-up that rewards and recognition, which ultimately help create a healthy and productive work environment, are big issues not just for employees but also for the managers of those employees. Although companies may set guidelines about how much each position or job is worth, it is the manager who has to implement those guidelines. The manager will make decisions about who gets paid what. And it is the manager's everyday interactions with the employees, within the culture of the organization (as discussed in Chapter 3), that influence how the employees feel about the organization. Therefore, it is important for a manager to understand rewards and recognition and their link to the success of the organization. It is also important for a manager to understand how compensation is derived and what factors influence the setting of the wage and benefits structure.

Literature and research indicate that important work-related variables leading to job satisfaction—besides interesting work, alignment of employee goals and organizational goals, participative management, and flexibility in work practices—are rewards and recognition, particularly in the form of wages and benefits, a supportive work environment, and demonstrated appreciation for employees.[1] Although other things might contribute, not many employees would continue working were it not for the money they earn. Compensation, therefore, is a major consideration in HRM. As mentioned earlier, the effectiveness of the manager has a large impact on an employee's job satisfaction, and it is usually the manager who is first to deal with any concerns or issues regarding compensation. Although an HR professional might be responsible for gathering compensation information and developing approaches to how the organization approaches compensation, the manager typically makes decisions on how much a person is compensated. Furthermore, due to ongoing changes within the economy, Canadian organizations will have to be strategic in their changes to base salary. Differences across industries are anticipated, with mining, oil, and gas extraction and public service employees receiving low to below-average increases.[2]

Both managers and scholars agree that the way rewards are allocated among employees sends a message about what management believes is important and the types of activities it encourages. Furthermore, for an employer, total rewards (direct and indirect) constitute a sizable operating cost. In manufacturing firms, compensation can account for 20% of total expenditures, and for in-service enterprises, it often exceeds 80%. A strategic rewards program, therefore, is essential so that compensation can serve to motivate employee production sufficiently to keep labour costs at an acceptable level.

Although the focus of this chapter is on pay and benefits, it is important to state that many organizations think about and create "reward strategies." The thrust of this approach is to develop an organizational mindset to recognize and reward people with links to the business strategy.[3] In doing so, organizations will tend to have components of the rewards program, particularly direct compensation, that are tied to the success of the organization and to the contributions of that success through individual (or team) performance.

REWARDS AS PART OF COMPANY STRATEGY

It is important to know that employee recognition and rewards include all forms of pay, rewards, and recognition received by employees for the performance of their jobs. **Direct compensation** includes wages and salaries, bonus payments, and commissions. **Indirect compensation** includes the benefits supplied by employers, such as extended health and dental plans, life insurance coverage, and *non-financial compensation*, which includes things such as employee recognition programs and services (i.e., free parking) offered to employees. Direct and indirect compensation are collectively referred to as "total compensation" or **total rewards**. The latter term helps communicate to employees that their compensation doesn't just have a monetary value but that it includes other forms of recognition and reward.

Direct compensation
Employee wages and salaries, bonuses, and commissions

Indirect compensation
All other forms of rewards, such as extended health and dental plans and other programs and plans that offer rewards or services to employees

Total rewards
Everything that the employee receives in terms of both direct and indirect compensation

LO1
Explain an organization's strategic considerations in developing a strategic rewards program.

Companies structure their rewards in ways that enhance employee motivation and growth while aligning employees' efforts with the objectives, philosophies, and culture of the organization. Designing the rewards and recognition system goes beyond determining what direct and indirect compensation to provide to employees. Research has shown that companies that make the rewards strategy a part of the overall organizational framework perform better than those that don't.[4] This finding is a compelling argument for the organization to take into consideration what employees see as important in the reward equation.

Looking at the reward system in a strategic fashion serves to align the overall rewards for employees with specific business objectives. Such a strategic approach can help the organization remain competitive.[5] For example, in the recruitment of new employees, the overall rewards for jobs can increase or limit the supply of applicants. Employers have adopted special reward strategies to attract job applicants with highly marketable skills, such as high-tech workers and engineers and scientists with financial knowledge and good people skills. Organizations also use rewards to attract and retain people with scarce skills. According to the 2018 report from Korn Ferry regarding reward trends, there was still concern about attracting and retaining a diverse workforce through equitable reward programs.[6] Therefore, organizations need to continue to evaluate diversity and equity goals and how reward programs can reinforce and enhance these.

If rewards are high, creating a large applicant pool, then organizations may choose to raise their selection standards and hire better-qualified employees. This, in turn, can reduce training costs for the employer. When employees perform at exceptional levels, their performance assessments may justify an increased pay rate. For these reasons and others, an organization should ensure that it has a systematic way to manage employee rewards that is linked to business performance. Recent research has demonstrated a strong link between a longer-term perspective on reward systems (for that particular organization) and achieving strong business results.[7]

It is important to remember that the concept of "total rewards" is a broader set of elements and includes not only the tangible rewards of pay, benefits, etc., but also factors such as career and development opportunities, work climate or culture, and work–life balance.[8] It is also important that the total rewards system be transparent to all employees.[9] For example, McDonald's redesigned its program so that there was a closer link to rewards and performance and that all employees were aware of the change and why.[10] At Work with HRM 8.1 discusses the importance of communicating the total rewards program and its various components.

AT WORK WITH HRM 8.1 — DOES THE REWARD SYSTEM MAKE SENSE?

Many organizations structure their rewards systems to ensure that employees are satisfied and motivated. But is that good enough? What about something as simple as the actual pay amount?

These are not easy questions, nor are the answers simple. Many factors go into structuring a company's reward system. A study by the Hay Group indicated that it is important for the organization to benchmark its reward system to ensure that a variety of factors are considered. Among them are the following:

- How aligned is the reward system with the business strategy?

- Are the total rewards above or below your competition?
- What is the number of employees compared to your competition?
- How motivated are your employees by the reward system?
- How aligned is your performance management system with the rewards system?

Although a total rewards system can go a long way in satisfying employees, if the base salary isn't at a certain level, no amount of additional items in a reward system can make up for it. It is also important that the organization be open and transparent about the rewards structure.

continued

This includes ensuring that employees know what the salary ranges are for any particular position. In this way, employees can be aware of opportunities for career advancement. Furthermore, by being more open about the rewards structure, employees may feel more trusting of the employer.

CRITICAL THINKING QUESTIONS:

1. If you are working, do you know the value of your total rewards? Would you think differently about the organization if you did?

2. Do you think that being provided with information about your total rewards would encourage you to remain with an employer? Why or why not?

Sources: Adapted from Robert Glazer, "3 Steps to Better Motivate Employees with Performance-Based Pay," *Entrepreneur*, October 18, 2017, accessed January 2, 2018, https://www.entrepreneur.com/article/302743; David Hoad and Nathalie Olds, "Finding Value in Rewards," *Canadian HR Reporter*, January 26, 2015, 23; Liz Bernier, "Putting a Price Tag on Employee Satisfaction," *Canadian HR Reporter*, November 3, 2014, 6; and Karl Aboud, "How Much Do You Pay Staff?," *Canadian HR Reporter*, May 5, 2014, 11.

LINKING REWARDS TO ORGANIZATIONAL OBJECTIVES

Rewards have been revolutionized by heightened domestic competition, globalization, increased employee skill requirements, and new technology. Therefore, an outcome of today's dynamic business environment is that managers need to change their reward philosophies from paying for a specific position or job title to rewarding employees on the basis of their individual competencies or group contributions to organizational success. For example, 1 study showed that 81% of responding organizations listed *improving employee's focus on achieving business goals* as a significant objective influencing reward changes (see Figure 8.1).[11] A total rewards program, therefore, must be tailored to the needs of the organization and its employees. And in doing so, it is important to ensure that employees feel they are being appropriately rewarded.

This same research suggests that there are 5 components of a total rewards program: compensation, benefits, work–life balance, recognition of performance, and learning and development and opportunities.

FIGURE 8.1 **Significant Goals Driving Pay and Reward Changes**

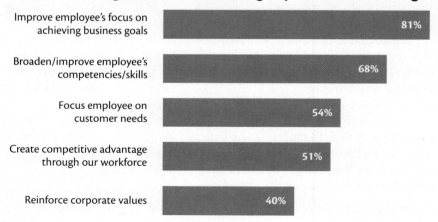

Fundamental to the framework of total rewards is the compensation component. It is not uncommon for organizations to establish specific goals for aligning their objectives with their compensation program.[12] Formal compensation goals serve as guidelines for managers to ensure that wage and benefit policies and practices produce the desired results. Some typical goals are as follows:

1. Rewarding employees' past performance.
2. Remaining competitive in the labour market.
3. Maintaining salary equity among employees.
4. Controlling the compensation budget.
5. Attracting, motivating, and retaining staff.[13]
6. Influencing employee work behaviours and job attitudes.[14]

THE MOTIVATING VALUE OF COMPENSATION

Pay is a quantitative or numerical way to measure an employee's value to the organization. Pay represents a reward received in exchange for an employee's contributions and therefore must be equitable, in terms of recognizing both the employee's work and the employee's work in relation to the contributions of others.

Equity Theory

Equity can be defined as anything of value earned through the investment of something of value. Equity theory is a motivation theory that explains how employees respond to situations in which they feel they have received less (or more) than they deserve.[15] Central to the theory is the role of perception in motivation and the fact that individuals make comparisons. The theory states that individuals look at their inputs (abilities, skills, experiences) compared to their outcomes (salary, benefits) and develop a ratio based upon these

Employees need to believe that they are being treated equitably by their manager.

measurements. Comparison with other individuals performing similar work, either internal or external to the organization, then occurs. If the value of their ratio equals the value of another person chosen as an appropriate comparison, the circumstances are thought to be equitable. However, if a person perceives that the input/output ratio is inequitable relative to that of others, the situation is corrected by lowering input (i.e., effort and work produced) or seeking greater rewards and recognition to bring the situation back into balance. As such, if a person feels that someone is getting more compensation for similar work, this perception can negatively affect that employee's view of the value of the employee's own work. HR practitioners who specialize in compensation systems are particularly concerned not only that employees are paid fairly for the work they do but also that they are paid equitably relative to other people in the organization.

Employees' perceptions of equity, or inequity, can have dramatic effects on their work behaviour, commitment to the organization, and productivity.[16] Although managers do not design compensation systems, they do have to respond to employee concerns about being paid equitably. Compensation policies are internally equitable when employees believe that the wage rates for their jobs approximate the worth of the jobs to the organization. Perceptions of external equity exist when the organization is paying wages and benefits that are relatively equal to what other employers are paying for similar types of work. At Work with HRM 8.2 provides an interesting perspective on pay for performance and equity in today's economic climate.

AT WORK WITH HRM 8.2 — AM I MOTIVATED?

Much has been written over the past several years about the use of incentives—particularly as a way to link employee performance to the overall success of the organization. Do incentives work, and will they motivate people?

The answer in recent studies suggests "yes," "no," or "it all depends." Whether it is as a result of the economic turmoil over the past few years or the changing expectations of the workforce, there is no simple solution, and one size does not fit all. The real issue is whether or not people are satisfied with their compensation and whether it motivates them to perform well.

According to a recent study, 75% of employers indicated that they have implemented some form of variable pay. But it isn't always easy to ensure that the metrics used to measure performance can be tied to corporate objectives. However, it is important not to overstate the link as employees may not always be able to see the link between their performance and that of the organization. The use of incentive pay as a way to provide more compensation than modest changes to base salary is increasing in all industries.

However, there is also contrary evidence suggesting that although pay is important, recognizing achievement is more memorable and creates a more engaged employee. Recognition has been shown to motivate employees to work harder.

What appears to be equally important when designing a pay-for-performance component is why the company is doing it. Although such plans don't give rewards unless performance results are achieved, the design has to fit the organization. This includes whether there is a threshold of performance before any additional payments are made and tracking payments over years to ensure that the costs are providing the retention and motivation as expected.

CRITICAL THINKING QUESTIONS:
1. Would you like to have your pay tied directly to your performance? Why or why not?
2. Would pay for performance motivate you? Why or why not?

Sources: Adapted from "Variable Pay: Is There a Difference Between a Bonus and an Incentive?," accessed January 2, 2018, https://www.payscale.com/compensation-today/2017/06/difference-bonus-incentive; Anne Fisher, "How to Get More Than a 3% Raise This Year," *Fortune*, February 20, 2015, accessed January 2, 2018, http://fortune.com/2015/02/12/salaries-raises-promotions; and Jo Faragher, "Show Me the Money," *People Management*, January 2015, 20–25.

PAY FOR PERFORMANCE

Pay for performance is used to increase results and lower labour costs in today's economic environment. In order to effectively implement variable pay, employee performance and the results produced should be linked to rewards. Furthermore, employees need to see and understand the link between their performance and the business's performance.[17]

The term "pay for performance" or "variable pay," as described by many consulting firms, such as Mercer and Willis Towers Watson, refers to a wide range of direct compensation options, including merit-based pay, bonuses, salary commissions, and team or group incentive programs. The overall objective is to distinguish pay given to average performers and employees who produce outstanding or exceptional results. Some companies may decide to focus on a specific corporate objective, such as energy conservation. For example, Co-operative Food (now Co-op Food) created a group incentive to achieve a reduction in its energy costs. It decided to do this to achieve a direct impact on its financial results.[18] Interestingly, productivity studies show that employees will increase their output by 15% to 35% when an organization institutes a pay-for-performance program.

Designing and implementing a pay-for-performance system is not simple. Considerations include how to accurately assess or measure employee performance, what funds will be available for pay increases, which employees will be eligible for variable pay, and how the funds will be paid. A critical issue concerns the size of the monetary increase and its perceived value to employees as a pay-for-performance program will lack its full potential when pay increases only approximate the rises in the cost of living.

A study by Deloitte, an international consulting firm, found that one of the key issues for organizations is not just the need to have variable pay but also that total rewards

Pay for performance
Standard by which managers tie direct compensation to employee or organizational outcomes and performance

Stuart O'Sullivan/Exactostock-1598

Pay for performance can be measured against specific objectives, such as energy conservation.

FIGURE 8.2 **Advantages and Disadvantages of Pay-for-Performance Systems**

Type of System	Advantages	Disadvantages
Individual	• Simple to compute. • Clearly links pay to organizational outcomes. • Motivates employees. • Employees focus on clear performance targets. • Distributes success among those responsible for producing success.	• Standards of performance may be difficult to establish. • May not be an effective motivator. • Difficult to deal with missed performance targets. • Available money may be inadequate. • Employees may be unable to distinguish merit pay from other types of pay increases.
Team	• Supports group planning. • Builds team culture. • Can broaden scope of contribution that employees are motivated to make. • Tends to reduce jealousies and complaints. • Encourages cross-training.	• Individuals may perceive that efforts contribute little to group success. • Intergroup social problems can limit performance. • Can be difficult to compute and therefore difficult to understand.
Organization	• Creates effective employee participation. • Can increase pride in organization. • Can be structured to provide tax advantages. • Has variable costs.	• Difficult to handle if organization's performance is low. • Can be difficult to compute and therefore difficult to understand. • More difficult for individual effort to be linked to organizational success.

must attract and keep top talent.[19] Furthermore, with ongoing economic uncertainty, some academics and practitioners have been advocating that the link between pay and performance be stopped. The basis for this criticism lies in the number of employees—particularly at senior management levels—who undertake business risk-taking actions that may actually harm the company. In addition, these individuals make reference to the incredibly high CEO compensation packages (as will be addressed later in this chapter in Ethics in HRM 8.1); that business challenges emerge daily, and, therefore, tying pay to performance isn't realistic; and that people will manipulate the criteria to achieve better results.[20] Figure 8.2 provides a summary of the advantages and disadvantages of different pay-for-performance systems.

BASES FOR COMPENSATION

Hourly work
Compensation based upon the number of hours worked

Piecework
Compensation based upon the number of units produced

Many employees are compensated on an hourly basis. This is referred to as **hourly work**, in contrast to **piecework**, in which employees are paid according to the number of units they produce.

Employees compensated on an hourly basis are called *hourly employees*, and those compensated based upon weekly, biweekly, or monthly pay periods are called *salaried employees*. Hourly employees are normally paid only for the time they work. Salaried employees, by contrast, are generally paid the same for each pay period, even though they occasionally may work more hours or fewer than the regular number of hours in a period. Salaried employees typically receive certain benefits not provided to hourly employees.

LO2

Identify the various factors that influence the setting of pay levels.

DETERMINING COMPENSATION

Both internal and external factors can influence, directly or indirectly, the rates at which employees are paid, as shown in Figure 8.3.

FIGURE 8.3 Factors Affecting Compensation

INTERNAL FACTORS
- Employer's compensation strategy
- Worth of a job
- Employee's performance
- Employer's ability to pay

Compensation

EXTERNAL FACTORS
- Economy
- Labour-market conditions
- Wage rates in specific geographic areas
- Cost of living
- Collective bargaining (unionized companies)
- Legal requirements

Internal Factors

The internal factors that influence wage rates are the employer's compensation policy, the worth of a job, an employee's performance, and an employer's ability to pay.

Employer's Compensation Strategy

Organizations will usually state objectives regarding compensation for their employees. For example, a public-sector employer may wish to pay fairly and at the market average. (Remember, "market" means the geographic area in which the organization typically finds qualified candidates for work.) On the other hand, a software development company may wish to pay fairly but be the industry leader to attract and retain high-calibre staff.

Employers may set pay policies with consideration to the following: the internal wage relationship among jobs and skill levels; compensation practices of competitors; strategic ways of rewarding performance; and decisions concerning administrative issues, such as overtime.

Worth of a Job

As discussed in Chapter 4, the design of work or of a job leads to the organization being able to achieve its objectives. Organizations without a formal compensation program generally base the worth of jobs on the subjective opinions of people familiar with the work employees perform. In such instances, pay rates may be influenced heavily by external factors, such as the labour market, or, in the case of unionized employees, by collective bargaining. Organizations with formal compensation programs, however, are more likely to use a formal job evaluation system to determine compensation.

Job evaluation is the systematic process of determining the *relative* worth of jobs in order to determine the correct compensation for each role, thereby ensuring equity. The worth of a job is usually measured by the following criteria: level of skill, effort, responsibility, and working conditions of the job. The relative worth of a job is then determined by using the criteria to compare it to other jobs in an organization. Four comparison methods are detailed later in the chapter in the section Job Evaluation Systems.

Job evaluation
Systematic process of determining the relative worth of jobs in an organization

Employee's Performance

An employee's output, or performance, can be used as a way to determine compensation increases. If an employee's relative worth, or results produced, are to be rewarded by compensation, an effective performance appraisal system that differentiates between those employees who deserve the raises and those who do not must be in place. (Chapter 7 detailed the various forms of performance management, and these should be reviewed to fully understand how best to evaluate an employee's performance.) Managers must be careful not to reward employees for just being present and instead should make changes to compensation based upon actual results achieved.

Employees' performance and contributions toward organizational goals can be used when making decisions on pay.

In some situations, managers will also compare the performance of one employee to that of another. Although proponents of performance stress that a person is to be assessed against standards of performance, there is a tendency to compare employees against each other. This is particularly true in the absence of any performance management system.

Employer's Ability to Pay

In the public sector, the amount of compensation (pay and benefits) employees can receive is limited by the funds budgeted for this purpose and by the willingness of taxpayers to provide them. Federal government employees had their pay frozen for 6 years in response

New services, such as home delivery, may be offered by companies that want to remain competitive.

to the drive to balance the budget and because of the public's perception of highly paid government workers. In the private sector, profits and other financial resources available to employers often limit pay levels. Economic conditions and competition faced by employers can also significantly affect the rates they are willing and able to pay. However, the manner in which an employer does this can have an impact on how the employees feel about their employer as well as a company's image in the marketplace.

For example, in 2017, Loblaws announced plans to close 22 unprofitable stores and introduce a home delivery service. Loblaws recognized that due to changing marketplace conditions, it would no longer be able to employ and pay employees as in previous times, and a great deal of public attention and discussion was given to this issue.[21]

External Factors

Key external factors that influence wage rates are the economy, labour-market conditions, wage rates in specific geographic areas, cost of living, collective bargaining (for unionized workplaces), and legal requirements.

Economy

Although Canada's economic woes are not as bad as elsewhere, given that it is an export-driven economy, businesses have to be sensitive to business projections. To deal with a possible labour shortage, particularly in key skill areas, companies are adopting a number of approaches. Surveys by the various consulting firms mentioned earlier have identified the following actions:

- designing variable pay to fit the organization and its industry
- providing meaningful pay increases even in a cost-reduction environment
- providing non-cash benefits
- improving workplace health and well-being
- aligning total rewards with the business strategy[22]

Labour-Market Conditions

The labour market is influenced by the demand and supply of qualified employees and impacts the wage rates required to recruit or retain competent employees. Even during times of oversupply, employers are often unable to lower wages due to collective agreements that are in place (in unionized workplaces) and to minimum wage requirements.

Wage Rates in Specific Geographic Areas

In addition to general economic conditions, employers review wages being paid by other employers for comparable jobs within a similar geographic area. This type of information is typically obtained through area wage surveys. Wage-survey data may also be obtained from consulting firms, such as Willis Towers Watson and the Hay Group. Smaller employers use government or local board of trade surveys to establish rates of pay. Many organizations conduct their own surveys. Others engage in a cooperative exchange of wage information or rely on various professional associations, such as Professional Engineers Ontario.

Cost of Living

Because of inflation, compensation rates tend to be adjusted upward periodically to help employees maintain their purchasing power. The **consumer price index (CPI)** is often used as a benchmarking tool by organizations. The CPI is a broad measure of the cost of living in Canada and measures the change in consumer prices over time.[23] The index is based on prices in a "shopping basket," and the contents of this basket can change over time depending on people's spending choices. Among the close to 600 items typically measured are food, clothing, shelter, and fuels; transportation fares; charges for medical services; and prices of other goods

Consumer price index (CPI)
Measure of the average change in consumer prices over time in a fixed "market basket" of goods and services

and services that people buy for day-to-day living. Statistics Canada collects price information monthly and calculates the CPI for Canada as a whole and for various Canadian city averages.

Using the CPI to determine changes in pay rates can also compress pay rates within a pay structure, creating inequities among those who receive the wage increase. For example, an increase of 50 cents an hour represents a 10% increase for an employee earning $5 per hour but only a 5% increase for someone earning $10 per hour.

Collective Bargaining

As you will see in Chapter 10, one of the primary functions of a labour union is to bargain collectively over conditions of employment, the most important of which is compensation. The union's goal in each new agreement is to achieve increases in **real wages**—wage increases larger than the increase in the CPI—thereby improving the standard of living of its members.

Further discussion of the collective bargaining process, including wage negotiations, is provided in Chapter 10.

Legal Requirements

As discussed in Chapter 2, legislation that either influences or requires certain pay rates is in place. For example, most provinces have a legislated minimum hourly wage, meaning that an employer cannot pay any worker less than the per-hour rate. However, numerous exceptions to this requirement exist. Read HRM and the Law 8.1 for further information about

> **Real wages**
> Wage increases larger than rises in the consumer price index; reflect actual purchasing power and have an impact on the standard of living

HRM AND **THE LAW** 8.1 — LEGAL CONSIDERATONS REGARDING MINIMUM WAGE

Under Canada's Constitution, responsibility for determining and enforcing labour laws—including the minimum wage—is given to each of the 10 provinces and 3 territories. They've been granted this authority through federal legislation. Every year each province and territory reviews its existing rates. The governing political party decides on whether to provide an increase or not. Factors such as inflation, unemployment, and developments in other jurisdictions are considered.

Across Canada, approximately 1.25 million people are earning minimum wage, or about 8% of the country's 15.3 million salaried employees. Furthermore, nearly 60% of minimum wage earners are youths aged 15 to 24, and almost as large a share of them live with family. Women are disproportionately represented in low-wage jobs— fully one-third of women earn less than $15/hour compared to only 22% of men.

Given the above-noted facts and the legal authority of provinces and territories to determine minimum wage rates, legal requirements for ongoing increases, or living wages, are expected. However, these increases are not without problems. For example, in Ontario, 2 Tim Hortons locations issued a notice to employees advising them that due to the requirement to pay higher wages, their benefits would be reduced or removed. The owners of Tim Hortons blamed the government of Ontario for not understanding the financial consequences to employers by forcing businesses to pay higher wages. In response, the premier of Ontario accused the Tim Hortons owners of bullying their employees and of improperly placing blame on the government and noted that people deserved to earn a living wage and that higher incomes would result in more expenditures, which, in turn, would be good for the Canadian economy overall.

CRITICAL THINKING QUESTIONS:

1. Do you think it is appropriate for different provinces and territories to have legal authority to determine a minimum wage rate? Why or why not?
2. What are some of the possible negative and positive consequences of legal requirements to continuously increase the minimum wage?

Sources: Adapted from Mark Swartz, "Minimum Wages across Canada In 2017," *Monster*, accessed January 3, 2018, https://www.monster.ca/career-advice/article/minimum-wages-across-canada-in-2017; "Tim Hortons' Franchisees Cut Back Staff Benefits After Minimum Wage Hike," *HRD Canada*, January 4, 2018, accessed January 6, 2018, https://www.hrmonline.ca/hr-news/tim-hortons-franchisees-cut-back-staff-benefits-after-minimum-wage-hike-235787.aspx; and Emily Douglas, "Ontario Premier Accuses Tim Hortons' Heirs of Bullying Workers," *HRD Canada*, January 5, 2018, accessed January 6, 2018, https://www.hrmonline.ca/hr-news/corporate-wellness/ontario-premier-accuses-tim-hortons-heirs-of-bullying-workers-235854.aspx.

minimum wage requirements across Canada. In addition, pay equity legislation obliges certain companies to pay the same wage rate for jobs of a dissimilar nature and is based on comparing jobs performed mostly by men to jobs performed mostly by women. Under pay equity, a company must use a "gender-neutral" system, comparing jobs based on the amount and type of skill, effort, and responsibility needed to perform the job and on the working conditions in which the job is performed. Some provinces also consider male–female pay rates under human rights legislation.

JOB EVALUATION SYSTEMS

As mentioned earlier in this chapter, job evaluation is a way to determine the relative worth of jobs in an organization. The most typical job evaluation systems are described below.

LO3

Describe the major job evaluation systems.

Job Ranking System

The most basic form of job evaluation is the job ranking system, which arranges jobs on the basis of their relative worth. As such, jobs are compared to one another and a listing, in decreasing order, is typically created based upon the worth of the various jobs in an organization. This ranking can be done by a single individual knowledgeable about all jobs within a company or by a committee composed of management and employee representatives. A key weakness of the job ranking system is that it does not examine jobs in great detail but instead compares the relative overall value of one job compared to another job.

Job Classification System

In the job classification system, jobs sufficiently alike with respect to duties and responsibilities are grouped and will have a common name and common pay. Jobs that require increasing amounts of job responsibility, skill, knowledge, ability, or other factors used to compare jobs would then be grouped with a different common name and a different common pay. For example, the "social science services group" classification of the federal government's Public Service Commission uses 9 different factors, including "very unpleasant working conditions," such as interactions with abusive individuals and possible threat to personal security.[24]

The descriptions of each of the job classes constitute the scale against which the specifications for the various jobs are compared. Managers then assess jobs by comparing job descriptions to the various wage grades in order to assign the job into the appropriate grade. This method of job evaluation is relatively simple but not very precise as it assesses the value of a job overall and does not examine the various tasks or components within each job.

Point System

The point system is a quantitative or numerical job evaluation process that determines a job's relative value by assigning points to various factors. The first step in a points evaluation is determining what factors or elements a group of jobs is expected to possess. These factors or elements are commonly called compensable factors. The skills, efforts, responsibilities, and working conditions that a job usually entails are the more common major compensable factors that serve to evaluate the worth of a job as more or less important than another. Points are assigned based on these characteristics that represent the importance of the job within the organization as a whole. Although point systems are rather complicated to create, once in place, they are relatively simple to understand and use. One advantage of the point system is that it provides a more defined and detailed basis for making judgments than either the ranking or the classification system, thereby producing results that are more valid and harder to manipulate.

Factor Comparison System

The factor comparison system, like the point system, permits the job evaluation process to be accomplished on a factor-by-factor basis. A factor comparison system is typically used for legislated pay equity purposes. It differs from the point system, however, in that the compensable factors of the jobs to be evaluated are compared against the compensable factors of key jobs within the organization that serve as the job evaluation scale.

Key jobs are evaluated against 5 compensable factors—skill, mental effort, physical effort, responsibility, and working conditions—resulting in a ranking of the different factors for each key job.

Regardless of the methodology used, all job evaluation methods require varying amounts of judgment made by individuals. Managers make decisions on the components of any job. Managers will also make decisions on how much responsibility and authority any particular job may have. Therefore, as careful as an organization is in having objective ways of measuring the value of a job, subjective decisions are made regarding the content of the job. As mentioned previously, organizations frequently use a committee or panel for job evaluation assessments to help ensure objectivity.

As well, regardless of the job evaluation method utilized, the following key points must be followed: it is the job that is being evaluated, not the job incumbent; the job is evaluated based upon the performance of tasks in a fully competent manner; the job is evaluated as it currently exists; and the current level of compensation associated with the job should not be considered.

To better understand the reasons behind having some type of job evaluation system, look at the considerations in Toolkit 8.1.

A proper job evaluation system needs to reflect the complexity within different roles.

TOOLKIT 8.1   **IS IT NECESSARY TO USE A JOB EVALUATION SYSTEM?**

Organizations that have formal job evaluation systems are often questioned about the reasons behind a particular system. It is helpful for managers to review the considerations companies give when making such a decision.

- Using a few salary ranges is easier than managing hundreds of individual salary ranges.
- A job evaluation system is a structured way to ensure internal equity.

- The system can inform employees about career requirements.
- A system can ensure pay equity considerations under legislated requirements.
- A job evaluation system can provide validity of market data.

Sources: Adapted from Susan Heathfield, "Why Would an Employer Perform a Job Evaluation?," *The Balance*, August 29, 2016, accessed January 3, 2018, https://www.thebalance.com/why-would-an-employer-perform-a-job-evaluation-1917851; and Karl Aboud, "How Much Do You Pay Staff?," *Canadian HR Reporter*, May 5, 2014, 11.

DETERMINING WAGE RATES

Job evaluation systems provide for internal equity and serve as a starting point for setting wages. However, *they do not in themselves determine the wage rate*. Information about the evaluated worth of each job needs to be expressed as hourly, daily, weekly, or monthly wages. In order to do this, salary surveys are used.

Salary Surveys

A **salary survey** provides information about what relevant competitors (determined by industry and/or geographic location) are paying employees who perform similar work. Using salary information from other organizations allows an employer to maintain external equity—that is, to pay wages to its employees that are equivalent to those of similar employees in other workplaces.

Collecting Survey Data

Although many organizations conduct their own salary surveys, a variety of resources are available to purchase information collected by third parties. For example, you might want to see what the average hourly rate is for an accounting clerk in the Toronto area. Or you might want to know the average hourly rate for a Web designer anywhere in Canada. Companies such as Willis Towers Watson, Aon, Mercer, and Hay Group conduct annual surveys and sell this information to employers. When using salary surveys, it is important that similar jobs are being compared. Therefore, using titles to compare jobs is not appropriate as a job title in one organization may represent a job that is significantly different in another workplace.

The Wage Curve

A wage curve displays the current pay rates for various jobs within a pay grade in relation to their company ranking. This visual picture helps ensure that employees receive fair compensation for their skill and education level. Wage curves sometimes depict a company's current salary rate in contrast to the salary rate of other companies in the same industry. When a curve is used for this purpose, it allows the company to see what competitors are paying their workers. Figure 8.4 provides an example of a wage curve.

LO4
Illustrate the compensation structure.

Salary survey
Survey of the wages paid to employees in other relevant, comparable organizations

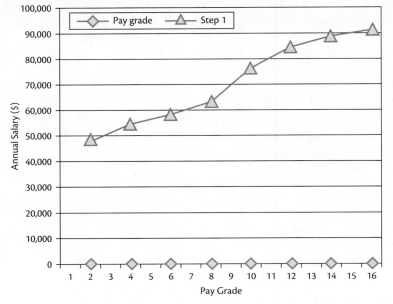

FIGURE 8.4 **Wage Curve Example**

Source: Treasury Board of Canada.

Pay Grades

A **pay grade** is a step within a compensation system that defines the amount of pay an employee will receive. Jobs that are determined to be equal or similar (i.e., through the job evaluation process) are typically grouped together in a pay rate or pay range.

Pay Ranges

Although a single rate may be created for each pay grade, providing a range of rates for each pay grade is more common. Progression through a pay range is typically based upon increased service with an organization. Figure 8.5 provides an example of pay rate ranges within various pay grades for court reporters employed at the Treasury Board of Canada.

Broadbanding

Broadbanding collapses numerous salary grades into a few wider salary bands. Broadbanding encourages employees to develop lateral skills while addressing the need to pay employees performing several different jobs with various skill-level requirements. Additionally,

FIGURE 8.5 **Salary Structure—Annual Rates of Pay: Court Reporters, Treasury Board of Canada, 2017**

Effective Date	Step 1	Step 2	Step 3	Step 4	Step 5	Step 6
A) June 2014	41,275	42,502	43,731	44,959	46,193	47,414
B) June 2015	41,791	43,033	44,278	45,521	46,770	48,007
C) June 2016	42,525	43,789	45,055	46,321	47,592	48,850
D) June 2017	43,057	44,336	45,618	46,900	48,187	49,461

Source: Treasury Board of Canada Secretariat, Pay Rate 8.5 Table; Subgroup: Court Reporter ST-COR-1 Annual Rates of Pay (in Dollars) Step 1 to 6, For Dates: June 2014, 2015, 2016, and 2017. http://www.tbs-sct.gc.ca/agreements-conventions/view-visualiser-eng.aspx?id=15.

broadbanding helps eliminate the obsession with pay grades and instead encourages employees to change jobs, develop their own careers, and seek different roles within an organization without the limitation of only seeking opportunities that provide higher pay rates.

Other Ways to Determine Wages

The most common way to determine an employee's compensation is to evaluate the worth of a job. However, this approach does not acknowledge or reward employees for their unique skills and knowledge. Furthermore, this approach does not encourage employees to learn new skills or to contribute to the work and accomplishments of others. To address these concerns, many organizations have introduced competency-based or skill-based pay plans.

Competency-based pay—also referred to as *knowledge-based pay*, *skill-based pay*, *pay for knowledge*, or *multiskill-based pay*—compensates employees for their knowledge and/or skills and for the work they perform, regardless of their formal job description.[25] This type of pay structure allows and encourages employees to earn higher wages by learning and performing a greater number of skills (or jobs) or by using a variety of competencies to achieve various organizational goals. For example, in an industrial setting, new tasks might include various welding activities, with an employee earning a higher base salary with each increasing level or type of welding that can be performed.

> **Competency-based pay**
> Pay based on how much knowledge or how many capabilities employees have or how many jobs they can perform

Competency-based pay systems allow an organization to differentiate between the performances of employees, provide increased flexibility in determining how work will be performed, and increase the recruitment and retention of a flexible workforce.[26] Competency-based pay also encourages employees to continuously update their knowledge and skills, thereby allowing an organization to maintain a competent workforce. Therefore, when considering the introduction of competency-based pay, it is important to address the following:

- link competencies to business objectives
- identify which jobs or types of work could benefit
- identify competencies that demonstrably affect performance
- devise methods to measure the achievement of each competency
- determine the appropriate amount of pay for an acquired skill
- provide mechanisms to review overall effectiveness[27]

The Government of Canada has developed a competency framework for talent management in the Office of the Comptroller General. Competency is defined as "measurable and observable skills, abilities or knowledge that enable an employee to perform satisfactorily in a position."[28]

Ethics in HRM 8.1 addresses ethical considerations when determining an employee's compensation.

ETHICS IN HRM 8.1 — DO LEADERS REALLY EARN THEIR PAY?

A recent study revealed that CEOs are receiving compensation that is 200 times more than the average Canadian worker, and the gap is increasing. Average annual compensation for the 100 highest-paid CEOs at TSX-listed companies hit a record $10.4 million, versus the average Canadian worker's $49,738. A CEO's base pay made up just 11% of income. Other elements of compensation included share grants (33%), bonuses (26%), and stock options (15%), which are payments that many Canadians do not have access to or an opportunity to earn. Carleton University believes CEOs' compensation is justifiable and should not be compared to the salary of an average worker. Based upon this compensation data, by the time they have lunch on their first day of work in the new year, some CEOs will have earned as much as an average employee's annual income.

continued

Another example of people in leadership positions receiving hefty compensation occurred when Sears Canada fired 2900 employees but provided the company's CEO and senior managers with extra compensation. This action was justified due to the requirement for managers to be given retention bonuses under Sears Canada's Key Employee Retention Plan (KERP). Sears argued that this action was necessary in order for the company to provide incentives for management to remain with the company while it was closing numerous stores, focus on operations, and maximize value for all stakeholders.

Some people believe that CEOs and top managers deserve every penny they earn. Key performers in many industries, from sports to entertainment to big business, always make far more than the average person because they offer rare and sought-after abilities and skills. The compensation of CEOs and other managers should therefore never be compared to those of typical employees as these people fulfill key leadership roles and have tremendous responsibilities.

CRITICAL THINKING QUESTIONS:
1. Are CEO salary levels appropriate in comparison with compensation received by other employees? Why or why not?
2. Should a company pay managers a retention bonus to ensure ongoing operations while other employees are losing their jobs? Why or why not?

Sources: Adapted from Adelle Chua, "Are CEOs' Incomes Unconscionable?," *HRD Canada*, January 4, 2018, accessed January 6, 2018, https://www.hrmonline.ca/hr-news/financial-wellness/are-ceos-incomes-unconscionable-235767.aspx; and Katie Dangerfield, "Sears Managers, Executives Get $9.2M in Bonuses While Thousands Laid Off," *Global News*, July 14, 2017, accessed January 6, 2018, https://globalnews.ca/news/3598469/sears-canada-lay-offs-management-bonuses.

INCENTIVE PLANS

LO5

List the types of incentive plans.

For several years, a trend in rewards has been the use of incentive plans, also called *variable pay programs*, for employees throughout the organization. However, with the continuing economic concerns, many companies are reexamining whether these are appropriate in the current circumstances. A study by Deloitte Consulting found that 38% of employers responding were focusing on variable pay as part of redesigning their rewards program. However, this same study also indicated that 19% of employers were also reexamining their base pay.[29]

Another study, by Towers Watson, identified that employers do not necessarily always understand that base pay and career advancement may be more important than other types of rewards in attracting and retaining employees.[30] And although incentive plans create an operating environment that champions a philosophy of shared commitment through the belief that every individual contributes to organizational performance and success, it is important that the components of such plans be well communicated.

Do incentive plans work? Research has shown a definite relationship between incentive plans and improved organizational performance. However, incentive plans must be customized for each organization, and employees must understand the impact of their performance on business results.[31]

A variety of individual and group incentive plans exist for both hourly and salaried employees. These include the following:

1. *Individual bonus*—an incentive payment that supplements the basic pay. It has the advantage of providing employees with more pay for exerting greater effort, while at the same time giving employees the security of a basic wage. Bonuses are common among managerial employees, but as indicated earlier, organizations are increasingly providing bonuses to front-line staff.
2. *Team- or group-based incentive*—a plan that rewards team members with an incentive bonus when agreed-upon performance standards are exceeded. Figure 8.6 provides the pros and cons of team incentive plans.
3. *Merit raises*—an incentive, used most commonly for salaried employees, based on achievement of performance standards. One problem with merit raises is that they may be perpetuated year after year even when performance declines.

FIGURE 8.6 The Pros and Cons of Team Incentive Plans

Pros	Cons
Team incentives support group planning and problem solving, thereby building a team culture.	Individual employees may not understand how their work contributes to the team's accomplishments.
The contributions of individual employees depend on group cooperation.	Reliance on 1 or few group members (i.e., social loafing) can occur, or employees may begin to display groupthink, with little questioning of decisions made and actions taken by the group.
Unlike incentive plans based solely on output, team incentives can broaden the scope of the contribution that employees are motivated to make.	Employees may not understand how group rewards are calculated.
Team bonuses tend to reduce employee jealousies and complaints over "tight" or "loose" individual standards.	
Team incentives encourage cross-training and the acquiring of new interpersonal competencies.	

4. *Profit sharing*—any plan by which an employer pays special sums based on the profits of the organization.
5. *Employee stock ownership plans (ESOPs)*—stock plans in which an organization contributes shares of its stock to an established trust for the purpose of stock purchases by its employees. With the recent economic turmoil, stock and stock options have not been as popular. There is also always the issue of what happens to stock ownership when there is a change in ownership.

But do incentive plans work? At Work with HRM 8.3 provides some insights.

AT WORK WITH HRM 8.3   **ARE INCENTIVE PLANS WORKING?**

Companies will use incentive pay as a strategic tool to attract, motivate, and retain employees and to improve organizational performance. And with ongoing economic issues, organizations want to keep key talent while keeping costs down. Is this goal achievable with incentive plans?

Yes, but careful attention has to be paid in the objectives, design, and implementation.

1. Companies will need to reward the most valued employees, which means that the organizations need to know who matters to business performance.
2. Companies need to determine the mix of short-term and long-term incentives.

3. Effective programs usually pay more to those who demonstrate better results.
4. Components need to be examined periodically to ensure that outcomes are being achieved.
5. To be effective, incentives must be linked to corporate goals, such as increased sales.
6. Plan design needs to address both short-term and long-term business performance.
7. The plan design needs to consider if there will be a threshold performance before any payouts are done.

For example, WestJet is proud to provide an employee share purchase plan for its employees—and refers to its

continued

staff as "owners." WestJet feels this type of recognition and reward has enabled it to be the most profitable North American airline.

CRITICAL THINKING QUESTION:
Would you like to have an incentive plan? Why or why not? Explain your reasons.

Sources: Adapted from Cassandra Carver, "2018 Compensation Budgeting Forecast Part 2: Trends in Incentive Compensation," *Astron Solutions*, September 5, 2017, accessed January 3, 2018, http://www.astronsolutions.net/2018-compensation-budgeting-forecast-part-2-trends-in-incentive-compensation; Paula Domm, "A Service Incentive Plan That Works," *Canadian Autoworld*, August 18, 2015, accessed January 3, 2018, http://www.canadianautoworld.ca/fixed -operations/a-service-incentive-plan-that-works; and "Great Jobs," *WestJet*, accessed January 3, 2018, www.westjet.com/guest/en/jobs.shtml.

EMPLOYEE BENEFITS

Employee benefits constitute an indirect form of compensation intended to improve the quality of the work and the personal lives of employees. The cost of benefits can be as high as 40% when you include premiums for health and welfare, government-mandated coverage such as workers' compensation, vacation, and paid sick leave. In return, employers generally expect employees to be supportive of the organization and to be productive. Since employees have come to expect an increasing number of benefits, the motivational value of these benefits depends on how the benefits program is designed and communicated. Once viewed as a gift from the employer, benefits are now considered rights to which all employees are entitled.

Too often, a particular benefit is provided because other employers are doing it, because someone in authority believes it is a good idea, or because there is union pressure. However, the contributions that benefits will make to the compensation package (and therefore to organizational performance) depend on how much attention is paid to certain basic considerations.

Linking Benefits to the Overall Rewards Program

Like any other component of the compensation plan, an employee benefits program should be based on specific objectives. The objectives an organization establishes will depend on many factors, including the size of the firm, its profitability, its location, the degree of unionization, and industry patterns. Most importantly, these objectives must be compatible with the organization's strategic rewards and recognition plan, including its philosophy and policies. The chief objectives of most benefits programs are to achieve the following:

- improve employee work satisfaction
- meet employee health, security, and environment concerns and requirements
- attract and motivate employees
- retain top-performing employees
- maintain a favourable competitive position

For example, OpenText Corporation, a software development company in Ontario, recognizes that there are many components in a benefits program. Its inclusion of sheltered bicycle parking and shower facilities resulted in the company being listed in Canada's Top 100 Employers for 2018.[32]

But it is important to remember that not all benefits work for everyone. As a result, it is important that organizations design their benefits program to fit the unique demographics of the company.[33] As with other good HR practices, it is a good idea to consult with employees when a new benefit is being considered. Many organizations establish committees composed of managers and employees to administer, interpret, and oversee their benefits policies. Opinion surveys are also used to obtain employee input. Having employees participate in designing benefits programs helps ensure that management is satisfying employee wants.

Cost Concerns

Organizations can typically spend about 35% to 45% of their annual payroll costs on benefits such as group health plans, pension contributions, EI premiums, CPP premiums, and workers' compensation premiums. The increasing costs, particularly of healthcare provisions, have made more and more organizations strive to manage those costs.

Since many benefits represent a fixed rather than a variable cost, management must decide whether it can afford this cost under less favourable economic conditions. As managers can readily attest, if an organization is forced to discontinue a benefit, the negative effects of cutting it may outweigh any positive effects that accrued from providing it.

To minimize negative effects and avoid unnecessary expense, many employers enlist the cooperation of employees in evaluating the importance of particular benefits. For example, Saint John Energy, the electrical distribution agency for the City of Saint John, decided that it needed to find a more cost-effective pension plan. Its existing plan had been around for 80 years and was potentially unsustainable in the future. Since pension plans can be quite important to employees, it involved both current and retired employees in the redesign, which not only met its cost concerns but also was endorsed by everyone.[34]

The escalating cost of healthcare benefits is a major concern to employers, who must strike an appropriate balance between offering quality benefits and keeping costs under control. Evidence suggests that organizations that take a more strategic and holistic approach to the design of its benefits can effectively keep costs down and employees well.[35]

Increasing use of data analysis regarding the most utilized drug or medical service enables employers to find tactics to reduce the costs or help employees with a different approach to managing the health issue.[36] Part of the reason for this is the use of generic drugs and the results of wellness programs initiated a number of years ago. In addition, some organizations are approaching their costs of healthcare benefits from a value-based perspective. Specifically, "value-based healthcare" is a systematic and holistic approach to creating a culture of health for employees. Value-based healthcare does this by promoting a healthier lifestyle, which can lead to better productivity and lower benefits costs.[37]

At Work with HRM 8.4 describes what 1 company has done to provide numerous innovative benefits that are valued by employees.

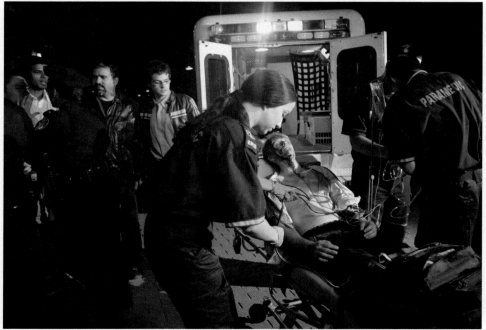

© Blue Images Online/Masterfile

The increasing cost of medical benefits to employees continues to be an issue for employers.

AT WORK WITH HRM 8.4   BENEFITS MATTER!

Labatt Brewing Company Limited was selected as one of Canada's Top 100 Employers in 2018 and one of Greater Toronto's Top Employers for 2018. The numerous and creative benefits offered to employees were a key reason that the company received this recognition. For example, Labatt Breweries supports employees who are new mothers with maternity top-up payments (to 75% of salary for up to 17 weeks) and the option to extend their leave into an unpaid leave of absence. The company also offers a subsidy for in vitro fertilization of up to $15,000 for employees who want to start a family. An adoption assistance subsidy, of up to $2000 per child, is also offered. These programs display the company's commitment to their employees and their families.

Other benefits that employees view as generous and valuable include academic scholarships of up to $2000 per child, flexible work hours, compressed work weeks, and 2 weeks of paid vacation after their first year on the job for new employees. As well, the company encourages employees to contribute to various charities and supports them by providing 1 paid day per year to do volunteer

work. In 2017, the total employee volunteer hours (on company time) was over 7500 hours, with involvement in over 100 charitable and community organizations. Some of the community organizations supported included Walk for Breast Cancer, Walk or Wheel for Cancer, Wildfire Relief in Alberta (the company's London brewery shipped over 200,000 cans of water last year), Water.org, Habitat for Humanity, World Environment Day, Thames River Cleanup (London), and numerous campaigns to encourage responsible drinking. Furthermore, the company encourages charitable giving by matching employee donations.

Employees recognize the value of the benefits they receive and appreciate Labatt's diverse way of recognizing workers and providing valuable support to them. This assistance clearly extends beyond a simple pay cheque.

CRITICAL THINKING QUESTIONS:

1. Do you think it is important for an employer to provide innovative or unique benefits? Why or why not?
2. If you could choose 1 unique benefit, what would it be?

Source: Adapted from Richard Yerema and Kristina Leung, "Labatt Brewing Company Recognized as One of Canada's Top 100 Employers (2018)," *Mediacorp Canada Inc.*, November 6, 2017, accessed January 6, 2018, https://content.eluta.ca/top-employer-labatt.

BENEFITS REQUIRED BY LAW

LO6

Explain the employee benefits that are required by law.

Legally required employee benefits can cost over 15% of an organization's annual payroll. These benefits include employer contributions to the Canada or Québec Pension Plan, Employment Insurance, workers' compensation (discussed in Chapter 3), and, in some provinces, provincial medicare. As legislated requirements can and do change, it is critical for managers to continuously review the appropriate employment standards act that governs the legally required benefits for their workplaces.

Canada and Québec Pension Plans (CPP/QPP)

The Canada and the Québec Pension Plans cover almost all Canadian employees between the ages of 18 and 70. Both plans require employers to match the contributions made by employees. The revenues generated by these contributions are used to pay 3 main types of benefits: retirement pensions, disability benefits, and survivors' benefits. With Canada's aging population, funds from the CPP will not be able to meet the needs of retirees unless those currently working, and their employers, significantly increase their contributions.

Employment Insurance (EI)

Employment Insurance (EI) benefits have been available for more than 50 years and were provided as income protection to employees who were between jobs. Employees and employers both contribute to the EI fund. The amount of benefit paid is a formula (which can change) based on the number of hours of employment in the past year and the regional unemployment rate. EI is also accessed for employees on parental leave. However, almost 40% of Canadian employers provide additional paid parental leave.[38]

Provincial Hospital and Medical Services

Most provinces fund healthcare costs from general tax revenue and federal cost sharing. Ontario, Québec, and Newfoundland also levy a payroll tax, whereas other provinces, such as Alberta and British Columbia, charge premiums payable by the resident or an agent, usually the employer (subsidies for low-income residents are provided).

The cost of the government providing healthcare has escalated to the point where major reform in Canada's healthcare system is occurring. As of 2017, 31% of the Canadian population was over 55, with those over 80 comprising just over 4%.[39] As has been discussed by policymakers, politicians, and journalists, the increasing longevity of people and the major health problems that do occur mean that our healthcare system will need significant redesign to be sustainable.[40]

Leaves without Pay

Most employers grant leaves of absence to employees who request them for personal reasons. In some provinces, legislation mandates that these types of leaves must be granted. For example, in 2017, Ontario and Alberta introduced changes to legislation requiring employers to grant employees unpaid leaves under certain conditions, such as caring for a sick child or dependent family member. The federal government also legislated enhanced changes to leaves for family caregivers, thereby providing increased access to, and length of, unpaid leaves for federally regulated employees. It should be noted that these types of leaves are usually taken without pay but also without loss of seniority or benefits.

Other Required Benefits

In addition to the benefits described, through provisions in employment standards legislation, provinces do require employers to pay for statutory holidays, minimum vacation pay, premiums when people work overtime, and, in some provinces, a severance payment when employees are terminated. Therefore, as noted previously, it is important that managers are always familiar with the specific employment standards act(s) that are applicable to their workplaces.

VOLUNTARY EMPLOYEE BENEFITS

In addition to the benefits required by legislation, employers can choose to provide more benefits as part of the overall compensation package. Organizations do this to ensure that they can attract and retain the kinds of employees they want. These benefits are called "voluntary benefits." Although there can be many types of these benefits, we will look at the more typical ones.

LO7
Describe voluntary benefits.

Health and Welfare Benefits

Due to sharply rising costs and employee concern, the benefits that receive the most attention from employers today are healthcare benefits. In the past, health insurance plans covered only medical, surgical, and hospital expenses. Today, employers include prescription drugs as well as dental, optical, and mental healthcare benefits in the package they offer their workers. As mentioned earlier in this chapter, employers are attempting to ensure that the benefit provided will be of value to the person. Listed below is a brief description of typical health and welfare benefits.

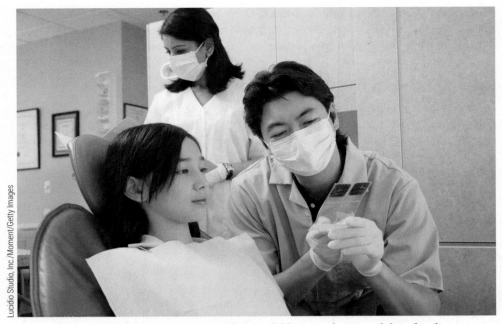

Lucidio Studio, Inc./Moment/Getty Images

Other benefits coverage, such as dental, is often available to employees and their families.

Dental Coverage

Dental plans are designed to help pay for dental-care costs and to encourage employees to receive regular dental attention. Typically, the insurance pays a portion of the charges and the employee pays the remainder.

Extended Health Coverage

This benefit provides for additional payments beyond the basic provincial medical coverage. It typically provides such things as semi-private or private hospital rooms, prescription drugs, private nursing, ambulance services, out-of-country medical expenses that exceed provincial limits, and vision care.

It should be noted that there could be duplication of coverage if both partners in a relationship have access to health coverage. In some cases, if there is better coverage in one plan than in another, the partner with the better coverage will enroll and include the partner.

One aspect of extended health coverage that is increasing greatly is the cost of prescription drugs. This situation becomes worse when provincial health plans reduce coverage or make use of generic drugs as private plans typically pick up the costs.[41] To counter this increase, many plans make use of generic drugs as well, but this only goes so far. Another way to help reduce costs is to ensure that employees can make informed decisions regarding their health care and to provide easy access to lower-priced pharmacies.[42] Employers and benefits carriers are also watching the increased use of genetic testing and its impact on all forms of insurance coverage. The concern is that as it becomes more widely available, insurance companies would deny coverage simply because there might be a genetic marker indicating the "potential" of a certain health risk that might never materialize.[43]

Life Insurance

Term life insurance provides death benefits to beneficiaries and may also provide accidental death and dismemberment benefits.

Retirement and Pension Plans

Retirement is an important part of life and requires sufficient and careful preparation. In convincing job applicants that theirs is a good organization to work for, employers usually emphasize the retirement benefits that can be expected after a certain number of years of employment.

Pension plans are classified into 2 primary categories: defined benefit and defined contribution. In a *defined benefit plan (DBP)*, a person receiving benefits receives a specific amount (usually based on years of service and average earnings), regardless of the amount of contributions. In a *defined contribution plan (DCP)*, the person gets an amount based on the accumulated funds and how much those funds can purchase (at the time of retirement) for retirement benefits.

Since defined benefit plans have to provide the specific payment whether or not the employee has made sufficient contributions, the organization becomes liable for the difference. With the aging workforce, more and more organizations and employees are expressing concern about whether their plan will be able to fund what has been promised. The continued economic uncertainty has increased concern about the viability of companies having a defined benefit plan. This concern had been magnified, and at one point, the Ontario government considered implementing legislation that would create a government-run required registered pension plan.[44] However, in response to enhancements to the Canada Pension Plan, in 2017, plans for the Ontario Registered Pension Plan (ORPP) were cancelled.[45] Unfortunately, the concerns about the value of pension plans are not new.[46] For some time, Canadian organizations have been faced with the dilemma of potentially having insufficient resources in the future to pay pensions to the people who will be retiring in the future. These concerns have led some employers to consider changing pension plan design from defined benefit to defined contribution. Within the private sector, companies are better understanding that the true cost of a defined benefit plan is much higher than employees would voluntarily wish to participate in.[47] Other suggestions to keep defined benefit plans viable are to have multi-employer pension plans, such as the Many Nations Pension Plan sponsored by 160 First Nations organizations or the Teamsters National Pension Plan.[48]

Given the current volatility of the stock market and the concern about future payments from pension plans, it is no wonder that there is a push to improve the performance of all pension plans, including government-funded ones.[49] For example, Air Canada discontinued a pension agreement with the federal government that is expected to save Air Canada about $300 million over 2 years.[50] Ethics in HRM 8.2 discusses the dilemma of pension plans when companies are faced with cost pressures.

ETHICS IN HRM 8.2 — BUT I THOUGHT MY RETIREMENT DOLLARS WERE SAFE!

Those people who have enjoyed working for employers who provide pension plans have assumed that these plans would always continue and that their retirement income would be secure based on the design of the pension plan. But that isn't always the case.

As Sears Canada faces bankruptcy, "16,000 retirees [are] uncertain about their futures amid fears they could lose out on almost 20 per cent of their underfunded defined-benefit pension plan. Pensioners hold little priority in Canadian law when it comes to dividing up assets during bankruptcy proceedings, so when a

pension plan is not fully funded, and an employer goes bust, the future of that pension is thrown into limbo."

According to Wanda Morris, vice-president of the Canadian Association of Retired Persons, 1.3 million Canadians on corporate defined benefit pension plans are potentially at risk. "The current plight of Sears Canada retirees has left many wondering why some pension plans are underfunded, why they are not given priority in the event of a bankruptcy and what could be done to better protect pensioners under the law." The problem isn't just with extreme situations,

continued

such as the impact of bankruptcy on pension plans. As retiree benefits become more expensive, employers are looking at a variety of ways to reduce their costs. To do so does pose legal risks to employers. For example, Weyerhaeuser, a forest products company with extensive operations in Canada, decided to reduce its contribution to the cost of medical benefits to its retirees. Several of the retired staff launched a claim based on the idea that through their years of employment and what had been promised, they were entitled to continue to have the cost of premiums paid for totally by the company. And the trial judge agreed. The judge determined that the premium costs were a type of deferred compensation that the retirees were entitled to as part of their retirement benefits.

In another case, GM Canada reduced healthcare and life insurance coverage for its retirees. The court judge ruled similarly to the judge in the Weyerhaeuser case, concluding that GM was contractually obligated to provide the original coverage.

CRITICAL THINKING QUESTIONS:

1. Is it ethical for companies to reduce retirement benefits? Why or why not?
2. What might employees do to ensure that this doesn't happen to them?

Sources: Adapted from Brennan MacDonald, "The Call to Protect Pensions Has Raised Questions: Here's a Look at 3 of Them," *CBC News*, October 28, 2017, accessed January 7, 2018, http://www.cbc.ca/news/politics/underfunded-pensions-sears-legislation-protections-1.4375483. Reproduced by permission of CBC Licensing; and Josée Dumoulin, "Grey Power," *Canadian HR Reporter*, June 2, 2014, accessed January 7, 2018, www.hrreporter.com/articleview/21319-grey-power.

Pay for Time Not Worked

The "pay for time not worked" category of benefits includes statutory holiday pay, vacation pay (above any legislated minimum), bereavement leave, rest periods, coffee breaks, sick leave, and parenting benefits (salary continuance). These benefits typically account for a large portion of overall benefit costs.

Vacations with Pay

Eligibility for vacations varies by industry, locale, and organization size. A recent study indicated that most organizations provide more paid vacation than is required by law.[51] To qualify for longer vacations of 3, 4, or 5 weeks, one may expect to work for 7, 15, and 20 years, respectively. However, some organizations may not tie paid vacation to any years of service. For example, Netflix provides unlimited vacation for its employees.[52]

Paid Holidays

Both hourly and salaried workers can expect to be paid for statutory holidays as designated in each province. The standard statutory holidays in Canada are New Year's Day, Good Friday, Canada Day (Memorial Day in Newfoundland and Labrador), Labour Day, and Christmas Day. Other holidays recognized by various provinces are Victoria Day, Thanksgiving Day, Remembrance Day, and Family Day. Additionally, each province may designate special holidays important to that province only. Many employers give workers an additional 1 to 3 personal days off. As noted earlier in this chapter, the appropriate employment standards act should be reviewed to determine if the company is legally required to pay an employee for a statutory holiday.

With the increasing diversity in culture and religions in the workforce, situations may arise in which governments feel a need to change the number and type of statutory holidays so that there are more general kinds of observations rather than holidays tied to any one faith. However, it creates a more inclusive and accepting environment, as well as not creating a discriminatory environment, if organizations provide opportunities for people to recognize their religious days.[53]

Sick Leave

Employees may continue to receive compensation when they are unable to work because of illness or injury. Most public employees, as well as many in private firms (particularly in white-collar jobs), receive a set number of sick days each year to cover such absences. Coverage through group insurance that provides some percentage of income protection during a longer-term disability is also becoming more common. As previously addressed in the chapter, absence from work and subsequent lost income due to job-related illness or injuries may be partially reimbursed through workers' compensation insurance.

According to Statistics Canada, workplace absences have remained stable over the past several years. In 2017, an average of almost 10 workdays (almost 2% of the work year) were lost due to illness or family responsibilities.[54] Much of this amount is due to the aging workforce. Workers aged 55 and over missed 13 days of work on average each year, whereas workers aged 25 to 34 missed only 7 days.[55]

Wellness Programs

In recent years, new types of services have been offered to make life at work more rewarding and to enhance employee well-being. Excellence Canada (formerly the National Quality Institute) provides annual awards for organizations that have outstanding wellness programs. ArcelorMittal Dofasco, a Hamilton, Ontario, producer of steel, won a gold-level award for a healthy workplace because it encourages each employee to support and participate in a variety of wellness activities.[56] Although there is uncertainty about the exact return on the investments in these types of programs, some employers have demonstrated that there is dollar value in them. For example, Bruce Telecom, a telecom services company in Ontario, convinced both employees and its union that having employees participate in a wellness program would be beneficial to everyone. In doing so, the company analyzed a number of metrics, such as health claims, drug claims, and sick days, and concluded that it saved over $136,000 in 1 year.[57]

Employee Assistance Programs

People's personal concerns and worries impact their job performance; therefore, to help workers deal with these issues, many organizations offer employee and family assistance programs (EFAPs). These programs typically provide diagnosis, counselling, and treatment when necessary for problems related to substance abuse (alcohol, drug), emotional difficulties, and financial or family difficulties. (EFAPs were discussed in detail in Chapter 3.) These programs are intended to help employees and their families solve their personal problems or at least prevent problems from turning into crises that affect their ability to work productively. One study determined that for every $1 invested in an EFAP, almost $9 was returned through less absence from work and improved productivity.[58]

Educational Assistance Plans

One of the benefits most frequently mentioned in the literature for employees is the educational assistance plan. The primary purpose of this plan is to help employees keep up to date with advances in their fields and to help them get ahead in the organization. Usually, the employer covers—in part or totally—the costs of tuition, books, and related fees, whereas the employee is required to pay for meals, transportation, and other expenses. Depending on the organization, some companies are willing to pay for courses not directly related to a specific job. Employers feel providing educational assistance enables them to attract and retain the key employees they need to be successful.[59]

Childcare and Eldercare

Consider these statistics:

1. Over 17% of the Canadian population is 65 or older.[60]
2. One-third of employees are caregivers.[61]
3. Annual lost productivity due to caregiving costs approximately $1.3 billion.[62]
4. The number of seniors requiring some type of help will double in the next 15 years.[63]

In the past, working parents had to make their own arrangements with sitters or with nursery schools for preschool children. Today, benefits may include financial assistance, alternative work schedules, and family leave. For many employees, on-site or near-site childcare centres are the most visible, prestigious, and desired solutions.

Responsibility for the care of aging parents and other relatives is another fact of life for more and more employees. **Eldercare** refers to situations in which an employee provides care to an elderly relative. This may occur while the employee continues actively working or may refer to situations where an employee requests time off to attend to this form of family responsibilities. According to Statistics Canada, at the end of 2017, just over 6 million Canadians were 65 or older.[64] By 2033, it is estimated that 23% will be 65 and older, and 7% of the population will be 80 or older.[65] As a consequence of the expected shortfall in eldercare facilities, the responsibility for the care of these seniors will be borne by their children and other relatives. The majority of caregivers are women.

To reduce the negative effects of caregiving on productivity, organizations may offer eldercare counselling, educational fairs and seminars, printed resource material, support groups, and special flexible schedules and leaves of absence. Interest in and demand for eldercare programs are increasing dramatically as the Canadian population ages and lives longer. It is also important to consider the impact of childcare on the Canadian workplace as well. Most people who are responsible for childcare are female. Given that the labour force is approximately 48% female,[66] significant issues can occur in the workplace when childcare duties need attention. Of the women working, 70% had children under 6 years old.[67] As mentioned earlier in this section, $1.3 billion is lost annually due to caregiving absences—a huge loss to the Canadian economy.

Eldercare
Care provided to an elderly relative by a person who continues actively working

Monkey Business Images Ltd/Thinkstock

Given the number of working parents, many companies want employees to have access to childcare.

Organizations have been involved in a number of initiatives to improve this situation. For example, BMO is working with its EAP supplier to develop a program for caregivers in which employees participate in support sessions facilitated by trained professionals. In this way, employees can feel and understand that many others have the same difficulties and that they can rely upon each other to provide support.[68] Experts in the field state that companies that do not have programs to help employees be caregivers are at risk of losing talent or having increased absenteeism.[69]

Employee Recognition Programs

Organizations may offer various programs to reward employees for their contributions. These range from long-service awards, to employee of the month initiatives, to peer recognition systems. When implemented properly (i.e., with clear and equitable criteria), these programs can enhance the overall workplace culture, enhance employee motivation, and increase employee retention.

Other Services

The variety of benefits and services that employers offer today could not have been imagined a few years ago. Some are fairly standard, which we have briefly covered. Some are unique and obviously grew out of specific concerns, needs, and interests. Some of the more creative and unusual benefits are group insurance for employee pets, free baseball tickets for families and friends, and summer boat cruises. At Work with HRM 8.5 describes a unique benefit at a software firm.

There are many emerging trends in relation to rewards and recognition. See Emerging Trends 8.1 for some of the more prominent ones.

AT WORK WITH HRM 8.5 — FIDO FRIENDLY!

Have you thought about bringing your dog to work? Have you done so?

If you work at Salesforce.com, you might have done so. It started some time ago when someone had a problem with how their dogs would be cared for during the day. And the company has always considered itself different by providing its employees with an uncommon work environment. The employees are very mobile, using smartphones and laptops at long tables instead of individual offices.

When the idea came up, discussions occurred among employees via social media. Although not everyone was keen for dogs at work, the company decided to run a trial program. It created a separate space—soundproof and with rubber flooring—with a fixed number of spaces for dogs. Reservations were required.

People with dogs find that they can be more productive when they don't have to worry about pet care. And people who don't have dogs also make use of the perk. The director of marketing has a busy travel schedule that doesn't allow for having a dog. However, if he feels particularly in need of canine support, he arranges to walk and spend time with a friend's dog. There is also evidence that people who bring their dogs to work are less stressed.

So many people think that it's such a great idea that the company is considering establishing similar facilities in its other offices.

CRITICAL THINKING QUESTIONS:
1. Do you think these special benefits are attractive? Why or why not?
2. Would the inclusion of unusual perks draw you to a specific employer? Why or why not?

Sources: Adapted from Josh McConnell, "Ease Stress – Just Bring Your Dog to Work," *The Globe and Mail*, March 25, 2017, accessed January 3, 2018, https://www.theglobeandmail.com/report-on-business/careers/career-advice/life-at-work/ease-stress-just-bring-your-dog-to-work/article20620317; Chris Morris, "The Pet Economy," *CNBC*, n.d., accessed January 3, 2018, https://www.cnbc.com/2014/02/11/10-companies-that-let-you-bring-your-dog-to-work.html; and Christopher Tkaczyk, "Bring Your Best Friend to Work," *Fortune*, August 11, 2014, 26.

EMERGING TRENDS 8.1

1. ***Legislative changes to ensure employees receive a living wage.*** As noted in this chapter, many governments are implementing legislated increases to minimum wage levels. Although not without controversy, these changes are meant to ensure that people earn a decent living and can support an acceptable standard of living. It is anticipated that these types of increases will continue.

2. ***Addressing the gender wage gap.*** Compensation data shows that disparity between wages for men and women continues to be a problem in Canada. Expressed as yearly income, women working full-time in Canada still earned 74.2 cents for every dollar earned by men employed full-time. Statistics Canada data shows that the pay gap exists in every province and in every major occupational group and that the gap in annual earnings between men and women has barely budged over the past 2 decades, even as education levels among women have surpassed those of men.

3. ***Ensuring that workers are properly classified.*** Careful review of independent contractor status. Hiring an independent contractor can be less expensive as these workers are not given benefits and must pay many of their own required expenses (i.e., CPP and EI). However, if a contractor is deemed to be an employee, both parties lose as unpaid taxes, penalties, interest, and CPP and EI premiums will all have to be paid. As such, many organizations are carefully reviewing the status of their independent contractors through the 4-point test developed through the Canada Revenue Agency.

4. ***Incentives and innovative programs for adopting a healthier lifestyle.*** As costs of health care—both publicly funded and through work benefits—continue to rise, employers are encouraging and supporting employees to be healthier. This includes providing health-risk assessments and specialized interventions such as smoking-cessation aids. Employers are concerned not just about the rising costs to health plans but also about a less productive workforce. More attention is also being paid to improving mental health in the workplace.

5. ***Increased use of and unusual non-financial rewards.*** Organizations are looking at new ways to reward and recognize employees in order to encourage creativity and innovation. Some of these include allowing employees to work remotely from anywhere in the world, providing for eldercare assistance, and helping employees enhance their education and/or qualifications. Another creative non-financial benefit that is gaining momentum is proving "pawternity" leave to employees by giving people paid time off when they adopt a new cat or dog.

6. ***Increased analysis of the costs of benefits.*** Primarily to deal with the changing demographics, employers will be looking at ways to ensure that drug plan costs are reasonable and that they are getting good value. Another way employers can improve the cost of benefits is by ensuring that the overall program is integrated, including use of sick leave, any injuries at work, etc.

Sources: Adapted from Sambhav Rakyan, "Top Five Trends in Compensation and Benefits for 2017," February 23, 2017, *Willis Towers Watson*, accessed January 11, 2018, https://www.towerswatson.com/en/Insights/Newsletters/Asia-Pacific/points-of-view/2017/top-five-trendsiin-compensation-and-benefits-for-2017; Tavia Grant, "Who Is Minding the Gap?," *The Globe and Mail*, November 12, 2017, accessed January 11, 2018, https://www.theglobeandmail.com/news/national/gender-pay-gap-a-persistent-issue-in-canada/article34210790; Susan Ward, "Independent Contractor vs Employee: Which One Are You?," *The Balance*, September 7, 2017, accessed January 11, 2018, https://www.thebalance.com/are-you-a-contractor-or-an-employee-2948639; Adelle Chua, "The Unlikely Staff Perk Taking Workplaces by Storm," *HRD Canada*, January 11, 2018, accessed January 11, 2018, https://www.hrmonline.ca/hr-general-news/the-unlikely-staff-perk-taking-workplaces-by-storm-236086.aspx; Nicola Middlemiss, "Could Eldercare Be the Next Employee Benefit?," *HRM Online*, February 10, 2015, accessed January 11, 2018, www.hrmonline.ca/hr-news/could-eldercare-be-the-next-employee-benefit-187989.aspx; "Push for Differentiation for Performance Yields Positive Results," *Compensation Strategies* 21, no. 8 (August 2014): 8–9; Elena Belogolovsky and Peter A. Bamberger, "Signaling in Secret," *Academy of Management Journal* 57, no. 6 (2014): 1706–1733; "The Downside of Financial Incentives," *HRM Online*, June 30, 2014; Willis Towers Watson, "2014 Global Talent Management and Rewards Study," accessed January 11, 2018, www.towerswatson.com/en-US/Insights/IC-Types/Survey-Research-Results/2014/08/2014-global-talent-management-and-rewards-study-making-the-most-of-employment-deal; Karen Welds, "Drug Plan Trends Report: Alarm About Costs Sparks 'Monumental Shift,'" *Benefits Canada*, March 21, 2017, accessed January 11, 2018, http://www.benefitscanada.com/news/drug-plan-trends-report-alarm-about-costs-sparks-monumental-shift-95051; and Mike Kennedy, "How to Help Employees Manage Drug and Disability Claims," *Benefits Canada*, February 1, 2015, accessed January 11, 2018, www.benefitscanada.com/benefits/health-benefits/how-to-help-employees-manage-drug-and-disability-claims-62245.

LEARNING OUTCOMES SUMMARY

1. Explain an organization's strategic considerations in developing a strategic rewards program.
   - *Companies structure compensation in ways that enhance employee motivation and growth*
   - *Compensation must be tailored to fit the needs of the company and its employees*
   - *Companies are concerned that employees believe the compensation to be equitable*

2. Identify the various factors that influence the setting of pay levels.
   - *There are internal and external factors*
   - *Internal factors include the organization's compensation policy, the perceived worth of the job, the performance of the employee, and the employer's willingness to pay*
   - *The external factors include labour-market conditions, cost of living, collective bargaining, and legal considerations*

3. Describe the major job evaluation systems.
   - *Job ranking system, which groups jobs on the basis of their relative worth*
   - *Job classification system, in which jobs are grouped according to a series of predetermined grades based on a number of factors*
   - *Point system, which determines a job's relative worth by using a quantitative system of points*
   - *Factor comparison system, in which a job is evaluated on a factor-by-factor basis; this type of system is typically used for legislated pay equity purposes*

4. Illustrate the compensation structure.
   - *Salary surveys, which provide information about average wage rates external to the organization*
   - *Development of a wage curve, which indicates the rates currently paid for jobs within the organization*
   - *Development of pay rates for paying individuals based on the job*

5. List the types of incentive plans.
   - *Individual bonus*
   - *Team or group based*
   - *Merit raises*
   - *Profit sharing*
   - *Employee stock ownership plan*

6. Explain the employee benefits that are required by law.
   - *Canada and Québec Pension Plans, which provide a pension for all employees working in Canada*
   - *Employment Insurance, which provides income protection to employees who are between jobs*
   - *Workers' compensation insurance, which pays people for work-related accidents or illnesses*

7. Describe voluntary benefits.
   - *Benefits considered indirect compensation*
   - *Benefits an organization chooses to provide*
   - *Can include health and welfare coverage, pay for time not worked (i.e., sick leave), wellness programs, recognition programs, and childcare assistance*

KEY TERMS

competency-based pay 259
consumer price index (CPI) 253
direct compensation 244
eldercare 270
hourly work 250
indirect compensation 244
job evaluation 251

pay grades 258
pay for performance 249
piecework 250
real wages 254
salary survey 257
total rewards 244

HRM CLOSE-UP APPLICATION

1. Monika Ille describes APTN's approach to total rewards as "holistic" in order to create a healthy work environment. What does Ille mean by this?
2. Why are employees at APTN motivated by the rewards and recognition they receive?
3. What could be some potential problems with the peer recognition program at APTN?
4. What additional benefits would you recommend that APTN offer employees? Why?

CRITICAL THINKING QUESTIONS

1. A large-chain retail store in your community has many part-time employees, primarily in the 18 to 25 years age range. The corporate office is considering providing a modest benefits program for part-time employees. The local manager knows you are taking an introductory course in human resources management and has approached you to give some ideas about what to include. What items would you suggest and why?
2. You were recently promoted to a management position. Your company is in the retail grocery business and has a policy that managers are paid a salary instead of an hourly wage. What are the advantages and disadvantages to you and your company?
3. You work for a yoga studio in your community as an instructor. The manager has approached you about your thoughts on introducing a bonus based on the number of classes taught and the total number of students who regularly attend. How would you respond and why?
4. You are the owner-operator of a bicycle rental company in a large city. You have decided that you need to hire someone who can assist you, particularly in taking telephone reservations and working with customers. However, you're not sure how much you might have to pay someone for this work. Where would you get the information, and what other factors might you need to consider?

BUILDING YOUR SKILLS

1. Think about your dream job. Do you know how much it pays? Working in pairs, go to Monster.ca (**www.monster.ca**) and use its Salary Wizard to find out how much that job would earn in the nearest large city to you. Is information about the methodology used provided? What would you need to do to determine whether the information was good data? Share your results with your classmates.
2. Assume that you have just been hired as the store manager for a high-volume discount store in Winnipeg. Other stores in Alberta are owned by the same person. The previous manager recently hired 10 part-time employees. The store has more than 50 full-time employees. Whereas the part-time employees in Alberta have a benefits program, the employees in Winnipeg do not. The store owner wants to know whether there should be consistency on benefits across the country. What would you need to consider in your response? Prepare a 1-page summary of your thoughts for the store owner.

3. Since pay for performance is an important factor governing compensation increases, managers must be able to defend the compensation recommendations they make for their employees. Merit raises granted under a pay-for-performance policy must be based on objective performance ratings if they are to achieve their intended purposes of rewarding outstanding employee performance. As managers know, however, they must deal with other factors that can affect compensation recommendations. These may include the opinions of the employee's peers or extenuating circumstances, such as illness or family responsibilities. The purpose of the following exercise is to provide you with the experience of granting salary increases to employees on the basis of their work performance and other information.

The following are the work records of 5 employees. As their manager, you have just completed their annual performance reviews, and it is now time to make recommendations for their future salaries. Your department budget has $10,000 allocated for salary increases. Distribute the $10,000 among your employees based on the descriptions for each person.

A. *John Acquin* currently earns $60,000. He is known as a strong team player, and coworkers often go to him for assistance and advice. He is single, with a daughter in university, whom he still supports.

B. *Jessica Simmons* earns a salary of $40,000. Her annual performance review was satisfactory. Several members of the work group have spoken to you about the complexity of her job and the numerous customers she regularly deals with. They feel it is a tough and demanding job and she is doing her best.

C. *Tabitha Tran* earns $40,000. Her performance review rating was below average, and she seems to have difficulty with other members of her team. Tabitha has had a difficult time this past year. Both her parents, with whom she lived, died recently.

D. *Simon Chan* earns $40,000. His performance review rating was above average. He is respected by his coworkers and is generally considered to be helpful and outgoing. He is single and has no dependants.

E. *Ray Bennett* earns $60,000. His performance review rating was very high. His peers resent him because he comes from a very wealthy family, and they feel he is trying to impress everyone. Ray is married, and his wife is a director at a local marketing company. They have 2 grown children who are self-sufficient.

Share your results with other class members. Be prepared to explain your allocation of money.

CASE STUDY 1

What Could I Have Done Differently?

Ravi Singh sat at his desk and wondered what his next steps should be. As the manager of the accounting department at Auto Parts Inc., he noticed that his employees were not as happy and engaged as they were just months ago and was troubled by the resignation letter he was just given from his senior accounting analyst, Tracey.

Auto Parts Inc. had been in business since 2008 and was 1 of 2 companies in Halifax that sold after-market car parts. The company was able to purchase these used products from car dealerships and salvage yards at a reasonable price. Therefore, a healthy profit margin was available, and the company had been very successful for numerous years. In total, 40 people were employed, and Ravi's accounting department had a staff of 6 people. This group of 6 included Ravi (as the manager), 2 clerks, 2 junior analysts, and 1 senior analyst. Tracey's resignation put Ravi in a difficult position as she had a lot of experience and knowledge that could not easily be replaced.

Ravi had recently hired a new junior analyst (Bob) who had a CPA designation and 5 years of relevant experience. Given the current economic conditions, it was difficult to attract a new person to this role, so Ravi had been given permission from the company CEO to offer Bob an extremely competitive salary. As it turned out, in order to hire Bob, he was given an annual salary that was only $5000 less than what Tracey was earning. When Tracey found out, she was furious. As she explained to Ravi, "I have been a loyal, productive employee for 5 years, and now you hire someone who is junior to me and who will be earning almost the same salary!" Ravi tried to explain to Tracey that he had to do this as the market was competitive and all funds currently available to him had to be allocated toward offering Bob a salary that would bring him to the company. No further money for other salary increases was currently available, and Ravi encouraged Tracey to think about her entire compensation package, including the benefits she earned at Auto Parts Inc. Tracey's response was that she didn't care at all about benefits and was extremely insulted about the salary situation. Tracey handed in her resignation the next day.

Ravi had also received complaints from the other junior analyst (Natasha) as she was not pleased that Bob, who was supposed to be a colleague whom she would have to train, was hired with a high salary. "How did employees find out about Bob's salary in the first place, and what if Natasha quits as well?" thought Ravi. "My department would not be able to function properly if I was short 2 employees and had to try to fill these positions in a very tight labour market." Ravi picked up the phone to call the HR director and book an urgent meeting. He needed some advice as to what his next steps should be as he didn't want to lose another staff member and was worried about the overall morale and lack of engagement from his employees.

Questions:

1. How do you think the other employees learned about Bob's salary? What could have been done to prevent this?
2. Why do you think Tracey did not care about her benefits? What should Ravi do to ensure that his other employees do not feel the same way?
3. Given that Ravi has no access to immediate funds and cannot give salary increases to other employees, what should he do next? Clearly outline a strategic plan of action that he should follow.

CASE STUDY 2

What Are the Right Ingredients for a Recognition and Rewards Program?

The answer to the question ought to be simple and straightforward. But it isn't. Depending on where they might be in their career or depending on their family status, people might want very different things in any recognition and rewards program. So how do employers make decisions?

One answer is to ask employees, although there might be concern that by asking, employees will have raised expectations as to what should be included. However, by not doing so, a company may put together a total rewards approach that is not meaningful to the employees and therefore may not achieve the total rewards strategy of the company. For example, a group of chief financial officers recently were asked to rate the total 3 components of a total rewards program. They listed a better benefit plan, more flexibility, and more vacation days. When a group of employees were asked the same question, their responses were more vacation days, more flexibility, and a better benefit plan. If the company could only do the first choice, it is possible that it would have missed the mark by following the views of the chief financial officer instead of the employees. It is also possible that the costs might have been more.

If a company focuses on providing more work flexibility as part of the rewards and recognition program, it needs to make it happen. Recent research found that although flexible work arrangements were available in many organizations, only about one-third of those organizations allowed more than 50% of the employees to use flexible work arrangements. Companies indicated that there was a limit on the amount of flexibility due to service delivery and adequate coverage of work activities. The same study also found that not all managers are comfortable with having employees on flexible arrangements, believing that better levels of productivity would be achieved at work rather than employees working from home.

Even though it is important to look at all ingredients in the total rewards package, companies need to ensure that their pay levels are competitive with the market if they want to attract and retain top talent. And depending on the geographic location of the company, the competitive pressures may be more severe. Although the decline in oil prices has led to a number of staff reductions in Alberta, it hasn't allowed Alberta companies to ease up on watching the salaries of their employees.

Whether it is 1 component or the entire total rewards program, organizations need to periodically review and ensure that they are meeting the needs of the employees and the organization.

Sources: Adapted from "What Is Total Rewards?," *World at Work*, accessed January 7, 2018, https://www.worldatwork.org/aboutus/html/aboutus-whatis.jsp; "Compensation Sense: 2018 Employee Compensation and Total Rewards Outlook," *Total Reward Solutions*, October 18, 2017, accessed January 7, 2018, http://www.totalrsolutions.com/compensation-sense-2018-employee-compensation-total-rewards-outlook; and "Other Than Better Pay, Workers Want More Vacation, Flexibility," *Canadian HR Reporter*, March 11, 2015, accessed January 7, 2018.

Questions:

1. If you could build your own total rewards program, what would be the components? Explain your answer.
2. How might employers ask employees about components of a total rewards program without creating unrealistic expectations?

NOTES AND REFERENCES

1. Lookman Buky Folami, Kwadwo Asare, Eillen Kwesiga, and Dennis Bline, "The Impact of Job Satisfaction and Organizational Context Variables on Organizational Commitment," *International Journal of Business & Public Administration* 11, no. 1 (Summer 2014): 1–18; Abdulmonem AlZalabani and Rajesh S. Modi, "Impact of Human Resources Management Practice and Perceived Organizational Support on Job Satisfaction: Evidence from Yanbu Industrial City, KSA," *IUP Journal of Organizational Behavior* 13, no. 3 (July 2014): 33–52; Valerie J. Vales, "Hawaii Government Employee Unions: How Do Salary, Benefits, and Environment Affect Job Satisfaction?," *Organization Development Journal* 32, no. 3 (Fall 2014): 41–55; and Claudine Kapel, "Lack of Acknowledgement Eroding Job Satisfaction," *Canadian HR Reporter*, October 20, 2014, accessed January 2, 2018, https://www.hrreporter.com/articleview/22558-lack-of-acknowledgement-eroding-job-satisfaction.

2. "Salaries Expected to Increase by 2.3 Per Cent in 2018: Survey," *Canadian HR Reporter*, August 9, 2017, accessed January 2, 2018, https://www.hrreporter.com/compensation-and-benefits/34221-salaries-expected-to-increase-by-23-per-cent-in-2018-survey.

3. David Hoad and Nathalie Olds, "Finding Value in Rewards," *Canadian HR Reporter*, January 26, 2015, accessed January 3, 2018, https://www.hrreporter.com/articleview/23321-finding-value-in-rewards.

4. Teresa M. Amabile and Steven J. Kramer, "The Power of Small Wins," *Harvard Business Review* 89, no. 5 (May 2011): 70–80; and Gretchen Spreitzer and Christine Porath, "Creating Sustainable Performance," *Harvard Business Review* 90, no. 1 (January/February 2012): 92–99.

5. David Hoad and Nathalie Olds, "Finding Value in Rewards."

6. "Compensation Trends and Strategies for 2018," presentation by Korn Ferry, September 2017.

7. James F. Waegelein, "The Influence of Long-Term Performance Plans on Corporate Performance & Investment," *Journal of Applied Financial Research* 1 (2014): 88–95.

8. "What Is Total Rewards?" *WorldAtWork*, accessed January 3, 2018, https://www.worldatwork.org/aboutus/html/aboutus-whatis.jsp.

9. "Compensation and Benefits," *HR Council*, accessed January 2, 2018, http://hrcouncil.ca/hr-toolkit/compensation-wages.cfm.

10. "Push for Differentiation for Performance Yields Positive Results," *Report on Salary Surveys* 21, no. 8 (August 2014): 8–9.

11. Towers Watson, "2014 Global Talent Management and Rewards Study," 3, accessed January 11, 2018, https://www.towerswatson.com/en-US/Insights/IC-Types/Survey-Research-Results/2014/08/2014-global-talent-management-and-rewards-study-making-the-most-of-employment-deal.

12. David Hoad and Nathalie Olds, "Finding Value in Rewards."

13. Elliot N. Dinkin, "Dust Off the Historical Approach to Total Compensation," *Benefits Quarterly*, First Quarter 2015, 43–50.

14. Richard E. Kopelman, Naomi A. Gardberg, and Ann Cohen Brandwein, "Using a Recognition and Reward Initiative to Improve Service Quality," *Public Personnel Management* 40, no. 2 (Summer 2011): 133–149.

15. Michaeline Skiba and Stuart Rosenberg, "The Disutility of Equity Theory in Contemporary Management Practices," *Journal of Business & Economic Studies* 17, no. 2 (Fall 2011): 1–19.

16. Ibid.

17. Beckett Frith, "Employees Don't See Link Between Pay and Performance," *HR Magazine*, October 16, 2017, accessed January 8, 2017, http://www.hrmagazine.co.uk/article-details/employees-dont-see-link-between-pay-and-performance.

18. Robert Crawford, "Co-operative Food Rewards Staff for Saving Energy," *Employee Benefits*, January 22, 2015, 1.

19. Deloitte, "2014 Global Top Five Total Rewards Priorities Survey."

20. Bruno S. Frey and Margit Osterloh, "Stop Tying Pay to Performance," *Harvard Business Review*, January/February 2012, 51.

21. Aaron Vincent Elkaim, "Loblaws Plans to Close 22 Unprofitable Stores and Launch Home Delivery," *CBC News*, November 15, 2017, accessed January 2, 2018, http://www.cbc.ca/news/business/loblaw-store-closure-1.4402838.

22. Deloitte, "2014 Global Top Five Total Rewards Priorities Survey"; Morneau Shepell, "2015 Survey on Compensation and Trends in Human Resources"; and Subeer Bakshi, "Is Your Variable Plan Working?," Towers Watson, 2014.

23. Statistics Canada, "Consumer Price Index," November 2017, accessed January 8, 2017, http://www23.statcan.gc.ca/imdb/p2SV.pl?Function=getSurvey&SDDS=.

24. Treasury Board of Canada Secretariat, "Classification Standard, Economics and Social Science Services Group," accessed January 3, 2018, https://www.tbs-sct.gc.ca/cla/snd/ec-eng.asp#Toc159814569.

25. Katerina Kashi, "Employees Training and Development: What Competencies Should Be Developed the Most?," *Proceedings of the European Conference on Management, Leadership and Governance* (2014): 452–459.

26. Candace L. Hawkes and Bart L. Weathington, "Competency-Based Versus Task-Based Job Descriptions: Effects on Applicant Attraction," *Journal of Behavioral and Applied Management* (2014): 190–211.

27. Vikram Singh Chouhan and Sandeep Srivastava, "Understanding Competencies and Competency Modeling," *Journal of Business and Management* 16, no. 1 (January 2014): 14–22.

28. Treasury Board of Canada Secretariat, "Talent Management for the Finance Community—Employee Guide to Competency-Based Management," accessed January 3, 2018, https://www.tbs-sct.gc.ca/fm-gf/tools-outils/guides/tm-gdt/tm-gdtpr-eng.asp.

29. Deloitte, "2014 Global Top Five Total Rewards Priorities Survey."

30. Towers Watson, "2014 Global Talent Management and Rewards Study," 3.

31. Subeer Bakshi, "Is Your Variable Plan Working?," Towers Watson, 2014.

32. "Canada's Top 100 Employers 2018," accessed January 6, 2018, http://www.canadastop100.com/national.

33. Kevin McFadden, "Benefits Trends: 3 Choices to Make Your Employee Benefits More Flexible," *Benefits Canada*, March 1, 2015, accessed January 3, 2018, https://www.benefitscanada.com/benefits/health-benefits/benefits-trends-3-choices-to-make-your-employee-benefits-more-flexible-62989.

34. Mel Bartlett and Paul Lai, "Collaboration Leads to Affordable Pension Plan Solution," *Benefits Canada*, February 20, 2014, accessed January 7, 2018, https://www.benefitscanada.com/pensions/db/collaboration-leads-to-affordable-pension-plan-solution-49757.

35. Chris Bonnett, "Making Connections to Improve Health Benefit Plans," *Canadian HR Reporter*, September 5, 2014, accessed January 3, 2018, https://www.hrreporter.com/articleview/22178-making-connections-to-improve-health-benefit-plans.

36. Ibid.

37. Catie Grigsby, "10 Employee Benefits Blog Posts to Read Before 2018," *Benefits Focus Blog*, December 20, 2017, accessed January 4, 2018, https://www.benefitfocus.com/blogs/benefitfocus/10-employee-benefits-blogs-to-read-before-2018.

38. "Time Off in Canadian Workplaces," *Canadian HR Reporter*, 2015, 15.

39. Statistics Canada, "Population by Sex and Age Group," accessed January 7, 2018, https://www.statcan.gc.ca/tables-tableaux/sum-som/l01/cst01/demo10a-eng.htm.

40. Information gathered by the current coauthor from a senior manager at Vancouver Coastal Health Authority, February 12, 2015.

41. Michael Biskey, "Reducing Drug Costs Using Behavioural Science," *Canadian HR Reporter*, April 7, 2014, accessed January 4, 2018, https://www.hrreporter.com/articleview/20751-reducing-drug-costs-using-behavioural-science.

42. Ibid.

43. Jacqueline Nelson, "Insurers Pressured over Genetic Tests," *The Globe and Mail*, July 11, 2014, B3.

44. Ashley Csanady, "Ontario to Start Implementing New Pension Plan in 2017, with Full Roll-Out Expected by 2020," *National Post*, August 11, 2015, accessed January 8, 2018, http://nationalpost.com/news/politics/orpp-ontario-to-start-implementing-new-pension-plan-in-2017; and "Ontario Pension Plan Could Cost Jobs, Hurt Economy: Survey," *Canadian HR Reporter*, February 19, 2015, accessed January 7, 2018, https://www.hrreporter.com/articleview/23576-ontario-pension-plan-could-cost-jobs-hurt-economy-survey.

45. Robert Benzie and Rob Ferguson, "Wynne Says CPP Deal Means No Need for Ontario Pension Plan," *The Star*, June 21, 2016, accessed January 8, 2018, https://www.thestar.com/news/queenspark/2016/06/21/wynne-says-cpp-deal-means-no-need-for-ontario-pension-plan.html; and Darryl Dyck, "A New Premium on Retirement," *The Globe and Mail*, November 12, 2017, accessed January 9, 2018, https://www.theglobeandmail.com/globe-investor/retirement/cpp-reform-whats-changing-and-how-it-will-affectyou/article30551445.

46. Julie Cazzin, "The Changing Face of Retirement in Canada," *Macleans*, June 27, 2017, accessed January 15, 2018, http://www.macleans.ca/economy/money-economy/the-changing-face-of-retirement-in-canada.

47. Fred Vettese, "The Biggest Myth About Defined Benefit Pensions Is How Much They Cost," *Financial Post*, September 6, 2014, accessed January 8, 2018, http://business.financialpost.com/2014/09/06/the-biggest-myth-about-defined-benefit-pensions-is-how-much-they-cost.

48. Many Nations Financial Services, "Pension Plans," accessed January 7, 2018, http://manynations.com/pension-plans.

49. Pete Evans, "Canada Pension Plan Assets Inch Up to $328.2B," *CBC News*, November 10, 2017, accessed January 9, 2018, http://www.cbc.ca/news/business/cppib-mark-machin-1.4396701.

50. Frederic Tomesco, "Air Canada Pension Exit Creates Potential Savings of About $310 Million," *The Globe and Mail*, May 28, 2015, B2.

51. "Time Off in Canadian Workplaces," 4.

52. "Not All Perks Are Created Equal," *HRM Online*, August 5, 2014, https://www.hrmonline.ca/hr-news/not-all-perks-are-created -equal-179321.aspx.

53. Stuart Rudner, "Holiday Season Requires Finesse," *Canadian HR Reporter*, October 20, 2014, accessed January 8, 2018, https://www .hrreporter.com/blog/Canadian-HR-Law/archive/2014/10/20/ holiday-season-requires-finesse.

54. Statistics Canada, "Work Absence Statistics of Full-Time Employees," Table 279-0029, accessed January 6, 2018, http://www5.statcan. gc.ca/cansim/a26?lang=eng&%20retrLang=eng&id=2790029& pattern=279-0029.279-0039&tabMode=dataTable&srchLan= -1&p1=-1&p2=31.

55. Ibid.

56. Excellence Canada, "2014 Canada Awards for Excellence," accessed January 9, 2018, http://www.excellence.ca/en/awards/2014-cae -recipients/2014-cae-profiles/2014-caeprofile-amd.

57. Alyssa Hodder, "Strategy: How Bruce Telecom's Focus on Wellness Saved $136,000," *Benefits Canada*, February 1, 2015, accessed January 8, 2018, https://www.benefitscanada.com/benefits/health-wellness/ strategy-how-bruce-telecoms-focus-on-wellness-saved-136000-62330.

58. "Employers See Significant ROI in EFAPs," *Canadian HR Reporter*, November 18, 2014, accessed January 8, 2018, https://www.hrreporter. com/articleview/22836-employers-see-significant-roi-in-efaps.

59. "Flex Hours, Education, T & D Top Retention Strategies: Survey," *Canadian HR Reporter*, August 28, 2014, accessed January 8, 2018, https://www.hrreporter.com/articleview/ 22089-flex-hours-education-td-top-retention-strategies-survey.

60. Statistics Canada, "Population by Sex and Age Group," accessed January 8, 2018, http://www.statcan.gc.ca/tables-tableaux/ sum-som/l01/cst01/demo31a-eng.htm.

61. Liz Bernier, "Do Employers Care About Caregivers?," *Canadian HR Reporter*, February 9, 2015, accessed January 8, 2018, https://www.hrreporter.com/articleview/23469-do-employers -care-about-caregivers.

62. Statistics Canada, "Canadians with Unmet Homecare Needs," accessed January 8, 2018, https://www.statcan.gc.ca/pub/ 75-006-x/2014001/article/14042-eng.htm.

63. Ibid.

64. Statistics Canada, "Population by Sex and Age Group," March 15, 2015, accessed January 8, 2018, http://www.statcan.gc.ca/tables -tableaux/sum-som/l01/cst01/demo31a-eng.htm.

65. Statistics Canada, "Population Projections for Canada (2013 to 2063)," Table 2.4, accessed March 9, 2015, https://www.statcan .gc.ca/pub/91-520-x/2014001/tbl-eng.htm.

66. Statistics Canada, "Employment by Age, Sex, Type of Work, Class of Worker and Province," December 2017, accessed January 8, 2018, https://www.statcan.gc.ca/tables-tableaux/sum-som/l01/cst01/ labr66a-eng.htm.

67. Statistics Canada, "Paid Work," December 2017, accessed January 8, 2018, https://www.statcan.gc.ca/pub/89-503-x/2010001/ article/11387-eng.htm.

68. Liz Bernier, "Do Employers Care About Caregivers?," *Canadian HR Reporter*, February 9, 2015, accessed January 4, 2018, https://www .hrreporter.com/articleview/23469-do-employers-care-about -caregivers.

69. Suzanne Bowness, "Caring for the Caregivers," *The Globe and Mail*, August 19, 2015, B12.

THIS MAKES SCENTS (PART 3)

The company was now in its second year of business. Sales and profits continued to grow, and more staff had been hired. There were now 8 sales clerks and 1 inventory specialist, in addition to Jessie and Ashton, who shared the responsibility of managing the store. Employees seemed to get along with one another, shifts were being split equally, and product was arriving in a timely manner, so all inventory concerns seemed to be addressed. Jessie and Ashton were convinced that the future was golden and that business would carry on as usual and the profits would continue to roll in.

Things were going so well that Jessie and Ashton were considering opening a second location. This new location would be in Cosmo Fair, a big, bright mall that was the talk of the town. Everyone was excited about the upcoming grand opening of this shopping haven, and Jessie and Ashton had a solid lead on leasing a beautiful spot in this new venue. They were thinking that they could each manage 1 store location, and given the current economy, it would be easy to hire sales clerks for the new location. The plan was to have new hires job-shadow current employees in order to learn how to be effective sales clerks. These new hires could then move to the new store after they had learned the ropes. However, plans for expansion were put on hold when unexpected news arrived.

You're Leaving Us?

Jessie was shocked when she arrived at work and opened the envelopes on her desk. Sandra, the most senior sales clerk who had been with the company since it opened, was giving 2 weeks' notice. The second envelope also contained a resignation letter from Jason, the inventory specialist. Jason indicated that he would be leaving the company next week. "How can this be happening?" thought Jessie, who picked up the phone to call Ashton for an emergency conversation.

The Conversations

Jessie and Ashton asked to meet with Sandra to inquire as to why she was leaving. Was it because of money? If they increased her hourly rate, would she stay? How much would it take? Sandra indicated that although the job she was moving to did pay slightly more per hour, she was mainly moving because the new role provided her with more responsibility and room for career growth and development. Her new employer promised to send her on leadership courses and invest in her future development. Sandra also indicated that her new job was in Cosmo Fair, and she was excited about working in a new, energized shopping mall.

When speaking with Jason, he indicated that he was tired of always showing sales clerks how to do inventory and that he wasn't really being paid for all the work he did. Jessie and Ashton explained to Jason that he was a valuable member of the team and that they didn't want him to leave, especially with expansion plans in the works. Jason was shocked and replied, "I have never been given any feedback or encouragement from either of you. How was I supposed to know any of this? Also, when you gave out bonuses last month, everyone got the same dollar amount. Why did I get the same money as sales clerks, when my salary is higher and my contributions are more meaningful? Also, everyone knows that the 2 of you took a sizeable bonus. I'm done. Consider this my last day!" Jason stormed out and slammed the office door behind him. That meeting had not gone as planned, and Jessie and Ashton were stunned. They knew they had to regroup and possibly rethink their expansion plans.

Questions:

1. Jessie and Ashton had offered Sandra more money to stay in her current role with the company. What problems could have occurred if Sandra had accepted their offer?
2. What unique benefits could This Makes Scents offer employees? Why did you select these items?
3. If a second location opens, how should new sales clerks be trained? Explain why this is the preferred method.
4. Is there anything wrong, from an HRM perspective, with the expansion plans?
5. What performance management plan should be implemented for sales clerks? What performance management plan should be implemented for the inventory specialist?
6. Is it time for Jessie and Ashton to hire an HR person? How should a company determine if it is time to hire someone with this specialized knowledge and/or experience?

9 Knowing Your Rights and Responsibilities

LEARNING OUTCOMES

After studying this chapter, you should be able to

1 Describe statutory rights, contractual rights, due process, and the legal implications of those rights.

2 Identify the job expectancy rights of employees.

3 Explain the process of establishing disciplinary practices, including the proper implementation of organizational rules.

4 Discuss the meaning of discipline and how to investigate a disciplinary problem.

5 Outline the differences between progressive and positive discipline.

6 Identify the different types of alternative dispute-resolution processes.

OUTLINE

Introduction
Management Rights and Responsibilities
Employee Rights
Employment Protection Rights
Job Expectancy Rights
Disciplinary Policies and Procedures
Setting Organizational Expectations
Defining Discipline
Investigating the Disciplinary Problem
Approaches to Disciplinary Action

Compiling a Disciplinary Record
Grounds for Termination
Terminating Employees
The Results of Inaction
Appealing Disciplinary Actions
Negotiation
Mediation
Ombudsperson
Arbitration

"Safeguarding employee privacy is really part and parcel of good employee relations."

JOHN JACAK is a busy man. As the privacy officer for Nutrien Ltd., the world's largest direct-to-grower provider of products, services, and solutions, which plays a critical role in helping global growers increase food production in a sustainable manner, Jacak is responsible for staying on top of the constantly evolving world of personal information privacy. With nearly 20,000 employees worldwide and the issue of privacy protection being a relatively new and constantly changing field, it's no mean feat.

"It is very much a fluid and dynamic environment, and it's an area of the law that's still evolving," Jacak explains. "I try to keep my finger on the pulse of developments and evolving areas of the law."

Although government legislation mandates what personal information can be collected and just what can be done with that information, Nutrien's robust and detailed Employee Privacy Policy has been driven by more than just legal compliance.

"Really, the bottom line behind it and the guiding principle is to maintain the trust of our employees," Jacak says. "The goal is to build their trust and confidence by respecting their privacy and their personal information. It's part of the trust process and the respect process."

And respect is something that Nutrien takes very seriously.

"Respect is a principle that really forms the bedrock to our employee relations practice, and it just carries right across into privacy and maintaining privacy," Jacak explains. "Safeguarding employee privacy is really part and parcel of good employee relations."

He adds: "The privacy policy gives people a good sense of what information we collect. It's a clear statement that we have a commitment to safeguard their personal information and retain it for only as long as needed. And in doing that, I think we build trust and confidence. It's a clear statement to our employees, prospective employees, and former employees of what we do with their personal information. What it's used for, how we protect it, how long we retain it, and lets them know that if they'd like to access it, they can do so. By doing that, I think it takes any questions out of their minds or potential concerns they may have."

Privacy of personal information is a topic of concern for many people in society today, including employees. Nutrien believes that the best approach with personal information is to be transparent and open. The company maintains that such an approach not only is the optimal way to help head off conflicts that might arise from a lack of understanding but also helps demonstrate respect for their employees.

"It's better from our standpoint to be transparent and just to lay it out on the table so everybody knows what the framework is for privacy practice,"

Nutrien Ltd.

Jacak explains. "By embracing a transparent approach, you really diffuse many concerns that people may otherwise have. When you don't address issues of safeguarding or retention, or when you don't have a clear statement that information collected will only be used for the purpose that was originally intended and consented to, [you open yourself up to problems]. So [transparency] just diffuses a whole lot of questions."

John Jacak believes that when it comes to the important area of employee privacy, the only advisable route is honesty and openness about your privacy practices.

"Starting from a point of transparency translates into a more positive feeling on the part of the employee from the outset, as opposed to having these lingering questions and perhaps concerns that you don't need and you can nicely sidestep."

INTRODUCTION

In this chapter, employee rights, management rights, workplace privacy, and employee discipline are discussed. Managers note that these topics have a major influence on the activities of both employees and themselves. Managers are discovering that the right to discipline and discharge employees—a traditional responsibility of management—is more difficult to exercise in light of the growing attention to employee rights. In addition, disciplining employees is a difficult and unpleasant task for most managers; many of them report that taking disciplinary action against an employee is the most stressful duty they perform. Balancing employee rights and employee discipline may not be easy, but it is a universal requirement and a critical aspect of good management. John Jacak, privacy officer at Nutrien, states in the HRM Close-up that openness and transparency are critical when it comes to gathering employee information.

Because the growth of employee rights issues may lead to an increase in the number of lawsuits filed by employees, this chapter includes a discussion of alternative dispute resolution as a way to foster a less legalistic approach to solving disagreements. As managers are the people who take disciplinary actions that are subject to challenge and possible reversal through governmental agencies or the courts, they should make a positive effort to prevent the need for such action.

When disciplinary action becomes impossible to avoid, however, that action should be taken in accordance with carefully developed HR policies and practices. Most of this chapter applies to both non-unionized and unionized workplaces. Where a concept applies only to a non-union workplace, this will be mentioned.

MANAGEMENT RIGHTS AND RESPONSIBILITIES

All companies have people, usually called "managers," who make fundamental decisions, such as how the business is run or how much the company should charge for its products or services. In making these decisions, they have both rights and responsibilities. One of the more basic rights is that the company can hire or terminate whomever it wants.

However, as discussed in both this chapter and Chapter 10, those rights now have to be exercised in certain ways, and managers now have more responsibility for how those rights are exercised. Managers function as representatives of the organization and therefore have the legal responsibilities and liabilities that go with that role.

In addition, employees and the public at large are demanding that employers demonstrate greater social responsibility in managing their people. Complaints that some jobs are deadening the spirit and injuring the health of employees are not uncommon. Complaints of discrimination against women, visible minorities, the physically and mentally challenged, and the elderly with respect to hiring, training, advancement, and compensation are being levelled against some employers. Issues such as comparable pay for dissimilar work, the high cost of health benefits, daycare for children of employees, and alternative work schedules are ones that many employers must address as our workforce grows more diverse.

In addition, managers are expected to behave and act in ways that acknowledge that employees also have certain rights. Managers are no longer able to make decisions or take actions without being aware of their obligations with respect to how an employee must be treated in today's workplace.

EMPLOYEE RIGHTS

Various human rights laws, wage and hour regulations, and safety and health legislation have secured basic employee rights and brought numerous job improvements to the workplace. Now employee rights litigation has shifted to such workplace issues as employees' rights to protest unfair disciplinary action, to refuse to take drug tests, to have access to their own personnel files, to challenge employer surveillance,[1] and to clarify an employer's use of information on social media.[2] All these things make it very important that managers act and behave in fair and objective ways.

The current emphasis on employee rights is a natural result of the evolution of societal, business, and employee interests. The term **employee rights** refers to the expectation of fair treatment from employers in the employment relationship. These expectations become rights when they are granted to employees by the courts, legislatures, or employers. Employee rights frequently involve an employer's alleged invasion of an employee's right to privacy. Unfortunately, the difference between an employee's legal right to privacy and the moral or personal right to privacy is not always clear. The confusion is due to the lack of a comprehensive and consistent body of privacy protection, whether from laws or from court decisions.

There can be a perceived invasion of privacy when the employer uses electronic monitoring or surveillance to observe or monitor employees while they are doing their work. Although such action is not illegal, employers are well advised to let employees know when and why they are doing it. For example, companies that have a call-centre operation frequently will use electronic means to monitor customer calls. However, employees are provided with full information about the purpose and, in some situations, given guarantees that the data will be used only to help employees learn and improve their customer-service skills.

Although the employee has certain rights, it is also the employer's obligation to provide a healthy and safe workplace for employees. At the same time, the employer also promises safe and quality products and services to its customers. For example, an employee may refuse to submit to a drug test based on the right of privacy. However, if that same employee is impaired at work and produces an inferior product or creates a safety hazard, the employer can be held liable. As a result, employers are expected to exercise a *duty of care* in the hiring and training of employees. This is particularly true in the field of emergency services, where there is also a public safety component. For example, in 2018, the RCMP was held liable for inadequate training on use-of-force equipment after a number of officers were shot and witnesses indicated that using a different weapon could have made a difference.[3] As mentioned earlier, without the exercise of reasonable care, employers can be held liable by outside parties or other employees injured by a dishonest, unfit, or violent employee.

It is at the point of liability where employer responsibilities and employee rights can collide. If an employer doesn't recognize employee rights, the employer's reputation can be damaged and the engagement of employees can suffer. On the other hand, if customer interests aren't protected, then employers can be sued. At Work with HRM 9.1 discusses the practical implications for managers of the balance between employee rights and employer responsibilities.

Employment Protection Rights

It should not come as a surprise that employees feel that having a job is a right—and a right that needs to be taken seriously. This line of reasoning has led to the emergence of 3 legal considerations regarding the security of one's job: statutory rights, contractual rights, and due process.

Employee rights
Expectations of fair treatment from employers

AT WORK WITH HRM 9.1 — THIS IS COSTLY!

For a number of years, 2 court cases* demonstrated the special recognition to the employer–employee relationship given through decisions of the Supreme Court of Canada. These decisions focused on the fair and individual treatment of each person. This meant that managers should pay greater attention to individual employees before, during, and at the end of employment.

One of the cases, *Wallace v. United Grain Growers*, pointed to the need for employers to pay more attention to how people are terminated. Besides compensation for lack of notice, employees were seeking damages if they felt they were poorly treated during the actual termination. This perspective meant that the manager's behaviour during the process could have a bearing on how much the termination would cost the employer.

However, a significant case decided by the Supreme Court in mid-2008 changed this approach. In *Honda Canada Inc. v. Keays*, the Court determined that earlier decisions had been inappropriate. In lower court decisions, the employee had been awarded $100,000 in punitive damages for the manner in which Honda conducted itself in the termination. The employee had been diagnosed with chronic fatigue syndrome, resulting in eventually being placed in Honda's disability program. That program required employees to provide Honda with medical information from a physician that absences were due to the medical condition. What the employee's physician provided was insufficient, so Honda requested that the employee meet with an occupational medical specialist. The employee refused.

Honda then terminated the employee. The employee sued for wrongful dismissal, stating that Honda had demonstrated bad faith. The court disagreed, saying that the employee had not been treated poorly—either in terms of compensation or behaviour.

This case eliminated a number of principles established through the *Wallace* case. The most significant was that employees were not entitled to additional severance or punitive damages but only to receive compensation for "actual" damages—that is, loss of wages. But the case maintained that employers must act in good faith when dismissing employees, and the employees must be treated respectfully. Any additional financial costs would occur only if the employee could prove that the way in which the employer terminated caused mental distress.

In an Ontario Court of Appeal decision, the judge upheld the ruling that Zochem Inc. failed to meet its obligations when it terminated an employee. Specifically, it did not act with fairness in the dismissal. The judge affirmed that when the employee raised safety concerns, the employee was not only ignored but was also demeaned. At this time, the employer knew it was restructuring and that the employee was going to be terminated. The employee subsequently launched a sexual harassment complaint, which the employer briefly investigated. The judge determined that the earlier decision of awarding moral damages in the amount of $60,000 would stand, in addition to the 10 months of salary and $25,000 in damages for sexual harassment. The judge stated, "Moral damages are awarded as a result of the manner of dismissal, where an employer engages in conduct during the course of dismissal that is unfair or is in bad faith...." This is one of the highest awards in Canada for the bad behaviour of an employer when terminating an employee.

CRITICAL THINKING QUESTIONS:

1. Do you believe that employees have too many rights? Why or why not?
2. What would you have decided in these cases and why?

Wallace v. United Grain Growers (1997), 152 DLR (4th) 1 (SCC); and *BC(PSERC) v. BCGSEU* [1999] SCJ No. 46 (SCC).

Sources: Adapted from Darren Stratton, "Bad Faith & Unfair Dealing in Employee Dismissal: 7 Lessons in 7 Years," *CanLII Connects*, February 2, 2015, accessed March 12, 2018, http://canliiconnects.org/en/commentaries/35631; Shreya Patel, "Court Upholds $60k Award for Bad Faith Dismissal," *HRD Canada*, October 17, 2018, accessed March 12, 2018, www.hrmonline.ca/hr-general-news/court-upholds-60k-award-for-bad-faith-dismissal-232498.aspx; and *Doyle v. Zochem*, January 13, 2017, 2017 ONCA 130.

LO1

Describe statutory rights, contractual rights, due process, and the legal implications of those rights.

Statutory Rights

Statutory rights are rights that derive from legislation. As we saw in Chapter 2, human rights legislation protects employees from discrimination and harassment on the basis of such grounds as age, sex, and race, and other prohibited grounds.

For example, a construction worker in Ontario was fired for displaying a Confederate flag on his truck and posing for photos outside his job site. The employer stated that it had zero tolerance for racism and discrimination. The CEO of the company, Yoke Group, stated, "We believe strongly in diversity, inclusiveness and acceptance." The CEO went on to say that the company was deeply offended by the employee's actions.[4]

Provincial employment standards acts establish basic rights for such things as overtime pay, minimum vacation pay, and leaves. The concept of basic rights changes over time as societal expectations change. For example, in early 2018, Alberta implemented changes to its employment standards that require employers to grant leaves of absence (unpaid) for a number of different purposes.[5] The leaves include such things as an employee taking time off to deal with domestic violence, taking time off to care for an ill or injured adult family member, and a parent taking up to 52 weeks off to deal with the disappearance of a child as a result of a crime.[6]

Labour relations laws (discussed in Chapter 10) give employees the right to form and belong to unions and to bargain for better working conditions.

Occupational health and safety legislation (discussed in Chapter 3) aims to ensure safe and healthy working conditions. Health and safety legislation has had a great deal of impact on both employers and employees, as well as at times challenging a person's right of privacy. The most notable of these issues intersecting is around random alcohol and drug testing. Employers want to do this to ensure a safe work environment, whereas employees feel this is an invasion of their privacy. This came to a head when the Alberta Court of Queen's Bench upheld a decision that Suncor Energy has the right to do random drug and alcohol testing at its Alberta oil-sands sites.[7] The union representing the workers, Unifor, maintained that this was "an invasive and degrading policy that violates the fundamental rights of workers." Suncor, on the other hand, maintained that its round-the-clock operation using heavy equipment that weighed in excess of 400 ton required the highest level of safety to minimize the risk of accidents.

All these laws are statutory and grant certain rights to people.

Contractual Rights

Whereas law establishes statutory rights, **contractual rights** are derived from contracts. A *contract* is a legally binding agreement; if 1 party breaches the contract, a remedy can be sought through an appeal to the courts. Although formal contracts between employers and full-time employees are rare, they are standard practice when it comes to contingent workers, a growing segment of the Canadian labour force. Such a contract, referred to as the *employment contract*, will deal with such items as the type of work, the length of work, the amount of pay for the work (including any benefits), and whether there is any obligation on the employer if the employee is terminated.

Not all contracts are written. An implied contract can occur when an employer continues to employ someone after a fixed-term contract has ended. Information on an application form or in an HR resource manual could be an implied contract. Even information provided during an interview or any written information given to applicants could be considered an implied right. Whether explicitly or implicitly, if an employee continues to work after the end of a fixed-term contract and no new contract has been entered into, or if multiple fixed-term contracts occur, courts will generally consider that the person continues to be an employee.

A case in Saskatchewan revolved around an employer's decision not to pay severance when the employment was terminated. A teacher began working in 1987 on a 1-year contract and was subsequently rehired on 1-year contracts for 27 consecutive years. The adjudicator determined that although the contracts didn't provide for automatic renewal, the actual contractual process was treated as automatic by both the employee and the school. The school was ordered to pay severance in the amount of 2 days' wages for each year of service.[8]

Sometimes an implied contract is binding on the employer. Here are some examples:

1. Communicating to employees that if they are loyal and do good work, their jobs are safe.
2. Expressing in an employee manual that if they are terminated, they have access to an appeal procedure (e.g., due process).
3. Enticing someone to leave another organization by promising a better job and then not following through after the person is hired.

Statutory rights
Rights that derive from legislation

Contractual rights
Rights that derive from contracts

In order for employers to minimize their risk of challenges on an implied contract, here are some suggestions:

1. Train managers about what to say to employees about pay or benefits.
2. Use a written employment letter or contract that explains the circumstances under which an employer may terminate the employee.
3. Have written information about the nature of the employment relationship, such as in employee manuals or the offer letter.
4. Ask the employee to read all documents and sign off that the materials have been read and understood.

It is important to remember that in a contractual situation, employees also have obligations and responsibilities. For example, an employer in Québec terminated an employee for refusing to participate in a harassment investigation. A subordinate made a harassment complaint about the employee. When the employer started the investigation into the complaint, the employee refused to answer certain questions, stating that privacy rights were paramount. Even when the employee brought a lawyer to attend any investigative meetings, the employee persisted in refusing to answer questions. As a result, the employer dismissed the person. The tribunal concluded that the employee had an obligation to participate in the investigation and answer questions that might be useful. To refuse is grounds for discipline, specifically termination.[9]

Due Process

Management has traditionally had the right to direct employees and to take corrective action when needed. Nevertheless, many individuals also believe a job is the property right of an employee and the loss of employment has such serious consequences that an employee should not lose employment without the protection of due process. Managers normally define **due process** as the employee's right to fair treatment in the handling of an employment matter.[10] Although due process is not a legal obligation, it does flow from common law history of fair treatment. As a result, proactive employers will additionally incorporate the following principles—or rights—into their interpretation of due process:

1. The right to know job expectations and the consequences of not fulfilling those expectations.
2. The right to consistent and predictable management action for the violation of rules.
3. The right to fair discipline based on facts, the right to question those facts, and the right to present a defence.
4. The right to appeal disciplinary action.
5. The right to progressive discipline—to be informed about an incident and be given a chance to improve.

Due process
Employee's right to a fair process in making a decision related to the person's employment relationship

Employment Rights Not a Guarantee

It should be understood that although employees might have cause to regard their jobs as an established right, there is no legal protection affording employees a permanent or continuous job. Furthermore, in general, the concept of due process does not guarantee employees any assurance of employment. However, the concepts of due process and of a job as a right do obligate management to act in a consistent and fair manner.

Employees *do* have the right to expect sound employment practices and to be treated respectfully as individuals. In Canada, in the absence of a formal contract specifying the duration of employment, the employment relationship can be construed as ongoing. Although employment is not necessarily considered permanent, the employer must provide reasonable notice and grounds for termination. Thus, Canada functions under statutory and common (contract) law.[11]

Job Expectancy Rights

Once hired, employees expect certain rights associated with fair and equitable employment. Employee rights on the job include those regarding substance abuse and drug testing, privacy, plant closing notification, and just-cause disciplinary and discharge procedures.

LO2

Identify the job expectancy rights of employees.

Substance Abuse and Drug Testing

In Canada, the social costs of substance abuse, including lost productivity, as well as health-care costs, have been estimated at more than $40 billion.[12] Most human rights legislation considers substance abuse to be a disability that therefore needs to be accommodated.[13]

According to a survey by Statistics Canada, almost 20% of the Canadian population aged 12 or older reported consuming more than 5 alcoholic drinks per occasion at least 12 times a year.[14] The trend in the general population continues to find daily and heavy drinking to be significantly higher for males than for females. Since illicit drugs are available and increasingly available in high quality throughout Canada, studies are finding that cannabis use is up among Canadian adults. With the legalization of cannabis in Canada in 2018, employers are very concerned about what impact this will have on the workplace. Recent student surveys in Ontario found use patterns increasing for most drug categories. Various studies have indicated that alcohol and other drug use (both prescription and non-prescription) contributes to issues of job performance, work productivity, absenteeism, increased workplace accidents, and problems with interpersonal relationships.[15]

As mentioned earlier in this chapter, the failure of an employer to ensure a safe and drug-free workplace can result in astronomical liability claims when consumers are injured because of a negligent employee or faulty product. Because of this, Canadian companies are ensuring that they have policies and programs on all types of potential substance abuse, including prescription drugs.[16] Although the Canadian government has not introduced legislation on drug testing, such legislation exists south of the border. Companies with drug-testing policies report reductions in absenteeism, sick days, and accidents. Some of the issues surrounding drug and alcohol testing are discussed in At Work with HRM 9.2.

AT WORK WITH HRM 9.2 WHAT CAN EMPLOYERS DO ABOUT CONCERNS OF SUBSTANCE DEPENDENCE IN THE WORKPLACE?

Many employers express concern about the impact of an employee being impaired at work. The concerns range from loss of productivity to safety for customers and employees. Although legislation exists in the United States to allow random and regular drug testing, no legislation in Canada allows this. And even though cannabis was legalized in Canada in 2018, a federal government task force (composed of employers and labour groups) was unable to agree on instituting "drug testing for jobs where impairment could pose a threat to public safety." Furthermore, since most human rights tribunals see drug or alcohol abuse as a disability, any testing for these substances can be a form of discrimination or a challenge to the rights to privacy.

So what can employers do? Some recent cases across Canada will help shed some light.

Suncor, an oil extractor and producer, has operations in the Alberta oil sands that use heavy equipment in sometimes dangerous circumstances. It implemented a random drug and alcohol testing policy for safety-sensitive positions. In introducing the policy, the union grieved the policy, stating that it was a violation of the employees' privacy rights and human rights. The arbitration board determined that Suncor had failed to show an existing problem and therefore determined that the policy was not appropriate. Suncor appealed, and the court determined that workplace safety in that type of environment is a broad concept; therefore, it did not need to prove that there was a problem. However, subsequently, the court issued an injunction against random tests, whereas the union (Unifor) attempted to take the appeal to the Supreme Court.

continued

In another case, the Toronto Transit Commission (TTC) was challenged by its union on the grounds of substance abuse testing being a violation of privacy rights and creating a psychological risk for employees. The Ontario Superior Court ruled that there wasn't evidence that harm would come to employees and that the TTC had demonstrated that random testing was necessary because of public safety, which outweighed any violation of privacy. The court allowed the TTC to continue with the testing, with the judge stating, "Drug testing will detect or deter people prone to using drugs or alcohol around their hours of work, which will increase public safety."

CRITICAL THINKING QUESTIONS:
1. Do you think employers ought to have the right to test for drug or alcohol use? Why or why not?
2. How would you feel if your employer did random drug and alcohol tests? Explain your answer.

Sources: "Drug-Testing Proposal Splits Group Helping Liberals on Workplace Policies," *Canadian HR Reporter*, March 16, 2018, accessed March 17, 2018, www.hrreporter.com/workplace-law/36297-drug-testing-proposal-splits-group-helping-liberals-on-workplace-policies; Shana French and Brian Wasyliw, "With Legalized Marijuana, What Drug and Alcohol Testing Is Permissible?," *Canadian HR Reporter*, June 12, 2017, accessed March 18, 2018, www.hrreporter.com/workplace-law/33695-with-legalized-marijuana-what-drug-and-alcohol-testing-is-permissible; *Suncor Energy Inc v Unifor Local 707A*, 2016 ABQB 269, May 18, 2016, accessed March 18, 2018, www.canlii.org/en/ab/abqb/doc/2016/2016abqb269/2016abqb269.html?resultIndex=1; Josee St-Onge, "Court Reserves Decision on Suncor's Random Drug Testing of Employees," *CTCX News*, February 8, 2018, accessed April 2, 2018, www.cbc.ca/news/canada/edmonton/suncor-drug-test-employees-1.4527361; "First Day of Drug and Alcohol Testing at TTC Produces Two Positive Tests," *Canadian HR Reporter*, May 11, 2017, accessed March 16, 2018, www.hrreporter.com/workplace-health-and-wellness/33389-first-day-of-drug-and-alcohol-testing-at-ttc-produces-two-positive-tests; and Amanda Jerome, "Court Upholds TTC's Drug Testing Policy," *The Lawyer's Daily*, April 5, 2017, accessed March 17, 2018, www.thelawyersdaily.ca/articles/2833/court-upholds-ttc-s-drug-testing-policy.

Employee Privacy

Consider these following practices:

1. General Electric installs fish-eye lenses behind pinholes in walls and ceilings to observe employees suspected of crimes.
2. DuPont uses long-distance cameras to monitor its loading docks.
3. An Alberta IDA drugstore requires cashiers to place their fingers on a pad that scans their fingerprints and allows them access to the cashiering system.
4. Agricultural employees wear devices that scan and track boxes of fruit and vegetables at the end of each picking row.[17]

Although these examples may seem a violation of privacy rights, it is not uncommon for employers to monitor employee conduct through surveillance techniques. Most retailers use some form of monitoring, and almost all of us have made a phone call in which we are informed that our call might be monitored.

Employees have no reasonable expectation of privacy in places where work rules that provide for inspections have been put into effect. They must comply with probable-cause searches by employers. They can be appropriately disciplined, normally for insubordination, for refusing to comply with search requests. It is advisable that employers inform new employees, at either the final employment interview or an orientation session, that mandatory or random searches are done. See Figure 9.1 for a variety of tools and techniques for monitoring employees.

Managers must be diligent when conducting employee searches. Improper searches can lead to employee complaints under various privacy legislation (see Chapter 2) and possible lawsuits claiming defamation of character and negligent infliction of emotional distress.

It is not uncommon for employers to monitor the conduct of employees through surveillance techniques. One of the most common means of electronic surveillance by employers is telephone surveillance to ensure that customer requests are handled properly or to prevent theft.

With the *Personal Information Protection and Electronic Documents Act* (PIPEDA), there is an expectation that employers be reasonable in their use of any type of surveillance technique. For example, 5 staff at a long-term care facility in Ontario were terminated for posting

FIGURE 9.1 Tools and Techniques for Monitoring Employees

Performance	Measure Internet use, keystrokes, and time Use of resources Examine communications content: email, social media, telephone calls, text messaging Identify location: cards, CCTV, GPS, RFID Use mystery shoppers
Behaviours	Examine communications content: email and social media, telephone calls, text messaging Identify location: cards, pages CCTV, GPS, RFID Use mystery shoppers Use psychometric testing, drug testing, biometrics Use lie detector tests Use audio and video surveillance Create open work spaces
Personal characteristics	Use mystery shoppers Use psychometric testing, drug testing, biometrics Use lie detector tests Use audio and video surveillance

Sources: Adapted from Kc Agu, "6 Software Tools for Monitoring Productivity," December 6, 2017, *Huffington Post*, accessed March 18, 2018, www.huffingtonpost.com/kc-agu/post_11966_b_10099296.html; "Managing Workplace Monitoring and Surveillance," *Society for Human Resource Management*, February 18, 2016, accessed March 18, 2018, www.shrm .org/resourcesandtools/tools-and-samples/toolkits/pages/workplaceprivacy.aspx; Office of the Information and Privacy Commission for British Columbia, "Employee Privacy Rights," November 2017; and Jeffrey R. Smith, "Smile for the Camera," *Canadian HR Reporter*, October 16, 2017, accessed March 19, 2018, www.hrreporter.com/columnist/employment-law/ archive/2017/10/16/smile-for-the-camera.

inappropriate photos of some of the residents on Snapchat. Although the app that was used deletes images quickly after being posted, the company indicated that it was a violation of its privacy policy and that the company expects a high standard of behaviour given that it has vulnerable residents in its care. The residence is highly regulated under the Ontario Ministry of Health and Long-Term Care, and as such, the local police were asked to investigate the incident.[18] When an employer is considering using surveillance, it is suggested that the following "best practices" be used:[19]

1. Establish, communicate, and enforce written policies, including codes of conduct.
2. Have up-to-date policies that include social media and any other technology that can be perceived as intruding on an employee's privacy.
3. Ensure that only information relating to employment is collected.
4. Ensure that personal information is kept secure.
5. Apply policies consistently.

Employers have the right to keep all types of information, but its access and use have to be handled very carefully. This is highlighted by recent breaches of private health records involving high-profile people whose personal health information was disclosed inappropriately. Specifically, the Ontario information and privacy commissioner stressed that as hospitals were moving toward electronic records, it was essential that employees understand that inappropriate disclosures of patient information are a serious breach of privacy.[20] As technology continues to change, privacy commissioners are requested to examine the appropriateness of the technology. Recently, the Canadian privacy commissioner was asked to consider whether employers could monitor an employee's social network sites.[21] The commissioner indicated that depending on the privacy settings of an individual user, many people and organizations could have access, including coworkers, future employers, and recruitment firms. Ethics in HRM 9.1 highlights some of these issues.

J.R. Bale / Alamy

Employees in a number of different organizations are video-monitored—sometimes for their own protection.

ETHICS IN HRM 9.1   IS THIS AN INVASION OF PRIVACY?

Many employers use a variety of electronic surveillance techniques to monitor employee activities in the workplace—everything from attendance reporting to controlling employee access to certain areas of work. Organizations with off-site assets use GPSs (global positioning systems) to monitor the use of company vehicles or video cameras to monitor employees on extended sick leave. There is the monitoring of a person's profile on any of the social networking sites, such as Twitter, Facebook, or LinkedIn, too. But when does this become an invasion of one's privacy? The answer is usually "it all depends." In March 2018, Facebook faced a potential financial crisis and public outcry when it was revealed that data mining companies may have inappropriately accessed and used personal information without the permission of users. Although the issue originated in the United States, it quickly spread to Canada when the privacy commissioner launched an investigation into whether Facebook allowed the

misuse of personal data, which is a violation of federal privacy laws.

A family business in British Columbia recently terminated an employee for deleting certain files from the employer's system as it was a violation of the company's code of conduct. The employee sued, claiming it was a breach of privacy as the deletion was found by accessing the employee's emails on the work computer. The court determined that there was no claim to privacy as the computer was not locked and the employer already had access to the computer as it was conducting an investigation anyway. The court did, however, rule in favour of the wrongful-dismissal claim.

With the introduction of "wearable technology" such as activity monitors, there are more possibilities of needing to balance an employer's right with the employee's privacy. For example, hockey teams use wearable monitors to assess fatigue and the potential for an increased risk of accidents. Mining companies use

continued

wearable technology that can provide critical alerts and warnings directly to employees. Other activity monitors help employees improve their overall health. When used appropriately, these are great tools for both the employees and the employer and need to be managed appropriately.

CRITICAL THINKING QUESTIONS:

1. Would you work differently if you knew your performance was continually monitored?
2. Is it ethical for employers to monitor employees this way? Why or why not?

Sources: Adapted from Tamsin McMahon, "Facebook Fallout: Data Misuse Revelations Engulf Company," *The Globe and Mail*, March 20, 2018, A1; Tamsin McMahon, "Canada's Privacy Commissioner Launches Investigation into Facebook Over Cambridge Analytica," *The Globe and Mail*, March 20, 2018, accessed March 20, 2018, www.theglobeandmail.com/report-on-business/international-business/us-business/canada-privacy-commissioner-facebook-cambridge-analytica/article38309030; Emily Douglas, "When Can HR Legally 'Snoop' on an Employee?," *HRD Canada*, March 19, 2018, accessed March 20, 2018, www.hrmonline.ca/hr-law/employment-agreements/when-can-hr-legally-snoop-on-an-employee-239289.aspx; and Olivia Solon, "Big Brother Isn't Just Watching: Workplace Surveillance Can Track Your Every Move," *The Guardian*, November 6, 2017, accessed March 20, 2018.

Access to Employee Files

The information kept in an employee's official employment record or employee file can have a significant impact—positive or negative—on career development. The personnel file, typically kept by the HR department, can contain performance reviews, salary information, investigatory reports, credit checks, criminal records, test scores, and family data.

In compliance with legislation, most employers give their employees access to their employment files. Virtually no organization is exempt from privacy legislation. PIPEDA also entitles employees to examine their own personnel file, including any information stored electronically.

In addition, any personal information cannot be used or disclosed without the prior knowledge and consent of the employee. For example, if you are seeking a car loan and the company wants confirmation of your employment, only you can authorize release of that information. The most important legal principle with regard to data privacy is the concept of consent—ahead of time—from the employee. Under PIPEDA, the person must be notified of the following before any information can be provided:

- that the employee is about to provide personal data
- the purposes for which the information is to be processed
- the people or bodies to whom the information might be disclosed
- the proposed transfer of information to other countries
- the security measures protecting the information

It is also important to remember that any medical information is not only personal but also confidential and potentially sensitive. Such information is to be accessed only by authorized people when required.[22]

Likewise, it is important to ensure that appropriate items reside in the employee file. For example, in its revised *Employment Standards Code*, Manitoba is allowing individual flextime agreements. The employer will need to have the employee sign the agreement, which will need to remain in the employee file until any changes occur. Employment professionals recommend that organizations develop a policy on employee files that includes, as a minimum, the points noted in Toolkit 9.1.

Electronic Privacy

The benefits of electronic communication, including email, voice mail, and social media, are many: they allow for collaboration on projects, enable the sharing of ideas, provide a way for employees to give input to the organization on any number of items, create professional networks, and aid in recruitment.[23]

TOOLKIT 9.1 — POLICY GUIDELINES ON HANDLING PERSONNEL FILES

- Ensure compliance with legislation.
- Define exactly what information is to be kept in employee files.
- Ensure that informed consent has been received from employees regarding the types of information that will be collected and stored.
- Develop different categories of personnel information, depending on legal requirements and organizational needs.
- Specify where, when, how, and under what circumstances employees may review or copy their files.

- Ensure that appropriate security measures are in place to safeguard information.
- Identify company individuals allowed to view personnel files.
- Prohibit the collection of information that might be viewed as discriminatory or form the basis of an invasion-of-privacy suit.
- Audit employment records regularly to remove irrelevant, outdated, or inaccurate information.

Unfortunately, the growth of management and financial information systems can create privacy problems by making personnel information more accessible to those with prying eyes, or to "hackers," who might use the information inappropriately. Even deleted messages can be accessed.

Furthermore, there is the issue of an employee using social media for inappropriate purposes. For example, an employee used Facebook to make offensive comments about the workplace and the boss. The company terminated the employee, indicating that the person's style of communicating was not appropriate for the company. The employee sued the company for wrongful dismissal, and the court determined that although the person ought to have been disciplined, the termination was excessive.[24]

Technology creates the need for a critical balance between employee privacy and the employer's need to know. Employees might assume that their right to privacy extends to email and voice-mail messages, but it does not. The *Freedom of Information and Protection of Privacy Act* (federal legislation) applies only to records in the custody or control of public bodies, such as a Crown corporation, a school board, or a government ministry. In many organizations, it does not apply to the employment relationship. That means that employers have the right to monitor performance and productivity and to prevent workplace harassment.[25] Employers are strongly encouraged to develop clear policies and guidelines that explain to employees how any form of electronic communication is to be used, including when and under what conditions employees can be monitored (see Toolkit 9.2). In addition, employees should be reminded of their responsibilities under the company's policy every time they log on to the company's computer system. More and more decisions by courts and arbitrators are reaffirming the organization's right to monitor email or any other electronic transmission on company-owned computers. This trend holds true for companies that monitor employee use of the Internet.

Therefore, it is important for managers, as well as employees, to understand that employers have the right to monitor any and all electronic transmissions at work. Where email and voice-mail policies do exist, employees should be required to sign a form indicating that they have read and understand the policy. In most cases, courts will find disciplining an employee for Internet abuse to be a reasonable action. However, as mentioned earlier in this chapter, the courts can decide that even when inappropriate materials are found on a work computer, the manner in which they are found can have a bearing on issues of privacy.

TOOLKIT 9.2 EMAIL, INTERNET, SOCIAL MEDIA, AND VOICE-MAIL POLICY GUIDELINES

- Decide on whether the policy will promote use or prohibit misuse.
- Ensure that other relevant policies, such as computer use, privacy, confidentiality, harassment/discrimination, and cyberbullying, are aligned.
- Ensure that the policy covers how it is applied when employees use their own devices for work purposes.
- Consistently apply the policy.
- Clearly specify anything prohibited, such as certain Internet sites or file sharing.
- Clearly specify use or non-use of social media sites and whether use on company equipment will be monitored, including any impact on work productivity.

- Communicate the consequences of breaches of policy.
- Through the organization's systems, block any sites the organization does not want employees to access.
- Inform employees that any confidential information is not to be shared or sent electronically.
- Advise employees that email and computer use, including any personal information stored on computer, is not private and therefore may be reviewed by others.
- Communicate the company's expectations on being connected after the workday.
- As technology changes, review, update, and communicate policy changes.

Sources: Adapted from Hootsuite, "How to Write a Social Media Policy for Your Company," July 27, 2017, accessed April 2, 2018, https://blog.hootsuite.com/social-media-policy-for-employees; "Social Media Policy," *SHRM*, accessed April 2, 2018, www.shrm.org/resourcesandtools/tools-and-samples/policies/pages/socialmediapolicy.aspx; Bernhard Warner, "Keeping Your Social-Media Policy in the Workplace and Out of the Courtroom," *Inc.com*, accessed April 2, 2018, https://www.inc.com/magazine/201407/bernhard-warner/how-to-keep-up-with-social-media-policy-in-the-workplace.html?cid=search; "Internet and Email Policy Sample," *The Balance*, accessed April 2, 2018, www.thebalance.com/internet-and-email-policy-sample-1918869; Tim Mitchell, "Offensive Material on Social Media Feeds," *Canadian HR Reporter*, December 11, 2017, accessed April 2, 2018, http://www.hrreporter.com/workplace-law/35408-offensive-material-on-social-media-feeds; and Michael Oliveira, "Right to Disconnect Talk Picks Up with Popularity of Workplace Message Apps," *Canadian HR Reporter*, March 27, 2018, accessed April 2, 2018, www.hrreporter.com/hr-trends/36389-right-to-disconnect-talk-picks-up-with-popularity-of-workplace-messaging-apps.

Image Source White/Thinkstock

Employees do not necessarily have a right to privacy on any of an organization's electronic devices.

Employee Conduct Outside the Workplace

Can an employer discipline, including terminate, an employee for off-duty activities? Like many other answers regarding the world of human resources, it all depends. Generally speaking, for an employer to successfully discipline the employee, there must be a direct connection between the action and the impact on the company. For example, several fire-fighters were disciplined (successfully) when they were seen on a Twitter post in their uniforms tweeting racist comments.[26]

New technologies enable employers to monitor staff very closely, even on their personal time. As well, with the widespread use of smartphones, pictures and videos can be taken; posted in blogs and on Facebook, Twitter, and Snapchat; and become very public. Although most courts uphold the right of the employer to monitor employees at the workplace, particularly if there is a justifiable reason to collect evidence, the question of monitoring employees outside the workplace is more complex.

To give you an example of what employers might do regarding off-duty activities, a CP rail conductor was terminated after the company investigated the employee's conduct and actions using social media. The reason for the termination is that the person had posted pictures posing in very unsafe situations at work, using both railway property and equipment and making very derogatory comments about the company. Although posting pictures or making comments was probably okay, the employee had done both in a very unsafe manner and made very negative comments about the investigation.[27] The entire case revolved around the expectation of safety at the workplace. This case highlights the issue of social media for both employees and employers and how the rights of the employee's privacy need to be balanced in relation to the employer's rightful business interests.[28]

For an employer to reasonably discipline an employee for behaviours and/or actions outside the work environment, the employer must establish that the behaviour or action is directly linked to the employment relationship. It also means that each situation has to be assessed on its own merits. The case mentioned above was directly linked to the occupational health and safety obligations and the employer's right to discipline an employee for publicly making offensive comments about the employer.[29]

Maria Savenko/Shutterstock.com

With the variety and number of electronic devices, everyone needs to understand that an employer can monitor your social media.

AT WORK WITH HRM 9.3 — **WHAT SHOULD AN EMPLOYER DO ABOUT MISBEHAVIOUR OUTSIDE THE WORKPLACE?**

As mentioned often, it all depends. With the widespread use of smart technology and social media, the lines between someone's work and life outside work can become blurred. Also, as societal norms change, what was acceptable a few years ago may not be acceptable now.

A good example of lines being blurred occurred at Hydro One when an employee was caught on video yelling inappropriate comments at a female news reporter. Not many years ago, it would be okay to yell at a news reporter and say rude things. Also, there is the recent case of an employee being terminated for a blog that expressed support of Nazi Germany in pictures, along with pictures of the person at work and showing the employer's name.

So what can employers do to ensure that employees know the boundaries? One of the more important things to do is create a policy regarding the use of electronic communications (such as blogs) and social media. The policy needs to include what type of enforcement will occur and what type of disciplinary action may be taken. The policy also needs to be simple and readily available at all times.

There is also a need to have a code of conduct so that it is clear how employees are to behave, including what is expected outside of work as it relates to the business. Furthermore, many companies are training all employees regarding behaviours and actions that are acceptable and not acceptable. Companies will also coach managers on how to deal with inappropriate behaviour. In some situations, it may be the employee who needs training regarding being more sensitive to others.

However an employer decides to approach the issue, employees do need to know that an employer may legally be able to discipline them for any misconduct outside the workplace.

CRITICAL THINKING QUESTION:

Do you think an employer should be able to discipline an employee for off-duty behaviours? Why or why not?

Sources: Adapted from Stuart Rudner, "What Do You Do If Your Employee Is 'One of Them'?," *Canadian HR Reporter*, August 21, 2017, accessed March 23, 2018, www.hrreporter.com/columnist/canadian-hr-law/archive/2017/08/21/what-do-you-do-if-your-employee-is-one-of-them; George Waggott and Chandra Ewing, "Social Media Policies: What Works Best in Light of Case Law?," *Canadian HR Reporter*, June 13, 2016, accessed March 23, 2018, www.hrreporter.com/article/27874-social-media-policies-what-works-best-in-light-of-case-law; and Cassandra Szklarski, "Train or Fire? Bosses Grapple with How to Handle Off-Hours Transgressions," *The Canadian Press*, August 17, 2017, accessed March 23, 2018, www.news1130.com/2017/08/16/train-or-fire-bosses-grapple-with-how-to-handle-off-hours-transgressions.

Ultimately, whether an employer can terminate someone for activities outside work will depend on the profession, the profession's code of conduct, and what role the profession plays in our general society.

Read At Work with HRM 9.3 to learn more about off-duty conduct.

DISCIPLINARY POLICIES AND PROCEDURES

The rights of managers to discipline and discharge employees are increasingly limited. There is thus a great need for managers at all levels to understand discipline procedures. Disciplinary action taken against an employee must be for justifiable reasons, and there must be effective policies and procedures to govern its use. Such policies and procedures serve to assist those responsible for taking disciplinary action and help ensure that employees receive fair and constructive treatment. Equally importantly, these guidelines help prevent disciplinary action from being voided or reversed through the appeal system.

LO3

Explain the process of establishing disciplinary practices, including the proper implementation of organizational rules.

If an organization has an HR department, it will have a major responsibility in developing disciplinary policies and procedures. Although the HR department will get top-management approval, it is also critical that managers be involved in the development of the policies and procedures. Managers will carry out the policies; their experiences can contribute to more effective coordination and consistency of disciplinary action throughout the organization. As part of the manager–HR partnership, the HR department will work with the manager to ensure that any actions taken against employees are consistent with any collective agreements and conform to current law.

It is the manager's responsibility to prevent or correct any disciplinary problems. Discussion is frequently all that is needed to correct the problem, and disciplinary action becomes unnecessary. However, when disciplinary action is needed, the manager should strive to use a problem-solving attitude. Causes underlying the problem are as important as the problem itself, and any attempt to prevent recurrence will require an understanding of them.

Admittedly, it is often difficult for managers to maintain an objective attitude toward employee infractions. But if managers can maintain a problem-solving stance, they are likely to come up with a diagnosis nearer the truth than if they used the approach of a trial lawyer. For example, if an employee is late for work several days in a row, the manager needs to discuss the situation with the employee and try to determine the reasons for the lateness. The manager needs to remember that the objective is to get the employee to work on time, not to discipline the individual. Therefore, by attempting to find out the reasons, the manager is in a better position to work with the employee to find an acceptable solution.

Setting Organizational Expectations

Clearly stating expectations of performance and behaviour is the foundation for an effective disciplinary system. These expectations govern the type of behaviour expected of employees. Since employee behaviour standards are established through the setting and communicating of organizational procedures and rules, the following suggestions may help reduce problems in this area:

1. Information about rules should be widely distributed and known to all employees. It should not be assumed that employees know what is expected of them.
2. Expectations regarding work success need to be reviewed on a regular basis.
3. Explain to employees the reasons for appropriate behaviour and expected performance.
4. Organization policies and rules should always be written. Ambiguity should be avoided because this can result in different interpretations by different managers.
5. Ensure that expectations regarding safe and efficient operations are reasonable and conform with safety legislation.
6. Ensure that managers enforce any policies and expectations of behaviours and performance.
7. Ask employees to sign a code of conduct or similar document, on an annual basis, indicating that they have read and understood organizational expectations.

When seeking reasons for unsatisfactory performance, managers must keep in mind that employees may not be aware of certain expectations. Before initiating any disciplinary action, therefore, it is essential that managers determine whether they have given their employees careful and thorough orientation in what is expected of them in relation to their jobs.

It is worth noting that organizations will change expectations if a significant crisis has undermined employee trust and that there is a culture that is no longer appropriate. This is what occurred after the widespread scandal of sexual harassment in the entertainment business and the #MeToo movement.[30]

Defining Discipline

In dictionaries, **discipline** normally has 3 meanings:

1. Treatment that punishes.
2. Orderly behaviour in an organizational setting.
3. Training that moulds and strengthens desirable conduct—or corrects undesirable conduct—and develops self-control.

LO4

Discuss the meaning of discipline and how to investigate a disciplinary problem.

Discipline
(1) Treatment that punishes, (2) orderly behaviour in an organizational setting, or (3) training that moulds and strengthens desirable conduct—or corrects undesirable conduct—and develops self-control

To some managers, discipline is synonymous with force. They equate the term with the punishment of employees who violate rules or regulations. Other managers think of discipline as a general state of affairs—a condition of orderliness in which employees conduct themselves according to standards of acceptable behaviour. Viewed in this manner, discipline can be considered positive when employees willingly practise self-control and respect organizational values and expectations.

The third definition considers discipline a management tool used to correct undesirable employee performance or behaviour. Discipline is applied as a constructive means of getting employees to conform to acceptable standards of behaviour and performance. Figure 9.2 provides examples of common disciplinary problems.

In most organizations, discipline is viewed as a way to correct poor employee performance and/or behaviour rather than simply to punish for an offence. As these organizations emphasize, discipline should be seen as a method of training employees to perform better or to improve their job attitudes or work behaviour. It is also interesting to note that the word "discipline" is derived from the word "disciple," which means follower or pupil. Figure 9.3 shows 1 disciplinary model, which consists of several steps that must be carried out to ensure that the termination is justifiable.

FIGURE 9.2 Typical Disciplinary Problems

Attendance Issues

- Unexplained absences.
- Persistent absenteeism.
- Ongoing tardiness.
- No approval to leave early.

Being Untruthful

- Stealing or committing fraud.
- Lying on resumé.
- Intentionally damaging company property.
- Being untruthful on work documents.

Performance at Work

- Not completing work activities.
- Not meeting production standards or customer expectations.
- Not meeting production metrics.

Behaviour Issues

- Using alcohol or drugs at work.
- Non-compliance when given a direction.
- Physical abuse.
- Performing or behaving unsafely.
- Being physically violent or hostile.
- Not using safety equipment.
- Not reporting a workplace injury.
- Harassing or bullying fellow workers.
- Having weapons.

FIGURE 9.3   An Approach to Discipline

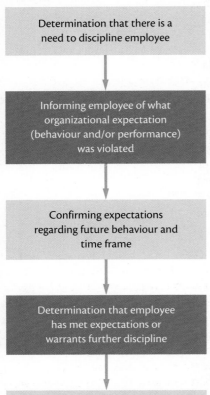

Determination that there is a need to discipline employee

↓

Informing employee of what organizational expectation (behaviour and/or performance) was violated

↓

Confirming expectations regarding future behaviour and time frame

↓

Determination that employee has met expectations or warrants further discipline

↓

If further discipline is warranted, determination if termination is appropriate action

Investigating the Disciplinary Problem

Managers often do not have a natural sense of how to investigate any situation with an employee. Too frequently, investigations are conducted in a haphazard manner; worse, they overlook 1 or more investigative concerns. In conducting an employee investigation, it is important to be objective and to avoid the assumptions, suppositions, and biases that often surround discipline cases.

Toolkit 9.3 lists things that need to be considered when doing workplace investigations. Paying attention to each item will help ensure a full and fair investigation while providing reliable information free from personal prejudice. And as mentioned in Chapter 2, many actions an organization would take in relation to an employment issue require a careful and full investigation. Furthermore, some employment concerns, such as substance abuse, may need "reasonable accommodation" (see Chapter 2); therefore, discipline would be an inappropriate action.[31]

When preparing documentation, it is important that the manager record the incident immediately after the infraction takes place. Then the memory of the incident is still fresh, and the manager can ensure that the record is complete and accurate. It is critical that the documentation be complete. This information will include whether there had been any previous warnings with an opportunity to improve. These documents are necessary to prove that the employer had the right to discipline.[32]

The Investigative Interview

One of the most important things to do when considering discipline is a thorough investigation of the incident, including interviewing the employee and the employee's manager. It is critical to gather facts and to understand that perceptions of what happened can differ. The discussion with the employee needs to focus on what standards were not met; it should avoid getting into personalities or areas unrelated to job performance. One of the key discussions during the interview is to ensure that the employee is given an opportunity to explain to ensure that there is nothing that is the fault of the company. In fact, it is critical to the outcome of any discipline to conduct a careful investigation as quickly as possible and to ensure that the investigation is approached thoughtfully and independently.[33] For example, it could be through an investigation of poor performance that the manager determines that the employee can be assisted by learning a different skill (Chapters 6 and 7).

TOOLKIT 9.3   WHAT MAKES AN EFFECTIVE INVESTIGATION?

1. Plan the investigation, including whether a particular process must be followed and whether the situation is serious enough to result in discipline.
2. Arrange for the investigation to be conducted by an individual who is trained and experienced and is appropriate for the subject of the investigation.
3. Ensure that the investigator is as independent as possible.
4. Identify all relevant issues and explore them as appropriate.
5. Ensure that the accused is informed of the accusation and investigation and provided with an opportunity to give their side of the story.
6. Ensure that all appropriate individuals are interviewed to gain their perspective of the situation and that the interviews are documented.
7. Ensure that all relevant documents (including any electronic records) are available and secure.
8. Ensure that the investigation has sufficient resources to be completed.

continued

9. Have the investigator prepare a full written report with conclusions.
10. Share the results of the investigation with the parties involved.
11. If the situation is serious, ensure that steps are taken to prevent it from occurring again, including training and counselling.
12. If the claim is not validated, explain to the parties how the conclusion was reached.
13. Ensure that there is closure for all involved, including any witnesses.
14. Maintain impartiality throughout the entire process.

Sources: Adapted from Ruth Mayhew, "How to Conduct an Effective Disciplinary Interview," *The Houston Chronicle*, accessed March 23, 2018, http://smallbusiness .chron.com/conduct-effective-disciplinary-interview-10327.html; Kellie Auld, "Handle with Care: The Impact of Workplace Investigations," *PeopleTalk*, Summer 2015, 32–33; and Lisa Bolton and Gerald Griffiths, "How to Conduct an Effective (and Defensible) Workplace Investigation," *Canadian HR Reporter*, March 2018, 5.

Approaches to Disciplinary Action

When taken against employees, disciplinary action should never be thought of as punishment. Discipline can embody a penalty as a means of obtaining a desired result; however, punishment should not be the intent of disciplinary action. Rather, discipline must have as its goal the improvement of the employee's future behaviour. To apply discipline in any other way—as punishment or as a way of getting even with employees—can only invite problems for management, including possible wrongful-dismissal suits. If a thorough investigation shows that an employee has violated some organization rule, disciplinary action must be imposed. Two approaches to disciplinary action are progressive discipline and positive discipline.

LO5
Outline the differences between progressive and positive discipline.

Progressive Discipline

Progressive discipline is imposed in a series of increasingly more formal and more consequential steps to improve behaviour and/or performance. By definition, it is a process for dealing with job-related behaviour and/or actions that do not meet expected standards. Its purpose is to help the employee understand the situation and create opportunities for

Progressive discipline
A series of steps to improve behaviour and/or performance

It is critical to investigate any workplace concerns before doing any type of discipline.

fizkes/Shutterstock.com

improvement.[34] However, the sequence and severity of the disciplinary action vary with the type of offence and the circumstances surrounding it. Since each situation is unique, a number of factors must be considered in determining how severe a disciplinary action should be.

To highlight the uniqueness of situations, a recent case involved an employee who was disciplined for going to the restroom too often.[35] Before any action is taken, it is important that the incident be investigated. It is also key to remember that the investigation can have an impact on the organization, and careful planning needs to take place. Therefore, creating a plan can help in identifying what steps have to be taken, by whom, and when. For example, with the rise of social media, confidentiality and privacy for those involved must be clearly spelled out.[36] Some of the factors to consider when conducting an investigation are listed in Toolkit 9.3.

The usual progressive discipline process has 4 or 5 steps: (1) meeting with the employee to inform and counsel about the situation and gain an understanding with the employee about the need to improve; (2) meeting with the employee and verbally warning that the situation cannot continue and that improvement must happen within a specified period of time; (3) sending the employee a written warning; (4) suspending the employee for a number of days; and (5) terminating the employee's employment. Depending on the situation, steps 1 and 2 may be combined.

The progressive discipline used by several organizations is described in At Work with HRM 9.4. The "capital punishment" of discharge is utilized only as a last resort. Organizations normally use lower forms of disciplinary action for less severe performance problems. It is important for organizations to follow "best practices" when documenting discipline, including:

1. Complete the documentation in a timely manner.
2. Ensure that all documents are dated.
3. Ensure that the documentation clearly identifies what occurred and what was expected.
4. Ensure that the investigation is documented, including an opportunity for the employee to provide their perspective.
5. Share the outcome of the investigation with the employee.
6. Share a copy of the investigative conclusions with the employee and the manager.[37]

AT WORK WITH HRM 9.4 — APPROACHES TO PROGRESSIVE DISCIPLINE

A number of organizations have readily available guidelines aimed at changing unwanted employee behaviour. Before discipline begins, it is expected that the manager can show that the employee is aware of desired behaviour and that he or she is choosing to act otherwise. Frequently, all that is needed is to let employees know that a particular behaviour is inappropriate. Employees usually react positively to this. Progressive discipline definitely is not used as a way of punishing an employee. Typical steps in a discipline process are the following:

Step 1: Establish cause for action. The employer needs to determine that an incident that warrants discipline has occurred. If the action is for performance, the employer must be able to prove to an arbitrator or judge that the employee knew of expectations and that supervision occurred to ensure the standard.

Step 2: Coaching. This is a supportive discussion in which the manager reinforces expectations of either performance or behaviour. It is important that this conversation is noted in the manager's calendar.

Step 3: Verbal warning. This is a private discussion between the employee and the manager that takes place if there has been a repetition of the incident after the coaching session. The manager describes the incident and ensures that all sides of the story are heard. Employment and Social Development Canada's verbal warning step also states that the manager needs to be very clear on outlining the consequences if expectations are not met.

Step 4: Written warning. If the employee's behaviour continues, a meeting is held with the manager and the employee. At the meeting, the manager describes the events, reviews expectations as discussed in step 1,

continued

seeks solutions from the employee, and indicates what will happen if the unacceptable behaviour continues. The meeting is summarized in writing and placed in the employee's personnel file. It is also helpful if the written warning includes a plan to ensure that the employee has sufficient time to improve.

Step 5: Suspension. If the inappropriate behaviour continues, the manager will next consider suspension. A meeting is held, similar to the meeting in step 2. At the conclusion of the meeting, a suspension may be imposed of a duration linked to the nature of the problem—it might be 1 day or several days. A letter of suspension is written and placed in the employee's file.

Step 6: Dismissal. This is a very serious step, taken only when all other options have been exhausted. Again, a meeting is held to review facts and expectations and to summarize previous meetings and actions. Even at this meeting, it is important to provide an opportunity for the employee to explain. At the end of the meeting, a letter of dismissal is presented. One copy is given to the employee, and one copy is put in the employee's file.

CRITICAL THINKING QUESTION:

Are there any other steps that ought to be taken in corrective discipline? Describe and explain.

Sources: Adapted from "Progressive Discipline," HR Council, accessed March 28, 2018, http://hrcouncil.ca/hr-toolkit/keeping-people-discipline.cfm#_secA2; "Progressive Discipline," go2HR, accessed March 25, 2018, www.go2hr.ca/articles/progressive-discipline; Jeffrey R. Smith, "Misconduct or Miscommunication?," *Canadian HR Reporter*, September 16, 2014, March 25, 2018, www.hrreporter.com/columnist/employment-law/archive/2014/09/16/misconduct-or-miscommunication; and Brian Kreissl, "Termination Should Never Be a Forgone Conclusion," *Canadian HR Reporter*, February 28, 2017, accessed March 26, 2018, www.hrreporter.com/columnist/hr-policies-practices/archive/2017/02/28/termination-should-never-be-a-foregone-conclusion.

Positive Discipline

Although progressive discipline is the most popular approach to correcting employee misconduct, some managers have questioned its logic. They have noted that it has certain flaws, such as being confrontational, which can create a situation that the employee reacts against. For these reasons, some organizations are using an approach called **positive discipline**. Positive discipline is based on the idea that employees are more likely to change the behaviour and/or performance when they participate and assume responsibility.[38]

Such an approach to discipline involves and motivates employees to change once they understand the consequences and accept responsibility. One of the more important features of positive discipline is to provide constructive criticism and encourage problem solving to resolve incidents of concern regarding the employee's performance and/or behaviour.[39] The approach focuses on the early correction of issues by ensuring that the employee fully understands what is expected and is provided with information regarding how the situation is impacting others.[40] Management imposes nothing; all solutions and affirmations are jointly reached. Although positive discipline appears similar to progressive discipline, its emphasis is on giving employees reminders rather than reprimands as a way to improve performance. Figure 9.4 illustrates the procedure for implementing the 3-step positive discipline procedure.

Positive discipline

Approach to discipline in which the employee assumes responsibility for changing behaviour and/or performance

Compiling a Disciplinary Record

In applying either progressive or positive discipline, it is important for managers to maintain complete records of each step of the procedure. When employees fail to meet the obligation of a disciplinary step, they should be given a warning, and their manager should document the warning. A copy of this warning is usually put in the employee's personnel file. After an established period—frequently 6 months—the warning is usually removed, provided that it has served its purpose; otherwise, it remains in the file to serve as evidence should a more severe penalty become necessary.

An employee's personnel file contains the employee's complete work history. It serves as a basis for determining and supporting disciplinary action and for evaluating the organization's disciplinary policies and procedures. Maintenance of proper records also provides management with valuable information about the soundness of the organization's policies

FIGURE 9.4   Positive Discipline Procedures

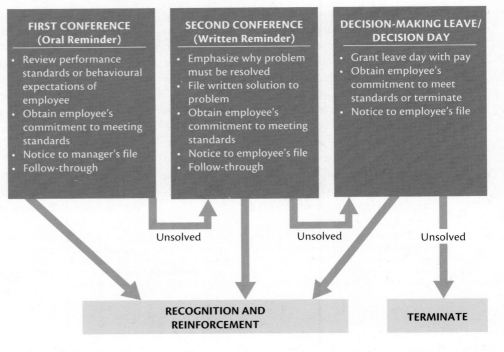

and procedures. Those rules that are violated most frequently should get particular attention because the need for them might no longer exist, or some change might be required to facilitate their enforcement. If the rule is shown to have little or no value, it should be revised or rescinded. Otherwise, employees are likely to feel they are being restricted unnecessarily.

Documentation of Concerns Regarding an Employee

"I don't know how to do this." "I didn't know this was part of my job." "I don't think anything will change." Managers make these statements as excuses when there has been no documentation of concerns about an employee's performance and/or behaviour. Often the frequent reason good documentation hasn't occurred, however, is that managers have no idea what constitutes good documentation. Unfortunately, the failure of managers to record employee misconduct accurately can result in the reversal of any subsequent disciplinary action. Written records are key in discipline.[41] Appropriate documentation needs to include the following:

1. Who is the employee? (name of employee and job title)
2. Who else is involved? (names of any witnesses or other employees)
3. When did the situation occur? (where it happened, time, date)
4. What occurred? Why is it an issue? (record of facts)
5. What was expected? (identification of which policies were breached, including code of conduct)
6. What was the impact on others? (information about the consequences)
7. What needs to change? (information about what must be done and when)
8. Has this happened before? (information about any previous conversations with the employee)
9. What happens if there is no improvement? (list of what the consequences will be if not resolved)[42]

It is critical that managers at all levels understand the guidelines for appropriate discipline, including the need for appropriate documentation.

The decision to terminate employment has consequences for both the employee and the organization and needs to be done thoughtfully.

Grounds for Termination

No matter how helpful and positive a manager is with an employee who is not abiding by the organization's policies and expectations or doesn't fit into the organizational culture, there may come a time when the employee must be terminated (dismissed). This is a decision that has serious impacts for both the employee and the organization and needs to be considered fairly and thoughtfully. Consider Ethics in HRM 9.2 about terminating an employee with a drug dependence.

ETHICS IN HRM 9.2   BUT WHAT ABOUT ACCOMMODATION?

In Chapter 2, there was a section on accommodation and the need for employers to potentially change certain aspects of the work environment to accommodate an individual to ensure that there is no discrimination. For example, a person may request to have the starting time changed so that the employee (a single parent) can pick up their child before the daycare closes. There was also information on accommodating those with disabilities.

So how can an employer terminate someone if the person has a disability? Isn't that discrimination? The Supreme Court of Canada determined that there might be a situation where a person with a disability could be terminated and there is no issue of discrimination.

The facts of the case concern a person with a drug addiction working as a heavy equipment operator in Alberta. The work environment is very safety sensitive and, as such, has a policy stating that employees are to inform the employer of any dependence or addiction issues. By doing so, the company offers employees treatment; the policy said that if the employee didn't disclose and subsequently had a drug-related accident, that person could be terminated.

The employee had an accident with a loader and subsequently tested positive for drugs. After the accident, the employee indicated that he thought he had a drug dependence. He stated that although he had signed

continued

the policy and understood the consequences, he didn't think there was a drug problem until after the safety-related accident. The union argued that the person was in denial; therefore, termination was not appropriate. The union grieved the termination on the basis that the person was being discriminated against and that accommodation was the more appropriate action.

Eventually, the case was heard by the Alberta Human Rights Tribunal, which concluded that the person was terminated for breach of the policy, not because of any drug dependence. The other higher courts in Alberta concluded the same thing prior to the case going to the Supreme Court. In all the decisions, the courts indicated that the onus was on the employee to disclose the drug dependence so that appropriate interventions could be taken to ensure safety in the workplace at all times.

CRITICAL THINKING QUESTIONS:

1. What is your perspective on the termination?
2. What would have happened if the employer had only suspended the employee and not terminated him?

Sources: Adapted from Sarah Dobson, "Supreme Court Confirms Employers Can Terminate Workers with Disabilities," *Canadian HR Reporter*, August 7, 2017, 1; Cristin Schmitz, "SCC Okays Zero Tolerance Drug Policy for Safety-Sensitive Workplaces," *The Lawyer's Daily*, June 15, 2017, accessed April 2, 2018, www .thelawyersdaily.ca/articles/3989/scc-okays-zero-tolerance-drug-policy-for-safety-sensitive-workplaces; Erin Brandt, "Safety and Accommodation: *Stewart v. Elk Valley Coal*," September 13, 2017, accessed April 2, 2018, https://kentemploymentlaw.com/2017/stewart-balancing-collective-individual-rights; and *Stewart v. Elk Valley Coal Corp.*, 2017 SCC 30, [2017] 1 S.C.R. 591.

Wrongful Dismissal

When an employer terminates an employee for not performing as expected or not following the company's policies, this is called dismissal for "just cause." To do this, the employer must document and prove serious misconduct or incompetence on the part of the employee. In recent years, a growing number of employees have sued their former employers for **wrongful dismissal**, claiming the termination was "without just or sufficient cause," implying a lack of fair treatment by management or insufficient reasons for the termination. Termination for cause also expects that the employee had been informed of this prior to termination and had an opportunity to change the behaviour or improve the performance. This means that a termination resulting from a job redefinition or redesign, downsizing, restructuring, or a lack of organizational fit is not just cause. However, poor performance, poor interpersonal relationships, and technical incompetence might be just cause if the employee had been informed of expectations and had been given a chance to improve but failed to conform. Figure 9.5 lists some "just cause" reasons.

Many managers are faced with having to terminate someone when there are sufficient and legitimate grounds for doing so. Some companies may suggest that just cause includes the organization's financial difficulties. It is important for managers to know that the

> **Wrongful dismissal**
>
> Terminating an employee's employment without just cause

FIGURE 9.5   Sample "Just Cause" Reasons

- Excessive lateness or absenteeism.
- Theft from the company.
- Improper or inappropriate conduct, such as fighting with a coworker.
- Continued and repeated failure to meet performance standards.
- Bullying and harassment.
- Continued workplace safety violations.
- Conflict of interest.
- Violence.

Depending on the seriousness of the wrongdoing, the individual may be terminated immediately, bypassing the steps of progressive discipline. For example, a hotel concierge who makes threatening statements to a guest could be terminated right away.

economic hardship of the company is not a justifiable reason to terminate someone's employment. HRM and the Law 9.1 gives 2 examples of wrongful-dismissal cases.

Managers must be able to document that any performance problems have been brought to the attention of the employee and that sufficient time, training, and assistance have been given to improve the weak performance. If the organization has an HR professional, the manager needs to work closely with the HR person to ensure that the appropriate type of documentation occurs. Other tips to prevent a challenge by a terminated employee are discussed later in the chapter.

If an employee termination is to be upheld for just cause, what constitutes fair employee treatment and valid reasons? This question is not easily answered, but standards governing just-cause dismissal have evolved from the field of labour arbitration. These standards are applied by arbitrators in dismissal cases to determine whether management had just cause. These guidelines are normally set forth in the form of questions, as provided in Toolkit 9.4. For example, before dismissing an employee, did the manager warn the person of possible

HRM AND **THE LAW** 9.1 — THE COURTS AND EMPLOYEE TERMINATIONS

Not all employment terminations are challenged by those terminated, and the ones that are always make interesting reading. As has often been mentioned before, whether or not a termination is upheld "all depends."

A case in New Brunswick involved the termination of a correctional officer for violating the employer's standard of professional conduct and its code of ethics. The employee, covered under the terms of a collective agreement, had been employed by the province for over 12 years and had never been disciplined, although the employee was exposed to any number of difficult situations, including inmates who harmed themselves. The person left and moved to the Correctional Service of Canada (CSC), where a situation that required force caused the employee anxiety and sleeplessness. The person did not seek treatment and began calling in sick. The CSC told the employee to bring in doctor's notes for the absences and was also referred to the EAP services. The employee made a self-diagnosis of PTSD and started using cannabis to help the symptoms. Plants were grown on a neighbour's property without the permission of the neighbour. Eventually, the police found the grow-op, plus several weapons on the property, and arrested the employee. The situation became very public, and the employee refused to cooperate with police. The CSC conducted its own investigation and, when the employee was uncooperative, decided to terminate the employment. The dismissal was grieved on the basis that the employee had PTSD and needed to be accommodated. The arbitrator determined that although the person had had a long career in corrections, the person's arrest for drugs and firearms was a serious issue as the employee dealt with people with similar charges. Such a role required the utmost level of trust and responsibility, which the employee violated. The dismissal was upheld.

Another case in Alberta had the opposite outcome. The courts determined that the employee had been wrongfully dismissed for non-performance. The employee was a safety training officer for a heavy truck parts and service vendor, responsible for managing safety requirements and maintaining its Fleet Brake certification of recognition. This certificate provided credibility for the company as a safety leader and a discount on workers' compensation premiums. After being employed for 3 years, the employee developed an autoimmune disease, which was discussed and accommodated by the employer. The employer also provided another employee to assist as the employee recovered from treatment. After several months, the employee's manager left, and the company opened several branches, which increased the workload of the safety training officer. The increased workload impacted the employee's recovery, and the assistant had to take on more work. Eventually, the company instructed the employee to fire the assistant; the employee disagreed as the assistant was vital to completing the various safety audits in progress.

Sources: Adapted from Jeffrey Smith, "Correctional Officer's Drug Bust Gives Employer Just Cause for Dismissal," *Canadian HR Reporter*, August 7, 2017, 5; and Jeffrey Smith, "Overworked, Sick Employee in Alberta Wrongfully Dismissed for Not Doing Job," *Canadian HR Reporter*, May 1, 2017, 5.

TOOLKIT 9.4   GUIDELINES FOR TERMINATION WITH CAUSE

1. Did the employee understand what was expected, and was the employee's situation considered independently of others?
2. How serious were the circumstances such that termination is the appropriate discipline?
3. Was the employee given sufficient time to improve and reach the standard of performance and/or behaviour?
4. Did the organization conduct an investigation?
5. Was the employee warned if unacceptable performance and/or behaviour continued?
6. Did the employer consistently apply standards to others?
7. Was termination the appropriate consequence?
8. Can the employer prove the employee's unacceptable performance and/or behaviour?

Sources: Adapted from "Fact Sheet," Employment Standards, Government of Manitoba, accessed March 27, 2018, www.gov.mb.ca/labour/standards/doc.just_cause,zfactsheet.html#q1802; Phil White, "Termination for Cause in Ontario: Overview," *Employment Law 101*, accessed March 27, 2018, http://employmentlaw101.ca/01-overview-termination-for-cause; and Karen Zvulony, "What Is Just Cause for Dismissal," Zvulony & Company, accessed March 27, 2018, https://zvulony.ca/2010/articles/employment-law/what-is-just-cause.

disciplinary action in the past? A "no" answer to any of these questions generally means that just cause was not established and that management's decision to terminate was arbitrary, capricious, or discriminatory. These guidelines are being applied not only by arbitrators in dismissal cases but also by judges in wrongful-dismissal suits.

Even when guidelines are used, the employer might not be able to prove just cause. For example, a senior manager at Walmart was terminated in 2010, but a final decision did not occur until the Ontario Superior Court in late 2017 determined that not only was the employee wrongfully dismissed, but also that "Walmart's conduct was misleading at best, and dishonest at worst, in the way [the employee] was treated. It was not just insensitive, it was mean." The court ordered Walmart to pay the individual $750,000 in moral and punitive damages—one of the largest awards in Canada.[43] Employers sometimes learn lessons the hard way: terminations are expected to be done with respect.

Constructive Dismissal

Constructive dismissal
Changing an employee's working conditions such that compensation, status, or prestige is reduced

Another type of dismissal is **constructive dismissal**, which occurs when an employer changes an employee's working conditions such that compensation, status, or prestige is reduced. Although employers have the right to make changes to employment conditions, there is an expectation that the employer provide appropriate notice. Even if the employee agrees to the changed conditions (the only other option might be unemployment) or resigns, the court may consider the employee to have been dismissed.[44]

To illustrate the concept and its relationship to wrongful dismissal, for some time the courts expected employees to return to work and undertake the work that fit "constructive dismissal" in order to minimize the employee's risk of not being able to sue for wrongful dismissal. Specifically, an employee had worked for the same employer for 38 years and was the vice president of operations. The company reorganized and moved the employee into the role of purchasing manager. The employee believed they had been constructively dismissed, quit, and then sued for wrongful dismissal. The lower court agreed that the person had been constructively dismissed. However, at the Ontario Court of Appeal, an issue arose as to whether the person would have been at work to minimize any damages. The appeal court upheld the lower court's decision: since the employee had not been asked to return to the demotion, there was no requirement that the employee go back to work to establish a claim.[45]

To access the latest information on constructive dismissals, Carswell's *The Wrongful Dismissal Handbook* is a helpful resource.

In a non-union setting, employers can give notice of future changes in compensation (wages and benefits), working hours, location, and other similar items as long as they provide notice equivalent to that given for dismissal. For example, if the company wished to reduce the amount of paid sick leave, it could do so with sufficient notice.

Terminating Employees

Since each discipline situation needs to be considered on its own, if an employee is to be terminated, the manager needs to be aware of how that individual will react. It is important that the employer handle the termination sensitively, recognizing the upheaval that may occur with the employee. The employer needs to be tactful and truthful regarding the reasons behind the termination.

This can also be a stressful situation for the manager, and it would be important and helpful for the manager to receive as much coaching as possible on what to say and how to say it. It is a good idea for managers to practise what they are going to say to make the termination as smooth as possible. Here are some helpful hints:

1. Hold the meeting as early in the week as possible and in a neutral meeting place.
2. Have the meeting in a private, neutral location.
3. Have the employee sit down so that you can quickly start the meeting and inform the employee directly of the termination.
4. Be open, honest, and direct; do not debate the decision.
5. Conduct the meeting calmly and be brief.
6. Take notes of the meeting.
7. Keep personal feelings out of the conversation; be considerate and polite.
8. Provide information about the final pay cheque, including any benefits coverage.
9. Inform the employee how references will be handled.
10. If the employee has any company property, ensure that arrangements are made for the return and for the employee to remove all personal items.

The prudent manager will also have determined, prior to the termination decision, that the dismissal does not violate any legal rights the employee may have.

Finally, when terminated employees are escorted off the premises, the removal must not serve to humiliate the employee. Managers should not give peers the impression that the terminated employee was dishonest or untrustworthy. Furthermore, managers are advised never to discuss the discharge with other employees, customers, or any other individual.

Providing Career Transition Assistance

Employers often use career transition or outplacement services to assist employees who are being dismissed. Assistance is especially likely to be provided for employees of long tenure. Although terminations do not have the negative stigma they once did, they are still traumatic for the employee.

Not just the usual organizations we think of provide help. For example, with the return of Canadian military staff who might have been deployed to a number of different countries, career transition services are being offered to veterans to help them secure work in an evolving economic environment.[46] Furthermore, educational institutions such as British Columbia Institute of Technology have programs that help advance their careers once they've returned to civilian life.[47]

Managers cite the following reasons for providing career transition services: concern for the well-being of the employees, protection against potential lawsuits, and the psychological effect on remaining employees. Career transition professionals assist employees being terminated by reducing their anger and grief and helping them regain self-confidence as they begin searching in earnest for a new job. Since many terminated workers have been out of the job market for some time, they may lack the knowledge and skills needed to look for a

People going through a career transition are encouraged to learn and/or upgrade their skills.

new job. Career transition specialists can coach them in how to develop contacts, probe for job openings through systematic letter and telephone campaigns, and handle employment interviews and salary negotiations.

The Results of Inaction

Failure to act implies that the performance or behaviour of the employee concerned is acceptable. If disciplinary action is eventually taken, the delay will make it more difficult to justify the action, if appealed. In defending against such an appeal, the employer is likely to be asked why an employee who had not been performing or behaving satisfactorily was kept on the payroll. An even more probing question might be "Why did that employee continue to receive pay adjustments if there was a question about the performance?"

Such contradictions in practice can only aid employees in successfully challenging management's corrective actions. Unfortunately, some managers try to build a case to justify their corrective actions only after they have decided that a particular employee should be dismissed. The following are common reasons given by managers for their failure to impose a disciplinary penalty:

1. The manager had failed to document earlier actions, so no record existed on which to base subsequent disciplinary action.
2. Managers believed they would receive little or no support from higher management for the disciplinary action.
3. The manager was uncertain of the facts underlying the situation requiring disciplinary action.
4. Failure by the manager to discipline employees in the past for a certain infraction caused the manager to forgo current disciplinary action in order to appear consistent.
5. The manager wanted to be seen as a likable person.

It is critical to remember that any grounds for discipline must be well documented. Failure to do so can result in the disciplinary action being invalid.

APPEALING DISCIPLINARY ACTIONS

With growing frequency, organizations are taking steps to protect employees from arbitrary and inequitable treatment by their managers. A particular emphasis is put on creating a climate in which employees are assured that they can voice their dissatisfaction with their superiors without fear of reprisal. This safeguard can be provided through the implementation of a formal procedure for appealing disciplinary actions.

Although employees covered by a collective agreement have a grievance procedure to use if there is a desire to appeal any disciplinary action, most non-unionized staff do not. However, more and more employers are using a number of **alternative dispute-resolution (ADR)** processes to enable non-unionized employees to challenge an employer's disciplinary decision. The employer's interest stems from the desire to meet employees' expectations for fair treatment in the workplace while guaranteeing them due process—in the hope of minimizing discrimination claims or wrongful-dismissal suits. The primary purpose of any dispute-resolution process is to keep the dispute out of the judicial (court) system.[48]

Some organizations prefer these procedures as an avenue for upward communication for employees and as a way to gauge the mood of the workforce. Others view these systems as a way to resolve minor problems before they mushroom into major issues, thus leading to improved employee morale and productivity.

The typical appeal procedures described in this chapter are negotiation, mediation, an ombudsperson, and arbitration. Helpful resources for additional information on ADR can be found at the ADR Institute of Canada.

> **LO6**
> Identify the different types of alternative dispute-resolution procedures.

> **Alternative dispute-resolution (ADR)**
> Term applied to different types of employee complaint or dispute-resolution processes

Negotiation

Most people think of negotiation in relation to unions and collective bargaining. However, in its simplest meaning, **negotiation** is people getting together to discuss an issue or problem and reaching a mutual agreement on the solution.

If you think about it, we all "negotiate" every day of our lives, whether it is with a friend, a parent, a partner, or a stranger. When people disagree, they will first attempt to reach a compromise themselves. For negotiations to be successful in resolving an issue, the individuals involved need to be prepared for the discussion, need to clarify what it is they're seeking, be positive, reach an agreement, and then implement the decision.[49] For example, if you are working on a group project, you may negotiate what part of the project you are working on.

> **Negotiation**
> People sorting out a problem between themselves

Mediation

Mediation is fast becoming a popular way to resolve employee complaints and labour disputes involving unions. The essence of mediation is facilitating face-to-face meetings so that the employee and the manager can reach an agreement. The people involved will look for someone who is impartial to help them with the discussions between themselves. The mediator can frequently ease any tensions or misunderstandings and help them get to an agreement. Mediation is popular as it helps the individuals (or organizations) reach a conclusion that is satisfactory to all involved.[50]

Conciliation is another form of mediation. It is used in labour relations, primarily in disputes involving governments as the employer or with federally regulated employers. For example, through the Federal Mediation and Conciliation Service offered by the federal government, the greatest number of disputes is in the road transportation sector (primarily trucking), and almost one-half of the disputes were settled through conciliation.[51]

> **Mediation**
> The use of an impartial third party to help facilitate a resolution to employment disputes

Ombudsperson

Ombudsperson
Person who helps in the resolution of a workplace issue

Someone who has been designated to help with the investigation and resolution of a workplace issue is referred to as an **ombudsperson**. Employers make use of this type of dispute-resolution process to quickly and efficiently deal with workplace conflicts. The person must be impartial and keep information confidential in order to help resolve the dispute.[52] In addition, such a system also allows the ombudsperson to make recommendations to improve workplace practices.[53]

Arbitration

There are times an employer may use arbitration to solve workplace disputes. Such a process tends to be a final and binding decision and is outside the court system. Arbitration can save court costs and avoid time delays and unfavourable publicity. Arbitration is fully explained in Chapter 10.

For trends in the areas covered in this chapter, see Emerging Trends 9.1.

EMERGING TRENDS 9.1

1. ***Increased attention to privacy issues.*** Companies have legitimate rights to protect their products and their employees through monitoring. However, recent incidents have highlighted the need to ensure that both customer and employee information is protected from inappropriate access and use. Furthermore, concerns are being raised about accessing one's social media as part of a screening step when considering someone for employment. As pilot projects using embedded technology gain acceptance, employers will need to be vigilant to ensure that employee information is kept private.

2. ***Employers making more use of alternative dispute resolutions.*** With the negative consequences of workplace conflicts and the increasing costs of litigation, employers are making more use of mediation to help resolve conflicts. Likewise, employers are reexamining their discipline approaches.

3. ***Better use of social media.*** Not too many years ago, organizations were creating very restrictive practices for the use of Internet access on work time. Now, as many organizations use the Internet as part of business information retrieval, companies have decided that social media sites might provide helpful contacts

and that the benefits can outweigh the risks of people wasting time. Social media is also being used to help bridge relationships between boomers and millennials in the workplace. Think about the backlash that occurred in 2018 regarding the use of personal information at Facebook, Amazon, and other companies with a large presence on the Internet.

4. ***Expectation of higher standards of workplace behaviour.*** With the heightened awareness of workplace issues such as sexual harassment, employers are being more diligent regarding holding all employees to a higher standard of behaviour. This includes everything from employees being fired for breaches of confidence to bullying.

5. ***More attention to after-work behaviour.*** Because of situations such as those discussed earlier involving the residential care staff and firefighters, more employers are willing to discipline employees, including termination, for off-duty behaviour that is considered inappropriate. Other real-life examples include a person working at a retail clothier who posted derogatory comments on Facebook and was fired and 2 individuals in Québec schools terminated for having been porn stars when they were younger.

Sources: Adapted from John Dujay, "Concerns Raised Over Tracking of Migrant Workers in British Columbia," *Canadian HR Reporter*, September 4, 2017, 10; Marcel Vander Wier, "Are Embedded Microchips the Future?," *Canadian HR Reporter*, September 4, 2017, 9; Julia Fioretti, "Facebook to Introduce New Privacy Controls in Wake of Data Scandal," *The Globe and Mail*, March 28, 2018, accessed March 29, 2018, www.theglobeandmail.com/business/article-facebook-to-introduce-new-privacy-controls-in-wake-of-data-scandal; Eric Atkins, "Canadian Pacific Overhauls Firing Policy," March 25, 2017, B1; Matthew Larsen, "'I Shouldn't Be Telling You This, But...': Court Rules Sharing Confidential Information Is Just Cause for Termination," *The HR Space*, March 23, 2018; Emily Douglas, "Staff Fired at Edmonton Prison Over Alleged Bullying," *HRD Canada*, January 10, 2018, accessed March 29, 2018, www.hrmonline.ca/hr-news/staff-fired-at-edmonton-prison-over-alleged-bullying-236057.aspx; "Managing a Multigenerational Workforce," *Canadian HR Reporter*, April 6, 2015, accessed March 29, 2018, www.hrreporter.com/articleview/23960-managing-a-multigenerational-workforce-toughest-hr-question; and "5 Cases of People Who Lost Jobs Over Off-Hours Conduct," *City News*, May 14, 2015, accessed March 29, 2018, http://toronto.citynews.ca/2015/05/13/five-cases-of-people-who-lost-their-jobs-over-off-hours-conduct.

LEARNING OUTCOMES SUMMARY

1. Describe statutory rights, contractual rights, due process, and the legal implications of those rights.
   - *Statutory rights derive from legislation, such as human rights legislation*
   - *Contractual rights are derived from contracts, such as an employment contract*
   - *Due process is the employee's right to be heard through a complaint process*
   - *Legal implications flow from how the employee is treated*

2. Identify the job expectancy rights of employees.
   - *Fair and equitable treatment*
   - *A workplace that is safe and drug-free*
   - *Reasonable treatment regarding privacy*
   - *Access to one's own personnel files*
   - *Not being subject to discipline for off-duty behaviour*
   - *Being notified of any plant closings*

3. Explain the process of establishing disciplinary practices, including the proper implementation of organizational rules.
   - *The primary purpose of having disciplinary procedures is to prevent or correct discipline problems*
   - *Failure to take disciplinary action serves only to aggravate a problem that eventually must be resolved*
   - *Organizations need to clearly outline rules and expectations regarding performance and behaviour*

4. Discuss the meaning of discipline and how to investigate a disciplinary problem.
   - *Discipline is action that results in desirable conduct or performance*
   - *If a problem occurs, the manager needs to determine when the situation occurred and to have a full discussion with the employee to get the employee's view of the situation*

5. Outline the differences between progressive and positive discipline.
   - *Progressive discipline is the application of corrective measures by increasing degrees*
   - *Progressive discipline is designed to motivate an employee to correct misconduct*
   - *Positive discipline is based on the concept that the employee must assume responsibility for personal conduct and job performance*
   - *Positive discipline requires a cooperative environment for joint discussion and problem solving between the manager and the employee*

6. Identify the different types of alternative dispute-resolution processes.
   - *Negotiation*
   - *Mediation*
   - *Ombudsperson*
   - *Arbitration*

KEY TERMS

alternative dispute-resolution (ADR) 311
constructive dismissal 308
contractual rights 287
discipline 298
due process 288
employee rights 285
mediation 311

negotiation 311
ombudsperson 312
positive discipline 303
progressive discipline 301
statutory rights 286
wrongful dismissal 306

HRM CLOSE-UP APPLICATION

1. What does John Jacak in the HRM Close-up say are the most important aspects in a privacy policy?
2. Jacak states that respect is the "bedrock" to employee relations practices. What does this mean?
3. According to Jacak, what does Nutrien's privacy policy provide to employees?
4. What is Nutrien's approach to handling personal information?

CRITICAL THINKING QUESTIONS

1. Suki frequently posts tweets about her unhappiness at work and makes derogatory comments about her manager. Does her employer have the right to control what she tweets? Why? What might the employer do?
2. Pardeep works as a millwright in a sawmill. The company is considering redesigning its discipline procedures to be oriented toward positive discipline. What would be the advantages and disadvantages of this change? What would the company want to include in the new procedure?
3. You were recently promoted to a management position. One of your first tasks is to discipline one of your staff for an ongoing tardiness problem. What information do you need prior to the discipline meeting, and how would you conduct the meeting?
4. Your professor is dealing with a case where a student was alleged to have cheated on the final exam. Would documentation be important? If so, what type of documentation would be necessary?

BUILDING YOUR SKILLS

1. Individually read the following scenarios. Then in groups of 4 to 5 students, determine if the situations are or are not fair. Explain your reasons. Be prepared to share your information with the rest of the class.
   A. Jane was using the company's access to the Internet to locate childcare facilities in her local community. Her manager observed this and then sought confirmation from the IT unit. Jane was given a written reprimand. Meanwhile, Kabir used his desk telephone to do his personal banking and bill paying. Kabir was not reprimanded.
   B. Sonita spent her lunch hour at the gym; she is following a strenuous workout program as she prepares for a triathlon event in the next several weeks. Meanwhile, Wang met his friends for lunch, sharing several beers at the local pub. Both employees felt fatigued in the afternoon, and their work performance decreased, which was noted by their manager. Wang was asked to meet with his manager to review performance expectations and received a verbal warning. Sonita did not.
2. Working in groups of 3 or 4, discuss the following questions:
   A. What would you do if you discovered that your employer was regularly following your tweets?
   B. Do you object to monitoring of employees? Why or why not?
   C. Would you object to being monitored? Why or why not?
3. Access the following sites, which discuss employee privacy rights in the workplace. Prepare a 1- to 2-page report summarizing what each site has to offer. Indicate if there are any areas of the site that might be more helpful to an employee rather than an employer.
   - www.priv.gc.ca
   - www.epic.org
   - https://cippic.ca/en/FAQ/workplace_privacy
4. Conduct your own Internet search, using any search engine, under the heading of "employee discipline." Share with your classmates what you learned and provide at least 2 URLs you found helpful.

CASE STUDY 1

But It's My Privacy!

There are many sides to the issue of workplace privacy. The employee side holds that employees have the right to privacy, that employers should respect and trust their employees, and that any issues regarding performance or conduct can be observed by the manager. The employer side holds that the workplace is a public environment; that the organization is responsible for the actions of its employees and for their interactions with clients, visitors, and other employees; and that it has the right to safeguard its business.

Many companies monitor email, voice mail, and employee computer use. Most employee monitoring is perfectly legal. The general legal view is that any equipment (computers, telephones, etc.) is company property and that employees should not be using them for personal reasons. Companies can trace deleted emails and voice mails, special software can track Internet use, and wireless video cameras are small enough to look like pagers. More and more employees are using technology, and this makes it even easier to monitor their work. Organizations monitor employees in order to deter crime, protect business secrets, and ensure a safe and supportive work environment.

A major reason for monitoring is to ensure that employees are actually working. Most employees waste at least a little time each day, however innocently. One company used a software tracking system to identify a group of employees who were selling Amway products from work. Another manager watched in horror as one of his top employees was led away by police, who had tracked his illegal activity (child pornography) through his email address, which contained the company name.

Some employers have abused their right to monitor employees—for example, by videotaping them in washrooms or hiring investigators to follow them. Another problem is the inferential misuse of the information obtained. For example, an employee may be visiting Internet sites on suicide, HIV, or substance dependence while doing research for a college paper. Employers may falsely infer from this that these issues personally affect the individual.

Now there is the popularity of social media sites such as Facebook, Twitter, and YouTube. Employers will sometimes monitor employees as they post information to see what is being communicated about the company or whether the employee is doing something that may create issues for the company. In addition, hiring managers may start searching social media sites when considering reviewing resumés to see what the applicant is posting.

Questions:

1. Employers usually do not have policies on using the telephone at work. Why, then, do employers need to develop policies on monitoring the use of email, the Internet, social media, and other forms of technology?
2. Few studies have considered the impact of monitoring on employee behaviour. Does it reduce crime and make workplaces safer and more productive? Or does it increase stress and result in an adversarial relationship? What do you think and why?
3. If an employer allows you to use your own smartphone at work for business purposes, should the employer be allowed to monitor emails? Why or why not?

CASE STUDY 2

Can't the Absence Be Ignored?

Most organizations have policies and practices regarding absence from the workplace. These same organizations usually track and monitor attendance and will take action when absence appears to be excessive. But what does the company do if a superior performer is frequently absent?

Caleb has been with a sales organization for about 10 years and has consistently met and exceeded his objectives each year. The company feels its success and growth have been accomplished partly through Caleb's good work.

Over the past several months, Caleb's manager, Anjana, has noticed that the times Caleb is late or absent have been increasing. The manager asked that an analysis be done of Caleb's attendance over the previous 12 months and discovered a consistent pattern of Caleb being absent on either a Friday or a Monday every few weeks. This information only provided full-day absences and didn't identify the number of times he was late. Anjana only had her anecdotal memories of the tardiness. With his superior performance, she was reluctant to bring it up with him.

After several months, other employees spoke to Anjana about Caleb's absences and the increased pressure it was putting on them to handle his clients. Anjana knew she had to do something as tensions in the work environment were increasing.

When Anjana met with Caleb about it, he immediately became defensive and explained that he wasn't absent very often, and even if he was, that shouldn't matter given his superior performance. Anjana decided it was important to clarify expectations about his attendance even with superior performance. Caleb wasn't happy but said he did understand and would improve.

However, the attendance didn't change, and Anjana had another discussion with him. She warned Caleb that any further patterns of absenteeism would result in his termination.

Unfortunately, Caleb's pattern of absences continued and, after another 3 months of repeated warnings, Anjana terminated him.

Questions:

1. Do you think Anjana was correct in deciding to terminate Caleb when she did? Why or why not?
2. Was there something else Anjana could have done? If so, what?
3. If you were Anjana, what would you have done?

NOTES AND REFERENCES

1. Adelle Chua, "Can You Make Your Workers Wear Surveillance Cameras," *HRD Canada*, November 13, 2017, accessed March 5, 2018, https://www.hrmonline.ca/hr-law/industrial-relations/can-you-make-your-workers-wear-surveillance-cameras-233821.aspx.
2. "Offensive Material on Social Media Feeds," *Canadian HR Reporter*, December 11, 2017, accessed March 5, 2018, https://www.hrreporter.com/workplace-law/35408-offensive-material-on-social-media-feeds.
3. Jeffrey R. Smith, "A High Bar for Protecting the Protectors," *Canadian HR Reporter*, January 29, 2018, accessed March 8, 2018, https://www.hrreporter.com/columnist/employment-law/archive/2018/01/29/a-high-bar-for-protecting-the-protectors.
4. "Ontario Worker Sacked Over Confederate Flag," *HRD Canada*, August 22, 2017, accessed March 12, 2018, https://www.hrmonline.ca/hr-news/ontario-worker-sacked-over-confederate-flag-229793.aspx.
5. Sarah Dobson, "Alberta Employers Face New Leaves," *Canadian HR Reporter*, January 10, 2018, accessed March 12, 2018, https://www.hrreporter.com/compensation-and-benefits/35617-alberta-employers-face-new-leaves.
6. Government of Alberta, "Employment Standards Code Change," accessed March 12, 2018, https://www.alberta.ca/employment-standards-changes.aspx.
7. Jason Franson, "Court Rules in Favour of Suncor in Employee Drug Testing Fight," *The Globe and Mail*, September 27, 2017, accessed March 14, 2018, https://www.theglobeandmail.com/report-on-business/court-rules-in-favour-of-suncor-in-employee-drug-testing-fight/article36422538.
8. Jeffrey Smith, "27 Consecutive 1-Year Contracts Make Teacher Permanent Employee," *Canadian HR Reporter*, November 28, 2016, accessed

March 14, 2018, https://www.hrreporter.com/article/31813-27-consecutive-1-year-contracts-make-teacher-permanent-employee.

9. "Refusing to Collaborate in an Employer's Psychological Harassment Investigation Can Be Grounds for Dismissal," *The HR Space*, Fasken Martineau, March 24, 2015.

10. *Business Dictionary*, accessed March 16, 2018, http://www.businessdictionary.com/definition/due-process.html.

11. Government of Canada, Department of Justice, "About Canada's System of Justice," accessed March 16, 2018, http://www.justice.gc.ca/eng/csj-sjc/just.

12. Rebecca Gowan, "3 Things Employers Should Know About Substance Dependence," *Canadian HR Reporter*, May 1, 2017, 14.

13. Canadian Human Rights Commission, "Impaired at Work: A Guide to Accommodating Substance Dependence," September 2017, accessed March 18, 2018, http://www.chrc-ccdp.gc.ca/eng/content/impaired-work-guide-accommodating-substance-dependence.

14. Statistics Canada, "Heavy Drinking, 2015," accessed March 16, 2018, https://www.statcan.gc.ca/pub/82-625-x/2017001/article/14765-eng.htm.

15. Dr. Anita Teslak, "Benefits Trend: How To Help with Substance Abuse," *Benefits Canada*, January 16, 2015, accessed March 16, 2018, https://www.benefitscanada.com/benefits/health-wellness/benefits-trends-how-hr-can-play-a-role-in-mental-health-issues-61152; and Nadine Wentzell, "Dealing with Prescription Drug Abuse in the Workplace," *Canadian HR Reporter*, September 8, 2014, accessed March 16, 2018, https://www.hrreporter.com/articleview/22175-dealing-with-prescription-drug-abuse-in-the-workplace.

16. Ibid.

17. John Dujay, "Concerns Raised Over Tracking of Migrant Workers in British Columbia," *Canadian HR Reporter*, September 4, 2017, 10.

18. "5 Pioneer Manor Staff Fired after 'Inappropriate' Snapchats," *CBC News*, June 28, 2017, accessed March 19, 2018, http://www.cbc.ca/news/canada/sudbury/pioneer-manor-staff-fired-1.4181269.

19. FairWork Ombudsman, "Workplace Privacy," accessed March 19, 2018, https://www.fairwork.gov.au/about-us/policies-and-guides/best-practice-guides/workplace-privacy; Erin Kuzz, "When Is an Employee's Off-Duty Conduct a Work-Related Issue?," *Canadian Lawyer*, February 29, 2016, accessed March 19, 2018, https://www.canadianlawyermag.com/article/when-is-an-employees-off-duty-conduct-a-work-related-issue-3195; and Laura McQuillan, "Can You Punish Employees for Off-Duty Tweets?," *HRD Canada*, September 17, 2017, accessed March 19, 2018, https://www.hrmonline.ca/hr-general-news/can-you-punish-employees-for-offduty-tweets-230970.aspx#.

20. Sarah Dobson, "Health-Care Privacy Breaches Highlight Staff Challenges," *Canadian HR Reporter*, March 9, 2015, 1.

21. Office of the Privacy Commissioner of Canada, "Privacy and Social Networking in the Workplace," accessed March 19, 2018, https://www.priv.gc.ca/en/privacy-topics/privacy-at-work/02_05_d_41_sn.

22. Susan M. Heathfield, "Learn What Medical Info Is In Employee Personnel Files," *The Balanced*, March 6, 2018, accessed March 20, 2018, https://www.thebalance.com/medical-file-contents-1918186.

23. Society for Human Resource Management, "Social Media: What Are the Advantages and Disadvantages of Using Social Media in the Workplace? What Should We Include in a Policy?," March 19, 2018, accessed March 21, 2018, https://www.shrm.org/resourcesandtools/tools-and-samples/hr-qa/pages/socialnetworkingsitespolicy.aspx; and Heather R. Huhman, "Employees Are Using Social Media at Work—Make the Most of It," *Entrepreneur*, August 8, 2016, accessed March 21, 2018, https://www.entrepreneur.com/article/280251.

24. Emily Douglas, "Ask a Lawyer: Can You Fire an Employee for a Social Media Rant?," *HRD Canada*, March 18, 2018, accessed March 21, 2018, https://www.hrmonline.ca/features/ask-a-lawyer-can-you-fire-an-employee-for-a-social-media-rant-239097.aspx.

25. Office of the Privacy Commissioner of Canada, "Privacy in the Workplace," accessed March 21, 2018, https://www.priv.gc.ca/en/privacy-topics/privacy-at-work/02_05_d_17.

26. Laura McQuillan, "Can You Punish Employees for Off-Duty Tweets?"

27. Sarah Dobson, "Full Steam Ahead," *Canadian HR Reporter*, January 31, 2018, accessed March 23, 2018, https://www.hrreporter.com/workplace-law/35828-full-steam-ahead.

28. Ibid.

29. Ibid.

30. Henry Chu, "#MeToo's Worldwide Moment: Global Industry Follows Hollywood's Lead in Combating Harassment," *Variety*, December 13, 2017, accessed March 23, 2018, https://variety.com/2017/film/news/sexual-harassment-global-entertainment-companies-metoo-1202637963; and "300 Hollywood A-Listers Launch Campaign Against Sexual Harassment," *CBC News*, January 1, 2018, accessed March 23, 2018, http://www.cbc.ca/news/entertainment/times-up-movement-hollywood-campaign-harassment-1.4469366.

31. Sarah Dobson, "Supreme Court Confirms Employers Can Terminate Workers with Disabilities," *Canadian HR Reporter*, August 7, 2017, 1.

32. Ethan Spielman, "How to Properly Handle a Workplace Investigation," *Business News Daily*, January 31, 2018, accessed March 24, 2018, https://www.businessnewsdaily.com/10562-handle-workplace-investigation.html.

33. Laura McQuillan, "Ask a Lawyer: What's the Best Way to Deal with Worker Misconduct?," *HRD Canada*, October 25, 2017, accessed March 24, 2018, https://www.hrmonline.ca/hr-law/terminations/ask-a-lawyer-whats-the-best-way-to-deal-with-worker-misconduct-232942.aspx.

34. Susan M. Heathfield, "What Is Progressive Discipline," *The Balance*, November 1, 2017, accessed March 25, 2018, https://www.thebalance.com/what-progressive-discipline-1918092.

35. Jon Hyman, "Pull Over the Potty Police," *Workforce*, September 3, 2014, accessed March 25, 2018, http://www.workforce.com/2014/09/03/pull-over-the-potty-police.

36. Kellie Auld, "Handle with Care: The Impact of Workplaces Investigations," *PeopleTalk*, Summer 2015, 32–33.

37. Jeffrey Kadlic, "Employee Discipline & Discharge Best Practices," Evolution Capital Partners website, February 3, 2014, accessed March 25, 2018, https://evolutioncp.com/blog/entrepreneurship/employee-discipline-discharge-best-practices; and June Yi, "Six Best Practices for HR Documentation, January 21, 2016, accessed March 25, 2018, https://www.polsinelliatwork.com/blog/2016/1/21/six-best-practices-of-hr-documentation.

38. Readers interested in the pioneering work on positive discipline should see James R. Redeker, "Discipline, Part 1: Progressive Systems Work Only by Accident," *Personnel* 62, no. 10 (October 1985): 8–12; and James R. Redeker, "Discipline, Part 2: The Nonpunitive Approach Works by Design," *Personnel* 62, no. 11 (November 1985): 7–14. See also Alan W. Bryant, "Replacing Punitive Discipline with a Positive Approach," *Personnel Administrator* 29, no. 2 (February 1984): 79–87; and Chimezie A.B. Osigweh Yg and William R. Hutchison, "Positive Discipline," *Human Resource Management* 28, no. 3 (Fall 1989): 367–383.

39. Stan Mack, "What Is Positive Discipline in the Workplace?," *The Houston Chronicle*, accessed March 26, 2018, http://smallbusiness.chron.com/positive-discipline-workplace-20774.html.

40. Ibid.

41. HR Council for the Nonprofit Sector, "Keeping the Right People: Discipline," accessed March 26, 2018, http://hrcouncil.ca/hr-toolkit/keeping-people-discipline.cfm#top.

42. Ibid.

43. Sarah Dobson, "No Discounts for Walmart," *Canadian HR Reporter*, March 2018, 1.

44. Stuart Rudner, "Deconstructing Constructive Dismissal," *Canadian HR Reporter*, June 30, 2015, accessed March 27, 2018, https://www

.hrreporter.com/columnist/canadian-hr-law/archive/2015/06/30/deconstructing-constructive-dismissal; and Province of Ontario, "Constructive Dismissal," accessed March 27, 2018, https://www.ontario.ca/document/your-guide-employment-standards-act/termination-employment#section-2.

45. Ken Krupat, "20 Month Wrongful Dismissal Award for Employee Upheld," July 19, 2017, accessed March 26, 2018, http://joblaw.ca/tag/constructive-dismissal.

46. Veterans Affairs Canada, "Career Transition Services," accessed March 27, 2018, http://www.veterans.gc.ca/eng/services/transition/career.

47. British Columbia Institute of Technology, "Legion Military Skills Conversion Program," accessed March 27, 2018, https://www.bcit.ca/legion.

48. Government of Canada, Department of Justice, "Resolving Disputes—Think About Your Options," accessed March 28, 2018, http://www.justice.gc.ca/eng/rp-pr/csj-sjc/dprs-sprd/dr-rd/index.html#dispute_resolution.

49. Skills You Need, "What Is Negotiation?," accessed March 28, 2018, https://www.skillsyouneed.com/ips/negotiation.html.

50. "Resolving Disputes—Think About Your Options."

51. Employment and Social Development Canada, "Federal Mediation and Conciliation Service Review of Fiscal Year 2016–17," 2017, 3–4.

52. Parisa Nikfarjam, "The Rise of the Workplace Ombudsman," *Canadian HR Reporter*, July 10, 2015, accessed March 28, 2018, https://www.hrreporter.com/article/24840-the-rise-of-the-workplace-ombudsman.

53. Ibid.

10 Understanding Labour Relations and Collective Bargaining

LEARNING OUTCOMES

After studying this chapter, you should be able to

1 Explain the federal and provincial legislation that provides the framework for labour relations.

2 Cite the reasons employees join unions.

3 Outline the process by which unions organize employees and gain recognition as their bargaining agent.

4 Illustrate the functions labour unions perform at international, national, and local levels.

5 Describe the bargaining process and the bargaining goals and strategies of a union and an employer.

6 List the forms of bargaining power that a union and an employer may utilize to enforce their bargaining demands.

7 Identify the major provisions of a collective agreement, including the issue of management rights.

8 Describe a typical grievance process and explain the basis for arbitration awards.

OUTLINE

HRM CLOSE-UP

"Transparency, understanding, making sure that you're focused on not just the interests of the company, but the interests of all involved are key."

IN EARLY 2015, Jazz Aviation reached an 11-year agreement with its almost 1200 unionized pilots. In a field as ever-changing as the airline industry, a contract of that duration was practically unheard of, but it was merely the latest in a history of labour accomplishments by one of the largest regional airlines in the world.

Established in 2001 after Air Canada merged its 4 regional airlines into 1 single entity initially known as Air Canada Regional, the wholly owned subsidiary was renamed, rebranded, and unveiled as Air Canada Jazz the following year.

The procedure had been a long and complex one that had involved no fewer than 20 collective agreements with unions representing everyone from pilots to maintenance staff. One of those most heavily involved in the process was Colin Copp, now Jazz's president.

"I had the responsibility to merge all these carriers from a labour relations perspective," he explains. "One of the things we started to do back then was to really look at…building a relationship with the unions that would be supportive of some of their interests and needs."

Having attended Trinity Western University's aviation program and holding a pilot's licence, Copp had entered the airline industry as a flight dispatcher in 1989 and worked his way up to director of operations at AirBC. Although originally drawn by an interest in aviation, he soon found himself equally captivated by labour relations.

"Once I was in the business, what got me interested in labour relations and senior management were the challenges," Copp explains. "The need for change and how you get through change; how you manage change; how you execute change; how you strategize around change. That's what has driven me into the labour relations world and then from there into the executive world, where we're really dealing with trying to find solutions around large global problems that are typically always related in some way to employees."

Although many may think of aircraft as the backbone of any airline,

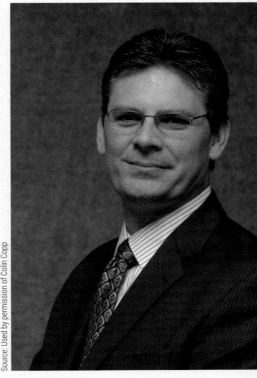

Source: Used by permission of Colin Copp

Colin Copp, President, Jazz Aviation LP

Copp quickly realized that the single biggest and most important asset was its people. "You really are dealing with a commodity product that's dependent on labour in all ways, so you're dependent on pilots, you're dependent on flight attendants, you're dependent on maintenance," he says.

"When you really look at it, all the airlines run basically the same type of business. There's very little difference except for employees and culture. Those are the 2 key differentiators that really make or break a business."

In 2006, Air Canada sold their Jazz assets, and the airline became an independent company trading on the Toronto Stock Exchange. Today, in addition to offering private charters and general services to other airline operators, Air Canada purchases all of Jazz's seat capacity, which is then operated under the name Air Canada Express.

"We have several masters," Copp explains of Jazz's structure. "We have Air Canada as a master; they're our customer. We have our unions, who are pretty much a key stakeholder for us, and as a subsidiary of our parent company, Chorus Aviation, we indirectly have a shareholder group that have [sic] a big say in things. So we're working with multiple stakeholders and … making sure that … it's important to understand their interests as well as our own in these things."

The historic agreement with the Air Line Pilots Association in January 2015 had not been accomplished overnight. Jazz and the pilots had spent 2 years discussing the plan for the company and the changes and challenges that lay ahead.

Once direct negotiations on the contract began, it had taken a further 2 months to reach a deal acceptable to both sides, but ultimately Copp attributes the completion of that agreement to understanding.

"Transparency, understanding, making sure that you're focused on not just the interests of the company, but the interests of all involved are key. Whoever the stakeholders are, you have to make sure you understand what's important to them. I would say that most of the success of the agreement can be attributed to the fact that the relationship was very strong and there was good understanding of what was important to both sides."

INTRODUCTION

What comes to your mind when someone mentions "union"? Does it suggest conflict and strikes, or does it suggest equality and that someone will look after you in relation to your employment? Many people feel that unions are necessary to counterbalance the power employers have, whereas others think that unions may have once served a purpose and are less relevant now.

Regardless of how people feel about them, unions have been an important force shaping organizational practices, legislation, and political thought in Canada since the mid-1800s. Consider Colin Copp's statements in the HRM Close-up. Some people might say that fears about unionization have helped employers become better at managing people. Today, unions remain of interest because of their influence on organizational productivity and competitiveness, the development of labour law, and HR policies and practices. Like business organizations themselves, unions are undergoing changes in both operation and philosophy. Unions grew out of the industrialization era and primarily were male dominated. Currently, it is more likely that the union member is a woman, working in a hospital or school. Likewise, there are fewer people employed in blue-collar jobs, which was a primary sector for unions.[1] Even though the rate of unionization continues to fall (from 38% in 1981 to 29% in 2014),[2] approximately 4.8 million people are unionized, or almost 32% of employees.[3] And with the continued shift in the workplace, as described in Chapter 1, new employees, such as millennials, want individual pay and rights, which can run contrary to the principles of any union.[4]

In spite of the long history of unions, the intricacies of labour relations are unfamiliar to many individuals. Therefore, this chapter describes government regulation of labour relations, the labour relations process, the reasons workers join labour organizations, the structure and leadership of labour unions, contemporary challenges to labour organizations, and the role a manager plays in labour relations.

Unions and other labour organizations can significantly affect the ability of managers to direct and control the various HR processes. For example, union seniority provisions in the labour contract may influence who is selected for job promotions or training programs. Pay rates may be determined through union negotiations, or unions may impose restrictions on management's employee evaluation methods. Therefore, it is essential that managers understand how unions operate and familiarize themselves with the growing body of laws governing labour relations. It is also important for the manager to understand how unionization affects the actions of the union and those of the HR professional.

THE LAWS GOVERNING LABOUR RELATIONS

Unions have a long history in North America, and the regulations governing labour relations have evolved over time. Initially, employers strongly opposed union growth, using court injunctions (e.g., court orders forbidding various union activities, such as picketing and strikes) and devices, such as the "yellow-dog contract"—an employers' anti-union tactic by which employees had to agree not to join a union while working for the employer's organization. Using strikebreakers, blacklisting employees (e.g., circulating the names of union supporters to other employers), and discriminating against those who favoured unionization were other anti-union tactics.

Today, the laws governing labour relations seek to create an environment in which both unions and employers can exercise their respective rights and responsibilities. Chapter 2 provided an overview of the various employment laws, including those governing labour relations. This chapter now looks at the laws in more detail.

Labour Relations Legislation

The first labour relations legislation, the *Trades Unions Act*, was passed by the federal Parliament in 1872. This act exempted unions from charges of criminal conspiracy, allowed them to pursue goals of collective bargaining without persecution, and gave them the ability to strike. Between 1872 and 1900, legislation to settle industrial disputes was enacted in a number of provinces, including Québec, Ontario, British Columbia, and Nova Scotia. Although these acts are no longer in effect, they did mark Canada's early recognition of the rights of unions.

Several different laws at the federal and provincial levels currently regulate labour relations. These laws make up a labour relations "system" consisting of government, unions, and employers. The government makes the laws that regulate how unions and employers behave with each other.[5] In making laws, the government will determine who can unionize and where they can unionize. There are specific laws, or acts, for different sectors, industries, and workers.

Canada's labour relations system is highly decentralized, whereas the US system is highly centralized. For example, in Canada, the federal law governs interprovincial transportation and communications, whereas provincial legislation governs manufacturing and mining. However, 90% of the workforce is governed by provincial legislation. As mentioned earlier in this book, the *Canada Labour Code* governs federally regulated companies such as Bell, Rogers, Canadian National Railway, and Telus, whereas the province in which they operate governs companies such as Molson Breweries. All labour legislation, whether federal or provincial, has certain features in common:

LO1

Explain the federal and provincial legislation that provides the framework for labour relations.

- the right of people to join unions
- the requirement that employers recognize a certified union as the rightful and exclusive bargaining agent for that group of employees
- the identification of unfair labour practices
- the right of unions to strike and the right of employers to lock out workers[6]

The Canada Industrial Relations Board (CIRB) was established to administer and enforce the *Canada Labour Code*. Similarly, each province has a labour relations board (LRB), whose members are appointed by the provincial government and who administer the labour law. (The exception is Québec, which has a labour court and commissioners.) The LRB is generally separate from the government and is composed of representatives from labour and management. The duties of the LRB include but are not limited to

- processing union applications to represent employees
- processing applications to terminate union bargaining rights
- hearing unfair labour practice complaints
- hearing complaints and issuing decisions regarding strikes, lockouts, and picketing[7]

TOOLKIT 10.1   **LABOUR RELATIONS BOARDS**

Labour relations boards are making it easier for employers and employees to access information. The following websites are a valuable resource for the manager and HR professional.

Jurisdiction	Name	Website
Federal government	Canada Industrial Relations Board	www.cirb-ccri.gc.ca
Alberta	Alberta Labour Relations Board	www.alrb.gov.ab.ca
British Columbia	Labour Relations Board	www.lrb.bc.ca
Manitoba	Manitoba Labour Board	www.gov.mb.ca/labour/labbrd
New Brunswick	Labour and Employment Board	www.gnb.ca/LEB-CTE/index-e.asp
Newfoundland and Labrador	Labour Relations Board	www.gov.nl.ca/lrb
Nova Scotia	Labour Board	www.novascotia.ca/lae/labourboard
Ontario	The Ontario Labour Relations Board	www.olrb.gov.on.ca
Prince Edward Island	Labour Relations Board	www.princeedwardisland.ca/en/information/workforce-and-advanced-learning/labour-relations-board
Québec	*Labour Code* administered through investigations and commissions created at the time of a complaint	
Saskatchewan	Labour Relations Board	www.sasklabourrelationsboard.com

It is important to remember that the administrative regulations are greatly influenced by the politics of any provincial government. Therefore, the legislation can be relatively similar, but the interpretation of the law can vary greatly from one province to another. The law typically gets interpreted by the decisions made by the respective labour boards, which then influence the actions a union or company can take in the future. To learn more about the administration of labour relations, see Toolkit 10.1, which lists the websites of the labour relations boards.

LO2

Cite the reasons employees join unions.

Labour relations system
A framework of the environment, the people, the processes, and the results

WHY EMPLOYEES UNIONIZE

Employees frequently feel that individually, they will be unable to exercise power regarding their employment conditions at any particular employer. The treatment and benefits they receive depend in large part on how their employers view their worth to the organization. Of course, if they believe they are not being treated fairly, they have the choice of quitting. However, another way to correct the situation is to organize and bargain with the employer collectively. When employees pursue this direction, the labour relations process begins. As Figure 10.1 illustrates, the **labour relations system** has a framework that recognizes the environment (economy, legal, political, etc.), the people involved (employers, unions,

FIGURE 10.1 Labour Relations System

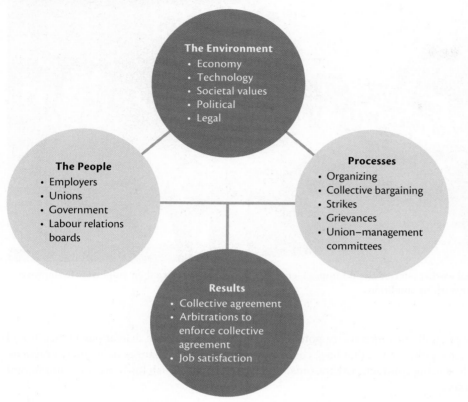

Source: Adapted from Larry Suffield, *Labour Relations*, 4th ed. Toronto: Pearson, 2016.

governments), the processes (union organizing, contract negotiations, strikes, grievances, etc.), and the results (collective agreement). Laws and administrative rulings influence each of these areas by granting special privileges to, or imposing defined constraints on, employees, employers, and union officials.[8]

A number of studies indicate that employees often join unions for better wages and benefits as well as for psychological reasons, such as feeling unfairly treated at work.[9] Furthermore, there might be a provision in the collective agreement that requires an employee to join: the employer is a **union shop**. Others join because the employer is a **closed shop**—only members of a union will be hired—or because they choose to under an **open shop** provision. Even when forced to join, many employees eventually accept the concept of unionism. The sections that follow look at some of the more specific reasons people unionize and what role the manager, the organization, or both play in the unionization process.

Pay, Benefits, and Working Conditions

Whether or not a union can become the bargaining agent for a group of employees will be influenced by the employees' degree of dissatisfaction, if any, with their overall employment conditions. For example, employees may feel their concerns about health and safety are ignored, or they may be required to wear uniforms without being reimbursed for the cost. It will also depend on whether the employees perceive the union as likely to be effective in improving these conditions. However, unhappiness with wages, benefits, and/or working conditions appears to be the strongest reason to join a union. Unions

Union shop
Clause in a collective agreement requiring employees to become a member of the union and retain membership to retain employment

Closed shop
Provision of the collective agreement that requires employers to hire only union members

Open shop
Provision of the collective agreement that allows employees to join or not join the union

Metal workers started the Winnipeg General Strike of 1919 to force their employers to improve their working conditions.

will generally try to convince potential members that they can deliver pay increases and benefits. Other issues that have concerned unions include changes in business practices, such as using contract workers, outsourcing, and paying much lower wages to immigrant workers.[10]

Dissatisfaction with Managers

Employees generally want to feel that their employer is concerned about their well-being; when the manager does something suggesting that the employer isn't concerned, they may feel the need to unionize. Likewise, they may feel the need for protection of their rights and working conditions and therefore want to unionize.[11] Unions will describe the structured complaint process in the collective agreement (the grievance process) as a formal way in which employees can have their complaints heard and acted on.

This book has noted that today's employees are better educated than those of the past and often express a desire to be more involved in decisions affecting their jobs. Chapter 3 discussed the concepts of employee engagement and highlighted various ways for managers to behave. The failure of employers to give employees an opportunity to participate in decisions affecting their welfare may encourage union membership. It is widely believed that one reason managers begin employee involvement programs and seek to empower their employees is to avoid collective action by employees.

Social and Status Concerns

If an employee needs to have constant reinforcement from the manager about doing a good job and the manager doesn't provide that, the person may feel that a union can provide the reinforcement they are seeking. In interactions with other union members, employees may also find common interests. In the final analysis, the deciding factor is likely to be whether employees perceive that the benefits of joining a union outweigh the costs associated with membership.

Sometimes employees in similar industries may feel they can improve their pay and working conditions only by joining a union. At Work with HRM 10.1 describes 2 situations in which employees in 2 different organizations are thinking of unionizing.

AT WORK WITH HRM 10.1 — A TALE OF 2 ORGANIZATIONS

It must be easy to unionize organizations if other organizations in the same industry are already unionized. Actually, it isn't. Read further to have a better appreciation of the issues in 2 distinct organizations: the RCMP and WestJet.

For many years, the *Canada Labour Code* restricted the RCMP from being unionized, making it the only major police force in Canada not unionized. However, that restriction was eliminated in early 2015 when the Supreme Court of Canada ruled that it did have the right to bargain collectively and that the *Charter of Rights* guaranteed the RCMP the freedom of association. Once the courts cleared the way for staff to unionize, several unions began to actively pursue certain job categories. For example, the Canadian Union of Public Employees (CUPE) will have a certification vote to represent more than 1000 of the RCMP members, mostly in the telecommunications area. Two different unions, the National Police Federation and the Mounted Police Professional Association, are attempting to certify the police.

Several small towns and municipalities are concerned about whether they will face higher policing costs if the RCMP is totally unionized. These communities have depended on the RCMP to provide contract policing, which in many cases was more cost-effective than the community having its own police force. This could change.

Then there was WestJet, a major company in the airline industry that had not been unionized. This, too, changed in 2017 when its pilots voted to form a union—the Air Line Pilots Association. It had only been in 2015 when a majority of pilots voted not to join a union. So what happened? Although there is no definitive answer, part of the rationale may have been because WestJet began flying to Europe and started a low-cost carrier. With changes in the business, pilots may have wanted something more secure when bidding for shifts: seniority.

Shortly after the pilots unionized, other unions began unionization drives for the flight attendants. For many years, WestJet boasted about the family-like culture and the relationship with all its employees. Many observers indicated that once the pilots were unionized, it was only a matter of time before the flight attendants also unionized. Then in early 2018, WestJet changed the way in which flight attendants were to be paid, which created a great deal of anger and unhappiness. Only time will tell if the attendants actually unionize.

CRITICAL THINKING QUESTION:

Why do you think these employees are unionizing?

Sources: Adapted from James Fitz-Morris, "RCMP Officers Have Right to Collectively Bargain Supreme Court Rules," *CBC News*, January 16, 2015, accessed April 2, 2018, www.cbc.ca/news/politics/rcmp-officers-have-right-to-collective-bargaining-supreme-court-rules-1.2912340; Alison Crawford, "CUPE Makes 1st Move to Unionize Some Members of RCMP," *CBC News*, January 13, 2017, accessed April 2, 2018, www.cbc.ca/news/politics/rcmp-cupe-unionization-1.3933300; Kathryn May, "Vote Called to Unionize Members of the RCMP," *iPolitics*, January 17, 2018, accessed April 2, 2018, https://ipolitics.ca/2018/01/17/vote-called-unionize-members-rcmp; Matthew McClearn, Collin Freeze, and Sunny Dhillon, "The RCMP's Thin Red Line: Is Contract Policing Unsustainable?," *The Globe and Mail*, March 8, 2018, accessed April 2, 2018, https://www.theglobeandmail.com/news/investigations/rcmp-contract-policing-investigation/article38085153; Tracy Johnson, "WestJet Pilots Vote in Favour of Forming a Union," *CBC News*, May 11, 2017, accessed April 2, 2018, www.cbc.ca/news/business/westjet-pilots-vote-in-favour-of-union-1.4110517; Alicja Siekierska, "Pilots Union May Hinder WestJet's Expansion Plans: Analysts," *Financial Post*, May 16, 2017, B1; Ian Bickis, "Two Groups Increase Efforts to Unionize WestJet Flight Attendants," *The Globe and Mail*, June 7, 2017, B5; and Ross Marowits, "WestJet Staff Eye Unionization Amid Pay Change," *The Globe and Mail*, March 17, 2018, A10.

HOW EMPLOYEES ORGANIZE

When employees decide to form a union, either the employees contact a union or a union may have approached the employees. In either case, the union will start what is called an "organizing drive." Larger unions, such as Unifor, the United Brotherhood of Carpenters, the United Steelworkers, and the Teamsters, have units within the union organization that help employees unionize. It has been no secret that the labour movement has targeted certain types of employers. Larger unions have moved out of their traditional industries into other areas. This has been due to changes from a goods-producing society to a service-based society and an overall decline in union membership. The decline in union membership has also created new opportunities for unions. One opportunity led to the creation of Unifor: the merger of the Canadian Auto Workers (CAW) and the Communication, Energy and Paperworkers Union of Canada (CEP), 2 large and influential labour unions.[12]

With the creation of Unifor, predictions were made that more low-wage employees would be targeted for becoming union members. This, coupled with some labour code changes, suggested that it would be easier for unions to sign up members and organize employees in sectors such as retail.[13] However, this doesn't appear to be happening to any great extent. Some observers believe this is occurring because of good people practices in various organizations as well as changes in the expectations and values of younger workers.

Since organizing campaigns can be expensive, union leaders carefully evaluate their chances of success and the possible benefits to be gained from their efforts. Important in this evaluation is the employer's vulnerability to unionization. Union leaders also consider the effect that allowing an employer to remain non-union might have on the strength of their union within the area. A non-union employer can impair a union's efforts to standardize employment conditions within an industry or geographic area and weaken the union's bargaining power with employers it has unionized. Unions will also assess whether there is a possibility that future employees may wish to decertify. Just as the costs of unionizing can be high, so can the challenges coming from employees wanting to cease having the union represent them.

LO3

Outline the process by which unions organize employees and gain recognition as their bargaining agent.

Membership cards

A document signed by an employee indicating that the union is able to act on the employee's behalf for collective bargaining and other union purposes

Organizing Steps

The typical organizing campaign follows a series of progressive steps that can lead to employee representation. Although each union has its own set of steps, as well as conforming with the appropriate provincial labour legislation, generally speaking, the steps include the following:

1. Employees contact a union and meet with an organizer to discuss next steps and timelines.
2. Employees sign **membership cards** and authorize the union to represent them.
3. The union submits the required minimum number of cards to the appropriate provincial labour board for a decision.
4. The labour board holds a secret ballot where all eligible employees vote.
5. The union informs the employer that it wishes to commence collective bargaining.

Richard Baker/Corbis News/Getty Images

When employees feel dissatisfied with treatment by their employer, they will often think about joining a union.

TOOLKIT 10.2   FREQUENTLY ASKED QUESTIONS

Many organizations find themselves unionized and are surprised that it has happened. There is also a mistaken belief that unions do not actively recruit new members. The following are the questions union organizers usually ask employees:

1. Do you think people get paid more in other organizations? (Unions will know how much people are paid in the industry and geographic area.)
2. Are decisions about how much employees are paid based on logic or favouritism? (Usually, unions will have received information that managers make decisions in an arbitrary fashion.)
3. Are decisions about promotions based on merit or favouritism? (Unions usually have information about a particular individual who was promoted for reasons other than merit.)
4. If something happens that you feel is unfair, do you have recourse? Can you get your complaint heard?

Who will hear it? Can they fix it? (Many small companies do not have a way to handle employee complaints. Unions will talk about the formal grievance process and the protections that can be provided to employees who feel helpless in dealing with a problem.)

5. How are shift schedules determined? (Unions will say that shifts ought to be determined by seniority.)
6. How are performance problems handled? (Unions will convince potential members that a union can ensure that people are treated fairly if there are performance issues.)
7. Do you feel your manager criticizes you unfairly? (Unions will describe the processes that can be used if employees feel they have not been treated fairly.)
8. Does your boss treat you with respect? (Unions will indicate that the power of a collective group of people will make the employer treat everyone respectfully.)

Recently, labour laws in Ontario were changed to allow off-site or electronic voting so that employees could express their true desires without influence from either the employer or the union.[14] Alberta also changed its labour code in 2018 to allow automatic certification, without a secret ballot, if the union has 65% or more signed membership cards from employees.[15] However, even changes of this nature do not always make it easy to unionize. For example, when Ontario raised the minimum hourly wage in early 2018, franchise owners of some Tim Hortons reduced pay and benefits for employees. Although the employees might have wanted to unionize, it is very difficult to unionize only 1 franchise, and an attempt to organize all franchises in Ontario is probably not likely.[16]

Managers can become familiar with the questions unions ask employees during organizing drives and therefore better assess the effectiveness of their management practices. Toolkit 10.2 presents these questions.

Legislation across Canada states that unions must have a majority of employees as members in a bargaining unit before they can apply for certification election. However, most jurisdictions now interpret this to mean that at least 50% of those voting constitute a majority. In other words, those who do not cast ballots are not assumed to be voting against the certification of the union. The union membership card, once signed, is confidential, and only the labour relations board has access to the cards.

Employer Tactics

Employers must not interfere with the certification process. They are prohibited by law from dismissing, disciplining, or threatening employees for exercising their rights to form a union. Employers cannot promise better conditions, such as increased vacation days, if the employees vote for no union or choose one union over another. Employers cannot unilaterally change wages and working conditions during certification proceedings or during collective bargaining. Like unions, they must bargain in good faith, meaning that they must

FIGURE 10.2 **Unfair Labour Practices**

Unfair labour practices by employers include the following:
- Helping to establish or administer a union.
- Changing the working conditions of the employees without the union's consent while a union is applying for certification.
- Intimidating, coercing, threatening, or exercising undue influence while a union is being organized.
- Failing to recognize or bargain with the authorized union.
- Hiring professional strikebreakers.

Unfair labour practices by unions include the following:
- Contributing financial or other support to an employees' organization.
- Not fairly representing the employees in the bargaining unit.
- Bargaining or negotiating a collective agreement with an employer while another union represents the employees in the bargaining unit.
- Calling or authorizing an unlawful strike or threatening to do so.

demonstrate a commitment to bargain seriously and fairly. In addition, they cannot participate in the formation, selection, or support of unions representing employees.

None of these prohibitions prevents an employer from making the case that the employees have a right not to join a union or that they can deal directly with the employer on any issue. Employer resistance to unionization is the norm in Canada; however, employers need to recognize that they cannot intimidate or coerce employees, but employers can express their views on the consequences of unionizing as long as they are not intimidating or coercive.[17] Attempts by employers to influence employees are scrutinized closely by officials of the organizing unions and the labour relations board.

Union Tactics

Unions also have a duty to act in accordance with labour legislation. Unions are prohibited from interfering with the operation of an employer's organization. They cannot intimidate or coerce employees to become or remain members of a union. Nor can they force employers to dismiss, discipline, or discriminate against non-union employees. They must provide fair representation for all employees in the **bargaining unit**, whether in collective bargaining or in grievance procedure cases. Unions cannot engage in activities such as strikes before the expiration of the union contract.

Any of the prohibited activities discussed above for both employers and unions are considered **unfair labour practices**. Charges of unfair labour practices are made to the labour relations board, whose duty is to enforce the applicable labour laws and decide if an unfair labour practice occurred. An example of an unfair labour practice by an employer would be to threaten to fire people who wanted to join a union. Similarly, a union cannot threaten harm to employees if they don't join the union. Figure 10.2 provides a list of unfair labour practices on both the union and the management sides.

CERTIFICATION PROCEDURES

The procedures for union **certification** vary across Canadian jurisdictions. As mentioned earlier, if an applicant union can present documentation that it has sufficient support in the proposed bargaining unit, labour boards will grant certification to the union or grant a vote. The labour relations board must certify a union before it can act as a bargaining unit for a

Bargaining unit
A group of employees represented by 1 union for the purposes of collective bargaining and other union processes

Unfair labour practices
Accusation that an employer, a union, or an individual has engaged in activity that is illegal in accordance with the appropriate labour code

Certification
Acquisition of exclusive rights by a union to represent the employees

group of employees. The union normally provides evidence by submitting signed application cards and proof that initiation dues or fees have been paid.[18] Recognition of a union may be obtained through voluntary recognition, regular certification, or a pre-hearing vote.

Voluntary Recognition

All employers, except those in the province of Québec, may voluntarily recognize and accept a union. This has not happened often, except in the construction industry, where there is a great reliance on union hiring halls. Recently, however, some university faculty members at major BC universities organized into trade unions, leaving the University of British Columbia as the only institution that had "voluntarily" recognized its faculty some years earlier.[19]

Regular Certification

The regular certification process begins with the union submitting the required minimum membership evidence to the labour relations board. Generally, if an applicant union can demonstrate that it has sufficient support in the proposed bargaining unit, labour boards may grant certification on that basis. (However, with changes in government, labour relations legislation is often reformed. Therefore, requirements for granting certification may change.) The labour relations board may order a representative vote if a sizable minority of workers have indicated either support for or opposition to the unionization.

There are times that employee associations eventually seek certification or decide to join another union. This occurred in 2017 when the pilots of WestJet Airlines voted to join an existing union instead of attempting to have the employee association certified. The 1400 pilots are now members of Air Line Pilots Association International.[20]

Pre-hearing Votes

If there is evidence of irregularities, such as unfair labour practices taking place during the organizing drive, a pre-hearing vote may be taken. The purpose of this vote is to establish the level of support among the workers. Depending on the particular labour relations legislation, votes can be called if less than 50% of the employees indicate support for a union.

Once a union has been certified, employees are part of a collective and can no longer individually make special arrangements on pay, hours of work, and so on. Likewise, this means that the manager can no longer treat individuals differently—that is, they can't make individual deals.

Contract Negotiations

Once a bargaining unit has been certified by the labour relations board, the employer and the union are legally obliged to bargain in good faith over the terms and conditions of a collective agreement. This process, known as collective bargaining, is discussed in greater detail later in the chapter. The collective agreement must have an end date and must be in place for at least 1 year. As the contract expiry date approaches, either party must notify the other of its intention to bargain for a renewal collective agreement or contract negotiation.

Decertification

All legislation allows for decertification of unions under certain conditions. If the majority of employees indicate that they do not want to be represented by the union or that they want to be represented by another union, or if the union has failed to bargain, an application for decertification can be made to the labour relations board. If a collective agreement has been reached with the employer, this application can be made only at specified times, such as a few months before the agreement expires. Either employees or the employer can initiate the application for decertification if the union fails to bargain.

The Canadian Press/Mark Spowart

Unifor, the largest private-sector union, can exert a great deal of influence during contract negotiations.

One of the more unusual decisions regarding decertification occurred in British Columbia when seasonal farm workers from Mexico wanted to decertify. The union charged that the Mexican government and Vancouver consulate had interfered; the labour board concurred. However, the Mexican government launched a lawsuit saying that the Mexican government had immunity. Although the Mexican government lost the case at the appeal court, it was concerned that employers would feel that Mexican workers were too much trouble and that workers from other Latin countries would be hired instead of from Mexico.[21]

IMPACT OF UNIONIZATION ON MANAGERS

The unionization of employees can affect managers in many ways. Perhaps most significant is the effect it can have on the ability of managers to make decisions about employees. A union can assist employees if they believe they haven't been treated in accordance with the agreed-on employment conditions. As an example, if a company doesn't have a formal complaint mechanism, there is now a structured grievance process. And the decisions of a structured grievance process can be enforced through the courts (as is discussed later in this chapter).

Challenges to Management Decisions

With the formation of a union, management decisions are often examined more closely by union members and/or union officials. Although there may be some sense that management can make certain decisions and employees have to go along with them, such as the introduction of new technology, this is often not accurate.[22] The involvement of a union does, however, mean that management decisions can be challenged, particularly if there is a clause in the collective agreement that requires union involvement in certain processes. For example, if there is language in a collective agreement stating that the most senior person with the required

AT WORK WITH HRM 10.2 — WHY CAN'T I MAKE THAT DECISION?

Part of the fabric of labour relations in Canada is the premise that management has the right to make decisions regarding the operation of the business. This can be restricted if language in the collective agreement requires union involvement and/or agreement before any action can be taken. Sometimes, however, it may not be clear.

A recent example occurred in Québec with a rail transportation company. Tshiuetin Rail Transportation Inc. is owned by a group of First Nations, and as it is federally regulated, all aspects of the company's labour relations are covered under the *Canada Labour Code*. The company determined that it needed to reduce the weekly hours of all full-time employees from 40 to 35 hours to assist with the company's financial problems. The action was to be temporary, although it wasn't clear at the time how long it might last. The language in the collective agreement was quite clear: all limitations on management rights were in the collective agreement. Nowhere in the agreement was there anything preventing the employer from temporarily reducing hours.

However, the union did grieve this management decision, which was arbitrated and subsequently reviewed by the Superior Court of Québec. The union maintained that when the employer reduced hours, it changed the employment of the employees from full-time to part-time. The employer declared that since the collective agreement did not limit changes in hours, it had the right to do so.

The arbitrator, and the court, did not agree with the employer and concluded that a full-time employee was one who worked 40 hours and that by changing the hours to 35, the employer had changed the working conditions and remuneration and was in violation of the collective agreement. The court upheld the decision of the arbitrator.

CRITICAL THINKING QUESTIONS:
1. Do you think the arbitrator made the correct decision? Why or why not?
2. If you were the arbitrator, how would you have decided?

Sources: Adapted from "Managerial Rights: An Endangered Notion?," *The HR Space*, November 2017; and Michael Babad, "What Companies, Unions Should Know about Quebec Ruling on Management Rights," *The Globe and Mail*, November 16, 2017, accessed April 5, 2018, www.theglobeandmail.com/report-on-business/top-business-stories/what-companies-unions-should-know-about-quebec-ruling-on-managementrights/article36936366.

skills and abilities is to be promoted, then management will have to be able to prove that the senior person did not have the required skills in order to promote a more junior employee. Read At Work with HRM 10.2 to gain a fuller understanding of challenges to the decisions of management.

Loss of Management Flexibility

Unions often cite the fact that basic working conditions of job security and pay are the most important items to their members. But for managers, the most important outcome of employees joining a union is the company's ability to operate effectively and efficiently. It is in the daily interactions of managers and employees where the collective agreement is real. For example, a manager may need to give a certain amount of advanced notice to require someone to work overtime. Likewise, a manager would need to have done a thorough investigation to prove that there was sufficient cause to discipline an employee. These actions can be challenged by the union, and a manager can be required to provide proof during a grievance hearing. If the challenge is upheld, the manager's effectiveness in making good business decisions may be impaired. In addition, the collective agreement may have specific language regarding shift assignments, hiring, pay, and other similar management activities.

The list provided in Toolkit 10.3 offers guidelines to help managers understand what they can do to create a work environment in which employees will see no need to unionize. You will note that these are all similar to the ideas presented in Chapter 3 about creating a culture of well-being.

TOOLKIT 10.3   CREATING A POSITIVE WORK ENVIRONMENT

1. If you have something to say to one of your employees, say it directly—and soon.
2. Praise employees publicly; criticize in private.
3. Remember that actions speak louder than words. Be sure your actions "say" what you want them to.
4. Be respectful of all your employees—even the poor performers.
5. Set up a file system for employee information, where you can keep documentation on pay raises, performance reviews, and the like. Allow employees access to their files and encourage them to review their files.
6. Create performance goals with each employee— goals that are challenging but attainable; monitor performance and provide feedback.
7. Share business information.
8. Seek input from employees when making changes that will affect them.
9. Ask employees for suggestions on how to improve business operations.

HOW UNIONS OPERATE

Unions that represent skilled craft workers, such as carpenters or masons, are called craft unions, such as the International Brotherhood of Electrical Workers (IBEW) and the Brotherhood of Boilermakers. Unions that represent unskilled and semi-skilled workers employed along industry lines are known as industrial unions—for example, the Canadian Union of Postal Workers and the Ontario Secondary School Teachers' Federation. Although the distinction between craft and industrial unions still exists, technological changes and competition among unions for members have weakened it. Today, skilled and unskilled workers, white-collar and blue-collar workers, and professional groups are being represented by both types of union.

Besides unions, there are also employee associations representing various groups of professional and white-collar employees. Examples of employee associations are the Québec Federation of Nurses and the Alberta Teachers' Association. In competing with unions, these associations may function as unions and become just as aggressive as unions in representing members. These associations are non-union; however, if the employee association met the necessary criteria under labour legislation, the association could become certified as a union.

Regardless of their type, labour organizations are diverse, each with its own method of governance and objectives. And it is important to remember that unions are primarily political organizations. That is, they have elected leaders who can be voted out of office if the wishes of the members are not met. Moreover, there can be situations in which unions are antagonistic toward each other, such as the dispute between Unifor and the Amalgamated Transit Union (ATU). At the root of the conflict is an allegation that Unifor planned to raid the ATU, which represents the employees at the Toronto Transit Commission. Unifor doesn't feel that the ATU, which is US based, can fairly represent employees in Canada. Unifor also contends that all the employees want to leave the ATU and join Unifor. Although Unifor acknowledged that it did attempt to raid, which is contrary to how unions are expected to behave, nothing has come of the attempt.[23]

Because of the political nature of unions, many have come together under an umbrella organization, called the Canadian Labour Congress (CLC). Through this organization, the CLC attempts to influence government policy by commenting on economic conditions, such as the unemployment rate. Also, since most of the major unions in Canada are members of the CLC, the CLC also helps referee between unions if they are seeking to organize the same group of workers. The CLC attempted to do this during the Unifor/ATU dispute. Observers feel this was the main reason Unifor withdrew its membership from the CLC.[24] Because of its size and resources, the CLC is a very influential organization in Canada and globally as well.

AT WORK WITH HRM 10.3 — FOR THE GOOD OF EVERYONE!

Unifor became the largest private-sector union in Canada when the former Canadian Auto Workers and the Communications, Energy and Paperworkers Union merged in 2013. At the time, union membership had steadily declined, especially in the private sector, while the nature of work was dramatically changing and the economy was more global than ever. Part of the objective of the new union was for it to better respond to these changes.

So how has it done? Jerry Dias was elected the president of the new organization with over 300,000 members. He has become the public face of the union, which claims that its membership is composed of almost every type of sector in the Canadian economy. Dias has taken great pride in being visible during the NAFTA renegotiations in 2017 and 2018, as well as linking NAFTA to the strikes in the Canadian auto industry. He believes in fighting for workers.

Dias argued that the reason GM went on strike in 2017 is a reflection of the problems with NAFTA. Specifically, the union wanted assurances that the plant in Ingersoll, Ontario, would be the lead manufacturer of a particular model and that no matter what happened to the economy or auto industry, work would not be relocated to Mexico. He felt very strongly that the plant was one of the most productive and yet was losing ground as wages in Mexico were cheaper. Dias blamed NAFTA when GM made the decision to shift production work to Mexico for the Terrain model even though GM said it was done to increase production at the Ingersoll plant.

He was directly involved in the NAFTA renegotiations, where he had ongoing discussions with the government during talks about the auto industry. He stated that he wasn't involved to keep quiet! He also indicated that the Liberal government sees unions as stakeholders and believes they have something to add.

Dias carries enough leverage in the labour movement that when Bombardier reached an agreement with Airbus to manufacture and sell the C Series jet, Dias met with the Bombardier president before the agreement was made public. Having worked in the aerospace industry, he knew what Bombardier was up against and also knew that Bombardier just couldn't fail.

CRITICAL THINKING QUESTIONS:

1. Do you think that Dias should be spending time on issues such as NAFTA? Why or why not?
2. Should Unifor take a more militant approach? Why or why not?

Sources: Adapted from "History & Mission," Unifor, accessed April 6, 2018, www.unifor.org/en/about-unifor/history-mission; Alicja Siekierska, "NAFTA Renegotiations Loom over General Motors Strike," *Vancouver Sun*, September 19, 2017, B1; Joanna Smith, "Unifor Leader 'Glad to Be in the Middle' of Action as Key Point Man," *Financial Post*, October 25, 2017, B3; and Kristine Owram, "GM Canada Cuts 600 Jobs as Production Shifts to Mexico," *Financial Post*, January 28, 2017, D2.

Canada's rate of unionization continues to fall and is currently at 28.4%.[25] The decline is most notable among men and younger employees.[26] Part of the reason or the decline is the shift in the Canadian economy from manufacturing and construction to professional services and retail trade.[27] Rates of unionization vary across the world, from over 80% in Iceland to 6% in Turkey, 26% in the United Kingdom, and 11% in the United States.[28] It is interesting to note that Germany, which has historically had high union involvement and co-management (as discussed in Chapter 11), only has a rate of 18%.[29]

Structure, Functions, and Leadership of International and National Unions

International unions tend to be affiliates of American unions, with headquarters in the United States. In Canada, there are 40 international unions (with membership of about 1.2 million workers) and 196 national unions (with membership of more than 33.3 million).[30] There are about the same number of international and national unions as there has been for many years, although the size and composition have changed.

Both international and national unions are made up of local unions. The objectives of these unions are to help organize local unions, to provide strike support, and to assist local unions with negotiations, grievance procedures, and the like. These unions also represent membership interest with internal and external constituents. By ensuring that all employers pay similar wages to their unionized workers, they fulfill the additional role of removing higher wages as a competitive disadvantage.

National unions can also have objectives that go beyond helping the local unions. Read At Work with HRM 10.3 to learn more about Unifor, the largest private-sector union in Canada.

Structure and Functions of Local Unions

LO4

Illustrate the functions labour unions perform at international, national, and local levels.

Employees of any organization can form their own union, with no affiliation to a national or international union. In this case, the local is the union. However, most local unions are members of national or international unions or the Canadian Labour Congress, which make financial resources and advice available to them. There are 12,227 locals in Canada—less than in previous years.[31] Some of the reduction is due to mergers between unions. For example, the merger of the CAW and the CEP created the third-largest union in Canada—Unifor—with over 300,000 members.[32]

Unionized employees pay union dues that finance the operation of the local union. The officers of a local union are usually responsible for negotiating the local collective agreement, for ensuring that the agreement is adhered to, and for investigating and processing member grievances. Read Ethics and HRM 10.1 to understand what can happen when there is conflict within a union.

ETHICS IN HRM 10.1 — ETHICS APPLY TO ALL!

Much attention is paid to business ethics in today's global economy. But does that also apply to union organizations? The answer is yes.

An issue arose recently with the BC Nurses' Union (BCNU) regarding the behaviour of its president. The union represents over 47,000 registered nurses in British Columbia, and an internal dispute arose during the campaign for electing a president. Due to the severity of the matter, including the actual conduct of the election, the Labour Relations Board of British Columbia had to conduct an investigation and make a decision.

Initially, the LRB was asked to appoint a mediator to settle a dispute between the union's nomination committee and 3 candidates who ran for key positions. The committee had decided to remove the names of the 3 candidates as they appeared to have mounted a smear and disinformation campaign against incumbents. The LRB determined that the nominations committee had acted fairly in removing the names. The LRB decision included a fine against the union of $75,000 and $15,000 against one of the candidates.

The strife then continued when one of the presidential nominees threatened to sue the union's nomination committee for allowing other candidates to make derogatory comments about her. This issue was also referred by the BCNU to the LRB as part of the overall issue of the election. This candidate was the incumbent president, and the behaviour toward the nominations committee was determined to be "a flagrant attempt to threaten, interfere with and manipulate the committee's processes." Subsequently, the incumbent president was re-elected by acclamation.

There has been internal conflict for a number of years, including the strike of its office staff, which are represented by different unions. The strike went on for about 6 months before a new collective agreement was reached. Furthermore, the former executive director left the organization after having been there for over 12 years for making improper comments.

CRITICAL THINKING QUESTIONS:

1. Do you think the LRB made the correct decision? Explain your answer.
2. Given the decision of the LRB regarding the incumbent president, do you think she ought to have been re-elected? Why or why not?

Sources: Adapted from Justin McElroy, "Challengers in B.C. Nurses' Union Election Disqualified Days before Voting Begins," *CBC News*, May 22, 2017, accessed April 7, 2018, www.cbc.ca/news/canada/british-columbia/challengers-in-b-c-nurses-union-election-disqualified-days-before-voting-begins-1.4127093; Charmaine de Silva, "BCNU President Files Complaints Against Own Union after Being Put on Leave," *Global News*, October 11, 2017, accessed April 7, 2018, https://globalnews.ca/news/3797697/bcnu-president-administrative-leave-complaint; Pamela Fayerman, "Embattled B.C. Nurses' Union President Grappling with Cancer, Complaints and Chaos," *Vancouver Sun*, October 25, 2017, accessed April 7, 2018, http://vancouversun.com/news/local-news/embattled-b-c-nurses-union-president-grappling-with-cancer-complaints-and-chaos; and Pamela Fayerman, "BCNU Must Pay $75K after 'Flagrant' Actions by Leader," *Vancouver Sun*, March 29, 2018, A1.

Role of the Shop (Union) Steward

The **shop (union) steward** represents union members in their relations with management. Shop stewards are employees of the company and are normally selected by union members within their department. This is typically an unpaid role.

A shop steward can be viewed as a "person in the middle," caught between conflicting interests and groups. It cannot be assumed that stewards will always champion union members and routinely oppose managerial objectives. Shop stewards are often insightful individuals working for the betterment of employees and the organization. Therefore, managers at all levels are encouraged to develop a positive working relationship with stewards and all union officials. This relationship can have an important bearing on union–management cooperation and on the efficiency and morale of the workers.

Shop (union) steward
An employee acting in an official union capacity representing other union members in their relations with management

Role of the Business Agent

Negotiating and administering the collective agreement and working to resolve problems arising in connection with it are major responsibilities of the **business agent**. In performing these duties, business agents must be all things to all people within their unions. They are frequently required to assume the role of counsellor in helping union members with both personal and job-related problems. They are also expected to satisfactorily resolve grievances that cannot be settled by the union stewards. Administering the daily affairs of the local union is another significant part of the business agent's job.

Business agent
Normally a paid labour official responsible for negotiating and administering the collective agreement and working to resolve union members' problems

Union Leadership Approaches and Philosophies

To evaluate the role of union leaders accurately, one must understand the nature of their backgrounds and ambitions and recognize the political nature of the offices they occupy. The leaders of many national unions have been able to develop political machines that enable them to defeat opposition and to perpetuate themselves in office. Tenure for the leaders of a local union, however, is less secure. If they are to remain in office, they must be able to convince a majority of the members that they are serving them effectively.

Although it is true that union leaders occupy positions of power within their organizations, rank-and-file members can and often do exercise a strong influence over these leaders, particularly with respect to the negotiation and administration of the collective agreement. It is important for managers to understand that union officials are elected to office and, like any political officials, must be responsive to the views of their constituency. The union leader who ignores the demands of union members may risk (1) being voted out of office, (2) having members vote the union out as their bargaining agent, (3) having members refuse to ratify the union agreement, or (4) having members engage in wildcat strikes or work stoppages.

To be effective leaders, union officials must also pay constant attention to the general goals and philosophies of the labour movement. Unions also have historically been politically active, backing such parties as the NDP. However, at times a union will lobby a government to achieve a particular aim. For example, the union representing the employees at the Bombardier manufacturing plant in Downsview, Ontario, pressured city officials not to allow any rezoning of the property. Bombardier was planning to sell the property as a way to help the debt of that particular plant. Part of the rationale for selling the property is that the company only used about 10% of the land. It was anticipated that the sale would conclude in 2018.[33]

One success story of union philosophy is a worker-owned pulp mill in British Columbia. Harmac Pacific, located in Nanaimo, was declared insolvent in 2008 and then put into receivership. A group of employees, including members of the then Pulp, Paper and Woodworkers of Canada, with the help of investors, put together an offer to take over the operation. The employees also agreed to buy into the mill at $25,000 per person, with employee ownership now at 25%.[34] The mill not only survived but has been upgraded, so now it is producing 365,000 tonnes of pulp per year. Its success is based on a new business model that is both responsive and adaptable to changing global conditions.

Labour Relations in the Public Sector

Collective bargaining among federal, provincial, and municipal government employees and among employees in parapublic agencies (private agencies or branches of the government acting as extensions of government programs) has increased dramatically since the 1960s. Over 71% of all public employees are now unionized, in contrast to 15% for the private sector.[35] The 2 largest unions in Canada represent public-sector employees. The Canadian Union of Public Employees (CUPE) is the largest union in Canada, representing more than 635,000 members, and the National Union of Provincial Government Employees (NUPGE) is the second largest union, with 360,000 members. As has been mentioned previously, Unifor, with over 300,000 members is the third largest union.[36] Growth in these unions is threatened by increased cost-cutting efforts of governments at all levels, resulting in employee reductions.

Although public- and private-sector collective bargaining have many features in common, a number of factors differentiate them. Two key distinctions are the political nature of the labour–management relationship and public-sector strikes.

Political Nature of the Labour–Management Relationship

Government employees are not able to negotiate with their employers on the same basis as their counterparts in private organizations. It is doubtful that they will ever be able to do so because of inherent differences between the public and private sectors.

One significant difference is that labour relations in the private sector have an economic foundation, whereas in government, their foundation tends to be political. Since private employers must stay in business in order to sell their goods or services, their employees are not likely to make demands that could bankrupt them. Governments, on the other hand, must stay in business because alternative services are usually not available. This assumption was recently challenged when the Supreme Court of Canada determined that the right to strike was a fundamental right protected by the Constitution.[37] Furthermore, as mentioned earlier, the Supreme Court of Canada decided that the RCMP could unionize—something not allowed by federal legislation. Again, the court determined that the law violated the fundamental right to freedom of association.[38] With these changes, there may be less ability for governments to legislate certain restrictions.

Strikes in the Public Sector

Strikes by government employees create a problem for lawmakers and for the general public. Because the services that government employees provide, such as police work and firefighting, are often considered essential to the well-being of the public, public policy is opposed to such strikes. However, various provincial legislatures have granted public employees the right to strike. Where striking is permitted, the right is limited to specific groups of employees—those performing non-essential services—and the strike cannot endanger the public's health, safety, or welfare.

Public-sector unions contend, however, that denying them the same right to strike as employees in the private sector greatly reduces their power during collective bargaining. (The union's power during collective bargaining, including the eventual right for employees to go on strike, is discussed in more detail later in the chapter.)

Public employees who perform essential services do, in fact, strike. Teachers, sanitation employees, police, transit employees, firefighters, and postal employees have all engaged in strike action. To avoid a potentially critical situation, various arbitration methods are used for resolving collective-bargaining deadlocks in the public sector. One is compulsory

Canadian Union of Public Employees workers strike to make people aware of the dispute.

binding arbitration for employees such as police officers, firefighters, and others in jobs in which strikes cannot be tolerated. Another method is final-offer arbitration, under which the arbitrator must select one or the other of the final offers submitted by the disputing parties. With this method, the arbitrator's award is more likely to go to the party whose final bargaining offer has moved the closest to a reasonable settlement. The government can also enact back-to-work legislation, an option being used more and more when concerns arise about public health or safety.

On the other hand, when public sector employees, such as college faculty, do strike, there are times when the public isn't supportive, and governments have to intervene. This occurred in Ontario when the provincial government tabled and passed back-to-work legislation that forced college faculty in 24 colleges to return to work. It was the first time in 50 years that faculty were forced back to work. The 5-week strike saw over 500,000 students prevented from attending classes.[39]

This particular legislation and the controversy surrounding it have specialists suggesting that a new model needs to be developed for disputes in the public sector. On the one hand, Supreme Court decisions have confirmed that public-sector employees have the right to join a union and bargain collectively. On the other hand, no matter how the dispute is settled, whether through back-to-work legislation or binding arbitration, taxpayers pay the costs—whether through disruption of service or higher wages.[40]

THE COLLECTIVE BARGAINING PROCESS

Once a union wins bargaining rights for employees, its 2 primary functions are to negotiate the collective agreement and resolve member complaints, usually through the grievance–arbitration process. Interestingly, according to labour law, once the union is certified to negotiate for bargaining-unit members, it must represent everyone in the unit equally, regardless of whether employees subsequently join the union or elect to remain

LO5

Describe the bargaining process and the bargaining goals and strategies of a union and an employer.

Bernard Weil/Toronto Star/Getty Images

FIGURE 10.3 Collective Bargaining Framework

Union gives notice to employer to commence collective bargaining (negotiations)

Employer and union each select their own bargaining (negotiation) teams

Employer and union each gather information to determine bargaining strategy and tactics, including assessing the other's goals

Bargaining (negotiation) teams meet to review/modify/compromise on the proposals from each and reach agreement on a new collective agreement

Employer and union each take agreement to the key decision makers for ratification of new collective agreement

non-members. The collective agreement ultimately negotiated establishes the wages, hours, employee benefits, job security, and other conditions under which represented employees agree to work.

Many of you may not be very familiar with collective bargaining and may see it as a passionate conflict between the employer and the union, with everything from all-night bargaining sessions to pounding on tables. There is no doubt that much effort goes into the preparation and conduct of negotiations, including the development of strategies and tactics. Both the employer and the union will also consider what kind of pressure, if any, it can exert on the other. Unions will typically use a strike, or threat of a strike, whereas an employer will consider a lockout.

For an overview of the collective bargaining framework, examine Figure 10.3.

Good-Faith Bargaining

Once a union has been recognized as the representative for employees, it will expect the employer to meet and negotiate in good faith. Employers as well as unions, by labour law, are required to do so; if not, either party could face consequences. For example, the employer would be expected to meet with the union representatives in a timely fashion to begin negotiations. Also, unions are expected not to withdraw agreement from something they had previously agreed to. Furthermore, an employer cannot override the bargaining process by making an offer directly to the employees. Figure 10.4 illustrates several common examples of bad-faith employer bargaining.

Preparing for Negotiations

As noted in Figure 10.3 (third box), both the union and the employer will gather information as well as develop strategies and tactics in preparation for collective bargaining. This allows a logical flow of the exchange of proposals, which creates a greater possibility of both parties' objectives being achieved. Negotiators often develop a bargaining book that serves as a cross-reference file to determine which contract clauses would be affected by a demand. Often preparation for the next round of collective bargaining will begin soon after the new collective agreement is signed. By doing so, both the employer and the union can assess what did occur or what should have occurred during negotiations.

FIGURE 10.4 Examples of Bad-Faith Bargaining

Employer
- Using delaying tactics, such as frequent postponements of bargaining sessions.
- Insisting that the union stop striking before resuming negotiations.
- Unilaterally changing bargaining topics.
- Negotiating with individual employees other than authorized union representatives.
- Going through the motions of bargaining rather than conducting honest negotiations.
- Refusing to meet with authorized union representatives.

Union
- Using delaying tactics, such as frequent postponements of bargaining sessions.
- Withdrawing concessions previously granted.
- Unilaterally changing bargaining topics.
- Going through the motions of bargaining rather than conducting honest negotiations.
- Refusing to meet with authorized employer representatives.

Gathering Bargaining Data

Any information relating to the administration of the collective agreement, such as grievances, shift assignments, arbitration decisions, and the amount of the labour payroll, is necessary to understand what proposals might be developed. In addition, information can be obtained from other collective agreements negotiated in the company's industry. These agreements are usually available through labour relations boards.

Managers are also actively involved in supplying information and suggestions as they work with the collective agreement on a daily basis. Furthermore, since they are frequently in contact with shop stewards, managers may also have some information about what the union's goals might be. Any concerns that managers might have with the collective agreement should be thoroughly understood, considered, and incorporated as appropriate into the overall bargaining approach. And since managers work with the collective agreement on a daily basis, it is important that they be involved in the data-collection process so that they understand and feel part of the bargaining process.

Bargaining Strategies

It is critical that the organization develop a strategy for negotiations. Without adequately planning what it wants to achieve, a company might end up with an unwanted outcome. Negotiators for an employer should develop a written plan covering their bargaining strategy. In addition, this plan ought to contemplate what the union's goals are likely to be, what might not have been achieved in the last round of collective bargaining, and whether the union would strike in order to achieve its goals. Likewise, it is essential that the company identify the point at which it is willing to let employees strike or to lock them out. Not knowing the organization's limits can create difficulties at negotiations and perhaps incur job action that could have been avoided.

It is important that both the employer's and the union's strategy include the following:

1. Determine what each party's goals are and how far each will go to achieve them.
2. Consider if the union will strike and/or the employer will lock out.
3. Separate issues into monetary and non-monetary.
4. Have sufficient and factual reasons to support what is being proposed.
5. Identify a likely timetable to conclude a new collective agreement without a dispute.
6. Identify the nature of the union–management relationship and the relationship the union has with its members and how employees view management.

Both the employer and the union typically will put forward more proposals than they expect to achieve. This happens so that compromises can be achieved, with each party feeling satisfied about the outcome.

Forms of Collective Bargaining

Traditionally, the collective bargaining relationship between an employer and a union has been adversarial. The union has held the position that although the employer has the responsibility for managing the organization, the union has the right to challenge certain actions of management. Unions also have taken the position that the employer has an obligation to operate the organization in a manner that will provide adequate compensation to employees. Moreover, unions maintain that their members should not be expected to subsidize poor management by accepting less than their full entitlement.

In traditional bargaining, with its give-and-take philosophy, negotiators usually begin with specific positions, and through a variety of tactics, such as trade, the teams work toward a resolution. However, the results may or may not be to the complete satisfaction of one or both parties. In fact, when one side feels it has gotten "the short end of the stick," bitter feelings may persist for the life of the agreement.

Integrative bargaining
A collaborative approach to negotiations that focuses on developing mutually favourable outcomes

To change how parties feel about the bargaining process, many support and use a less confrontational approach. **Integrative bargaining** (or interest based) is based on creating value and determining what is best for everyone. The approach seeks to understand by asking questions and really listening to the answers. Often, by asking a "what if?" scenario, an opportunity to brainstorm is also created.[41] In addition, it is important that the individuals involved in the negotiations trust each other. To achieve this, and to bring different perspectives to the problem, it may be necessary to have others at the negotiations.[42]

Interest-based bargaining is novel in both its philosophy and its process. Also distinct are the bargaining tools used to expedite a successful non-adversarial negotiating experience. This style of negotiation was pioneered by Roger Fisher and William Ury, 2 professors at the Harvard Business School, and published in their highly successful book *Getting to Yes*. Fry and Ury stressed the need to focus on the problem (not the positions of the parties), to separate the people from the problem, and to create options for mutual benefit. In this fashion, the parties strive to find solutions and thus improve their overall relationship.[43]

Conducting the Negotiations

Among the factors that tend to make each bargaining situation unique are the economic conditions under which negotiations take place, the experience and personalities of the negotiators on each side, the goals they are seeking to achieve, and the strength of the relative positions. Some collective agreements can be negotiated informally in a few hours, particularly if the contract is short and the terms are not overly complex. Other agreements, such as those negotiated with large organizations, such as Air Canada and CP Rail, require months before settlements are reached.

Bargaining Teams

The composition and size of bargaining teams are often a reflection of the desires and practices of the parties. There is no set number for the teams, although it needs to be small enough to get the work done and large enough to demonstrate the importance of the process—frequently 4 to 6 people. The chief negotiator is usually the senior HR person for management and the business agent for the union. The others can be people from HR, finance, and operations (for the employer) and local union officials such as the president and potentially a person from the national union. In some cases, the representative from the national union will be the chief negotiator for the local union.

Labour negotiations have become increasingly complex and legalistic. Therefore, it is advisable that the parties have an experienced negotiator.

The initial meeting of the bargaining teams is particularly important because it establishes the climate that will prevail during the negotiations that follow. A cordial attitude, with perhaps the injection of a little humour, can contribute much to a relaxation of tensions and help the negotiations to begin smoothly.

Analyzing the Proposals

As with sellers who will try to get a higher price for their products if they think the prospective buyer strongly desires them, negotiators will try to get greater concessions in return for granting those their opponents want most. In traditional win-lose or adversarial bargaining, negotiators will do the same thing: the employer will try to find out what is important to the union without revealing what is important to it and vice versa.

As they develop their collective bargaining proposals, astute negotiators know that some demands are more important to their side than others—for either economic or political reasons. Therefore, the proposals that each side submits generally may be divided into those it feels it must achieve, those it would like to achieve, and those it is submitting primarily for trading purposes. As bargainers discuss the proposals from each side, they are constantly trying to determine the intensity with which each side is committed to its demands. The ability to accurately gauge "commitment" to various proposals can spell the difference between an agreement and an impasse.

Resolving the Proposals

For a collective agreement to be achieved, the various issues eventually need to be resolved to the satisfaction of all parties. This occurs within a range, is called the "bargaining zone," and has some overlap, which is why an agreement can be reached.[44] If the resolution for either the union or the employer is outside the acceptable range, and there is no more willingness to compromise, a deadlock will occur. For example, if the employer is insisting that it be allowed 24 hours to issue notice of mandatory overtime and the union's lowest limit is 24 hours—the zone—then a settlement can occur. If, however, the union's bottom limit is 36 hours, then the parties won't be able to reach an agreement.

The Union's Power in Collective Bargaining

During negotiations, it is necessary for each party to retreat sufficiently from its original position to permit an agreement to be achieved. If this does not occur, the negotiations will become deadlocked, and the union may resort to the use of economic power, such as a strike, to achieve its demands. Otherwise, the only alternative will be to have members continue working without a collective agreement once the old one has expired. As managers know well, the ability to engage in or even threaten to engage in such activities also can serve as a form of pressure. In some cases, employees do not actually strike but slow down their work and create pressure on the company. Or the employees will "work to rule"—strictly follow the terms of the collective agreement. This means that if the collective agreement specifies that employees will have a 45-minute lunch break, yet most employees take only 30 and work the other 15 minutes, in a work-to-rule situation, the employees would take the full 45 minutes.

> **LO6**
> List the forms of bargaining power that a union and an employer may utilize to enforce their bargaining demands.

Striking

A **strike** is a situation in which unionized workers refuse to perform their work during labour negotiations. It is legal only during negotiations, after the collective agreement has expired. Employees cannot strike during the collective agreement as proscribed by labour legislation. Although strikes account for only a small portion of total workdays lost in industry each year, they are a costly and emotional event for all concerned. For example, in early 2017, 175,000 construction workers in Québec unions went on strike. Initially, the government was reluctant to table legislation.[45] Because of the potential economic fallout from a lengthy strike, estimated at $45,000,000 per day, it only took a few days before the provincial government legislated the striking construction workers back to work.[46]

> **Strike**
> A situation in which unionized workers refuse to perform their work during labour negotiations

Unions do not use a strike or the threat of a strike casually. It is a very serious matter as union members are not working and therefore have no wages being paid. Even if striking employees are on a picket line and receive pay from the union for that purpose, it does not replace what the employee was earning. Because of the seriousness of the situation, unions will seek approval from their membership before striking. Although this vote is frequently used as a threat to show strength to the employer, the threat of a strike creates as much of a problem as an actual strike.

Since a strike can have serious effects on the union and its members, the union must analyze the prospects for its success carefully. For example, in mid-2018, all the workers at the Caesars Windsor hotel-casino in Windsor, Ontario, went on strike after the membership rejected a new collective agreement by a vote of 59%. This is a risky decision by the union as the local president stated that although employees liked much of what was in the new agreement, the 2300 dealers, cooks, housekeepers, and janitors went on strike because they felt disrespected by the employer.[47] It is unusual for a union membership to reject an agreement that is being recommended by the union officials that negotiated the agreement. Typically, the strike occurs, and then a new agreement is reached and recommended to the membership. This is what occurred when the employees at GM's CAMI assembly plant went on strike in the fall of 2017. During the strike, GM also issued layoff notice to employees at another plant, stating that the work was being shifted to Mexico. The issue of job security became prominent, and the union, Unifor, presented a comprehensive new agreement to GM after about a week of the workers being on strike.[48] Although a deal was reached and the strike was settled about 3 weeks later, it isn't clear as to whether the employees achieved their objectives given the work disruption.[49] The agreement did have some additional assistance to help employees in the event of layoffs, but the overall improvements to job security did not happen. GM retained the right to move production from the CAMI plant to Mexico.[50]

Work stoppages continue to create issues for the Canadian economy. The federal government is now publishing monthly statistics, and for 2017, there were 1.2 million person-days lost, of which 60% were in the private sector—a change from previous years when most of the days lost were in the public sector.[51] Strikes can be disruptive and challenging to the organizations struck. As noted in the section under preparation for negotiations, it is important to assess whether the employer can continue to operate with management staff. For example, if the organization uses a great deal of automation to conduct its business, such as a manufacturer, it may be able to do so. If the employer is able to maintain operations during a strike, then the strike tactic of the union may not achieve the desired outcome.

To understand more about the issues over which unions will strike, check out the websites of the International Association of Machinists and Aerospace Workers, the Canadian Union of Public Employees, and the International Brotherhood of Electrical Workers.

Picketing

Picket

A situation in which unionized workers stand in front of entrances to the employer to prevent people from conducting business with the employer

Almost always during a strike, the union will have its members **picket** the employer. It does this by having its members (the employees) stand in front of entrances to prevent people from conducting business with the employer. Even when the strikers represent only a small proportion of the employees within the organization, they can cause shutdown of an entire organization if enough of the organization's remaining employees (i.e., sympathy strikers) refuse to cross their picket line. In addition, if there are other unionized employees that deliver or pick up goods from the struck employer, those employees may refuse to cross the picket line.

If a strike fails to stop an employer's operations, the picket line may serve as more than a passive weapon. Employees who attempt to cross the line may be subjected to verbal insults and even physical violence. Mass picketing, in which large groups of pickets try to block the path of people trying to enter an organization, may also be used. However, the use of picket lines to exert physical pressure and incite violence is illegal and may harm more than help the union's cause.

The Employer's Power in Collective Bargaining

For the employer, any power it has during negotiations is a function of whether or not it can continue operating. The employer can transfer these operations to other locations or can subcontract them to other employers through outsourcing. General Motors outsources to foreign manufacturers many parts used in the assembly of North American cars. In exercising their economic freedom, however, employers must be careful that their actions are not interpreted by the provincial labour relations board to be an attempt to avoid bargaining with the union.

Winnipeg Free Press-Joe Bryksa/The Canadian Press

A strike for workers is a significant situation, and the union needs to be sure it will be successful as a bargaining tactic.

Operating during Strikes

When negotiations become deadlocked, typically, the union initiates action and the employer reacts. In reacting, employers must balance the cost of taking a strike against the long- and short-term costs of agreeing to union demands. They must also consider how long operations might be suspended and the length of time that they and the unions will be able to endure a strike. An employer who chooses to accept a strike must then decide whether to continue operating if it is possible to do so. CP Rail uses its managers and office staff to operate locomotives during any strike. This is a situation that the Teamsters, which represents unionized train crews, is not happy with, and the union wants the new president to stop the practice. Even though the new president wants to improve the overall labour relations climate, he feels strongly that the company needs to continue to operate.[52]

Should employees go on strike, employers in certain jurisdictions are limited in their ability to hire replacement workers. Québec and British Columbia have passed "anti-scab" laws, forbidding the use of replacement workers during a strike. Employers have the right to dismiss workers who engage in sabotage or violence during a strike.

Workers are entitled to return to their jobs, but not necessarily their previous positions, once a strike is settled. The right to return to work is often an issue to be negotiated. Although laws vary, in many cases, employees must submit, in writing, their intention to return to their job once a strike is finalized.

Using the Lockout

Lockout
Strategy by which the employer denies employees the opportunity to work by closing its operations

Much like the union carefully assessing whether or not it strikes to achieve its objectives, so, too, is the situation for an employer in relation to a **lockout** of employees. Employers use this tactic much less frequently than unions use the strike tactic. Not only does it create hardship for its employees, but it also might damage the company's reputation.

Although this approach hasn't been used often, the *Chronicle Herald* in Halifax locked out its pressroom workers for almost 3 weeks before an agreement was reached.[53]

Under labour relations board provisions, an employer cannot enforce a lockout within a prescribed number of hours (48 to 72) of a strike vote. Lockouts affect non-striking workers. For example, when miners at Inco are locked out, administrative work ceases, and office staff are also locked out or laid off.

Resolving Bargaining Deadlocks

When a strike or a lockout occurs, both parties are soon affected by it. The employer will suffer a loss of profits and customers and possibly of public goodwill. The union members suffer a loss of income that is likely to be only partially offset by strike benefits or outside income. The union's leaders risk the possibility of losing members, of being voted out of office, of losing public support, or of having the members vote to decertify the union as their bargaining agent. As the losses to each side mount, the disputing parties usually feel more pressure to achieve a settlement.

Mediation and Arbitration

Mediator
Third party in a labour dispute who meets with one party and then the other in order to suggest compromise solutions or to recommend concessions from each side that will lead to an agreement

When the disputing parties are unable to resolve a deadlock, a third party serving in the capacity of a conciliator, a mediator, or an arbitrator may be called on to provide assistance. In many jurisdictions, conciliation is compulsory before a legal strike or lockout. The conciliator, appointed by the provincial ministry of labour, helps the parties reconcile their differences in an attempt to reach a workable agreement. If the conciliation effort is unsuccessful, a report is filed with the ministry of labour, which, in rare instances, may appoint a conciliation board that accepts presentations from both parties and makes non-binding formal recommendations. If a settlement cannot be reached at this stage, a strike is permitted, except in Manitoba, Alberta, Saskatchewan, and Québec, where strikes are permissible during conciliation. This 2-stage conciliation process is normally reserved for high-profile cases in which significant social and economic consequences would result from a strike.

Mediation is similar to conciliation except that it is voluntary (the 2 parties contract a neutral third party to help them), and the mediator assumes a more active role as a negotiator. A **mediator** serves primarily as a fact finder and someone to open up a channel of communication between the parties. Typically, the mediator meets with one party and then the other in order to suggest compromise solutions or to recommend concessions from each side that will lead to an agreement without causing either to lose face. Mediators have no power or authority to force either side toward an agreement. They must have the ability to understand the perspectives of all parties and to help each party involved to understand those perspectives. Other skills include active listening, empathy, and the ability to reframe the problem or issues.[54]

One of the newer forms of mediation is online mediation. Through using Internet-based help, ways can be found to use experts in helping solve the dispute without having the expert present. Check out some of these resources by visiting the following sites: Mediate.com, ADR Resources, and ADR Institute of Canada.

Arbitration is the only third-party resolution form that results in binding decisions. The arbitrator is a neutral individual who is retained to hear the dispute and make a decision. As mentioned in Chapter 9, arbitration is an alternative dispute-resolution process. Arbitration is a type of judicial process as the decision is final and binding. The arbitrator will ask for evidence from each party so that the new collective agreement can be determined. Although mediation is frequently used to settle a collective agreement, arbitration is not often used, and if it is, it is usually in the public sector. There are situations in the public sector where strikes may be prohibited if the employees are in an essential service area, such as fire-fighting. If this is the case, then **interest arbitration** is used to resolve negotiations. Often the union, the employer, or both are not anxious to have a third party determine the collective agreement, and, frequently, the only issue at an interest arbitration is a key item such as compensation. Even this can be problematic for both parties.

Interest arbitration
A mechanism to renew or establish a new collective agreement for parties

THE COLLECTIVE AGREEMENT

At the conclusion of negotiations, a collective agreement is put in writing and ratified by the union membership. The union typically does this by asking that the members vote on the new terms. The representatives of both parties then sign the agreement—a legal, binding contract. The scope of the agreement (and the length of the written document) will vary with the size of the employer and the length of the bargaining relationship.

Although each collective agreement is unique to the employer and the union, all collective agreements have many similarities. Toolkit 10.4 lists some of the standard employment conditions that you would find in a collective agreement. What is typically also of critical importance to the union is its security clause and to the employer is the management rights language.

LO7

Identify the major provisions of a collective agreement, including the issue of management rights.

TOOLKIT 10.4   **STANDARD EMPLOYMENT CONDITIONS IN A COLLECTIVE AGREEMENT**

- Pay and benefits, including pensions, overtime, etc.
- Various leaves, such as vacation, sick leave, and legislated holidays.
- Health and safety policies.
- Scope of the bargaining unit, that is, which employee categories are included.
- Employees who are required to join the union in order to be or remain employed (i.e., union security).
- Role and scope of management decisions (i.e., management rights).
- Extent of management rights.
- Grievance process.
- Definition of seniority and how it is acquired.
- Shift schedules and how changes are made.
- Just-cause discipline, particularly in relation to termination.
- Labour–management relationships, for example, an ongoing committee to deal with issues during the life of the collective agreement.
- Layoff/recall.
- Term of the collective agreement (the dates the agreement is in force).

The Issue of Management Rights

When employers refer to "management rights," they are referring to a range of choices they have to manage the enterprise. This includes everything from strategic direction to operational decisions such as hiring. Since virtually every management right can and has been challenged successfully by unions, the ultimate determination of these rights will depend on the relative bargaining power of the 2 parties. Furthermore, to achieve union cooperation or concessions, employers have had to relinquish some of these time-honoured rights.

Residual Rights

Residual rights

Concept that management's authority is supreme in all matters except those it has expressly conceded to the union in the collective agreement

In the collective agreement, management rights may be treated as **residual rights** or as defined rights. The residual rights concept holds that management's authority is supreme in all matters except those it has expressly conceded in the collective agreement, or in those areas where its authority is restricted by law. Put another way, management does not look to the collective agreement to ascertain its rights; it looks to the agreement to find out which and how much of its rights and powers it has conceded outright or agreed to share with the union.[55]

Residual rights might include the right of management to determine the product to produce or to select production equipment and procedures. Employers who subscribe to the residual rights concept prefer not to mention management rights in the collective agreement on the grounds that they possess such rights already. To mention them might create an issue with the union.

Defined Rights

Defined rights

Concept that management's authority should be expressly defined and clarified in the collective agreement

The **defined rights** concept, on the other hand, is intended to reinforce and clarify which rights are exclusively those of management. This concept means that the employer has only those rights that are written into the collective agreement. It serves to reduce confusion and misunderstanding and to remind union officers, union stewards, and employees that management never relinquishes its right to operate the organization. For example, a defined right would include the right of management to take disciplinary action against problem employees. The great majority of collective agreements contain provisions covering management rights. The following is an example of a general statement defining management rights in 1 collective agreement:

ARTICLE 7 - PLANT MANAGEMENT

7.01 The Management of the Plant, and the direction of the working force, the maintenance of order, discipline and efficiency, including the right to direct, plan, and control plant operations, to schedule working hours, and the right to select, hire, promote, demote, transfer, suspend or discharge employees for just and sufficient cause, or to release employees because of lack of work or for other legitimate reasons, the right to establish work or job assignments and the output of machines and operators, and to decide the number of employees needed by the Company at any time, the right to introduce new and improved methods and facilities, or to change existing production methods and facilities and to determine the products to be manufactured are vested exclusively in the Company.

7.02 The Company agrees that the above functions will be exercised in a manner not inconsistent with the terms of this Agreement, and that an employee who feels he has been unjustly treated within the terms of this Agreement may make such complaint, subject to the Grievance Procedure in the manner and to the extent as provided for in this Agreement.[56]

Forms of Union Security

As mentioned earlier in this chapter, there are provisions in collective agreements that may require an employee to become a union member as a condition of employment. This type of clause (union shop) would be considered a form of union security. Other forms of union security were also presented: a closed shop (must be a union member to be hired) and an open shop (the employee chooses to become a union member or not).

The type of union security clause can be very controversial as it can restrict where an employer can recruit. Although rare, closed-shop clauses are perhaps the most adversarial because they require employers to recruit employees from a union hiring hall.

Working in conjunction with the union shop clause are the various seniority provisions of the collective agreement. Unions prefer that many personnel decisions (e.g., promotions, job transfers, shift assignments, vacations) be based on seniority, a criterion that limits the discretion of managers to make such decisions on the basis of merit.

Read Ethics in HRM 10.2 regarding an example of how strongly unions feel about union security.

ETHICS IN HRM 10.2   **CAN A UNION REALLY DO THIS?**

Most people would think that individuals volunteering as firefighters in their own community would be a very good and noble thing to do. However, some firefighters' unions think this is wrong.

Specifically, some firefighter unions in Ontario have rules stating that professional firefighters cannot volunteer during their days off in their own community. This is referred to as "double-hatting," and it is common in many rural communities. In order to ensure that this doesn't happen, some firefighters have been accused of double-hatting and could face sanctions for doing so, including costly fines. Why the concern?

The unions, including the parent organization, the International Association of Fire Fighters (IAFF), are against the practice as it is a threat to union growth. These unions feel there should be growth of professional (and therefore paid) firefighters and no reliance on volunteers. Furthermore, because their constitutions have a clause that prevents members from doing so, unions feel allowing it violates the very core of the organization.

The individuals involved feel strongly that they want to give back to their community and that the union doesn't have the right to tell them what to do or not do in their off-duty time. The communities that have a volunteer fire service cannot afford to increase tax revenue— estimated to be over 25%—just to have a larger, paid fire service. Furthermore, some of the communities say that the need for fire service support isn't large enough to justify any paid staff.

In these communities, there are many more volunteer firefighters than just professional firefighters. For example, in Caledon and its surrounding small communities, there are 250 volunteer firefighters and 22 full-time (paid) firefighters. These communities also cite a lack of population density as a barrier to any more full-time firefighters. There is no doubt that the large majority of volunteers receive all the proper training and support to be effective. These volunteers also state that having professional firefighters working alongside them provides invaluable experience.

When a union tribunal determined that these individuals had "double-hatted," the IAFF suspended their union membership and indicated that it will start fining them if they continue the practice. These firefighters will appeal, with Caledon paying for the appeal and any fines the firefighters may be assessed.

CRITICAL THINKING QUESTIONS:

1. Do you agree with what the union is doing? Why or why not?
2. Do you think these rural communities ought to hire more professional firefighters? Why or why not?

Sources: Adapted from Eric Andrew-Gee, "Five Firefighters Face Union Charges for Double-Hatting," *The Globe and Mail*, May 16, 2017, A6; "Double-Hatting Criticized by Firefighters' Union," *CBC News*, May 17, 2017, accessed April 12, 2018, www.cbc.ca/news/canada/windsor/double-hatting-criticized-by-firefighter -s-union-1.4118961; and Eric Andrew-Gee, "Ontario Firefighters Vow to Appeal Union's 'Double-Hatting' Verdict," *The Globe and Mail*, June 15, 2017, accessed April 12, 2018, www.theglobeandmail.com/news/national/ontario-firefighters-vow-to-appeal-unions-double-hatting-verdict/article35324068.

TOOLKIT 10.5 — CLAUSES FROM COLLECTIVE AGREEMENTS

1. Leave With or Without Pay for Other Reasons

At its discretion, the Employer may grant:

   a. leave with pay when circumstances not directly attributable to the employee prevent his or her reporting for duty; such leave shall not be unreasonably withheld;

   b. leave with or without pay for purposes other than those specified in this Agreement. (Between Canada Revenue Agency and the Public Service Alliance of Canada)

2. Layoffs

The Employer shall give all permanent Employees with one (1) or more years of service, two (2) consecutive working days' notice of lay off or two (2) days' pay.

(Between Communications, Energy, and Paperworkers Union and A.B.C. Press [1979] Limited)

3. Seniority

SENIORITY LIST The Company shall at least once every six (6) months, post in a conspicuous place on its premises an up-to-date list of all employees covered by this Agreement showing the date when each commenced his employment with the Company. The Company shall forward to the Union a copy of each list on the date of its posting.

LAYOFFS In the event of layoffs, seniority shall be recognized. The principle of last man on, first man off, shall prevail, subject to job classification. The Company shall give at least forty-eight (48) hours' notice on layoffs, exclusive of Saturdays, Sundays, and General Holidays.

(Between Robinson Rentals and Sales and International Union of Operating Engineers.)

Administration of the Collective Agreement

Although there is much publicity around labour negotiations, the day-to-day use of the collective agreement is the bulk of labour relations activities. Managers became very familiar with the terms of the collective agreement as these will set both the tone and the substance of managing their employees. Sometimes the administration of the collective agreement has to be done through the union itself. For example, the Windsor police were called in to investigate a hate crime when a worker at Fiat Chrysler found nooses around his work stage. Since this is considered a hate crime, the union met with all its members to remind them that this is totally unacceptable and that if caught, they will lose union membership.[57]

Toolkit 10.5 provides examples of clauses from collective agreements.

GRIEVANCE PROCESS

LO8

Describe a typical grievance process and explain the basis for arbitration awards.

Grievance process
Formal process that provides the union with a way to handle a complaint that something within the collective agreement has been violated

In the daily course of using the collective agreement, sometimes the employer and the union will interpret the same provision differently. If the parties decide to pursue the differences, they can make use of the **grievance process**. Almost all grievances are initiated by the union, usually alleging that some term of the collective agreement was violated. Furthermore, by law, a grievance process precludes a union from striking during the term of a collective agreement. When negotiating a grievance process, an important concern for both sides is how effectively the system will serve the needs of employees and management. A well-written grievance process will allow grievances to be heard quickly and with as little red tape as possible. Furthermore, it should serve to foster cooperation, not conflict, between the employer and the union.

Although each grievance process is distinctive for each employer–union relationship, it is required under Canadian labour relations codes. Grievance processes are negotiated to address the organization's structure and labour–management philosophy and the specific desires of the parties.

Although each process is unique, there are common elements among systems. For example, grievance processes normally specify how the grievance is to be initiated, the number and timing of steps that are in the process, and the identity of representatives from each side who are to be involved in the hearings at each step (see Figure 10.5). The purpose of this multistep process is to allow higher levels of union and management representatives to look at the issue from different perspectives. If the grievance cannot be resolved between the union and management, most grievance processes allow the dispute to go to arbitration for a binding decision. It is not the function of an arbitrator to help the 2 parties reach a compromise solution. Rather, it is the arbitrator's job to mandate how the grievance is to be resolved.

Initiating the Formal Grievance

The first step of the grievance process can be either in writing or done in person to the employee's manager. If the employee feels unable to communicate effectively with the manager, the grievance may be taken to the shop steward, who will discuss it with the manager. Often the situation in question is the result of an error or misinterpretation and can be fixed quickly. For this to happen, the manager must be willing to discuss it with the employee and the shop steward. Managers should be trained formally in resolving grievances. This training should include familiarization with the terms of the collective agreement and the development of counselling skills to facilitate a problem-solving approach.

There are times when the situation cannot be resolved at the initial step. This can be because there are real differences in the interpretation of the collective agreement or the manager doesn't have the power to make a decision to the satisfaction of the employee. Furthermore, feelings and conflicts can also get in the way of finding a resolution without an arbitration.

FIGURE 10.5 **Grievance Process**

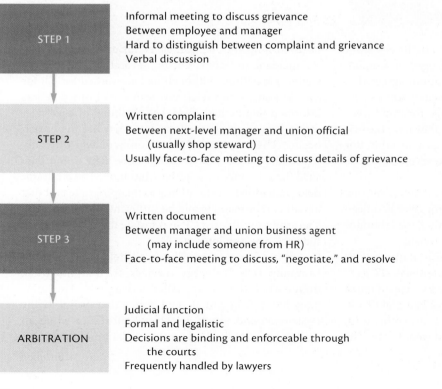

STEP 1
Informal meeting to discuss grievance
Between employee and manager
Hard to distinguish between complaint and grievance
Verbal discussion

STEP 2
Written complaint
Between next-level manager and union official
(usually shop steward)
Usually face-to-face meeting to discuss details of grievance

STEP 3
Written document
Between manager and union business agent
(may include someone from HR)
Face-to-face meeting to discuss, "negotiate," and resolve

ARBITRATION
Judicial function
Formal and legalistic
Decisions are binding and enforceable through
the courts
Frequently handled by lawyers

Grievance Resolution

If a grievance is to be resolved successfully, representatives of both management and the union must be able to discuss the problem in a rational and objective manner. A grievance should not be viewed as something to be won or lost. Rather, both sides must view the situation as an attempt to solve a problem. Throughout the process, both parties will try to resolve the issue. However, if the conflict cannot be resolved through discussion and compromise, all collective agreements in Canadian jurisdictions contain a provision for arbitration, or **grievance resolution**. An arbitrator (usually a lawyer or professional skilled in the arbitration process) or a board or panel (consisting of a union nominee, a management nominee, and a neutral chair) hears the case and submits a decision, including the rationale. The decision is final, and the parties are legally bound to accept the decision unless there is serious concern over the arbitrator's competence or integrity.

Grievance resolution
Process in which a neutral third party makes a decision on a grievance

Rights Arbitration

Rights arbitration
A mechanism to resolve disputes about the interpretation and application of a collective agreement during the term of that collective agreement

A **rights arbitration** is the final step in any grievance process. The arbitration is conducted by someone neutral who makes a final and binding decision—which is enforceable through the courts.

One criticism of the arbitration process is that it is slow (up to 2 years) and costly. Although arbitration hearings at one point had 3 individuals serving as an arbitration panel (1 selected by the employer, 1 selected by the union, and a third selected by the other 2), this does not happen as frequently due to the costs involved. Now, most arbitrations are done by a single arbitrator. Another solution is expedited arbitration, which is an agreement to bypass some steps in the grievance process when the issue is particularly important or urgent, as in the case of employee dismissals or layoffs of employees.

Read HRM and the Law 10.1 for 2 different outcomes when employees were terminated.

HRM AND **THE LAW** 10.1   FIRED!

You might think that terminating an employee's work is an action that ought not to be challenged by a union, but that is rarely the case. Even if a union agrees that the person was appropriately terminated, it will usually always launch a grievance to challenge the employer's action. Employers want to be sure that they have the evidence to prove that wrongdoing occurred as an arbitrator might decide that termination was too severe and reinstate the employee with full back pay.

Two recent cases had different outcomes: in one case, the arbitrator decided that the employer had been wrong in the termination, and in the other, the arbitrator decided that the termination was appropriate.

One case involved Canadian Pacific Railway (CP) and the Teamsters Canada Rail Conference (TCRC). One of the railway's locomotive engineers stepped into a gopher hole shortly before finishing his late-night shift. Although he had immediate pain, he finished his shift, warned a coworker about the hole, and went home. The

next morning, the engineer called his manager to report the incident and saw a doctor. Several weeks later, the engineer was fired. Although he had worked for CP for over 34 years, with a relatively clean work history, he was informed that he had "breached the bond of trust necessary for continued employment." How did the breach occur? The employee did not immediately officially report the accident or the safety issue. The union pursued the grievance through to arbitration. The arbitrator determined that termination was inappropriate and that a written reprimand would be sufficient for the incident. The arbitrator ordered CP to reinstate the employee with full back pay (and interest).

In another case, an Alberta oil-field transportation company, D & D Energy Services, fired a pilot truck driver when the worker failed a drug test. The company has a drug and alcohol policy that prohibits the possession and use of any illegal substance while on shift in any vehicle. To do so is a violation of the policy.

continued

Furthermore, the policy provides for a leave for treatment if any employee tested positive for either alcohol or drugs. The employee had signed a document acknowledging understanding of the policy. For several years prior to the incident, the employee had several written warnings for accidents with trucks. A further accident occurred when the driver lost control of the pilot truck, rolling it into a ditch. Another truck driver came along to help, and as the first truck driver was getting out of the truck cab, the helping driver smelled marijuana. The helping employee reported the incident, including the smell of marijuana at the scene of the accident. The employee was ordered to take a drug test, which was determined to be falsified when it indicated negative.

On a subsequent test, the employee did test positive for THC. The employee was then fired. The grievance was submitted to arbitration, where the arbitrator determined that there was no evidence of impairment at the time of the accident. However, the arbitrator did confirm that the employee falsified the urine sample and that dishonesty constituted serious misconduct, and therefore upheld the termination.

CRITICAL THINKING QUESTIONS:
1. If you were the arbitrator, what decisions would you make? Explain your answers.
2. Is there any other information you would want before a decision was made? If so, what?

Sources: Adapted from Eric Atkins, "'Oh My God, It's So Brutal,'" *The Globe and Mail*, March 4, 2017, B7; Canadian Railway Office of Arbitration & Dispute Resolution, *Canadian Pacific Railway Company and Teamsters Canada Rail Conference, Case No. 4522*, accessed April 9, 2018, http://arbitrations.netfirms.com/croa/50/CR4522.htm; and Jeffrey Smith, "Falsified Post-Incident Drug Test Worse Than Having Marijuana at Work," *Canadian HR Reporter*, October 16, 2017, accessed April 9, 2018, www.hrreporter.com/workplace-law/34855-falsified-post-incident-drug-test-worse-than-having-marijuana-at-work.

The Decision to Arbitrate

If a grievance cannot be resolved through the grievance procedure, each disputing party must decide whether to use arbitration to resolve the case. The alternatives would be for the union to withdraw the grievance or for the employer to agree to union demands.

Typically, the union forwards the dispute to arbitration. In doing so, the union and the employer then determine how important the matter is in relation to the cost of an arbitration and the likely outcome. There are times a union will want something arbitrated even though there is a high probability of the award being in favour of the employer in order to demonstrate that it is representing the interests of its members. In fact, in British Columbia, the labour code requires the union to fairly represent all members, or the members can challenge the union through the labour relations board.

However, the employer may also let a grievance proceed to arbitration to show strength to the union. Sometimes lower-level managers may agree with the union's position and will not go against senior management for fear of reprisal. And sometimes the personalities of the people get in the way of a sound resolution and the dispute goes to arbitration even though it ought not to.

The Arbitration Process

The issues to be resolved through arbitration may be described formally in a statement. Each party makes a joint submission to the arbitrator, indicating the rationale for the grievance. The submission to arbitrate must state the nature of the dispute with reference to the section of the collective agreement that has allegedly been breached. Such a statement might read: "Was the 3-day suspension of Alex Hayden for just cause? If not, what is the appropriate remedy?" However, the 2 parties at the beginning of the hearing also present grievable issues orally to the arbitrator. The purpose of an arbitration hearing is to provide a full and fair hearing of the matter in dispute, including statements from witnesses. If minutes and memoranda covering the meetings held at earlier stages of the grievance process have been prepared, these are sometimes submitted prior to the formal hearing to acquaint the arbitrator with the issues.

The procedures for conducting arbitration hearings and the restrictions governing the evidence that may be introduced during these hearings are more flexible than those

The final stage of the grievance process is arbitration, which is a final and binding decision.

permitted in a court of law. However, it is still the responsibility of the arbitrator to ensure that both the employer and the union have a fair hearing as each side presents evidence to support its case. Hearsay evidence, for example, may be introduced, assuming that it is described as such. The objective of the hearing is to enable the arbitrator to gather information necessary to resolve the problem—which is a people problem in the organization, not a legal problem. Because the process is more flexible, the arbitrator can ask for additional information and question any witnesses.

Depending on the importance of the case, the hearings may be conducted either in an informal way or in a very formal way, not unlike that of a court trial. If the proceedings have witnesses who will testify, they are sworn in. In all grievance arbitrations except those involving any form of discipline, the "burden of proof" rests with the union—that is, the union must prove that the employer violated the written collective agreement. Finally, the costs associated with the arbitration are usually shared equally between the employer and the union.

The Arbitration Award

Once the hearing is finished, the arbitrator will provide a written decision as soon as possible. Some collective agreements even specify the length of time the arbitrator has to make the decision. If for whatever reason the written decision isn't ready in a timely fashion, the arbitrator can inform the parties of the decision with reasons to follow. This can happen in cases such as terminations. The decision usually includes the reasons for the arbitrator's determination. By providing the reasons behind the decision, hurt feelings can be minimized. In short, tact and objective reasoning can help reduce disappointment and hard feelings.

The foundation for an arbitrator's decision is the collective agreement and the rights it establishes for each party. In many instances, the decision may hinge on whether management's actions were justified under the terms of this agreement. Sometimes it may depend on the arbitrator's interpretation of the wording of a particular provision. Established HR policies and past practices can also provide the basis for determining the award. And it must be remembered that an arbitration decision, if need be, is enforceable through the courts.

In many grievances, such as those involving employee performance or behaviour on the job, the arbitrator must determine whether the evidence supports the employer's action against the griever. The evidence must also indicate whether the employee was accorded the right of due process, which is the employee's right to be informed of unsatisfactory performance and to have an opportunity to respond to these charges. Under most collective agreements, an employer is required to have just cause (i.e., a good reason) for the action it has taken, and such action should be justified by the evidence presented.

If the arbitration hearing indicates that an employee was accorded due process and the disciplinary action was for just cause, the severity of the penalty must then be assessed. Where the evidence supports the discipline imposed by the employer, the arbitrator will probably let the discipline stand intact. However, it is within the arbitrator's power, unless denied by the submission agreement, to reduce the penalty. It is not uncommon, for example, for an arbitrator to reduce a discharge to a suspension without pay for the period the griever has been off the payroll.

The outcome of an **arbitration award** can have a significant impact on either or both the employer and the union. Therefore, it is important to have some understanding of what an arbitrator considers when making a decision, which are typically the following:

1. The language in the collective agreement.
2. The issue(s) in the dispute presented, including what section of the collective agreement has been violated.
3. The testimony of witnesses regarding what the section of the collective agreement in dispute means or is interpreted to mean.
4. The use of similar arbitral decisions and precedents.

> **Arbitration award**
> Final and binding award issued by an arbitrator in a labour–management dispute

Depending on the issue, all or only some of these factors would be taken into consideration. However, in a termination grievance, the arbitrator looks at slightly different factors, primarily whether the employer proved that discipline was appropriate and that the termination was appropriate. For example, in a recent termination case, 2 employees (janitorial staff at a university) were terminated for smoking marijuana in one of their cars during a shift break. Campus police approached the car and smelled marijuana. The employees denied that they had smoked any and said they had none in their possession. However, once the employees were advised that the police would have to be called, they acknowledged that they had smoked and provided a small bag of marijuana to the officer. During the investigation, the employer concluded that the employees had been smoking during their shift. As a result, they were terminated for consuming an illegal substance on the employer's premises and for being dishonest about their behaviour. Since as janitorial staff they were usually not directly supervised, they were in a position of trust, particularly since the jobs were safety sensitive. Although the union argued that termination was too severe, the arbitrator did not agree. Even though the arbitrator stated that any case involving drug use had to be determined on the evidence and the context, the arbitrator did conclude that the dishonesty of the employees and the breach of trust the employer felt were sufficient to uphold the termination.[58]

Given the ongoing global challenges, labour relations and collective bargaining continue to undergo many changes. See Emerging Trends 10.1 for some of the more important ones.

EMERGING TRENDS 10.1

1. ***Changes in bargaining rights.*** With changes to employment legislation in several provinces, labour law is changing bargaining rights for certain workers (such as contract employees) and also changes for how unionization can occur. Many of the changes are occurring due to changes at the provincial political level, such as in British Columbia, where the relatively new government wanted to eliminate secret balloting when making a decision on a union certification.

continued

2. ***Changes in the length of agreements.*** As the economy changes and as collective negotiations become costlier, the term of many collective agreements is getting longer. Furthermore, as the relationship with the union and the employer matures and there is more trust between the parties, both are becoming more comfortable with longer agreements. It used to be that unions frequently wanted to have shorter agreements to deal with changes in the economic environment. Now, with the inflation rate being relatively stable for a long time, there is less need to have more frequent negotiations to improve wage rates.

3. ***Union leadership publicly commenting on a wide range of economic issues.*** Due to the political nature of unions, they have periodically made public statements regarding issues that really only affected their members. However, unions are now making public statements regarding issues such as the potential impacts of raising minimum wages, NAFTA negotiations, and whether certain laws are too complex to be effective. For example, the Canadian Labour Congress stated that raising minimum wages could force more employers to find ways to automate work.

4. ***Potential changes in the overall model of Canadian labour relations.*** The existing system and model of labour relations have been around for over 100 years. Although some changes have occurred, many involved in labour relations are wondering if a fundamental shift in the model needs to occur. As noted earlier, unionization for public sector workers is now only about 16%, so workers rely upon either legislation or caring employers. Likewise, the workplace is changing dramatically as more technological advances occur in a worldwide economy and shifting demographics.

5. ***Continuing decline in unionization rates.*** Union density in Canada continues to decline—currently, it is less than 30%. Much of the decline is due to the shift from an industrial economy to one of service and knowledge. People in these sectors are usually more educated and therefore tend to resist collective action. Furthermore, some provinces have enacted labour legislation that restricts the union certification process. Although Gen X and Gen Y, as well as millennials, have different expectations and views of their role in the workplace, millennials are also almost 40% of the working population of Canada. Given the "gig" economy and the lack of job stability, many are now turning to unions to find that stability.

Sources: Derrick Penner, "Unions and Employers Divided on Use of Secret-Ballot Votes," *Vancouver Sun*, March 29, 2018, A9; "Unions Looking to Millennials as Alberta Workforce Grows Younger," *Teamsters*, August 3, 2016, accessed April 13, 2018, www.teamsters362.com/unions-looking-to-millennials-as-alberta-workforce-grows-younger; Ross Marowits, "Rising Minimum Wages Inevitable, Could Speed Up Automation: Labour Leaders," *Financial Post*, January 11, 2018, C3; Keith Fraser, "Unions Applaud Asbestos Ruling Reversal," *Vancouver Sun*, January 31, 2017, A7; Greg Keenan, "Striking GM Workers Face Threat of Production Shift to Mexico," *The Globe and Mail*, September 19, 2017, B1; Richard Chaykowski, Maurice Mazerolle, and Rafael Gomez, "Is a 21st-Century Model of Labour Relations Emerging in Canada?," *The Globe and Mail*, September 3, 2017, accessed April 13, 2018, www.theglobeandmail.com/report-on-business/rob-commentary/is-a-21st-century-model-of-labour-relations-emerging-in-canada/article36159190; Employment and Social Development Canada, *Labour Organizations in Canada 2015*; Statistics Canada, "Unionization Rate, Canada and Provinces, 2016," *The Daily*, September 8, 2017, accessed April 7, 2018, www.statcan.gc.ca/daily-quotidien/170908/cg-a004-eng.htm; John Dujay, "Are Longer-Term Agreements the New Normal?," *Canadian HR Reporter*, September 4, 2017, 26; and "How Millennials Are Trying to Revive the Labor Movement," *Fast Company*, November 16, 2017, accessed April 13, 2018, www.fastcompany.com/40497318/how-millennials-are-trying-to-revive-the-labor-movement.

LEARNING OUTCOMES SUMMARY

1. Explain the federal and provincial legislation that provides the framework for labour relations.
   - *Laws determine who can unionize*
   - *Laws require that unions and employers bargain in good faith*
   - *Laws provide for unions to strike and for employers to lock out*
2. Cite the reasons employees join unions.
   - *Dissatisfaction with pay and benefits*
   - *Dissatisfaction with managerial practices*
   - *Desire for recognition and status*
3. Outline the process by which unions organize employees and gain recognition as their bargaining agent.
   - *Employees make contact with a union representative*
   - *The union schedules a meeting with other employees*

- *Application is made to a labour relations board*
- *The labour relations board grants bargaining rights*

4. Illustrate the functions labour unions perform at international, national, and local levels.
   - *National unions help organize local unions*
   - *National unions help train and educate local unions*
   - *Local unions negotiate collective agreements and process member grievances*

5. Describe the bargaining process and the bargaining goals and strategies of a union and an employer.
   - *Each side will prepare a list of goals it wishes to achieve while also trying to anticipate the goals desired by the other side*
   - *Both employer and union negotiators will be sensitive to current bargaining patterns within the industry, general cost-of-living trends, and geographic wage differentials*
   - *The collective bargaining process includes not only the actual negotiations but also the power tactics used to support negotiating demands*

6. List the forms of bargaining power that a union and an employer may utilize to enforce their bargaining demands.
   - *The union's power in collective bargaining comes from its ability to picket, strike, or boycott the employer*
   - *The employer's power during negotiations comes from its ability to lock out employees or to operate during a strike by using managerial or replacement employees*

7. Identify the major provisions of a collective agreement, including the issue of management rights.
   - *Typical collective agreements will contain numerous provisions governing the labour–management employment relationship*
   - *Major areas of interest concern wages (rates of pay, overtime differentials, holiday pay), hours (shift times, days of work), and working conditions (safety issues, performance standards, retraining)*
   - *"Management rights" refers to the supremacy of management's authority in all issues except those shared with the union through the collective agreement*

8. Describe a typical grievance process and explain the basis for arbitration awards.
   - *The process will consist of 3 to 5 steps—each step having specific filing and reply times*
   - *Higher-level managers and union officials will become involved in disputes at the higher steps of the grievance process*
   - *The final step of the grievance process may be arbitration*
   - *Arbitrators render a final decision for problems not resolved at lower grievance steps*
   - *Arbitrators consider the wording of the collective agreement, testimony, and evidence offered during the hearing, including how the parties have interpreted the collective agreement*

KEY TERMS

HRM CLOSE-UP APPLICATION

1. What are the reasons for success in Jazz reaching a long-term collective agreement with its pilots?
2. What does Copp say is the most important asset of any airline?
3. What was the primary reason Copp became involved in labour relations?
4. What were the reasons the collective agreement was achieved?

CRITICAL THINKING QUESTIONS

1. One of your friends is a manager in a Canada-wide retail chain. All the stores in Ontario have just become unionized, and your friend is not sure how to treat the staff. What advice would you give?
2. What approach might an employer take to discourage employees from joining a union? What response might a union make?
3. Your best friend has recently been appointed a shop steward of their work unit. You know the friend's manager and feel the manager has always been fair in dealing with staff. What advice might you give your friend in their new role?
4. The negotiations between Grand Plumbing Services International and its union have become deadlocked. What form of bargaining power does each side possess to enforce its bargaining demands? What are the advantages and disadvantages of each form of bargaining power for both the union and the employer?
5. Sam Wong has decided to file a grievance with the shop steward, alleging that he was not promoted and a more junior (in seniority) employee was. Describe the steps in the grievance process and what information would be necessary.

BUILDING YOUR SKILLS

1. *Welcome aboard CUPE*, a media story produced by the Canadian Union of Public Employees, tells the story of what unionized flight attendants can look for from their union and is probably a union membership recruiting tool. Watch the YouTube clip at **www.youtube.com/watch?v=dZnYTYQcxyA** and then in groups of 3 or 4 determine whether you support this type of recruitment tool. Give reasons for your response.
2. Access to technology has been changing the dynamics in bargaining. Go to UNI Global Union at **www.uniglobalunion.org** and explore the various items in a global union in 150 countries that represents over 20 million workers in jobs ranging from graphics, to entertainment, to sport, and to tourism. Prepare a 2- or 3-page summary explaining how the use of social media can affect people's perspectives on labour relations.
3. A group of students wants a health-food restaurant on their college campus. College administrators want a Tim Hortons franchise. Resources allow for only 1 food outlet. Divide the class into bargaining teams, with 1 team representing the students and the other team representing the college administrators. The objective is for each side to negotiate from that perspective and reach an agreement. (If there is another issue on your campus, use the real and current issue instead.)
4. During a union organizing drive, labour and management will develop a plan to present their perspectives to employees. A goal of each side will be to collect information on the other that can be used to build a case for or against the union. In addition, each side will seek to avoid committing unfair labour practices. Working in teams of union and management representatives, answer the following questions. Be prepared to present your findings during a discussion period.
   A. What information might the union collect on management in order to obtain employee support?
   B. What information might management want to collect on the union?

    C. What methods might unions and management use to tell their story to employees? What illegal actions will the union and management want to guard against?

    D. Are there any new developments (such as concerns about privacy) that either the union or management need to be concerned about?

5. Access the Canadian Industrial Relations Board website, where decisions of cases can be found. Also access the site of your provincial labour relations board (see Toolkit 10.1 above) and the link to decisions. Retrieve 1 from each site. Prepare a 2- to 3-page report describing the decisions, including any comparison if the issue in dispute is the same.

CASE STUDY 1

But Isn't My Union Supposed to Protect Me?

Perhaps the biggest stories about unions and the work environment over the past couple of years has been the issue of sexual harassment and how widespread it still is. When the behaviours of a former CBC host, Jian Ghomeshi, made the news, CBC decided that it needed to investigate the situation and develop an approach that would prevent something similar in the future. The report from an independent investigator noted that the union, the Canadian Media Guild (CMG), knew of the complaints about Ghomeshi, and other situations of sexual harassment, yet did nothing. After the report was released, the union issued a statement that it welcomes the recommendations in the report, it supports workplaces that are free from harassment, and it is committed to working with the CBC to ensure that the CBC is harassment-free.

    Although this was a high-profile case, other stories of sexual harassment and the role of the union also made headlines. In a case in Saskatchewan, 3 women working at the City of Regina landfill filed over 40 sexual harassment complaints against male coworkers in accordance with the City's harassment policy. In fact, since the harassment had been going on for several years (along with the complaints), with no significant changes, 2 of the women began to feel their physical safety was at risk. In 2014, when the harassment started, one of the women even informed the union (CUPE Local 21) that a complaint was going to be filed. The union president asked that she not do so, indicating that since one of the harassers was a friend, he would speak to him and get him to stop. Eventually, the women did file official complaints, and the union indicated that it would wait until the employer had completed the investigation before it did anything. The harassing continued, and eventually the women were diagnosed with medical conditions that were a result of the harassment and quit their jobs. Then, in 2015, they filed an application of "unfair representation due to discriminatory treatment" against the union at the Saskatchewan Labour Relations Board. A decision was finally made in late 2017, and the board concluded that indeed the union was more concerned about any discipline the men might receive and had driven the women from the workplace. The arbitrator went on to state that both the local CUPE representation and the national CUPE representation didn't take the concerns seriously. The remedy for the employees was that the union post the decision in a very public place so that all employees would see the order.

Questions:

1. Is posting the decision in a place for all employees to see a sufficient consequence for the union? Why or why not?

2. Should there be consequences for the employer for not dealing with the matter sooner? Why or why not?

3. What should the union do now? Explain your answer.

Sources: Adapted from Janice Rubin and Parisa Nikfarjam, "Report: CBC Workplace Investigation regarding Jian Ghomeshi," April 13, 2015; "The Canadian Media Guild Committed to Working with CBC to Ensure a Safe and Harassment-Free Workplace," The Canadian Media Guild, April 16, 2015, accessed April 14, 2018, www.cmg.ca/en/2015/04/16/the-canadian-media-guild-committed-to-working-with-cbc-to-ensure-a-safe-and-harassment-free-workplace; "Union Discriminated Against Women Who Filed Sexual Harassment Claims: Sask. Labour Board," *CBC News*, October 31, 2017, accessed April 14, 2018; and Saskatchewan Labour Relations Board, LRB File No. 034-15, 035-15 & 037-15, October 3, 2017, accessed April 14, 2018, www.sasklabourrelationsboard.com/pdfdoc/034-15%20035-15%20%20037-15%20Oct3%202017GM.

CASE STUDY 2

What's Wrong with Body Piercings?

With the variety and extent of body piercings on many people, one would think that it is okay to have and display them in any work environment. However, this may not always be true.

A residential care facility for older people developed a new dress code policy that specifically stated that clothing needed to be able to cover any and all body piercings. The facility argued that the policy was necessary due to the number of elderly people who were uncomfortable around individuals with piercings. This new policy was grieved by its union and went to arbitration for a decision.

For 50 years, in a unionized workplace, arbitrators have held that any dress code must be "reasonable." Of course, what was "reasonable" in 1965, when the first ruling was made, may not be reasonable in 2018. The original arbitration had a number of tests for any new policy: (1) it must not be inconsistent with terms of collective agreement, (2) it must not be unreasonable, (3) it must be clear, (4) it must be made known to the employees, (5) employees must be notified of any breach of policy, and (6) the policy must be consistently enforced.

During the arbitration hearing, the union argued that these tests were not met. The care facility also argued that the tests were outdated and need to be revised, particularly in a healthcare setting.

Although the arbitrator did acknowledge that some patients might not have positive impressions of body piercings, the arbitrator also stated that the patients also might not have positive impressions of any other particular staff member. Furthermore, the arbitration determined that there was no human rights issue but a simple one of an employer wanting to prevent any complaints.

The arbitrator ruled in favour of the union, indicating that there was no business case or evidence for the policy. The arbitrator also stated that there was no apparent connection between how staff looked and any health outcomes.

Questions:

1. Do you think an employer ought to be able to institute any type of dress code, including one dealing with body piercings? Why or why not?

2. Since the "test" for implementing a policy is only applicable to unionized work environments, do you think "personal appearance" ought to be a prohibited ground in human rights legislation? Why or why not?

Sources: Adapted from Dr. D. Doorey, "Should Employers Be Permitted to Discriminate on the Basis of Appearance?," October 14, 2014, accessed June 14, 2015, http://lawofwork.ca/?p=7688; and In the Matter of an Arbitration Between: The Ottawa Hospital and Canadian Union of Public Employees, Local 4000, January 14, 2013.

NOTES AND REFERENCES

1. Statistics Canada, "Unionization Rates Falling," *The Daily*, March 3, 2017, accessed March 30, 2018, https://www.statcan.gc.ca/pub/11-630-x/11-630-x2015005-eng.htm.

2. Ibid.

3. Employment and Social Development Canada, "*Labour Organizations in Canada 2015*," August 16, 2016, 2.

4. Graeme McFarlane, "New Challenges for Unions," *Canadian HR Reporter*, March 2018, 22.

5. For a more complete understanding of the labour relations system in Canada, refer to Morley Gunderson and Daphne G. Taras, *Canadian Labour and Employment Relations*, 6th ed. (Toronto: Pearson, 2009); Larry Suffield, *Labour Relations*, 4th ed. (Toronto: Pearson, 2016); and William H. Holley, William H. Ross, and Roger S. Wolters, *The Labor Relations Process*, 11th ed. (Toronto: Nelson 2017).

6. Justice Laws website, "Canada Labour Code," accessed March 30, 2018, http://laws-lois.justice.gc.ca/eng/acts/L-2/index.html.

7. Suffield, *Labour Relations*, 82.

8. To read more about the labour relations process, consult Gunderson and Taras, *Canadian Labour and Employment Relations*; Suffield, *Labour Relations*; Richard Hyman and Rebecca Gumbrell-McCormick, "Resisting Labour Market Insecurity: Old and New Actors, Rivals or Allies?," *Journal of Industrial Relations* 59, no. 4 (August 2017): 538–561.

9. Jennifer Newman, "The Psychological Reasons Why People Join Unions," *CBC News*, April 18, 2016, accessed March 30, 2018, http://www.cbc.ca/news/canada/british-columbia/jennifer-newman-the-psychological-reasons-why-people-join-unions-1.3540147.

10. Joseph Bonney, "A Win for Unionization," *Journal of Commerce* 16, no. 3 (February 2015): 20; and Victor Silverman, "Victory at Pomona College: Union Strategy and Immigrant Labor," *Labor Studies Journal* 40, no. 1 (March 2015): 8–31.

11. Jennifer Newman, "The Psychological Reasons Why People Join Unions."

12. Unifor. "Unifor History and Mission," accessed March 30, 2018, https://www.unifor.org/en/about-unifor/history-mission.

13. Todd Humber, "Good HR Makes Union Growth Tough," *Canadian HR Reporter*, June 12, 2017, accessed April 4, 2018, https://www.hrreporter.com/workplace-law/33704-good-hr-makes-union-growth-tough.

14. John Dujay, "New Tools for Unions in Ontario," *Canadian HR Reporter*, January 2018, 1.

15. Birch Miller and Bruce Graham, "Strengthening Union Activity in Alberta," *Canadian HR Reporter*, September 4, 2017, 27.

16. Marty Warren, "Tim Hortons Workers Need a Union," *The Star*, January 11, 2018, accessed April 4, 2018, https://www.thestar.com/opinion/contributors/2018/01/11/tim-hortons-workers-need-a-union.html.

17. Go2HR, "Unfair Labour Practices and Employer Free Speech," accessed April 4, 2018, https://www.go2hr.ca/articles/unfair-labour-practices-and-employer-free-speech.

18. Canada Industrial Relations Board regulations and *Ontario Labour Relations Act*.

19. University of British Columbia Faculty Association, "About Us," accessed April 5, 2018, https://www.facultyassociation.ubc.ca/about-us.

20. Greg Keenan, "WestJet Pilots Vote to Unionize as Airline Looks to Form Discount Service," *The Globe and Mail*, May 12, 2017, accessed April 5, 2018, https://www.theglobeandmail.com/report-on-business/westjet-pilots-vote-to-form-first-union/article34970319.

21. Sunny Dhillon, "B.C. Court Rules Against Mexico in Dispute over Seasonal Farm Workers," *The Globe and Mail*, February 3, 2015, accessed April 5, 2018, https://www.theglobeandmail.com/news/british-columbia/bc-court-rules-against-mexico-in-dispute-over-seasonal-farm-workers/article22777687.

22. Annette Davies, "Industrial Relations & New Technology," *The Economics and Business of Technology*, 10 (2018): 3.

23. Antonella Artuso, "Labour Pains," *National Post*, April 11, 2017, NP3.

24. "Unifor Leaves CLC Over Rights," *Vancouver Sun*, January 18, 2018, C1; and "Unifor Splits with Canadian Labour Congress over Lack of Action regarding U.S.-Based Unions," *Global News*, January 17, 2018, accessed, April 6, 2018, https://globalnews.ca/news/3971669/unifor-canadian-labour-congress-split.

25. Statistics Canada, "Unionization Rate, Canada and Provinces, 2016," *The Daily*, September 8, 2017, accessed April 7, 2018, https://www.statcan.gc.ca/daily-quotidien/170908/cg-a004-eng.htm.

26. Statistics Canada, "Unionization Rates Falling."

27. Ibid.

28. Jelle Visser, Susan Hayter, and Rosina Gammarano "Trends in Collective Bargaining Coverage: Stability, Erosion or Decline?," *ILO Issue Brief* No. 1, accessed April 7, 2018, http://www.ilo.org/wcmsp5/groups/public/---ed_protect/---protrav/---travail/documents/publication/wcms_409422.pdf.

29. Ibid.

30. Employment and Social Development Canada, *Labour Organizations in Canada 2015*, 8.

31. Ibid.

32. Ibid, 11.

33. Frederic Tomesco, "Bombardier Union Seeks to Block Toronto Plant Sale," *The Globe and Mail*, March 12, 2018, B3.

34. Harmac Pacific, "Employees," accessed April 7, 2018, http://www.harmacpacific.com/employees.php; and "Harmac Pacific Pulp Mill: A Local Success Story," Forestry Friendly Communities website, March 16, 2017, accessed April 7, 2018, https://forestryfriendly.ca/harmac-pacific-pulp-mill-local-success-story.

35. Statistics Canada, "Unionization Rates Falling."

36. *Labour Organizations in Canada 2015*, 11.

37. Sean Fine, "Court Protects Public-Sector Workers' Right to Strike," *The Globe and Mail*, January 31, 2015, A14.

38. Douglas Quan, "Mounties Keenly Await Decision on Union Bid," *Vancouver Sun*, January 14, 2015, B2; and James Fitz-Morris, "RCMP Officers Have Right to Collective Bargain, Supreme Court Rules," *CBC News*, January 16, 2015, accessed April 7, 2018, http://www.cbc.ca/news/politics/rcmp-officers-have-right-to-collective-bargaining-supreme-court-rules-1.2912340.

39. Simona Chiose, "Instructors' Strike Looms over Ontario Colleges," *The Globe and Mail*, October 14, 2017, A7; Simona Chiose, "Ontario Tables Bill to End College Teachers' Strike," *The Globe and Mail*, November 17, 2017, A5; and Jill Mahoney, "Back-to-Work Legislation Ends Ontario College Faculty Strike," *The Globe and Mail*, November 20, 2017, A7.

40. Ake Blomqvist, "Canada Needs a New Model for Public Sector Labour Disputes," *Report on Business*, November 27, 2017, B4.

41. Pon Staff, "Use Integrative Negotiation Strategies to Create Value at the Bargaining Table," *Harvard Law School Daily Blog*, December 21, 2017, accessed April 7, 2018, https://www.pon.harvard.edu/daily/negotiation-skills-daily/find-more-value-at-the-bargaining-table.

42. Ibid.

43. Roger Fisher and William Ury, *Getting to Yes* (Toronto: Penguin Books, 1991).

44. "Negotiation Bargaining Zone," Negotiation Experts website, accessed April 7, 2018, https://www.negotiations.com/definition/bargaining-zone.

45. Benjamin Singler and Kalina Laframboise, "'Nobody Is Winning': Quebec Construction Projects Halt as Workers Stage General Strike," *CBC News*, May 24, 2017, accessed April 7, 2018,

http://www.cbc.ca/news/canada/montreal/quebec-construction
-worker-strike-1.4128886.

46. "Quebec Government Tables Bill Forcing Construction Workers Back to Work," *The Globe and Mail*, May 30, 2017, A4.

47. "All Bets Are Off: Caesars Windsor Workers on Strike after Rejecting Agreement," *HRD Canada*, April 6, 2018, https://www.hrmonline.ca/business-news/all-bets-are-off-caesars-windsor-workers-on-strike-after-rejecting-agreement-240562.aspx.

48. Alicja Siekierska, "Strike at Ontario GM Plantsparks Layoffs at 3 Sites in U.S., Canada," *Vancouver Sun*, September 22, 2017, B1; and Greg Keenan, "Cami Union Pitches New Deal Amid Strike," *The Globe and Mail*, September 25, 2017, B3.

49. Eric D. Lawrence, "Strike Ends at Plant Where Chevy Equinox Is Made, but Did Workers Get What They Wanted?," *Detroit Free Press*, October 16, 2017, accessed April 8, 2018, https://www.freep.com/story/money/cars/2017/10/16/workers-ok-new-contract-cami-assembly/768781001.

50. Kristine Owram, "GM Ends Canada Plant Strike After Workers Cave on Mexico Demands," *Bloomberg*, October 16, 2017, accessed April 8, 2018, https://www.bloomberg.com/news/articles/2017-10-16/gm-ends-canada-plant-strike-after-workers-cave-on-mexico-demands.

51. "Work Stoppages by Sector and Year," Labour Program, Government of Canada, April 3, 2018, accessed April 8, 2018, https://www.canada.ca/en/employment-social-development/services/collective-bargaining-data/work-stoppages/work-stoppages-year-sector.html#H2_1.

52. Eric Atkins, "Canadian Pacific Rail Crews Hold Strike Vote," *The Globe and Mail*, March 14, 2018, B5.

53. Robert Devet, "Locked Out Herald Workers Reach Tentative Agreement," *Halifax Media Co-op*, March 6, 2015, accessed April 8, 2018, http://halifax.mediacoop.ca/fr/story/locked-out-herald-workers-reach-tentative-agreemen/33226.

54. TMG The Mediation Group, "Mediator Skills," accessed April 8, 2018, http://www.themediationgroup.org/news/mediator-skills.

55. For an expanded discussion of management's residual rights, termed "reserved rights" in the United States, see Paul Prasow and Edward Peters, *Arbitration and Collective Bargaining*, 2nd ed. (New York: McGraw-Hill, 1983): 33–34. This book is considered an authority on management rights issues.

56. Collective Agreement, Westrock Company of Canada, Inc. and USW-IWA Local 1-500, April 1, 2017 to March 31, 2023.

57. Dave Battagello, "Police Investigate Hate Crime at Auto Plant," *Vancouver Sun*, March 31, 2015, B2.

58. Mike MacLellan, "Employees' Termination for Smoking Dope at Work Upheld," *Canadian HR Reporter*, March 22, 2018, accessed April 11, 2018, https://www.hrreporter.com/article/36338-employees-termination-for-smoking-dope-at-work-upheld.

THIS MAKES SCENTS (PART 4)

Jessie and Ashton managed to weather the storm around their expansion plans and are now in several different locations. It is 5 years later, and they hired an HR person about 2 years ago to help them with future business and employee needs.

As the business has grown, so have certain employee issues. For example, they've had to ensure that all employees understand appropriate behaviours toward customers even when customers are rude or aggressive. Jessie suggests that surveillance cameras be installed in all stores to ensure the safety of employees as well as to be able to observe how some managers treat staff. Ashton isn't sure this is a good idea and suggests that a code of conduct be initiated as well as a discipline process. He feels a softer approach would work better and not be as intrusive as cameras. Both Ashton and Jessie feel staff need to be informed as to what is occurring and why.

With the assistance of the HR person, Ashton develops a discipline process that includes an informal meeting with the employee to discuss the issue and a time frame for improvement; a second, more formal meeting to explain that the employee's behaviour must change or more serious discipline would be considered; and a final meeting with the employee where the employee is asked to make a decision to resign or else be terminated. The code of conduct and discipline process are communicated to all employees, including at workshops, to help them understand what it means in practice. Since the implementation of the code of conduct and discipline process, they've had a few occurrences when an employee at one location was rude to customers and had to be disciplined. The store manager isn't confident that the employee's behaviour will improve.

Consideration for a New Store

Even with the concerns about how to handle certain employee issues, Jessie and Ashton are considering opening a store in a very exclusive part of the city that is not close to any of the existing stores. The other locations are still in shopping malls, and this would be a departure from the current business model. They realize that the actual working location and store environment might be much nicer and more attractive than the mall locations. This has them concerned about how to staff the new location: should they offer everyone an opportunity to express interest and then select the best people, or should they just pick the individuals they feel have the best skills for the new location, without allowing all staff to be considered?

At the same time that Jessie and Ashton are thinking about opening another store, they've received information that some employees at one of the stores are unhappy about how they are treated by their manager and have been speaking with a union representative. This situation, along with the employee discipline, has them concerned about opening another store and what might happen if their staff become unionized.

Questions:

1. What can Jessie and Ashton do to ensure that staff understand the reasons for creating a code of conduct and a discipline process?
2. What are some other aspects of a discipline process that need to be included in the process?
3. What else could the store manager do to help the disciplined employee improve and be successful?
4. What could Jessie and Ashton say to employees regarding unionizing?
5. What might be other reasons that the employees are considering unionizing?
6. What could the HR person do to help Jessie and Ashton with these issues?

11 Learning About International Human Resources Management

After studying this chapter, you should be able to

1. Describe the types of organizational forms used by companies with international operations.

2. Explain the economic, political-legal, and cultural factors in different countries that need to be considered from an HR perspective.

3. Describe recruitment and selection for international operations.

4. Discuss the unique training and development needs of employees working in international locations.

5. Discuss the considerations when managing the performance of employees working in international locations.

6. Outline the characteristics of a good international reward and recognition program.

7. Explain how labour relations practices differ around the world.

OUTLINE

HRM CLOSE-UP

"Recognizing other people's different expectations, cultures, and laws is critical."

IMAGINE A world of darkness where you could not see the faces of your loved ones or enjoy the beauty of nature. What if you were unable to work and contribute to your family's well-being? How would this impact your self-esteem? How would you survive if shunned by those within your community?

Aly Bandali, CEO of Operation Eyesight, invites everyone to consider these questions as they illuminate the important work that this organization does. With its bold vision to eliminate avoidable blindness, Operation Eyesight contributes at every level throughout the eye health continuum. The primary beneficiaries of the organization's services are people in developing countries (within Africa and South Asia) suffering from a variety of eye conditions and eye diseases. Secondary beneficiaries include support staff and community-based health workers who function within the healthcare systems in these locations.

Operation Eyesight's impact is clear as in 2017, over 3 million people were examined for eye health problems, over 250,000 people received new prescription eyeglasses, over 200,000 surgeries were performed, and over 3000 front-line staff and volunteers were trained. "Each day that we exist and focus our work and efforts, we make a difference in lives around the world," says Bandali. He stresses that when helping people living with avoidable blindness, Operation Eyesight addresses not only the symptoms but the causes as well. As such, part of the organization's mandate is to build eye health care capacity through partner hospitals and to educate people about the importance of eye healthcare and proper eye care–seeking behaviours. In Africa in particular, there is an emphasis on hygiene and the provision of access to safe, healthy environments (i.e., clean drinking water) so that communities can work together to sustain the overall health of the population.

In recognition of its achievements, Operation Eyesight was named as one of the top 23 Canadian charities in the *Financial Post*'s 2017 Canadian Charities of the Year. Also in 2017, Operation Eyesight received a Sustainable Development Goal Award from Global Compact Network Canada for embedding sustainable principles into their sight-saving work. Building on this momentum, Bandali wants to enhance partnerships and continue collaborating with others around the world in order to further expand the organization's reach and impact. "Surrounding yourself with people who know what they are doing is critical," he says. "The front-line people on the ground keep the operations running in a successful way, and my role as a leader, even from a geographical distance, is to support them and remove any barriers they encounter."

However, in an international organization, this isn't always simple. "Think about the challenges that telecommuting presents. Then add the complexity of a few different time zones and a couple of oceans." Bandali recognizes that trying to connect with people and build relationships with his team is complicated by these matters; therefore, he leverages technology where possible. "7:30 a.m. Skype calls every Monday morning have become part of my routine. It doesn't matter what type of weekend I've had or what type of week is ahead of me. I have to be available early each Monday in order to connect with my team members in their respective locations. I need to focus on these

Aly Bandali, CEO, Operation Eyesight

people and build trusting relationships with them."

Different standards of behaviour and varying expectations of how an employer and how colleagues should behave must also be taken into account. "This all comes back around to keeping the proper perspective. A Western approach to an issue that needs addressing in our project countries might not provide the solution they need. Recognizing other people's different expectations, cultures, and laws is critical. Things we take for granted are not necessarily how business is conducted in other locations, and it is important to pay attention to these issues." Something as basic as benefits can be vastly different and only be provided to an employee (not their family) and only if an accident at work occurs. Determining appropriate compensation plans is further complicated by a lack of relevant data and differing legal requirements. How people expect to be trained and how they expect to receive feedback can also vary across locations.

Even with the complexities of leading an international organization, Bandali enjoys the challenges and opportunities to make a difference in the lives of others. When asked what advice he would share having led such a dynamic organization and travelling to different countries to meet with staff and volunteers, he notes, "If you ever get the opportunity to work abroad, you must. This will jolt your system and expose you to an entirely different way of thinking about business and about life in general. Getting out of your comfort zone will enhance your self-development in ways that you cannot even begin to imagine."

INTRODUCTION

There are many examples of companies operating in a global environment. These examples might include acquisitions of international companies, such as when Burger King acquired Canada's iconic Tim Hortons. Or they might highlight companies expanding into other markets, such as Operation Eyesight in developing countries, Bombardier in Asia, or BMO in the United States. Or examples might focus on international companies gaining dominance here in Canada, such as Starbucks, Walmart, and Lowes. Lastly, the examples might include companies acquiring a Canadian company and shutting it down, such as the acquisition of Future Shop by Best Buy, resulting in the eventual shutdown of all Future Shops.

Whatever the angle, we see clearly that globalization is a chief factor driving Canadian business. Nearly all organizations today are influenced by international competition. Some handle the challenge well, whereas others fail miserably when they try to manage across borders. More often than not, as noted by Aly Bandali in the HRM Close-up, a critical element for international organizations boils down to how people are managed and the flexibility of organizations. Because of this, many organizations are focusing on their human resources management practices.[1]

The importance of globalization notwithstanding, we have—for the most part—emphasized HRM practices and systems as they exist in Canada. This is not so much an oversight on our part as a deliberate decision to explain the HR practices in the most fundamental way. However, the topic of international HRM is so important that an entire chapter is dedicated to this discussion. Our thinking is that now after you have read (and, we hope, discussed) some of the best practices for managing people at work, it might be appropriate to see how some of these practices may need to change for companies operating in the international arena.

MANAGING ACROSS BORDERS

LO1

Describe the types of organizational forms used by companies with international operations.

A company must determine how to structure its operations in various countries in order to be efficient and effective. Some organizations choose to have limited operations in foreign countries, whereas others have many locations and employ numerous people in places outside of their home country. Think about the many places throughout the world where the golden arches can be seen. This is a clear example of how McDonalds operates in many countries and must ensure that all locations address unique customer needs while still taking advantage of standard company operating procedures and processes to ensure a profitable outcome.

The following 4 terms are mainly used to describe any company doing business in another country: multinational, international, transnational, and global. Each term is distinct and has a specific meaning that defines the scope and degree of interaction with the operations outside of the "home" country.

- *Multinational companies* have investment in other countries but do not have coordinated product offerings in each country. They are more focused on adapting their products and service to each local market.

- **International companies** are importers and exporters; they have no investment outside of their home country.
- **Transnational companies** are much more complex organizations. They have invested in foreign operations and have a central corporate facility but give decision-making, research and development, and marketing powers to each foreign market.
- **Global companies** have invested and are present in many countries. They market their products through the use of the same coordinated image or brand in all markets. Generally, 1 corporate office is responsible for global strategy. The emphasis is on volume, cost management, and efficiency.[2]

Although there are various ways that an organization can operate within global markets, in this chapter, we refer to any company that conducts business outside of its home country as an international business. Canada, of course, is not the only country that conducts international business. International organizations operate throughout the world. Figure 11.1 shows a list (as of 2018) of the world's 10 biggest public companies as documented by *Forbes*. These companies are in a strong position to affect the world economy in the following ways:

1. Production and distribution extend beyond national boundaries, making it easier to transfer technology.
2. They have direct investments in many countries, affecting the balance of payments.
3. They have a political impact that leads to cooperation among countries and to the breaking down of barriers of nationalism.

Although Figure 11.1 is showing financial measures to demonstrate "top" or "best," there are other lists. For example, there is the world's "Most Admired Companies" list. This list, created jointly by *Fortune* and the Hay Group, was determined by surveying executives, directors, and industry analysts in a methodological "peer review" of reputation. It was done this way because of a belief that a company's reputation is positively related to measurable outcomes, such as innovation, social responsibility, financial soundness, and global competitiveness. Interestingly enough, 3 companies receiving a higher ranking on the list, Apple, Google, and Amazon, had only recently started when the list was originally compiled 18 years ago.[3]

FIGURE 11.1 World's Largest Public Companies (2018 *Forbes* Ranking)

Rank	Company	Country	Sales	Profits
#1	ICBC	China	$165.3 B	$43.7 B
#2	China Construction Bank	China	$143.2 B	$37.2 B
#3	JPMorgan Chase	United States	$118.2 B	$26.5 B
#4	Berkshire Hathaway	United States	$235.2 B	$39.7 B
#5	Agricultural Bank of China	China	$129.3	$29.6 B
#6	Bank of America	United States	$103 B	$20.3 B
#7	Wells Fargo	United States	$102.1 B	$21.7 B
#8	Apple	United States	$247.5 B	$53.3 B
#9	Bank of China	China	$118.2 B	$26.4 B
#10	Ping An Insurance Group	China	$141.6 B	$13.9 B

Source: Adapted from *Forbes Magazine*, "The World's Largest Public Companies 2017," accessed February 2, 2018, http://www.forbes.com/global2000/list/#tab. © 2018 Forbes. All rights reserved.

FIGURE 11.2 **The Complete Ranking of Canada's Fastest-Growing Companies (2017)***

Rank	Company	Industry	City
1	Gillam Group	Construction	Toronto
2	Buyatab Online	Software	Vancouver
3	Maropost	Software	Toronto
4	IOU Financial	Financial Services	Montréal
5	SendtoNews	Marketing & Media	Victoria
6	Milo Enterprises	Manufacturing	Vancouver
7	Eden Park	Financial Services	Toronto
8	Canada Drives	Financial Services	Vancouver
9	FixMeStick	Manufacturing	Montréal
10	Bronte Construction	Construction	Oakville

*These are the 10 fastest-growing companies in Canada, measured by their revenue growth over the last 5 years.

Source: "PROFIT 500: The Complete Ranking of Canada's Fastest-Growing Companies," *Canadian Business*, September 14, 2017, accessed February 2, 2018, http://www.canadianbusiness.com/profit500/2017-ranking-p500.

Another, more recent list measures the world's most sustainable organizations—those equipped to prosper in the long term because of their approach to relationship building with all the various stakeholders. This 2017 list included the following Canadian companies: Tim Hortons, Teck Resources, Telus, Bombardier, Enbridge Inc., Toronto-Dominion Bank, Celestica, Bank of Montreal, Encana Corporation, Suncor Energy, and Intact Financial.[4] It is important to remember that Canada is an export nation; therefore, most of our major companies do business outside Canada. For example, Hudson Bay purchased a very profitable German department store chain both for its name in Germany and its vast real estate holdings.[5] It sees this acquisition as a method to launch its other high-profile store, Saks Fifth Avenue, in Europe.[6] So how are Canadian companies doing? Figure 11.2 lists the top 10 fastest-growing Canadian companies in 2017 and provides examples of Canadian organizations that can continue to expand by exploring options for international expansion.

How Does the Global Environment Influence Management?

LO2

Explain the economic, political-legal, and cultural factors in different countries that need to be considered from an HR perspective.

In Chapter 1, we highlighted some of the challenges facing business and therefore affecting human resources management. One of the major economic issues we discussed was the creation of free trade zones within Europe, North America, and the Pacific Rim. However, there has been ongoing concern with the economic health of some of the members, as can be seen by the financial problems being experienced in Greece.[7] Further issues can be seen as the United Kingdom has voted to leave the European Union on Friday, March 29, 2019.[8] This issue, known as *Brexit*, adds further complications to international operations and dealings with the United Kingdom and other European countries. Further complexities with international business operations are arising due to problems with NAFTA.[9] Changes to this agreement with the United States, Mexico, and Canada have far-reaching implications and the potential to drastically alter, and potentially limit or diminish, business conducted among these countries. It is also important to note that the United States is Canada's largest partner, the EU is Canada's second-largest economic partner, and China is now the third-largest trading partner.[10]

Similar to NAFTA, numerous trade associations, including the Association of Southeast Asian Nations (ASEAN), East Asia Economic Group, and Asia-Pacific Economic Cooperation (APEC), have significantly facilitated trade among Asian countries, making Asia the fastest-growing region in the world. China—Asia's fastest-growing country—has emerged as a dominant trade leader since instituting trade reforms in the late 1970s. In the past 18 years, China's economy has grown fourfold, drastically altering political and trading relations among nations.[11] Some industry analysts estimate that the country now produces 50% of the world's cameras, 30% of air conditioners and televisions, 25% of washing machines, and 20% of refrigerators. In addition, China's 1.4 billion people represent a massive, largely untapped consumer market for global companies. Today, more cars are sold in China than in Europe. Driving this trend are multinational corporations, such as General Electric, Toyota, and Intel, which are building or expanding their manufacturing units in the country.

Furthermore, in January 2018, Canada agreed to a deal to renew the Trans-Pacific Partnership.[12] This agreement is intended to enhance economic relationships among the 12 countries that border the Pacific Ocean by slashing tariffs and fostering trade to boost growth.[13] The specific outcomes for the Canadian economy will have to be monitored as the deal and international relationships evolve.

The auto industry has undergone tremendous global change as well. Fiat, which purchased a portion Chrysler automaker a few years ago, recently acquired the remaining 42%.[14] Likewise, a German transmission maker acquired a Livonia, Michigan–based automotive company, and Volkswagen acquired the remaining shares of Scania, a truck manufacturer in Sweden.[15] Also, General Motors and Isuzu (Japan) have an agreement to collaborate on the production of medium-duty trucks.[16]

In addition to China, other key countries for trade are Brazil, Russia, India, and South Africa. With China, these countries are called "BRICS" and are considered to have the fastest-growing economies. As of 2017, BRICS can be broken into 2 groups: those that took advantage of globalization's march to integrate themselves into global supply chains (primarily China and India) and those that took advantage of globalization to sell their abundant natural resources (primarily Brazil, Russia, and South Africa).[17] The fact that international corporations can choose the countries in which they do business or relocate operations generally results in the selection of countries that have the most to offer. For example, several

China represents an important part of the consumer market within the global economy.

Canadian forestry companies have bought mills in the United States as lumber in Canada is being devastated by a pest infestation.[18] In addition to economic factors, political-legal factors are a huge consideration. In many countries, particularly those in Africa, governments poorly protect property rights. Whoever has the political power or authority can seize others' property with few or no consequences. Civil unrest can also lead to the poor enforcement of property rights. This situation gives companies less incentive to locate factories or invest in those countries. Another issue relates to intellectual property rights—rights related to patents, trademarks, and so forth. Despite the fact that private property rights are now generally enforced in China, intellectual property rights have seen little protection. For example, when General Motors formed a joint venture with a Chinese company to produce and sell a new automobile in the country, a knock-off version of the car could be seen on China's streets even before GM and its partner were able to manufacture their first car.

Beyond the economic and political-legal issues just mentioned, a country's **cultural environment** (communications, religion, values and ideologies, education, and social structure) also has important implications when it comes to a company's decision about when and how to do business in another country. Language similarities to the home country are another consideration.

Hofstede's cultural dimensions are a useful resource for understanding important differences when conducting business in different countries. Figure 11.3 summarizes Hofstede's work. It is important to acknowledge and respond to cultural variances in the country where a company is doing business, also known as the **host country**, as different cultural environments require different approaches to human resources management.

Cultural environment
Descriptions of the values, norms, communication standards, and religion of a country; includes social structure and general way of life

Host country
Country in which an organization is conducting business

FIGURE 11.3 Hofstede's Cultural Dimensions

Cultural dimension	Definition	Examples
Power distance	*Power distance* is the extent to which the less powerful members of institutions and organizations within a country expect and accept that power is distributed unequally.	**Low:** US and Canada **High:** Japan and Singapore
Individualism and collectivism	*Individualism* describes the cultures in which the ties between individuals are loose. *Collectivism* describes cultures in which people are integrated into strong, cohesive groups that protect individuals in exchange for unquestioning loyalty.	**Individualistic:** US, Australia, and Great Britain **Collectivistic:** Singapore, Hong Kong, and Mexico
Masculinity-femininity	*Masculinity* pertains to cultures in which social gender roles are clearly distinct. *Femininity* describes cultures in which social gender roles overlap.	**Masculinity:** Japan, Austria, and Italy **Femininity:** Sweden, Norway, and the Netherlands
Uncertainty avoidance (UAI)	*Uncertainty avoidance* is the extent to which the members of a culture feel threatened by uncertain or unknown situations.	**Low:** Singapore, Jamaica, and Denmark **High:** Greece, Portugal, and Japan
Confucian dynamism	*Confucian dynamism* denotes the time orientation of a culture, defined as a continuum with long-term and short-term orientations as its 2 poles.	**Long-term:** China and Japan **Short-term:** US and Canada
Indulgence versus restraint	*Indulgence* refers to having fun and seeking out good times. *Restraint* refers to delayed or suppressed gratification and happiness.	**Indulgence:** Mexico **Restraint:** China

Source: Geert Hofstede, Gert Jan Hofstede, Michael Minkov, *Cultures and Organizations, Software of the Mind*, Third Revised Edition, McGraw-Hill 2010, ISBN 0-07-166418-1. © Geert Hofstede B.V. quoted with permission.

AT WORK WITH HRM 11.1 — NOT AMAZON!

With the worldwide presence of Amazon, it is hard to imagine it might not understand that the cultural environment in any country makes a big difference in how business is conducted.

Just before a holiday shopping rush, Amazon learned the hard way that Germany has certain expectations regarding who speaks for employees. Amazon, as part of its operating style, is used to dealing directly with its employees—not through a union. However, in Germany, unions are very powerful and used to having a collaborative relationship with companies, which has led to sector-wide labour agreements.

Although there had been a series of walkouts at the Amazon warehouse for almost a year, the action escalated when the employees staged a strike in Amazon's busiest shopping season. The union, Verdi, wanted to begin collective bargaining to establish a collective agreement that would result in wages higher than in other retail sectors. Amazon, however, believed its wages were in line and competitive for the type of work being done in the warehouse.

Amazon had been doing business in Germany for almost 20 years and didn't see the need to make changes in how it dealt with its employees. The company felt that anything coming between it and its staff slowed down operations and innovation. Amazon has about 10,000 German workers in its distribution centres throughout the year and then hires an additional 10,000 during seasonal activity.

The union, on the other hand, felt there is a social partnership between unions and employers and that Amazon was being unreasonable.

All this was particularly troubling because Germans tend to be eager online shoppers, and Germany is Amazon's largest market after the United States. Many experts saw it as a clash of German society and US arrogance.

CRITICAL THINKING QUESTIONS:

1. Do you think Amazon ought to conform to the culture of relationships with unions in Germany? Why or why not?
2. What might happen if the strikes and confrontation continue? Explain your answer.

Source: Adapted from Joanna Slater, "Amazon.com's German Culture Clash," *The Globe and Mail*, December 23, 2014, B1.

Strategies, structures, and management styles appropriate in 1 cultural setting may lead to failure in another. For example, in India, promotional opportunities are more highly valued than compensation. And Japan recently introduced a 4-day workweek to motivate employees so that businesses outcomes can improve.[19] Read At Work with HRM 11.1 to learn more about the cultural implications of doing business in another country.

CANADIAN VERSUS INTERNATIONAL HRM

International HRM presents its own complexities and challenges. Issues such as relocating employees to foreign offices and hiring local employees in different countries must be addressed. Because of the complexity of HR when doing business in other countries, larger companies will have HR professionals devoted solely to assisting with the globalization process. Furthermore, some companies will also hire international staffing firms, such as Boston Consulting Group. These firms have expertise when it comes to relocating employees, establishing operations abroad, and helping with import/export and foreign tax issues.

HR management systems have come a long way in terms of helping firms improve their international coordination. A good HR management system can facilitate communication, record keeping, and a host of other activities worldwide. Some HRM systems are designed to track the whereabouts of employees travelling or on assignment. This can be important in the event of a transportation accident, a natural disaster such as a tsunami, a terrorist attack, or civil strife when evacuation plans may have to be implemented.

LO3

Describe recruitment and selection for international operations.

Expatriates
Employees from an organization's home country who move to the international country where the organization does business

Host-country nationals
Employees who are natives of the country where an organization conducts international business

Third-country nationals
Employees who are natives of a country other than the home country of the organization or the country in which the international business is being conducted

To review how Canadian and International HRM practices differ, it is useful to examine some of the topics we have addressed throughout this text through the viewpoint of global operations. This is the focus of the following sections.

INTERNATIONAL RECRUITMENT

International management poses many problems in addition to those faced by a domestic operation. Because of geographic distance and a lack of close, day-to-day relationships with headquarters in the home country, problems must often be resolved with little or no counsel or assistance from others. It is essential, therefore, that special attention be given to planning how overseas companies will function, how many employees will be needed for effective operation, where these employees will be located, and how these workers need to function. In fact, research suggests that the inability to successfully integrate cultural differences is a major reason global mergers and acquisitions fail.[20]

There are 3 main sources of people to hire to work in international operations. As 1 option, a company can relocate employees from its home country; these workers are referred to as **expatriates**. Or a company can hire people from the country in which the business is being conducted; these employees are known as **host-country nationals**. The third option is to hire employees from another country altogether; these people are called **third-country nationals**.

Four Seasons Hotels and Resorts (described in At Work with HRM 11.2) uses all 3 sources for staffing multinational operations.

Expatriate assignments cost companies, on average, $1 million over a 3-year period, which can be 3 to 5 times what a domestic assignment costs. To reduce the costs, some

AT WORK WITH HRM 11.2   WORLD-CLASS HIRING

Four Seasons Hotels and Resorts, with a staff of 44,000, has grown in 50 years to 94 hotels in 39 countries. The Four Seasons brand is synonymous with luxury and first-class service standards. The execution of the strategy of being the best in the world starts with leaders who are passionate about the corporation's customer service and employee relations' values. These leaders can take a concept such as "We have chosen to specialize within the hospitality industry by offering only experiences of exceptional quality" and paint a picture for employees that is clear and motivational and results in the delivery of that exceptional personal service.

Does the perception of service excellence depend on the country or culture in which Four Seasons operates? Four Seasons trains service staff to be sensitive to guests' needs and to minimize or avoid culture and language problems. It also has an ethical culture that focuses on doing business according to the applicable laws in the country in which it has hotels.

So that employees can meet these performance expectations, Four Seasons selects employees based on

their service attitudes. Candidates for employment must undergo 4 behaviourally based interviews (including 1 with the general manager) to determine their service attitudes and current skills and knowledge.

Four Seasons does not have a rigid formula for selecting home-country nationals or expatriates for any given country. The ratios depend on 3 factors: regulations, economics, and corporate management development needs. For example, Indonesia used to have a rule that no more than 3 expatriates could be employed per hotel, and it set expatriate reduction targets to meet this regulation. Economically, it made sense because an expatriate general manager could cost as much as 75 or 80 local employees. Finally, Four Seasons will choose candidates on the basis of their need for global exposure and professional development, to match the company's targeted needs for international expansion.

The biggest challenge in international HR is management development. Four Seasons needs to develop culturally appropriate leadership in preparation for specific new locations on a defined timeline. If managers cannot

continued

be found who can speak the language and understand the culture, the ability to grow is limited.

This attention to the selection and development of high-performance employees has resulted in *Fortune* magazine naming Four Seasons one of the 100 best employers in the world for many years. Consequently, Four Seasons is now able to attract more and better applicants. Four Seasons is also widely recognized as the best luxury hotel chain in the world. Furthermore, the turnover rate at Four Seasons is one of the lowest in the hospitality sector. Even those employees who have left are often recaptured as they elect to return to the kind of culture that treats them as they treat the guests.

CRITICAL THINKING QUESTION:
Do you think Four Seasons ought to focus more on developing local managers? Why or why not?

Sources: Adapted from "The 100 Best Companies to Work For," *Fortune*, March 15, 2015, 148; "About Four Seasons," Four Seasons, accessed February 2, 2018, https://www.fourseasons.com/about_four_seasons/service-culture; and "Supporting Sustainability," Living Values Four Seasons, accessed February 2, 2018, http://livingvalues.fourseasons.com/category/supporting-sustainability/#.

companies are considering short-term and "commuter" assignments. A short-term assignment lasts 6 to 12 months, with the employee remaining under a home-country employment contract. Companies will also take into account the "quality of life" in another country when deciding whether to use local talent or an expatriate.[21]

Given the ever-expanding global environment, more and more people appear to be open to working in another country. Many individuals, especially in Canada, feel this work experience is an asset to their future career opportunities.[22]

At later stages of internationalization, there is typically a steady shift toward the use of host-country nationals, which accomplishes the following: lowered relocation costs for expatriates, meeting local government requirements for hiring of local workers, and enhanced marketing to customers who wish to do business with local businesses.

Bombardier and Four Seasons, which have strong regional organizations, tend to replace their expatriate managers with local managers as quickly as possible. The use of third-country nationals is also becoming more common as these employees often have the required language skills and a deeper understanding of the culture within the host country. It can also be less costly to relocate a third-country national who lives closer to the host country instead of sending an expatriate on an international assignment that is far from the employee's home location. At Work with HRM 11.3 tells the story of a British Columbia company entering into a partnership with a Chinese conglomerate.

It is important to note, however, that although top managers may prefer 1 source of employees to another, the host country may put pressure on them that restricts their choices. Such pressure takes the form of sophisticated government persuasion through administrative or legislative decrees designed to employ host-country individuals, and these types of requirements must be built into the HR planning process of international operations. To encourage local hiring, the host country frequently implements tax incentives, tariffs, and quotas.

Advances in technology and increased mobility make it easier to find employees from all over the world to work in different international locations. For example, Rolls-Royce, which is headquartered in the United Kingdom, hires a quarter of its workers from locations outside of the United Kingdom. The trend of global hiring is likely to continue as the populations in developed countries age and companies search for talent elsewhere. Even China, despite its massive population, will face labour shortages because laws from 1979 to 2015 prohibited couples from having more than 1 child.

Companies must ensure that employees who are hired can adapt to the legal, political, and behavioural expectations of the company they operate within. For example, Starbucks creates specialized codes of conduct so that employees throughout the world understand

AT WORK WITH HRM 11.3   THE FLOAT PLANE LANDS!

Doing business with Chinese companies is not simple, nor does it happen quickly. Take Harbour Air, a Vancouver-based float plane company that has undertaken a strategic partnership with a large Chinese firm to provide float-plane services and knowledge in a new venture.

The firm will help Zongshen Industrial Group set up the first float-plane operation in China. Given the 1.4 billion people in China and the many waterways, it is hard to imagine that there are no planes in operation. The expertise Harbour Air brings to the relationship will provide a solid launching pad for services in Shanghai and other South Asian places.

Part of the deal allows for the purchase of 49% of shares of Harbour Air from its current owner and CEO, Greg McDougall. McDougall indicated that he had been approached for a number of years to export the expertise but resisted for fear of bureaucracy and lethargy as regulators dealt with expansion of low-flying aircraft. However, he felt the time was now to move into another market. There is a need to have fast and efficient transportation services along China's coastal routes, and Zongshen indicated that local governments are strongly supporting the new endeavour.

Besides the expertise and knowledge Harbour Air will bring, the new company will be called Harbour Air China. Another reason for utilizing this approach is to generally introduce more aviation into China. Part of the long-term plan is to build its own seaplanes as the business expands into Malaysia and Vietnam.

This relationship will also allow Harbour Air to expand into the northern area of British Columbia, where oil and gas development is creating more demand for coastal plane services.

CRITICAL THINKING QUESTIONS:

1. Besides expertise, what other advantages might Harbour Air have in partnering with Zongshen?
2. What might be some disadvantages for Harbour Air in the future with the current ownership arrangement?

Sources: Adapted from Iain Marlow, "Harbour Air's Commuter Seaplanes Soon to Be Tried in Chinese Market," *The Globe and Mail*, June 18, 2015, B2; Jeff Lee, "Harbour Air Partners with Chinese Company," *Vancouver Sun*, June 17, 2015, A1; and Jeff Lee, "Harbour Air Deal with Zuo Zongshen Larger Than First Thought," *Vancouver Sun*, June 17, 2015, accessed February 2, 2018, http://blogs.vancouversun.com/2015/06/17/harbour-air-deal-with-zuo-zongshen-%e5%b7%a6%e5%ae%97%e7%94%b3-larger-than-first-thought.

the requirements regarding ethical and legal behaviour. It is important to recognize local cultures in relation to implementing ethical codes in other countries.

In general, however, employee recruitment in other countries is subject to more government regulation than it is in Canada. Regulations governing the employment of foreign workers or requiring the employment of the physically disabled, war veterans, or displaced persons vary from country to country. Appropriate interview questions and bona fide occupational requirements also vary. For example, the United States has a less restrictive definition of safety-sensitive positions than we do in Canada; therefore, many more positions require an employee to be able to meet these requirements and meet bona fide requirements in order to meet health and safety restrictions.

Multinational companies (MNCs) tend to use the same kinds of internal and external recruitment sources as are used in their home countries. Although unskilled labour may be readily available in a developing country, recruitment of skilled workers may be more difficult. As such, organizations use targeted recruitment techniques such as radio advertisements or asking current employees for referrals. Hiring a search firm that specializes in international recruitment is another strategy that is used.

Guest workers
Foreign workers who are hired to work in a country where there is a shortage of labour

When there are not enough local workers to meet a company's demand for labour, foreign workers may be recruited, and these are typically referred to as **guest workers**. Although hiring guest workers usually provides a company with lower labour expenses, other expenses, such as accommodation, transportation, and enhanced benefits, result in a high cost to employ these individuals. As such, recruitment of any foreign employees must be done in a strategic and well-thought-out manner that accounts for all associated expenses.

Even though international recruitment is still strong, there are restrictions in some countries about the number of non-resident people who can be hired. For example, in late 2014, the United Kingdom changed its regulations for hiring skilled workers so that there was more opportunity for residents before immigrants were brought in specifically for certain jobs.[23] With situations like this and the increasing complexity in the world, companies are using a number of different approaches to have the talent they need.[24]

In order to ensure that global talent is attracted and retained in other countries, organizations need to focus on the following:

1. Brand—having a reputation as an employer where people can excel.
2. Compensation—ensuring that the rewards program is competitive and fits the local circumstances as well as what applies in the home country.
3. Development—increasing employees' skills and competencies.
4. Culture—understanding the local environment and what additional supports might be necessary to attract and retain employees[25].

Transnational Teams

Instead of focusing on recruiting individual workers to work in international locations, some companies form teams of employees who move from one international project or location to another. These **transnational teams**, composed of people from various national backgrounds, are mobile employees who work as a group and move where the company requires their knowledge, skills, and abilities.

Research indicates that the ability to communicate effectively between different nationalities is critical to the success of the team.[26] Therefore, one of the key considerations when creating a transnational team is choosing the right people, based not only upon their competencies but also upon who can work effectively together. The different nationalities of employees within a transnational team create further complexity in managing group dynamics to ensure that employees are able to effectively produce the desired work outcomes.

> **Transnational teams**
> Teams made up of people from various nationalities who work on different international projects in various international locations

People with different national backgrounds can work together as part of transnational teams.

INTERNATIONAL SELECTION

As you might imagine, selection practices vary around the world. In Canada, managers tend to emphasize merit, with the best-qualified person getting the job. In other countries, however, firms tend to hire on the basis of family ties, social status, language, and common origin. The candidate who satisfies these criteria may get the job even if otherwise unqualified. Much of this is changing as there has been a growing realization among organizations in other nations that greater attention must be given to hiring those most qualified. In addition to a person's qualifications, various other hiring laws are enforced around the world. Labour union restrictions, which are discussed later in this chapter, can also have an impact on hiring.

The Selection Process

Selecting people to work in international locations requires unique considerations beyond a person's abilities to perform the required work. The ability to work with people from a different culture, the ability to live within a different culture, language skills, and adaptability are some examples of qualities required from people working outside of their home country. Cultural norms and the requirements of the country the business is operating within must also be considered. For example, some countries stress the importance of building connections with local communities that a business operates within; as such, employees need to be willing and able to do this when working in these foreign locations. Other factors that might be different in a foreign environment include the way in which business is conducted, including a more informal or easygoing pace of work, and employees selected to work in these locations must be able to adapt to this style of operation.[27]

Therefore, selecting people to work in international locations requires careful deliberation and exploration of various factors. The following section addresses issues that should be considered when selecting home-country employees to work in international locations.

Selecting Expatriate Employees

One of the toughest jobs facing many organizations is finding employees who can meet the demands of working in a foreign environment. Therefore, this requires careful planning and attention to critical components within this specific type of selection process. Strategic selection of expatriates requires the following actions:

1. *Encourage self-identification.* The process of finding home-country employees to work in international locations, in international roles, should begin well before a specific need ever arises. Employees should be encouraged to think about their career plans and ability and desire to move to international locations as part of an organization's ongoing performance management and coaching conversations. Employees need to be made aware of possible future opportunities and then discuss their suitability and interest with their managers. Various assessment instruments are available for employees to use to help them assess if this type of work is suitable for them, and employees should be encouraged to engage in this type of reflection and discuss outcomes with managers.

2. *Create a pool of candidates.* After employees have that they are interested in international work, a company can create a database of this information. Further details about potential expatriates, including language skills and technical abilities, can also be stored in this resource. An organization's succession planning should also document and plan for employee assignments to international locations based upon employees' capabilities and interest in this type of work. Although self-identification is a critical first step in selecting expatriates, managers should also initiate discussions with employees to explore their career interests and suitability for this type of work.

Effective succession planning, particularly to fulfill the demand created by international work, requires managers to take an active role in the process.

3. *Ensure person–job fit.* Based upon the specific requirements of each international job, managers need to assess the knowledge, skills, and abilities of potential candidates to ensure that, from a technical aspect, the employee would be capable of performing the required work. Although many factors determine success abroad, the initial focus should be on the requirements of the job. One of the key skills that can create success is the language skills of the host country.[28]

4. *Ensure person–location fit.* As detailed in Figure 11.4, selecting an expatriate employee involves much more than considering the employee's ability to do the job. The employee's ability to adapt and live in a different culture is also important. Skills such as decision making, team building, negotiating, and flexibility are critical for an expatriate to be successful. It is worth noting that many of these skills are not significantly different from those required for managerial success at home. As well, participating in a variety of different activities, such as athletic or social programs, can be very helpful in assisting the person in adapting to the host country.

FIGURE 11.4 Considerations When Selecting an Expatriate Employee

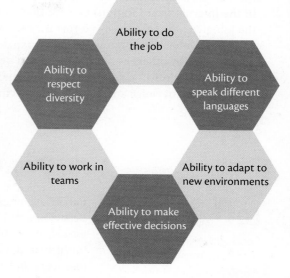

Failure rate
Percentage of expatriates who are not successful in their international assignments

Even when expatriates have been carefully selected, an employee can be unsuccessful in this type of role, and a company must pay special attention to the **failure rate** of expatriates. One of the primary reasons for an assignment failure is the person's family—spouse and children. Studies on this topic determined that inadequate attention was paid to ensuring that the family could adapt to the new conditions. Besides family issues, failures also occurred due to the person's lack of job knowledge, poor relational leadership skills, and lack of cultural openness and adaptability.[29] Samsung, another global electronics manufacturing company, has found that the most common reasons for an unsuccessful foreign assignment were inability to adapt to the different culture, lack of appropriate skills, and lack of communication skills.[30]

There are a number of ways to improve the success of expatriates. One important step is to involve spouses and children early in the process. As well, providing specific training and development for both expatriates and their families can help minimize failure rates. (This matter is discussed next.) As an example of how companies can prepare employees and their families, Shell created an online information centre called the Outpost Expatriate Support Network. This resource provides a handy tool that expatriates and their families can use to adapt to living in a new country.

To decrease the failure rates of international assignments, some companies also offer employment to the spouse of the expatriate. Ethics in HRM 11.1 outlines some of the concerns and issues that can happen with this type of arrangement.

ETHICS IN HRM 11.1 — BUT THE JOB WAS SUPPOSED TO BE MINE!

In order to entice employees to take an international assignment and to ease the relocation for the entire family, some companies offer both the employee and his or her spouse employment in the new location. This is seen as decreasing financial and emotional costs to the employee and the family, as well as providing the company with 2 sources of talent and expertise. Having both spouses work in the new country can also help the family adjust to living in a unique culture.

continued

However, when this occurs, other employees (both those in the home country and those currently working in the international location) can become annoyed as the job given to the spouse is a role they were hoping to have. At other times, the spouse of an expatriate can be perceived by others as not being the best person for the job or can also be seen to be given "make-work projects," both of which are unfair to current employees.

Actions taken by a company to be strategic and helpful to relocating employees may, in fact, be seen as unjust and unfavourable to other employees.

CRITICAL THINKING QUESTION:

Is it fair for a company to offer the spouse of an expatriate a job in the new location, even if they are not the best person for the job? Why or why not?

INTERNATIONAL TRAINING AND DEVELOPMENT

LO4

Discuss the unique training and development needs of employees working in international locations.

Expatriate employees require specialized training and development opportunities. Behaviours such as negotiations, conducting meetings, providing feedback, and work performance vary based upon specific cultural norms. To illustrate this point, Finning International, in its desire to provide global exposure to its key staff, has had to ensure that Canadian managers understand that the concept of time is very relaxed in its operations in Chile. Expatriates cannot assume that acceptable behaviour in their home country will be appropriate in an international location. Therefore, for a company to operate in a foreign country successfully, expatriates need to receive training that goes beyond the technical aspects of how to perform their job.

Content of Training Programs

Expatriates, and ideally their families, need training to help them adapt to working and living in a new country. Opportunities to learn about the following topics is critical to helping people succeed in foreign assignments:

1. The country's history, politics, religion(s), and economy.
2. The country's culture and values.
3. The country's currency and banking system.
4. The country's transportation and housing.
5. The country's laws and issues pertaining to safety and security.
6. The country's availability of, and preferences for, food.
7. The country's expectations regarding social and business etiquette.

Other types of training can include fundamentals of the international business and its strategy, as DHL Express has done to ensure a common understanding of the business throughout the world.[31]

Language Training

Communication with individuals who have a different language can be very challenging. In order for expatriates to effectively work in a foreign country, and for these employees and their families to effectively immerse themselves and live in these environments, understanding the language(s) is critical. As such, many companies provide language training prior to and during the international assignment.[32]

Even when English is spoken in the host country, words can have different meanings. For example, in England, an elevator is called a lift and the trunk of a car is called the boot. It is a mistake to assume that just because English is spoken in a different country, expatriates and their families will not encounter difficulties and therefore do not require language training.

It is important to train expatriates and their families about social and business etiquette in a foreign country.

Cultural Sensitivity Training

Cross-cultural differences, although subtle and potentially difficult to recognize, must be acknowledged and respected when conducting international business. As previously noted in this chapter, Hofstede's model outlines key areas of difference across cultures. Employees' behaviours and attitudes about work are largely influenced by the country in which they grew up and first joined the workforce.

This is often referred to as cultural conditioning. As such, organizations are finding that by developing a global mindset and providing cultural sensitivity training, people are better equipped for an international assignment.[33]

One important dimension of leadership, whether we are talking about international or domestic situations, is the degree to which managers invite employee participation in decision making. Although finding hard data on employee participation across different countries is difficult, careful observers report that Canadian managers are about in the middle on a continuum of autocratic to democratic decision-making styles. Scandinavian and Australian managers also appear to be in the middle. South American and European managers, especially those from France, Germany, and Italy, are toward the autocratic end of the continuum, whereas Japanese managers are at the most participatory end. These differences in participatory work cultures serve as an important reminder that employees working in international locations need to be aware of, and sensitive to, norms and standards of behaviour within the host country.

Training the Entire Family

As discussed earlier in this chapter, one of the most frequent causes of an employee's failure to be successful in an international assignment is personal and family stress. Employees and their family members who accompany them on international assignments may experience **culture shock**, which is ongoing stress and unhappiness due to the inability to adapt to an unfamiliar way of life in a new country. Language barriers, not knowing how to access transportation, being unable to determine where stores and restaurants are, and feelings of isolation are some indicators of culture shock. Simple actions and basic freedoms that are

Culture shock
Ongoing stress and unhappiness due to the inability to adapt to a new way of life in a foreign country

The ability of an employee's family to adapt to living in a new location is key to the success of an international assignment.

taken for granted in a home country, when no longer within easy access in a foreign land, can overwhelm employees and their family members.

Many industry studies have indicated that the #1 reason people refuse international assignments or the assignment fails is partner/spousal issues.[34] To address these issues, many organizations ensure that an expatriate's spouse has appropriate training (regarding all the topics previously discussed in training content) as well as access to support resources and counselling in the new country. As well, companies have processes in place to ensure that school-age children have access to proper education, various sporting activities, and numerous social events. The overall goal is to minimize culture shock, for expatriate employees and their families, and ensure that the international assignment can be completed with minimal problems or issues within and for the family unit.

Career Development

The opportunity to work in an international location may assist employees to enhance their career opportunities. Exposure to new cultures, new work environments, and new people provides the opportunity for developing technical abilities and other, softer skills. With this in mind, any international assignments must be given to employees with a purpose, or end goal, in mind. Companies such as SAP inform candidates when they are first employed that a global assignment may be part of their overall career development; it then seeks specific information at the appropriate time about interests and what the employee wants out of the global assignment.[35]

Organizations need to strategically plan how employees can use their international experiences, whether it be in different or new international assignments or when returning to a job back in their home country after the international assignment is finished. Employees will be more willing to become expatriates when they can envision how international work will benefit their overall career progression and future employment opportunities. Employees often complain that their organizations are unclear about what their roles within the company will be upon returning from an international assignment. In many cases, employees working in another country have learned how to run an entire international operation and upon returning home find that the scope and depth of their work may be significantly diminished. In fact, the evidence suggests that only a fraction of employees are promoted and that the knowledge, skills, and abilities developed by employees during an international assignment are not fully used by the organizations.[36] This is detrimental to both employees and companies as they are not using people to their full, competitive advantage.

It is also not uncommon for employees to return home after a few years to find *no* position for them in the firm and no one they know who can help them. Therefore, a company must give careful thought to how long an international assignment should be and what job an employee should return to upon completion of this work. Furthermore, consideration should be given to what support employees and their families will need when returning to their home country. Therefore, thinking about the conclusion of an international assignment is a key part of an employee's career development, and this is addressed in the next section.

Repatriation

It may seem strange that employees and their families require assistance when returning back to their home country, but after significant time away, the original home location can seem foreign. As such, organizations need to help employees and their families with **repatriation**, which is the process of returning to their original home country or country of original citizenship.

When being repatriated, employees and their families can experience culture shock, even though they are returning home. As an example, an employee who repatriated from Colombia walked outside his Edmonton office and waited for his driver, not remembering that he had driven his own car to work. Another family, repatriated from Kazakhstan, had to be restrained from purchasing all the fresh vegetables at the supermarket because over there, if there was fresh produce, you hoarded it because it might not be there next week.

Companies with good repatriation processes ensure that employees and their families are given information about how the expatriate experience may have changed them and readily acknowledge that transitioning back to a home country may not be an easy process. Research shows that the following needs to occur:

1. Issues need to be planned before the employee has left for their assignment.
2. Support has to be ongoing.
3. The returning assignee cannot be neglected after returning.
4. The repatriation process should begin at least 6 months prior to the return.[37]

To ease repatriation, some organizations take extra steps to ensure that employees keep in touch with home-based employees and are regularly updated about work processes and changes in the home country's business as this will lessen the shock and disorientation when returning from an international assignment. However, many firms are now allocating fewer dollars to processes that support international assignments and thereby spending less time and attention on employees working in foreign countries. Over time, this could make repatriation even more difficult and could influence the number of people willing to accept international work.[38]

INTERNATIONAL PERFORMANCE MANAGEMENT

As with other HRM practices, different countries have different standards and expectations regarding how, and even if, performance should be managed. In less formal or casual cultures, the idea of conducting a formal, written review of an employee's performance would be absurd. As well, some cultures would only expect feedback to be given on an individual basis (regardless of the teamwork that is occurring), whereas other environments would only expect comments to be given to entire groups of employees. Furthermore, local cultures

Repatriation
Process of moving back to the home country, or original country of citizenship, after an international assignment

LO5
Discuss the considerations when managing the performance of employees working in international locations.

may influence one's perception of how well an individual is performing. Therefore, careful attention to cultural norms is required while still meeting a company's need to be successful and ensure that workers, regardless of location, are effectively and efficiently doing their jobs. This is a complex issue and means that managers in international locations must balance company requirements for overall performance and must be familiar with what is and is not appropriate performance feedback, based upon the specific cultural norms of the international operation.

Reviewing Expatriate Employees' Performance

Expatriate employees' work is often best observed and assessed by other people working in the same international location. However, this is not always possible, and expatriates often want feedback from managers back in their home offices or countries. Expatriates want to ensure that they are staying connected to their home operations, with the eventual goal of having increased career progression upon repatriation. Providing frequent updates on projects and achievements, either through written reports or via video conferencing, allows expatriates to stay connected to their home operations.

Furthermore, although host-country employees are in a good position to view day-to-day activities, in many cases, an expatriate's promotion, pay, and other administrative decisions are determined by the home office, and as a consequence, the home-country manager usually handles the written evaluation. Nevertheless, the review should be completed only after vital input has been gained from a host-country manager.

Performance Criteria

Expatriate assignments are costly, and organizations are under pressure to ensure that money spent sending employees to work abroad was worth it. Using a return-on-investment (ROI) approach, similar to what was discussed in Chapter 6, for determining the value of training and development can be lacking. Productivity, profits, and market share, although valid, may not capture the full range of an expatriate's responsibility. Leadership development, for example, involves a much longer-term value proposition. In many cases, an expatriate is an

Using video conferencing is a good way to have contact with staff working in other countries.

ambassador for the company, and a significant part of the job is cultivating relationships with citizens of the host country. As discussed at the beginning of this chapter, an individual's success or failure is affected by a host of technical and personal factors. For example, as one might guess, it is much easier to adjust to similar cultures than to dissimilar ones. A Canadian can usually travel to the United Kingdom or Australia and work with locals almost immediately. Send the same individual to Hungary or Malaysia and the learning curve is steeper.

Providing Feedback

In providing feedback to expatriates, here are some tips:

1. Create and maintain a trusting relationship between the employee and the manager.
2. Help employees identify and focus on the most important objectives.
3. Be involved in all aspects of employees' lives to ensure that no external issues are creating problems.
4. Establish regular meetings, whether in person or via technology.
5. Hold employees accountable for outcomes.[39]

If the performance is not successful after review and coaching, careful attention needs to be paid to the local environment before terminating an employee. In some cases, such as China, employees can be terminated only for cause (discussed in Chapter 9); in other cases, such as in France, a prescribed procedure must be followed. Read HRM and the Law 11.1 to learn about legal considerations and consequences when dealing with people from different cultural backgrounds.

HRM AND **THE LAW** 11.1　　DOES THE LAW CHANGE BECAUSE OF CULTURE?

Many organizations would not tolerate any form of sexual harassment, and yet, according to a 2017 report by CNN, harassment continues to be prevalent in companies all over the world. Inappropriate behaviour is often ignored, or even deemed acceptable, due to cultural standards and norms. Why do some employees think that certain behaviours are acceptable and other employees tolerate these actions, all due to the premise that there are different cultural standards of acceptable behaviour?

A case in point occurred when Dominique Strauss-Kahn, a prominent French politician, was arrested and prosecuted for assaulting a maid in his New York hotel room. During his trial, there was considerable speculation about the different national approaches to sexual violence and sexual harassment in the United States and France. Was this a story of a clash of sexual cultures? Did it reflect different legal traditions regarding sexual violence?

The case was eventually closed with a non-disclosed settlement, but financial loss was not the only consequence for Strauss-Kahn. In addition to losing his job at the International Monetary Fund (IMF), it ended any realistic chance Strauss-Kahn had at a run at the French presidency as further lurid details of his lifestyle later emerged. Ultimately, Strauss-Kahn could not use cultural differences, and different acceptable standards of behaviour, as a defence for his actions.

CRITICAL THINKING QUESTIONS:

1. Given the diversity of cultures across the world, is it possible for companies to have a global standard of behavioural expectations for all employees, regardless of where they are working?
2. How can companies ensure that all employees adhere to company standards, regardless of national culture and work location?

Sources: Adapted from Meera Senthilingam, "Sexual Harassment: How It Stands around the Globe," *CNN*, November 29, 2017, accessed February 5, 2018, https://www.cnn.com/2017/11/25/health/sexual-harassment-violence-abuse-global-levels/index.html; Matt Williams, "Dominique Strauss-Kahn Settles Sexual Assault Case with Hotel Maid," *The Guardian*, December 10, 2012, accessed February 5, 2018, https://www.theguardian.com/world/2012/dec/10/dominique-strauss-kahn-case-settled; and Abigail C. Saguy, "French and U.S. Legal Approaches to Sexual Harassment," Cairn.info, accessed February 5, 2018, https://www.cairn-int.info/article-E_TGS_028_0089--french-and-u-s-legal-approaches-to.htm.

INTERNATIONAL REWARDS AND RECOGNITION

LO6

Outline the characteristics of a good international reward and recognition program.

Compensation is one of the most complex areas of international HRM. Different countries have different laws and standards regarding how employees should be paid. Managers should carefully consider the motivational use of incentives and rewards in foreign countries.

Some cultures emphasize monetary rewards, whereas others focus on job security, respect, work–life balance, or time off from work. Some countries believe in public recognition of accomplishments, whereas in other countries, this would be considered boastful and inappropriate. A company's overall rewards and recognition strategy must still align with and support the organization's overall objectives and yet be flexible enough to respond to the specific requirements and norms within a foreign location. The next section addresses compensation practices for host-country employees and managers and is followed by an overview of important considerations when dealing with the compensation of expatriates.

Compensation of Host-Country Employees

As Figure 11.5 shows, compensation can vary dramatically from country to country. Host-country employees are typically paid based upon productivity, with piece-rate compensation being quite common in industrialized countries. When companies commence operations in a foreign country, they usually set their wage rates at or slightly higher than the prevailing wage for local companies. Eventually, however, they are urged to conform to local practices to avoid "upsetting" local compensation practices.

FIGURE 11.5 **Hourly Compensation Costs in Manufacturing, in US Dollars and as a Percentage of Costs in the United States (US = 100)**

Hourly Compensation Costs						
Country	in US dollars			US = 100		
	1997 (2)	2015	2016 (3)	1997 (2)	2015	2016
Switzerland	30.43	61.01	60.36	132	161	155
Norway	25.88	50.96	48.62	112	135	125
Belgium	28.95	47.96	47.26	126	127	121
Denmark	23.72	44.57	45.32	103	118	116
Germany	28.86	42.27	43.18	125	112	111
Sweden	25.05	41.64	41.68	109	110	107
Austria	24.88	38.99	39.54	108	103	101
United States	23.04	37.81	39.03	100	100	100
Finland	22.36	38.44	38.72	97	102	99
Australia	19.29	38.59	38.19	84	102	98
France	24.87	37.31	37.72	108	99	97
Ireland	17.42	35.84	36.23	76	95	93
Netherlands	22.71	35.02	34.60	99	93	89
Italy	19.77	32.40	32.49	86	86	83

continued

Canada	18.49	30.74	30.08	80	81	77
United Kingdom	19.30	33.01	28.41	84	82	73
Singapore	12.16	25.87	26.75	53	68	69
Japan	22.00	23.60	26.46	96	62	68
New Zealand	12.04	23.23	23.67	52	61	61
Spain	13.96	23.40	23.44	61	62	60
South Korea	9.24	22.54	22.98	40	60	59
Israel	11.62	21.85	22.63	50	58	58
Greece	11.61	16.01	15.70	50	42	40
Estonia	NA	11.00	11.60	NA	29	30
Slovakia	2.84	11.08	11.57	12	29	30
Argentina	7.55	20.20	16.77	33	53	43
Portugal	6.44	10.99	10.96	28	29	28
Czech Republic	3.25	10.39	10.71	14	27	27
Taiwan	7.07	9.49	9.82	31	25	25
Hungary	3.05	8.21	8.60	13	22	22
Poland	3.29	8.52	8.53	14	23	22
Brazil	7.03	7.73	7.98	31	20	20
Mexico	2.62	4.38	3.91	11	12	10

For complete definitions, notes, and country information, see www.conference-board.org/ilcprogram/compensation.

Source: The Conference Board, "International Comparisons of Hourly Compensation Costs in Manufacturing, 2016," online: www.conference-board.org/ilcprogram/compensation. © 2018 The Conference Board, Inc. Content reproduced with permission.

Large companies such as McDonald's or Walmart can almost dictate what they pay. For example, a few years ago, McDonald's US decided to raise pay by more than 10% and include some additional benefits.[40] However, at the same time, Walmart was cutting health insurance for part-time employees as a way to manage costs.[41] Benefits provided to host-country employees are also a key consideration within international compensation. More companies are now creating targeted benefits packages for people working in global assignments so that costs can be better managed, such as using hired drivers in Singapore because drivers' licences are so expensive.[42] In Sweden, for example, paid maternity leave remains at 480 days, whereas some countries, such as the United Kingdom and Greece, have reduced benefits due to economic concerns.[43] Then you have situations such as in India, where 45 law officers in Chandigarh (a city in northern India) had not been paid for almost a year as the government had no money, whereas other parts of India reduced the retirement age from 60 to 58.[44]

Labour costs are one of the biggest motivators for international expansion, but many managerial and administrative issues must be addressed when an organization establishes operations overseas. For example, bad press can be generated for charging hundreds of dollars for individual products while the people who make them—sometimes children in developing countries working under poor conditions—earn only a few cents. Bad press can also be generated when an organization does not pay employees inappropriately. See Ethics in HRM 11.2 for the story about a company's payroll errors.

ETHICS IN HRM 11.2   I NEED TO BE PAID FAIRLY!

Tesco, Britain's largest supermarket chain, provided incorrect compensation to almost 140,000 employees due to errors in its payroll system. Almost £10m is owed to current and former workers after a system error led to them being paid less than the national living wage.

The company found that calculation errors were made when staff made voluntary contributions from their wages to benefits such as pensions, childcare vouchers, and cycle-to-work schemes. Chief Executive Matt Davies noted that as soon as the errors were discovered, action was taken to correct the underpayments, and apologies were issued. Tesco is not denying these errors and, going forward, is working to ensure that fair and appropriate compensation is provided to all employees.

Employees are anxious to receive money owed to them as they need to meet their own financial obligations. As well, employees want to know that their employer is paying them fairly and accurately.

CRITICAL THINKING QUESTIONS:

1. What other actions should Tesco take to rectify this situation?
2. Beyond legal obligations, why should a company ensure that employees are being paid properly?

Source: Adapted from Ben Chapman, "Tesco to Pay Back Staff Almost £10m after Massive Payroll Blunder," *Independent*, March 9, 2017, accessed February 16, 2018, http://www.independent.co.uk/news/business/news/tesco-pay-back-staff-10-million-error-less-than-minimum-wage-a7620806.html.

Compensation of Host-Country Managers

Compensation of host-country managers has typically been based upon local salary standards; however, increased competition among different companies with subsidiaries in the same country has led to a gradual upgrading of host-country managers' salaries. Overall, international firms are moving toward a narrowing of the salary gap between the host-country manager and the expatriate. For example, the expected salary for a warehouse manager in either Shanghai or Beijing ranges from $3000 to $6000 per month.[45] There is a recognition that talent is scarce and competition is intense.

The ongoing global economic challenges are putting pressure on companies to attract and retain the top talent. A number of studies have suggested that this translates into a better link between global performance expectations—both of the company and the individual—and an appropriate rewards package. Talent is mobile, and organizations are learning that there is a wide spectrum of approaches for compensating people in an international environment.[46]

Compensation of Expatriate Employees

If an international assignment is going to be enticing and successful, the expatriate's compensation plan must be competitive, fair, easy to understand and explain, consistent with international pay and taxation policies, and simple to administer.

Expatriates are typically paid either in their home-country currency (regardless of where the international assignment is) or in the currency of the location of the assignment. For example, an airline pilot working for KLM Royal Dutch Airlines and living in Vancouver is paid in euros. When paid in the local currency, fluctuations in currency exchange can affect the value of the expatriate employee's pay; therefore, this must be carefully monitored to ensure that the worker is receiving fair compensation.[47] Whether a company uses home-based or host-based pay depends on whether the employee may also depend on the cost of living within a particular country. For example, Switzerland and Norway are very expensive countries, whereas India and Serbia are the least expensive.[48]

Taxation, required deductions from pay, and provision of appropriate benefits are just some of the other complex issues that need to be addressed for expatriate employees. Due to the many considerations that must be addressed when compensating an expatriate, a company usually provides this employee with a tax and financial advisor along with assistance in filing the required tax returns.

INTERNATIONAL LABOUR RELATIONS

Labour relations in countries outside Canada differ significantly from those here. Differences exist not only in the collective bargaining process but also in the political and legal conditions. China has only 1 officially recognized organization of workers, the All-China Federation of Trade Unions, but as China's economy slows, more workers and foreign companies are seeing more labour unrest and more aggression on the part of workers.[49]

Other examples of the labour environment in other countries include the investigation into the deaths of over 1000 people at a Bangladeshi factory. What is unusual is that the owner of the factory has now been formally charged with murder.[50] Furthermore, labour laws in India are being blamed for poor economic performance as it is almost impossible to fire anyone without agreement between the unions and the company.[51] To gain a basic idea about labour–management relations in an international setting, we will look at 4 primary areas: (1) the role of unions in different countries, (2) collective bargaining in other countries, (3) international labour organizations, and (4) the extent of labour participation in management.

The Role of Unions in Other Countries

The role of unions varies from country to country and depends on many factors, such as the level of employee participation, per capita labour income, mobility between management and labour, homogeneity of labour (racial, religious, social class), and unemployment levels. These and other factors determine whether the union will have the strength it needs to represent labour effectively. Nearly all of Sweden's workers are organized, giving the unions in

Labour unrest exists, at different levels, throughout global operations.

this country considerable strength and autonomy. By contrast, in countries with relatively high unemployment, low pay levels, and no union funds with which to support social welfare systems, unions are driven into alliance with other organizations: political party, church, or government. This kind of relationship is in marked contrast to Canada, where the union selected by the majority of employees bargains only with the employer, not with other institutions. As mentioned earlier in this section, China has a central union that is more aligned with employers than employees.

There are many examples of union unrest in the global economy. For example, the rail union in Germany, GDL, shut the entire system down in early May 2015, which is estimated to have cost the German economy many hundred million euros.[52] On the other hand, Chile boosted the power of its unions to ensure that there is no labour unrest and improve its income inequality.[53] Unions in India decided not to stage a sit-in at a state legislature to protest the decision to remove a tax on natural gas when the companies decided to restart the gas plants and bring people back to work.[54] As well, unions in the United States are targeting fast-food franchisers in a bid to help the franchise owner have more protection from the corporation.[55] Lastly, union activists in France physically attacked 2 managers at Air France when an announcement was made that the company would be laying off 3000 staff as it restructured.[56]

Collective Bargaining in Other Countries

Chapter 10 reviewed typical collective bargaining processes in Canada, but this can be drastically different in other countries, especially with regard to the role of government. For example, in the United Kingdom and France, the government is involved in every aspect of collective bargaining. Also, in countries where nationalization is heavy, government involvement is more likely to be accepted, even in non-nationalized companies.

International Labour Organizations

The most active of the international union organizations has been the International Confederation of Free Trade Unions (ICFTU), which is headquartered in Brussels. Numerous International Trade Secretariats (ITSs) work with the ICFTU, and these are essentially international federations of national trade unions operating in the same or related industries. The ICFTU also cooperates with the European Trade Union Confederation, which represents over 90 national trade organizations in 39 countries plus 10 EU trade union federations.[57] As well, the International Labour Organization is a specialized agency of the United Nations and has had a big influence. on the rights of workers throughout the world. Read At Work with HRM 11.4 to learn more about the ILO from one of Canada's representatives.

AT WORK WITH HRM 11.4   **WHAT A PRIVILEGE!**

What's it like being one of Canada's representatives to the International Labour Organization (ILO)? Just ask John Beckett, vice-president of training, safety and recruitment for the BC Maritime Employers Association, and he will describe the privilege it is to be one of Canada's employer representatives on one of the ILO's committees.

The ILO, as an agency of the United Nations, is funded by the United Nations, which is funded by member countries. The ILO is considered to be the "house of labour," with labour, employer, and government representatives. Although it started in the early 1900s, it wasn't until after World War II that it really took off. As Beckett states, "The primary mandate is for continuous improvement

continued

on social issues throughout the world." Much of its focus has been on labour issues.

Typically, the ILO identifies 3 or 4 areas every year in which active work occurs by the members. Beckett, as a representative of Canada, sits on one of the ILO's subcommittees. This particularly committee, labour inspection protocols, has about 400 members. Although it might seem that this is quite a few for getting things done, in fact, things do get done, and new standards, called "conventions," are agreed to. Then each member country can choose to adopt or accept the convention and develop legislation to support it. Canada has a good track record of adopting the various conventions over the years.

What's the most interesting aspect of Beckett's work? "It is the international reach of the ILO in social programs and reforms," says Beckett. "And it is great being part of the changes that happen."

CRITICAL THINKING QUESTION:
Why else might John Beckett consider his role privilege? Explain.

Labour Participation in Management in Other Countries

In many European countries. there is a legal requirement for employees to have representation on health and safety committees and worker councils. Although their responsibilities vary from country to country, worker councils basically provide a communication channel between employers and workers.

Germany requires more intense participation from workers as there is a legal requirement for workers to be represented on the board of directors of a company. This is known as **codetermination** and often by its German word, *Mitbestimmung*, and it requires that company shareholders and employees are equally represented on the boards of all companies with more than 2000 employees.

> **Codetermination**
> Representation of labour on the board of directors of a company

CONCLUDING COMMENTS

Managing human resources in different international locations involves complex and multi-faceted processes. One approach will not work across all situations as customization is required to meet different cultural norms and various legal requirements. Throughout this book, we have noted that different situations call for different approaches to managing people, and nowhere is this point more clearly evident than in international HRM.

As the discussion on international HRM draws to a close, remember that whether the world is less volatile or not, today's organizations will need to be vigilant about employee engagement in a global context. There is, and will continue to be, competition for global talent, and companies will need to monitor and take actions to motivate and engage employees all over the world.[58] Furthermore, as already demonstrated, multinational companies will relocate operations that provide a competitive advantage—whether in terms of natural resources, cost of labour, or inducements by governments.

Are the factors in employee engagement, recruitment, and selection different for global assignments than for domestic ones? No, all organizations are concerned with the motivation, attraction, and retention of talent.[59] After that, the differences depend on the country, although flexibility and appropriate compensation for the assignments are also important.[60]

Moving forward with a still struggling global economy, organizations will have to continue with an emphasis on talent management in order to succeed in the global marketplace. Consider the other areas to watch in Emerging Trends 11.1.

EMERGING TRENDS 11.1

1. *Identifying skills on a local level.* Companies that can identify skills beyond those presented in traditional CVs and resumés will have a competitive advantage. Finding the right people to work in complex international environments, especially when entering new markets and geography areas, will continue to present challenges.

2. *Adhering to legislative requirements, particularly for part-time workers.* Workforce planning, with a focus on the laws and customs in each of the regions where a company operates, will continue to be important, with a special focus on part-time and temporary workers. Indonesian law, for example, does not recognize the concept of part-time workers, who are consequently entitled to the same rights as full-time workers. Temporary workers must also receive the same benefits as permanent workers.

3. *Capitalizing on advances in technology.* With ongoing technological advancements in communication, it is easier to have a global workforce feel and act more connected.

4. *Preparing a new set of globally prepared leaders.* Managers need to be trained on how to take advantage of the cultural differences while mitigating any friction among employees. Creating practices for promoting collaboration among diverse workers and communicating values and policies across countries and ethnicities, and developing leaders who are able to do this, will be important to driving success within global organizations.

5. *Aligning HR practices throughout global companies.* Although there is always a need to customize HR practices to a specific geographic environment, there is a continuing desire to align practices such as tracking employees, managing performance, and identifying future leaders to take advantage of economies of scale.

6. *Focusing on employee engagement.* Even global companies have concerns about employee engagement; therefore, developing strategies for its international operations to keep employees engaged and operating at their peak will continue to be important.

7. *Reforming pensions.* With the continual sluggish world economy, more countries are examining public pensions, and pensioners are becoming more vocal when their funds have been invested in organizations that appear to have excessive pay for executives.

Sources: Adapted from "What's Next: Future Global Trends Affecting Your Organization Engaging and Integrating a Global Workforce," Society of Human Resource Management Foundation, accessed February 4, 2018, http://futurehrtrends.eiu.com/report-2015/challenges-for-human-resource-management-and-global-business-strategy; Karen Higgenbottom, "Top Challenges Facing HR Directors of Global Firms in 2017," *Forbes*, December 28, 2016, accessed February 4, 2018, https://www.forbes.com/sites/karenhigginbottom/2016/12/28/challenges-facing-hr-directors-of-global-firms-in-2017/#290091fa4f95; "International Pension Regulatory Services," Morneau Shepell, accessed February 4, 2018, https://www.morneaushepell.com/ca-en/international-pension-regulatory-services; Tari Ellis, Chiara Marcati, and Julia M. Sperling, "Promoting Gender Diversity in the Gulf," *McKinsey Insights*, February 2015, accessed February 4, 2018, www.mckinsey.com/insights/organization/promoting_gender_diversity_in_the_gulf?cid=other-eml-alt-mkq-mck-oth-1502&p=1; Takeo Yamaguchi, "Standardizing HR Practices around the World," *Harvard Business Review*, September 2014, 5; "How Is Global Uncertainty Impacting Employee Engagement Levels? (2017)," *AON*, accessed February 4, 2018, http://www.aon.com/engagement17; and Chris Flood, "Pensions Group Calls for Shareholder Action," *Financial Times*, December 8, 2014, 2.

LEARNING OUTCOMES SUMMARY

1. Describe the types of organizational forms used by companies with international operations.
   - *Multinational—fully autonomous units operating in multiple countries*
   - *International—domestic firm that uses existing capabilities to move into global markets*
   - *Transnational—firm that attempts to balance local responsiveness with the efficiencies of a global firm*
   - *Global—multinational firm that maintains control back in the home office*
2. Explain the economic, political-legal, and cultural factors in different countries that need to be considered from an HR perspective.
   - *Trade agreements can shift jobs from one location to another*

- *Companies will move or expand operations depending on which country provides best economic return*
- *Cultural factors include language, religion, values, education, and social structure*

3. Describe recruitment and selection for international operations.
   - *Companies must develop strategic plans for effective operations of international operations, including how best to manage and coordinate a culturally diverse workforce*
   - *Companies can send people from the home country (expatriates)*
   - *Firms can hire employees who are natives to the host country*
   - *Employee recruitment in other countries is subject to more government regulation than in Canada*

4. Discuss the unique training and development needs of employees working in international locations.
   - *Content needs to have information about the country and the country's culture*
   - *Language training may be necessary*
   - *Cultural sensitivity training may be necessary*
   - *Special attention needs to be paid to helping employees, and their families, manage personal circumstances*
   - *Some development programs are designed to facilitate repatriation*

5. Discuss the considerations when managing the performance of employees working in international locations.
   - *Decisions need to be made on who will be involved in the performance management process*
   - *Domestic managers may not fully understand the expatriate's experiences, so it is a good idea to involve the host-country manager*
   - *Performance criteria need to include more than just financial goals*
   - *It is important to provide feedback regularly to the expatriate*

6. Outline the characteristics of a good international reward and recognition program.
   - *Different cultures value recognition and rewards differently*
   - *Determine whether the employee will be paid through the policies of the home or host country and in what currency*

7. Explain how labour relations practices differ around the world.
   - *Labour laws differ from one country to another*
   - *Government may be more involved in determining wage rates even with unionized staff*
   - *Some countries, such as Germany, have a high degree of worker participation*

KEY TERMS

codetermination 389

cultural environment 370

culture shock 379

expatriates 372

failure rate 377

guest workers 374

host country 370

host-country nationals 372

repatriation 381

third-country nationals 372

transnational teams 375

HRM CLOSE-UP APPLICATION

1. Operation Eyesight, as described in the HRM Close-up at the beginning of this chapter, is a thriving charitable organization with global operations. What are 3 challenges, as described by Aly Bandali, in managing such a complex organization?
2. Where should Operation Eyesight recruit future employees? What specific skills and abilities would these workers need?

3. What training opportunities should Operation Eyesight offer employees?
4. Aly Bandali encourages people to obtain global experience. Would you ever want to work for an organization outside of Canada? Why or why not?

CRITICAL THINKING QUESTIONS

1. RBC operates in over 40 countries and employs both Canadians and local staff. What are the advantages of employing Canadians with roots in the host country? Would you use expatriate managers or host-country nationals to staff RBC offices? Explain.
2. How can Canadian managers minimize any difficulties in relationships with employees in a foreign operation?
3. How can learning about different cultures be incorporated into a manager's professional development plan, and how could the organization assess the learning?
4. Bombardier Inc. once fired an employee for accepting confidential information about a Dutch train contract in which the Dutch company was going to purchase a new fleet of trains. Since selling and receiving confidential information occur throughout the world, do you think the employee ought to have been fired? Why or why not?

BUILDING YOUR SKILLS

1. Think of a foreign country where you would like to work. Make a list of 6 specific resources that you would want from an employer before taking on an international assignment in this location. List 6 specific resources that you would want for your family if they accompanied you to this location.
2. Access WageIndicator.org (**https://wageindicator.org**) and find a country that is of interest to you for possible work. Think of a type of work you are interested in and see what the wages are for that work in that country. Is it what you thought? Explain.
3. Using any search engine, do a search on "resources for expatriates." Examine the top 5 different resources. What might be the most useful if you were thinking of working in another country?
4. Access the Expatriate Foundation website (**https://expatriatefoundation.org**) and review the information provided. Was it useful? Why or why not?

CASE STUDY 1

A Great Adventure!

What are the challenges and opportunities that await a leader who has relocated to a foreign country? Just ask Erica Sanyo, a leader in a global company with a variety of business lines. She recently accepted an expatriate assignment in an emerging market.

Erica has been with the company for over 12 years in a variety of different positions. There is no doubt that she was identified as someone for international opportunities some time ago, and she has moved, along with her family, to a number of different countries, taking on more extensive responsibilities with each move. Her current assignment takes her to an emerging country in Africa—far from her home country, Canada—and into another new role.

In this new assignment, she is responsible for the marketing and sales staff in all the businesses that operate in a large region in southern Africa. The company has only been present with any significant employee base for the past 7 years and as such has a relatively young workforce. The staff are eager to learn and succeed and do not always understand the highs and lows of business cycles and what that means for them. Erica not only has to pay attention to her career, she is also responsible for her staff and their career paths.

Since the company is based in North America, there is the challenge of understanding and adapting her leadership style to the local context yet driving forward the desired broader company culture of candour, transparency, humility, and employee trust—which is not easy in a country with a geopolitical culture that typically does not support or reinforce these qualities. Erica learned some time ago that people need to be resilient in order to adapt to changes around them. So how does she help her staff gain the resilience they need in order to adapt and move ahead?

On top of this, Erica has also had to prepare herself for such a role in a region that has a complex political and labour environment as well as being knowledgeable about the company's social investment in the country. Almost every country in her region is undergoing significant political changes, which impacts the operating environment, especially from a commercial perspective. This means that Erica needs to be aware of the local context and all the subtleties that come with it.

For Erica, it isn't just about herself; her family has moved with her. Her husband and 3 small children have also relocated to a physical environment, as well as a cultural environment, that is very different from where they had been living. To be successful in her role, her family also needs to succeed. To do so, they need to draw upon their resilience as they adapt to their new surroundings.

Erica is excited about her role and location but also recognizes the hurdles and challenges she faces in being effective in her role—both for the organization and in terms of her impact as a leader. She is on a steep learning curve and relies on those around her for support. Like her staff and family, she draws upon her resilience to adapt to her environment and be an effective leader.

Questions:

1. What are some of the challenges facing Erica?
2. What are some of the opportunities for Erica?
3. What advice would you give Erica?

CASE STUDY 2

Is Global Competition Good?

What happens when 2 entrepreneurs start selling coconut water at the same time in the same place? Two great companies are competing internationally 10 years later.

Vita Coco, founded by Michael Kirban, and ZICO, founded by Mark Rampolla, discovered quite accidentally that both started selling coconut water in Manhattan in 2004. Both men were athletically active and found that coconut water was useful in rehydrating. But at the time, this was not friendly competition, and soon the tactics that each used garnered the name "coconut wars." Each started out simply: Kirban going around on in-line skates with samples in a backpack and Rampolla driving around in an old van with samples to stores. The reason both picked Manhattan is that it has a very large number of independent stores where the owners can quickly make decisions.

When each discovered that there was a competitor, both entrepreneurs were in shock. Kirban had discovered coconut water in Brazil and was anxious to bring it to the United

States; Rampolla discovered coconut water in Costa Rica and also wanted to build a business selling it in the United States. With consumers not only being exposed to coconut water for the first time but also having choices of brands, competition soon became quite visible. Some salespeople learned phrases in Spanish, Arabic, Korean, and Hebrew to pitch to certain audiences.

This competition went on until 2009, when Coca-Cola bought 20% of ZICO. Vita Coco responded by selling 10% of its company to a group of celebrities that included Madonna and Demi Moore. Both investments created much media attention, and sales were expected to rise.

But like any deal, the outcomes depend on the details. Vita Coco was able to continue accessing distributors that it felt could make a difference. On the other hand, ZICO was restricted to how Coca-Cola handled distribution—which did not include sales staff that were focused only on ZICO.

Where are things today? Rampolla sold all the remaining shares to Coca-Cola in late 2014 but is still seen as the face of ZICO. Vita Coco continues as a strong independent brand, with sales in dozens of countries. Vita Coco also recently announced that it was getting rid of its celebrity ambassadors. Both are embarking on large marketing campaigns as the trend for increased sales continues. Kirban would like to have strong competition, which he believes is good for business, but without having the wars, as he did in the beginning.

Sources: Adapted from K. Divan, "The Coconut Wars," *Gladrags Magazine*, December 2014, 88–90; "Our Story," Vita Coco, accessed February 5, 2018, http://vitacoco.com/our-story; Seth Stevenson, "Gatorade Is the Antichrist," *Slate*, accessed February 5, 2018, www.slate.com/articles/business/branded/2011/11/coconut_water_why_is_it_suddenly_so_popular_.html; and Declan Harty, "Jessica Alba Returns for Zico as Vita Coco Ditches Celebs," *Advertising Age*, June 6, 2015, accessed February 5, 2018, http://adage.com/article/advertising/zico-coconut-water-vita-coco-launch-summer-campaigns/298899.

Questions:

1. What helped make this a global success?
2. If you were asked to become a sales representative for either company in Asia, what might you need to know about the national culture?

NOTES AND REFERENCES

1. Liz Bernier, "Canada Tops in Attracting Talent," *Canadian HR Reporter*, November 3, 2014, 1; M. Rajendran, "More Indians to Head Global Cos: Top Headhunter," *Hindustan Times*, November 25, 2014, 13; and Sarah Dobson, "Following a Not-So-Linear Path," *Canadian HR Reporter*, May 4, 2015, 19.
2. "Difference between a Global, Transnational, International and Multinational Company," accessed February 8, 2018, https://leeiwan.wordpress.com/2007/06/18/difference-between-a-global-transnational-international-and-multinational-company.
3. "Methodology: World's Most Admired Companies," *Fortune*, accessed February 8, 2018, http://fortune.com/worlds-most-admired-companies.
4. Richard Blackwell, "A Dozen Canadian Firms Crack List of World's Top 100 Sustainable Companies," *The Globe and Mail*, March 25, 2017, accessed February 2, 2018, https://www.theglobeandmail.com/report-on-business/a-dozen-canadian-firms-crack-list-of-worlds-top-100-sustainable-companies/article22554162.
5. Marina Strauss, "Hudson's Bay Set to Buy German Chain," *The Globe and Mail*, June 15, 2015, B1.
6. Marina Strauss, "HBC Eyes European Launch for Saks," *The Globe and Mail*, June 16, 2015, B1.
7. James Kanter, Alison Smale, and Niki Kitsantonis, "EU Urged to Plan for Greece to Default," *The Globe and Mail*, June 16, 2015, B9.
8. Alex Hunt and Brian Wheeler, "Brexit: All You Need To Know About the UK Leaving the EU," *BBC News*, January 30, 2018, accessed February 8, 2018, http://www.bbc.com/news/uk-politics-32810887.
9. "NAFTA Talks Have Hit a Wall After Mexico and Canada Resist U.S. Demands," *Reuters*, November 22, 2017, accessed February 8, 2018, http://fortune.com/2017/11/21/america-mexico-canada-nafta-talks.
10. Foreign Affairs and International Trade Canada, "International Commerce—By Country," 2014, accessed February 8, 2018, http://w03.international.gc.ca/Commerce_International/Commerce_Country-Pays.aspx?lang=eng.
11. "GDP Growth in China 1952-2014," China Ability website, accessed February 8, 2018, http://chinability.com/GDP.htm.
12. "Canada Reaches Deal on Revised Trans-Pacific Partnership," *CBC News*, January 23, 2018, accessed February 16, 2018, http://www.cbc.ca/news/politics/tpp-champagne-deal-1.4499616.
13. "TPP: What Is It and Why Does It Matter?," *BBC News*, January 23, 2018, accessed February 16, 2018, http://www.bbc.com/news/business-32498715.
14. Brent Snavely, "Pace of Auto Industry Mergers Hits Seven-Year High," *Detroit Free Press*, November 4, 2014, accessed February 8, 2018, https://www.freep.com/story/money/cars/2014/11/04/automotive-merger-acquisition-pricewaterhousecoopers-fiat-chrysler/18487615.
15. Ibid.

16. "GM, Isuzu Partner on Truck Line," *Vancouver Sun*, June 17, 2015, C1.

17. Ian Bremmer, "The Mixed Fortunes of the BRICS Countries, in 5 Facts," *Time*, September 1, 2017, accessed February 8, 2018, http://time.com/4923837/brics-summit-xiamen-mixed-fortunes.

18. Christopher Donville and Willem Marx, "Beetle Plague Pushes Canadian Firms to buy U.S. Mills," *The Globe and Mail*, June 24, 2015, B7.

19. "Japanese Firms are Improving Results by Boosting Motivation," *Vancouver Sun*, January 17, 2015, F6.

20. Iulian Warter and Liviu Warter, "The New Face of Global M & A: Intercultural Issues in the Banking Industry," *Forum Scientiae Oeconomia* 3, no. 1 (2015): 127–138.

21. Sarah Dobson, "A Tale of 2 Cities," *Canadian HR Reporter*, July 14, 2014, accessed February 8, 2018, https://www.hrreporter.com/articleview/21712-a-tale-of-2-cities.

22. Mark Swartz, "The Benefits of Working in a Foreign Country," Monster.ca website, accessed February 8, 2018, https://www.monster.ca/career-advice/article/working-in-a-foreign-country-ca.

23. Lubna Kably, "Strict UK Laws Seek to Scan Migrants' Job Role," *The Times of India*, December 8, 2014, 17.

24. "Adopting New Approaches within Recruitment," *The Talent Boom*, April 21, 2017, accessed February 8, 2018, http://www.thetalentboom.com/adopting-new-approaches-within-recruitment.

25. Luc Minguet, "Creating a Culturally Sensitive Corporation," *Harvard Business Review*, September 2014, 101–103; Charles Doucot, "Mining for Talent," *Canadian HR Reporter*, February 9, 2015, accessed February 8, 2018, https://www.hrreporter.com/articleview/23466-mining-for-talent; and Sarah Dobson, "Following a Not-So-Linear Path."

26. Ana Langovic Milicevic, Vladimir Tomasevic, and Smiljka Isakovic, "The Importance of Successful Project Team Communication in Agribusiness," *Economics of Agriculture*, 61, no. 2 (2014): 367–379.

27. Eduardo Caride, "Diversifying Talent to Suit Market," *Harvard Business Review*, September 2014, 4–5.

28. Jan Seimer and Jakob Lauring, "Host Country Language Ability and Expatriate Adjustment: The Moderating Effect of Language Difficulty," *The International Journal of Human Resource Management* 26, no. 3 (2015): 401–420.

29. Information supplied to current coauthor by Doug Whitehead, chair of the board of directors, April 2015.

30. "Why Do So Many Expatriates Fail on Foreign Assignments?," *UK Essays*, January 10, 2018, accessed February 8, 2018, https://www.ukessays.com/essays/management/why-do-so-many-expatriates-fail-on-foreign-assignments-management-essay.php.

31. "DHL," accessed February 8, 2018, http://www.dhl.com/en.html.

32. Managers who are interested in setting up a language-training program, wish to evaluate commercially available language-training programs, or wish to find appropriate cross-cultural training can use the following resources: Rosetta Stone, https://www.rosettastone.com; Berlitz, https://www.berlitz.com; Global Integration, http://www.global-integration.com; and Dean Foster Global Cultures, http://deanfosterglobal.com. Additional resources can be found through continuing education at many local universities or community colleges.

33. "Importance of cross cultural awareness," *Forum for Expatriate Management*, July 26, 2017, accessed February 8, 2018, https://www.forum-expat-management.com/users/50831-sirva/posts/18869-importance-of-cross-cultural-awareness.

34. Dawn S. Onley, "Avert Assignment Failure: Support Spouses in Overseas Relocations," Society of Human Resource Management website, March 13, 2014, accessed February 8, 2018, https://www.shrm.org/hrdisciplines/global/articles/pages/spouses-overseas-relocations.aspx.

35. SAP. "SAP Careers," accessed February 8, 2018, https://www.sap.com/canada/about/careers.html.

36. "Does an expat assignment really help your career progression?," *FIDI*, April 20, 2017, accessed February 8, 2018, https://www.fidi.org/blog/does-expat-assignment-help-career.

37. CAI Editor, "Repatriation: Challenges Faced when Coming Home," *Cultural Awareness International*, July 13, 2017, accessed February 8, 2018, https://culturalawareness.com/repatriation-challenges-faced-coming-home.

38. T.W. Coppler, "Why Are Companies Failing with Expats in Angola?," April 19, 2017, accessed February 8, 2018, https://www.couplertw.com/why-are-companies-failing-with-expats-in-angola.

39. Jane F. Maley and Miriam Moeller, "Global Performance Management Systems: The Role of Trust as Perceived by Country Managers," *Journal of Business Research* 67, no. 1 (2014): 2803–2810; and Annamarie Mann and Ryan Darby, "Should Managers Focus on Performance or Engagement?," *Gallup Business Journal*, August 2014, 1.

40. "McDonald's to Offer Raises, Paid Time Off," *The Globe and Mail*, April 2, 2015, B4.

41. Shelly Banjo and Stephanie Armour, "Wal-Mart to Cut Health Coverage for More Workers," *The Globe and Mail*, October 5, 2014, B10.

42. Tim McDonald, "Is Singapore Really the World's Most Expensive City?," *BBC*, April 7, 2017, accessed February 8, 2018, http://www.bbc.com/capital/story/20170407-is-singapore-really-the-worlds-most-expensive-city.

43. "Quick Facts: Sweden," accessed February 5, 2018, https://sweden.se/quickfact/parental-leave.

44. Ajay Sura, "$5 Law Officers Not Paid Salaries Since Last Year," *The Times of India*, November 28, 2014, P3; and Geentanjali Gayatri, "Haryana Staff Retirement Age Back at 58," *The Tribune*, November 26, 2014, 1.

45. "Guide to China Market Salaries 2nd Quarter 2015," J.M. Gemini Personnel Ltd.

46. "5 Important Considerations for Your Global Mobility Program," Mercer, 2015, 20.

47. "ECA International," accessed February 8, 2018, https://www.eca-international.com/services.

48. "Cost of Living Index, Updated June 2017," Expatistan, accessed February 8, 2018, https://www.expatistan.com/cost-of-living/index.

49. Kent D. Kedl, "Forbes: With Labor Disputes in China on the Rise, Companies Must Tread Carefully," *China Labour Bulletin*, March 24, 2015, accessed February 10, 2018, http://www.clb.org.hk/en/content/forbes-labor-disputes-china-rise-companies-must-tread-carefully.

50. "Murder Charges Filed in 2013 Factory Collapse," *The Globe and Mail*, June 2, 2015, B8.

51. Unni Krishnan, "How Decades-Old Labour Laws Strangle Growth," *Vancouver Sun*, August 18, 2014, A14.

52. Joanna Slater, "Rail Strike Brings Germany to a Halt," *The Globe and Mail*, May 6, 2015, A3.

53. "Chile Boosts Power of Unions, Leaders," *Vancouver Sun*, December 31, 2014, B1.

54. "FACT Unions Withdraw Plans for Protest in State Capital," *The Hindu*, December 1, 2014, 3.

55. Candice Choi, "Unions Woo Fast-Food Franchisees," *Vancouver Sun*, May 1, 2015, D5.

56. Lori Hinnant, "Union Attacks Air France Bosses," *The Globe and Mail*, October 6, 2015, A15.

57. European Trade Union Confederation, accessed February 9, 2018, https://www.etuc.org.

58. Ibid.

59. "5 Important Considerations for Your Global Mobility Program," 5.

60. Ibid.

THIS MAKES SCENTS (PART 5)

Three more years have passed, and Jessie and Ashton are pleased with how the business is doing. They avoided unionization, and all the stores are profitable. In addition, the human resource polices, practices, and systems they have implemented are helping to retain and engage employees. They have a very low turnover rate for a retail business.

The store they opened in an exclusive part of town has done well but is not as profitable as their shopping mall–based operations. Jessie and Ashton wonder if this is because clients in this part of the city prefer to, and can afford to, purchase actual products in lieu of mock perfumes. They also wonder if this is even a problem because this location is still making a slight profit, although not at the same level as other locations. While contemplating the future of the non–shopping mall location, they were approached by a consumer research company that offered to do some fact finding and investigation for them. This would cost them money but could, in the long term, result in better decision making and profits.

Una Buena Idea?

Just as Jessie and Ashton were contemplating the future of one of the stores, an old school friend, whom they hadn't heard from in years, reconnected with them on social media. Juanita had moved back to Mexico City after they had all finished university and was enjoying life back in her home city. Juanita had heard about the success of the various stores and was encouraging Jessie and Ashton to open up a shop in Mexico City, especially since the mock perfume products were produced in Mexico. Juanita was convinced that there was a need for this type of product and that both locals and tourists would want to purchase mock perfumes. Furthermore, Juanita had told them that she knew many people (mainly her friends and family members) who were looking for jobs and would be able to work at the Mexican store. As such, Juanita offered to do all the recruitment and selection for them, including finding a local person to manage the store.

So Many Questions

Although the idea of an international location was exciting, there were many unanswered questions and considerations. Instead of spending money on local consumer research, the least profitable store could be shut down and the funds could be expended on developing a shop in Mexico City. However, Jessie and Ashton wondered if they really could just rely on Juanita to do all the recruitment and selection. Was it a good idea to hire locals, or should one of them go and manage the store, at least for the first year or so? Or perhaps they could send one of their current employees to do this job? They weren't even sure about the legal requirements and how many locals they would have to hire.

What Next?

Jessie and Ashton felt they were at a crossroad in their business. They had accomplished so much and knew that the next move would be pivotal. Although it was exciting, it was also scary. "The next move we make could make or break us," said Jessie. Ashton agreed, and they sat down together to discuss and plan their next steps.

Questions:

1. Should Jessie and Ashton allow Juanita to do all of the recruitment and selection for them if they open a store in Mexico City? Why or why not?
2. What other legal considerations (i.e., other than the number of locals they must hire) that have human resources management implications should Jessie and Ashton investigate if they open a store in Mexico City?

3. If Jessie and Ashton want to send a current employee to manage the store in Mexico City, what competencies and skills should this person have?

4. What type of training should be provided to this employee before leaving for Mexico City?

5. What type of support should be provided to this employee when returning home from working in Mexico City?

6. What would you suggest to Jessie and Ashton as their next steps? Why did you select these steps?

Glossary

360-degree review
Provides employees with performance feedback from a variety of people or sources (page 226)

Achievement tests
Measures of what a person knows or can do right now (page 165)

Alternative dispute-resolution (ADR)
Term applied to different types of employee complaint or dispute-resolution processes (page 311)

Apprenticeship training
System of training in which a worker entering the skilled trades is given thorough instruction and experience, both on and off the job, in the practical and theoretical aspects of the work (page 189)

Aptitude tests
Measures of a person's capacity to learn or acquire skills (page 165)

Arbitration award
Final and binding award issued by an arbitrator in a labour–management dispute (page 355)

Balanced Scorecard (BSC)
A measurement framework that helps managers translate strategic goals into operational objectives (page 232)

Bargaining unit
A group of employees represented by 1 union for the purposes of collective bargaining and other union processes (page 330)

Behaviour modification
Belief that the consequences of behaviour determine if it will be repeated or discontinued (page 188)

Behavioural description interview (BDI) question
Question about what a person actually did in a given situation (page 161)

Behaviourally anchored rating scale (BARS)
A performance review method that consists of a series of scales for each performance dimension or component within a job (page 231)

Benchmarking
(1) Finding the best practices in other organizations that can be brought into a company to enhance performance (page 18); (2) evaluating and comparing processes and practices against those that represent high standards or those that deliver strong performance outcomes (page 197)

Bona fide occupational qualification (BFOQ)
Job qualifications that may be discriminatory due to business or safety reasons (page 44)

Bullying
Actions and verbal comments that can hurt or isolate a person in the workplace (page 51)

Business agent
Normally a paid labour official responsible for negotiating and administering the collective agreement and working to resolve union members' problems (page 337)

Certification
Acquisition of exclusive rights by a union to represent the employees (page 330)

Closed shop
Provision of the collective agreement that requires employers to hire only union members (page 325)

Co-operative programs
Training programs that combine practical, on-the-job experience with formal education (page 190)

Coaching
A more experienced employee closely observes a less experienced worker over a short period of time and provides ongoing feedback to improve work performance (page 194)

Codetermination
Representation of labour on the board of directors of a company (page 389)

Competency-based pay
Pay based on how much knowledge or how many capabilities employees have or how many jobs they can perform (page 259)

Constructive dismissal
Changing an employee's working conditions such that compensation, status, or prestige is reduced (page 308)

Consumer price index (CPI)
Measure of the average change in consumer prices over time in a fixed "market basket" of goods and services (page 253)

Contractual rights
Rights that derive from contracts (page 287)

Core competencies
A combination of knowledge, skills, and characteristics needed to effectively perform a role in an organization (page 20)

Cultural environment
Descriptions of the values, norms, communication standards, and religion of a country; includes social structure and general way of life (page 370)

Culture
Consistent and observable pattern of behaviours in organizations (page 24)

Culture shock
Ongoing stress and unhappiness due to the inability to adapt to a new way of life in a foreign country (page 379)

Customer review
Performance review that seeks information from both external and internal customers (page 226)

Cyberbullying
Bullying by using communication technology and information (page 98)

Defined rights
Concept that management's authority should be expressly defined and clarified in the collective agreement (page 348)

Designated groups
Women, members of visible minorities, Aboriginal peoples, and persons with disabilities who have been disadvantaged in employment (page 56)

Development
The acquisition of skills, behaviours, and abilities to perform future work or to solve an organizational problem (page 180)

Direct compensation
Employee wages and salaries, bonuses, and commissions (page 244)

Disability management
Integrated approach to managing disability-related benefits (page 104)

Discipline
(1) Treatment that punishes, (2) orderly behaviour in an organizational setting, or (3) training that moulds and strengthens desirable conduct—or corrects undesirable conduct—and develops self-control (page 298)

Diversity
The combination of organizational policies and practices that supports and encourages employee differences in order to reach business objectives (page 59)

Downsizing
A strategic approach to decreasing the number of employees in a company (page 12)

Due process
Employee's right to a fair process in making a decision related to the person's employment relationship (page 288)

Duty to accommodate
Requirement that employers adjust employment practices to avoid discrimination (page 45)

E-learning
Training that uses computers and/or online resources (page 192)

Eldercare
Care provided to an elderly relative by a person who continues actively working (page 270)

Employee assistance programs (EAP)
Program to provide short-term counselling and referrals to appropriate professionals (page 104)

Employee empowerment
Granting employees power to initiate change, thereby encouraging them to take charge of what they do (page 128)

Employee engagement
Amount of commitment and dedication an employee has toward the job and the organization (page 81)

Employee rights
Expectations of fair treatment from employers (page 285)

Employee teams
An employee-contributions technique in which work functions are structured for groups rather than for individuals and team members are given discretion in matters traditionally considered management prerogatives, such as process improvements, product or service development, and individual work assignments (page 130)

Employment branding
An organization's reputation as an employer (page 147)

Employment equity
A distinct Canadian process for achieving equality in all aspects of employment (page 55)

Ethics
Things that matter to us that motivate our behaviour (page 64)

Expatriates
Employees from an organization's home country who move to the international country where the organization does business (page 372)

Failure rate
Percentage of expatriates who are not successful in their international assignments (page 377)

Gig economy
Environment in which employees have many part-time jobs instead of 1 permanent full-time role (page 27)

Globalization
Moving local or regional business into the global marketplace (page 10)

Graphic rating scale
A trait approach to performance review where an employee is rated, typically on a numerical scale, regarding key elements within the job (page 229)

Grievance process
Formal process that provides the union with a way to handle a complaint that something within the collective agreement has been violated (page 350)

Grievance resolution
Process in which a neutral third party makes a decision on a grievance (page 352)

Guest workers
Foreign workers who are hired to work in a country where there is a shortage of labour (page 374)

Harassment
Any conduct or comment that a reasonable person would consider objectionable or unwelcome (page 48)

Host country
Country in which an organization is conducting business (page 370)

Host-country nationals
Employees who are natives of the country where an organization conducts international business (page 372)

Hourly work
Compensation based upon the number of hours worked (page 250)

Human capital
The value that employees provide to an organization through their knowledge, skills, and abilities (page 19)

Human resource planning
Process to ensure that an organization has people available (employed) who have the right competencies and that these people are being effectively utilized in the right capacities in order for the company to achieve its desired objectives (page 142)

Human resources management (HRM)
An integrated set of systems, practices, and policies in an organization that focuses on the effective deployment and development of its employees (page 5)

Human resources management strategy
Identifying key HRM systems, practices, and policies and linking them to the overall business strategy (page 29)

Inclusion
Putting the concept of diversity into action (page 59)

Independent contractor
A person who is hired by contract to perform a specific job and is not considered part of the employee base (page 14)

Indirect compensation
All other forms of rewards, such as extended health and dental plans and other programs and plans that offer rewards or services to employees (page 244)

Industrial disease
A disease resulting from exposure relating to a particular process, trade, or occupation in industry (page 83)

Instructional goals
Desired outcomes of a training program (page 187)

Integrative bargaining
A collaborative approach to negotiations that focuses on developing mutually favourable outcomes (page 342)

Interest arbitration
A mechanism to renew or establish a new collective agreement for parties (page 347)

Internship programs
Programs jointly sponsored by colleges, universities, and other organizations that offer students the opportunity to gain real-life experience while allowing them to find out how they will perform in work organizations (page 190)

Job
A group of related activities and duties (page 116)

Job analysis
Process of obtaining information about jobs by determining the duties, tasks, or activities and the skills, knowledge, and abilities associated with the jobs (page 117)

Job characteristics model
An approach to job design that recognizes the link between motivational factors and components of the job to achieve improved work performance and job satisfaction (page 128)

Job description
A document that lists the tasks, duties, and responsibilities of a job to be performed along with the skills, knowledge, and abilities or competencies needed to successfully perform the work (page 119)

Job design
Process of defining and organizing tasks, roles, and other processes to achieve employee goals and organizational effectiveness (page 127)

Job evaluation
Systematic process of determining the relative worth of jobs in an organization (page 251)

Job incumbent
The employee hired to do a job (page 117)

Job specifications
Statement of the needed knowledge, skills, and abilities of the person who is to perform the position (page 121)

Labour market
Area from which applicants are recruited (page 150)

Labour relations system
A framework of the environment, the people, the processes, and the results (page 324)

Lean
Organizational system of improvements that maximize customer value and minimize waste (page 18)

Learning
A relatively permanent change in knowledge or behaviour (page 184)

Lockout
Strategy by which the employer denies employees the opportunity to work by closing its operations (page 346)

Management by objectives (MBO)
Employees and managers agree on an individual's goals, which support the organization's objectives, and employee performance is assessed upon results achieved in relation to these goals (page 232)

Management forecasts
Asking managers for their predictions regarding the future demand for employees (page 144)

Manager review
Performance review done by the employee's manager (page 225)

Markov analysis
Description of how employees typically move into, within, and out of the organization (page 145)

Mediation
The use of an impartial third party to help facilitate a resolution to employment disputes (page 311)

Mediator
Third party in a labour dispute who meets with one party and then the other in order to suggest compromise solutions or to recommend concessions from each side that will lead to an agreement (page 346)

Membership cards
A document signed by an employee indicating that the union is able to act on the employee's behalf for collective bargaining and other union purposes (page 328)

Mentors
Experienced employees who provide advice and guidance to encourage and support less experienced workers (page 203)

Negotiation
People sorting out a problem between themselves (page 311)

Occupational illness
Abnormal condition or disorder resulting from exposure to environmental factors in the workplace (page 83)

Occupational injury
Any cut, fracture, sprain, or amputation resulting from a workplace accident (page 83)

Ombudsperson
Person who helps in the resolution of a workplace issue (page 312)

On-the-job training (OJT)
Method by which employees are given hands-on experience with instructions from their manager or another trainer (page 189)

Open shop
Provision of the collective agreement that allows employees to join or not join the union (page 325)

Organizational culture
Collective understanding of beliefs and values that guide how employees act and behave (page 78)

Orientation
A structured process for new employees to become familiar with the organization and their work; critical to socialization, which is the embedding of organizational values, beliefs, and accepted behaviours (page 180)

Outsourcing
Hiring an external person (or a company) to do work that had previously been done by an internal employee (page 12)

Oversupply of labour
Occurs when an organization's demand for employees is less than the number of employees currently employed (page 146)

Panel interview
An interview in which a board of interviewers questions and observes a single candidate (page 160)

Pay equity
The practice of equal pay for work of equal value (page 58)

Pay for performance
Standard by which managers tie direct compensation to employee or organizational outcomes and performance (page 249)

Pay grades
Groups of jobs within a specific class that are paid the same rate or rate range (page 258)

Peer review
Performance feedback collected from an employee's colleague (page 226)

Performance management system
A set of integrated management practices designed to help employees maximize performance, thereby allowing the organization to reach its goals (page 212)

Picket
A situation in which unionized workers stand in front of entrances to the employer to prevent people from conducting business with the employer (page 344)

Piecework
Compensation based upon the number of units produced (page 250)

Position
Specific duties and responsibilities performed by only 1 employee (page 116)

Positive discipline
Approach to discipline in which the employee assumes responsibility for changing behaviour and/or performance (page 303)

Progressive discipline
A series of steps to improve behaviour and/or performance (page 301)

Promotion
Moving an employee into a job that is more complex, has increased responsibilities, and therefore typically provides increased compensation and status (page 202)

Psychological harassment
Repeated and aggravating behaviour that affects an employee's dignity or psychological or physical integrity that makes the work environment harmful (page 51)

Real wages
Wage increases larger than rises in the consumer price index; reflect actual purchasing power and have an impact on standard of living (page 254)

Recruitment
The process of locating and encouraging people to apply for jobs (page 147)

Reliability
The degree to which selection procedures provide consistent and comparable outcomes over time (page 156)

Repatriation
Process of moving back to the home country, or original country of citizenship, after an international assignment (page 381)

Residual rights
Concept that management's authority is supreme in all matters except those it has expressly conceded to the union in the collective agreement (page 348)

Reverse discrimination
Giving preference to members of certain groups such that others feel they are the subjects of discrimination (page 47)

Rights arbitration
A mechanism to resolve disputes about the interpretation and application of a collective agreement during the term of that collective agreement (page 352)

Role
The part played by an employee within an organization and the associated expected behaviours (page 117)

Safety data sheets (SDS)
Documents supplied by the supplier containing detailed information regarding hazardous material (page 93)

Salary survey
Survey of the wages paid to employees in other relevant, comparable organizations (page 257)

Selection
Selection is the process of choosing from the pool of applicants and hiring individuals who are best able to fulfill the requirements of the job (page 155)

Self-review
Performance review done by the employee being assessed, generally on a form completed by the employee prior to the performance interview (page 255)

Shop (union) steward
An employee acting in an official union capacity representing other union members in their relations with management (page 337)

Shortage of labour
Occurs when an organization's demand for employees is greater than the number of employees employed (page 147)

Situational question
Question in which an applicant is given a hypothetical incident and asked how he or she would respond to it (page 162)

Six Sigma
A process used to translate customer needs into a set of optimal tasks performed in concert with one another (page 16)

Skills inventory
Information about the education, experiences, skills, etc., of employees (page 145)

Staffing table
Graphs displaying the jobs in an organization and showing the number of people currently in these jobs. Anticipated demand for the number of people to fill each job in the organization may be shown as well (page 145)

Standards of performance
Set out the expected results of the job (page 125)

Statutory rights
Rights that derive from legislation (page 287)

Stress
Physiological, mental, and/or emotional tension caused in response to a demanding environment (page 99)

Strike
A situation in which unionized workers refuse to perform their work during labour negotiations (page 343)

Subordinate review
Performance review of a superior by an employee, which is more appropriate for developmental than for administrative purposes (page 225)

Systemic discrimination
The exclusion of members of certain groups through the application of employment policies or practices based on criteria that are not job related (page 43)

Talent management
Leveraging competencies to achieve high organizational performance (page 21)

Telecommuting
Conducting work activities away from the office (typically at home) through the use of technology (page 15)

Third-country nationals
Employees who are natives of a country other than the home country of the organization or the country in which the international business is being conducted (page 372)

Total rewards
Everything that the employee receives in terms of both direct and indirect compensation (page 244)

Trainee readiness
The consideration of trainees' skills and experiences when assessing their ability to benefit from training (page 187)

Training
The acquisition of skills, behaviours, and abilities to perform current work (page 180)

Transfer
Moving an employee to a different role in the organization. The new job is typically similar to the previous role in terms of responsibility and complexity (page 202)

Transfer of training
Applying what is learned to enhance performance on the job (page 195)

Transnational teams
Teams made up of people from various nationalities who work on different international projects in various international locations (page 375)

Trend analysis
Using past numerical data to look for patterns in order to predict future demand for employees (page 144)

Unfair labour practices
Accusation that an employer, a union, or an individual has engaged in activity that is illegal in accordance with the appropriate labour code (page 330)

Union shop
Clause in a collective agreement requiring employees to become a member of the union and retain membership to retain employment (page 325)

Validity
How well a selection procedure measures what it is intended to measure (page 156)

Virtual team
A team with widely dispersed members linked through computer and telecommunications technology (page 130)

Whistleblowing
Reporting unethical behaviour outside the organization (page 65)

Work
Tasks or activities that need to be completed (page 116)

Workplace stressors
A workplace event, process, or practice that has the potential to cause worker stress (page 100)

Wrongful dismissal
Terminating an employee's employment without just cause (page 306)

Name Index

Subject Index